Handbook of Adolescent Digital Media Use and Mental Health

Digital media, including social media, has fundamentally changed how the human species communicates with, relates to, and influences one another. Adolescents use digital media extensively. Researchers, scholars, teachers, parents, and teens themselves have many questions about the effects of digital media on young people's psychological development. This handbook offers a comprehensive synthesis of scientific studies that explain what we know so far about digital media and its effects on youth mental health. With chapters from internationally renowned experts in the fields of psychology, psychiatry, media, and communications, the book offers a broad overview of the positive and negative implications of youths' engagement with digital media for brain development, relationships, identity exploration, daily behaviors, and psychological symptoms. Chapters include a discussion of the current state of knowledge, directions for future research, and practical suggestions for parents, educators, and teens themselves. This title is also available as Open Access on Cambridge Core.

JACQUELINE NESI is an Assistant Professor in the Department of Psychiatry and Human Behavior at the Warren Alpert Medical School of Brown University.

EVA H. TELZER is an Associate Professor of Psychology and Neuroscience at the University of North Carolina at Chapel Hill and Co-Director of the Winston National Center on Technology Use, Brain, and Psychological Development.

MITCHELL J. PRINSTEIN is the John Van Seters Distinguished Professor of Psychology and Neuroscience at the University of North Carolina at Chapel Hill, the Chief Science Officer at the American Psychological Association, and Co-Director of the Winston National Center on Technology Use, Brain, and Psychological Development.

Handbook of Adolescent Digital Media Use and Mental Health

Edited by

Jacqueline Nesi
Brown University

Eva H. Telzer
University of North Carolina at Chapel Hill

Mitchell J. Prinstein
University of North Carolina at Chapel Hill

CAMBRIDGE
UNIVERSITY PRESS

CAMBRIDGE
UNIVERSITY PRESS

University Printing House, Cambridge CB2 8BS, United Kingdom

One Liberty Plaza, 20th Floor, New York, NY 10006, USA

477 Williamstown Road, Port Melbourne, VIC 3207, Australia

314–321, 3rd Floor, Plot 3, Splendor Forum, Jasola District Centre,
New Delhi – 110025, India

103 Penang Road, #05–06/07, Visioncrest Commercial, Singapore 238467

Cambridge University Press is part of the University of Cambridge.

It furthers the University's mission by disseminating knowledge in the pursuit of
education, learning, and research at the highest international levels of excellence.

www.cambridge.org
Information on this title: www.cambridge.org/9781108838726
DOI: 10.1017/9781108976237

First published 2022

A catalogue record for this publication is available from the British Library.

Library of Congress Cataloging-in-Publication Data
Names: Nesi, Jacqueline, 1988– editor. | Telzer, Eva H., editor. | Prinstein, Mitchell J., 1970- editor.
Title: Handbook of adolescent digital media use and mental health / edited by Jacqueline Nesi, Brown
    University, Rhode Island, Eva H. Telzer, University of North Carolina, Chapel Hill, Mitchell J.
    Prinstein, University of North Carolina, Chapel Hill.
Description: Cambridge, United Kingdom ; New York, NY : Cambridge University Press, 2022. |
    Includes bibliographical references and index.
Identifiers: LCCN 2021058050 (print) | LCCN 2021058051 (ebook) | ISBN 9781108838726 (hardback) |
    ISBN 9781108972277 (paperback) | ISBN 9781108976237 (epub)
Subjects: LCSH: Internet and teenagers–Psychological aspects. | Mass media and teenagers–Psychological
    aspects. | Digital media–Psychological aspects. | Teenagers–Mental health. | Adolescent psychology. |
    BISAC: PSYCHOLOGY / Clinical Psychology
Classification: LCC HQ799.2.I5 H36 2022 (print) | LCC HQ799.2.I5 (ebook) | DDC 004.67/80835–
    dc23/eng/20220211
LC record available at https://lccn.loc.gov/2021058050
LC ebook record available at https://lccn.loc.gov/2021058051

ISBN 978-1-108-83872-6 Hardback
ISBN 978-1-108-97227-7 Paperback

To the many adolescents who have generously shared their time with me across therapy rooms, research labs, and classrooms: thank you for everything you have taught me. – JN

To my newborn son Henry. I can't imagine what digital media will be like when you're a teen, but I hope the science we continue to do will equip parents to help teens thrive in digital spaces. – EHT

To my own children, Samara and Max, who will ask me for smartphones soon, and to my wife, Tina, who will remind me of this book and help me say "no." – MJP

Contents

Figures

Tables

About the Editors

JACQUELINE NESI, PHD, is an assistant professor in the Department of Psychiatry and Human Behavior at the Warren Alpert Medical School of Brown University. Nesi earned her BA in Psychology at Harvard University and her PhD in Clinical Psychology at the University of North Carolina at Chapel Hill. She completed her internship and postdoctoral fellowship at the Brown University Clinical Psychology Training Consortium. Nesi's research examines the role of social media in adolescents' peer relationships and mental health, with a focus on depression and suicidal thoughts and behavior. Her research has been funded by the National Institute of Mental Health, the Eunice Kennedy Shriver National Institute of Child Health and Development, the American Foundation for Suicide Prevention, and the National Science Foundation. She has published in numerous peer-reviewed journals, including *Clinical Psychology Review* and the *Journal of the American Academy of Child and Adolescent Psychiatry*, and her work has been featured in popular media outlets such as *The Wall Street Journal* and *Teen Vogue*. She has also served as an invited speaker for the Society for Research on Adolescence and the National Academies of Sciences, Engineering, and Medicine. She is passionate about understanding how and for whom social media influences adolescents' mental health, so as to identify and intervene with youth most at risk.

EVA H. TELZER, PHD, is an associate professor of psychology and neuroscience at the University of North Carolina at Chapel Hill. She received her PhD in Developmental Psychology from University of California–Los Angeles. Her research examines how social and cultural processes shape adolescent brain development, with a focus on both prosocial and risk-taking behaviors, family and peer relationships, and long-term psychological well-being. She is an associate editor for *Child Development* and *Social Cognitive Affective Neuroscience*. She has authored more than 160 publications in peer-reviewed journals, 9 book chapters, and an edited book on culture and biology interplay. Telzer has received numerous awards for her work, including a NARSAD Young Investigator Grant, a Jacobs Foundation Early Career Research Fellowship, an Early Career Award from the Society for Research on Adolescence, and the Boyd McCandless Award for Early Career Contributions to Developmental Psychology from the American Psychological Association Division 7, and she was named a Rising Star by the Association for Psychological Science. Her research is supported by the National Science Foundation, Brain and Behavior Research Foundation, National Institute of Drug Abuse, National Institute of Mental Health, and the Jacobs Foundation. In her free time she enjoys drawing biological illustrations, hiking with her dog, and baking sourdough.

MITCHELL J. PRINSTEIN, PHD, is the John Van Seters Distinguished Professor of Psychology and Neuroscience at the University of North Carolina at Chapel Hill and Chief Science Officer at the American Psychological Association. He received his PhD in Clinical Psychology from the University of Miami and completed his internship and postdoctoral fellowship at the Brown University Clinical Psychology Training Consortium. Prinstein's research examines interpersonal models of internalizing symptoms and health risk behaviors among adolescents, with a specific focus on the unique role of peer relationships in the developmental psychopathology of depression and self-injury. He is the PI on several past and active grants from the National Institute of Mental Health, the National Institute of Child and Human Development, and several private foundations. He served as the editor for the *Journal of Clinical Child and Adolescent Psychology* and is an editorial board member for several developmental psychopathology journals. He has received several national and university-based awards recognizing his contributions to research (American Psychological Association Society of Clinical Psychology Theodore Blau Early Career Award; Columbia University/Brickell Award for research on suicidality; American Psychological Association Fellow of the Society of Clinical Child and Adolescent Psychology and the Society of Clinical Psychology), teaching (UNC Chapel Hill Tanner Award for Undergraduate Teaching; Psi Chi Professor of the Year), and professional development of graduate students (American Psychological Association of Graduate Students Raymond D. Fowler Award) and undergraduate students (Psychology Club Department Research Mentor Award).

Contributors

KATIE AVERY, BS, Department of Psychology, Central Michigan University

GLORIA ROJAS BARAJAS, BA, Department of Psychology, Central Michigan University

SUSANNE E. BAUMGARTNER, PHD, Amsterdam School of Communication Research, University of Amsterdam

AUBREY L. BORGEN, MA, Department of Psychology, Central Michigan University

MORGAN T. BROWN, BA, Department of Psychology, University of North Carolina Greensboro

MATTHEW M. CARPER, PHD, Department of Clinical Psychology, William James College

LINDA CHARMARAMAN, PHD, Wellesley Centers for Women, Wellesley College

JASON CHEIN, PHD, Department of Psychology, Temple University

MICHELLE CHIU, MA, Department of Psychology, Temple University

SOPHIA CHOUKAS-BRADLEY, PHD, Department of Psychological and Brain Sciences, University of Delaware

SARAH E. DOMOFF, PHD, Department of Psychology, Central Michigan University

SAMUEL E. EHRENREICH, PHD, Department of Human Development, Family Science and Counseling, University of Nevada, Reno

ISABELA GRANIC, PHD, Department of Developmental Psychopathology, Behavioral Science Institute, Radboud University

NASTASIA GRIFFIOEN, MSC, Department of Developmental Psychopathology, Behavioral Science Institute, Radboud University

JESSICA L. HAMILTON, PHD, Department of Psychology, Rutgers University

J. MAYA HERNANDEZ, MA, Department of Social Ecology, University of California, Irvine

RACHEL HODES, BA, Wellesley Centers for Women, Wellesley College

CARRIE JAMES, PHD, Project Zero, Harvard Graduate School of Education

MICHAELINE JENSEN, PHD, Department of Psychology, University of North Carolina Greensboro

ANNA F. JOLLIFF, MS, Department of Pediatrics, University of Wisconsin–Madison

KAYLEE PAYNE KRUZAN, PHD, Center for Behavioral Intervention Technologies, Northwestern University

BRIANNA A. LADD, BA, Department of Psychological and Brain Sciences, University of Delaware

CHELLY MAES, MS, School for Mass Communication Research, Katholieke Universiteit Leuven

ANNE J. MAHEUX, MS, Department of Psychological and Brain Sciences, University of Delaware

ADRIANA M. MANAGO, PHD, Department of Psychology, University of California, Santa Cruz

JESSICA MCKENZIE, PHD, Department of Child and Family Science, California State University, Fresno

MINAS MICHIKYAN, PHD, Department of Psychology, California State University – Los Angeles and Children's Digital Media Center, Los Angeles

MEGAN A. MORENO, MD, MSED, MPH, Department of Pediatrics, University of Wisconsin–Madison

HIROMITSU MORITA, MSC, Department of Developmental Psychopathology, Behavioral Science Institute, Radboud University

JESSICA NAVARRO, MS, MSW, Department of Human Development and Family Studies, University of North Carolina Greensboro

JOHANNA M. F. VAN OOSTEN, PHD, Amsterdam School of Communication Research, University of Amsterdam

SAVANNAH R. ROBERTS, BS, Department of Psychological and Brain Sciences, University of Delaware

BONNY RYE, MA, Department of Psychology, Central Michigan University

DAVID M. SIEGEL, MA, Graduate School of Applied and Professional Psychology, Rutgers University

KAVERI SUBRAHMANYAM, PHD, Department of Psychology, California State University – Los Angeles, and Children's Digital Media Center, Los Angeles

PATTI M. VALKENBURG, PHD, Amsterdam School of Communication Research, University of Amsterdam

LAURA VANDENBOSCH, PHD, School for Mass Communication Research, Katholieke Universiteit Leuven

EMILY WEINSTEIN, EDD, Project Zero, Harvard Graduate School of Education

MARIANI WEINSTEIN, MA, Department of Psychology, University of North Carolina Greensboro

JANIS WHITLOCK, PHD, MPH, Bronfenbrenner Center for Translational Research, Cornell University

Acknowledgments

We wish to sincerely thank the contributors of this volume for their hard work and generosity. It is a privilege to work with such talented scholars, all of whom have made incredible contributions to the study of digital media use and adolescent mental health. This work was made possible through the generosity of the Winston Family Foundation, which has supported the Winston Family Initiative in Technology and Adolescent Brain Development, codirected by Dr. Eva Telzer and Dr. Mitch Prinstein; see www.teensandtech.org.

Introduction

The experience of contemporary adolescents is one that differs profoundly from that of earlier generations. Research on adolescence has also endured substantial change, and the concept of change is central to the topics addressed in this handbook. Change, for example, is key to the very definition of adolescence as a developmental time period marked by rapid physical, social, and psychological transformation. Accumulating evidence in developmental neuroscience over the past decades reveals a complexity of change not previously understood. Mental health is also an evolving concept – both in definition and in practice – with our understanding of what constitutes "good" mental health subject to fluctuating societal norms and stigmas, emerging diagnostic categories and dimensions, and increasing prevalence rates. Yet perhaps most closely tied to the concept of change is digital media – inextricably linked with evolution, adaptation, and transformation. To understand digital media is to recognize and wrestle with a constantly evolving phenomenon – an entity that changes within a world that changes around it, both as a cause and a consequence of it.

Research on digital media must enter into this complex exchange. As researchers aim to make sense of digital media, to describe its usage and effects, to catalogue where it is, where it was, and where it will be, scientists must themselves become embedded in this changing context. In this volume, we strive to embrace the complexities brought on by phenomena that are so closely tied to change. We bring together the foremost experts in digital media and adolescent mental health, to work toward an understanding of what we currently do and do not, can and cannot, know; what prior research has taught us; and, perhaps most importantly, how to approach the future of this field.

Digital Media: Defining an Evolving Concept

It is challenging to define a concept for which change is such a central component. Attempts at characterizing digital media often become quickly outdated, seeming alternatively to rely on classifications that are either so narrow as to preclude the inevitable arrival of new technologies, or so broad as to miss the essence of the term itself. Adding complexity to this endeavor is a variety of terms often used interchangeably – new media, interactive media, social media, screen media, social technologies, interactive communication technologies. Although it seems clear what digital media are *not* – that is, they stand in stark contrast to *mass* media tools that rely on "one-to-many" communication (see Subrahmanyam & Michikyan, Chapter 1 in this volume; Valkenburg, Chapter 2 in this volume) – what digital media *are* remains somewhat elusive, and there has been much confusion in the literature regarding the use of these terms. For the purposes of this handbook, we define digital media broadly to include the range of tools used to store and share information in a digital (i.e., computer-readable) format, including hardware (e.g., computers, mobile devices), software (e.g., operating systems, smartphone applications), and online platforms. We have chosen to use the term "digital media" in this volume's title, so as to promote a broad consideration of the many electronic tools that may influence the mental health of contemporary adolescents, including smartphones, mobile applications, and social media. Most authors have adopted this terminology in their chapters.

However, when it comes to understanding the effects of digital media on adolescents' mental health, and vice versa, we are interested not only in the *what* of digital media, but also in the *how*. That is, we are interested both in the smartphone's operating system itself and also in how adolescents use that system. And when it comes to adolescents, that means a key area of focus must be on the *social*. It has long been recognized that adolescence is a period of increased interest and engagement in social interactions, particularly with peers, and is accompanied by heightened biological sensitivity to peer evaluation and social rewards. It is perhaps no surprise, then, that the vast majority of digital media tools adopted by adolescents are social or interactive in nature. Thus, for the purposes of this handbook, we devote considerable attention to *social media*, or "Internet-based channels that allow users to opportunistically interact and selectively self-present, either in real-time or asynchronously with both broad and narrow audiences who derive value from user-generated content and the perception of interaction with others" (Carr & Hayes, 2015, p. 51). We define this to include social networking sites (e.g., Instagram, Snapchat, WeChat, and Facebook), messaging tools (e.g., text messaging and messaging apps), online forums and communities, video- and image-sharing platforms (e.g., YouTube and TikTok), and video games with a social component.

Of course, the challenge of defining what digital and social media *are* is complicated by the constantly – and quickly – evolving nature of the technical landscape. From MySpace to TikTok, desktop computer to iPhone, video games to virtual reality, the tools that encompass digital media change frequently and often drastically. While it is important to recognize the specific affordances of platforms that may influence their use and effects, research efforts that focus on a single platform often become quickly outdated and can lack generalizability to future work. In this volume, we strive to unify prior research from a perspective that is agnostic to specific platforms or tools; in doing so, our goal is to provide a reference and guide for future scholarship that remains relevant beyond the existence of a given site or app. We recognize that, by necessity, we can only capture the state of this research at a very specific snapshot in time. Yet it is our hope that by approaching the topic with both historical and forward-looking lenses, we may integrate the idea of an evolving digital media into our very definition of this concept moving forward.

Theoretical Foundations: A Developmental Psychopathology Perspective

Understanding the role of digital media in adolescent mental health requires a revisiting of prior frameworks, models, and theories. For several decades, developmental psychopathology has been the predominant framework for examining the onset and course of youth mental illness, and we draw on this framework for defining and understanding "mental health" in the context of this volume. Developmental psychopathology perspectives emphasize both typical and atypical trajectories of development at the multiple levels (e.g., biological, psychological, social, and cultural) at which developmental processes take place (Cicchetti, 1993), suggesting that mutually reciprocal transactions between youth and their environments continuously shape pathways toward adaptation and maladaptation (Sameroff, 2000). The developmental psychopathology perspective encapsulates ideas about evolution and change – of individuals, their external environments, and the interactions between them – and it is essential to return to such seminal theories as we consider the intersection of digital media and adolescent mental health.

Yet digital media represents a paradigm shift of magnitude not previously encountered since the introduction of the developmental psychopathology approach. Digital media challenges our traditional ideas about environmental contexts (Nesi et al., 2018a, 2018b). Social media, for example, may be considered a unique social-developmental context within which adolescents are embedded. Yet given the nature of social media, prior work suggests that youth also co-construct this context, designing it in such a way as to meet their needs, values, and desires (Subrahmanyam & Greenfield, 2008; Subrahmanyam et al., 2006). Furthermore, digital media integrates aspects of many other external contexts – from the macro (i.e., cultural and mass media influences) to the micro (i.e., dyadic social interactions), and often represents a melding of various contexts. The degree to which these overlapping contexts are influencing youth during a given use of digital media – and the degree to which youth themselves are alternatively shaping these contexts – is not always clear. As research progresses in the area of digital media use and adolescent mental health, investigators must aim to draw on existing theoretical frameworks that may inform this work, while also working to build on and adapt these frameworks to account for the changing digital world in which contemporary adolescents are living. In this handbook, we aim to strike this balance, using the developmental psychopathology perspective as our guiding framework.

Part I of the volume begins with a consideration of theoretical perspectives from the fields of developmental psychology, media effects, and communications, with Chapter 1 (Subrahmanyam & Michikyan) and Chapter 2 (Valkenburg) each building on these historical perspectives to offer innovative new theoretical approaches that begin to account for the complexity of the digital media environment. In line with developmental psychopathology perspectives, Part II examines relevant developmental processes and mechanisms at various levels of analysis, including cultural, systemic, biological, and social factors. Part III examines potential risks and benefits of digital media for a range of adolescent mental disorders, and examines factors that may mitigate or exacerbate these influences. Finally, Part IV concludes with a brief consideration of mental health intervention and prevention efforts in the digital age.

Developmental psychopathology is an interdisciplinary approach, and to thoroughly understand the role of digital media in adolescent mental health requires integrating perspectives from multiple fields. In this volume, we bring together experts from a range of disciplines, including clinical, developmental and social psychology, neuroscience, medicine, communications, and media studies. As such, the volume aims to synthesize and advance research on this topic, appealing to scholars, educators, and students across a range of fields.

Research in the Digital Age

Change has characterized not only the topics of consideration in this handbook, but also the larger research landscape surrounding the investigation of these topics. The body of research on the topic of adolescent digital media use and mental health has grown exponentially in recent years. A search of the key term "social media" in APA PsycInfo in June of 2021 reveals 20,551 academic journal articles. Remarkably, nearly one-quarter of these have been published since 2019, nearly one-half in the last five years, and over 85% in just the past ten years. As the digital media landscape has transformed youths' lives rapidly and dramatically, the topic has evoked intense emotions among the general public, the media, and the research community. As change often does, the topic has alternatively engendered excitement, curiosity, and fear. Heated debates have arisen over the risks – or lack thereof – of youths' "screen time." Researchers have both urgently warned against the dangers of the digital world and have lauded the potential for digital media to solve a variety of societal ills.

At the same time, the methods and tools that research has brought to bear on this topic have also evolved. From retrospective self-reports, to daily ecological momentary assessments, to passive sensing technologies, to innovative experimental paradigms, numerous tools are now readily available to researchers aiming to answer questions about digital media and youth mental health. Investigators themselves increasingly turn to social media – Twitter, ResearchGate, even TikTok – to share their recent findings and connect with the scientific community, no doubt a factor in increasing calls for scientific transparency and public accessibility. And as the field progresses, the newest generation of scientists can themselves be considered "digital natives."

There has never been a more urgent need to synthesize what is known about digital media and adolescent mental health – to make sense of an evolving landscape and provide a roadmap for the future of the field. The authors of the chapters of this handbook – representing the leading voices on this topic – do just that. Despite the challenges inherent in such a rapidly changing field, so too does such challenge offer an opportunity for growth. The message of the authors in this handbook is one of progress – toward identifying the mechanisms by which digital media use impacts youths' well-being, toward innovation in research methodology to understand these mechanisms, and, ultimately, toward supporting and improving the mental health of youth living in the digital age.

References

Carr, C. T., & Hayes, R. A. (2015). Social media: Defining, developing, and divining. *Atlantic Journal of Communication, 23*(1), 46–65. https://doi.org/10.1080/15456870.2015.972282

Cicchetti, D. (1993). Developmental psychopathology: Reactions, reflections, projections. *Developmental Review, 13*(4), 471–502. https://doi.org/10.1006/drev.1993.1021

Nesi, J., Choukas-Bradley, S., & Prinstein, M. J. (2018a). Transformation of adolescent peer relations in the social media context: Part 1 – A theoretical framework and application to dyadic peer relationships. *Clinical Child and Family Psychology Review, 21*(3), 267–294. https://doi.org/10.1007/s10567-018-0261-x

Nesi, J., Choukas-Bradley, S., & Prinstein, M. J. (2018b). Transformation of adolescent peer relations in the social media context: Part 2 – Application to peer group processes and future directions for research. *Clinical Child and Family Psychology Review, 21*(3), 295–319. https://doi.org/10.1007/s10567-018-0262-9

Sameroff, A. J. (2000). Developmental systems and psychopathology. *Development and Psychopathology, 12*(3), 297–312. https://doi.org/10.1017/S0954579400003035

Subrahmanyam, K., & Greenfield, P. M. (2008). Online communication and adolescent relationships. *The Future of Children, 18*(1), 119–146. https://doi.org/10.1353/foc.0.0006

Subrahmanyam, K., Šmahel, D., & Greenfield, P. M. (2006). Connecting developmental constructions to the internet: Identity presentation and sexual exploration in online teen chat rooms. *Developmental Psychology, 42*(3), 395–406. https://doi.org/10.1037/0012-1649.42.3.395

PART I

Theoretical and Methodological Foundations in Digital Media Research and Adolescent Mental Health

1 Methodological and Conceptual Issues in Digital Media Research

Kaveri Subrahmanyam and Minas Michikyan

Decades of research on adolescence has demonstrated that contexts such as families, peer groups, schools, and neighborhoods play an important role in adolescent development (Petersen, 1993; Steinberg & Morris, 2001). To these well-accepted contextual influences, we should add media – both mass media (e.g., television, films, and music) as well as new digital media, which include the Internet (e.g., websites, online forums and communities, and video- and image- sharing platforms), communication applications/platforms (e.g., social media and messaging apps), and electronic games. Survey data suggest that digital media have become ubiquitous in young people's lives (Anderson & Jiang, 2018; Rideout & Robb, 2019); of particular note is that a majority of US adolescents now have access to a computer or smartphone, with 95% reporting access to a smartphone and 45% reporting that they are online almost all the time (Anderson & Jiang, 2018).

Research to date suggests that adolescents primarily use digital media for information, communication, and entertainment, with peer interaction and communication becoming especially popular (Anderson & Jiang, 2018; Subrahmanyam & Greenfield, 2008; Valkenburg & Peter, 2011). In prior work, we have suggested that new digital worlds should be considered an important developmental context during adolescence (Subrahmanyam & Šmahel, 2011; Subrahmanyam et al., 2006). Not only are digital media an important social context, but they have also become instrumental in adolescents' interactions with other key contexts such as friends and families. Relationships with friends and families are predictive of health and well-being during adolescence (Moore et al., 2018) and it is important to understand the impact of youths' digital media use on their psychological well-being and mental health.[1] This handbook brings together the multidisciplinary scholarship on adolescent social media use and mental health, and critically evaluates the extant research to provide a blueprint for future research. In this introductory chapter, we first provide an overview of the definitions and terminology related to digital media and social media, an overview of adolescents' digital media use at the time of this writing, and a brief historical account of the study of adolescents' social media use. In the second part of the chapter, we describe some of the key methodological and conceptual issues pertaining to adolescent digital media use research.

Overview of Definitions and Terminology

When reviewing the literature on new digital media, one sees a confusing array of terminology and labels with little consistency in how the terms are used. Thus, it is important to begin by defining the terminology that will be used in this chapter and more *generally in this handbook*. At the most general level, the term mass media is used to refer to legacy media forms such as television, films, and music, where the communication is "one-to-many"; in other words, a media producer creates the content, which is then consumed by many people, often using specific hardware (e.g., television set, boombox, record player). In contrast to mass media are new media, also called interactive media, screen media, or digital media, the term used in the title of this book. Although there are many definitions of interactive media, we adopt the one proposed by England and Finney (2002) that states: "interactive media is the integration of digital media including combinations of electronic text, graphics, moving images, and sound, into a structured digital computerised environment that allows people to interact with the data for appropriate purposes" (p. 2). There are two key elements to note in this definition of interactive media – first is that the user interacts with the electronic data to construct and co-construct the content; second, the digital environment includes a variety of hardware components (e.g., computers, mobile devices, smartphones) and software platforms (operating systems, internet browsers, and specialized applications/apps).

The term digital media is a broad umbrella term for a variety of media forms including electronic/video games, online messaging, social media, and other digital communication applications/digital tools. Social media are the primary focus of this book and we adopt the definition put forth by Carr and Hayes (2015): "Social media are Internet-based channels that allow users to opportunistically interact and selectively self-present, either in real-time or asynchronously, with both broad and narrow audiences who derive value from user-generated content and the perception of interaction with others" (p. 51). As clarified by Nesi, Prinstein, and Telzer (see the Introduction to this volume), "We define this to include social networking sites (e.g., Instagram, Snapchat, WeChat, and Facebook), messaging tools (e.g., text messaging and messaging apps), online forums and communities, video- and image-sharing platforms (e.g., YouTube and TikTok), and video games with a social component." In this chapter, we use the terms social media and digital media interchangeably.

Overview of Adolescents' Digital Media Use

Adolescent respondents to the 2019 Common Sense Census reported an average of 7 hours and 22 minutes of daily screen use that was not for school or homework; furthermore, they reported spending 39% of their screen time watching TV/videos, 22% of their time on gaming, 16% on social media, and 8% browsing websites (Rideout & Robb, 2019). Among the adolescent respondents in the 2018 Pew report, YouTube (85%), Instagram (72%), and Snapchat (69%) were the most popular online platforms, and only 51% reported that they used Facebook (Anderson & Jiang, 2018). According to a 2021 Pew report, TikTok is gaining popularity among younger social media users – 55% of its users are between the ages of 18 and 24 (Auxier & Anderson, 2021. Overall, the survey data suggest that adolescents spend a considerable portion of their day with screen media.

History of the Study of Adolescents' Social Media Use

In this section, we present a brief historical account of the study of adolescents' use of digital media, including social media. The Internet as we know it has only been used widely by youth for about a decade and a half, and so it might seem strange to use a "historical lens" to describe research on it. Nonetheless, the lessons learned from examining the historical context and arc of the extant body of work can help researchers adapt to the changes in social media that are inevitable in the years to come. Research on youth digital media use has been conducted by scholars coming from a range of disciplinary traditions including psychology, communication studies, media studies, education, computer science, and human–computer interaction.

The disciplines of psychology and developmental psychology / developmental science were slow to recognize the growing importance of digital media in the lives of children and adolescents. Researchers who first worked in this area (Subrahmanyam & Manago, 2012) found it challenging to publish in mainstream journals in the field unless the papers were part of a special issue or a special collection (Greenfield et al., 2012; Greenfield & Yan, 2006; Michikyan & Suárez-Orozco, 2016; Subrahmanyam & Greenfield, 2008; Yan & Hardell, 2018). In fact, it was not until 2016 that the Society for Research in Child Development hosted its first special topics conference on the role of technology in child development. The constantly changing and fluid nature of the digital landscape presents unique methodological challenges to digital media researchers, and we address them in a later section. For ease of communication, we divide research on adolescents' social media use into three phases. The first phase of research focuses on the use of the Internet and on early online communication contexts such as text-based chat rooms, bulletin boards, and blogs. The second phase investigates the first generation of digital media platforms, which were referred to as "social networking sites" in the literature. The third phase encompasses research on the social media platforms/applications that are in vogue at the time of writing this chapter.

The First Phase: Research on Internet Use and Early Online Communication Contexts

The Internet became available to the public in 1991, and we see survey reports and journal articles on youths' internet use starting around the late 1990s and early 2000s (Finkelhor et al., 2000; Kraut et al., 1998; Roberts et al., 1999; Sanders et al., 2000; Stahl & Fritz, 2002; Subrahmanyam et al., 2001; Turow, 1999). Given the novelty of the Internet and that youth were among the early adopters of it, studies generally focused on two questions – what youth did online (Roberts et al., 1999; Turow, 1999) and how their internet use related to their safety and psychological well-being (Kraut et al., 1998; Sanders et al., 2000; Stahl & Fritz, 2002; Subrahmanyam et al., 2001). The majority of studies used self-report survey designs and showed that from the very beginning, youth who had access to the Internet used it for communication, with popular applications including email and chat rooms (Turow, 1999).

Each new media technology such as radio, film, and television has been greeted by concerns about its negative effects on youth (Wartella & Jennings, 2000; Wartella & Robb, 2009), and the Internet was no different. Early concerns centered on risky behaviors related to visiting problematic content (e.g., pornography), having contact with strangers, inappropriate/unsafe interactions (e.g., sexual solicitation, threatening or harassing contact) (e.g., Finkelhor et al., 2000; Stahl & Fritz, 2002), and psychological well-being (Kraut et al., 1998; Sanders et al., 2000). The latter concern stemmed from two related elements of youths' internet use at that time – first, computer-mediated interactions were text-based, and users were disembodied, so they did not have access to face-to-face cues such as gaze, gestures, emotional tone, and body language. Thus, online interactions were perceived to be lower in quality. Additionally, internet use was not very diffuse and so youths' online interactions mostly occurred with strangers and others from outside their offline social networks. Given these elements of youths' online interactions, the concern was that lower quality online interactions with strangers were displacing/replacing higher quality face-to-face interactions with friends and acquaintances; thus, early scholarship examined the implications of adolescents' internet use for social isolation, loneliness, and depression. A detailed description of this research is beyond the scope of this chapter, and the interested reader is referred to the papers above and a monograph on digital youth coauthored by the first author (Subrahmanyam & Šmahel, 2011).

This body of work suggested that the relation between internet use and psychological well-being was complex with contradictory results. For instance, the HomeNet study, a longitudinal field study conducted in Pittsburgh between 1995 and 1998 (Kraut et al., 1996, 1998) found that during the first two years of the study, increased time spent online was associated with declines in well-being (social involvement, loneliness, and depression). However, in the third year of the study, internet use was associated with smaller declines and even reversals (i.e., improvements) in well-being (Subrahmanyam et al., 2001). The HomeNet study was unique in that a diverse sample of 93 families (208 adults and 110 children and adolescents) were given computers and internet access in 1995. They were then surveyed on several measures and their online activities were automatically recorded whenever they went online. The seminal study was conducted at a time when people had little exposure to technology, and thus the researchers were able to get a detailed picture of youths' online activities and well-being from their first exposure to this technology and for a short period of time thereafter. Despite the study's contradictory findings, the appeal of online settings for youth was clear – a 16-year-old HomeNet participant declared, "I really want to move to Antarctica – I'd want my cat and Internet access and I'd be happy." The HomeNet study was conducted in 1995 – not much seems to have changed in that regard since that time!

Other studies in the first phase of research were more qualitative and focused on obtaining a rich picture of what adolescents and emerging adults (college students) were doing online (Greenfield & Subrahmanyam, 2003; Turkle, 1995a). Recall that youth were among the early adopters of the most common communication venues of that era, including internet relay chat rooms, multiuser dungeons (MUDs), and the commercially available chat rooms hosted by AOL, Yahoo, and instant messaging (also hosted by AOL). These spaces were significantly different from the social media apps were available when this chapter was written. They were text-based, accessed via computers and low-speed internet, and users were disembodied and largely anonymous (Subrahmanyam & Šmahel, 2011).

Adult researchers were not using these venues, and thus were unfamiliar with the text-based language and code that digital media users were constructing and coconstructing within them; using qualitative methods from a variety of disciplines including ethnography, participant observation, and discourse analysis, these researchers provided a rich picture of the structure, content, modes of online communication, and youth subculture that was emerging within new online venues such as MUDS, chat rooms, blogs, bulletin boards, and webpages (Greenfield & Subrahmanyam, 2003; Huffaker & Calvert, 2005; Šmahel & Subrahmanyam, 2007; Subrahmanyam et al., 2004; Suzuki & Calzo, 2004). These studies provided a window into adolescents' emerging online lives and showed that youth used these spaces in the service of core developmental issues, including identity exploration, intimacy, health, and sexuality. Whereas youths' online lives were psychologically connected to their offline counterparts, they were not mirror images of each other. Given the features of new online environments such as anonymity, disembodiedness, and lack of face-to-face cues, youths' communication within them was often exaggerated and were observed with new intensities (Šmahel & Subrahmanyam, 2007; Subrahmanyam, 2007). For instance, within online chat rooms, there was one sexual comment per minute, and one obscene comment every two minutes (Subrahmanyam et al., 2006).

The Second and Third Phase: Research on Digital Communication Tools from Social Networking Sites to Social Media Apps

The next wave of online communication tools included the now defunct MySpace and Friendster, as well as Facebook. They were the first generation of social networking sites and were introduced in the early to mid-2000s. Social network sites were defined by boyd and Ellison (2007) as "web-based services that allow individuals to (1) construct a public or semi-public profile within a bounded system, (2) articulate a list of other users with whom they share a connection, and (3) view and traverse their list of connections and those made by others within the system" (p. 211). For a detailed history of social networking sites, we refer the reader to boyd and Ellison's 2007 article published in the special volume of the *Journal of Computer-Mediated Communication*, which was the first collection of research on social networking sites. Since then, there have been dramatic advances in hardware (e.g., smartphones and tablets), software, and internet access (e.g., high speed Wi-Fi), and the term "social media" has come to replace the term "social networking sites." It is difficult to pinpoint who coined the term social media and when it began to be used in popular culture (Bercovici, 2010). As noted earlier, this handbook uses the term social media to refer to digital tools that can be used for social interaction and selective self-presentation.

Compared to the early text-based online communication tools, social networking sites and social media apps are multimodal and allow users to interact and communicate via text, images, audio, and video. They make it possible to have both private and public interactions, and they vary in the extent to which users are disembodied and anonymous (Subrahmanyam & Greenfield, 2008). As access to the Internet and mobile devices became widespread, users were also more likely to interact with people they knew from their offline lives. In contrast to the earlier generation of online venues, where youth primarily interacted with people they met online, research revealed that youth used social networking sites and then social media platforms/applications to interact and make plans with friends from their offline lives and to keep in touch with peers they were not able to meet in person (Pempek et al., 2009; Subrahmanyam et al., 2008). Social media platforms also allowed users to easily engage in self-expression and self-presentation via text and audiovisual content such as status updates, emojis, pictures and videos (Manago et al., 2008; Michikyan & Subrahmanyam, 2012).

As found in the first studies of online communication venues, youths' offline and online social media lives were psychologically connected; online behaviors were again exaggerated, with youth reporting wider online networks (Manago et al., 2012). Given many adolescents' 24/7 access to social media and, by extension, their immersion in elevated levels of peer interaction, self-disclosure, and self-presentation, research has examined the implications of social media use for the intrapersonal need for identity and the interpersonal need for intimacy as well as for psychological well-being. The chapters of this handbook will give the reader a detailed picture of the theoretical and empirical scholarship related to adolescents' use of social media and their mental health. In the remaining part of this chapter, we draw on lessons learned from the extant research on youths' use of social media to identify methodological challenges and conceptual issues pertaining to adolescent digital media use research.

Methodological Challenges in Adolescent Digital Media Research

New online contexts presented many unique challenges to researchers when they burst on the scene and adolescents flocked to them. Researchers have now become adept with technology and are social media users themselves; in fact, within their ranks are those who are referred to as digital natives – or individuals who have grown up with technology their entire lives (Prensky, 2001). Here we examine some of the key methodological challenges confronting researchers who seek to investigate the implications of youths' digital media use. As before, we use a historical lens, as it helps to illustrate both the challenges that researchers faced and will continue to face.

Fluid Digital Media Landscape

The fluid nature of technology and rapid pace of change has always been an intrinsic element of the digital media landscape. During the first phase of digital media research, researchers not only had to contend with changes in hardware, but also in internet speed, software, and communication applications, and widening of users to include both strangers as well as friends and acquaintances. Additionally, there were constant shifts in the communication applications that were popular among adolescents at any given time, and changes in the features and elements within applications. MySpace, which was at one time a favored social networking site, was eventually supplanted by Facebook. There were also constant changes in elements of social media apps such as the top 8 list in MySpace or the Like button on Facebook. Rapid change in technology and rates of adoption also meant that there were changes in who was online. As noted earlier, initially youth mostly interacted online with strangers, including adults and peers who they did not know from their offline lives. Subsequently, as technology became more diffuse and widespread, more of their peers were online. Simultaneously there was an explosion in the popularity of more private and closed systems via social networking sites, within which people created profiles and chose who they interacted with and who could see the information they shared on their profiles. They were thus more likely to interact online with peers from their offline lives.

Perhaps the most challenging issue was how frequently changes occurred – there was often a lag between when a digital media platform emerged and gained popularity and when researchers began to investigate its use in earnest. In some cases, researchers found themselves investigating a platform that was no longer in vogue, as youth had moved on to the next new context that had appeared on the digital scene. This fluidity of digital platforms is particularly challenging for longitudinal studies as it complicates comparisons between different waves of data. Logistically, this meant that researchers had to focus broadly on a category of applications (e.g., chat rooms or social networking sites) and not target specific applications (e.g., AOL chat rooms, MySpace, or Facebook). This is also the approach adopted in this handbook. Given the fundamentally transient nature of digital platforms, even focusing on application categories does not ensure continued relevance after a platform's eventual demise; so, we used a developmental lens for our early studies and focused on developmental tasks including identity, sexuality, and intimacy. Such a developmental approach ensures that study results are relevant long after the shelf life of a particular digital media platform or category of platforms/applications. An additional approach to ensure the continued relevance of research on an application is to focus on elements or features of digital platforms and the activities that they support. This issue also relates to conceptual considerations and is discussed in further detail in the latter part of this chapter.

A related methodological challenge that arose in early digital media studies was that each new platform had different communication features or capabilities. From the earliest studies of online communication, communication scholars interested in computer-mediated communication investigated how communicative cues in online settings shape interaction within them (Culnan & Markus, 1987; Walther, 1992). Subsequently, drawing from this body of work and Gibson's notion of affordances in the context of object perception (Gibson, 1979), the term media affordances (Hutchby, 2001) has been used to refer to the qualities of different digital platforms, including mobile phones and social media (boyd, 2011; Ellison & Vitak, 2015; Reid & Reid, 2007; Subrahmanyam & Šmahel, 2011; Treem & Leonardi, 2013). Because different platforms have different affordances, it is important for researchers to be flexible and use different approaches when studying youths' use of these technologies.

In our own work at the Children's Digital Media Center @ Los Angeles, techniques from discourse analysis and participant observation were adapted to investigate how adolescent digital media users utilize the communication cues available in online chat rooms to construct and co-construct conversational coherence (Greenfield & Subrahmanyam, 2003; Subrahmanyam & Manago, 2012) in the service of key developmental tasks such as identity and sexuality (Subrahmanyam et al., 2004). These studies were qualitative in design and used a single chat transcript to analyze the online culture that adolescent digital media users were co-constructing. Subsequent studies utilized a combination of qualitative and quantitative analysis to examine a larger number of utterances in chat rooms as well posts on online blogs (Subrahmanyam et al., 2006, 2009). When social networking sites and text messaging became popular and youths' digital communication occurred in private spaces, we shifted to self-report measures and adapted techniques from social network analysis (Reich et al., 2012; Subrahmanyam et al., 2008), mixed-method (Michikyan, 2019; Michikyan et al., 2015), and daily diary (Subrahmanyam et al., 2020) designs to better investigate the developmental implications of youths' digital media use for their well-being. Thus, it is important for researchers investigating youths' social media to be flexible and adapt their methodological and analytical approaches based on an analysis of the digital media platform's affordances, how youth use it, and its potential mental health implications.

Measuring Digital Media Use

Researchers investigating youths' digital media use must make decisions about how they measure usage and the research designs they adopt. These decisions have methodological as well as conceptual implications, and in this section, we address them from a methodological perspective. Using the "historical lens" that we have adopted heretofore in this chapter, we see that from the earliest studies of youths' internet use and continuing into extant social media apps, amount of time spent online has been researchers' favored measure of operationalizing social media usage. This was influenced by prior research on mass media such as television, and research on the first generation of electronic media, including computers and games, when computers were often in common spaces and shared among members of the family. Thus, it was reasonable that digital media users would be able to estimate the time they spent on average during a given period (day or week). With youths' widespread access to mobile technologies and high-speed internet, the issue of time use has become considerably complicated. As with all retrospective self-report measures, internet time use measures are susceptible to inaccurate/distorted/biased estimates (Parry et al., 2021; Scharkow, 2016). An alternative way of obtaining an estimate is to use software to automatically record internet use, as in the HomeNet study; however, given that multitasking with multiple windows on a screen or with multiple devices is ubiquitous, it is important to distinguish between open/active windows and applications to which a user may or may not actually be paying attention.

Another approach to studying digital media use is by analyzing the actual content of digital communication. In fact, this was the method by which researchers analyzed conversation in the first generation of digital media platforms such as online teen chat rooms, blogs, and bulletin boards

(Subrahmanyam et al., 2006, 2009; Suzuki & Calzo, 2004). These applications were publicly available and so accessing the content was relatively easy for researchers. As the digital landscape moved toward closed networks with private (e.g., private messaging on Facebook, direct messaging on Twitter, private messaging on smartphones) and public communication (e.g., Facebook wall, publicly available tweets), researchers deployed automatic means to capture the content of youths' digital communication (Negriff, 2019; Underwood et al., 2012). Underwood et al. (2012) pioneered this technique by providing adolescent participants in a longitudinal study with BlackBerry devices and automatically recording text messages and other contents of their private communication. While this approach provides an unfiltered window into adolescents' digital worlds, it is logistically challenging, as it provides a vast amount of data that then has to be analyzed by researchers, machine learning models, or a combination of the two (Dinakar et al., 2014). The biggest concern of this approach, of course, is that the analytical technique – whether human or machine – may impute intentions, emotions, biases, and motives that were not intended by the social media user.

While there is no easy remedy for the measurement challenges outlined above, some possible solutions are briefly described next. This is not intended to be an exhaustive list, but to provide a selective sampling to illustrate how to approach measurement of youths' social media use. First, researchers should consider a mixed-methods design to capture users' intentions; in one study on online self-presentation, we asked participants to describe a picture they posted, and their identity-related meaning making was coded and then quantitatively analyzed. Note that codes were based on participants' own descriptions of the picture and their reasons for posting instead of the researchers trying to deconstruct the image and post (Michikyan et al., 2015). Second, we encourage researchers to consider daily diary designs and ecological momentary assessment techniques to get more accurate estimates of users' social media use and activities over several days at a time. Daily diary studies have been used extensively in social psychology to study frequent everyday interactions (Bolger et al., 2003); at the end of each day, participants are asked to report on their interactions that day and about other variables such as well-being, conflict, etc. In the experience sampling method, participants are asked to self-report what they are doing, feeling, and thinking at random points during times they are awake (Larson & Csikszentmihalyi, 2014). In both methods, participants report about their social media use when it is fresh in their mind, helping to limit memory distortions that are more likely when asked to estimate or recall use and activities on average. Both designs have the added advantage of yielding multiple data points over time, which are essential to address key questions regarding the longer-term implications of social media use and for the examination of within-person effects (Gonzales, 2014; Jelenchick et al., 2013; Kross et al., 2013; Pouwels et al., 2021; Subrahmanyam et al., 2020).

Finding Equivalent Comparison Groups

A final methodological challenge stems from the widespread use of social media among adolescents. Typically, when studying the influence or impact of a variable, psychologists compare groups of people with varying levels of the variable in question. This is true whether the comparison group is naturally occurring in a correlational or descriptive study (e.g., coffee drinkers and nondrinkers, alcohol drinkers and nondrinkers, and video-game players and nonvideo-game players) or created by the experimenter's manipulation in an experimental design. Because digital media have become ubiquitous in adolescents' lives, it is virtually impossible to find a group of youth who do not use social media and are truly equivalent to a group of youth who use them, at least in the Global North. The lack of a naturally occurring control or comparison group is an intractable design challenge facing social media researchers, and correlational designs have dominated the literature to date. A few researchers have conducted clever experiments to test the effects of digital communication (Gross, 2009; Sherman et al., 2013, 2016; Vogel et al., 2015; Weinstein, 2017); given the dearth of such studies, there is an urgent need for more experimental designs to help unearth the mechanisms by which social media use shapes well-being.

Conceptual Considerations for Adolescent Digital Media Research

As the foregoing section demonstrates, the novelty, variability, and fluidity of the digital landscape presents methodological challenges for researchers investigating adolescents' digital media use. This section discusses some of the conceptual issues that should guide research on the implications of adolescents' social media use for their well-being.[2] Specifically, researchers examining youths' digital media use must make decisions about how they conceptualize and operationalize digital media usage. The following three conceptual considerations can help to guide researchers as they make these decisions:

(1) Conceptualizing the role of digital media in adolescent development and well-being: digital media as a developmental context.
(2) Conceptualizing youths' digital media usage: reimagining and operationalizing digital media use.
(3) Conceptualizing pathways between digital media usage and well-being: considering mediators and moderators.

Figure 1.1 presents a schematic of the conceptual considerations that researchers should keep in mind when studying adolescent digital media use and psychological well-being.

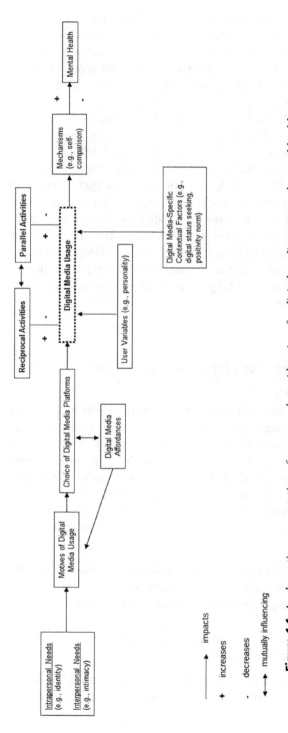

Figure 1.1 *A schematic representation of conceptual considerations for digital media usage and mental health*

Note: As indicated in the figure, intrapersonal needs and interpersonal needs drive adolescents' motives of digital media usage and impact their choice of digital media platforms. The selection of specific digital media platform and its affordances shape adolescents' use and motives as well as the levels and types of activities; these in turn influence the different mechanisms through which adolescents make meaning of their digital media use, impacting their psychological well-being and mental health. Individual factors as well as contextual factors both within and outside of the digital media context can influence digital media usage; only digital media-specific contextual factors (e.g., digital status seeking and positivity norm) are shown in the schematic.

20

Consider Digital Media as a Developmental Context

There is wide agreement in the literature that human behavior across developmental time can only be fully understood in context (Bronfenbrenner & Morris, 2006; Vygotsky, 1978). With regard to adolescent development, the role of contexts such as families, peer groups, schools, and neighborhoods has been well documented (Petersen, 1993; Steinberg & Morris, 2001), and as noted at the start of this chapter, digital media should be viewed as an important context in the lives of adolescents. Digital media broadly, and social media more specifically, are incredibly diverse, and a variety of applications are available, each with its own unique communication contexts and affordances. An important question is the extent to which researchers should focus on particular social media platforms in any study. As an example, consider the case of Twitter and Snapchat, which share similar features such as photo sharing, but also differ in their affordances and how they are used (Alhabash & Ma, 2017). From an affordances perspective (Treem & Leonardi, 2013), both social media platforms – Twitter and Snapchat – allow for *visibility* (i.e., the ability to make information about oneself, once fully or partly invisible, visible to others), *editability* (i.e., the ability to construct, reconstruct, and coconstruct the information intended to convey to others), and *association* (i.e., the ability to establish a relationship with others and with a specific content), but they differ in terms of *persistence* (i.e., the ability to access and review the information in its original form after the user has completed the communication or interaction). Empirical evidence also suggests that the specific digital media platform matters to the user in terms of *how* and *why* it is used (Alhabash & Ma, 2017; Madden et al., 2013; Utz et al., 2015); if it matters to the user, then it seems that it should matter to researchers' conceptualizations of digital media both when investigating and disseminating their results.

At the same time, social media platforms are adopting similar features – Snapchat Stories vs. Instagram Stories vs. Facebook Stories. What was once unique to Snapchat – the limited time feature – is no longer the case, as Instagram and Facebook now afford the ability to automatically vanish videos and images. The most recent trends – similarities across social media platforms and the emergence of newer platforms like TikTok – push us to consider whether and how we need to distinguish between the various social media platforms that youth use when investigating implications for development and well-being. Given how quickly digital media platforms evolve and the variety of affordances and activities possible on each platform, it is challenging for researchers to remain consistent in their conceptualization as the platforms themselves change. Perhaps one way to reconcile this conundrum – a lack of consistency in conceptualizing and operationalizing specific digital media platforms – is to be consistent in the recognition and articulation of digital media platforms as unique developmental contexts with specific affordances through which users influence and are influenced by the context (Subrahmanyam & Greenfield, 2008; Subrahmanyam et al., 2006).

Researchers should also be mindful of both the contextual factors outside of the digital world (e.g., race, socioeconomic status, immigration generation status) as well as within the specific social media context (i.e., implicit and explicit norms and expectations shared among users within a specific digital media context) (De Choudhury et al., 2017; Elsaesser et al., 2021; Michikyan & Suárez-Orozco, 2017; Nesi & Prinstein, 2019; Valkenburg & Peter, 2007). For brevity, we only discuss contextual factors within social media, and provide two examples to illustrate the potential role of social media–specific contextual factors that could shape psychological well-being and mental health. One example is the *positivity norm* found within many social media platforms, where the unspoken expectation is for users to engage in a set of behaviors in an attempt to put their best "face" forward (Qui et al., 2012). Another example is *digital status seeking* – wherein users engage in specific behaviors to obtain peer status (Nesi & Prinstein, 2019). These examples illustrate that just as researchers take into account key features of particular developmental contexts such as peer groups and schools, they should take into account the contextual characteristics of the specific digital media platform studied – including its affordances and unique cultural elements (e.g., positivity norm), even when such contextual characteristics may not be analytical variables. Taken together, these examples suggest that consistency in the recognition and articulation of digital media can provide a more complete understanding of digital media usage in the service of development and mental health.

Reimagine Digital Media Usage

Another critical issue concerns the conceptualization and operationalization of digital media *usage*. Digital media usage has been conceptualized and operationalized in myriad ways (see Kross et al., 2020; Schønning et al., 2020, for a review). Extant research has mostly operationalized digital media usage in terms of the extent to which users engage in different activities via digital platforms, for example through self-presentation and self-disclosure using social media and the frequency and time spent on these activities (e.g., Gil-Or, 2015; Manago et al., 2008; Masur & Scharkow, 2016; Michikyan, 2019; Michikyan, Dennis, & Subrahmanyam, 2014a; Michikyan et al., 2015; Qui et al., 2012; Twomey & O'Reilly, 2017; Wright et al., 2018). In the next subsections, we discuss the different ways that digital media usage has been operationalized and make recommendations for how usage can be conceptualized to study adolescent digital media use more accurately and meaningfully.

Digital Screen Time: As noted earlier in the methodological challenges section, digital screen time is frequently used in investigations of youths' digital media use, and as a retrospective self-report measure, it is susceptible to both over- and underreporting (Parry et al., 2021; Scharkow, 2016). Here we examine whether total digital screen time, on its own, is a meaningful and accurate measure of digital media usage as related to psychological well-being (see Meier & Gray, 2014; Orben & Przybylski, 2019a, for a similar argument). Scholars (e.g., Orben, 2020) have asked whether self-reported measures of digital screen time should be "retired." The arguments for retiring self-reported measures of total digital screen time seem valid given that the size of the negative effects of digital media use on mental health is either non-existent (Coyne et al., 2020) or too small to have a practical significance or to warrant a meaningful scientific debate (Orben & Przybylski, 2019b). In fact, some have argued that adolescent digital media users would need to spend a physically impossible amount of time using digital media – more than 63 hours per day – to experience noticeable decline in their well-being (see Orben & Przybylski, 2019a). While it might be premature to "retire" the concept of self-reported measures of digital screen time without more research, it is important to "reimagine" it. A more meaningful approach to conceptualizing and operationalizing digital screen time would be to combine – the amount of time + activity + specific time frame + motive of use – within a single item or question (e.g., "How much time did you spend today chatting with friends on Instagram to tell them about your problems and troubles?"). Doing so would increase the meaningfulness and accuracy of measuring digital screen time. Another possibility is to combine objective measures of screen time (e.g., via tracking apps) with objective measures of content or activity, and a subjective measure of motivation (see Subrahmanyam et al., 2020; Underwood et al., 2012). Future research should aim to tease apart the role of these different components – for instance, examining whether chatting with friends on Instagram about problems improves mental health when it happens for short durations of time, but undermines mental health when it happens for longer periods of time. Taken together, it appears that it might not the amount of digital screen time in and of itself that matters for psychological well-being, but rather, how adolescents use their time engaging with digital media.

Digital Activities: Social media platforms afford users a range of possible digital activities, and there is empirical evidence that different activities may differentially impact psychological well-being (Kross et al., 2020). For instance, digital activities that involve interacting with existing friends via text messaging can enhance well-being (Valkenburg & Peter, 2007), because certain features of text-based content may serve as "digital affiliative cues" that can facilitate emotional bonding (Sherman et al., 2013). Similarly, digital activities that involve visual cues or image-based content (e.g., photos) can also enhance well-being by decreasing loneliness and by increasing happiness and life satisfaction (Pittman & Reich, 2016), likely because photos can foster increased social connectedness (Bakhshi et al., 2014; Goh et al., 2009); it is worth noting that image-based content can also negatively impact well-being by increasing social comparisons, particularly those focused on appearance and body image (e.g., Lewallen & Behm-Morawitz, 2016).

Other aspects of digital media activities that are relevant in adolescent social media use research are the *type of activity* and *level of interactivity* – or exchanges between users and between users and specific digital media features (see Stromer-Galley, 2004, for a detailed argument). Research examining youths' digital media usage and psychological well-being has focused on the distinction between two types of social activities: "active" use vs. "passive" use (Kross et al., 2020; Schønning et al., 2020); "active" use (e.g., commenting on or responding to someone else's content) has been found to enhance well-being (Escobar-Viera et al., 2018; Liu et al., 2019), whereas "passive" use (e.g., reading comments or newsfeeds of hundreds of friends and followers without any participation or lurking) has been found to undermine psychological well-being (Escobar-Viera et al., 2018; Tandoc et al., 2015; Underwood & Ehrenreich, 2017).

Although the terms "active" and "passive" capture some aspects of social media use that are relevant to mental health and well-being, other aspects of use are not captured by these terms. Consider one example of self-presentation via posting photos, which is considered an "active" use of digital media (Wang et al., 2017). Missing from the current conceptualization of "active" digital media usage, however, is whether and how *interactive* "active" usage is. For instance, when a user posts a picture, does the self-presentation occur during an interaction with other users, or does the user engage in self-presentation outside of an interaction, as a result of an exchange between the user and specific digital media features, or some combination of both? The current conceptualization of "passive" digital media usage places significant emphasis on content consumption with minimum interactivity (e.g., lurking) (Underwood & Ehrenreich, 2017). Even with content consumption, "passive" activities such as viewing humorous or inspiring social media content might improve mood and well-being. An important question is how passive "passive" digital media usage is. Is reading someone else's comments *really* passive?

This begs the question of what "active" use and "passive" use in the current paradigm *really* capture (Valkenburg et al., 2021). It appears that the active- vs. passive-use paradigm emphasizes the *behavioral* component of digital media usage, while mostly ignoring its *cognitive* and *affective* components. A focus on the behavioral component of digital media usage assumes that "passive" use (e.g., lurking) is psychologically passive. Drawing from Bandura that "a theory that denies that thoughts can regulate actions does not lend itself readily to the explanation of complex human behavior" (Bandura, 1986, p. 15), we reject the premise that digital media usage is passive. Even "passive" digital media usage wherein the user chooses to observe other users' activities online without any participation (e.g., reading someone else's comments) involves some level of psychological activity (e.g., encoding, interpretation, and processing) (see Sherman et al., 2018; see also Bandura, 1997). Instead, we propose that digital media usage be viewed on an interactivity continuum with exchanges between users and between users and specific digital media features (Stromer-Galley, 2004). In this conceptualization of digital media usage, digital activities are assumed to be inherently active, although the level of interactivity might vary. Drawing from the developmental literature on peer interactions (Rubin et al., 2006), the terms *reciprocal activities* and *parallel activities* may better capture the distinction between different kinds of social media activities that are relevant to mental health and well-being.

Reciprocal activities involve exchanges via digital media platforms wherein users can take turns to respond and react to one another (e.g., texting, chatting, commenting on another user's post, liking another user's photo, etc.). Parallel activities involve actions via digital media platforms that do not engage other users in a particular exchange, or actions that do not involve reciprocity or response from other users (posting a status, a comment, or a photo to express one's thoughts and feelings, watching a video/film, etc.). Reciprocal and parallel activities vary across the interactivity continuum, with reciprocal activities at the high end of the interactivity continuum and parallel activities at the low end. Given the complexity of digital media usage, reciprocal activities and parallel activities may also be dynamic – influencing one another and at varying levels of intensity. For instance, a user can engage in both high or low levels of reciprocal *and* parallel activities simultaneously (e.g., texting while reading someone else's comment, or posting more than one photo and chatting with one or more persons at the same time). This distinction is one possibility and not intended to comprehensively capture all aspects of digital/social media activities. Another distinction proposed in the research is between content creation, production, and consumption (see Schønning et al., 2020); content curation and/or content distribution are increasingly important aspects of social media use. The point here is that when considering social media usage, researchers must capture the nuances when conceptualizing digital activities. The continuum of parallel to reciprocal activities can help as it can capture both the level and the characteristic of digital media usage – whether and how actively the user is interacting with others online and/or whether and how actively the user is "interacting" with a digital media platform and with themselves.

Consider a Variety of Mechanisms and User Variables as Mediators and Moderators

As noted elsewhere in the literature (Beyens et al., 2020; Subrahmanyam et al., 2020) and in this handbook, extant research on the relation between adolescent digital media use and psychological well-being has revealed no clear or consistent patterns, suggesting that the relation is complex. Thus, it is important for researchers to also consider underlying mechanisms as well as individual factors that may shape the pathways between digital media usage and mental health.

Possible Mechanisms: Digital media usage has been linked with different mechanisms that can either enhance or undermine mental health and well-being (Escobar-Viera et al., 2018; Yoon et al., 2019). For instance, researchers have demonstrated that specific digital activities (e.g., reading someone else's comments without any participation), on the one hand, can undermine well-being through upward social comparison (i.e., comparing oneself with someone better off than oneself), negative self-evaluation (Wang et al., 2017), and rumination (Feinstein et al., 2013), as well as through feelings of envy (Appel et al., 2015) and fear of missing out (Oberst et al., 2017; Przybylski et al., 2013). On the other hand, digital activities wherein users peruse their own photos on social media might also improve psychological well-being through self-affirmation (see Toma & Hancock, 2013) and perhaps through downward comparison (i.e., comparing oneself with someone worse off than oneself).

Depending on the type of self-comparison, social media users may experience decreases or increases in their mental health and well-being. Not only do people compare themselves with others, but they also compare their "current self" with their "past self" and generally view themselves as improving over the years, despite how illusory this view may be (M. Ross & Wilson, 2003). Applying this to digital media usage, it is to be expected that users who engage in downward comparison (i.e., viewing the current self as better than the past self when comparing recent online photos with the earlier photos) may experience increases in their mental health. Although it remains to be seen, the effects of downward comparison may be of even greater significance for adolescent digital media users who are undergoing the task of developing a personal fable (Elkind, 1967; Erikson, 1959; Granic et al., 2020a, 2020b).

Possible User Variables: Examining user variables that may moderate the pathway between social media usage and well-being can also yield more nuanced insights about the ways that digital media use can enhance or undermine mental health. As an example, we focus on one variable, personality, to illustrate why researchers should consider individual factors as moderators and mediators when studying the relation between digital media usage and psychological well-being and mental health (Ehrenberg et al., 2008; Kircaburun et al., 2020; Michikyan et al., 2015; C. Ross et al., 2009). Other potential moderators identified in prior research include age and gender (Booker et al., 2018; Correa et al., 2010; Simoncic et al., 2014), offline support (Hatchel et al., 2019), and social anxiety (Hatchel et al., 2018; Subrahmanyam et al., 2020).

Personality can be defined as a collection of generally stable characteristics that define the self across time and context (Zuckerman, 1991) – including traits such as extroversion, introversion, neuroticism, and openness to new experiences (Costa & McCrae, 2008). Social media users who are extroverted (e.g., outgoing, talkative) and who are open to new experiences (reflecting curiosity and novelty-seeking) appear to engage in self-enhancing digital activities (e.g., via posting selfies) (Sorokowska et al., 2016, Zywica & Danowski, 2008), which can further enhance their interpersonal skills and psychological well-being. However, even among extroverts, users who are also experiencing psychological well-being concerns (e.g., lower life satisfaction) may be prone to problematic social media use such as addiction (Nikbin et al., 2020).

Like their extroverted peers, introverted users who are shy or less outgoing and users who are moody (indicative of high neuroticism) also benefit from using social media (Simoncic et al., 2014); however, these groups of users appear to utilize social media to compensate for a lack of offline social networks and a lack of confidence in their interpersonal skills (Ehrenberg et al., 2008; C. Ross et al., 2009). Since neuroticism can be manifested as loneliness and anxiety (Cattell & Mead, 2008), it is also not uncommon for social media users with high trait neuroticism to engage in frequent parallel activities involving self-presentation (e.g., posting comments and photos) (C. Ross et al., 2009), which tend to be more elaborate (Bai et al., 2012), more negative (Kern et al., 2014), and more socially desirable and less truthful (Michikyan et al., 2014). It appears that the reluctance to engage other users via digital media might reflect social anxiety or the fear of being negatively evaluated by other users that is typically experienced by social media users with high trait neuroticism (Bowden-Green et al., 2021). A major complication in the search for user variables is that different individual factors may interact both with one another as well as with contextual factors, often in a nonlinear way. Thus, the various ways in which different individual factors and contextual factors as well as different mechanisms interact with one another should be considered when conceptualizing the multiple ways digital media usage impacts adolescents' psychological well-being and mental health.

Conclusions

As digital media are now entrenched in the lives of adolescents, they have become an important contextual influence along the lines of families, peer groups, and schools. Considerable research demonstrates the importance of friends and families in adolescent health and well-being, and it is similarly important to investigate the impact of digital media on adolescent well-being and mental health. This introductory chapter presented an overview of the terms and history of research on this topic and described some of the pressing methodological and conceptual issues confronting researchers investigating this topic. Our discussion highlighted two main themes: (1) Changes in technology are inevitable, and thus researchers will need to be flexible in the methodological approaches they adopt to investigate the short- and long-term implications of youths' social media use; (2) Researchers must clearly articulate how they conceptualize and operationalize digital media, its role, usage, and pathways of influence. We present a few ways that researchers can adapt to the methodological challenges and clarify how they should innovate when conceptualizing and measuring adolescents' digital media use. These are but a few suggestions, and we encourage researchers to build and expand on them as they investigate the growing presence of social media in adolescents' lives.

Notes

[1] Researchers examining digital media use frequently use the term "psychological well-being" and "mental health" interchangeably to refer to different psychological outcomes such as depression, anxiety, distress, life satisfaction, self-esteem, loneliness, etc. (see Orben, 2020, for a review). In this chapter, we use these terms interchangeably as both psychological well-being outcomes (e.g., life satisfaction) and mental health outcomes (e.g., depression) are interrelated; however, we do recognize that substantive differences distinguish these constructs especially concerning digital media use (Verduyn et al., 2015).

[2] Throughout this section the terms well-being and mental health are used interchangeably; when describing research findings, we have adopted the particular terms used by the study authors themselves.

References

Alhabash, S., & Ma, M. (2017). A tale of four platforms: Motivations and uses of Facebook, Twitter, Instagram, and Snapchat among college students? *Social Media + Society*, *3*(1), 1–13. https://doi.org/10.1177/2056305117691544

Anderson, M., & Jiang, J. (2018). *Teens, social media & technology.* Pew Research Center. https://www.pewresearch.org/internet/2018/05/31/teens-social-media-technology-2018/

Appel, H., Crusius, J., & Gerlach, A. L. (2015). Social comparison, envy, and depression on Facebook: A study looking at the effects of high comparison standards on depressed individuals. *Journal of Social and Clinical Psychology*, *34*(4), 277–289. https://doi.org/10.1521/jscp.2015.34.4.277

Auxier, B., & Anderson, M. (2021). *Social media use in 2021.* Pew Research Center. https://www.pewresearch.org/internet/2021/04/07/social-media-use-in-2021/

Bai, S., Gao, R., & Zhu, T. (2012). Determining personality traits from RenRen status usage behavior. In *International conference on computational visual media* (pp. 226–233). Springer.

Bakhshi, S., Shamma, D. A., & Gilbert, E. (2014). Faces engage us: Photos with faces attract more likes and comments on Instagram. In *Proceedings of the SIGCHI conference on human factors in computing systems* (pp. 965–974). https://doi.org/10.1145/2556288.2557403

Bandura, A. (1986). *Social foundations of thought and action.* Princeton Hall.

Bandura, A. (1997). *Self-efficacy.* Freeman.

Bercovici, J. (2010, December 9). Who coined "social media"? Web pioneers compete for credit. *Forbes*. https://www.forbes.com/sites/jeffbercovici/2010/12/09/who-coined-social-media-web-pioneers-compete-for-credit/?sh=98501d351d52

Beyens, I., Pouwels, J. L., van Driel, I. I., Keijsers, L., & Valkenburg, P. M. (2020). The effect of social media on well-being differs from adolescent to adolescent. *Scientific Reports, 10*(1), 10763. https://doi.org/10.1038/s41598-020-67727-7

Bolger, N., Davis, A., & Rafaeli, E. (2003). Diary methods: Capturing life as it is lived. *Annual Review of Psychology, 54*, 579–616. https://doi.org/10.1146/annurev.psych.54.101601.145030

Booker, C. L., Kelly, Y. J., & Sacker, A. (2018). Gender differences in the associations between age trends of social media interaction and well-being among 10–15-year-olds in the UK. *BMC Public Health, 18*(1), 1–12. https://doi.org/10.1186/s12889-018-5220-4

Bowden-Green, T., Hinds, J., & Joinson, A. (2021). Understanding neuroticism and social media: A systematic review. *Personality and Individual Differences, 168*, 110344. https://doi.org/10.1016/j.paid.2020.110344

boyd, d. m. (2011). Social network sites as networked publics: Affordances, dynamics, and implications. In Z. Papacharissi (Ed.), *A networked self: Identity, community, and culture on social network sites* (pp. 39–58). Routledge. https://doi.org/10.4324/9780203876527-8

boyd, d. m., & Ellison, N. B. (2007). Social network sites: Definition, history, and scholarship. *Journal of Computer-Mediated Communication, 13*(1), 210–230. https://doi.org/10.1111/j.1083-6101.2007.00393.x

Bronfenbrenner, U., & Morris, P. (2006) The bioecological model of human development. In W. Damon & R. M. Lerner (Series Eds.) & R. M. Lerner (Vol. Ed.) *Handbook of child psychology: Vol. 1. Theoretical models of human development* (6th ed.; pp. 793–828). John Wiley.

Carr, C. T., & Hayes, R. A. (2015). Social media: Defining, developing, and divining. *Atlantic Journal of Communication, 23*(1), 46–65. https://doi.org/10.1080/15456870.2015.972282

Cattell, H. E. P., & Mead, A. D. (2008). The sixteen personality factor questionnaire (16PF). In G. J. Boyle, G. Matthews, & D. H. Saklofske (Eds.), *The SAGE handbook of personality theory and assessment: Vol. 2. Personality measurement and testing* (pp. 135–159). Sage Publications, Inc. https://doi.org/10.4135/9781849200479.n7

Correa, T., Hinsley, A. W., & De Zuniga, H. G. (2010). Who interacts on the web?: The intersection of users' personality and social media use. *Computers in Human Behavior, 26*(2), 247–253. https://doi.org/10.1016/j.chb.2009.09.003

Costa, P. T., Jr., & McCrae, R. R. (2008). The revised NEO personality inventory (NEO-PI-R). In G. J. Boyle, G. Matthews, & D. H. Saklofske (Eds.), *The SAGE handbook of personality theory and assessment: Vol. 2. Personality measurement and testing* (pp. 179–198). Sage Publications, Inc. https://doi.org/10.4135/9781849200479.n9

Coyne, S. M., Rogers, A. A., Zurcher, J. D., Stockdale, L., & Booth, M. (2020). Does time spent using social media impact mental health?: An eight-year longitudinal study. *Computers in Human Behavior, 104*, 106160. https://doi.org/10.1016/j.chb.2019.106160

Culnan, M., & Markus, M. L. (1987). Information technologies. In F. Jablin, L. L. Putnam, K. Roberts, & L. Porter (Eds.), *Handbook of organizational communication: An interdisciplinary perspective* (pp. 420–444). Sage.

De Choudhury, M., Sharma, S. S., Logar, T., Eekhout, W., & Nielsen, R. C. (2017). Gender and cross-cultural differences in social media disclosures of mental illness. In *Proceedings of the 2017 ACM conference on computer supported cooperative work and social computing* (pp. 353–369). ACM.

Dinakar, K., Weinstein, E., Lieberman, H., & Selman, R. (2014). Stacked generalization learning to analyze teenage distress. *Proceedings of the 8th international AAAI conference on web and social media, ICWSM 2014, 8*(1). https://ojs.aaai .org/index.php/ICWSM/article/view/14527

Ehrenberg, A., Juckes, S., White, K. M., & Walsh, S. P. (2008). Personality and self-esteem as predictors of young people's technology use. *Cyberpsychology & Behavior, 11*(6), 739–741. https://doi.org/10.1089/cpb.2008.0030

Elkind, D. (1967). Egocentrism in adolescence. *Child Development, 38*(4), 1025–1034. https://www.jstor.org/stable/1127100

Ellison, N. B., & Vitak, J. (2015). Social network site affordances and their relationship to social capital processes. In S. S. Sundar (Ed.), *The handbook of the psychology of communication technology* (pp. 205–227). Wiley Blackwell. https://doi.org/10.1002/9781118426456.ch9

Elsaesser, C., Patton, D. U., Weinstein, E., Santiago, J., Clarke, A., & Eschmann, R. (2021). Small becomes big, fast: Adolescent perceptions of how social media features escalate online conflict to offline violence. *Children and Youth Services Review, 122*, 105898. https://doi.org/10.1016/j.childyouth.2020.105898

England, E., & Finney, A. (2002). *Interactive media – What's that? Who's involved?* ATSF White Paper – Interactive Media UK. http://www.atsf.co.uk/atsf/interactive_media.pdf

Erikson, E. H. (1959). *Identity and the life cycle: Selected papers.* International Universities Press.

Escobar-Viera, C. G., Shensa, A., Bowman, N. D., et al. (2018). Passive and active social media use and depressive symptoms among United States adults. *Cyberpsychology, Behavior and Social Networking, 21*, 437–443. https://doi .org/10.1089/cyber.2017.0668

Feinstein, B. A., Hershenberg, R., Bhatia, V., Latack, J. A., Meuwly, N., & Davila, J. (2013). Negative social comparison on Facebook and depressive symptoms: Rumination as a mechanism. *Psychology of Popular Media, 2*(3), 161–170. https://doi.org/10.1037/a0033111

Finkelhor, D., Mitchell, K. J., & Wolak, J. (2000). Online victimization: A report on the nation's young people. In *ERIC (Educational Resources Information Center)*. https://files.eric.ed.gov/fulltext/ED442039.pdf

Gibson, J. (1979). *The ecological approach to visual perception.* Erlbaum.

Gil-Or, O., Levi-Belz, Y., & Turel, O. (2015). The "Facebook-self": Characteristics and psychological predictors of false self-presentation on Facebook. *Frontiers in Psychology, 6*, Article 99. https://doi.org/10.3389/fpsyg.2015.00099

Goh, D., Ang, R., Chua, A., & Lee, C. (2009). Why we share: A study of motivations for mobile media sharing. *Lecture Notes in Computer Science, 5820*, 195–206. https://doi.org/10.1007/978-3-642-04875-3_23

Gonzales, A. L. (2014). Text-based communication influences self-esteem more than face-to-face or cellphone communication. *Computers in Human Behavior*, *39*, 197–203. https://doi.org/10.1016/j.chb.2014.07.026

Granic, I., Morita, H., & Scholten, H. (2020a). Beyond screen time: Identity development in the digital age. *Psychological Inquiry*, *31*(3), 195–223. https://doi.org/10.1080/1047840X.2020.1820214

Granic, I., Morita, H., & Scholten, H. (2020b). Young people's digital interactions from a narrative identity perspective: Implications for mental health and wellbeing. *Psychological Inquiry*, *31*(3), 258–270. https://doi.org/10.1080/1047840X.2020.1820225

Greenfield, P. M., & Subrahmanyam, K. (2003). Online discourse in a teen chatroom: New codes and new modes of coherence in a visual medium. *Journal of Applied Developmental Psychology*, *24*(6), 713–738. https://doi.org/10.1016/j.appdev.2003.09.005

Greenfield, P. M., Subrahmanyam, K., & Eccles, J. S. (2012). Special section: Interactive media and human development. *Developmental Psychology*, *48*(2), 343–355.

Greenfield, P. M., & Yan, Z. (2006). Children, adolescents, and the Internet: A new field of inquiry in developmental psychology. *Developmental Psychology*, *42*(3), 391–394. https://doi.org/10.1037/0012-1649.42.3.391

Gross, E. F. (2009). Logging on, bouncing back: An experimental investigation of online communication following social exclusion. *Developmental Psychology*, *45*(6), 1787–1793. https://doi.org/10.1037/a0016541

Hatchel, T., Negriff, S., & Subrahmanyam, K. (2018). The relation between media multitasking, intensity of use, and well-being in a sample of ethnically diverse emerging adults. *Computers in Human Behavior*, *81*, 115–123. https://doi.org/10.1016/j.chb.2017.12.012

Hatchel, T., Subrahmanyam, K., & Negriff, S. (2019). Adolescent peer victimization and internalizing symptoms during emerging adulthood: The role of online and offline social support. *Journal of Child and Family Studies*, *28*(9), 2456–2466. https://doi.org/10.1007/s10826-018-1286-y

Huffaker, D. A., & Calvert, S. L. (2005). Gender, identity, and language use in teenage blogs. *Journal of Computer-Mediated Communication*, *10*(2). https://doi.org/10.1111/j.1083-6101.2005.tb00238.x

Hutchby, I. (2001). Technologies, texts and affordances. *Sociology*, *35*(2), 441–456. https://doi.org/10.1177/S0038038501000219

Jelenchick, L. A., Eickhoff, J. C., & Moreno, M. A. (2013). "Facebook depression?" Social networking site use and depression in older adolescents. *Journal of Adolescent Health*, *52*(1), 128–130. https://doi.org/10.1016/j.jadohealth.2012.05.008

Kern, M. L., Eichstaedt, J. C., Schwartz, H. A., et al. (2014). The online social self: An open vocabulary approach to personality. *Assessment*, *21*(2), 158–169. https://doi.org/10.1177/1073191113514104

Kircaburun, K., Alhabash, S., Tosuntaş, Ş. B., & Griffiths, M. D. (2020). Uses and gratifications of problematic social media use among university students: A simultaneous examination of the Big Five of personality traits, social media platforms, and social media use motives. *International Journal of Mental Health and Addiction*, *18*(3), 525–547. https://doi.org/10.1007/s11469-018-9940-6

Kraut, R., Patterson, M., Lundmark, V., Kiesler, S., Mukopadhyay, T., & Scherlis, W. (1998). Internet paradox: A social technology that reduces social involvement and psychological well-being? *American Psychologist*, *53*(9), 1017–1031. https://doi.org/10.1037/0003-066X.53.9.1017

Kraut, R., Scherlis, W., Mukhopadhyay, T., Manning, J., & Kiesler, S. (1996). The HomeNet field trial of residential internet services. *Communications of the ACM*, *39*(12), 55–63. https://doi.org/10.1145/240483.240493

Kross, E., Verduyn, P., Demiralp, E., et al. (2013). Facebook use predicts declines in subjective well-being in young adults. *PLoS ONE*, *8*(8), e69841. https://doi.org/10.1371/journal.pone.0069841

Kross, E., Verduyn, P., Sheppes, G., Costello, C. K., Jonides, J., & Ybarra, O. (2020). Social media and well-being: Pitfalls, progress, and next steps. *Trends in Cognitive Sciences*, *25*(1), 55–66. https://doi.org/10.1016/j.tics.2020.10.005

Larson, R., & Csikszentmihalyi, M. (2014). The experience sampling method. In *Flow and the foundations of positive psychology: The collected works of Mihaly Csikszentmihalyi* (pp. 21–34). Springer. https://doi.org/10.1007/978-94-017-9088-8_2

Lewallen, J., & Behm-Morawitz, E. (2016). Pinterest or thinterest?: Social comparison and body image on social media. *Social Media+ Society*, *2*(1), 1–9. https://doi.org/10.1177/2056305116640559.

Liu, D., Baumeister, R. F., Yang, C. C., & Hu, B. (2019). Digital communication media use and psychological well-being: A meta-analysis. *Journal of Computer-Mediated Communication*, *24*(5), 259–273. https://doi.org/10.1093/jcmc/zmz013

Madden, M., Lenhart, A., Cortesi, S., et al. (2013). *Teens, social media, and privacy*. Pew Research Center. https://www.pewresearch.org/internet/2013/05/21/part-1-teens-and-social-media-use/

Manago, A. M., Graham, M. B., Greenfield, P. M., & Salimkhan, G. (2008). Self-presentation and gender on MySpace. *Journal of Applied Developmental Psychology*, *29*(6), 446–458. https://doi.org/10.1016/j.appdev.2008.07.001

Manago, A. M., Taylor, T., & Greenfield, P. M. (2012). Me and my 400 friends: The anatomy of college students' Facebook networks, their communication patterns, and well-being. *Developmental Psychology*, *48*(2), 369–380. https://doi.org/10.1037/a0026338

Masur, P. K., & Scharkow, M. (2016). Disclosure management on social network sites: Individual privacy perceptions and user-directed privacy strategies. *Social Media + Society*, *2*(1). https://doi.org/10.1177/2056305116634368

Meier, E. P., & Gray, J. (2014). Facebook photo activity associated with body image disturbance in adolescent girls. *Cyberpsychology, Behavior, and Social Networking*, *17*(4), 199–206. https://doi.org/10.1089/cyber.2013.0305

Michikyan, M. (2019). Depression symptoms and negative online disclosure among young adults in college: A mixed-methods approach. *Journal of Mental Health*, *29*(4), 392–400. https://doi.org/10.1080/09638237.2019.1581357

Michikyan, M., Dennis, M., & Subrahmanyam, K. (2014). Can you guess who I am? Real, ideal, and false self-presentation on Facebook among emerging adults. *Emerging Adulthood*, *3*(1), 55–64. https://doi.org/10.1177/2167696814532442

Michikyan, M., Hatchel, T., Kennison, R., & Subrahmanyam, K. (2014). Relation between daily self-esteem and online self-presentation among minority emerging adults. In K. Subrahmanyam (Chair), *Social media use among minority youth – Social support, self-presentation, and cyberbullying*. Symposium conducted at the 2014 SRA Biennial Meeting, Austin, TX, USA. (March, 2014).

Michikyan, M., & Suárez-Orozco, C. (2016). Adolescent media and social media use: Implications for development. *Journal of Adolescent Research, 31*(4), 411–414. https://doi.org/10.1177/0743558416643801

Michikyan, M., & Suárez-Orozco, C. (2017). Enacted identities of immigrant-origin emerging adult women in online contexts: Capturing multiple and intersecting identities using qualitative strategies. *Identity, 17*(3), 138–155. https://doi.org/10.1080/15283488.2017.1340161

Michikyan, M., & Subrahmanyam, K. (2012). Social networking sites: Implications for youth. In Z. Yan (Ed.), *Encyclopedia of cyber behavior* (pp. 132–147). IGI Global.

Michikyan, M., Subrahmanyam, K., & Dennis, J. (2015). A picture is worth a thousand words: A mixed methods study of online self-presentation in a multiethnic sample of emerging adults. *Identity, 15*(4), 287–308. https://doi.org/10.1080/15283488.2015.1089506

Moore, G. F., Cox, R., Evans, R. E., et al. (2018). School, peer and family relationships and adolescent substance use, subjective wellbeing and mental health symptoms in Wales: A cross sectional study. *Child Indicators Research, 11*(6), 1951–1965. https://doi.org/10.1007/s12187–017-9524-1

Negriff, S. (2019). A pilot study examining risk behavior in Facebook posts for maltreated versus comparison youth using content analysis. *Child Abuse and Neglect, 96*, 104091. https://doi.org/10.1016/j.chiabu.2019.104091

Nesi, J., & Prinstein, M. J. (2019). In search of likes: Longitudinal associations between adolescents' digital status seeking and health-risk behaviors. *Journal of Clinical Child & Adolescent Psychology, 48*(5), 740–748. https://doi.org/10.1080/15374416.2018.1437733

Nikbin, D., Iranmanesh, M., & Foroughi, B. (2020). Personality traits, psychological well-being, Facebook addiction, health and performance: Testing their relationships. *Behaviour & Information Technology, 40*(7), 1–17. https://doi.org/10.1080/0144929X.2020.1722749

Oberst, U., Wegmann, E., Stodt, B., Brand, M., & Chamarro, A. (2017). Negative consequences from heavy social networking in adolescents: The mediating role of fear of missing out. *Journal of Adolescence, 55*, 51–60. https://doi.org/10.1016/j.adolescence.2016.12.008

Orben, A. (2020). Teenagers, screens and social media: A narrative review of reviews and key studies. *Social Psychiatry and Psychiatric Epidemiology, 55*(4), 407–414. https://doi.org/10.1007/s00127–019-01825-4

Orben, A., & Przybylski, A. K. (2019a). Screens, teens, and psychological well-being: Evidence from three time-use-diary studies. *Psychological Science, 30*(5), 682–696. https://doi.org/10.1177/0956797619830329

Orben, A., & Przybylski, A. K. (2019b). The association between adolescent well-being and digital technology use. *Nature Human Behaviour, 3*(2), 173–182. https://doi.org/10.1038/s41562–018-0506-1

Parry, D. A., Davidson, B. I., Sewall, C. J., Fisher, J. T., Mieczkowski, H., & Quintana, D. S. (2021). A systematic review and meta-analysis of discrepancies between logged and self-reported digital media use. *Nature Human Behaviour, 5*(11), 1535–1547. https://doi.org/10.1038/s41562–021-01117-5

Pempek, T. A., Yermolayeva, Y. A., & Calvert, S. L. (2009). College students' social networking experiences on Facebook. *Journal of Applied Developmental Psychology*, *30*(3), 227–238. https://doi.org/10.1016/j.appdev.2008.12.010

Petersen, A. C. (1993). Presidential address: Creating adolescents: The role of context and process in developmental trajectories. *Journal of Research on Adolescence*, *3*(1), 1–18. https://doi.org/10.1207/s15327795jra0301_1

Pittman, M., & Reich, B. (2016). Social media and loneliness: Why an Instagram picture may be worth more than a thousand Twitter words. *Computers in Human Behavior*, *62*, 155–167. https://doi.org/10.1016/j.chb.2016.03.084

Pouwels, J. L., Valkenburg, P. M., Beyens, I., van Driel, I. I., & Keijsers, L. (2021). Social media use and friendship closeness in adolescents' daily lives: An experience sampling study. *Developmental Psychology*, *57*(2), 309–323. https://doi.org/10.1037/dev0001148

Prensky, M. (2001). Digital natives, digital immigrants Part 1. *On the Horizon*, *9*(5), 1–6. https://doi.org/10.1108/10748120110424816

Przybylski, A. K., Murayama, K., DeHaan, C. R., & Gladwell, V. (2013). Motivational, emotional, and behavioral correlates of fear of missing out. *Computers in Human Behavior*, *29*(4), 1841–1848. https://doi.org/10.1016/j.chb.2013.02.014

Qiu, L., Lin, H., Leung, A. K., & Tov, W. (2012). Putting their best foot forward: Emotional disclosure on Facebook. *Cyberpsychology, Behavior, and Social Networking*, *15*(10), 569–572. https://doi.org/10.1089/cyber.2012.0200

Reich, S. M., Subrahmanyam, K., & Espinoza, G. (2012). Friending, IMing, and hanging out face-to-face: Overlap in adolescents' online and offline social networks. *Developmental Psychology*, *48*(2), 356–368. https://doi.org/10.1037/a0026980

Reid, D. J., & Reid, F. J. M. (2007). Text or talk? Social anxiety, loneliness, and divergent preferences for cell phone use. *Cyberpsychology and Behavior*, *10*(3), 424–435. https://doi.org/10.1089/cpb.2006.9936

Rideout, V. J., & Robb, M. B. (2019). *The Common Sense census: Media use by tweens and teens, 2019.* Common Sense Media. https://www.commonsensemedia.org/research/the-common-sense-census-media-use-by-tweens-and-teens-2019

Roberts, D. F., Foehr, U. G., Rideout, V. J., & Brodie, M. (1999). *Kids & media@ the new millennium.* Kaiser Family Foundation. https://www.kff.org/wp-content/uploads/2013/01/kids-media-the-new-millennium-report.pdf

Ross, C., Orr, E. S., Sisic, M., Arseneault, J. M., Simmering, M. G., & Orr, R. R. (2009). Personality and motivations associated with Facebook use. *Computers in Human Behavior*, *25*(2), 578–586. https://doi.org/10.1016/j.chb.2008.12.024

Ross, M., & Wilson, A. E. (2003). Autobiographical memory and conceptions of self: Getting better all the time. *Current Directions in Psychological Science*, *12*(2), 66–69. https://doi.org/10.1111/1467-8721.01228

Rubin, K. H., Bukowski, W. M., & Parker, J. G. (2006). Peer interactions, relationships, and groups. In N. Eisenberg, W. Damon, & R. M. Lerner (Eds.), *Handbook of child psychology: Vol. 3. Social, emotional, and personality development* (6th ed., pp. 571–645). Wiley.

Sanders, C. E., Field, T. M., Diego, M., & Kaplan, M. (2000). The relationship of Internet use to depression and social isolation among adolescents. *Adolescence*,

35(138), 237–242. https://search.proquest.com/docview/195940231?pq-origsite=gscholar&fromopenview=true

Scharkow, M. (2016). The accuracy of self-reported internet use: A validation study using client log data. *Communication Methods and Measures*, *10*(1), 13–27. https://doi.org/10.1080/19312458.2015.1118446

Schønning, V., Hjetland, G. J., Aarø, L. E., & Skogen, J. C. (2020). Social media use and mental health and well-being among adolescents: A scoping review. *Frontiers in Psychology*, *11*, Article 1949. https://doi.org/10.3389/fpsyg.2020.01949

Sherman, L. E., Greenfield, P. M., Hernandez, L. M., & Dapretto, M. (2018). Peer influence via Instagram: Effects on brain and behavior in adolescence and young adulthood. *Child Development*, *89*(1), 37–47. https://doi.org/10.1111/cdev.12838

Sherman, L., Michikyan, M., & Greenfield, P. (2013). The effects of text, audio, video, and in-person communication on bonding between friends. *Cyberpsychology: Journal of Psychosocial Research on Cyberspace*, Article 3. https://doi.org/10.5817/CP2013-2-3

Sherman, L. E., Payton, A. A., Hernandez, L. M., Greenfield, P. M., & Dapretto, M. (2016). The power of the like in adolescence: Effect of peer influence on neural and behavioral responses to social media. *Psychological Science*, *27*(7), 1027–1035. https://doi.org/10.1177/0956797616645673

Simoncic, T. E., Kuhlman, K. R., Vargas, I., Houchins, S., & Lopez-Duran, N. L. (2014). Facebook use and depressive symptomatology: Investigating the role of neuroticism and extraversion in youth. *Computers in Human Behavior*, *40*, 1–5. https://doi.org/10.1016/j.chb.2014.07.039

Šmahel, D., & Subrahmanyam, K. (2007). "Any girls want to chat press 911": Partner selection in monitored and unmonitored teen chat rooms. *Cyberpsychology & Behavior: The Impact of the Internet, Multimedia and Virtual Reality on Behavior and Society*, *10*(3), 346–353. https://doi.org/10.1089/cpb.2006.9945

Sorokowska, A., Oleszkiewicz, A., Frackowiak, T., Pisanski, K., Chmiel, A., & Sorokowski, P. (2016). Selfies and personality: Who posts self-portrait photographs?. *Personality and Individual Differences*, *90*, 119–123. https://doi.org/10.1016/j.paid.2015.10.037

Stahl, C., & Fritz, N. (2002). Internet safety: Adolescents' self-report. *Journal of Adolescent Health*, *31*(1), 7–10. https://doi.org/10.1016/S1054-139X(02)00369-5

Steinberg, L., & Morris, A. S. (2001). Adolescent development. *Annual Review of Psychology*, *52*(1), 83–110. https://doi.org/10.1146/annurev.psych.52.1.83

Stromer-Galley, J. (2004). Interactivity-as-product and interactivity-as-process. *The Information Society*, *20*(5), 391–394. https://doi.org/10.1080/01972240490508081

Subrahmanyam, K. (2007). Adolescent online communication: Old issues, new intensities. *Cyberpsychology: Journal of Psychosocial Research on Cyberspace*, *1*. https://cyberpsychology.eu/article/view/4199/3235

Subrahmanyam, K., Frison, E., & Michikyan, M. (2020). The relation between face-to-face and digital interactions and self-esteem: A daily diary study. *Human Behavior and Emerging Technologies*, *2*(2), 116–127. https://doi.org/10.1002/hbe2.187

Subrahmanyam, K., Garcia, E. C. M., Harsono, L. S., Li, J. S., & Lipana, L. (2009). In their words: Connecting on-line weblogs to developmental processes.

British Journal of Developmental Psychology, 27(1), 219–245. https://doi.org/10.1348/026151008X345979

Subrahmanyam, K., & Greenfield, P. (2008). Online communication and adolescent relationships. *The Future of Children, 18*(1), 119–146. https://www.jstor.org/stable/20053122

Subrahmanyam, K., Greenfield, P., Kraut, R., & Gross, E. (2001). The impact of computer use on children's and adolescents' development. *Journal of Applied Developmental Psychology, 22*(1), 7–30. https://doi.org/10.1016/S0193-3973(00)00063-0

Subrahmanyam, K., Greenfield, P. M., & Tynes, B. (2004). Constructing sexuality and identity in an online teen chat room. *Journal of Applied Developmental Psychology, 25*(6), 651–666. https://doi.org/10.1016/j.appdev.2004.09.007

Subrahmanyam, K., & Manago, A. (2012). The Children's Digital Media Center @ Los Angeles. In *Encyclopedia of cyber behavior* (pp. 64–76). https://doi.org/10.4018/978-1-4666-0315-8.ch005

Subrahmanyam, K., Reich, S. M., Waechter, N., & Espinoza, G. (2008). Online and offline social networks: Use of social networking sites by emerging adults. *Journal of Applied Developmental Psychology, 29*(6), 420–433. https://doi.org/10.1016/j.appdev.2008.07.003

Subrahmanyam, K., & Šmahel, D. (2011). *Digital youth: The role of media in development.* Springer. https://doi.org/10.1177/110330881202000304

Subrahmanyam, K., Šmahel, D., & Greenfield, P. (2006). Connecting developmental constructions to the internet: Identity presentation and sexual exploration in online teen chat rooms. *Developmental Psychology, 42*(3), 395–406. https://doi.org/10.1037/0012-1649.42.3.395

Suzuki, L. K., & Calzo, J. P. (2004). The search for peer advice in cyberspace: An examination of online teen bulletin boards about health and sexuality. *Journal of Applied Developmental Psychology, 25*(6), 685–698. https://doi.org/10.1016/j.appdev.2004.09.002

Tandoc, E. C., Ferrucci, P., & Duffy, M. (2015). Facebook use, envy, and depression among college students: Is Facebooking depressing? *Computers in Human Behavior, 43*, 139–146. https://doi.org/10.1016/j.chb.2014.10.053

Toma, C. L., & Hancock, J. T. (2013). Self-affirmation underlies Facebook use. *Personality and Social Psychology Bulletin, 39*(3), 321–331. https://doi.org/10.1177/0146167212474694

Treem, J. W., & Leonardi, P. M. (2013). Social media use in organizations: Exploring the affordances of visibility, editability, persistence, and association. *Annals of the International Communication Association, 36*(1), 143–189. https://doi.org/10.1080/23808985.2013.11679130

Turkle, S. (1995). *Life on the screen: Identity in the age of the internet.* Simon & Schuster.

Turow, J. (1999). *The internet and the family: The view from parents the view from the press.* Annenberg Public Policy Center. https://cdn.annenbergpublicpolicycenter.org/wp-content/uploads/19991201_Internet_and_family2.pdf

Twomey, C., & O'Reilly, G. (2017). Associations of self-presentation on Facebook with mental health and personality variables: A systematic review.

Cyberpsychology, Behavior, and Social Networking, 20(10), 587–595. https:// doi.org/10.1089/cyber.2017.0247

Underwood, M. K., & Ehrenreich, S. E. (2017). The power and the pain of adolescents' digital communication: Cyber victimization and the perils of lurking. *American Psychologist, 72*(2), 144–158. https://doi.org/10.1037/a0040429

Underwood, M. K., Rosen, L. H., More, D., Ehrenreich, S. E., & Gentsch, J. K. (2012). The BlackBerry project: Capturing the content of adolescents' text messaging. *Developmental Psychology, 48*(2), 295–302. https://doi.org/10 .1037/a0025914

Utz, S., Muscanell, N., & Khalid, C. (2015). Snapchat elicits more jealousy than Facebook: A comparison of Snapchat and Facebook use. *Cyberpsychology, Behavior, and Social Networking, 18*(3), 141–146. https://doi.org/10.1089/ cyber.2014.0479

Valkenburg, P. M., & Peter, J. (2007). Online communication and adolescent well-being: Testing the stimulation versus the displacement hypothesis. *Journal of Computer-Mediated Communication, 12*(4), 1169–1182. https://doi.org/10 .1111/j.1083-6101.2007.00368.x

Valkenburg, P. M., & Peter, J. (2011). Online communication among adolescents: An integrated model of its attraction, opportunities, and risks. *Journal of Adolescent Health, 48*(2), 121–127. https://doi.org/10.1016/j.jadohealth.2010.08.020

Valkenburg, P. M., van Driel, I. I., & Beyens, I. (2021, May 7). Social media and well-being: Time to abandon the active-passive dichotomy. https://doi.org/10 .31234/osf.io/j6xqz

Verduyn, P., Lee, D. S., Park, J., et al. (2015). Passive Facebook usage undermines affective well-being: Experimental and longitudinal evidence. *Journal of Experimental Psychology General, 144*(2), 480–488. https://doi.org/10.1037/ xge0000057

Vogel, E. A., Rose, J. P., Okdie, B. M., Eckles, K., & Franz, B. (2015). Who compares and despairs? The effect of social comparison orientation on social media use and its outcomes. *Personality and Individual Differences, 86*, 249–256. https:// doi.org/10.1016/j.paid.2015.06.026

Vygotsky, L. (1978). *Mind in society*. Harvard University Press.

Walther, J. B. (1992). Interpersonal effects in computer-mediated interaction: A relational perspective. *Communication Research, 19*(1), 52–90. https://doi .org/10.1177/009365092019001003

Wang, J. L., Wang, H. Z., Gaskin, J., & Hawk, S. (2017). The mediating roles of upward social comparison and self-esteem and the moderating role of social comparison orientation in the association between social networking site usage and subjective well-being. *Frontiers in Psychology, 8*, Article 771. https://doi.org/10.3389/fpsyg.2017.00771

Wartella, E. A., & Jennings, N. (2000). Children and computers: New technology – old concerns. *Future of Children, 10*, 32–43. https://doi.org/10.2307/1602688

Wartella, E. A., & Robb, M. (2009). Historical and recurring concerns about children's use of the mass media. In S. L. Calvert & B. J. Wilson (Eds.), *The handbook of children, media, and development* (pp. 5–26). Blackwell Publishing Ltd. https://doi.org/10.1002/9781444302752.ch1

Weinstein, E. (2017). Adolescents' differential responses to social media browsing: Exploring causes and consequences for intervention. *Computers in Human Behavior, 76*, 396–405. https://doi.org/10.1016/j.chb.2017.07.038

Wright, E. J., White, K. M., & Obst, P. L. (2018). Facebook false self-presentation behaviors and negative mental health. *Cyberpsychology, Behavior, and Social Networking, 21*(1), 40–49. https://doi.org/10.1089/cyber.2016.0647

Yan, Z., & Hardell, L. (2018). Contemporary mobile technology and child and adolescent development (Special Section). *Child Development, 89*(1), 1–331.

Yoon, S., Kleinman, M., Mertz, J., & Brannick, M. (2019). Is social network site usage related to depression? A meta-analysis of Facebook–depression relations. *Journal of Affective Disorders, 248*, 65–72. https://doi.org/10.1016/j.jad.2019.01.026

Zuckerman, M. (1991). *Psychobiology of personality* (Vol. 10). Cambridge University Press.

Zywica, J., & Danowski, J. (2008). The faces of Facebookers: Investigating social enhancement and social compensation hypotheses; predicting Facebook™ and offline popularity from sociability and self-esteem, and mapping the meanings of popularity with semantic networks. *Journal of Computer-Mediated Communication, 14*(1), 1–34. https://doi.org/10.1111/j.1083-6101.2008.01429.x

2 Theoretical Foundations of Social Media Uses and Effects

Patti M. Valkenburg

Empirical work into the cognitive, affective, and behavioral effects of media use started in the 1920s under the umbrella concept of mass communication. The term mass communication arose as a response to the new opportunities of reaching audiences via the mass media (e.g., film, radio; McQuail, 2010). In early mass communication theories, the *mass* did not only refer to the "massness" of the audience that media could reach, but also to homogenous media use and powerful media effects, notions that apply increasingly less to the contemporary media landscape (Valkenburg et al., 2016). In the past two decades, media use has undergone a rapid evolution. It has become increasingly individualized, and, with the introduction of social media, undeniably more dynamic and ubiquitous. It is no surprise, therefore, that communication and media effects theories have undergone important adjustments. And it is also no surprise that the mass has turned increasingly obsolete in contemporary media effects theories (Valkenburg & Oliver, 2019).

The aim of this chapter is to discuss the communication and media effects theories that may serve as the foundations for research into the effects of *social* media use on adolescents. To define social media, I follow the definition of Bayer et al. (2020, p. 472): Social media are "computer-mediated communication channels that allow users to engage in social interaction with broad and narrow audiences in real time or asynchronously." Social media use thus entails the active (e.g., posting) or passive (e.g., browsing), private (one-to-one) or public (e.g., one-to-many), and synchronous or asynchronous usage of social media platforms, such as Instagram, Facebook, Snapchat, TikTok, WeChat, and WhatsApp.

The first section of this chapter focuses on three important paradigms of general media effects theories that may help us understand the effects of social media, namely the selectivity, transactionality, and conditionality paradigms. The second section reviews computer-mediated communication theories, which originated in the 1970s, and are still relevant to understand the effects of social media. The third section introduces a transactional affordance theory of social media uses, which is inspired by transactional theories of development

The first part of this chapter is largely based on Valkenburg, Peter, and Walther (2016), Media effects: Theory and research. *Annual Review of Psychology, 67*, 315–338.

(Bronfenbrenner, 2005; Sameroff, 2009), Self-effects theory (Valkenburg, 2017), and affordance theories of social media use (e.g., boyd, 2011; McFarland & Ployhart, 2015). A fourth and final section presents some avenues for future research into the effects of social media on adolescents.

Media Effects Theories

In this chapter, I define media effects as the deliberate and nondeliberate short- and long-term within-person changes in cognitions, emotions, attitudes, and behavior that result from media use (Valkenburg et al., 2016). And I define a (social) media effects *theory* as a theory that attempts to explain the uses and effects of (social) media use on individuals, groups, or societies as a whole (Valkenburg & Oliver, 2019). To be labeled a (social) media effects theory, a theory at least needs to conceptualize media use, and the potential changes that this use can bring about within individuals, groups, or societies (i.e., the media effect).

Over the past decades, dozens of media effects theories have been developed. These theories differ substantially in how they conceptualize the media effects process. Some theories, particularly the early ones, focus primarily on unidirectional linear relationships between media use and certain outcomes. Other, more comprehensive theories pay more attention to the interactive effects of media use and nonmedia factors (e.g., dispositions, social contexts) on certain outcomes. Valkenburg et al. (2016) argued that media effects theories can be organized along five paradigms that specify the conditions under which media effects can (or cannot) occur. This chapter discusses the three paradigms that are most relevant to our understanding of the effects of social media use, the selectivity, transactionality, and conditionality paradigm. The term "message" in this chapter refers to all textual, auditory, visual, and audiovisual content that is shared on social media.

The Selectivity Paradigm

The selectivity paradigm of media effects theories states that: (a) individuals can only attend to a limited number of media messages out of the wealth of media messages that can potentially attract their attention, (b) they select these media messages in response to dispositions, needs, and desires that differ from person to person, and (c) only those media messages they select have the potential to influence them. The selectivity paradigm is represented by two different communication theories: uses and gratifications theory (Katz et al., 1973) and selective exposure theory (Zillmann & Bryant, 1985). Both theories argue that a variety of cognitive and psychosocial factors guide and filter one's selective media use. An important difference between the theories is that uses and gratifications theory conceives of media users as rational and conscious of their selective media use, whereas selective exposure theory argues that media users are often not aware, or at least not fully aware, of their selection motives.

The Transactionality Paradigm

The transactionality paradigm is an extension of the selectivity paradigm. Early studies into the selectivity paradigm have predominantly focused on the extent to which the dispositions of media users (e.g., needs, moods, attitudes) predict their tendency to select media. In other words, these studies conceptualized selective media use as the outcome, whereas the effects of this media use received less attention. In more recent transactional media effects theories (e.g., Slater, 2007; Valkenburg & Peter, 2013a), the selectivity paradigm has become an integrated part of the media effects process. Transactional media effect theories argue that (a) the media user, rather than the media, is the starting point of a process that leads to selective media use, (b) this selective media use may bring about a transaction (i.e., change) in the media user, which is the media effect, and (c) this media effect may, in turn, reciprocally influence media use and the antecedents of media use. For example, it has been shown that adolescents high in trait aggressiveness are more likely to selectively expose themselves to violent websites, which may further enhance their trait aggressiveness (Slater, 2003).

The propositions in transactional media effects theories have important implications for theories and research on the effects of *social* media. First, in comparison with mass media, social media have more filters and algorithms to cater to the preferences of adolescent users, which may stimulate their selective exposure to messages that match these preferences. Second, social media platforms typically allow adolescents to make their posts more personal, vivid, and emotional, which may enhance the likelihood of effects. Third, since 2017, adolescents can not only search for messages related to a specific hashtag but can also follow one or more hashtags, after which posts under these hashtags start to show up more prominently in the users' timelines or feeds (Scherr et al., 2020). In comparison with mass media content, such posts may be more effective both in attracting the selective attention of recipients of these posts, and in influencing their cognitions, attitudes, and behavior (e.g., Parmelee & Roman, 2020).

Following transactional theories, social media use may thus result in selective exposure to messages that match with individuals' preexisting dispositions (e.g., needs, moods, attitudes), more so than mass media use. These theories thus imply that social media users may also more than mass media users be able to shape their own media effects via this targeted selective social media use. Hence, if we want to understand the effects of social media use on adolescents, we may need to study the antecedents that shape their selective social media use. Selective exposure theories have mostly focused on dispositional antecedents, such as mood and preexisting attitudes. But according to

Valkenburg & Peter's (2013a) differential susceptibility to media effects model (DSMM), three types of antecedents may predict adolescents' selective (social) media use and, thus, the effects of this use: dispositional, developmental, and social-context factors.

Dispositional Factors

Dispositions that may lead to selective social media use range from more stable factors (e.g., temperament, personality) to more transient and situational ones (e.g., needs, desires, moods). Both types of antecedents have received some support. For example, fear of missing out (FOMO, a more stable anxiety of missing out on rewarding experiences that others are having) has been linked to adolescents' (problematic) social media use (Franchina et al., 2018). Furthermore, some (but not all) adolescents experiencing low mood turn to social media to look for funny clips or supportive feedback (Rideout & Fox, 2018).

Developmental Factors

As for development, research has shown that children and adolescents typically prefer media messages that are only moderately discrepant from their age-related comprehension schemata and level of psychosocial development (Valkenburg & Cantor, 2000). If they encounter media content that is too discrepant, they will allocate less attention to it or avoid it. This moderate-discrepancy hypothesis explains, for example: (a) why toddlers are typically attracted to audiovisual material with a slow pace, simple characters, and familiar contexts, and why they can be mesmerized by buttons on tablets; (b) why preschoolers typically like to attend to faster-paced, more adventurous contexts, and more sophisticated fantasy characters; (c) why children in middle childhood typically enjoy computer games and virtual worlds that allow collecting and saving, and identify with real-life idols; and (d) why adolescents are the most avid users of social media for interacting with their friends, and seek online entertainment that presents irreverent humor or risky behavior (for a more elaborate review of developmentally related media preferences, see Valkenburg and Piotrowski (2017).

Social Context Factors

Social context refers to the surroundings within which individuals or groups act or interact, and whose norms and affordances may influence the cognitions, emotions, attitudes, and behaviors that occur within it. On the macro level, structural aspects of the media system (e.g., platform availability) can affect media choices (e.g., Webster, 2009), whereas on the micro level, parents and schools can forbid adolescents from spending time on social media during dinner or in the classroom (Valkenburg & Piotrowski, 2017). In addition, especially in adolescence, peer groups can exert a strong influence on certain preferences and behaviors (Brechwald & Prinstein, 2011), including media preferences (Valkenburg & Cantor, 2000). Members of a peer group share norms that they have created themselves. Adolescents typically form strong social antennas for these norms, including those pertaining to social media use. Environmental influences on social media use can thus occur overtly (e.g., by parental restriction or monitoring) or more covertly, for example through adolescents' sensitivity to the prevailing norms in their peer group.

The Conditionality Paradigm

The conditionality paradigm is closely linked with the selectivity and transactionality paradigms. After all, in both paradigms it is argued that only the messages that individuals select in response to person-specific antecedents have the potential to influence them. Theories that propose conditional media effects share the notion that media effects (a) do not equally hold for all media users, and (b) can be enhanced or reduced by dispositional, developmental, and social-context factors (Valkenburg & Peter, 2013a). In line with earlier media effects theories (e.g., Bandura, 2009), Valkenburg and Peter's DSMM postulates that dispositional, developmental, and social-context factors may have a double role in the media effects process: They not only predict media use, but they also influence the way in which media messages are processed and subsequent distal media outcomes. This twofold influence results in three types of differential susceptibility to media effects: dispositional, developmental, and social-context susceptibility.

Dispositional Susceptibility

Dispositional susceptibility refers to the degree to which certain dispositions influence media processing and media outcomes. It has been shown, for example, that trait aggressiveness can increase the effects of media violence on cognitive and emotional processing of violent media content (Schultz et al., 2004), which may, in turn, result in enhanced aggression (Krcmar, 2009). As for social media, it has been shown that Facebook users who scored high on FOMO, experience more hurtful comments, and more stalking and harassment (Buglass et al., 2017). In addition, sensation seeking is an important predictor of risky behavior on social media, whereas a lack of inhibitory control can result in more negative feedback on these media (Koutamanis et al., 2015). Finally, specific affordances of social media may particularly stimulate online disinhibition among self-conscious and socially anxious adolescents (e.g., Schouten et al., 2007). This online disinhibition has been shown to result in positive (e.g., friendship closeness; Valkenburg & Peter, 2009) or negative effects of social media use (e.g., cyberbullying; Nesi et al., 2018b).

Developmental Susceptibility

Developmental susceptibility refers to the degree to which developmental level influences media processing and media outcomes. Evidence for developmental susceptibility is relatively scarce. It has been shown that younger children react with stronger physiological arousal to violent and frightening audiovisual content than adolescents, even if this content is unrealistic, which may enhance the effects of such content (Cantor, 2009). In addition, online sexual risk behavior seems to reach a peak in middle adolescence, after which it levels off again (Baumgartner et al., 2012). This developmentally induced inverted U-shaped trajectory is often explained by dual-system theories of brain development (e.g., Steinberg, 2010), which argue that the parts of the adolescent brain that are responsible for reward sensitivity to social stimuli may develop more quickly than the parts that are responsible for regulation of this reward sensitivity.

Social-Context Susceptibility

Social-context susceptibility refers to the degree to which social context factors influence media processing and media outcomes. Evidence for social-context susceptibility comes from studies showing that when physical violence is normative in families, children may learn to interpret media violence differently (Schultz et al., 2004), making them more susceptible to media effects on aggression (Fikkers et al., 2013). Social-context susceptibility can be explained by the context-convergence hypothesis (Valkenburg & Peter, 2013a), which posits that individuals are more susceptible to media messages if these messages converge with the values and norms in their social context. In cultivation theory (Gerbner et al., 1980, p. 15), an early media effects theory, this phenomenon has been named resonance: When something experienced in the media is similar to the norms that prevail in one's social environment, it creates a "double dose" of the message, which enhances the likelihood of media effects.

Social Media as a Social Context in Its Own Right

As discussed earlier on in the chapter, social context refers to the environment within which individuals or groups act or interact, and whose norms and affordances may influence the cognitions, emotions, attitudes, and behaviors that occur within it. An important theoretical question is whether we need to conceptualize social media as a social context in its own right that may shape both social media uses and their effects. Authors differ in their conceptions of whether social media should be seen as a social context in itself. Some scholars adhere to a "Mirroring Framework" (Nesi et al., 2018a, p. 268), that is, the notion that adolescents' experiences on social media simply mirror their offline experiences.

Several other scholars, including the author of this chapter, believe that social media is not merely a technology, but a social context, whose norms and affordances may influence social media use, as well as the changes among users that result from this use. These scholars do acknowledge that the social media context overlaps with other contexts, such as the family, peer, and school context. But such overlap also applies to other social contexts (e.g., family with school; peer group with school). Coconstruction theory (Subrahmanyam et al., 2006) and the transformation framework (Nesi et al., 2018a, 2018b) both discuss how the social media context differs from equivalent offline interaction contexts. Coconstruction theory proposes that even though adolescents construct the same developmental issues online as they do offline, they use specific affordances of social media that do not exist in offline situations (e.g., cue manageability and scalability) to construct and coconstruct their identity, intimacy, and sexuality. Finally, following affordance theories of social media (e.g., boyd, 2011; McFarland & Ployhart, 2015; Peter & Valkenburg, 2013), the transformation framework considers social media as a context that differs in important ways from face-to-face and earlier digital interactions (e.g., email). As a result, this context may affect social media uses and their effects in different ways than face-to-face and earlier digital interactions (Nesi et al., 2018a, 2018b).

A telling example of a defining norm of the social media context is its positivity bias, which refers to the observation that public social media interactions (e.g., Instagram, Facebook) are typically more positive than equivalent offline interactions (e.g., Reinecke & Trepte, 2014; Waterloo et al., 2017). This positivity bias may influence both message recipients and message senders positively or negatively. Message recipients can be exposed to positively biased messages of happy, successful, and popular peers. Among some recipients this exposure may result in envy and negative psychosocial effects (e.g., Vogel et al., 2014). And among other recipients it may lead to inspiration, and positive psychosocial effects (e.g., Meier et al., 2020).

The positivity bias may also influence message senders in opposite ways. Firstly, their positively biased self-presentations may increase their own psychological well-being (Burnell et al., 2020), a phenomenon that has been named a self-effect (Valkenburg, 2017). But when these self-presentations are exaggerated (e.g., too emotional) they may create embarrassment and guilt, and decrease psychological well-being (Stern, 2015). Apparently, the perceptions and consequences of the positivity bias on social media differ from adolescent to adolescent, an idea that will be elaborated upon when discussing affordance theories of social media.

Computer-Mediated Communication Theories

Studies into the cognitive, affective, and behavioral effects of social media have often been inspired by theories of computer-mediated communication (CMC). CMC theories and research emerged in the 1970s, long before the Internet became widespread. Unlike media effects research, which evolved from the study of mass communication, CMC research originated from a mixture of interpersonal communication, teleconferencing, and organizational behavior. In addition, whereas media effects research is more survey-oriented, the approach of CMC research is mostly experimental. CMC research has typically focused on comparing the cognitive, affective, and behavioral effects of face-to-face communication to those of CMC. It has often centered on questions such as whether and how certain CMC properties, such as anonymity or the lack of audiovisual cues, influence the quality of social interaction among dyads or group members, and the impressions these dyads or group members form of one another.

In the 1970s, some early, rather pessimistic CMC theories compared the "lean" text-only CMC with the "rich" communication in face-to-face settings. In doing so, they tried to explain, for example, why CMC leads to less intimacy and more disinhibited behavior (Walther, 2011). In the early 1990s, a new cluster of theories emerged, with a more optimistic view on CMC. That was the time that individuals started emailing, and the Internet became available for personal use. During this time, Walther's social information processing theory became influential. This theory explains how CMC partners can gradually overcome the presumed limitations of CMC by creatively employing strategies to exchange and understand social and emotional messages in CMC. In this way, with sufficient time and message exchanges, CMC partners could develop intimacy levels comparable to those in face-to-face communication (Walther, 1992).

In the second half of the 1990s, Walther extended his theory with an even more optimistic perspective, which predicted that CMC messages could lead to greater intimacy than face-to-face communication. According to his hyperpersonal communication model (Walther, 1996), the relative anonymity and reduced audiovisual cues in CMC encourage individuals to optimally present themselves, for instance, by pretending to be kinder and more beautiful than they actually are. Meanwhile, the recipients of these optimized self-presentations are free to fill in the blanks in their impressions of their partners, which may encourage them to idealize these partners. In doing so, CMC relationships could become "hyperpersonal," that is, more intimate than offline relationships (Walther, 1996). In the same period, another influential CMC theory emerged, the social identity model of deindividuation effects, whose major focus was to explain how the anonymity in CMC groups affects normative and anti-normative behavior among their members (Postmes et al., 2000).

The focus of early CMC theories on anonymity and limited audiovisual cues fitted well in the 1990s and the first half of the 2000s, when CMC was predominantly text-based and typically took place in anonymous chatrooms or newsgroups (Valkenburg et al., 2016). However, most current CMC technologies popular among adolescents, such as Instagram and Snapchat, are much less anonymous than their predecessors, and rely heavily on a range of audiovisual cues. Therefore, it has become less relevant to experimentally compare their specific CMC properties with face-to-face communication (Scott & Fullwood, 2020). Moreover, the "computer" part of CMC applications has become more portable and ubiquitous, and has diluted into a multitude of mobile devices and apps (Xu & Liao, 2020, p. 32). Indeed, the devices with which we communicate have gotten closer and closer to our bodies. They moved from our desks (desktop), to our bags (laptop), to our pockets (smartphone), and to our wrists (Valkenburg & Piotrowski, 2017). It is no surprise that these rapid developments provide contemporary CMC theorists with many new conceptual, theoretical, and empirical challenges (Carr, 2020).

An important strength of CMC theories and research, certainly when compared with media effects theories, has been their strong focus on the dynamic give-and-take interactions between message senders and recipients. CMC theories are, by definition, transactional theories that acknowledge that message exchanges are shaped by both message senders and receivers (Valkenburg, 2017). However, possibly due to its experimental orientation, CMC research has often focused on the unidirectional, across-the-board effects of CMC properties (i.e., anonymity, reduced audiovisual cues) on the recipients of these properties. Although both media effects and CMC theories like to describe recipients as active in the sense that they have autonomy over the way they interpret media or CMC characteristics, the empirically investigated influence in both research traditions is still all too often unidirectional: from the media or technology to the recipients.

However, if we accept that the current generation of social media are not merely technologies, but a social context whose norms and affordances differ from offline social contexts, such as the peer group or the neighborhood (Sameroff, 2009), we may need an updated theorization on the uses and effects of social media. Such an update needs to address the transactional relationships between social media users and the social media context, as well as the interactions between the social media context and other, offline, contexts. In the next section, I will make a preliminary start on such an update, by introducing a transactional affordance theory of social media uses. I deliberately use the term "uses" to refer to the many possible uses of social media.

Three types of theories might offer inspiration to such an updated theorization: transactional theories of development (e.g., Bronfenbrenner, 2005; Sameroff, 2009), Gibson's (1979) affordance theory, which later evolved into affordance theories of social media (e.g., boyd, 2011; Treem & Leonardi, 2013), and self-effects theory (Valkenburg, 2017). Transactional theories of development propose that change within an adolescent is a product of their continuous dynamic interactions with their experienced social contexts (Bronfenbrenner, 2005; Sameroff, 2009). Gibson's affordance theory is a learning theory that explains how different perceptions of an object or environment can result in different actions toward or uses of this object or environment. Finally, self-effects are the effects of messages on message senders themselves. As will be clear, social media use cannot only result in transactions (i.e., changes) within message *recipients*, but also within the senders of these messages.

A Transactional Affordance Theory of Social Media Uses

A transactional affordance theory of social media uses elaborates on three related propositions raised in transactional theories and/or affordance theories and/or self-effects theory: These propositions are: (1) social media users (co)create their own social media context, and this (co)created context shapes their experienced effects; (2) just like the family, school, and peer context, the social media context is a micro-level social context, in which transactional effects are more likely than in the mass media context; (3) the experiences with the social media context differ from adolescent to adolescent; thus, the unique way in which an adolescent experiences the norms, affordances, and messages in this context is the driving force of social media effects on this adolescent.

Social Media Users Shape Their Own Effects

The first proposition is that (1) social media users can individually (or collectively) shape their social media context, and (2) their experiences within this social media context can shape the effects of this context. The first part of this proposition is in line with transactional theories of development and Gibson's (1979) affordance theory. Transactional theories of development agree that children can shape and be shaped by their experienced social contexts (Bronfenbrenner, 2005; Sameroff, 2009). Likewise, Gibson argued that individuals tend to alter their environment by adjusting its affordances to better suit their needs and desires. In other words, an individual's perceptions of the affordances of a context may lead to specific uses of this context, which in turn shape the experienced effects of this context. A similar proposition has been raised in self-effects theory (Valkenburg, 2017), which proposes that social media users carefully craft their messages (e.g., social media posts), which may influence the recipients of these messages (i.e., the social environment) but also the message senders themselves, directly via internalization of overt behavior (Bem, 1972), or indirectly, via the feedback that their messages elicit.

The first part of this proposition, that social media users can individually (or collectively) shape their social media context, has received support. Adolescents can (co)create both the affordances and norms of the social media contexts in which they participate. It has been found, for example, that the sharing of intimate, self-related information is more accepted in the social media context than in equivalent offline contexts (Christofides et al., 2009). Another (co)created norm is that the sharing of negative emotions is more accepted in private (e.g., WhatsApp) than public social media contexts (e.g., Instagram; Waterloo et al., 2017). And if adolescents do want to share intimate, self-related information on a public social medium like Instagram, they sometimes turn to a Finsta (a Fake Instagram account where they can be honest and show their true self) in addition to a Rinsta (a Real Instagram account used to post their positive experiences). Finally, overly emotional expressions on in public social media are considered norm violations (Waterloo et al., 2017).

The second part of this proposition, that adolescents' *unique* experiences within their (co) created social media context can shape the effects of this context, has also received support. For example, message recipients can selectively and autonomously expose themselves to uplifting or depressing social media messages, which may subsequently affect their well-being in unique ways. In a qualitative study of Rideout and Fox (2018), one adolescent reported: "If I'm feeling depressed, getting on Twitter and seeing funny tweets or watching funny videos on YouTube can really brighten my mood" (p. 20). In this example, a transient dispositional variable (low mood) shaped this adolescent's selective exposure, which in turn positively shaped their experienced effect (i.e., a brightened mood). In the same study, another adolescent's preexisting low mood resulted in an opposite effect of social media browsing (i.e., a worsened low mood): "Social media makes me feel worse when I'm scrolling through feeds and seeing news headlines and posts about how terrible something is" (Rideout & Fox, 2018, p. 19). And yet another adolescent with a preexisting low mood reacted with selective avoidance: "Usually friends post happy things – getting together with others, accomplishments, bragging. I don't always want to see it when I'm feeling down about myself so I stay off social media" (p. 20).

These qualitative finding illustrate the complex nature of the associations between preexisting disposition (i.e., low mood), selective exposure to social media messages, and postexposure mood. Mood-induced selective exposure to social media messages can enhance mood (adolescent 1), worsen mood (adolescent 2), and it can lead to selective avoidance (adolescent 3). Such unique differences have also been reported in two recent experience sampling studies by Beyens et al. (2020, 2021), who found considerable differences in experienced effects of social media use. In one study, they found that 46% of the participating adolescents felt better after social media browsing in the past hour, while 44% did not feel better or worse, and 10% felt worse after such use (Beyens et al., 2020).

Such uniquely experienced social media effects also seem to hold for message senders. Several studies have shown that message sending (e.g., posting) can improve the well-being of message senders (Verduyn et al., 2017), a result that has often been explained by the positive feedback that message senders receive (Verduyn et al., 2017). However, social media–induced improvements in well-being can also occur without any involvement of fellow users (Pingree, 2007; Valkenburg, 2017). Self-expressions on social media, especially when their intended audience is sizeable, may lead to internalization of these self-expressions, for example, via self-perception. Self-perception theory (Bem, 1972) argues that individuals infer their internal self-concept from retrospectively observing their own overt behavior. If these individuals share positive self-expressions induced by the positivity norm in public social media, these individuals may, due to a desire for a consistency between their overt behavior and their self-concept, adjust their self-concept to match their behavior. For a discussion of self-effects in social media, and the mechanisms that may explain such effects, such as cognitive reframing, biased scanning, and public commitment, see Valkenburg (2017).

Social Media as a Micro- and Mesosystem

A second proposition of a transactional affordance theory of social media uses is that the social media context is a micro-level context, in which effects on participants are more likely than in the mass media context. Bronfenbrenner was one of the first to conceptualize the relationship between individuals and their social contexts. He distinguished between four types of contexts: the micro-, meso-, macro-, and exosystem (Bronfenbrenner, 1979, 2005). The microsystem involves direct interactions of the child with their most proximal circle, such as the family, peer group, or neighborhood. The mesosystem represents the possible interactions among these microsystems (e.g., between the family and peer group), whereas the macrosystem refers to the overarching culture or subculture of children. Bronfenbrenner's fourth context, the exosystem, refers to social contexts that do not allow the child as an active participant but that have the potential to affect the child. An example of an exosystem is the work context of one of the parents of the child. A child cannot actively participate in this context but can in many ways be influenced by it.

At the time of the development of his theory, Bronfenbrenner identified the mass media as an exosystem because it did not allow for active involvement of adolescents, even though it could shape their experiences. Although valid at the time, Bronfenbrenner (1917–2005) could not have foreseen the rapid developments within the media landscape. If he could have, he would probably have categorized the social media context as a microsystem rather than an exosystem. After all, unlike before, the media landscape now does allow for, and even stimulates, direct interactions among participants. For example, idols, an important source of identity formation in adolescence, have been transferred from the exosystem to the microsystem: Whereas movie stars or pop singers used to be celebrities that adolescents could admire from an unsurmountable distance, social media now provide them with ample opportunity for direct communication with their idols. In fact, many of their contemporary idols *are* YouTubers or Instagram influencers with whom they can directly interact.

If Bronfenbrenner could, he may now also have identified the social media context as part of the mesosystem because it allows for, or even stimulates, interactions with other microsystems (e.g., the family or the peer contexts). Although every traditional microsystem is in part "permeable" to the influences from other microsystems (e.g., family to peers and vice versa; family to school and vice versa), the social media context might be much more permeable to such influences. Conversely, the social media context seems to have penetrated all other microsystems in which adolescents participate, ranging from the family and peer context to the school.

However, if we accept the social media context as a microsystem, we must acknowledge that this context may, due to its proximity, dynamic, and ubiquitous nature, enhance the likelihood of effects on its participants, certainly when compared to the traditional mass media context. And if we accept the social media context as a part of the mesosystem (interactions among microsystems), we need to acknowledge that it may interact with the norms and affordances of other microsystems, such as parents or the school. And such interactions do occur. For example, preventing or counteracting possible negative consequences of social media interactions, and explaining to adolescents that the social media context may not be as perfect as it often appears, are important ingredients of today's media-specific parenting and school-based prevention and intervention programs (Valkenburg & Piotrowski, 2017).

It Is the Subjective Experience That Counts

A third and final proposition of a transactional affordance theory of social media uses is that the unique way in which individuals *experience* the norms and affordances of the social media context is the driving force of transactional effects between individuals and this context. This proposition is consistent with both transactional theories of development (Bronfenbrenner, 2005; Sameroff, 2009) and Gibson's affordance theory (Gibson, 1979). Affordances, according to Gibson, are the unique ways in which individuals experience the utility of objects. For example, distinct individuals may all perceive another utility of a bottle (e.g., as a water container, a vase, a candle holder, or a weapon). However, to understand such individual differences in experiences of the affordances of social media, I first specify some of these affordances and argue how and why these affordances differ from other micro-level social contexts, such as the family or peer contexts.

A growing number of social media scholars have ventured to identify specific affordances of social media (boyd, 2011; McFarland & Ployhart, 2015; Nesi et al., 2018a, 2018b; Sundar et al., 2015; Treem & Leonardi, 2013; Valkenburg & Peter, 2011; Valkenburg & Piotrowski, 2017). Some of these scholars have identified four affordances (Treem & Leonardi, 2013), others have focused on seven (Nesi et al., 2018a; Valkenburg & Piotrowski, 2017) or even eight affordances (McFarland & Ployhart, 2015). Many comparable affordances appear in different studies but sometimes under different names (e.g., identifiability vs. cue absence; scalability vs. publicness). In this chapter, the focus is on three affordances that have been mostly identified in earlier literature. For each affordance, I discuss the scarce evidence of individual differences in the perceptions of its utility, as well as its potential consequences for both senders and recipients of social media messages. A more elaborate discussion of these consequences can be found in Nesi et al. (2018a, 2018b)

Asynchronicity

Most social media are asynchronous, that is, they afford their users the possibility to edit and reflect on their messages and pictures before uploading them. Even in more synchronous apps, such as WhatsApp, users must press the send button before they can transmit their message or photo to partners or group members. Asynchronous communication allows message senders to carefully craft, refine, and optimize their self-presentations. Adolescents differ significantly in the importance they attach to this affordance. In one of our survey studies, we asked (pre)adolescents (10–17-year-olds) how much importance they attached to the idea that they have more time to think about what they share on social media than in face-to-face encounters (this part of data not published). Thirty-seven percent of them attached importance or high importance to this affordance, 25% did not attach any importance to this affordance, and a remaining 38% reported that they did not care. The asynchronicity affordance seemed particularly valuable for early and middle adolescents (12–15-years-olds), socially anxious, and lonely adolescents, who apparently benefit most from the extra time to optimize their self-presentations (Peter & Valkenburg, 2006).

The asynchronicity affordance may influence both senders and recipients of social media messages. The optimized self-presentations of senders could lead to self-effects through internalization of these self-presentations (Valkenburg, 2017). Such optimized self-presentations can also influence message recipients in both positive and negative ways. They can evoke empathy, laughter, or a positive mood, but in case they are optimized to hurt recipients, they can also lead to painful experiences among recipients (Rideout & Fox, 2018; Valkenburg & Peter, 2013a).

Cue Manageability

Most social media offer their users the possibility to show or hide visual or auditory cues about the self. Social media users can decide whether they present themselves only through textual descriptions or whether they add more cues, such as pictures or video clips. Moreover, by means of specific software, they can edit, manipulate, and optimize these cues. Adolescents differ greatly in the importance they attach to the cue-manageability affordance. For example, in one of our studies, 8% of adolescents deemed it important or very important that others cannot see them while communicating on social media, whereas 55% deemed it as unimportant, and 37% reported that they did not care (this part of the data not published). The cue-manageability affordance seems particularly valuable for female adolescents, socially anxious adolescents, and adolescents high in private self-consciousness (e.g., I am generally attentive to my inner feelings), and public self-consciousness (e.g., I usually worry about making a good impression; Schouten et al., 2007).

Like the asynchronicity affordance, cue management affords adolescents possibilities to optimize their online self-presentations, which can lead to positive self-effects, for example via self-perception (Bem, 1972) or to cognitive reframing (an intra-individual change in how previous experiences are viewed). However, when the self-presentations are exaggerated (e.g., too intimate or childish), they can violate the norms of the social media context, and they may trap adolescents in uncomfortable situations, in which they may become ridiculed or socially rejected (Peter & Valkenburg, 2013).

Scalability

Scalability offers social media participants the ability to articulate self-related messages and photos to any size and nature of audiences. It thus provides message senders with ample forums to commit themselves to realistic or imagined social media audiences. This may be preeminently attractive to adolescents, whose egocentrism (i.e., their inability to distinguish between their perception of what others think and what others actually think of them) may result in their perception of an imaginary audience that is constantly observing their actions (Elkind, 1967).

To my knowledge, no research has demonstrated individual differences in the value attached to the scalability affordance, and this may, therefore, be an interesting question for future research. The scalability affordance may enhance self-effects through public commitment. When individuals believe that their self-presentations are public, the likelihood of internalization enhances (Kelly & Rodriguez, 2006), not only because other people can see their presentations, but also because individuals do not like to appear inconsistent in their public self-presentations (Tice, 1992).

The three affordances of social media are all important in their own right but they have an important overarching affordance in common: They offer social media users greater controllability of their self-presentations than face-to-face interactions or older technologies do (Valkenburg & Peter, 2011). This controllability means that social media users can choose not only what, but also how, when, and to whom in the global village they can present themselves. This controllability may offer social media users a sense (or an illusion) of security, which makes some of them feel freer in their interpersonal interactions than they can experience in other micro-level social contexts. This sense (or illusion) of security and freedom is particularly important for adolescents, who typically experience enhanced uncertainty about their identity (i.e., how to define who they are and will become), intimacy (i.e., how to form and maintain meaningful relationships), and sexuality (e.g., how to cope with sexual desire and define their sexual orientation; Steinberg, 2011). This enhanced controllability of self-presentations may, therefore, be a major explanation of adolescents' attraction to social media (Valkenburg & Peter, 2011).

Conclusions and Avenues for Future Research

In this chapter, I conceptualized social media as a social context in its own right, and borrowing from Bronfenbrenner's (1979) typology, as a social context that frequently interacts with other micro-level contexts, such as the family, peer group, and school. I also explained how the social media context differs from the traditional mass media context and why it can lead to stronger effects on both message senders and recipients. The social media context is not only more proximal and ubiquitous than the mass media context, but it is also more dynamic in the sense that everyone can actively participate in and contribute to it. Whereas the "effects" of mass media have mostly been conceptualized as recipient effects in earlier research, social media inherently point our attention to self-effects: the messages produced by the sender on themself. The emphasis on self-effects is important for future social media research because it implies a focus on theories accounting for intra-individual transactions as a result of one's own affordance-induced behavior, next to theories explaining intra-individual transactions among recipients that occur as a result of selective attention and perception of messages sent by others.

Consistent with Gibson's (1979) affordance theory, this chapter revealed that adolescents differ greatly in their perceptions of some of the affordances of social media. Preliminary work also suggest that they also differ greatly in the effects they experience in the social media context (Pouwels et al., 2021; Valkenburg et al., 2021). Unfortunately, social media effects research still all too often focuses on universal effects. This may in part be due to the experimental focus of the CMC research tradition, in which individual differences are typically disregarded, because they are assumed to be canceled out by random assignment (Bolger et al., 2019). If such individual differences are measured at all, they are often included as covariates rather than as factors that may interact with the experimental condition (Valkenburg & Peter, 2013b).

There is a need for future research focusing on transactional and person-specific effects of social media use. Qualitative studies have repeatedly demonstrated that adolescents can differ substantially in their media use, their experiences on social media, and the effects of social media use (e.g., Rideout & Fox, 2018). However, most *quantitative* studies into the psychosocial effects of social media still adopt a group-differential approach, in which potential differences in susceptibility are conceptualized by group-level moderators, such as gender or age (Beyens et al., 2020; Howard & Hoffman, 2017). However, due to technological advancements, it has become feasible to collect masses of intensive longitudinal data from masses of individuals on the uses and effects of social media (e.g., through experience sampling or tracking). Moreover, rapid developments in data mining and statistical methods now also enable researchers to analyze highly complex $N = 1$ time series data, and by doing so, to develop and investigate media effects and other communication theories bottom up (i.e., from the individual adolescent to the population or subpopulation) rather than top down (i.e., from the population to the adolescent; Lerner et al., 2019).

In our recent and current experience sampling studies, we have adopted such a person-specific, $N = 1$ time series approach (McNeish & Hamaker, 2020). Up to now, our results show striking differences in adolescents' susceptibility to the momentary effects of social media on well-being (Beyens et al., 2020), self-esteem (Valkenburg et al., 2021), and friendship closeness (Pouwels et al., 2021). In all these studies, the effect sizes of social media use on outcomes ranged from moderately or strongly negative to moderately or strongly positive. For example, the within-person effect sizes of social media browsing on well-being ranged from $\beta = -0.24$ to $\beta = +0.68$ across adolescents. Likewise, the effects of Instagram use on friendship closeness ranged from $\beta = -0.57$ to $\beta = +0.45$. And the effects of social media use on self-esteem led to lagged effect sizes ranging from $\beta = -0.21$ to $\beta = +0.17$.

Unfortunately, we still do not know how these short-term effects of social media use accumulate into longer-term effects, and this is an important avenue for future research. Moreover, up to now we do not know whether the person-specific effects that we found can be attributed to (stable or transient) dispositional, developmental, and/or (situational or structural) social-context factors. An important avenue for future research is to explain why social media use can lead to "positive susceptibles" (i.e., adolescents who mainly experience positive effects of social media use), "negative susceptibles" (adolescents who mainly experience negative effects of social media use, and "nonsusceptibles" (adolescent who are predominantly unaffected by social media use). After all, only if we know which, when, how, and why adolescents may be influenced by certain types of social media use will we be able to adequately target prevention and intervention strategies to these adolescents.

References

Bandura, A. (2009). Social cognitive theory of mass communication. In J. Bryant & M. B. Oliver (Eds.), *Media effects: Advances in theory and research* (pp. 94–124). Routledge.

Baumgartner, S. E., Sumter, S. R., Peter, J., & Valkenburg, P. M. (2012). Identifying teens at risk: Developmental pathways of online and offline sexual risk behavior. *Pediatrics, 130*(6), E1489–E1496. https://doi.org/10.1542/peds.2012-0842

Bayer, J. B., Triệu, P., & Ellison, N. B. (2020). Social media elements, ecologies, and effects. *Annual Review of Psychology, 71*, 471–497. https://doi.org/10.1146/annurev-psych-010419-050944

Bem, D. J. (1972). Self-perception theory. In L. Berkowitz (Ed.), *Advances in experimental social psychology* (Vol. 6; pp. 1–62). Academic Press.

Beyens, I., Pouwels, J. L., van Driel, I. I., Keijsers, L., & Valkenburg, P. M. (2020). The effect of social media on well-being differs from adolescent to adolescent. *Scientific Reports, 10*, Article 10763. https://doi.org/10.1038/s41598-020-67727-7

Beyens, I., Pouwels, J. L., van Driel, I. I., Keijsers, L., & Valkenburg, P. M. (2021). Social media use and adolescents' well-being: Developing a typology of person-specific effect patterns. *PsyArXiv.* https://doi.org/10.31234/osf.io/ftygp

Bolger, N., Zee, K., Rossignac-Milon, M., & Hassin, R. (2019). Causal processes in psychology are heterogeneous. *Journal of Experimental Psychology: General, 148*(4), 601–618. https://doi.org/10.1037/xge0000558

boyd, d. (2011). Social network sites as networked publics: Affordances, dynamics and implications. In Z. Papacharissi (Ed.), *A networked self: Identity, community, and culture on social network sites* (pp. 39–58). Routledge.

Brechwald, W. A., & Prinstein, M. J. (2011). Beyond homophily: A decade of advances in understanding peer influence processes. *Journal of Research on Adolescence, 21*(1), 166–179. https://doi.org/10.1111/j.1532-7795.2010.00721.x

Bronfenbrenner, U. (1979). *The ecology of human development.* Harvard University Press.

Bronfenbrenner, U. (2005). The bioecological theory of human development. In U. Bronfenbrenner (Ed.), *Making human beings human: Bioecological perspectives on human development* (pp. 3–15). Sage.

Buglass, S. L., Binder, J. F., Betts, L. R., & Underwood, J. D. M. (2017). Motivators of online vulnerability: The impact of social network site use and FOMO. *Computers in Human Behavior, 66*, 248–255. https://doi.org/10.1016/j.chb.2016.09.055

Burnell, K., George, M. J., & Underwood, M. K. (2020). Browsing different Instagram profiles and associations with psychological well-being. *Frontiers in Human Dynamics, 2*, Article 6. https://doi.org/10.3389/fhumd.2020.585518

Cantor, J. (2009). Fright reactions to mass media. In J. Bryant & D. Zillmann (Eds.), *Media effects: Advances in theory and research* (pp. 287–303). Erlbaum.

Carr, C. T. (2020). CMC is dead, Long live CMC!: Situating computer-mediated communication scholarship beyond the digital age. *Journal of Computer-Mediated Communication, 25*(1), 9–22. https://doi.org/10.1093/jcmc/zmz018

Christofides, E., Muise, A., & Desmarais, S. (2009). Information disclosure and control on Facebook: Are they two sides of the same coin or two different

processes? *CyberPsychology & Behavior, 12*(3), 341–345. https://doi.org/10
.1089/cpb.2008.0226

Elkind, D. (1967). Egocentrism in adolescence. *Child Development, 38*(4), 1025–1034.
https://doi.org/10.2307/1127100

Fikkers, K. M., Piotrowski, J. T., Weeda, W. D., Vossen, H. G. M., & Valkenburg,
P. M. (2013). Double dose: High family conflict enhances the effect of media
violence exposure on adolescents' aggression. *Societies, 3*(3), 280–292. https://
doi.org/10.3390/soc3030280

Franchina, V., Vanden Abeele, M., van Rooij, A. J., Lo Coco, G., & De Marez, L.
(2018). Fear of missing out as a predictor of problematic social media use
and phubbing behavior among Flemish adolescents. *International Journal of
Environmental Research and Public Health, 15*(10), 1–18. https://doi.org/10
.3390/ijerph15102319

Gerbner, G., Gross, L., Morgan, M., & Signorielli, N. (1980). The "mainstreaming" of
America: Violence profile no. 11. *Journal of Communication, 30*(3), 10–29.
https://doi.org/10.1111/j.1460-2466.1980.tb01987.x

Gibson, J. J. (1979). *The ecological approach to visual perception*. Houghton-Mifflin.

Howard, M. C., & Hoffman, M. E. (2017). Variable-centered, person-centered, and
person-specific approaches. *Organizational Research Methods, 21*(4), 846–876.
https://doi.org/10.1177/1094428117744021

Katz, E., Blumler, J. G., & Gurevitch, M. (1973). Uses and gratifications research.
Public Opinion Quarterly, 37(4), 509–523. http://www.jstor.org/stable/
2747854

Kelly, A. E., & Rodriguez, R. R. (2006). Publicly committing oneself to an identity.
Basic and Applied Social Psychology, 28(2), 185–191. https://doi.org/10.1207/
s15324834basp2802_8

Koutamanis, M., Vossen, H. G. M., & Valkenburg, P. M. (2015). Adolescents'
comments in social media: Why do adolescents receive negative feedback
and who is most at risk? *Computers in Human Behavior, 53*, 486–494. https://
doi.org/10.1016/j.chb.2015.07.016

Krcmar, M. (2009). Individual differences in media effects. In R. L. Nabi & M. B.
Oliver (Eds.), *The SAGE handbook of media processes and effects*
(pp. 237–250). Sage.

Lerner, R. M., Lerner, J. V., & Chase, P. A. (2019). Toward enhancing the role of
idiographic-based analyses in describing, explaining, and optimizing the
study of human development: The sample case of adolescent ←→ family
relationships. *Journal of Family Theory & Review, 11*(4), 495–509. https://
doi.org/10.1111/jftr.12347

McFarland, L. A., & Ployhart, R. E. (2015). Social media: A contextual framework to
guide research and practice. *Journal of Applied Psychology, 100*(6),
1653–1677. https://doi.org/10.1037/a0039244

McNeish, D., & Hamaker, E. L. (2020). A primer on two-level dynamic structural
equation models for intensive longitudinal data in Mplus. *Psychological
Methods, 25*(5), 610–635. https://doi.org/10.1037/met0000250

McQuail, D. (2010). *McQuail's mass communication theory*. Sage.

Meier, A., Gilbert, A., Börner, S., & Possler, D. (2020). Instagram inspiration:
How upward comparison on social network sites can contribute to

well-being. *Journal of Communication*, *70*(5), 721–743. https://doi.org/10.1093/joc/jqaa025

Nesi, J., Choukas-Bradley, S., & Prinstein, M. J. (2018a). Transformation of adolescent peer relations in the social media context: Part 1 – A theoretical framework and application to dyadic peer relationships. *Clinical Child and Family Psychology Review*, *21*(3), 267–294. https://doi.org/10.1007/s10567-018-0261-x

Nesi, J., Choukas-Bradley, S., & Prinstein, M. J. (2018b). Transformation of adolescent peer relations in the social media context: Part 2 – Application to peer group processes and future directions for research. *Clinical Child and Family Psychology Review*, *21*(3), 295–319. https://doi.org/10.1007/s10567-018-0262-9

Parmelee, J. H., & Roman, N. (2020). Insta-echoes: Selective exposure and selective avoidance on Instagram. *Telematics and Informatics*, *52*, Article 101432. https://doi.org/10.1016/j.tele.2020.101432

Peter, J., & Valkenburg, P. M. (2006). Research note: Individual differences in perceptions of internet communication. *European Journal of Communication*, *21*(2), 213–226. https://doi.org/10.1177/0267323105064046

Peter, J., & Valkenburg, P. M. (2013). The effects of internet communication on adolescents' psychological development. In E. Scharrer (Ed.), *The international encyclopedia of media studies: Media psychology/media effects* (pp. 686–697). Wiley-Blackwell. https://doi.org/10.1002/9781444361506.wbiems136

Pingree, R. J. (2007). How messages affect their senders: A more general model of message effects and implications for deliberation. *Communication Theory*, *17*(4), 439–461. https://doi.org/10.1111/j.1468-2885.2007.00306.x

Postmes, T., Lea, M., Spears, R., & Reicher, S. D. (2000). *SIDE issues centre stage: Recent developments in studies of de-individuation in groups*. KNAW.

Pouwels, J. L., Valkenburg, P. M., Beyens, I., van Driel, I. I., & Keijsers, L. (2021). Social media use and friendship closeness in adolescents' daily lives: An experience sampling study. *Developmental Psychology*, *57*(2), 309–323. https://doi.org/10.1037/dev0001148

Reinecke, L., & Trepte, S. (2014). Authenticity and well-being on social network sites: A two-wave longitudinal study on the effects of online authenticity and the positivity bias in SNS communication. *Computers in Human Behavior*, *30*, 95–102. https://doi.org/10.1016/j.chb.2013.07.030

Rideout, V., & Fox, S. (2018). *Digital health practices, social media use, and mental well-being among teens and young adults in the US*. https://www.commonsensemedia.org/

Sameroff, A. (2009). The transactional model. In A. Sameroff (Ed.), *The transactional model of child development: How children and contexts shape each other* (pp. 3–22). American Psychological Association. https://doi.org/10.1037/11877-001

Scherr, S., Arendt, F., Frissen, T., & Oramas M. J. (2020). Detecting intentional self-harm on Instagram: Development, testing, and validation of an automatic image-recognition algorithm to discover cutting-related posts. *Social Science Computer Review*, *38*(6), 673–685. https://doi.org/10.1177/0894439319836389

Schouten, A. P., Valkenburg, P. M., & Peter, J. (2007). Precursors and underlying processes of adolescents' online self-disclosure: Developing and testing an "internet-attribute-perception" model. *Media Psychology*, *10*(2), 292–314. https://doi.org/10.1080/15213260701375686

Schultz, D., Izard, C. E., & Bear, G. (2004). Children's emotion processing: Relations to emotionality and aggression. *Development and Psychopathology, 16*(2), 371–387. https://doi.org/10.1017/S0954579404044566

Scott, G. G., & Fullwood, C. (2020). Does recent research evidence support the hyperpersonal model of online impression management? *Current Opinion in Psychology, 36*, 106–111. https://doi.org/10.1016/j.copsyc.2020.05.005

Slater, M. D. (2003). Alienation, aggression, and sensation seeking as predictors of adolescent use of violent film, computer, and website content. *Journal of Communication, 53*(1), 105–121. https://doi.org/10.1093/joc/53.1.105

Slater, M. D. (2007). Reinforcing spirals: The mutual influence of media selectivity and media effects and their impact on individual behavior and social identity. *Communication Theory, 17*(3), 281–303. https://doi.org/10.1111/j.1468-2885.2007.00296.x

Steinberg, L. (2010). A dual systems model of adolescent risk-taking. *Developmental Psychobiology, 52*(3), 216–224. https://doi.org/doi.org/10.1002/dev.20445

Steinberg, L. (2011). *Adolescence* (Vol. 9). McGraw-Hill.

Stern, S. (2015). Regretted online self-presentations: U.S. college students' recollections and reflections. *Journal of Children and Media, 9*(2), 248–265. https://doi.org/10.1080/17482798.2015.1024000

Subrahmanyam, K., Smahel, D., & Greenfield, P. (2006). Connecting developmental constructions to the internet: Identity presentation and sexual exploration in online teen chat rooms. *Developmental Psychology, 42*(3), 395–406. https://doi.org/10.1037/0012-1649.42.3.395

Sundar, S. S., Jia, H., Waddell, T. F., & Huang, Y. (2015). Toward a theory of interactive media effects (TIME). In S. S. Sundar (Ed.), *The handbook of the psychology of communication technology* (pp. 47–86). Wiley. https://doi.org/10.1002/9781118426456.ch3

Tice, D. M. (1992). Self-concept change and self-presentation: The looking glass self is also a magnifying glass. *Journal of Personality and Social Psychology, 63*(3), 435–451. https://doi.org/10.1037//0022-3514.63.3.435

Treem, J. W., & Leonardi, P. M. (2013). Social media use in organizations: Exploring the affordances of visibility, editability, persistence, and association. *Annals of the International Communication Association, 36*(1), 143–189. https://doi.org/10.1080/23808985.2013.11679130

Valkenburg, P. M. (2017). Understanding self-effects in social media. *Human Communication Research, 43*(4), 477–490. https://doi.org/10.1111/hcre.12113

Valkenburg, P. M., Beyens, I., Pouwels, J. L., van Driel, I. I., & Keijsers, L. (2021). Social media and adolescents' self-esteem: Heading for a person-specific media effects paradigm. *Journal of Communication, 71*(1), 56–78. https://doi.org/10.1093/joc/jqaa/039

Valkenburg, P. M., & Cantor, J. (2000). Children's likes and dislikes of entertainment programs. In D. Zillmann & P. Vorderer (Eds.), *Media entertainment: The psychology of its appeal* (Vol. 11; pp. 135–152). Lawrence Erlbaum Associates.

Valkenburg, P. M., & Oliver, M. B. (2019). Media effects theories: An overview. In *Media effects: Advances in theory and research: Fourth Edition* (4th ed.; pp. 16–35). Routledge.

Valkenburg, P. M., & Peter, J. (2009). The effects of instant messaging on the quality of adolescents' existing friendships: A longitudinal study. *Journal of Communication, 59*(1), 79–97. https://doi.org/10.1111/j.1460-2466.2008.01405.x

Valkenburg, P. M., & Peter, J. (2011). Online communication among adolescents: An integrated model of its attraction, opportunities, and risks. *Journal of Adolescent Health, 48*(2), 121–127. https://doi.org/10.1016/j.jadohealth.2010.08.020

Valkenburg, P. M., & Peter, J. (2013a). The differential susceptibility to media effects model. *Journal of Communication, 63*(2), 221–243. https://doi.org/10.1111/jcom.12024

Valkenburg, P. M., & Peter, J. (2013b). Five challenges for the future of media-effects research. *International Journal of Communication, 7*, 197–215.

Valkenburg, P. M., Peter, J., & Walther, J. B. (2016). Media effects: Theory and research. *Annual Review of Psychology, 67*, 315–338. https://doi.org/10.1146/annurev-psych-122414-033608

Valkenburg, P. M., & Piotrowski, J. T. (2017). *Plugged in: How media attract and affect youth.* Yale University Press.

Verduyn, P., Ybarra, O., Résibois, M., Jonides, J., & Kross, E. (2017). Do social network sites enhance or undermine subjective well-being? A critical review. *Social Issues and Policy Review, 11*(1), 274–302. https://doi.org/10.1111/sipr.12033

Vogel, E. A., Rose, J. P., Roberts, L. R., & Eckles, K. (2014). Social comparison, social media, and self-esteem. *Psychology of Popular Media Culture, 3*(4), 206–222. https://doi.org/10.1037/ppm0000047

Walther, J. B. (1992). Interpersonal effects in computer-mediated interaction: A relational perspective. *Communication Research, 19*(1), 52–90. https://doi.org/10.1177/009365092019001003

Walther, J. B. (1996). Computer-mediated communication: Impersonal, interpersonal, and hyperpersonal interaction. *Communication Research, 23*(1), 3–43. https://doi.org/10.1177/009365096023001001

Walther, J. B. (2011). Theories of computer-mediated communication and interpersonal relations. In M. L. Knapp & J. A. Daly (Eds.), *The handbook of interpersonal communication* (pp. 443–479). Sage.

Waterloo, S. F., Baumgartner, S. E., Peter, J., & Valkenburg, P. M. (2017). Norms of online expressions of emotion: Comparing Facebook, Twitter, Instagram, and WhatsApp. *New Media & Society, 20*(5), 1813–1831. https://doi.org/10.1177/1461444817707349

Webster, J. G. (2009). The role of structure in media choice. In T. Hartmann (Ed.), *Media choice: A theoretical and empirical overview* (pp. 221–233). Routledge.

Xu, K., & Liao, T. (2020). Explicating cues: A typology for understanding emerging media technologies. *Journal of Computer-Mediated Communication, 25*(1), 32–43. https://doi.org/10.1093/jcmc/zmz023

Zillmann, D., & Bryant, J. (1985). Affect, mood, and emotion as determinants of selective exposure. In D. Zillmann & J. Bryant (Eds.), *Selective exposure to communication* (pp. 157–190). Erlbaum.

PART II

Digital Media in the Adolescent Developmental Context

3 Digital Media and the Dual Aspect of Adolescent Identity Development

The Effects of Digital Media Use on Adolescents' Commitments and Self-Stories

Hiromitsu Morita, Nastasia Griffioen, and Isabela Granic

Concerns abound about the impact of social media on adolescents as it increasingly becomes an integral part of their social lives. One of the concerns that has received a great deal of attention is the impact of social media on adolescents' mental health (Gordon, 2020). A large number of studies have been conducted to investigate the impact; however, the findings are mixed, showing both positive and negative impact (Baker & Algorta, 2016; Best et al., 2014; Seabrook et al., 2016). What is clear in this growing body of research with seemingly contradictory findings is that the relation between social media use and adolescent mental health is much more complex than originally thought. In line with the recognition of this complexity, more and more researchers examine the mechanism of this relation within the framework of a psychological theory (Keles et al., 2019).

Adolescent Identity Development on Social Media

In a recent theoretical review, Granic et al. (2020) suggested that, in order to understand the impact of digital media on adolescents' mental health, it is essential to consider their core developmental concern: identity development. For decades, developmental psychologists have studied the challenging transition adolescents are expected to make in order to become functional members of society – that is, moving past identifying with the roles and values of others and toward making social commitments that are in accord with their own interests, aptitudes, and values (Erikson, 1968; Kroger, 2004). Whether or not adolescents successfully make this transition has important implications for their mental health (e.g., Azmitia et al., 2013; Kuiper et al., 2016). Since a considerable proportion of identity development processes is now taking place on social media, it is important to examine how the use of social media affects these processes.

A Model of Adolescent Identity Development

To present a model of adolescent identity development, we build on the theoretical framework proposed by Granic et al. (2020). In this framework, progression toward (a) commitment to person–society integrated values and (b) the construction of a coherent life story constitutes adolescent identity development. The framework specifies key factors at intrapersonal, interpersonal, and cultural levels that shape adolescent identity development. Key factors at the intrapersonal level are psychological needs that drive adolescents to uphold and unite personal and social values and form a coherent life story. Key interpersonal factors are the characteristics of narrative partners that affect how adolescents construct and develop stories about themselves. Finally, key cultural factors are cultural values, norms, and narratives that set the boundaries within which adolescents explore and make commitment choices. This chapter focuses on processes at the interpersonal level, where intrapersonal and cultural factors intersect, as these processes are most pertinent to social media. Specifically, we discuss narrative and dialogical processes as an interpersonal mechanism of identity development (Hammack, 2008; McLean & Pasupathi, 2012). Through sharing self-stories with others, individuals encounter various perspectives, reflect on and learn about themselves, and consolidate or change their commitments, values, and narratives. Furthermore, we clearly differentiate between the subjective and objective aspects of identity by drawing on McAdams's (1998) exposition of the self-as-subject (meaning-making process) and the self-as-object (product of the meaning-making process). We explain how the two aspects of identity develop together through narrative and dialogical processes (see Figure 3.1).

Chapter Overview

We begin by describing the subjective aspect of identity development: changes in *commitments* and *values*.[1] We explain how conventional commitments change to self-evaluated commitments during adolescence and the key role of introspection in this transition. We then describe the objective aspect of identity development: changes in a self-story, or *narrative identity*. We explain the process of constructing a coherent life story during adolescence and the function of narrative partners in this process. After the description of each aspect of adolescent identity development, we discuss how the use of social media may facilitate or hinder the key processes involved. Since the field of identity development is just beginning to incorporate social media in its research, our discussion will consist mainly of hypothetical links between social media use and adolescent identity development. However, the paucity of research in this area also means there are many avenues for future research. Therefore, the chapter concludes with future directions for studying the impact of social media use on adolescent identity development.

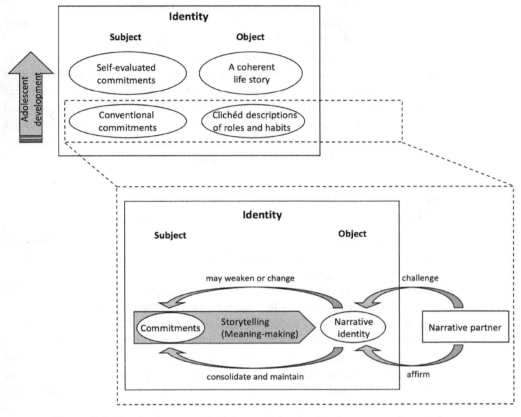

Figure 3.1 *The dual aspect of adolescent identity development and narrative and dialogical processes*

The Subjective Aspect of Identity Development: Changes in Commitments and Values

Identity is first and foremost the self as subject. Although developmental psychologists have taken different approaches to conceptualizing and studying the subjective self and its changes, there are some commonalities in their descriptions (Kroger, 2004). In this chapter we focus on Erikson's (1968) theory of the life cycle and Loevinger's (1976) theory of ego development. Erikson laid out a series of crises that people face in their lifetime and must resolve for proper functioning and development. Although he described all the crises as having some bearing on identity, he characterized the fifth one – which takes place in adolescence – as a major crisis for identity. Erikson conceptualized identity in several different ways. However, later psychologists have focused on his conception of identity as ideological and occupational commitments and expanded it to include interpersonal commitments (e.g., Luyckx et al., 2006; Marcia, 1966).

Loevinger (1976) also developed a theory of changes in the subjective self, namely ego development theory. Unlike Erikson's theory, Loevinger's theory is not built around chronological age, and therefore the ego stages are not tied to age-related challenges and tasks. The theory describes changes in various aspects of the self, such as impulse control, conscious preoccupations, and cognitive and interpersonal styles. At its core, ego development theory is about changes in an individual's frame of reference, the values in accordance with which an individual makes experience meaningful and coherent (Hy & Loevinger, 1996). In short, changes in commitments and values constitute the subjective aspect of identity development.

The Formation of Self-Evaluated Commitments in Adolescence

Identity development is a lifelong process. Throughout life, identity undergoes qualitative changes (Kroger, 2004). However, particular attention has been paid to the type of identity that is thought to mark the entrance to adulthood. According to Erikson's (1968) theory of the life cycle, childhood is a period in which individuals learn the roles of adults around them and focus on becoming skillful at preparatory tasks provided by their family, school, and community. Children are therefore identified with the roles and values of others in the immediate environment. In adolescence, psychological needs and social demands drive individuals to explore different occupations and ideologies in the larger society and commit to occupations and ideologies that match their own interests, aptitudes, and values to find their niche in society. This serves as the foundation for adulthood.

It is now widely recognized that identity exploration and commitment are iterative processes (Bosma & Kunnen, 2001; Grotevant, 1987; Kerpelman et al., 1997; Luyckx et al., 2006). For example, Luyckx et al. (2006, 2013) suggested that identity formation involves two cycles. The first one consists of exploration in breadth and commitment-making. In this cycle, individuals explore various values and goals and make initial commitments. The second cycle consists of exploration in depth and identification with commitment. Specifically, current commitments are continually re-evaluated through self-reflection and interpersonal dialogue, and if individuals feel confident about their commitments, they identify with them.

A similar developmental sequence can be found in Loevinger's (1976) ego development theory: progression from the Conformist stage to the Conscientious stage via the Self-Aware stage. At the Conformist stage, social belonging is of paramount importance, and most effort is put into gaining acceptance by a social group. Individuals at this stage conform to the norms and values of their social groups, which are based on external characteristics (e.g., physical appearance, outward behavior). Thus, they seek social acceptance and recognition by trying to look or behave in a socially desirable manner. At the next, Self-Aware stage, individuals begin to explore inner aspects of themselves, and conformity starts to become less rigid. When the next, Conscientious stage is reached, individuals have gained a rich understanding of their motives and personality traits. Individuals at this stage therefore evaluate and commit to social values based on their internal characteristics (i.e., the formation of self-evaluated commitments; Loevinger, 1987). Although ego development was conceptualized independently of chronological age, research has shown that the progression from the Conformist stage toward the Conscientious stage commonly takes place during adolescence (Syed & Seiffge-Krende, 2015; Westenberg & Gjerde, 1999).

In sum, the transition from conventional commitments to self-evaluated commitments constitutes the subjective aspect of adolescent identity development. This transition is marked by changes in the mode of commitment – from conformity to self-evaluated commitment – and the nature of commitments – from external to internal characteristics.

Identity Exploration and Introspection

Exploration to gain an understanding of one's environment and oneself is considered a key mechanism of identity development (Grotevant, 1987). Erikson (1968) emphasized the importance of psychosocial moratorium, the period during which adolescents explore different ideologies and occupations in society and find suitable ones. Such exploration entails introspection to find out one's own interests, values, and aptitudes. In Loevinger's (1976) ego development, we have seen that progression from the Conformist stage to the Conscientious stage goes through the Self-Aware stage, where individuals begin introspection to gain a deeper understanding of their internal characteristics. In order to move on from rigid conformity, individuals must shift their focus from external to internal aspects of themselves to understand their own interests and values, which they can then use to evaluate and choose social values to commit to. Indeed, introspection was found to be the most common factor in identity development (Kroger & Green, 1996).

The capacity for introspection begins to develop in adolescence (Sebastian et al., 2008), making it a sensitive period for cultivating the capacity. Counseling, psychotherapy, and educational programs have been used to aid adolescents' identity exploration (Kroger, 2004). Marcia (1989) suggested that it is important to create an open and safe environment that encourages free exploration and serves as a safety net if adolescents' choices go awry. Indeed, it has long been noted that open and accepting relationships are crucial in facilitating self-exploration (Rogers, 1961). As we discuss later in the chapter, identity exploration and introspection often happen during or following interpersonal dialogue, and the characteristics of conversational partners greatly affect the extent to which individuals engage in self-exploration and gain insights into themselves.

Social Media and the Adolescent Development of Commitments and Values

We have explained the adolescent development of commitments and values: the transition from conventional to self-evaluated commitments. We now discuss how the use of social media may affect this transition. To reiterate, identity exploration and introspection inherent in the exploration are a key mechanism through which adolescents move on from conformity and preoccupation with external characteristics and form self-evaluated commitments. Therefore, the use of social media would facilitate the transition if it supports identity exploration and introspection. Conversely, the use of social media would hinder the transition if it prevents identity exploration and introspection, increases conformity, and makes adolescents fixated on appearance.

A Playground for Identity Exploration

Social media provides the opportunity for people to try out different versions of themselves and see what feels right (Casserly, 2011). When asked about who they are on social media, people often report that they have different personas depending on the platform (Zhong et al., 2017). This may be because different platforms tend to attract different audiences by virtue of their design and functionality. For example, Instagram may be well suited to expressing people's artistic side and therefore popular among artists, while Reddit may cater to their contemplative, intellectual side and attract curious minds and experts. The beauty of social media is therefore that all platforms taken together serve as a playground in which individuals can explore different aspects of themselves. However, there is also the downside of a plethora of options: Too many options can create paralysis and lead to ruminative explor- ation, keeping adolescents from completing the cycle of identity formation (Beyers & Luyckx, 2016). As we have discussed, successful adolescent identity development requires not only exploration of commitment options but also introspection to evaluate whether these options fit one's personality. Therefore, social media platforms that provide space for identity exploration as well as self-reflection may be more conducive to identity development than those that provide space for the former only.

Potent Social Norms and Values

While social media offers plenty of opportunities for identity exploration, the large scale of social media also enables potent social norms and values, potentially making it more difficult for adolescents to move on from conform- ity. Most adolescents in the pre–social media era are likely to have negotiated with trends and conventions that manifested themselves in a relatively small social group, at most on a national scale. With social media, however, adolescents now have the possibility to observe trends on a much larger global scale, likely experiencing greater pressure to conform to these trends. Indeed, norms and values on social media may have stronger influence than those offline because they are more widely shared and more readily accessed (Nesi et al., 2018).

Social attitudes that currently prevail in Western cultures and may be magnified by social media are anti-mainstream sentiments (Vinh, 2021). Those who follow counterculture movements are usually called hippies or hipsters, going against what – in their eyes – everyone else is doing. One reflection of this trend is the popularity of prank videos on social media, in which people violate social conventions and norms for entertainment. The anti-mainstream sentiments have appealed to so many people that they themselves have become the norm and the source of conformity. Thus, social media can spread and magnify trends rapidly to create potent social norms and values, including those that espouse anti-mainstream sentiments.

Inescapable Past Selves

An essential condition for identity development is the freedom to leave behind old identities and explore new ones. Unfortunately, such freedom is not always guaranteed on the Internet. What people say and do on the Internet is permanently recorded and often remains on the Internet for future generations to unearth (Eichhorn, 2019; Nesi et al., 2020). This permanence of information on the Internet, especially on social media, can be problematic for identity development (see Davis & Weinstein, 2017). Traces of old identities on social media can mislead others into thinking that the old identities still hold true and make it difficult for individuals to change or to fully embrace the change. There is the increasing occurrence of people being criticized or getting fired for what they said or did on the Internet in the past even though these views or deeds no longer reflect them (e.g., Arora, 2021). Accordingly, there are signs of adolescents and young adults erasing their social media posts for fear of repercussions (Davis & Weinstein, 2017; Jargon, 2020; Smith, 2013). These privacy issues therefore seem to be making it difficult for individuals to free themselves from the past and move forward.

However, reminders of one's past selves may also benefit identity development. In adolescent years, individuals may go through many different phases. For example, an adolescent may experience the "goth" phase from age 15 to 16 years, reflected in a series of photos of a black-clothed self with plaid skirts and chains. From age 17 to 18 years, this adolescent may be absorbed in environmentalism, reflected in posts and photos depicting community efforts and environmental protests. Transition between such phases may sometimes feel fluent and smooth and may be easily forgotten. Snippets of social media content and interactions in the past can help individuals recall parts of their past selves that they may otherwise have forgotten. Being reminded of past selves can also help individuals reflect on the development they have gone through and understand that identity is never permanent and continues to change over time (Pasupathi et al., 2007). It is nonetheless important that the right to social media data belong to users so that they can access their past data when they want to and they can erase them if they deem them harmful to their current identity.

A Tool for Distraction or Introspection?

One of the concerns that social media has generated is that it may act as a distraction from oneself (The School of Life, n.d.). Social media is filled with information about people's lives and world events, and passive usage of social media (e.g., reading news feeds) is more common than active usage (e.g., posting status updates; Verduyn et al., 2015). The implication is that people are focused mainly on other people's lives on social media, leaving little room to reflect on their own lives and gain insights into themselves. Furthermore, information overload on social media, which has been shown to lead to "social media fatigue" in some (Bright et al., 2015; Dhir et al., 2019), may deplete cognitive resources necessary for digesting information and integrating it into a sense of self. Indeed, Misra and Stokols (2012) found that individuals who experienced an overload of digital information spent less time on contemplative activities such as self-reflection.

Nevertheless, social media has some functionalities that could help people gain insights into themselves. For example, Facebook's "Year in Review" posts provide users with a chance to reflect on their life experiences in the past year. Such reflection may bring people insights into what kind of things they value and are interested in and what they are good at. Furthermore, as we discuss later, social media significantly increases the chance to receive feedback about oneself from others (e.g., boyd & Heer, 2006), thereby deepening self-understanding.

Emphasis on Appearance

Another important issue to consider is the extent to which social media promotes preoccupation with appearance. Although social media can be used for a variety of purposes, posting pictures of one's physical appearance (i.e., selfies) is popular among adolescents, and many adolescents are preoccupied with how others perceive their physical appearance on social media (Boursier & Manna, 2018; Choukas-Bradley et al., 2020). The increasing use of clickbaits to attract followers on social media may also be contributing to their perceived importance of appearance and superficial impressions. Preoccupation with appearance on social media is associated with a number of negative mental health indices among adolescents (Choukas-Bradley et al., 2020). While having a healthy body image is important, adolescent identity development entails a shift in the source of self-esteem from external to internal attributes. Therefore, social media is likely to be harmful to adolescents to the extent that it makes them fixated on appearance.

The design and affordances of social media platforms may affect the degree to which adolescents focus on external aspects of themselves. For example, photo-based social media platforms such as Instagram may attract those who are concerned with physical appearance, and consequently social values and norms that revolve around physical appearance may be more prevalent on these platforms. Therefore, the use of photo-based platforms may put adolescents at higher risk of being influenced by appearance-based values and norms. Furthermore, given that individuals can explore and express their internal characteristics more easily using concepts and words rather than images, text-based platforms such as Reddit and Tumblr might be more conducive to introspection and the expression of inner qualities. It is nonetheless important to note that the nonverbal expression of internal characteristics is possible (e.g., an expression of creativity in dancing), and photo-based platforms can also serve as a place for more mature expressions of identity.

The Objective Aspect of Identity Development: Changes in a Narrative Identity

Thus far, we have discussed the subjective aspect of identity development: changes in commitments and values. We now turn to the objective aspect, manifestations of the changes. Commitments and values manifest themselves in several ways. For example, people strive to fulfill their commitments and values; therefore, commitments and values are manifested in goal-striving (Maslow, 1970; Schwartz, 1996). Moreover, values act as a frame of reference in perception to create "coherent meanings in experience" (Hy & Loevinger, 1996, p. 4). Thus, they are reflected in the meanings that individuals assign to objects and events. When this meaning-making process is applied to past experiences, it often takes the form of storytelling. A story about the self that an individual creates based on their past experiences has been termed "narrative identity" (McAdams, 2018; Singer, 2004). In storytelling, individuals make sense of and organize their past experiences by relating them to important aspects of themselves (Pasupathi et al., 2007). In other words, past experiences that are relevant to one's goals and values (i.e., *self-defining memories*) make up the main contents of a narrative identity (Blagov & Singer, 2004; Singer et al., 2013). In short, commitments and values (identity-as-subject) act as the guiding principles of storytelling to make sense of and organize past experiences into a narrative identity (identity-as-object; see Figure 3.1).

The Construction of a Coherent Life Story in Adolescence

As adolescents' commitments change from conventional to self-evaluated commitments, corresponding changes likely occur in their narrative identities. During adolescence, a narrative identity changes from relatively disjointed descriptions of roles and habits to an autobiographical narrative, which demonstrates more complex reflective thinking and a causal understanding of one's life experiences (Habermas & de Silveira, 2008; McAdams, 1998). Specifically, adolescents' narrative identities increasingly take the form of a life story, which tells how the past self has grown into the present self, which may then become an envisioned future self (McAdams, 2018; McAdams & McLean, 2013). Their past, present, and future become clearly differentiated and yet causally connected to form a temporally coherent life story (Habermas & Bluck, 2000; Pasupathi et al., 2007). In addition to temporal coherence, there is another type of coherence that likely emerges in adolescents' narrative identities: person–society coherence (Syed & McLean, 2016). This type of coherence shows alignment between individuals' personal attributes and their social contexts. As discussed earlier, adolescent identity development is progression toward commitment to social values that match personal interests, values, and talents. Therefore, narrative identities likely exhibit temporal and person–society coherence toward the end of adolescent development, weaving together the past self that was identified with the roles and values of others, the present self that commits to person–society integrated values, and the future self that will fulfill these values.

Besides these structural changes, adolescent identity development is likely to be accompanied by related changes in the theme of a narrative identity. Granic et al. (2020) suggested that the dynamics of the needs for agency and communion shift during adolescence and that this shift may be reflected in the relative prominence on agency versus communion themes in a narrative identity. Specifically, as adolescents start to engage in self-exploration and gain better insight into their own interests and values, a predominance of communion themes may give way to a predominance of agency themes (see Van Doeselaar et al., 2020, for some indirect support for this). Toward the end of adolescent identity development, when the needs for agency and communion become more balanced, agency and communion themes may become relatively equalized and united in a narrative identity.

Another theme that is relevant to adolescent identity development is external versus internal focus. As discussed earlier, the nature of commitments changes from external to internal characteristics during adolescence. Therefore, the theme of adolescents' narrative identities is likely to change from that of trying to look good and behave properly to that of cultivating their inner traits.

Dialogue and the Function of Narrative Partners

Storytelling is inherently a social activity and therefore usually involves dialogue (Hammack, 2008; Hermans, 2004). A narrative identity expressed in storytelling can be affirmed or challenged, which may in turn consolidate, weaken, or change commitments and values (McLean & Pasupathi, 2012; Thorne, 2000; see Figure 3.1). Thus, storytelling and dialogue are an important mechanism of identity development. Whether storytelling and dialogue contribute meaningfully to identity development depends heavily on the characteristics of their narrative partners (McLean et al., 2007; Pasupathi & Hoyt, 2009). There are three essential functions that narrative partners serve: (a) elaboration, (b) grappling, and (c) attention and validation (Granic et al., 2020).

First, narrative partners help people elaborate on their stories (Fivush et al., 2006; Pasupathi et al., 2007). To construct a meaningful and coherent life story from past experiences, you must derive meaning from these experiences, and a simple recounting of past experiences is often insufficient (Blagov & Singer, 2004; Singer et al., 2013). Therefore, narrative partners' requests for elaboration are essential. Blagov and Singer (2004) specified four dimensions of self-defining memories, which have implications for elaboration requests. Specifically, elaboration requests are likely to be especially helpful if they use a time frame most conducive to meaning-making in a given situation (e.g., "Tell me exactly what happened in that moment"; "How did you change during your college years?") and ask about affect, or more specifically, emotional valence and intensity (e.g., "How did the experience make you feel?"; "How much impact did the experience have on you?"), content, or the relevance to values and goals (e.g., "Why is the experience important to you?"; "How does the experience help you achieve your goals?"), and meaning, or learning and growth (e.g., "What did you learn from the experience?"; "How did the experience change you as a person?").

The second important function of narrative partners is "grappling", which is an act of supporting identity exploration in a dialogue while maintaining an attitude of open-mindedness and patience (Granic et al., 2020). Engaging in dialogue with others is essentially identity exploration because different people uphold different values and you are encouraged to take others' perspectives in dialogue (Hermans, 2004). Your values and narratives may sometimes be challenged in the process, and listening to alternative views may bring new insights and weaken or change your values and commitments. However, such a challenge is likely most fruitful when it is done in an open and accepting relationship (Rogers, 1961). Moreover, it is important that narrative partners remain patient despite unexpected perspective changes and contradictions, which are due to occur during identity exploration (Granic et al., 2020).

Finally, narrative partners provide attention and affirmation. When narrative partners listen attentively and affirm your life story, your values and goal endeavors are reflected back to you and become consolidated (McLean & Pasupathi, 2012; Pasupathi & Rich, 2005). Those who show interest and give you affirmation are usually the ones who share your values and commitments. As discussed earlier, adolescent identity development is considered complete when they find their niche in society, where like-minded others share the interests and values that adolescents have discovered through self-exploration (Erikson, 1968). Therefore, finding narrative partners who share personal values and aspirations is important especially toward the end of adolescent identity development.

Social Media and the Adolescent Development of a Narrative Identity

We have discussed how commitments and a narrative identity develop together through storytelling and dialogue in adolescence. In this section we explore different ways in which social media can support or obstruct storytelling and dialogue, thereby facilitating or hindering the adolescent development of a narrative identity.

Dialogue with Diverse Groups of People

Social media emerged with the advent of the Web 2.0, a dramatic change of the Internet from a place for passive consumption to active participation, interaction, and collaboration (Peters, 2020). Anyone who has access to the Internet can express and share their views and stories on social media, and there are usually others – sometimes hundreds and thousands of people – who validate or reject their views and stories. Storytelling and dialogue in such a large, interconnected social environment have never existed before. Social media has made it easy to have dialogue with people who come from different cultures and backgrounds, thus significantly increasing the chance of encountering different perspectives. Since taking different perspectives during social interaction is essential for identity development (Hermans, 2004; Kroger, 2004), social media can be a great tool for adolescents' identity development. While there is some concern about the increasing frequency of conflicts resulting from the increased contact with diverse groups of people, conflicts can be meaningful experiences and contribute to identity development, especially if they are managed with understanding (Rogers, 1961). Therefore, the presence of moderators who are discerning but also empathetic would be valuable.

Censorship

There has been growing concern and controversy surrounding censorship on social media (Heins, 2014). Social media platforms such as Twitter and YouTube recently came under fire after deleting posts or banning users and channels that express certain ideological views (e.g., BBC News, 2020; Zaru, 2021). Social media companies have long suggested that their platforms provide a space for the free exchange of views and ideas. However, it has become apparent that these platforms are not neutral public platforms, but rather, just like traditional media, they promote certain content and suppress others according to their interests and ideologies (Lewis, 2021). Although social media companies began to acknowledge such editorial actions, it remains largely unclear how they are curating content. As we have just discussed, dialogue with diverse groups of people plays an essential role in identity development. Therefore, if social media platforms exercise editorial power, it is important that they make their decisions transparent so that people can make informed decisions about which platforms to use for a meaningful dialogue.

Narrative Elaboration on Social Media

Social media platforms generally support the elaboration of narratives as they provide comment sections and encourage dialogue between users. However, the unique affordances of social media platforms may affect the extent to which users elaborate on their stories. For example, Twitter sets a strict character limit for posts and comments and may therefore hinder the elaboration of narratives and deep dialogue compared to platforms like Facebook, Reddit, and Tumblr. Indeed, in an in-depth interview with activists, Comunello et al. (2016) found that the activists perceived platform affordances as having a significant impact on their ability to express themselves, with one of them reporting that the possibility to write longer texts allowed him to better articulate his opinions. Misunderstandings between users may be more common on platforms that restrict the length of posts and comments because short posts and comments do not easily allow clarification of meaning. Such platforms might predispose users to insult each other instead of asking each other questions to elaborate on their self-stories.

Attention and Validation on Social Media

Social media offers unprecedented opportunities to be listened to and validated by others. Before social media, individuals whose values and beliefs deviated from the norm had difficulty finding someone who would listen to or affirm their views (e.g., Gray, 2009). It is now much easier to find like-minded others because social media platforms such as Facebook and Reddit enable people to search for various communities. This is, for example, reflected in online activism by various groups of people (Bennett, 2014; Buell Hirsch, 2014; Sandoval-Almazan & Gil-Gracia, 2014). However, the downside of such diverse and specific communities is that they can create echo chambers and shun interaction outside the communities (Singer, 2020). An optimal social media environment may therefore be that which makes it easy to find like-minded people while encouraging communication and interaction between diverse groups.

Attention and validation are most effective if they come from close people (Carr et al., 2016). Hayes et al. (2016) found that people experienced more personal support on platforms that allowed them to easily narrow their audience and share posts with close friends (e.g., Snapchat). Therefore, adolescents who are in the phase of identity consolidation may benefit more by using platforms that make it easy to target posts to close friends.

Future Research Directions

Now that we have presented a theoretical model of adolescent identity development and discussed how the use of social media may facilitate or hinder the development, we suggest a few directions for future research. First, it is important to study how narrative identities typically develop during adolescence. Since many adolescents currently use social media for identity expressions (i.e., narrative identities), it is possible to examine the adolescent development of a narrative identity on social media (Granic et al., 2020). Although social media platforms have tightened restrictions on data access over the past few years (e.g., Facebook Business, 2018; Hemsley, 2019), private data download options and application programming interfaces remain a viable avenue for collecting social media data for research (Lomborg & Bechmann, 2014; Taylor & Pagliari, 2018). Adolescents' social media posts can be analyzed with research methods that have been developed to study narrative identities (Adler et al., 2017). The narrative research framework specifies how to code narrative identities in terms of structure (e.g., coherence) and theme (e.g., agency, communion). New coding manuals need to be developed for themes that are relevant to adolescent identity development but not included in the framework (e.g., external versus internal focus). It is important to note, however, that people are not given narrative prompts to elicit detailed information on social media. Therefore, it may be necessary to use an additional method such as an interview to fully understand what is being expressed in social media posts. Alternatively, researchers may develop an application to add narrative prompts to social media posts. Once the methods are developed, researchers can conduct longitudinal studies to examine how the structure and theme of narrative identities change during adolescence.

Another important direction for future research is to study how the design and affordances of social media platforms affect key processes of identity development (introspection, elaboration, grappling, attention, and validation). For this line of research, it is important to first examine the unique affordances and features of different social media platforms. For example, researchers may assess the diversity of communities on social media platforms (see, e.g., Bisgin et al., 2012; De Salve et al., 2018, for the methods). To assess the processes of identity development, researchers can code adolescents' posts as well as others' comments and reactions by using or adapting existing methods for studying these processes (e.g., Pasupathi & Hoyt, 2009; Pasupathi & Rich, 2005) or developing new ones.

However, like the analysis of narrative identities, the study of identity development processes may require more than social media data (especially introspection, which does not easily manifest itself). It would therefore be best to combine the coding of social media content with other methods that probe individuals' experiences on social media (e.g., interviews). One useful approach is the stimulated recall method, in which interviews are conducted around objective data to aid the recollection of experiences associated with the data (Bloom, 1953). Using social media data as memory cues can facilitate the recollection of thoughts and feelings that occurred during the use of social media (Griffioen et al., 2020).

Finally, a worthwhile research direction is to develop applications that support key identity development processes and examine whether they facilitate adolescents' identity development. For example, researchers may design an application based on the four dimensions of self-defining memories (Blagov & Singer, 2004) to help the meaning-making and organization of past experiences:

- Affect: Users can rate the emotional valence and intensity of social media posts so that they can gain insights into what kind of events have an impact on them and the nature and degree of the impact.
- Content: Users can assign value and commitment tags to their social media posts so that they can make explicit connections between their values and commitments and their life experiences.
- Meaning: Social media posts are accompanied by narrative prompts so as to help users derive meaning from their experiences and construct a meaningful and coherent narrative identity.[2]
- Time specificity: Users' social media posts can be displayed in different time frames (e.g., a given moment in time, day, week, month, year, and life stage) so that users can create narratives in these different time frames and later integrate these narratives into a life story.

After applications are developed, researchers can conduct studies (e.g., randomized control trials) to evaluate their efficacy in facilitating adolescent identity development. It is recommended that researchers take person-specific effects into account when evaluating the effects of social media (e.g., see Valkenburg et al., 2021).

Conclusion

In this chapter we have suggested that it is important to study how the use of social media affects adolescent identity development in order to under-stand the mechanism of the impact of social media on adolescent mental health. We presented a model of the dual aspect of adolescent identity development – progression toward the formation of self-evaluated commitments and values and the construction of a coherent life story – and discussed how the use of social media may facilitate or hinder the key processes involved, namely introspection, storytelling, and dialogue. It was suggested that future research should devise methods for studying narratives on social media and discover how narrative identities develop during adolescence. We also suggested examining the design and affordances of social media platforms and how they affect the key processes of identity development. We hope that this chapter will provide a useful framework for future research on the impact of social media on adolescents and encourage media developers to design social media environments that support identity development.

Notes

[1] Although values are generally more abstract than commitments, we use these terms interchangeably for our current purposes.

[2] Although Blagov and Singer (2004) discussed meaning primarily in terms of personal growth, individuals can also create meaning by linking life experiences to current goal aspirations and values without the growth element (which is discussed by the authors as "content"). Therefore, narrative prompts asking about the implications of the life experience for personal growth (value change) and those asking about the relevance to current goals and values would both be helpful in facilitating meaning-making.

References

Adler, J. A., Dunlop, W. L., Fivush, R., et al. (2017). Research methods for studying narrative identity: A primer. *Social Psychological and Personality Science*, *8*(5), 519–527. https://doi.org/10.1177/1948550617698202

Arora, R. (2021, March 27). If Teen Vogue can fire an editor for her teenage tweets, no one is safe. *New York Post*. https://nypost.com/2021/03/27/if-alexi-mccammond-can-be-fired-for-teenage-tweets-nobodys-safe/

Azmitia, M., Syed, M., & Radmacher, K. (2013). Finding your niche: Identity and emotional support in emerging adults' adjustment to the transition to college. *Journal of Research in Adolescence*, *23*(4), 744–761. https://doi.org/10.1111/jora.12037

Baker, D. A., & Algorta, G. P. (2016). The relationship between online social networking and depression: A systematic review of quantitative studies. *Cyberpsychology, Behavior, and Social Networking*, *19*(11), 638–648. https://doi.org/10.1089/cyber.2016.0206

BBC News. (2020, February 27). *YouTube 'not a public forum' with guaranteed free speech*. https://www.bbc.com/news/technology-51658341

Bennett, L. (2014). 'If we stick together we can do anything': Lady Gaga fandom, philanthropy and activism through social media. *Celebrity Studies*, *5*(1–2), 138–152. https://doi.org/10.1080/19392397.2013.813778

Best, P., Manktelow, R., & Taylor, B. (2014). Online communication, social media and adolescent wellbeing: A systematic narrative review. *Children and Youth Services Review*, *41*, 27–36. https://doi.org/10.1016/j.childyouth.2014.03.001

Beyers, W., & Luyckx, K. (2016). Ruminative exploration and reconsideration of commitment as risk factors for suboptimal identity development in adolescence and emerging adulthood. *Journal of Adolescence*, *47*, 169–178. https://doi.org/10.1016/j.adolescence.2015.10.018

Bisgin, H., Agarwal, N., & Xu, X. (2012). A study of homophily on social media. *World Wide Web*, *15*, 213–232. https://doi.org/10.1007/s11280-011-0143-3

Blagov, P. S., & Singer, J. S. (2004). Four dimensions of self-defining memories (specificity, meaning, content, and affect) and their relationships to self-restraint, distress, and repressive defensiveness. *Journal of Personality*, *72*(3), 481–511. https://doi.org/10.1111/j.0022-3506.2004.00270.x

Bloom, B. S. (1953). Thought-processes in lectures and discussions. *Journal of General Education*, *7*(3), 160–169.

Bosma, H. A., & Kunnen, E. S. (2001). Determinants and mechanisms in ego identity development: A review and synthesis. *Developmental Review*, *21*(1), 39–66. https://doi.org/10.1006/drev.2000.0514

Boursier, V., & Manna, V. (2018). Selfie expectancies among adolescents: Construction and validation of an instrument to assess expectancies toward selfies among boys and girls. *Frontiers in Psychology*, *9*, Article 839. https://doi.org/10.3389/fpsyg.2018.00839

boyd, d., & Heer, J. (2006, January 4–7). *Profiles as conversation: Networked identity performance on Friendster* [Paper presentation]. Proceedings of the 39th Annual Hawaii International Conference on System Sciences, Kunai, HI, United States. https://doi.org/10.1109/HICSS.2006.394

Bright, L. F., Kleiser, S. B., & Grau, S. L. (2015). Too much Facebook? An exploratory examination of social media fatigue. *Computers in Human Behavior*, *44*, 148–155. https://doi.org/10.1016/j.chb.2014.11.048

Buell Hirsch, P. (2014). Clicks or commitment: activism in the age of social media. *Journal of Business Strategy*, *35*(5), 55–58. https://doi.org/10.1108/JBS-07-2014-0086

Carr, C. T., Wohn, D. Y., & Hayes, R. A. (2016). 👍 as social support: Relational closeness, automaticity, and interpreting social support from paralinguistic digital affordances in social media. *Computers in Human Behavior*, *62*, 385–393. https://doi.org/10.1016/j.chb.2016.03.087

Casserly, M. (2011, January 26). Multiple personalities and social media: The many faces of me. *Forbes*. https://www.forbes.com/sites/meghancasserly/2011/01/26/multiple-personalities-and-social-media-the-many-faces-of-me/

Choukas-Bradley, S., Nesi, J., Widman, L., & Galla, B. M. (2020). The Appearance-Related Social Media Consciousness Scale: Development and validation with adolescents. *Body Image*, *33*, 164–174. https://doi.org/10.1016/j.bodyim.2020.02.017

Comunello, F., Mulargia, S., & Parisi, L. (2016). The 'proper' way to spread ideas through social media: Exploring the affordances and constraints of different social media platforms as perceived by Italian activists. *The Sociological Review*, *64*(3), 515–532. https://doi.org/10.1111/1467-954X.12378

Davis, K., & Weinstein, E. C. (2017). Identity development in the digital age: An Eriksonian perspective. In M. F. Wright (Ed.), *Identity, sexuality, and relationships among adults in the digital age* (pp. 1–7). IGI Global.

De Salve, A., Guidi, B., Ricci, L., & Mori, P. (2018). Discovering homophily in online social networks. *Mobile Networks and Applications, 23*(6), 1715–1726. https://doi.org/10.1007/s11036–018-1067-2

Dhir, A., Kaur, P., Chen, S., & Pallesen, S. (2019). Antecedents and consequences of social media fatigue. *International Journal of Information Management, 48*, 193–202. https://doi.org/10.1016/j.ijinfomgt.2019.05.021

Eichhorn, K. (2019). *The end of forgetting: Growing up with social media.* Harvard University Press.

Erikson, E. H. (1968). *Identity: Youth and crisis.* Norton.

Facebook Business. (2018, April 4). *Restricting data access and protecting people's information on Facebook.* https://www.facebook.com/business/news/restricting-data-access-and-protecting-peoples-information-on-facebook

Fivush, R., Haden, C. A., & Reese, E. (2006). Elaborating on elaborations: Role of maternal reminiscing style in cognitive and socioemotional development. *Child Development, 77*(6), 1568–1588. https://doi.org/10.1111/j.1467-8624.2006.00960.x

Gordon, S. (2020, July 13). *5 ways social media affects teen mental health.* Verywell Family. https://www.verywellfamily.com/ways-social-media-affects-teen-mental-health-4144769

Granic, I., Morita, H., & Scholten, H. (2020). Beyond screen time: Identity development in the digital age. *Psychological Inquiry, 31*(3), 195–223. https://doi.org/10.1080/1047840X.2020.1820214

Gray, M. L. (2009). *Out in the country: Youth, media, and queer visibility in rural America.* New York University Press.

Griffioen, N., Van Rooij, M. M., Lichtwarck-Aschoff, A., & Granic, I. (2020). A stimulated recall method for the improved assessment of quantity and quality of social media use. *Journal of Medical Internet Research, 22*(1), Article e15529. https://doi.org/10.2196/15529

Grotevant, H. D. (1987). Toward a process model of identity formation. *Journal of Adolescent Research, 2*(3), 203–222. https://doi.org/10.1177/074355488723003

Habermas, T., & Bluck, S. (2000). Getting a life: The emergence of the life story in adolescence. *Psychological Bulletin, 126*(5), 748–769. https://doi.org/10.1037/0033-2909.126.5.748

Habermas, T., & de Silveira, C. (2008). The development of global coherence in life narratives across adolescence: Temporal, causal, and thematic aspects. *Developmental Psychology, 44*(3), 707–721. https://doi.org/10.1037/0012-1649.44.3.707

Hammack, P. L. (2008). Narrative and the cultural psychology of identity. *Personality and Social Psychology Review, 12*(3), 222–247. https://doi.org/10.1177/1088868308316892

Hayes, R. A., Carr, C. T., & Wohn, D. Y. (2016). It's the audience: Differences in social support across social media. *Social Media + Society, 2*(4), 1–12. https://doi.org/10.1177/2056305116678894

Heins, M. (2014, June 20). The brave new world of social media censorship. *Harvard Law Review.* https://harvardlawreview.org/2014/06/the-brave-new-world-of-social-media-censorship

Hemsley, J. (2019, July 11). Social media giants are restricting research vital to journalism. *Columbia Journalism Review*. https://www.cjr.org/tow_center/facebook-twitter-api-restrictions.php

Hermans, H. J. M. (2004). Introduction: The dialogical self in a global and digital age. *An International Journal of Theory and Research, 4*(4), 297–320. https://doi.org/10.1207/s1532706xid0404_1

Hy, L. X., & Loevinger, J. (1996). *Measuring ego development* (2nd ed.). Erlbaum.

Jargon, J. (2020, February 20). Teens are deleting Instagrams almost as fast as they post them. *Wall Street Journal*. https://www.wsj.com/articles/teens-are-deleting-instagrams-almost-as-fast-as-they-post-them-11582021801

Keles, B., McCrae, N., & Grealish, A. (2019). A systematic review: The influence of social media on depression, anxiety and psychological distress in adolescents. *International Journal of Adolescence and Youth, 25*(1), 79–93. https://doi.org/10.1080/02673843.2019.1590851

Kerpelman, J. L., Pittman, J. F., & Lamke, L. K. (1997). Toward a microprocess perspective on adolescent identity development: An identity control theory approach. *Journal of Adolescent Research, 12*(3), 325–346. https://doi.org/10.1177/0743554897123002

Kroger, J. (2004). *Identity in adolescence: The balance between self and other* (3rd ed.). Routledge.

Kroger, J., & Green, K. E. (1996). Events associated with identity status change. *Journal of Adolescence, 19*(5), 477–490. https://doi.org/10.1006/jado.1996.0045

Kuiper, N., Kirsh, G., & Maiolino, N. (2016). Identity and intimacy development, humor styles, and psychological well-being. *Identity, 16*(2), 115–125. https://doi.org/10.1080/15283488.2016.1159964

Lewis, B. (2021, January 17). The Trump ban across social media wasn't censorship – it was a series of editorial decisions by media companies that call themselves social platforms. *Business Insider*. https://www.businessinsider.com/trump-ban-wasnt-censorship-it-was-an-editorial-decision-2021-1?international=true&r=US&IR=T

Loevinger, J. (1976). *Ego development: Conceptions and theories*. Jossey-Bass.

Loevinger, J. (1987). *Paradigms of personality*. Freeman.

Lomborg, S., & Bechmann, A. (2014). Using APIs for data collection on social media. *The Information Society, 30*(4), 256–265. https://doi.org/10.1080/01972243.2014.915276

Luyckx, K., Goossens, L., & Soenens, B. (2006). A developmental contextual perspective on identity construction in emerging adulthood: Change dynamics in commitment formation and commitment evaluation. *Developmental Psychology, 42*(2), 366–380. https://doi.org/10.1037/0012-1649.42.2.366

Luyckx, K., Klimstra, T. A., Duriez, B., Van Petegem, S., Beyers, W. (2013). Personal identity processes from adolescence through the late 20s: Age trends, functionality, and depressive symptoms. *Social Development, 22*(4), 701–721. https://doi.org/10.1111/sode.12027

Marcia, J. E. (1966). Development and validation of ego-identity status. *Journal of Personality and Social Psychology, 3*(5), 551–558. https://doi.org/10.1037/h0023281

Marcia, J. E. (1989). Identity and intervention. *Journal of Adolescence, 12*(4), 401–410. https://doi.org/10.1016/0140-1971(89)90063-8

Maslow, A. H. (1970). *Motivation and personality* (2nd ed.). Harper & Row.

McAdams, D. P. (1998). Ego, trait, identity. In P. M. Westenberg, A. Blasi, & L. D. Cohn (Eds.), *Personality development: Theoretical, empirical, and clinical investigations of Loevinger's conception of ego development* (pp. 27–38). Erlbaum.

McAdams, D. P. (2018). Narrative identity: What is it? What does it do? How do you measure it? *Imagination, Cognition, and Personality*, *37*(3), 359–372. https://doi.org/10.1177/0276236618756704

McAdams, D. P., & McLean, K. C. (2013). Narrative identity. *Current Directions in Psychological Science*, *22*(3), 233–238. https://doi.org/10.1177/0963721413475622

McLean, K. C., & Pasupathi, M. (2012). Processes of identity development: Where I am and how I got there. *Identity*, *12*(1), 8–28. https://doi.org/10.1080/15283488.2011.632363

McLean, K. C., Pasupathi, M., & Pals, J. L. (2007). Selves creating stories creating selves: A process model of self-development. *Personality and Social Psychology Review*, *11*(3), 262–278. https://doi.org/10.1177/1088868307301034

Misra, S., & Stokols, D. (2012). Psychological and health outcomes of perceived information overload. *Environment and Behavior*, *44*(6), 737–759. https://doi.org/10.1177/0013916511404408

Nesi, J., Choukas-Bradley, S., & Prinstein, M. J. (2018). Transformation of adolescent peer relations in the social media context: Part 2 – Application to peer group processes and future directions for research. *Clinical Child and Family Psychology Review*, *21*(3), 295–319. https://doi.org/10.1007/s10567–018-0262-9

Nesi, J., Telzer, E. H., & Prinstein, M. J. (2020). Adolescent development in the digital media context. *Psychological Inquiry*, *31*(3), 229–234. https://doi.org/10.1080/1047840X.2020.1820219

Pasupathi, M., & Hoyt, T. (2009). The development of narrative identity in late adolescence in emergent adulthood: The continued importance of listeners. *Developmental Psychology*, *45*(2), 558–574. https://doi.org/10.1037/a0014431

Pasupathi, M., Mansour, E., & Brubaker, J. R. (2007). Developing a life story: Constructing relations between self and experience in autobiographical narratives. *Human Development*, *50*(2–3), 85–110. https://doi.org/10.1159/000100939

Pasupathi, M., & Rich, B. (2005). Inattentive listening undermines self-verification in personal storytelling. *Journal of Personality*, *73*(4), 1051–1085. https://doi.org/10.1111/j.1467-6494.2005.00338.x

Peters, K. (2020, October 20). *Web 2.0*. Investopedia. https://www.investopedia.com/terms/w/web-20.asp

Rogers, C. R. (1961). *On becoming a person: A therapist's view of psychotherapy*. Houghton Mifflin.

Sandoval-Almazan, R., & Gil-Garcia, J. R. (2014). Towards cyberactivism 2.0? Understanding the use of social media and other information technologies for political activism and social movements. *Government Information Quarterly*, *31*(3), 365–378. https://doi.org/10.1016/j.giq.2013.10.016

Schwartz, S. H. (1996). Value priorities and behavior: Applying a theory of integrated value system. In C. Seligman, J. M. Olson, & M. P. Zanna (Eds.), *The Ontario Symposium: Vol. 8. The psychology of values* (pp. 1–24). Erlbaum.

Seabrook, E. M., Kern, M. L., & Rickard, N. S. (2016). Social networking sites, depression, and anxiety: A systematic review. *JMIR Mental Health*, *3*(4), Article e50. https://doi.org/10.2196/mental.5842

Sebastian, C., Burnett, S., & Blakemore, S.-J. (2008). Development of the self-concept during adolescence. *Trends in Cognitive Sciences, 12*(11), 441–446. https://doi.org/10.1016/j.tics.2008.07.008

Singer, J. A. (2004). Narrative identity and meaning making across the life span: An introduction. *Journal of Personality, 72*(3), 437–460. https://doi.org/10.1111/j.0022-3506.2004.00268.x

Singer, J. A. (2020). Narrative identity in a digital age: What are the human risks? *Psychological Inquiry, 31*(3), 224–228. https://doi.org/10.1080/1047840X.2020.1820217

Singer, J. A., Blagov, P., Berry, M., & Oost, K. M. (2013). Self-defining memories, scripts, and the life story: Narrative identity in personality and psychotherapy. *Journal of Personality, 81*(6), 569–582. https://doi.org/10.1111/jopy.12005

Smith, C. (2013, August 5). Three out of four young adults delete social media posts over fears they could harm their careers. *Business Insider.* https://www.businessinsider.com/young-adults-delete-social-media-posts-2013-8?international=true&r=US&IR=T

Syed, M., & McLean, K. C. (2016). Understanding identity integration: Theoretical, methodological, and applied issues. *Journal of Adolescence, 47*, 109–118. https://doi.org/10.1016/j.adolescence.2015.09.005

Syed, M., & Seiffge-Krenke, I. (2015). Change in ego development, coping, and symptomatology from adolescence to emerging adulthood. *Journal of Applied Developmental Psychology, 41*, 110–119. https://doi.org/10.1016/j.appdev.2015.09.003

Taylor, J., & Pagliari, C. (2018). Mining social media data: How are research sponsors and researchers addressing the ethical challenges? *Research Ethics, 14*(2), 1–39. https://doi.org/10.1177/1747016117738559

The School of Life (n.d.). *How to live more wisely around our phones.* https://www.theschooloflife.com/thebookoflife/how-to-live-more-wisely-around-our-phones/

Thorne, A. (2000). Personality memory telling and personality development. *Personality and Social Psychology Review, 4*(1), 45–56. https://doi.org/10.1207/S15327957PSPR0401_5

Valkenburg, P. M., Beyens, I., Pouwels, J. L., van Driel, I. I., & Keijsers, L. (2021). Social media and adolescents' self-esteem: Heading for a person-specific media effects paradigm. *Journal of Communication, 71*(1), 56–78. https://doi.org/10.1093/joc/jqaa039

Van Doeselaar, L., McLean, K. C., Meeus, W., Denissen, J. J. A., & Klimstra, T. A. (2020). Adolescents' identity formation: Linking the narrative and the dual-cycle approach. *Journal of Youth and Adolescence, 49*(4), 818–835. https://doi.org/10.1007/s10964-019-01096-x

Verduyn, P., Lee, D. S., Park, J., et al. (2015). Passive Facebook usage undermines affective well-being: Experimental and longitudinal evidence. *Journal of Experimental Psychology: General, 144*(2), 480–488. https://doi.org/10.1037/xge0000057

Vinh, N. (2021, February 10). *Does counter culture still exist?* The Western Front. https://www.westernfrononline.com/2021/02/10/does-counterculture-still-exist/

Westenberg, P. M., & Gjerde, P. F. (1999). Ego development during the transition from adolescence to young adulthood: A 9-year longitudinal study. *Journal of Research in Personality, 33*(2), 233–252. https://doi.org/10.1006/jrpe.1999.2248

Zaru, D. (2021, January 13). *Trump Twitter ban raises concerns over 'unchecked' power of big tech*. ABC News. https://abcnews.go.com/US/trump-twitter-ban-raises-concerns-unchecked-power-big/story?id=75150689

Zhong, C., Chang, H. W., Karamshuk, D., Lee, D., & Sastry, N. (2017, May 15–18). *Wearing many (social) hats: How different are your different social network personae?* Proceedings of the 11th International Conference on Web and Social Media, Montreal, QC, Canada.

4 Peer Relationship Processes in the Context of Digital Media

Samuel E. Ehrenreich

Peer relationships have always served an important role in adolescent development. The quality of peer relationships is a driving force in adolescents' academic functioning (Wentzel et al., 2021), sense of self (Bellmore & Cillessen, 2006), and mental health (La Greca & Harrison, 2005). Furthermore, many – if not most – of the core developmental tasks that adolescents must traverse require navigating the peer context. Adolescents obviously cannot establish intimate peer relationships or explore romantic feelings and sexuality without engaging with their peers. Even experimenting with different versions of the self often requires feedback from peers to help understand how the external world will receive a potential internal self (Erikson, 1968).

Digital communication and social media have likely reshaped adolescents' peer relationships and social environment more than any other force in the 21st century. Digital communication is adolescents' preferred method for engaging with peers (Anderson & Jiang, 2018), beyond even face-to-face interaction (Lenhart et al., 2010). Nearly 90% of adolescents report using social media platforms every single day (Lenhart, 2015), primarily to interact with the same peers and friends they interact in their offline lives. It is not surprising then that adolescents' digital peer interactions are related to a range of outcomes similar to in-person peer interactions: self-concept and self-esteem (Steinsbekk et al., 2021), involvement in risk behavior (Ehrenreich et al., 2014), and mental health (Vannucci & McCauley Ohannessian, 2019). Digital communication is a critically important context that has transformed the way that the peer process unfolds and impacts adolescents (Nesi et al., 2018a, 2018b).

This chapter will begin with an examination of the features of social media that make it such a powerful context in which peer interaction occurs, briefly reviewing the theoretical underpinnings of this context. We will review recent research on how three important peer constructs unfold and are shaped by digital media: peer influence, social connectedness (vs. isolation), and popularity and social status. We will then discuss challenges and opportunities for studying peer relationships in the context of digital media. Finally, we will conclude with a discussion of the future directions in this field.

Theoretical Considerations

Much of the early research examining how digital communication relates to peer relationships was guided by existing, "offline" developmental theory. This perspective coalesced in co-construction theory (Subrahmanyam et al., 2006), which suggested that adolescents use social interaction in digital spaces as a means to explore the same developmental issues occurring in their offline lives. Accordingly, adolescents are active participants in the construction of the online content that they consume and create, building environments that can facilitate their developmental needs. Subrahmanyam and colleagues viewed these on- and offline environments as being "psychologically continuous" (Subrahmanyam et al., 2008, p. 421). In line with this perspective, many early studies of peer relations in the digital sphere sought to examine whether important peer processes truly did translate between realms. For example, do adolescents' offline social deficits translate into online spaces (i.e., the rich-get-richer hypothesis) or are online contexts used as a more comfortable space to compensate for their offline deficits (social compensation; Kraut et al., 1998, 2002; Valkenburg & Peter, 2007)? Alternatively, considerable research examined the extent to which individuals who engaged in offline bullying behaviors or were subjected to offline victimization were also involved in these aggressive relations online (Kowalski et al., 2014), and whether there was similar overlap in offline and online prosocial behavior (Wright & Li, 2011).

Co-construction was an important advancement, in that it promoted the application of existing developmental theory to the study of adolescents' online interactions, which had previously functioned with a fractured combination of theories emerging from a variety of disciplines (see Underwood et al., 2018). However, co-construction theory placed great emphasis on the overlap between adolescents' on- and offline worlds, highlighting that adolescents are creating these spaces in an effort to fulfill their offline developmental needs (Subrahmanyam et al., 2008). Although co-construction does not suggest that these spaces are the same (despite being psychologically connected), little focus was placed on systematically identifying the ways in which digital communication functionally changes adolescents' peer interactions. To bridge this gap, the transformational framework (Nesi et al., 2018a, 2018b), sought to systematically identify specific ways that social media transforms peer experiences, proposing five specific methods. First, social media increases the frequency and immediacy of peer interactions, allowing (and encouraging) near-constant contact with peers. Second, and relating to this, social media also amplifies the demands of peer interactions, creating new expectations to be available and responsive to peers. Third, social media changes the qualitative nature and feel of peer interactions, for example by changing the access to various social cues, and placing a greater emphasis on quantitative peer metrics such as number of likes and followers. Fourth, social media affords youth new opportunities for compensating behaviors, such as the opportunity to maintain relationships despite physical distance. Finally, social media also provides adolescents with the potential to engage in entirely new social behaviors, such as virtually stalking romantic partners, or passively viewing the entire peer network.

Although this recently proposed framework has received limited empirical examination to date, initial findings examining the role of social media on women's body image have generally supported the model (Choukas-Bradley et al., 2019). Additional research is needed, but the transformation framework builds on existing developmental theory to highlight specific – and testable – ways that peer interactions should differ in, and be affected by, these digital contexts. Perhaps most importantly for its continued utility, the transformational framework highlights seven specific aspects of the social media environment (asynchronicity, permanence, publicness, availability, cue absence, quantifiability, and visualness) that transcend specific digital media platforms and tools (e.g., Facebook vs. Snapchat vs. text messaging). Given the incredible pace in which digital platforms rise and fall in popularity, emphasizing broader features of these platforms is critically important for a cohesive study of peer interactions in digital spaces over time.

Transformed Peer Constructs in Digital Communication

Guided by co-construction and the transformational framework, researchers have established the importance of digital communication in both promoting and inhibiting a variety of peer processes, and at times fundamentally transforming these processes altogether. In the following sections, we will review recent research on the role of social media on three of these important peer processes and constructs: peer influence, social connectedness versus isolation, and popularity/status. These sections will not serve as a comprehensive review but will instead highlight recent trends and future directions.

Peer Influence in Digital Realms

Susceptibility to peer influence peaks during the adolescent years (Steinberg & Monahan, 2007), due to an increased importance of peer relationships and status during this period (Prinstein & Dodge, 2008), as well as neurological development (Sommerville, 2013; Steinberg, 2008). Adolescents look to their peers as informative models for what behaviors are considered acceptable and desirable (injunctive norms), and to assess the how frequent various behaviors are (descriptive norms; Kallgren et al., 2000). Due to the highly public nature of many social media platforms, adolescents are able to spend hours examining the posted lives of their close friends and more distant peers. Because adolescents' social media feeds display the content produced by their wide social networks, this could also serve to blur the line between proximal norms (their immediate friends) and more distal or global norms (peers in general). A great deal of research on peer influence has focused on how it can affect the development of problematic behaviors such as substance use (Geusens & Beullens, 2017a, 2017b). Adolescents who believe that their friends and peers are using substances (or hold positive views of substance use) are more likely to engage in this behavior themselves. Depictions of substance use are viewed on social media by both adolescents (Boyle et al., 2017; Carrotte et al., 2016) and college-aged adults (Moewaka Barnes et al., 2016; Morgan et al., 2010), and these depictions in turn relate to individuals' perception of injunctive norms (Boyle et al., 2016; Yoo et al., 2016) and their own substance use (Geusens & Beullens, 2017b). Substance use presentations on social media likely influence adolescents by changing their perception of the acceptability and prevalence of these behaviors. In one study, viewing peers' posts about substance use improved the perceived desirability and positive expectancies of substance use behaviors (Huang et al., 2014). Another study found that viewing friends' substance use posts on social media predicted elevated drinking one year later, and this relationship was mediated by more positive injunctive peer norms about alcohol (Nesi et al., 2017).

However, social media does not only influence adolescents by allowing them to observe their peers, but also permits adolescents to *be observed* by their peers as well. Adolescents are heavily influenced by the notion (accurate or inaccurate) that their activities are being viewed and judged by peers. Although the impact of the *imaginary audience* has been discussed for decades (Elkind, 1967), recent fMRI studies support the neurological underpinnings for this influence process. Simply being in the presence of peers increases adolescents' susceptibility to peer influence by increasing functioning in the regions of the brain responsible for social cognition and reward seeking (primarily the amygdala, striatum, and prefrontal cortex; Somerville, 2013; Steinberg, 2008). This increased focus on reward seeking in turn leads to greater risk-taking behavior (Chein et al., 2011; O'Brien et al., 2011). In offline contexts, peer presence is a fairly objective variable (for both adolescents themselves and inquiring researchers), but many of the features of social media outlined in the transformation framework (Nesi et al., 2018a) may amplify this experience. The availability and the publicness of social media means that peers can be "present" even when the adolescent is physically alone. Furthermore, the quantifiability of these networks, with a numeric quantity of followers and likes, could intensify peer influence. Recent fMRI studies have found that the neurological activation patterns underpinning peer influence when peers are physically present (Chein et al., 2011, Steinberg, 2008) also occur when peers are "present" via Instagram (Sherman, Hernandez, et al., 2018; Sherman et al., 2016), and the impact of digital peer influence is stronger for adolescents compared to young adults (Sherman, Greenfield, et al., 2018).

The studies highlighted above suggest that social media can extend the reach of peer influence beyond physical presence and interaction with peers. Future research can leverage the networked data available on these platforms to better understand the role of proximal and distal peers in influencing adolescents' behavior, and to operationalize different levels of peer connection and degrees of separation from each other in more detailed ways. For example, frequency of communication with a peer or even frequency of viewing a peer's posts might objectively and accurately assess proximity to that peer. Alternatively, metrics used in social network analyses such as network closure and centrality can be used to more clearly define proximal and distal peers (Hanneman & Riddle, 2011). This would allow researchers to go beyond simply asking adolescents to identify and rate their friends and peers, to directly assess with whom an adolescent digitally interacts and is connected. Directly assessing interactions (and observation) at the network level could greatly enhance our understanding of peer influence for a variety of important variables such as mental health, academic performance, and body image issues.

Social Connectedness and Isolation via Social Media

The role of social media in promoting (or inhibiting) social connectedness has received increasing research interest over the past several years. Social connectedness and a feeling of belonging is one of the primary benefits of peer relationships during adolescence, promoting positive psychosocial outcomes (Bradley & Inglis, 2012) and protecting against both externalizing and internalizing problems (Newman et al., 2007). As social media and digital communication increased in popularity, there was a great deal of speculation about whether these technologies would foster intimacy and connection with peers, or if the reductions in face-to-face interaction would actually diminish adolescents' sense of belongingness with peers (Allen et al., 2014). Some proposed that specific features of social media would provide opportunities to better connect with peers. In a series of interviews conducted with adolescents, Davis (2012) identified that frequent communication with friends through a variety of digital platforms promoted a sense of closeness with these peers. The ability to connect with peers despite physical distance is identified by adolescents as one of the primary benefits of digital communication (Ling, 2005). Indeed, adolescents exchange a great deal of emotionally supportive communication via social media (Siriaraya et al., 2011), using these platforms to reach out to peers in times of need (Ehrenreich et al., 2020).

Beyond using social media to directly interact with peers, there is also some evidence that posting broadly to social media platforms without directly connecting with a specific peer (such as a tweet or a status post on Facebook) can reduce loneliness in undergraduate samples (große Deters & Mehl, 2013; Lou et al., 2012). These findings highlight that the availability of the peer network that social media affords adolescents translates into increases in connection and belongingness, and reductions in loneliness. Indeed, a meta-analysis examining 63 studies found that social media use was positively correlated with perceived social resources from peers (Domahidi, 2018). Interestingly, a recent study examining specific features of social media platforms found that image-based platforms in particular (e.g., Instagram and Snapchat) reduced users' loneliness (Pittman & Reich, 2016). The authors speculate that the emphasis on images facilitates the sense of a "social presence" with peers that is better able to promote connection, aligning with the perspective that the visualness of social media (Nesi et al., 2018a) may be an important feature for subsequent research into the role of social media in connection.

In contrast to the potential benefits of social media on adolescents' peer connection, a separate body of research has suggested that smartphones and social media use are actually reducing social connection and well-being, and account for overall increases in social isolation and loneliness among adolescents (Twenge, 2019). Population-level studies have indeed identified increasing trends in both suicidality and depression over the past decade (Mojtabai et al., 2016) that coincided with similar rises in cellphone ownership and social media use (Twenge et al., 2018). One meta-analysis found that social media use does indeed correlate with perceived loneliness (although the authors suggest that loneliness predicting social media use is the most likely direction of effect; Song et al., 2014). One large-scale cross-sectional study of young adults found that social media usage was a significant predictor of social isolation (Primack et al., 2017), and a micro-longitudinal study also found that time spent on social media predicts momentary feelings of social isolation (Kross et al., 2013). Furthermore, a few experimental studies have also supported the hypothesis that social media causally predicts maladjustment. College students who were instructed to limit their social media use to no more than 30 minutes per day reported lower levels of depression and loneliness compared to the control group (Hunt et al., 2018). Similarly, individuals randomly assigned to abstain from Facebook for one week reported being happier and less depressed by the end of the week (Tromholdt, 2016).

Although the immediate and constant connection that social media provides is appealing to adolescents (Davis, 2012), there is concern that time spent on these digital platforms comes at the cost of more intimate and socially valuable face-to-face time (Kraut et al., 1998). The conflicting evidence on the role of social media in supporting or inhibiting social connection likely reflects methodological limitations for disentangling direction of effect (but see George et al., 2021 and Twenge, 2019 for contrasting perspectives on this). However, it also likely reflects the reality that the way adolescents are using these technologies may be more important than the overall time spent online. In particular, it appears *passive social media use* (time spent scrolling through peers' posts without actually interacting or engaging with peers) may be especially harmful for adolescents' well-being and sense of connection, compared to actively engaging with peers via social media. Time spent passively viewing peers' social media content indeed predicts reductions in perceived peer support (Frison & Eggermont, 2015), increases in social loneliness (Amichai-Hamgurger & Ben-Artzi, 2003; Matook et al., 2015) and a sense of disconnection from peers (Amichai-Hamgurger & Ben-Artzi, 2003) that likely grows out of feelings of envy and negative social comparison (de Vries et al., 2018; Vogel et al., 2015; Weinstein, 2017).

In contrast to the consistently negative correlates of passive social media use, active social media use (posting and directly interacting with peers) appears to have much more positive outcomes. Adolescents' public Facebook posts elicit positive feedback from peers, which in turn increases the perception of peer support (Frison & Eggermont, 2015). Similarly, experimentally increasing the frequency of posting publicly on Facebook reduced loneliness among college students (große Deters & Mehl, 2013). Social media can also facilitate more private, dyadic interactions among peers, which in turn predicts social connection and support (Frison et al., 2019; Frison & Eggermont, 2015). It is not surprising that the opportunities for actual peer interaction (active use) promote feelings of connection and support among adolescents; indeed this was identified by adolescents as a primary benefit (Davis, 2012). However, the conflicting findings between social media contributing to connection versus isolation highlights the importance of *how* adolescents are using these media. Future research must continue to focus on the specific online behaviors and usage patterns that foster connection, rather than simply assessing the amount of time spent using these platforms. The transformational framework model (Nesi et al., 2018a) may be especially useful in disentangling the conflicting findings that have emerged in this research area. By focusing on the specific features of social media platforms that may be shaping peer interactions in these contexts, researchers can better understand what promotes a sense of connection and peer support, and what may undermine it.

Popularity and Social Status

Because of its highly public nature and constant availability, social media may be especially important in shaping adolescent social status (Nesi & Prinstein, 2019). Although social status has always been an important component of adolescent peer relationships (Harter et al., 1996), social media both intensifies that importance and salience of peer status, and also provides new tools for managing and promoting status (Nesi et al., 2018b). The quantifiability of social networks makes social media especially important for adolescents' perceptions of status. Adolescents are highly aware of a variety of social media metrics assessing popularity (e.g., number of friends, number of likes or retweets; Madden et al., 2013).

Indeed, the preoccupation with popularity on social media may have reframed adolescents' traditional desire for popularity into aspirations for fame and stardom. Content analysis of movies and television viewed by adolescents has found that fame is increasingly portrayed as an important – and achievable – goal (Uhls & Greenfield, 2012), and adolescents who use social networking sites more frequently report a greater emphasis on the value of fame (Uhls et al., 2014). This emphasis on fame is somewhat attributable to the rise in popularity of reality television, wherein "ordinary people" ostensibly become famous for simply living their day-to-day lives (Rui & Stefanone, 2016). But adolescents are also highly cognizant of the potential to achieve celebrity simply by acquiring enough social media followers (e.g., "Instagram famous"; Marwick, 2015).

Although social media has made peer status and popularity much more salient, it has also provided a variety of tools adolescents can use in their attempt to improve their status. Prior to the advent of social media, many adolescents no doubt spent their free time envisioning moving up the social hierarchy. However, with the help of smartphones and social networking sites, adolescents can actively work toward improving their number of friends, and curating their self-presentation at all times. Adolescents are quite strategic in leveraging social media to promote a positive and popular image. Many adolescents go to great lengths to ensure that their self-presentation on social media receives positive peer response, including taking numerous photos to select the best image for posting (Yau & Reich, 2019), heavily editing photos to present an attractive image (Bell, 2019), curating the activities they disclose to create a fun and glamorous identity (Fardouly & Vartanian, 2016), and timing posts to maximize peer likes (Nesi & Prinstein, 2019). Indeed in her analyses of adolescents' digital presentations, Marwick (2013) suggests adolescents are engaging in "self-branding," designed to market themselves using techniques similar to consumer products.

Although social media may provide a variety of new tools for managing one's social status, that does not mean that all adolescents leverage social media to achieve higher status. Using social media in ways that will promote one's social status requires a significant amount of social competence (Reich, 2017) and a great deal of effort (Yau & Reich, 2019). Popular adolescents are more likely to engage with their peers in ways that will promote their existing status, including both positive and aggressive behaviors. Furthermore, popular adolescents who are better able to self-monitor and regulate the online interactions are less likely to be the target of cybervictimization (Ranney & Troop-Gordon, 2020).

Opportunities and Challenges for Studying Peer Relationships in Digital Communication

As social media increases as an important context for adolescents to interact with their peers, it presents both opportunities and challenges for researchers seeking to better understand peer relationships. Perhaps the greatest advantage of social media is that it permits researchers to connect with adolescents where their peer interactions are unfolding. While observing peer interactions used to require artificial lab settings (Piehler & Dishion, 2007) or naturalistic observation that was restricted in time and location (Snyder et al., 2010), researchers can now potentially observe peer interactions in digital spaces unobtrusively for extended periods of weeks, months, or years (Hendriks et al., 2018; Underwood et al., 2012). Furthermore, because much of adolescents' digital communication is centered around their smartphones, a variety of additional data collection technologies can be connected with peer relationships and interactions, including ecological momentary assessment (Duvenage et al., 2019), geolocation (Boettner et al., 2019), and even physical functioning such as sleep patterns (George et al., 2019). These technologies provide researchers with a unique opportunity to stitch together a more comprehensive understanding of how peer relationships are impacting adolescents' functioning and development.

Although the potential for these research methods is truly exciting, they are not without challenges and risk. First, there are important ethical considerations for researchers to capture the volume of data available in adolescents' digital spaces. Although adolescents seem fairly comfortable with digital observation (Meter et al., 2019), capturing digital communication nonetheless involves novel ethical considerations. Because this data collection can be conducted subtly from smartphones and social media apps, it is important that researchers clearly explain the details of digital data collection. Similarly, since social media data is inherently networked information, challenges arise for navigating when it is necessary to obtain peer consent (and whether that is even possible). This may require a dialogue with IRBs and granting institutions to better reflect the digital contexts in which adolescents live their lives. With tens of millions of adolescents permitting third parties to observe their social media data, these research activities are likely the very definition of minimal risk (see Ehrenreich et al., 2021 for a discussion about this).

Another challenge for researchers is understanding the hidden, guiding hand of the algorithms that decide what is presented on social media platforms. These algorithms constantly evaluate the adolescents' social media behavior to provide a stream of content tailored to the adolescent (and the marketing forces underlying many of these platforms). The role of these artificial intelligence and machine learning algorithms obfuscates peer processes occurring in these platforms. For example, one long-running research inquiry has examined whether adolescents' similarity to peers is best explained by socialization (learning how to behave from our peers) or selection (choosing peers who behave as we do). Evidence suggests that both of these processes likely work in tandem: adolescents select peers who are similar to them, who in turn further socialize their attitudes and behaviors. However, on social media these two processes become further intertwined (and blurred), as the content an adolescent views and posts themselves will in turn affect who and what is highlighted in their social media feeds. In this way, the content that is social-izing the adolescent is also being used to select the peers who will be suggested to them or featured on their feed, and the selection of this network is in turn dictating what content will be presented (and will thus socialize the adolescent further). And all of these "decisions" are being conducted by computer algorithms that are likely hidden to the adolescent. Indeed, much of TikTok's explosion in popularity during 2020 is attributed to the advanced artificial intelligence recommendation engine that rapidly tailors what videos are suggested based on the user's previous preferences (see Wang, 2020 for an overview of this technology). Much of the research outlined above highlights investigations into how social media features and content impact adolescents peer relationships. But *why* adolescents are exposed to features and content (e.g., why this specific video is presented at the top of their feed) is being guided by algorithms that are likely poorly understood by both adolescents and developmental scientists.

Future Directions

In their presentation of the transformational framework, Nesi and colleagues (2018a, 2018b) highlight seven features of the social media context that are important to understanding how peer relationships operate in these environments (asynchronicity, permanence, publicness, availability, cue absence, quantifiability, and visualness). Future research must move away from examining specific social media platforms, and instead focus on their features. Not only do social media platforms rise and fall in popularity, but they also change their form and features over time. Not only is Facebook less popular among adolescents than it was in 2012 (Rideout & Robb, 2018), but the platform itself is also quite different, with new features constantly being added. By focusing on features of social media that can be assessed on a variety of platforms (e.g., the emphasis on visual content versus textual, the degree of asynchronicity; Nesi et al., 2018a), researchers can better understand how the broader social media context is shaping adolescents' peer relation-ships, and these impacts can be assessed more consistently across time.

But the importance of these features of the social media context may not just be limited to assessing the social media platforms themselves. Perhaps some (or all) of these features of the *context* are now reflected in fundamental changes in the *relationships* themselves. For example, prior to the advent of social media, moving into new stages of life often meant losing contact with peers from previous stages. Although an adult may have retained friends from middle or high school, it was perhaps unlikely that they kept tabs on the broader peer network from those years. However, with Facebook, Instagram, and other social networking sites, it is quite common for individuals to maintain a (perhaps tenuous) connection with these earlier peer networks.

Although the transformational framework suggests that a feature of the Facebook context is its permanence (e.g., photos and subsequent comments are retained indefinitely), by extension, relationships themselves may now reflect this feature (the relationship itself is now retained indefinitely).

It is possible that other features of social media may be redefining the features of peer relationships as well. For example, perhaps the cue absence permitted in social media is redefining how adolescents want to experience all relationship interactions. Alternatively, perhaps the publicness of social media has fostered the perception that relationships themselves should be experienced publicly. If this were the case, it would challenge the conventional adolescent developmental task of navigating intimate relationships traditionally characterized as a dyadic process. Similarly, there has been a great deal of concern about how digital communication may be undermining youth's development of more general social skills, such as navigating small talk and interpersonal interactions (Turkle, 2012). Whereas periods of downtime (e.g., waiting for a class to begin, standing in line at the supermarket) used to be opportunities to strike up a conversation with the stranger next to you, these moments are now often spent checking in with peers on one's phone. A student of mine once shared that she used her phone to avoid getting drawn into a conversation with her classmates, because she worried she wouldn't be able to end the conversation if it was awkward or boring. While the asynchronicity and availability of digital communication may permit adolescents to have social interactions on their own terms, perhaps it comes at the cost of learning to navigate challenging, awkward (and even boring) interactions. The seven features of social media outlined by the transformation framework (Nesi et al., 2018a, 2018b) provide an important advancement for the study of adolescents' interactions occurring via digital media, but they also provide guidance for future research seeking to understand how peer relationships themselves are fundamentally changing.

Finally, future research must increasingly focus on the behaviors and processes that are occurring in these platforms. In many ways, researchers' initial focus on the *quantity* of social media use has obfuscated our understanding of these contexts (such as the conflicting associations between social media and subsequent loneliness and mental health). Current research is illuminating the fact that time spent on social media is less important than how adolescents are using these platforms (e.g., Swirsky, Rosie & Xie, 2021). Researchers must continue to move away from overly simplistic metrics of social media use. Examinations about the amount of time spent on social media should be reframed into *how time is spent* on social media. Evaluating the number of friends and followers is likely less important than evaluating the interactions (and observation) of those peer networks. Luckily social media platforms provide a unique opportunity to naturalistically observe adolescents in these more nuanced ways.

Conclusion

Social media platforms have become an increasingly important context for adolescents' peer relationships. These platforms are reshaping the way that adolescents interact with and observe their peers. In many ways, social media has accomplished what social scientists have sought to do for years: it has established a platform that makes peer relationships quantifiable, networked, available to outside observers, and permanent so interactions can be scrutinized and analyzed after the fact. It is perhaps somewhat ironic that the features that make these platforms ideal for studying peer relationships are driving many of the changes occurring in these relationships. The publicness of these data allows researchers to observe teens more easily but does it come at the cost of intimate connections with peers? The quantifiability of social media may allow researchers to better understand social status hierarchies. But in doing so, does it change what these hierarchies mean to adolescents? Researchers are now presented with the opportunity to leverage these powerful new social tools to better understand adolescents' relationships but must simultaneously address how these tools are shifting how these relationships unfold and impact adolescents.

References

Allen, K. A., Ryan, T., Gray, D. L., McInerney, D. M., & Waters, L. (2014). Social media use and social connectedness in adolescents: The positives and the potential pitfalls. *Australian Educational & Developmental Psychologist*, *31*(1), 18–31. https://doi.org/10.1017/edp.2014.2

Amichai-Hamburger, Y., & Ben-Artzi, E. (2003). Loneliness and internet use. *Computers in Human Behavior*, *19*(1), 71–80. https://doi.org/10.1016/S0747-5632(02)00014-6

Anderson, M., & Jiang, J. (2018). *Teens, social media & technology 2018*. Pew Research Center. http://publicservicesalliance.org/wp-content/uploads/2018/06/Teens-Social-Media-Technology-2018-PEW.pdf

Bell, B. T. (2019). "You take fifty photos, delete forty nine and use one": A qualitative study of adolescent image-sharing practices on social media. *International Journal of Child-Computer Interaction*, *20*, 64–71. https://doi.org/10.1016/j.ijcci.2019.03.002

Bellmore, A. D., & Cillessen, A. H. (2006). Reciprocal influences of victimization, perceived social preference, and self-concept in adolescence. *Self and Identity*, *5*(3), 209–229. https://doi.org/10.1080/15298860600636647

Boettner, B., Browning, C. R., & Calder, C. A. (2019). Feasibility and validity of geographically explicit ecological momentary assessment with recall-aided space-time budgets. *Journal of Research on Adolescence*, *29*(3), 627–645. https://doi.org/10.1111/jora.12474

Boyle, S. C., Earle, A. M., LaBrie, J. W., & Ballou, K. (2017). Facebook dethroned: Revealing the more likely social media destinations for college students' depictions of underage drinking. *Addictive Behaviors, 65,* 63–67. https://doi .org/10.1016/j.addbeh.2016.10.004

Boyle, S. C., LaBrie, J. W., Froidevaux, N. M., & Witkovic, Y. D. (2016). Different digital paths to the keg? How exposure to peers' alcohol-related social media content influences drinking among male and female first-year college students. *Addictive Behaviors, 57,* 21–29. https://doi.org/10.1016/j.addbeh.2016.01.011

Bradley, G. L., & Inglis, B. C. (2012). Adolescent leisure dimensions, psychosocial adjustment, and gender effects. *Journal of Adolescence, 35*(5), 1167–1176. https://doi.org/10.1016/j.adolescence.2012.03.006

Carrotte, E. R., Dietze, P. M., Wright, C. J., & Lim, M. S. (2016). Who 'likes' alcohol? Young Australians' engagement with alcohol marketing via social media and related alcohol consumption patterns. *Australian and New Zealand Journal of Public Health, 40*(5), 474–479. https://doi.org/10.1111/1753-6405.12572

Chein, J., Albert, D., O'Brien, L., Uckert, K., & Steinberg, L. (2011). Peers increase adolescent risk taking by enhancing activity in the brain's reward circuitry. *Developmental Science, 14*(2), F1–F10. https://doi.org/10.1111/j.1467-7687 .2010.01035.x

Choukas-Bradley, S., Nesi, J., Widman, L., & Higgins, M. K. (2019). Camera-ready: Young women's appearance-related social media consciousness. *Psychology of Popular Media Culture, 8*(4), 473–481. https://doi.org/10.1037/ppm0000196

Davis, K. (2012). Friendship 2.0: Adolescents' experiences of belonging and self-disclosure online. *Journal of Adolescence, 35,* 1527–1536. https://doi.org/10 .1016/j.adolescence.2012.02.013

de Vries, D. A., Möller, A. M., Wieringa, M. S., Eigenraam, A. W., & Hamelink, K. (2018). Social comparison as the thief of joy: Emotional consequences of viewing strangers' Instagram posts. *Media Psychology, 21*(2), 222–245. https://doi.org/10.1080/15213269.2016.1267647

Domahidi, E. (2018). The associations between online media use and users' perceived social resources: A meta-analysis. *Journal of Computer-Mediated Communication, 23*(4), 181–200. https://doi.org/10.1093/jcmc/zmy007

Duvenage, M., Uink, B. N., Zimmer-Gembeck, M. J., Barber, B. L., Donovan, C. L., & Modecki, K. L. (2019). Ambulatory assessment of adolescent coping: It's a complicated process. *Journal of Research on Adolescence, 29*(3), 578–594. https://doi.org/10.1111/jora.12468

Ehrenreich, S. E., Beron, K. J., Burnell, K., Meter, D. J., & Underwood, M. K. (2020). How adolescents use text messaging through their high school years. *Journal of Research on Adolescence, 30*(2), 521–540. https://doi.org/10.1111/jora.12541

Ehrenreich, S. E., George, M., Burnell, K., & Underwood, M. K. (2021). Importance of digital communication in adolescents' development: Theoretical and empir-ical advancements in the last decade. *Journal of Research on Adolescence, 31*(4), 928–943. https://doi.org/10.1111/jora.12643

Ehrenreich, S. E., Underwood, M. K., & Ackerman, R. A. (2014). Adolescents' text message communication and growth in antisocial behavior across the first year of high school. *Journal of Abnormal Child Psychology, 42*(2), 251–264. https://doi.org/10.1007/s10802-013-9783-3

Elkind, D. (1967). Egocentrism in adolescence. *Child Development, 38*(4), 1025–1034. https://doi.org/10.2307/1127100

Erikson, E. (1968). *Identity: Youth and crises.* W. W. Norton & Company.

Fardouly, J., & Vartanian, L. R. (2016). Social media and body image concerns: Current research and future directions. *Current Opinion in Psychology, 9,* 1–5. https://doi.org/10.1016/j.copsyc.2015.09.005

Frison, E., Bastin, M., Bijttebier, P., & Eggermont, S. (2019). Helpful or harmful? The different relationships between private Facebook interactions and adolescents' depressive symptoms. *Media Psychology, 22*(2), 244–272. https://doi.org/10.1080/15213269.2018.1429933

Frison, E., & Eggermont, S. (2015). Toward an integrated and differential approach to the relationships between loneliness, different types of Facebook use, and adolescents' depressed mood. *Communication Research, 47*(5), 701–728. https://doi.org/10.1177/0093650215617506

George, M. J., Beron, K., Vollet, J., Burnell, K., Ehrenreich, S. E., & Underwood, M. K. (2021). Frequency of text messaging and adolescents' mental health symptoms across four years of high school. *JAMA Pediatrics, 68*(2), 324–330. https://doi.org/10.1016/j.jadohealth.2020.06.012

George, M. J., Rivenbark, J. G., Russell, M. A., Ng'eno, L., Hoyle, R. H., & Odgers, C. L. (2019). Evaluating the use of commercially available wearable wristbands to capture adolescents' daily sleep duration. *Journal of Research on Adolescence, 29*(3), 613–626. https://doi.org/10.1111/jora.12467

Geusens, F., & Beullens, K. (2017a). Strategic self-presentation or authentic communication? Predicting adolescents' alcohol references on social media. *Journal of Studies on Alcohol and Drugs, 78*(1), 124–133. https://doi.org/10.15288/jsad.2017.78.124

Geusens, F., & Beullens, K. (2017b). The reciprocal associations between sharing alcohol references on social networking sites and binge drinking: A longitudinal study among late adolescents. *Computers in Human Behavior, 73,* 499–506. https://doi.org/10.1016/j.chb.2017.03.062

große Deters, F., & Mehl, M. R. (2013). Does posting Facebook status updates increase or decrease loneliness? An online social networking experiment. *Social Psychological and Personality Science, 4*(5), 579–586. https://doi.org/10.1177/1948550612469233

Hanneman, R. A., & Riddle, M. (2011). Concepts and measure for basic network analysis. In J. Scott & P. J. Carrington (Eds.), *The Sage handbook of social network analysis* (pp. 364–367). Sage.

Harter, S., Stocker, C., & Robinson, N. S. (1996). The perceived directionality of the link between approval and self-worth: The liabilities of a looking glass self-orientation among young adolescents. *Journal of Research on Adolescence, 6* (3), 285–308.

Hendriks, H., Van den Putte, B., Gebhardt, W. A., & Moreno, M. A. (2018). Social drinking on social media: Content analysis of the social aspects of alcohol-related posts on Facebook and Instagram. *Journal of Medical Internet Research, 20*(6), e226. https://doi.org/10.2196/jmir.9355

Huang, G. C., Unger, J. B., Soto, D., et al. (2014). Peer influences: The impact of online and offline friendship networks on adolescent smoking and alcohol use. *Journal of Adolescent Health, 54*(5), 508–514. https://doi.org/10.1016/j.jadohealth.2013.07.001

Hunt, M. G., Marx, R., Lipson, C., & Young, J. (2018). No more FOMO: Limiting social media decreases loneliness and depression. *Journal of Social & Clinical Psychology*, *37*(10), 751–768. https://doi.org/10.1521/jscp.2018.37.10.751

Kallgren, C. A., Reno, R. R., & Cialdini, R. B. (2000). A focus theory of normative conduct: When norms do and do not affect behavior. *Personality and Social Psychology Bulletin*, *26*(8), 1002–1012. https://doi.org/10.1177/01461672002610009

Kowalski, R. M., Giumetti, G. W., Schroeder, A. N., & Lattaner, M. R. (2014). Bullying in the digital age: A critical review and meta-analysis of cyberbullying among youth. *Psychological Bulletin*, *140*(4), 1072–1137. https://doi.org/10.1037/a0035618

Kraut, R., Patterson, M., Lundmark, V., Kiesler, S., Mukophadhyay, T., & Scherlis, W. (1998). Internet paradox: A social technology that reduces social involvement and psychological well-being? *American Psychologist*, *53*(9), 1017–1031. https://doi.org/10.1037/0003-066X.53.9.1017

Kraut, R., Kiesler, S., Boneva, B., Cummings, J., Helgeson, V., & Crawford, A. (2002). Internet paradox revisited. *Journal of Social Issues*, *58*(1), 49–74. https://doi.org/10.1111/1540-4560.00248

Kross, E., Verduyn, P., Demiralp, E., et al. (2013). Facebook use predicts declines in subjective well-being in young adults. *PLoS ONE*, *8*(8), Article e69841. https://doi.org/10.1371/journal.pone.0069841

La Greca, A. M., & Harrison, H. M. (2005). Adolescent peer relations, friendships, and romantic relationships: Do they predict social anxiety and depression?. *Journal of Clinical Child and Adolescent Psychology*, *34*(1), 49–61. https://doi.org/10.1207/s15374424jccp3401_5

Lenhart, A. (2015, April 9). *Teens, social media and technology overview 2015*. Pew Research Center. http://www.pewinternet.org/2015/04/09/teens-social-media-technology-2015/

Lenhart, A., Ling, R., Campbell, S., & Purcell, K. (2010). *Teens and mobile phones*. Pew Research Center. http://pewinternetorg/Reports/2010/Teens-and-Mobile-Phones.aspx

Ling, R. (2005). Mobile communications vis-à-vis teen emancipation, peer group integration, and deviance. In R. Harper, L. Palen, & A. Taylor (Eds.), *The inside text: Social, cultural, and design perspectives on SMS* (pp. 175–193). Springer.

Lou, L. L., Yan, Z., Nickerson, A., & McMorris, R. (2012). An examination of the reciprocal relationship of loneliness and Facebook use among first-year college students. *Journal of Educational Computing Research*, *46*(1), 105–117. https://doi.org/10.2190/EC.46.1.e

Madden, M., Lenhart, A., Cortesi, S., et al. (2013, May 21). *Teens, social media, and privacy*. Pew Research Center. http://www.pewinternet.org/2013/05/21/teens-social-media-and-privacy/

Marwick, A. E. (2013). *Status update: Celebrity, publicity, and branding in the social media age*. Yale University Press.

Marwick, A. E. (2015). Instafame: Luxury selfies in the attention economy. *Public Culture*, *27*(75), 137–160. https://doi.org/10.1215/08992363-2798379

Matook, S., Cummings, J., & Bala, H. (2015). Are you feeling lonely? The impact of relationship characteristics and online social network features on loneliness.

Journal of Management Information Systems, 31(4), 278–310. https://doi.org/10.1080/07421222.2014.1001282

Meter, D. J., Ehrenreich, S. E., Carker, C., Flynn, E., & Underwood, M. K. (2019). Older adolescents' understanding of participant rights in the BlackBerry Project, a longitudinal ambulatory assessment study. *Journal of Research on Adolescence, 29*(3), 662–674. https://doi.org/10.1111/jora.12461

Moewaka Barnes, H., McCreanor, T., Goodwin, I., Lyons, A., Griffin, C., & Hutton, F. (2016). Alcohol and social media: Drinking and drunkenness while online. *Critical Public Health, 26*(1), 62–76. https://doi.org/10.1080/09581596.2015.1058921

Mojtabai, R., Olfson, M., & Han, B. (2016). National trends in the prevalence and treatment of depression in adolescents and young adults. *Pediatrics, 138*(6), Article 320161878. https://doi.org/10.1542/peds.2016-1878

Morgan, E. M., Snelson, C., & Elison-Bowers, P. (2010). Image and video disclosure of substance use on social media websites. *Computers in Human Behavior, 26*(6), 1405–1411. https://doi.org/10.1016/j.chb.2010.04.017

Nesi, J., Choukas-Bradley, S., & Prinstein, M. J. (2018a). Transformation of adolescent peer relations in the social media context: Part 1 – A theoretical framework and application to dyadic peer relationships. *Clinical Child and Family Psychology Review, 21*(3), 267–294. https://doi.org/10.1007/s10567-018-0261-x

Nesi, J., Choukas-Bradley, S., & Prinstein, M. J. (2018b). Transformation of adolescent peer relations in the social media context: Part 2 – Application to peer group processes and future directions for research. *Clinical Child and Family Psychology Review, 21*(3), 295–319. https://doi.org/10.1007/s10567-018-0262-9

Nesi, J., & Prinstein, M. J. (2019). In search of likes: Longitudinal associations between adolescents' digital status seeking and health-risk behaviors. *Journal of Clinical Child and Adolescent Psychology, 48*(5), 740–748. https://doi.org/10.1080/15374416.2018.1437733

Nesi, J., Rothenberg, W. A., Hussong, A. M., & Jackson, K. M. (2017). Friends' alcohol-related social networking site activity predicts escalations in adolescent drinking: Mediation by peer norms. *Journal of Adolescent Health, 60*(6), 641–647. https://doi.org/10.1016/j.jadohealth.2017.01.009

Newman, B. M., Lohman, B. J., & Newman, P. R. (2007). Peer group membership and a sense of belonging: Their relationship to adolescent behavior problems. *Adolescence, 42*(166), 241–263. http://www.ncbi.nlm.nih.gov/pubmed/17849935

O'Brien, L., Albert, D., Chein, J., & Steinberg, L. (2011). Adolescents prefer more immediate rewards when in the presence of their peers. *Journal of Research on Adolescence, 21*(4), 747–753. https://doi.org/10.1111/j.1532-7795.2011.00738.x

Piehler, T. F., & Dishion, T. J. (2007). Interpersonal dynamics within adolescent friendships: Dyadic mutuality, deviant talk, and patterns of antisocial behavior. *Child Development, 78*(5), 1611–1624. https://doi.org/10.1111/j.1467-8624.2007.01086.x

Pittman, M., & Reich, B. (2016). Social media and loneliness: Why an Instagram picture may be worth more than a thousand Twitter words. *Computers in Human Behavior, 62*, 155–167. https://doi.org/10.1016/j.chb.2016.03.084

Primack, B. A., Shensa, A., Sidani, J. E., et al. (2017). Social media use and perceived social isolation among young adults in the U.S. *American Journal of Preventative Medicine, 53*(1), 1–8. https://doi.org/10.1016/j.amepre.2017.01.010

Prinstein, M. J., & Dodge, K. A. (2008). *Understanding peer influence in children and adolescents.* Guilford Press.

Ranney, J. D., & Troop-Gordon, W. (2020). The role of popularity and digital self-monitoring in adolescents' cyberbehaviors and cybervictimization. *Computers in Human Behavior, 102,* 293–302. https://doi.org/10.1016/j.chb.2019.08.023

Reich, S. M. (2017). Connecting offline social competence to online peer interactions. *Psychology of Popular Media Culture, 6*(4), 291–310. https://doi.org/10.1037/ppm0000111

Rideout, V., & Robb, M. B. (2018). *Social media, social life: Teens reveal their experiences.* Common Sense Media. https://www.commonsensemedia.org/research/social-media-social-life-2018

Rui, J. R., & Stefanone, M. A. (2016). The desire for fame: An extension of uses and gratifications theory. *Communication Studies, 67*(4), 399–418. https://doi.org/10.1080/10510974.2016.1156006

Sherman, L. E., Hernandez, L. M., Greenfield, P. M., & Dapretto, M. (2018). What the brain 'likes': Neural correlates of providing feedback on social media. *Social Cognitive and Affective Neuroscience, 13*(7), 699–707. https://doi.org/10.1093/scan/nsy051

Sherman, L. E., Greenfield, P. M., Hernandez, L. M., & Dapretto, M. (2018). Peer influence via instagram: Effects on brain and behavior in adolescence and young adulthood. *Child Development, 89*(1), 37–47. https://doi.org/10.1111/cdev.12838

Sherman, L. E., Payton, A. A., Hernandez, L. M., Greenfield, P. M., & Dapretto, M. (2016). The power of the like in adolescence: Effects of peer influence on neural and behavioral responses to social media. *Psychological Science, 27*(7), 1027–1035. https://doi.org/10.1177/0956797616645673

Siriaraya, P., Tang, C., Ang, C. S., Pfeil, U., & Zaphiris, P. (2011). A comparison of empathic communication pattern for teenagers and older people in online support communities. *Behaviour & Information Technology, 30*(5), 617–628. https://doi.org/10.1080/0144929X.2011.582146

Snyder, J., McEachern, A., Schrepferman, L., et al. (2010). Contribution of peer deviancy training to the early development of conduct problems: Mediators and moderators. *Behavior Therapy, 41*(3), 317–328. https://doi.org/10.1016/j.beth.2009.05.001

Somerville, L. H. (2013). The teenage brain sensitivity to social evaluation. *Current Directions in Psychological Science, 22*(2), 121–127. https://doi.org/10.1177/0963721413476512

Song, H., Hayeon, S., Anne, Z. S., et al. (2014). Does Facebook make you lonely? A meta analysis. *Computers in Human Behavior, 36,* 446–452. https://doi.org/10.1016/j.chb.2014.04.011

Steinberg, L. (2008). A social neuroscience perspective on adolescent risk-taking. *Developmental Review, 28*(1), 78–106. https://doi.org/10.1016/j.dr.2007.08.002

Steinberg, L., & Monahan, K. C. (2007). Age differences in resistance to peer influence. *Developmental Psychology*, *43*(6), 1531–1543. https://doi.org/10.1037/0012-1649.43.6.1531

Steinsbekk, S., Wichstrøm, L., Stenseng, F., Nesi, J., Hygen, B. W., & Skalická, V. (2021). The impact of social media use on appearance self-esteem from childhood to adolescence: A 3-wave community study. *Computers in Human Behavior*, *114*, Article 106528. https://doi.org/10.1016/j.chb.2020.106528

Subrahmanyam, K., Reich, S. M., Waechter, N., & Espinoza, G. (2008). Online and offline social networks: Use of social networking sites by emerging adults. *Journal of Applied Developmental Psychology*, *29*(6), 420–433. https://doi.org/10.1016/j.appdev.2008.07.003

Subrahmanyam, K., Smahel, D., & Greenfield, P. (2006). Connecting developmental constructions to the internet: Identity presentation and sexual exploration in online teen chat rooms. *Developmental Psychology*, *42*(3), 395–406. https://doi.org/10.1037/0012-1649.42.3.395

Swirsky, J. M., Rosie, M., & Xie, H. (2021). Adjustment correlates of social media engagement among early adolescents. *Journal of Youth and Adolescence*, *50*, 2265–2278. https://doi.org/10.1007/s10964-021-01421-3

Tromholt, M. (2016). The Facebook experiment: Quitting Facebook leads to higher levels of well-being. *Cyberpsychology, Behavior, and Social Networking*, *19*(11), 661–666. https://doi.org/10.1089/cyber.2016.0259

Turkle, S. (2012). *Alone together: Why we expect more from technology and less from each other*. Basic Books.

Twenge, J. M. (2019). More time on technology, less happiness? Associations between digital-media use and psychological well-being. *Current Directions in Psychological Science*, *28*(4), 372–379. https://doi.org/10.1177/0963721419838244

Twenge, J. M., Joiner, T. E., Rogers, M. L., & Martin, G. N. (2018). Increases in depressive symptoms, suicide-related outcomes, and suicide rates among U.S. adolescents after 2010 and links to increased new media screen time. *Clinical Psychological Science*, *6*(1), 3–17. https://doi.org/10.1177/2167702617723376

Uhls, Y. T., & Greenfield, P. M. (2012). The value of fame: Preadolescent perceptions of popular media and their relationship to future aspirations. *Developmental Psychology*, *48*(2), 315–326. https://doi.org/10.1037/a0026369

Uhls, Y. T., Zgourou, E., & Greenfield, P. M. (2014). 21st century media, fame, and other future aspirations: A national survey of 9–15 year olds. *Cyberpsychology: Journal of Psychosocial Research on Cyberspace*, *8*(4). https://doi.org/10.5817/CP2014-4-5

Underwood, M. K., Brown, B. B., & Ehrenreich, S. E. (2018). Social media and peer relations. In K. H. Rubin, W. M. Bukowski, & B. Laursen (Eds.), *Handbook of peer interactions, relationships, and groups* (2nd ed.; pp. 533–551). Guilford Press.

Underwood, M. K., Rosen, L. H., More, D., Ehrenreich, S. E., & Gentsch, J. K. (2012). The BlackBerry project: Capturing the content of adolescents' text messaging. *Developmental Psychology*, *48*(2), 295–302. https://doi.org/10.1037/a0025914

Valkenburg, P. M., & Peter, J. (2007). Preadolescents' and adolescents' online communication and their closeness to friends. *Developmental Psychology*, *43*(2), 267–277. https://doi.org/10.1037/0012-1649.43.2.267

Vannucci, A., & McCauley Ohannessian, C. M. (2019). Social media use subgroups differentially predict psychosocial well-being during early adolescence. *Journal of Youth and Adolescence, 48*(8), 1469–1493. https://doi.org/10.1007/s10964-019-01060-9

Vogel, E. A., Rose, J. P., Okdie, B. M., Eckles, K., & Franz, B. (2015). Who compares and despairs? The effect of social comparison orientation on social media use and its outcomes. *Personality and Individual Differences, 86*, 249–256. https://doi.org/10.1016/j.paid.2015.06.026

Wang, C., (2020, June 7). *Why TikTok made its user so obsessive? The AI algorithm that got you hooked.* Towards Data Science. https://towardsdatascience.com/why-tiktok-made-its-user-so-obsessive-the-ai-algorithm-that-got-you-hooked-7895bb1ab423

Weinstein, E. (2017). Adolescents' differential responses to social media browsing: Exploring causes and consequences for intervention. *Computers in Human Behavior, 76*, 396–405. https://doi.org/10.1016/j.chb.2017.07.038

Wentzel, K. R., Jablansky, S., & Scalise, N. R. (2021). Peer social acceptance and academic achievement: A meta-analytic study. *Journal of Educational Psychology, 113*(1), 157–180. https://doi.org/10.1037/edu0000468

Wright, M. F., & Li, Y. (2011). The associations between young adults' face-to-face prosocial behaviors and their online prosocial behaviors. *Computers in Human Behavior, 27*, 1959–1962. https://doi.org/10.1016/j.chb.2011.04.019

Yau, J. C., & Reich, S. M. (2019). "It's just a lot of work": Adolescents' self-presentation norms and practices on Facebook and Instagram. *Journal of Research on Adolescence, 29*(1), 196–209. https://doi.org/10.1111/jora.12376

Yoo, W., Yang, J., & Cho, E. (2016). How social media influence college students' smoking attitudes and intentions. *Computers in Human Behavior, 64*, 173–182. https://doi.org/10.1016/j.chb.2016.06.061

5 Digital Media and the Developing Brain

Michelle Chiu and Jason Chein

The pervasiveness of modern digital media in the lives of children and teens has raised important questions about how exposure to, and involvement with, such media might interact with the developing brain. The framing of these questions reflects differing implicit beliefs about the direction of causality in this relationship. Some questions assume that facets of brain development can predispose youth to digital media involvement. It is tempting to ask, for example, whether maturational processes taking place within the brain might prejudice a given age group to become especially enmeshed with digital media, or whether individuals whose brain development lags behind (or is relatively more precocious than) that of their peers also incur greater vulnerability to the consequences of digital media use. Conversely, questions can be posed with the underlying assumption that digital media environments can themselves impact subsequent brain development. We might wonder, for instance, whether digital media experiences have the potential to fundamentally "rewire" the cabling patterns in developing brains, or to stunt or alter the normative developmental processes that lead to a "mature" functional brain. Seeking answers to questions like these carries obvious importance in informing how we, societally and individually, approach the introduction and management of digital media in the lives of our children and teens.

In this chapter, we explore evidence that shapes our current understanding of the relationship between the developing brain and digital media experiences. Although there are many tools that can be applied to the question of how the developing brain affects, and is affected by, digital media behaviors, noninvasive magnetic resonance imaging (MRI) methods have produced many of the key insights, and are the central source of evidence discussed in this chapter. Broadly, MRI methods can be broken down into structural and functional approaches. Structural MRI methods are used to characterize the static anatomical and structural properties of an individual's brain, and include morphometric methods that detail the specific qualities (e.g., thickness, volume) of the gray matter that comprises the brain's outer cortex and major subcortical nuclei, and diffusion-weighted imaging methods that can characterize the cabling patterns formed by the brain's white matter pathways. Meanwhile, functional MRI methods, including task-based functional MRI (fMRI) and intrinsic connectivity approaches such as resting-state fMRI (rsfMRI), allow us to observe dynamic temporal variation in the activation of individual brain regions, and in the coactivation of regions cooperating as part of interconnected brain networks. The evidence from these MRI-based approaches can be considered alongside data derived from complementary methods that render a sharper view of the temporal structure and dynamics of key neural events, especially electroencephalography (EEG).

Combining evidence obtained from these different modalities allows us to consider where and how the findings coalesce, and to evaluate the extent to which various perspectives on the relationship between brain development and digital media behaviors are supported. We focus on three emergent perspectives on the developmental factors that drive, and may be influenced by, digital media habits, and attempt to link these perspectives to evidence on the specific brain networks implicated in these facets of development. One perspective derives from theoretical and empirical work suggesting that the differences in the ability to exert self-regulatory control might account for variation in digital media involvement. Broadly, the idea is that those who struggle to control their thoughts, actions, and the orientation of their attention may be more prone to form digital media habits and be more vulnerable to any impacts of the behavior (Brand et al., 2014; Wei et al., 2017; Wilmer et al., 2017). As we will detail in the next section of the chapter, there are specific brain regions thought to support the capacity for self-regulatory control, and evidence suggesting that the structure and function of these regions might be relevant in the development of digital media habits. A second perspective on digital media involvement focuses on variation across age groups and individuals in the valuation of, and responsiveness to, environmental rewards. Under this view, normative developmental shifts in reward-relevant processes may introduce periods of particular susceptibility to the appetitive, novel, and arousing properties of digital media interactions, especially for those who possess (or who come to develop) a particularly acute sensitivity to those rewards (Firth et al., 2019). Once again, this perspective orients us to the specific brain regions we know to be involved in the coding of reward value and in processing the outcomes of pursuing (or not pursuing) environmental rewards. A third perspective arises from evidence highlighting conspicuous developmental shifts in the importance of nonfamilial social relationships, and associated changes in orientation and response to social influence (Blakemore, 2018; Mills et al., 2014; Sutter et al., 2019). Since digital media, and especially social media, have become such an important source of socially relevant information, some argue that developmental changes in the structure and function of the "social brain" might be especially important for understanding what motivates digital media behaviors, and how they might impact subsequent brain development (Meshi et al., 2020).

Importantly, the brain systems that support control, reward, and social information processes are thought to follow distinct trajectories of development. Whereas the mechanisms involved in self-regulatory control mature in a gradual and protracted manner across the period from middle childhood into early adulthood, the brain regions that subserve valuation of, and sensitivity to, rewards are thought to undergo more rapid reconfiguration during early adolescence, in response to the hormonal changes of puberty (Sisk & Zehr, 2005; Smith et al., 2013; Spear, 2010). This asynchronous developmental timing has important implications for how these systems interact with one another, and may be fundamental to understanding their roles in relation to emerging digital media behaviors. Meanwhile, regions associated with social information processing evince mixed developmental timing patterns (Atzil et al., 2018; Kilford et al., 2016; Mills et al., 2021; Richardson et al., 2018), with some areas showing marked change in periods of childhood and adolescence, and others showing a more protracted developmental trajectory resembling that of self-regulatory control regions.

While this is a quickly advancing area of scientific inquiry, and the tools of modern neuroimaging have afforded valuable insights into the structure and function of the developing human brain, the reader should be warned from the outset that conclusive answers to the types of questions we posed in the opening paragraph of this chapter are still on the horizon. Rather, perspectives on how digital media experiences might interact with brain development currently derive from only a sparse corpus of fundamentally limited research. Perhaps the most obvious limitation is that very few studies are able to address the directionality of observed relationships. This is because, at present, the vast majority of relevant data originates from purely cross-sectional or correlational work, and very few true experiments or longitudinal studies exist to more adequately clarify causal patterns. It is worth noting, however, that the patterns of association and group differences observed in correlational and cross-sectional studies do help to guide alternative causal hypotheses, and the absence of predicted patterns can serve as key counter-evidence against causal claims. Another clear limitation of the literature is that surprisingly few neuroinvestigative studies explore the brain correlates of digital media habits as they arise during the course of development. Rather, most of the evidence derives from studies of brain–behavior relationships observed at a relatively late point in development (in late adolescent and young adult cohorts). This state of affairs is due, in part, to the fact that many digital media behaviors (e.g., smartphone and social media account ownership, online gaming) often only begin to take hold in middle to later adolescence (Lauricella et al., 2016), and also to the inherent challenges involved in collecting neuroimaging data from younger participants (e.g., excessive movement and difficulty with task compliance). In our consideration of the brain systems implicated in digital media habits, we therefore rely primarily on the findings from later developmental periods, with the hope that this work contains reliable clues to how digital media experiences might interact with earlier brain development. Finally, as is discussed elsewhere in this handbook, the ever-changing technological landscape makes it difficult to conduct studies on digital media and the brain in a way that sufficiently addresses developmental cohort effects (i.e., the specific digital milieu available to a given developing cohort) and that anticipates consequential changes in the character and function of the digital media environment (e.g., the introduction of new social media forms). As such, much of what we can conclude to date is based on untested assumptions about the stability of observed brain–behavior relationships across varying digital media modalities and ecosystems.

With these caveats in mind, we can consider what the brain science tells us about the brain–behavior relations that surround digital media use. In the sections that follow, we consider, in turn, whether the brain regions and networks implicated in control, reward, and social processing are specifically relevant to digital media experiences. For each perspective, we weigh whether the extant neuroinvestigative evidence is corroborative or not, and consider how the specific pattern of evidence might sharpen or refine current explanatory theories. Rather than attempt an exhaustive review, we walk the reader through some seminal and informative findings, focusing first on studies from mostly nondevelopmental samples of adults, and then visiting the sparse but instructive patterns that have emerged in the developmental neuroscientific literature.

Digital Media and the Brain's Control and Attention Networks

A growing body of work points to associations between digital media behaviors and the capacity for top-down self-regulatory control over thoughts, emotions, and behavior. Behavioral scientists often subdivide this skillset into separate psychological constructs with different labels (e.g., executive functioning, response inhibition, working memory, attention control, emotion regulation), and use a varied array of tasks and surveys to index its subcomponents. The general finding from across behavioral studies is that groups (and individuals) who demonstrate a weaker capacity for control also tend to exhibit higher levels of digital media use and more problematic involvements (e.g., excessive or addiction-like[1] use) with various media forms. This is presumably because the inability to reliably exert control makes one more prone to impulsive engagement with digital media (e.g., frequent phone checking), greater attentional distractibility in response to media-associated cues (e.g., notifications), and greater difficulty with sustaining goal-relevant behaviors in the presence of digital media (Ward et al., 2017). In our own lab, we have found that poorer performance on self-report and behavioral measures of response and impulse control is associated with increased smartphone and social media use habits among young adults (Wilmer & Chein, 2016) and that early signs of this relationship are already present in much earlier stages of development (i.e., in a cohort of 6- to 8-year-olds, unpublished data). Several other studies detail similar relationships between poorer cognitive and attentional control and varying forms of digital media involvement,

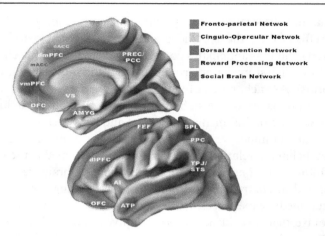

Figure 5.1 *Visualization of regions comprising the brain networks thought to be associated with digital media behaviors. Key* control *regions are shown for the* fronto-parietal *"executive" network, the* cingulo-opercular control network, *and the* dorsal attentional network, *including the frontal eye fields (FEF) and superior parietal lobule (SPL). Also shown are regions strongly implicated in* reward *processing and those thought to be connected to* social *processing in the brain.*

including greater social media use (Alloway & Alloway, 2012), internet dependency (Choi et al., 2014; Dong et al., 2011), increased media-multitasking (the concurrent use of alternate digital media modalities; Baumgartner et al., 2014; Lopez et al., 2020; Minear et al., 2013; E. Ophir et al., 2009), and excessive smartphone habits (Liebherr et al., 2020), at various points in development.

Given the apparent links between the behavioral expression of self-regulatory control processes and a range of digital media behaviors, an obvious place to begin looking for brain–behavior relationships tied to digital media use is within the brain regions and networks thought to support control processes. Considerations of where "control" arises in the brain often emphasize the lateral prefrontal cortex, but a more extensive characterization of how control is enacted might consider three complementary brain networks (Cole & Schneider, 2007; Dixon et al., 2018; Dosenbach et al., 2008; Gratton et al., 2018). The most prominent of these networks, the fronto-parietal "executive" network (FP; see Figure 5.1), is comprised of the dorsolateral prefrontal cortex (dlPFC, found in the middle frontal gyrus), the posterior parietal cortex (PPC, spanning the supramarginal gyrus and neighboring cortex extending into the intraparietal sulcus), and a dorsomedial prefrontal (dmPFC) region covering the dorsal extent of the anterior cingulate cortex (dACC) and extending into the midline superior frontal gyrus. While the FP network is thought to orchestrate the initiation and adjustment of control, the cingulate component of this network, along with a mid-anterior cingulate (mACC) area found slightly more rostral (in front of) and inferior to (below) the dACC, also functions as a hub region that dynamically coordinates its activity with the bilateral operculum (including the anterior insula and the neighboring posterior segment of the inferior frontal gyrus) to form a cingulo-opercular network (CO; see Figure 5.1). The CO network is thought to drive sustained control over behavior, and to orchestrate reactions to salient (goal-relevant or attention-grabbing) external and interoceptive (coming from inside the body) events, thus giving the network its alternative name – the "salience" network (Menon, 2015). The ability to intentionally orient attention toward specific external and internal (mental) events is also known to involve an additional attention control network that has been dubbed the dorsal attentional network (also shown in Figure 5.1), which includes superior portions of the bilateral parietal association cortex (superior parietal lobule) as well as the bilateral frontal eye fields (found where the middle frontal gyrus intersects with the precentral gyrus). The brain regions encompassed in these control networks are generally understood to undergo a gradual, and particularly protracted, period of maturation that extends from childhood into at least the mid-twenties, which may explain why the ability to exert self-regulatory control over arousing and distracting stimuli is not fully formed until young adulthood (Sherman et al., 2016).

These control and attentional networks in the brain may be important to the manifestation of digital media behaviors. Some research implicating the neural correlates of control in digital media habits relies on basic structural MRI measurements of regional gray matter volume/density in the brain. Various studies on excessive internet use and online gaming behaviors, for example, offer evidence of reduced gray matter in key regions of the FP and CO networks, including the lateral prefrontal cortex (Q. He et al., 2020; Yuan et al., 2011), the dACC (X. Lin et al., 2015; Yuan et al., 2011), and the insula (Turel et al., 2020); though studies in these populations occasionally show the opposing pattern of relationship (cf. Li et al., 2015). Decreased gray matter volume has also been observed in the lateral prefrontal cortex, dACC, and anterior insula of individuals with smartphone "addiction" (Horvath et al., 2020; Y. Wang et al., 2016), and in the dACC of individuals exhibiting a strong tendency to engage in media-multitasking (Loh & Kanai, 2014). While some investigators interpret these associations as evidence of consequential long-term impacts of digital media habits on the structural maturation of the brain's control centers, such causal conclusions are simply untenable on the basis of this correlational evidence (e.g., we cannot know whether different habits lead to differentiated brain maturation, or whether different brains lead to differentiated habits). Moreover, it is challenging to translate evidence of altered structure into functional terms. For instance, while reduced gray matter volume does at times coincide with disrupted functioning, decreases in gray matter over the course of adolescent development are also thought to reflect the normative and desirable removal of unneeded neuronal connections through synaptic pruning (Gogtay & Thompson, 2010).

To try to clarify the nature of the relationship, we can consider evidence from studies of brain activity and connectivity, many of which highlight the same control-relevant brain regions. One early study on the functional correlates of internet gaming (Sun et al., 2012) found that visual cues designed to elicit cravings among heavy video-gamers induced activation of the bilateral dlPFC and dACC. Subsequent work found that heavy media-multitasking was linked to both poorer performance and relatively increased right lateralized PFC activity when attempting an attentionally demanding task, which suggested that media-multitaskers might experience more difficulties when recruiting cognitive control resources (Moisala et al., 2016). More recently, similarly aberrant lateral and dorso-medial PFC activation was reported in association with excessive smartphone usage (Schmitgen et al., 2020), with smartphone addicts exhibiting increased activity in these areas when viewing smartphone-relevant visual cues (perhaps indicative of a need for greater effort in order to inhibit cue-related responses). Studies examining functional connectivity within and between the brain's control networks provide further clarification of the relationship between control and digital media behaviors. The same group of smartphone addicts studied in Schmitgen et al. (2020) also evinced weaker coordination between the dmPFC and the left PPC, and between the anterior insula and the right lateralized PPC (Horvath et al., 2020). Other recent work in heavy and excessive smartphone users has likewise indicated weaker intra-network connectivity in the FP and CO networks (Chun et al., 2020), and decreased functional (Chun et al., 2020) and structural (Wilmer et al., 2019) connectivity between key centers of the brain's control networks and the ventral striatum (VS), a region of the brain where mesolimbic dopamine is released to signal the value of potential rewards. Thus, studies of brain activity and connectivity suggest that individuals who are more enmeshed with digital media also have a harder time (or need to devote more effort) initiating and sustaining self-regulatory processes, and may not be as facile at controlling responses to appetitive and potentially rewarding cues.

Evidence from EEG studies conducted on groups of heavy and addicted digital media users provides further support for the involvement of self-regulatory control mechanisms in these behaviors. Early work demonstrated that deficient executive abilities (assessed behaviorally) found in heavy internet users were paralleled by differences in the evoked potentials produced during a "Go/NoGo" response inhibition task (Dong et al., 2011). The specific pattern exhibited by the heavy-use group reflected a relatively lower amplitude N2 (a frontally generated electrical potential that the authors associated with the conflict monitoring process that triggers the need to engage control), followed by a higher amplitude and delayed latency P3 (an evoked potential often associated with attention and response control). The authors interpreted these findings as evidence that the addicted group was less efficient at engaging control mechanisms during the task. Some subsequent work on internet use has replicated the reduced N2 potential during inhibitory control (Chen et al., 2016), while recent studies in excessive social media network users (Q. Gao et al., 2019) and problematic smartphone users (L. Gao et al., 2020) point to a reversed pattern in which the more digitally engaged groups were found to evince a *higher* amplitude N2, and *weaker* P3 (specifically in the smartphone group) when trying to inhibit impulsive responses. While it can be challenging, even for experts in the field, to interpret the meaning of these differentiated components in the electrophysiological record, they do provide yet another source of evidence connecting digital media habits with the mechanisms underlying control.

So, though far from conclusive and based exclusively on correlational observations, the evidence seems to be broadly consistent with the notion that relative weaknesses in the brain systems supporting control may act as a gateway to digital media habit formation, and that diminished control could be a downstream consequence of prolonged or intensive periods of digital media involvement. However, some variation in the particular sites that emerge as significant across studies, and the occasionally reversed directionality of the findings (e.g., increases vs. decreases in regional volume, activity, connectivity, or evoked potentials), certainly warrant further consideration. One plausible explanation is that this variability is the result of unique brain-behavior relationships that exist for the diverse digital media experiences covered in this work. While the findings most consistently implicate key anterior and frontal nodes of the FP and CO networks, there is also considerably less evidence pointing to the involvement of parietal subregions of the FP and DAT networks (cf. Kei et al., 2020). This might indicate that digital media use is more closely tied to frontally mediated aspects of control – such as the establishment and maintenance of goal-state representations, and less connected to the parietal processes that dictate the shifting and orientation of attention (Chein & Schneider, 2005).

Digital Media and the Brain's Reward Circuitry

A somewhat different perspective stems from the belief that digital media habits are connected to approach motivational and reinforcement processes. Under this view, the appetitive and rewarding features of digital media technologies – often embedded intentionally into digital platforms by their developers in order to stimulate more intense usage habits (Harris, 2016) – might drive increased engagement with these platforms, disrupt the normal development of reward circuits, and at the extremes, give rise to maladaptive and addiction-like behaviors. Indeed, much of the work on digital media use draws upon the language and theories of addiction and reward dysregulation, and such diagnostic labels as internet-use disorder, internet addiction, internet gaming disorder, social network use disorder, and smartphone addiction are commonly applied in the literature to groups and individuals who exhibit seemingly excessive, problematic, or dependent use habits (Griffiths et al., 2014; Gutiérrez et al., 2016; Kirby et al., 2020; Yao et al., 2017).

As with claims regarding control, theories linking aberrant reward processing and responsivity to digital media habits also gain some purchase in correlational behavioral evidence. Across several studies exploring the behavioral and trait correlates of different digital media modalities, there is compelling evidence that individuals who tend to be more engaged with these media also tend to exhibit greater general reward sensitivity and responsivity (Sanbonmatsu et al., 2013) – particularly with respect to more immediate rewards (Hadar et al., 2017; Tang et al., 2017; Wilmer & Chein, 2016), and have greater difficulty with reward reinforcement learning (Meshi et al., 2019).

If the development of reward-relevant processes plays a role in the formation of digital media habits, or results in reward dysregulation that causes greater vulnerability to relevant problematic outcomes, then we might expect to observe such effects within the brain's reward circuitry (see Figure 5.1). This circuitry includes the dopaminergic pathways that connect the ventral tegmental area of the brainstem (where dopamine is produced) to the nucleus accumbens of the VS, the amygdala, and the ventromedial prefrontal cortex (vmPFC) – especially its ventral-most extent comprising the orbitofrontal cortex (OFC), a region linked to aberrant reward processes in patients with other substance-related and behavioral addictions (Kuss et al., 2018). From a developmental perspective, these reward-processing structures are known to undergo a rapid period of change around the onset of puberty, which is thought to explain why adolescence constitutes a period of particularly heightened reward responsivity (Blakemore & Robbins, 2012; Sisk & Zehr, 2005; Spear, 2010).

Neuroimaging work suggests that the dysregulation of reward-relevant regions, especially the OFC, VS, and amygdala, may indeed be a hallmark for the addiction-like behaviors found in association with a range of digital media forms (Kuss et al., 2018; Lin & Lei, 2015; Turel et al., 2014). A study on addicted players of the online video game *World of Warcraft* (Ko et al., 2009) was among the first to show this relationship. Specifically, the study found that excessive gamers, relative to a comparison group of game novices, evinced increased activity not only in self-regulatory processing regions (dlPFC, dmPFC), but also in the OFC and VS, when presented with game-related cues that aroused the urge to play. Several subsequent studies examining brain structure in participants engaged in especially high levels of internet and smartphone use have found corroborating evidence of gray matter abnormalities in the OFC (Hong et al., 2013; Lee et al., 2019; Lin & Lei, 2015; Zhou et al., 2019).

Studies examining the number of social relationships that one forms by way of online social networking sites also point to the relevance of reward processing centers in the brain. Building on prior work examining the neural correlates of both online and offline social network size (Bickart et al., 2011; Kanai et al., 2012), Von der Heide and colleagues demonstrated that having a larger online social network, as measured by participants' actual number of Facebook friends, was associated with *greater* gray matter volume in multiple reward-relevant brain regions, including the bilateral amygdala and OFC (Von der Heide et al., 2013). A related study on the structural brain correlates of actual Facebook use – this time indexed by participants' mobile device Facebook use over a five-week period (Montag et al., 2017) – found that higher frequency and duration of mobile Facebook use were both associated with decreased gray matter volume of the bilateral VS. Other related work has found evidence of decreased gray matter volume in the bilateral amygdalae of those reporting generally heavier use of social networking sites (i.e., not focused on a particular platform; W. He et al., 2017). As we noted earlier, relative increases and decreases in the volume of regional gray matter can be difficult to interpret in functional terms, but such findings, at the very least, suggest that there are relevant linkages between digital media habits and the processes enacted within these reward-processing centers.

Here again, we can turn to fMRI studies involving task-based manipulations of the digital media environment to corroborate and clarify the structural findings. In one early neuroimaging study on social media behavior (Turel et al., 2014), heavy Facebook users were scanned while performing a task that required them to respond to Facebook-relevant cues (iconography taken from the Facebook platform) while withholding responses to irrelevant cues (traffic signs), or vice versa. Among the regions tested, only one exhibited a pattern of activity that predicted individual differences in Facebook addiction – the VS. That is, the level of one's Facebook addiction selectively related to how strongly this central reward value processing center responded in association with Facebook images. The importance of the VS in social media behaviors was similarly underscored in another early study of Facebook users in which social feedback given to participants was experimentally manipulated in a simulated social media environment (Meshi et al., 2013). In this study, the authors found that actual Facebook usage was associated with how active the VS became when participants received positive social feedback for themselves (compared to others) in the simulated platform. Another widely cited neuroimaging study deployed a simulated version of the Instagram social networking platform (Sherman et al., 2016). In the study, high school students submitted photos from their own actual Instagram accounts and were told that their photos, along with photos provided by others, would be viewed by the participants in the study, and either liked or not liked; in reality, the number of likes and the content (neutral or risky behaviors) of the photos were manipulated by the researchers as part of their experimental design. FMRI evidence showed increased activation in the VS, along with several other regions, when participants saw that their own images had received a higher number of likes, and also when viewing neutral photos that were more liked by others. These findings suggest that receiving positive social feedback via social media, and evaluating the relative social value of the information (e.g., photos) others post on these platforms, engages the same brain processes that generally signal rewarding experiences. A related study conducted in adolescents (Cascio et al., 2015) investigated whether these same processes might influence online decisions about whether or not to conform with others' expressed preferences. During a scanning session, subjects were shown the recommendations (ratings) that they and others had given for a set of smartphone apps, and were then given the chance to revise their own prior rating. Analyses indicated greater activation in both the VS and OFC when participants changed, rather than maintained, their initial rating, which suggests once again that reward valuation signals play a role in dictating this facet of online behavior. Indeed, two recent companion studies exploring the neural processes underlying the selection and sharing of digital media content likewise implicate this same reward valuation network (Baek et al., 2017; Scholz et al., 2017). Specifically, these studies found that the VS and OFC were among the most strongly engaged regions when participants opted to share news headlines via social media in a simulated task, and in association with headlines that are actually the most "viral" (i.e., shared in real-life media) at the population level.

Functional and structural connectivity approaches provide still further evidence of reward circuitry involvement in mediating the nature and intensity of one's digital media habits, though the directionality of these findings is somewhat nuanced. While some studies suggest that heavier digital media involvement is tied to disrupted (weaker) integration among the brain regions that process reward-relevant information (e.g., functional connectivity with the VS is reduced in internet addicts; Zhang et al., 2015), other studies find that heavier digital media use is associated with *stronger* interconnectivity among reward regions (e.g., the integrity of white matter pathways connecting the VS and OFC is stronger in heavy smartphone users [Wilmer et al., 2019]; functional connectivity of the amygdala to other regions is a correlate of adolescent smartphone dependence [Tymofiyeva et al., 2020]).

EEG studies examining online gaming and smartphone addiction also lend support to the idea that heavy digital media use is associated with altered neural activity in the reward system. Relevant studies on internet behavior have found, for instance, that online gaming addicts produce an attenuated P300 in response to receiving rewards (Duven et al., 2015), and that individuals who report excessive internet use evince both a smaller feedback-related negativity in response to reward gains, and a larger P300 in response to losses (W. He et al., 2017), which could indicate stronger reinforcement sensitivity and weaker punishment sensitivity, respectively. Recent work on smartphone habits similarly observed an altered reward positivity potential among heavier smartphone users, but no association between intensity of use and the amplitude of the parietal P3 (which the authors considered an index of higher-level decision processing), leading to the conclusion that smartphone addiction may be selectively correlated with reward processing, and not higher-level deliberative processes (Kirby et al., 2020).

Overall, the behavioral and imaging findings connect reward-related brain systems to a range of digital media behaviors. This work spans early forms of digital media, including video gaming and internet use habits, but also harnesses one of digital media's currently most widespread and time-consuming manifestations – social media networking. While some studies find that digital media behaviors are selectively associated with reward-related signals and locations in the brain (e.g., Kirby et al., 2020), many of the relevant studies also contain evidence for the involvement of regions thought to undergird other, more disparate, functions (e.g., Ko et al., 2009; Sherman et al., 2016). Indeed, as we consider in greater depth in the next section, several studies highlighting the relevance of reward circuitry in digital media habits (e.g., Cascio et al., 2015; Horvath et al., 2020; Sherman et al., 2016) also indicate the relevance of regions more typically associated with social information processes (rather than reward processes, per se).

Digital Media and the Brain's Social Processing Systems

Increasingly, many of our day-to-day social interactions take place on digital platforms, and it has been argued that social networking sites now serve as an independent medium for developing and maintaining social connectedness despite being devoid of direct face-to-face interactions (Grieve et al., 2013; Spies Shapiro & Margolin, 2014). As such, researchers have leveraged the quantification of social interactions supported by online social networking sites like Facebook and Instagram to explore whether, and how, this type of digital social context relates to psychological and brain functioning.

The strength and directionality of the influence of digital screen engagement and social media networking on psychosocial functioning in developmental populations is a subject of significant debate (Coyne et al., 2020; Przybylski et al., 2020; Twenge et al., 2020), and evidence from both longitudinal and large-scale secondary data analysis suggests that the relationship is likely smaller and more nuanced than has sometimes been claimed (Coyne et al., 2020; Przybylski et al., 2020). Any impact of social media behaviors is also likely to vary across different social networking platforms. For example, some studies in adolescent and young adult samples find that heavier use of Facebook, but not YouTube or Twitter, is related to higher self-reported levels of social connectedness (Alloway et al., 2013; Alloway & Alloway, 2012), potentially due to the built-in features in Facebook that facilitate more sharing of personal content.

The expectation that aspects of digital media involvement could be motivated by, or have an impact on, social exchange, has led some investigators to pursue evidence of associations between the brain's social information processing networks (see Figure 5.1) and digital media habits. There is, however, only partial consensus regarding which specific brain regions participate selectively in social information processes. The brain regions most consistently implicated in social information processing are the temporoparietal junction and neighboring (posterior) superior temporal sulcus along with the midline (ventromedial) prefrontal cortex. Some treatments of the "social brain" also variably include the precuneus and adjacent posterior cingulate cortex, and the anterior temporal poles (Adolphs, 2009; Becht et al., 2021; Mills et al., 2014). Together, these regions are thought to support empathy, mentalizing, social perspective taking, and the processing of social feedback. The conspicuous proximity of the medial prefrontal areas implicated in social feedback processing and those associated with the valuation of primary rewards, such as food and sex (Bartra et al., 2013; Lieberman & Eisenberger, 2009) has led some researchers to emphasize the functional overlap between these systems (Bhanji & Delgado, 2014; Braams et al., 2014), as have studies showing engagement of mesolimbic "reward" regions in putatively "social" tasks. Likewise, colocalization of regions implicated in social information processing tasks with areas that also exhibit increased engagement when our minds are supposed to be at rest – comprising a so-called default mode network – has spurred additional theorizing on the specific operations that are supported by these brain areas (Mars et al., 2012).

Work exploring the links between the magnitude of one's online social network size and brain structure points not only to the involvement of nodes in the brain's reward system, as was noted earlier, but also to the involvement of social processing areas such as the temporoparietal junction (Kanai et al., 2012). The involvement of the social brain in digital media experiences is further suggested by work examining the association between intrinsic functional organization in the brain and individual differences in the sharing of personal (self-related) information on Facebook (Meshi et al., 2016). Specifically, analyses focused on how social processing centers in the vmPFC and precuneus connect up with the rest of the brain. The study revealed that the strength of connectivity between these regions and the lateral PFC predicted a greater tendency to share information with others on Facebook, while stronger connectivity between the precuneus and ATP predicted less sharing. Such findings suggest that the decision to broadcast personally relevant information via social media may depend in part on how one mentally represents social relationships (interactions between the self and others) in these regions.

Other recent work has explicitly investigated whether the structure of social brain regions might also explain the overall amount of time one spends on social media (Turel et al., 2018). Based on behavioral findings establishing that the effort to maintain and navigate online social relationships is subjectively perceived as demanding (Turel et al., 2018, Exp. 1), the authors wondered whether the social skills used to keep up with these demands might also be reflected in the neuroanatomical correlates of social information processing. Seeming to confirming this hypothesis, structural MRI analyses revealed a significant positive correlation between overall Facebook usage and the gray matter volume of a superior temporal site near the temporoparietal junction (Turel et al., 2018, Exp. 2). That is, those with more gray matter in a temporal region of the social brain network reported spending more time on Facebook, which the authors thought could reflect the relative sophistication of the social skills that they rely on to maintain extended online social networks, or their relative adeptness at deploying these skills.

The idea that possessing stronger social skills might promote greater digital media involvement is, however, in an interesting juxtaposition with findings suggesting that individuals with *lower* social empathy also tend to be more enmeshed with certain digital media (Decety & Lamm, 2006; Engelberg & Sjöberg, 2004; Melchers et al., 2015). As such, while heavier media use might coincide with a stronger ability to understand others' perspectives (i.e., advanced social processing skills), it may also coincide with less actual concern for others' emotional states. Evidence from EEG studies aimed at investigating the neural basis of empathic processing among individuals who report heavy internet use reinforces this speculation. Specifically, multiple studies have found that participants with high internet addiction scores (compared to healthy controls) exhibit an undifferentiated electrical response when viewing images of others in painful versus nonpainful circumstances, whereas the EEG record in healthy controls shows discrimination of these conditions (Jiao et al., 2017; T. Wang et al., 2014). That is, internet-addicted individuals exhibit (at least in their EEGs) a relative absence of empathy for others' discomfort.

The evidence considered above demonstrates that some digital media experiences are associated with brain regions and patterns implicated in social information processing. Namely, they show that key nodes in the social brain, including the temporoparietal junction, the precuneus, and the vmPFC, are likely to play a role in determining how digital media users navigate through the complexities of online social networking space and how they form representations of others' perspectives and feelings. We note, however, that the supportive findings in this domain may be less abundant in the literature than those implicating self-regulatory control and reward-relevant processes. This state of affairs could indicate the differential contributions of these systems to digital media behaviors, or could simply reflect the fact that few studies have thus far deliberately tried to disentangle the social facets of digital media interactions from its inherent rewards and high-level processing demands. We anticipate that this will be a focal aim of future work in this space.

Digital Media Use in the Developing Brain

Above, we harnessed evidence from the young adult literature in order to establish the involvement of control, reward, and social brain systems in digital media experiences. Guided by this evidence, and with some knowledge of the expected trajectory of development within these systems, we turn now to a limited body of developmental neuroscientific work that might help us to understand how these brain–behavior relationships manifest in earlier stages of development: to discern whether the patterns observed in young adulthood are already present in earlier life, whether brain–behavior relationships emerge specifically in conjunction with the maturation of the three systems (or with other brain systems), or whether the patterns discussed above are only characteristic of later stages of development.

Studies in Early Life and Childhood

While early childhood screen and digital media exposure is a widely researched topic, only a handful of studies have deployed noninvasive brain imaging methods in the effort to illuminate potential interrelationships with brain development. Perhaps the earliest developmental glimpse comes from MRI and EEG studies conducted in preschoolers (Hutton et al., 2020; Zivan et al., 2019). One MRI-based diffusion tractography study (Hutton et al., 2020) found that, already by preschool (ages 3–5), screen time exposure is associated with widespread reductions in white matter integrity, a sign that these children have less well-developed structural connections between brain regions. While several tracts (pathways) exhibited this association, those associated with executive function, multimodal association, visual processing, and language were especially implicated. The same research group also conducted an EEG study of children aged 4–6 (Zivan et al., 2019), which found that six weeks of exposure to screen-based, digitally recorded, stories, compared to live human storytelling, resulted in weaker attentional gains and a resting-state EEG pattern characteristic of attentional disruption (increased theta/beta power ratio). Meanwhile, a study exploring screen-based media habits in a group of older children (aged 8–12; Horowitz-Kraus & Hutton, 2018) indicated that increased media exposure might be associated with decreased resting-state connectivity between both cognitive control and language regions of the brain and the visual word form area, a region known to be important in the acquisition and execution of reading skills. The authors speculated that this pattern might have arisen because substantial screen time disrupts the normal development of the regions that support reading skill in the brain. Recently, Horowitz-Kraus and colleagues (2020) followed up on this discovery to investigate whether functional connectivity patterns in this age range might also relate to the ratio of time that children spend in front of screens versus reading; this time considering these relationships for both typical readers and children with reading difficulties. The two reading ability groups exhibited similar screen-to-reading time ratios but, selectively for the children with reading difficulties, a relatively greater proportion of screen time activity was related to increased functional connectivity in the salience and executive control networks. The authors suggested that this pattern might reflect inefficient engagement of control processes when reading (and presumably when engaging in other cognitively challenging tasks), which might ultimately lead these children to greater screen dependency (though see Y. Ophir et al., 2020). Through we still only have correlational evidence from these studies, the findings are at least consistent with the idea that screen time exposure, particularly during earlier stages of dynamic brain growth and development, might be intertwined with the processes supporting self-regulatory control, especially among those with existing developmental deficits.

Paulus and colleagues (2019) recently reported findings from the first large-scale investigation aimed at relating screen media activity to structural brain characteristics in prepubescent youth (ages 9 and 10 at recruitment), using the structural imaging and survey data from a 4,277-participant subset of the first cross-sectional release of the Adolescent Brain Cognitive Development (ABCD) study (Volkow et al., 2018). The authors characterized and quantified screen media activity via multivariate analyses of survey responses provided by parents and youth. Overall, these analyses produced significant but complex patterns of relationship between structural brain indices (cortical thickness, sulcal depth, and gray matter volume) and screen media activity. In particular, the factor accounting for the most variance in screen media activity showed that greater screen involvement was linked to widespread cortical thinning and gray matter volume reductions (along with greater levels of externalizing psychopathology and lower crystallized intelligence). Interestingly, this pattern held for regions supporting both early sensory processing and higher order functions. However, the specific pattern of relationship was also found to depend on the type of screen media behavior (e.g., social media vs. gaming) – for instance, greater exposure to gaming-related activities was associated with thinner cortex, but also *larger* regional volume (e.g., OFC) and *higher* crystallized intelligence. Moreover, other latent factors capturing variance in the screen media activity data suggested disparate patterns of relationship between screen activity and brain structure. In light of this diversity of findings, the authors cautioned that screen media activity cannot be reduced to being simply "good" or "bad" for brain structure and function.

Studies in Adolescents

There is a widely observed rise in digital media involvement during adolescence. With adolescence, pubertal processes advance the brain into a period characterized by rapid change in both the midline dopaminergic reward system and in the extended network of brain regions involved in social information processing (Blakemore, 2008, 2012). It is, accordingly, tempting to speculate that the changes taking place in these brain systems might explain the escalation of digital media use during this period, and earlier in this chapter we presented some relevant and corroborative findings (e.g., Cascio et al., 2015; Sherman et al., 2016; Tymofiyeva et al., 2020; Yuan et al., 2011). Unfortunately, much of the additional literature on brain-to-digital-media relationships during "adolescence" has involved either very late adolescent cohorts, or participant samples spanning a wide age range that may include some younger adolescents but also extends into young adulthood (i.e., participants in their early to mid- twenties; F. Lin et al., 2012; Moisala et al., 2016, 2017; Von der Heide et al., 2013; H. Wang et al., 2015). Thus, it can be difficult to draw meaningful developmental conclusions from this corpus of work.

The few studies using somewhat more constrained age cohorts (i.e., including only adolescents aged 18 or under) produce intriguing, but varied outcomes. One study, for instance, observed that internet gaming habits among a group of 14- to 17-year-olds related to disrupted blood flow patterns (as measured by MRI-based arterial spin labeling) in a large number of brain areas, including some linked to reward-relevant processing (e.g., amygdala) (Feng et al., 2013). Using functional connectivity methods, another study found that a group of gaming addicts, aged 12–17, also evince relatively increased connectivity between the posterior cingulate cortex and several other social- and reward-relevant regions, including the precuneus and the nucleus accumbens (Ding et al., 2013). However, more recent work (Chun et al., 2018) on excessive smartphone use among adolescents aged 12–18 found that smartphone usage intensity related to significantly *weaker* intrinsic resting-state connectivity within the reward network (OFC to VS) and between the control and reward systems (OFC to mACC), with weakened OFC–VS functional connectivity also found to be predictive of the severity of smartphone withdrawal symptoms reported by the group. Thus, evidence on the relationship between digital media behaviors and functional connectivity across regions of the reward and social processing networks appears to be nuanced, and difficult to align neatly with specific theories of development.

Age Group Comparisons and Longitudinal Studies of Youth

Cross-sectional evidence comparing digital media use among different age cohorts could help us to determine whether observed brain–behavior relationships simply track with the trajectory of normative brain development, or rather, contain evidence for a causative effect of digital media behavior on brain development. Unfortunately, the literature is almost completely lacking studies that directly compare one age group to another. The only notable exception is Sherman et al.'s (2018) replication and extension of their earlier work in adolescents (Sherman et al., 2016), in which they leveraged the same simulated Instagram paradigm to collect comparison data from an older young adult cohort comprised of university students (Sherman et al., 2018). Similar to their prior findings in adolescents, the young adults evinced greater activation in social- and reward-relevant brain regions, including the precuneus, vmPFC, and VS, when viewing images from their own Instagram accounts that had received more versus fewer likes. Indeed, the direct contrast between adolescents' and young adults' brain activity when these groups received social feedback on their own images produced no significant differences, other than a small region of the visual cortex. This congruency across the two age cohorts suggests that adolescents' elevated concerns toward "popularity" likely persist into young adulthood. That is, the sensitivity of the brain's social and reward circuitry might rise with adolescence, but then plateau in young adulthood. When viewing others' images, however, important age differences did emerge in control-relevant regions of the brain. Namely, while the adolescent sample had exhibited diminished engagement of control regions when viewing risky compared to non-risky/neutral images, young adults showed equivalent activity in the two conditions. In other words, the young adults responded to the images of risky activities by activating the self-regulatory control regions that inhibit actual involvement in such behaviors, while the adolescents did not appear to do so. Indeed, a direct contrast across the two age groups indicated significantly greater activation for young adults in both the dmPFC and dlPFC when viewing risky images. Together, these findings accord with a dual systems framework (Shulman et al., 2016; Steinberg, 2008), wherein the sensitivity of reward circuitry levels off as the brain's control and attention systems reach young adult maturity, and show that changes in these interacting systems likely hold relevance for developing digital media habits.

Longitudinal examinations of brain structure and function spanning different stages of development could be especially fertile territory for furthering our understanding of the origins and effects of digital media use. Though relevant longitudinal studies are currently underway (e.g., ABCD; Volkow et al., 2018), the findings available to date generally come from relatively short-term longitudinal investigations that are not specifically informative with respect to development. In one study, for instance, a six-week internet gaming exposure enacted with naïve and experienced young adult gamers resulted in short-term longitudinal reductions in left OFC volume (Zhou et al., 2019), which could be interpreted as evidence that video game play affects one of the important centers for reward processing. Another short-term intervention study found that when internet-naïve adults were given four weeks of increased internet access, they started to exhibit higher rates of media-multitasking, but there were no significant changes detected in brain structure (Loh et al., 2019). A more extended longitudinal undertaking involved a three-year study conducted in a large sample of Japanese children and adolescents (aged 5–18) aimed at exploring how various digital media behaviors (TV viewing, video gaming, internet use) might prospectively impact brain development (Takeuchi et al., 2015, 2016, 2018). While the basic prospective longitudinal approach represents the type of method that could inform our understanding of digital media's causal impacts on brain development, the outcomes are quite challenging to put into a coherent narrative. Notably, the work assessed digital media behaviors only at the start of the study, with no follow-up assessment of how habits may have changed over the longitudinal period. There was also no consistency or specificity in the findings with respect to the particular brain areas whose longitudinal change was predicted by baseline digital media habits, and disparate MRI modalities (gray/white matter volume, mean diffusivity of diffusion MRI) were needed to obtain significant brain–behavior relationships across media types. Most important, there was no reported attempt to delineate specific developmental patterns, despite the longitudinal nature of the data and the wide age range of the participants at entry to the study. Finally, as was alluded to by the authors themselves, the cohort project began in 2008, which predates the widespread availability and popularity of smartphones, social media, and online games in Japan. This observation underscores how work of this nature may be subject to cohort effects introduced by the ever-changing technology climate.

Conclusions: What We Know Now and Where We May Be Headed

Alongside rapid advancements in digital technology, recent years have witnessed a growing body of work dedicated to understanding the potential impact of digital media behaviors on psychological and brain functions. In this chapter, we reviewed a growing literature deploying various MR imaging and complementary electrophysiological methods that might inform our understanding of the links between brain development and digital media behaviors. Broadly, we sought to examine whether the data accord with current perspectives on digital media involvement that emphasize maturing self-regulatory control skills, a heightened sensitivity to rewards, and shifts in responsivity to socially relevant inputs. Acknowledging important limitations in the available developmental evidence, we first considered how well these perspectives address the body of data obtained primarily from young adult populations, and then surveyed the findings from earlier life for evidence that might provide traction in clarifying the developmental origins of observed brain–behavior relationships.

Overall, there is corroborative evidence denoting each of the three highlighted systems (control, reward, social). That is, for each perspective, there appear to be an ample number of supportive findings from across different types of digital media (e.g., internet behaviors, smartphone use, social media involvement, media-multitasking, etc.) and from multiple neuroinvestigative modalities (various MRI-based approaches, EEG). There are, likewise, some examples from research conducted in younger developmental samples pointing to digital media interactions with some of the same neural substrates of control, reward, and social processes that are featured in the young adult literature.

However, we also come across findings that compel more nuanced accounting of the relationships between digital media involvement and brain development. First, across studies, modalities, and age groups, even the most affirming observations – that is, those implicating expected neural correlates of control, reward, or social processing – place differential emphasis on separate regions/subcomponents within a given brain system, and moreover, at times appear to indicate opposing directional patterns (e.g., increases vs. decreases in regional volume/activity/connectivity, positive vs. negative correlations with digital media involvement, stronger vs. weaker engagement across development). These differences may just be the consequence of noisy measurement approaches (e.g., in the characterization of digital media behaviors or the indexing of brain structure/function), but could also reflect actual, and potentially meaningful, differences in the brain–behavior relationships that exist for certain digital media experiences and particular populations. The outcomes may depend, for example, on whether one is examining the addiction-like or excessive digital media behaviors that are emphasized in the disease-oriented approach that dominates much of the field, or whether one is examining more normative day-to-day patterns of engagement with digital media technologies.

We should also be mindful of some specific limitations in how we have approached this review. First, while we present the findings as though each of the three emphasized systems (control, reward, social) can be considered independently, this assumption is plainly fraught, not only because there is imperfect agreement about which specific regions contribute to each system as well as some neuroanatomical overlap between them (e.g., medial PFC, parietal cortex), but more importantly, because the real story of digital media's relationship with brain development almost certainly lies in the complex and dynamic interactions that take place between these systems, and in how these interactions shift over the course of development. Second, this approach to review reflects a form of confirmation bias. That is, with the expectation that the brain areas associated with control, reward, or social information processing might be relevant to the link between brain development and digital media behaviors, we sought out examples in the literature that could affirm this expectation, while being less attentive to evidence that could potentially lead us toward a different, perhaps overlooked, explanation. By way of example, though we proffered the work conducted by Horvath et al. (2020), Sherman et al. (2016), and Turel et al. (2018) as examples implicating control, reward, and social mechanisms, respectively, each of these studies also reported significant findings in the medial temporal lobe (the hippocampus or neighboring cortices), which might encourage us to consider the relevance of episodic memory mechanisms enacted within the medial temporal lobe in the relationship between digital media habits and brain development. Likewise, our review could have devoted greater attention to emerging evidence of digital-media-dependent effects on primary visual and somatosensory cortices, and the possibility that daily intensive digital media use is leading to the plastic reshaping of these cortical areas (Gindrat et al., 2015).

Despite the negative attitudes toward digital media involvement often emphasized in public outlets (Bennett, 2017; Parks, 2020), the causal impacts of digital media habits on the developing brain remain unclear, due in part to the relative absence of longitudinal work and largely correlational nature of cross-sectional studies, and to the challenges that naturally arise with neuroscientific work conducted with younger populations. Emerging technologies beyond fMRI and EEG could be helpful in circumventing some of these practical limitations. For instance, functional near-infrared spectroscopy, a wearable and relatively low-cost tool that is used across a wide range of populations from preterm infants to the elderly (Pinti et al., 2020; Rahimpour et al., 2018) could be fruitfully applied to examine the brain correlates of digital media habits as they arise in real-world settings. Meanwhile, noninvasive brain stimulation methods could help us to close the causal chain by revealing how experimentally induced alteration of brain states affects digital media behaviors. Findings demonstrative of behavioral change following brain stimulation in other relevant contexts, such as inhibitory control (Cai et al., 2016; Stramaccia et al., 2015) and risk taking (Figner et al., 2009; Gilmore et al., 2018), suggest that it may even be possible to use brain stimulation technologies to alter the course of digital media habit formation or to ameliorate impacts on other behaviors (Hadar et al., 2017).

So, where does this leave us? To put it plainly, despite a now sizable literature on associations between the brain and digital media behavior, it is clear that there is much still to be learned. Within an ever-changing media technology landscape, it has proven challenging to address the essential questions that motivate work in the field. Are there specific brain markers present during the course of development that can reliably predict subsequent digital media habits, or that might signal greater susceptibility to any harmful outcomes of these habits? Is brain development influenced in any particularly meaningful way by earlier, or more extended, exposure to digital media technologies? As much as we would like to forward conclusive answers to these questions, the only answer we can justifiably offer as a field is that we do not yet know. But, armed with the many valuable insights provided by the extant literature, and with clarifying evidence that will most certainly emerge through longitudinal and convergent methodology studies on the near horizon, we are optimistic that the field will continue to narrow the gaps in our understanding, and bring us closer to more edifying answers.

Notes

[1] Whether excessive or problematic digital media habits should be considered as true addictions is a matter of some debate among clinicians and researchers (Kuss & Billieux, 2017; Yao et al., 2017). While we use the term "addiction" when referencing work in which the authors apply this label to the group(s) under investigation, we do so largely as a matter of convenience, while remaining agnostic to the appropriateness of this diagnostic label.

References

Adolphs, R. (2009). The social brain: Neural basis of social knowledge. *Annual Review of Psychology*, *60*(1), 693–716.

Alloway, T. P., & Alloway, R. G. (2012). The impact of engagement with social networking sites (SNSs) on cognitive skills. *Computers in Human Behavior*, *28*(5), 1748–1754. https://doi.org/10.1016/j.chb.2012.04.015

Alloway, T. P., Horton, J., Alloway, R. G., & Dawson, C. (2013). Social networking sites and cognitive abilities: Do they make you smarter? *Computers & Education*, *63*, 10–16. https://doi.org/10.1016/j.compedu.2012.10.030

Atzil, S., Gao, W., Fradkin, I., & Barrett, L. F. (2018). Growing a social brain. *Nature Human Behaviour*, *2*(9), 624–636. https://doi.org/10.1038/s41562-018-0384-6

Baek, E. C., Scholz, C., O'Donnell, M. B., & Falk, E. B. (2017). The value of sharing information: A neural account of information transmission. *Psychological Science*, *28*(7), 851–861. https://doi.org/10.1177/0956797617695073

Bartra, O., McGuire, J. T., & Kable, J. W. (2013). The valuation system: A coordinate-based meta-analysis of BOLD fMRI experiments examining neural correlates of subjective value. *Neuroimage*, *76*, 412–427. https://doi.org/10.1016/j.neuroimage.2013.02.063

Baumgartner, S. E., Weeda, W. D., van der Heijden, L. L., & Huizinga, M. (2014). The relationship between media multitasking and executive function in early adolescents. *The Journal of Early Adolescence*, *34*(8), 1120–1144. https://doi.org/10.1177/0272431614523133

Becht, A. I., Wierenga, L. M., Mills, K. L., et al. (2021). Beyond the average brain: Individual differences in social brain development are associated with friendship quality. *Social Cognitive and Affective Neuroscience*, *16*(3), 292–301. https://doi.org/10.1093/scan/nsaa166

Bennett, B. (2017). *The internet is destroying society, sobering research shows.* CNET.

Bhanji, J. P., & Delgado, M. R. (2014). The social brain and reward: Social information processing in the human striatum. *Wiley Interdisciplinary Reviews: Cognitive Science*, *5*(1), 61–73. https://doi.org/10.1002/wcs.1266

Bickart, K. C., Wright, C. I., Dautoff, R. J., Dickerson, B. C., & Barrett, L. F. (2011). Amygdala volume and social network size in humans. *Nature Neuroscience*, *14*, 163–164. https://doi.org/10.1038/nn.2724

Blakemore, S.-J. (2008). The social brain in adolescence. *Nature Reviews Neuroscience*, *9*, 267–277. https://doi.org/10.1038/nrn2353

Blakemore, S.-J. (2012). Development of the social brain in adolescence. *Journal of the Royal Society of Medicine*, *105*(3), 111–116. https://doi.org/10.1258/jrsm.2011.110221

Blakemore, S.-J. (2018). Avoiding social risk in adolescence. *Current Directions in Psychological Science*, *27*(2), 116–122. https://doi.org/10.1177/0963721417738144

Blakemore, S.-J., & Robbins, T. W. (2012). Decision-making in the adolescent brain. *Nature Neuroscience*, *15*, 1184–1191. https://doi.org/10.1038/nn.3177

Braams, B. R., Peters, S., Peper, J. S., Güroğlu, B., & Crone, E. A. (2014). Gambling for self, friends, and antagonists: Differential contributions of affective and social brain regions on adolescent reward processing. *Neuroimage*, *100*, 281–289. https://doi.org/10.1016/j.neuroimage.2014.06.020

Brand, M., Young, K. S., & Laier, C. (2014). Prefrontal control and internet addiction: A theoretical model and review of neuropsychological and neuroimaging findings. *Frontiers in Human Neuroscience*, *8*, Article 375. https://doi.org/10.3389/fnhum.2014.00375

Cai, Y., Li, S., Liu, J., et al. (2016). The role of the frontal and parietal cortex in proactive and reactive inhibitory control: A transcranial direct current stimulation study. *Journal of Cognitive Neuroscience*, *28*(1), 177–186. https://doi.org/10.1162/jocn_a_00888

Cascio, C. N., O'Donnell, M. B., Bayer, J., Tinney, F. J., & Falk, E. B. (2015). Neural correlates of susceptibility to group opinions in online word-of-mouth recommendations. *Journal of Marketing Research*, *52*(4), 559–575. https://doi.org/10.1509/jmr.13.0611

Chein, J. M., & Schneider, W. (2005). Neuroimaging studies of practice-related change: fMRI and meta-analytic evidence of a domain-general control network for learning. *Cognitive Brain Research*, *25*(3), 607–623. https://doi.org/10.1016/j.cogbrainres.2005.08.013

Chen, J., Liang, Y., Mai, C., Zhong, X., & Qu, C. (2016). General deficit in inhibitory control of excessive smartphone users: Evidence from an event-related potential study. *Frontiers in Psychology*, *7*, Article 511. https://doi.org/10.3389/fpsyg.2016.00511

Choi, J.-S., Park, S. M., Roh, M.-S., et al. (2014). Dysfunctional inhibitory control and impulsivity in internet addiction. *Psychiatry Research*, *215*(2), 424–428. https://doi.org/10.1016/j.psychres.2013.12.001

Chun, J.-W., Choi, J., Cho, H., et al. (2018). Role of frontostriatal connectivity in adolescents with excessive smartphone use. *Frontiers in Psychiatry*, *9*, Article 437. https://doi.org/10.3389/fpsyt.2018.00437

Chun, J.-W., Park, C.-H., Kim, J.-Y., et al. (2020). Altered core networks of brain connectivity and personality traits in internet gaming disorder. *Journal of Behavioral Addictions*, *9*(2), 298–311. https://doi.org/10.1556/2006.2020.00014

Cole, M. W., & Schneider, W. (2007). The cognitive control network: Integrated cortical regions with dissociable functions. *Neuroimage*, *37*(1), 343–360. https://doi.org/10.1016/j.neuroimage.2007.03.071

Coyne, S. M., Rogers, A. A., Zurcher, J. D., Stockdale, L., & Booth, M. (2020). Does time spent using social media impact mental health?: An eight year longitudinal study. *Computers in Human Behavior*, *104*, Article 106160. https://doi.org/10.1016/j.chb.2019.106160

Decety, J., & Lamm, C. (2006). Human empathy through the lens of social neuroscience. *The Scientific World Journal, 6*, 1146–1163. https://doi.org/10.1100/tsw.2006.221

Ding, W., Sun, J., Sun, Y., et al. (2013). Altered default network resting-state functional connectivity in adolescents with internet gaming addiction. *PLoS ONE, 8*(3), e59902. https://doi.org/10.1371/journal.pone.0059902

Dixon, M. L., De La Vega, A., Mills, C., et al. (2018). Heterogeneity within the frontoparietal control network and its relationship to the default and dorsal attention networks. *Proceedings of the National Academy of Sciences, 115*(7), E1598–E1607. https://doi.org/10.1073/pnas.1715766115

Dong, G., Zhou, H., & Zhao, X. (2011). Male internet addicts show impaired executive control ability: Evidence from a color-word Stroop task. *Neuroscience Letters, 499*(2), 114–118. https://doi.org/10.1016/j.neulet.2011.05.047

Dosenbach, N. U. F., Fair, D. A., Cohen, A. L., Schlaggar, B. L., & Petersen, S. E. (2008). A dual-networks architecture of top-down control. *Trends in Cognitive Sciences, 12*(3), 99–105. https://doi.org/10.1016/j.tics.2008.01.001

Duven, E. C. P., Müller, K. W., Beutel, M. E., & Wölfling, K. (2015). Altered reward processing in pathological computer gamers: ERP-results from a semi-natural gaming-design. *Brain and Behavior, 5*(1), e00293. https://doi.org/10.1002/brb3.293

Engelberg, E., & Sjöberg, L. (2004). Internet use, social skills, and adjustment. *Cyberpsychology & Behavior, 7*(1), 41–47. https://doi.org/10.1089/109493104322820101

Feng, Q., Chen, X., Sun, J., et al. (2013). Voxel-level comparison of arterial spin-labeled perfusion magnetic resonance imaging in adolescents with internet gaming addiction. *Behavioral and Brain Functions, 9*(1), 1–11. https://doi.org/10.1186/1744-9081-9-33

Figner, B., Mackinlay, R. J., Wilkening, F., & Weber, E. U. (2009). Affective and deliberative processes in risky choice: Age differences in risk taking in the Columbia Card Task. *Journal of Experimental Psychology: Learning, Memory, and Cognition, 35*(3), 709–730. https://doi.org/10.1037/a0014983

Firth, J., Torous, J., Stubbs, B., et al. (2019). The "online brain": How the internet may be changing our cognition. *World Psychiatry, 18*(2), 119–129. https://doi.org/10.1002/wps.20617

Gao, L., Zhang, J., Xie, H., Nie, Y., Zhao, Q., & Zhou, Z. (2020). Effect of the mobile phone related-background on inhibitory control of problematic mobile phone use: An event-related potentials study. *Addictive Behaviors, 108*, Article 106363. https://doi.org/10.1016/j.addbeh.2020.106363

Gao, Q., Jia, G., Zhao, J., & Zhang, D. (2019). Inhibitory control in excessive social networking users: Evidence from an ERP-based Go-Nogo task. *Frontiers in Psychology, 10*, Article 1810. https://doi.org/10.3389/fpsyg.2019.01810

Gilmore, C. S., Dickmann, P. J., Nelson, B. G., Lamberty, G. J., & Lim, K. O. (2018). Transcranial direct current stimulation (tDCS) paired with a decision-making task reduces risk-taking in a clinically impulsive sample. *Brain Stimulation, 11*(2), 302–309. https://doi.org/10.1016/j.brs.2017.11.011

Gindrat, A.-D., Chytiris, M., Balerna, M., Rouiller, E. M., & Ghosh, A. (2015). Use-dependent cortical processing from fingertips in touchscreen phone users. *Current Biology, 25*(1), 109–116. https://doi.org/10.1016/j.cub.2014.11.026

Gogtay, N., & Thompson, P. M. (2010). Mapping gray matter development: Implications for typical development and vulnerability to psychopathology. *Brain and Cognition*, *72*(1), 6–15. https://doi.org/10.1016/j.bandc.2009.08.009

Gratton, C., Sun, H., & Petersen, S. E. (2018). Control networks and hubs. *Psychophysiology*, *55*(3), e13032. https://doi.org/10.1111/psyp.13032

Grieve, R., Indian, M., Witteveen, K., Anne Tolan, G., & Marrington, J. (2013). Face-to-face or Facebook: Can social connectedness be derived online? *Computers in Human Behavior*, *29*(3), 604–609. https://doi.org/10.1016/j.chb.2012.11.017

Griffiths, M. D., Kuss, D. J., & Demetrovics, Z. (2014). Social networking addiction: An overview of preliminary findings. In K. P. Rosenberg & L. Curtiss Feder (Eds.), *Behavioral addictions: Criteria, evidence, and treatment* (pp. 119–141). Elsevier Academic Press. https://doi.org/10.1016/B978–0-12-407724-9.00006-9

Gutiérrez, J. D. S., de Fonseca, F. R., & Rubio, G. (2016). Cell-phone addiction: A review. *Frontiers in Psychiatry*, *7*, Article 175. https://doi.org/10.3389/fpsyt.2016.00175

Hadar, A., Hadas, I., Lazarovits, A., Alyagon, U., Eliraz, D., & Zangen, A. (2017). Answering the missed call: Initial exploration of cognitive and electrophysiological changes associated with smartphone use and abuse. *PLoS ONE*, *12*(7), e0180094. https://doi.org/10.1371/journal.pone.0180094

Harris, T. (2016, May 18). How technology hijacks people's minds – from a magician and Google's design ethicist. *Medium Magazine*. https://medium.com/thrive-global/how-technology-hijacks-peoples-minds-from-a-magician-and-google-s-design-ethicist-56d62ef5edf3

He, Q., Turel, O., & Bechara, A. (2017). Brain anatomy alterations associated with social networking site (SNS) addiction. *Scientific Reports*, *7*, Article 45064. https://doi.org/10.1038/srep45064

He, Q., Turel, O., Wei, L., & Bechara, A. (2020). Structural brain differences associated with extensive massively-multiplayer video gaming. *Brain Imaging and Behavior*, *15*, 361–374. https://doi.org/10.1007/s11682-020-00263-0

He, W., Qi, A., Wang, Q., et al. (2017). Abnormal reward and punishment sensitivity associated with internet addicts. *Computers in Human Behavior*, *75*, 678–683. https://doi.org/10.1016/j.chb.2017.06.017

Hong, S. B., Kim, J. W., Choi, E. J., et al. (2013). Reduced orbitofrontal cortical thickness in male adolescents with internet addiction. *Behavioral and Brain Functions*, *9*, Article 11. https://doi.org/10.1186/1744-9081-9-11

Horowitz-Kraus, T., DiFrancesco, M., Greenwood, P., et al. (2020). Longer screen vs. reading time is related to greater functional connections between the salience network and executive functions regions in children with reading difficulties vs. typical readers. *Child Psychiatry and Human Development*, *52*(4), 681–692. https://doi.org/10.1007/s10578–020-01053-x

Horowitz-Kraus, T., & Hutton, J. S. (2018). Brain connectivity in children is increased by the time they spend reading books and decreased by the length of exposure to screen-based media. *Acta Paediatrica, International Journal of Paediatrics*, *107*(4), 685–693. https://doi.org/10.1111/apa.14176

Horvath, J., Mundinger, C., Schmitgen, M. M., et al. (2020). Structural and functional correlates of smartphone addiction. *Addictive Behaviors*, *105*, Article 106334. https://doi.org/10.1016/j.addbeh.2020.106334

Hutton, J. S., Dudley, J., Horowitz-Kraus, T., Dewitt, T., & Holland, S. K. (2020). Associations between screen-based media use and brain white matter integrity in preschool-aged children. *JAMA Pediatrics*, 174(1), e193869–e193869. https://doi.org/10.1001/jamapediatrics.2019.3869

Jiao, C., Wang, T., Peng, X., & Cui, F. (2017). Impaired empathy processing in individuals with internet addiction disorder: An event-related potential study. *Frontiers in Human Neuroscience*, *11*, Article 498. https://doi.org/10.3389/fnhum.2017.00498

Kanai, R., Bahrami, B., Roylance, R., & Rees, G. (2012). Online social network size is reflected in human brain structure. *Proceedings of the Royal Society B: Biological Sciences*, *279*, 1327–1334. https://doi.org/10.1098/rspb.2011.1959

Kei, K., Naoya, O., Sayaka, Y., et al. (2020). Relationship between media multitasking and functional connectivity in the dorsal attention network. *Scientific Reports (Nature Publisher Group)*, *10*(1), Article 17992. https://doi.org/10.1038/s41598-020-75091-9

Kilford, E. J., Garrett, E., & Blakemore, S.-J. (2016). The development of social cognition in adolescence: An integrated perspective. *Neuroscience & Biobehavioral Reviews*, *70*, 106–120. https://doi.org/10.1016/j.neubiorev.2016.08.016

Kirby, B., Dapore, A., Ash, C., Malley, K., & West, R. (2020). Smartphone pathology, agency and reward processing. *Lecture Notes in Information Systems and Organisation*, *43*, 321–329. https://doi.org/10.1007/978-3-030-60073-0_37

Ko, C.-H., Liu, G.-C., Hsiao, S., et al. (2009). Brain activities associated with gaming urge of online gaming addiction. *Journal of Psychiatric Research*, *43*(7), 739–747. https://doi.org/10.1016/j.jpsychires.2008.09.012

Kuss, D. J., & Billieux, J. (2017). Technological addictions: Conceptualisation, measurement, etiology and treatment. *Addictive Behaviors*, *64*, 231–233. https://doi.org/10.1016/j.addbeh.2016.04.005

Kuss, D. J., Pontes, H. M., & Griffiths, M. D. (2018). Neurobiological correlates in internet gaming disorder: A systematic literature review. *Frontiers in Psychiatry*, *9*, Article 166. https://doi.org/10.3389/fpsyt.2018.00166

Lauricella, A. R., Cingel, D. P., Beaudoin-Ryan, L., Robb, M. B., Saphir, M., & Wartella, E. A. (2016). *The Common Sense census: Plugged-in parents of tweens and teens*. Common Sense Media. https://www.commonsensemedia.org/sites/default/files/uploads/research/common-sense-parent-census_executivesummary_for-web.pdf

Lee, D., Namkoong, K., Lee, J., Lee, B. O., & Jung, Y. C. (2019). Lateral orbitofrontal gray matter abnormalities in subjects with problematic smartphone use. *Journal of Behavioral Addictions*, *8*(3), 404–411. https://doi.org/10.1556/2006.8.2019.50

Li, W., Li, Y., Yang, W., et al. (2015). Brain structures and functional connectivity associated with individual differences in internet tendency in healthy young adults. *Neuropsychologia*, *70*, 134–144. https://doi.org/10.1016/j.neuropsychologia.2015.02.019

Lieberman, M. D., & Eisenberger, N. I. (2009). Pains and pleasures of social life. *Science*, *323*(5916), 890–891. https://doi.org/10.1126/science.1170008

Liebherr, M., Schubert, P., Antons, S., Montag, C., & Brand, M. (2020). Smartphones and attention, curse or blessing? A review on the effects of smartphone usage on attention, inhibition, and working memory. *Computers in Human Behavior Reports*, *1*, Article 100005. https://doi.org/10.1016/j.chbr.2020.100005

Lin, F., & Lei, H. (2015). Structural brain imaging and internet addiction. In C. Montag & M. Reuter (Eds.), *Internet addiction* (Studies in Neuroscience, Psychology and Behavioral Economics; pp. 21–42). Springer. https://doi.org/10.1007/978-3-319-07242-5_2

Lin, F., Zhou, Y., Du, Y., et al. (2012). Abnormal white matter integrity in adolescents with internet addiction disorder: A tract-based spatial statistics study. *PLoS ONE*, *7*(1), e30253. https://doi.org/10.1371/journal.pone.0030253

Lin, X., Dong, G., Wang, Q., & Du, X. (2015). Abnormal gray matter and white matter volume in 'internet gaming addicts.' *Addictive Behaviors*, *40*, 137–143. https://doi.org/10.1016/j.addbeh.2014.09.010

Loh, K. K., Chakraborty, P., Sadhu, A., et al. (2019). Longitudinal cognitive and brain changes associated with one-month of increased internet access. Preprint. https://doi.org/10.31234/osf.io/p927z

Loh, K. K., & Kanai, R. (2014). Higher media multi-tasking activity is associated with smaller gray-matter density in the anterior cingulate cortex. *PLoS ONE*, *9*(9), Article e106698. https://doi.org/10.1371/journal.pone.0106698

Lopez, R. B., Heatherton, T. F., & Wagner, D. D. (2020). Media multitasking is associated with higher risk for obesity and increased responsiveness to rewarding food stimuli. *Brain Imaging and Behavior*, *14*(4), 1050–1061 https://doi.org/10.1007/s11682-019-00056-0

Mars, R. B., Neubert, F.-X., Noonan, M. P., Sallet, J., Toni, I., & Rushworth, M. F. S. (2012). On the relationship between the "default mode network" and the "social brain." *Frontiers in Human Neuroscience*, *6*, Article 189. https://doi.org/10.3389/fnhum.2012.00189

Melchers, M., Li, M., Chen, Y., Zhang, W., & Montag, C. (2015). Low empathy is associated with problematic use of the internet: Empirical evidence from China and Germany. *Asian Journal of Psychiatry*, *17*, 56–60. https://doi.org/10.1016/j.ajp.2015.06.019

Menon, V. (2015). Salience network. In A. W. Toga (Ed.), *Brain mapping: An encyclopedic reference* (Vol. 2, pp. 597–611). Academic Press. https://doi.org/10.1016/B978-0-12-397025-1.00052-X

Meshi, D., Elizarova, A., Bender, A., & Verdejo-Garcia, A. (2019). Excessive social media users demonstrate impaired decision making in the Iowa Gambling Task. *Journal of Behavioral Addictions*, *8*(1), 169–173. https://doi.org/10.1556/2006.7.2018.138

Meshi, D., Mamerow, L., Kirilina, E., Morawetz, C., Margulies, D. S., & Heekeren, H. R. (2016). Sharing self-related information is associated with intrinsic functional connectivity of cortical midline brain regions. *Scientific Reports*, *6*(1), 1–11. https://doi.org/10.1038/srep22491

Meshi, D., Morawetz, C., & Heekeren, H. R. (2013). Nucleus accumbens response to gains in reputation for the self relative to gains for others predicts social media use. *Frontiers in Human Neuroscience*, *7*, Article 439. https://doi.org/10.3389/fnhum.2013.00439

Meshi, D., Turel, O., & Henley, D. (2020). Snapchat vs. Facebook: Differences in problematic use, behavior change attempts, and trait social reward preferences. *Addictive Behaviors Reports*, *12*, Article 100294. https://doi.org/10.1016/j.abrep.2020.100294

Mills, K. L., Lalonde, F., Clasen, L. S., Giedd, J. N., & Blakemore, S.-J. (2014). Developmental changes in the structure of the social brain in late childhood and adolescence. *Social Cognitive and Affective Neuroscience*, *9*(1), 123–131. https://doi.org/10.1093/scan/nss113

Mills, K. L., Siegmund, K. D., Tamnes, C. K., et al. (2021). Individual variability in structural brain development from late childhood to young adulthood. *BioRxiv*. https://doi.org/10.1016/j.neuroimage.2021.118450

Minear, M., Brasher, F., McCurdy, M., Lewis, J., & Younggren, A. (2013). Working memory, fluid intelligence, and impulsiveness in heavy media multitaskers. *Psychonomic Bulletin & Review*, *20*(6), 1274–1281. https://doi.org/10.3758/s13423-013-0456-6

Moisala, M., Salmela, V., Hietajärvi, L., et al. (2016). Media multitasking is associated with distractibility and increased prefrontal activity in adolescents and young adults. *NeuroImage*, *134*, 113–121. https://doi.org/10.1016/j.neuroimage.2016.04.011

Moisala, M., Salmela, V., Hietajärvi, L., et al. (2017). Gaming is related to enhanced working memory performance and task-related cortical activity. *Brain Research*, *1655*, 204–215. https://doi.org/10.1016/j.brainres.2016.10.027

Montag, C., Markowetz, A., Blaszkiewicz, K., et al. (2017). Facebook usage on smartphones and gray matter volume of the nucleus accumbens. *Behavioural Brain Research*, *329*, 221–228. https://doi.org/10.1016/j.bbr.2017.04.035

Ophir, E., Nass, C., & Wagner, A. D. (2009). Cognitive control in media multitaskers. *Proceedings of the National Academy of Sciences*, *106*(37), 15583–15587. https://doi.org/10.1073/pnas.0903620106

Ophir, Y., Tikochinski, R., & Rosenberg, H. (2020). Science has not proven that screen use impacts children's brain development. *JAMA Pediatrics*, *174*(8), 805. https://doi.org/10.1001/jamapediatrics.2020.0635

Parks, M. (2020). Social media usage is at an all-time high: That could mean a nightmare for democracy. National Public Radio. https://www.npr.org/2020/05/27/860369744/social-media-usage-is-at-an-all-time-high-that-could-mean-a-nightmare-for-democr

Paulus, M. P., Squeglia, L. M., Bagot, K., et al. (2019). Screen media activity and brain structure in youth: Evidence for diverse structural correlation networks from the ABCD study. *NeuroImage*, *185*, 140–153. https://doi.org/10.1016/j.neuroimage.2018.10.040

Pinti, P., Tachtsidis, I., Hamilton, A., et al. (2020). The present and future use of functional near-infrared spectroscopy (fNIRS) for cognitive neuroscience. *Annals of the New York Academy of Sciences*, *1464*(1), 5–29. https://doi.org/10.1111/nyas.13948

Przybylski, A. K., Orben, A., & Weinstein, N. (2020). How much is too much? Examining the relationship between digital screen engagement and psychosocial functioning in a confirmatory cohort study. *Journal of the American Academy of Child & Adolescent Psychiatry*, *59*(9), 1080–1088. https://doi.org/10.1016/j.jaac.2019.06.017

Rahimpour, A., Noubari, H. A., & Kazemian, M. (2018). A case-study of NIRS application for infant cerebral hemodynamic monitoring: A report of data analysis for feature extraction and infant classification into healthy and unhealthy. *Informatics in Medicine Unlocked, 11*, 44–50. https://doi.org/10.1016/j.imu.2018.04.001

Richardson, H., Lisandrelli, G., Riobueno-Naylor, A., & Saxe, R. (2018). Development of the social brain from age three to twelve years. *Nature Communications, 9*(1), 1–12. https://doi.org/10.1038/s41467-018-03399-2

Sanbonmatsu, D. M., Strayer, D. L., Medeiros-Ward, N., & Watson, J. M. (2013). Who multi-tasks and why? Multi-tasking ability, perceived multi-tasking ability, impulsivity, and sensation seeking. *PLoS ONE, 8*(1), e54402. https://doi.org/10.1371/journal.pone.0054402

Schmitgen, M. M., Horvath, J., Mundinger, C., et al. (2020). Neural correlates of cue reactivity in individuals with smartphone addiction. *Addictive Behaviors, 108*, Article 106422. https://doi.org/10.1016/j.addbeh.2020.106422

Scholz, C., Baek, E. C., O'Donnell, M. B., Kim, H. S., Cappella, J. N., & Falk, E. B. (2017). A neural model of valuation and information virality. *Proceedings of the National Academy of Sciences, 114*(11), 2881–2886. https://doi.org/10.1073/pnas.1615259114

Sherman, L. E., Greenfield, P. M., Hernandez, L. M., & Dapretto, M. (2018). Peer influence via Instagram: Effects on brain and behavior in adolescence and young adulthood. *Child Development, 89*(1), 37–47. https://doi.org/10.1111/cdev.12838

Sherman, L. E., Payton, A. A., Hernandez, L. M., Greenfield, P. M., & Dapretto, M. (2016). The power of the like in adolescence: Effects of peer influence on neural and behavioral responses to social media. *Psychological Science, 19*(1), 39–64. https://doi.org/10.1177/0956797616645673

Shulman, E. P., Smith, A. R., Silva, K., et al. (2016). The dual systems model: Review, reappraisal, and reaffirmation. *Developmental Cognitive Neuroscience, 17*, 103–117. https://doi.org/10.1016/j.dcn.2015.12.010

Sisk, C. L., & Zehr, J. L. (2005). Pubertal hormones organize the adolescent brain and behavior. *Frontiers in Neuroendocrinology, 26*(3–4), 163–174. https://doi.org/10.1016/j.yfrne.2005.10.003

Smith, A. R., Chein, J., & Steinberg, L. (2013). Impact of socio-emotional context, brain development, and pubertal maturation on adolescent risk-taking. *Hormones and Behavior, 64*(2), 323–332. https://doi.org/10.1016/j.yhbeh.2013.03.006

Spear, L. (2010). *The behavioral neuroscience of adolescence*. W.W. Norton & Company.

Spies Shapiro, L. A., & Margolin, G. (2014). Growing up wired: Social networking sites and adolescent psychosocial development. *Clinical Child and Family Psychology Review, 17*(1), 1–18. https://doi.org/10.1007/s10567-013-0135-1

Steinberg, L. (2008). A social neuroscience perspective on adolescent risk-taking. *Developmental Review, 28*(1), 78–106. https://doi.org/10.1016/j.dr.2007.08.002

Stramaccia, D. F., Penolazzi, B., Sartori, G., Braga, M., Mondini, S., & Galfano, G. (2015). Assessing the effects of tDCS over a delayed response inhibition task by targeting the right inferior frontal gyrus and right dorsolateral prefrontal cortex. *Experimental Brain Research, 233*(8), 2283–2290. https://doi.org/10.1007/s00221-015-4297-6

Sun, Y., Ying, H., Seetohul, R. M., et al. (2012). Brain fMRI study of crave induced by cue pictures in online game addicts (male adolescents). *Behavioural Brain Research, 233*(2), 563–576. https://doi.org/10.1016/j.bbr.2012.05.005

Sutter, M., Zoller, C., & Glätzle-Rützler, D. (2019). Economic behavior of children and adolescents: A first survey of experimental economics results. *European Economic Review, 111*, 98–121. https://doi.org/10.1016/j.euroecorev.2018.09.004

Takeuchi, H., Taki, Y., Asano, K., et al. (2018). Impact of frequency of internet use on development of brain structures and verbal intelligence: Longitudinal analyses. *Human Brain Mapping, 39*(11), 4471–4479. https://doi.org/10.1002/hbm.24286

Takeuchi, H., Taki, Y., Hashizume, H., et al. (2015). The impact of television viewing on brain structures: Cross-sectional and longitudinal analyses. *Cerebral Cortex, 25*(5), 1188–1197. https://doi.org/10.1093/cercor/bht315

Takeuchi, H., Taki, Y., Hashizume, H., et al. (2016). Impact of videogame play on the brain's microstructural properties: Cross-sectional and longitudinal analyses. *Molecular Psychiatry, 21*(12), 1781–1789. https://doi.org/10.1038/mp.2015.193

Tang, Z., Zhang, H., Yan, A., & Qu, C. (2017). Time is money: The decision making of smartphone high users in gain and loss intertemporal choice. *Frontiers in Psychology, 8*, Article 363. https://doi.org/10.3389/fpsyg.2017.00363

Turel, O., He, Q., Brevers, D., & Bechara, A. (2018). Social networking sites use and the morphology of a social-semantic brain network. *Social Neuroscience, 13*(5), 628–636. https://doi.org/10.1080/17470919.2017.1382387

Turel, O., He, Q., Wei, L., & Bechara, A. (2020). The role of the insula in internet gaming disorder. *Addiction Biology, 26*(2), e12894. https://doi.org/10.1111/adb.12894

Turel, O., He, Q., Xue, G., Xiao, L., & Bechara, A. (2014). Examination of neural systems sub-serving Facebook "addiction." *Psychological Reports, 115*(3), 675–695. https://doi.org/10.2466/18.PR0.115c31z8

Twenge, J. M., Haidt, J., Joiner, T. E., & Campbell, W. K. (2020). Underestimating digital media harm. *Nature Human Behaviour, 4*(4), 346–348. https://doi.org/10.1038/s41562-020-0839-4

Tymofiyeva, O., Yuan, J. P., Kidambi, R., et al. (2020). Neural correlates of smartphone dependence in adolescents. *Frontiers in Human Neuroscience, 14*, Article 428. https://doi.org/10.3389/fnhum.2020.564629

Volkow, N. D., Koob, G. F., Croyle, R. T., et al. (2018). The conception of the ABCD study: From substance use to a broad NIH collaboration. *Developmental Cognitive Neuroscience, 32*, 4–7. https://doi.org/10.1016/j.dcn.2017.10.002

Von der Heide, R., Vyas, G., & Olson, I. R. (2013). The social network-network: Size is predicted by brain structure and function in the amygdala and paralimbic regions. *Social Cognitive and Affective Neuroscience, 9*(12), 1962–1972. https://doi.org/10.1093/scan/nsu009

Wang, H., Jin, C., Yuan, K., et al. (2015). The alteration of gray matter volume and cognitive control in adolescents with internet gaming disorder. *Frontiers in Behavioral Neuroscience, 9*, Article 64. https://doi.org/10.3389/fnbeh.2015.00064

Wang, T., Ge, Y., Zhang, J., Liu, J., & Luo, W. (2014). The capacity for pain empathy among urban internet-addicted left-behind children in China: An event-related potential study. *Computers in Human Behavior, 33*, 56–62. https://doi.org/10.1016/j.chb.2013.12.020

Wang, Y., Zou, Z., Song, H., & Xu, X. (2016). Altered gray matter volume and white matter integrity in college students with mobile phone dependence. *Frontiers in Psychology, 7*, Article 597. https://doi.org/10.3389/fpsyg.2016.00597

Ward, A. F., Duke, K., Gneezy, A., & Bos, M. W. (2017). Brain drain: The mere presence of one's own smartphone reduces available cognitive capacity. *Journal of the Association for Consumer Research, 2*(2), 140–154. https://doi .org/10.1086/691462

Wei, L., Zhang, S., Turel, O., Bechara, A., & He, Q. (2017). A tripartite neurocognitive model of internet gaming disorder. *Frontiers in Psychiatry, 8*, Article 285. https://doi.org/10.3389/fpsyt.2017.00285

Wilmer, H. H., & Chein, J. M. (2016). Mobile technology habits: Patterns of association among device usage, intertemporal preference, impulse control, and reward sensitivity. *Psychonomic Bulletin and Review, 23*(5), 1607–1614. https://doi.org/10.3758/s13423–016-1011-z

Wilmer, H. H., Hampton, W. H., Olino, T. M., Olson, I. R., & Chein, J. M. (2019). Wired to be connected? Links between mobile technology engagement, intertemporal preference and frontostriatal white matter connectivity. *Social Cognitive and Affective Neuroscience, 14*(4), 367–379. https://doi.org/10.1093/ scan/nsz024

Wilmer, H. H., Sherman, L. E., & Chein, J. M. (2017). Smartphones and cognition: A review of research exploring the links between mobile technology habits and cognitive functioning. *Frontiers in Psychology, 8*, Article 605. https://doi .org/10.3389/fpsyg.2017.00605

Yao, Y. W., Liu, L., Ma, S. S., et al. (2017). Functional and structural neural alterations in internet gaming disorder: A systematic review and meta-analysis. *Neuroscience and Biobehavioral Reviews, 83*, 313–324. https://doi.org/10 .1016/j.neubiorev.2017.10.029

Yuan, K., Qin, W., Wang, G., et al. (2011). Microstructure abnormalities in adolescents with internet addiction disorder. *PLoS ONE, 6*(6), e20708. https://doi .org/10.1371/journal.pone.0020708

Zhang, Y., Mei, S., Li, L., Chai, J., Li, J., & Du, H. (2015). The relationship between impulsivity and internet addiction in Chinese college students: A moderated mediation analysis of meaning in life and self-esteem. *PLoS ONE, 10*(7), e0131597. https://doi.org/10.1371/journal.pone.0131597

Zhou, F., Montag, C., Sariyska, R., et al. (2019). Orbitofrontal gray matter deficits as marker of internet gaming disorder: Converging evidence from a cross-sectional and prospective longitudinal design. *Addiction Biology, 24*(1), 100–109. https://doi.org/10.1111/adb.12570

Zivan, M., Bar, S., Jing, X., Hutton, J., Farah, R., & Horowitz-Kraus, T. (2019). Screen-exposure and altered brain activation related to attention in preschool children: An EEG study. *Trends in Neuroscience and Education, 1*(1), 32–42. https://doi.org/10.1016/j.tine.2019.100117

6 Adolescents' Digital Media Interactions within the Context of Sexuality Development

Chelly Maes, Johanna M. F. van Oosten, and Laura Vandenbosch

Digital media interactions have become an integral part of adolescents' everyday lives as a wide range of evolving technological tools (e.g., smartphones) allow adolescents to be online almost continually (Davis, 2013). As such, the context in which teens mature has now expanded from the traditional offline context to the online environment (Lerner et al., 2010). One of the most significant developmental tasks, which is facilitated through the use of digital media, is the construction of one's sexuality (Collins et al., 2010).

Within the current chapter, the uses of different digital media applications are discussed in the context of the establishment of a sexual identity. In particular, the chapter focuses on social media, sexting, and online pornography. The literature has explained that the unique affordances of these media (i.e., accessibility, anonymity, and asynchronous communication) invite adolescents to use them for the construction of a sexual identity (e.g., Valkenburg & Peter, 2011).

The current chapter situates adolescents' sexually oriented digital media use by first describing adolescents' sexuality development. Then, the chapter delves into (1) adolescents' varying sexually oriented digital media activities, (2) motivators for these activities, and (3) outcomes of such uses with attention for potential underlying processes, and the possible conditional nature of such outcomes. The chapter concludes with recommendations for future research that should help to bolster our understanding of adolescents' digital media interactions and their impact on sexuality.

Adolescent Sexuality Development

Adolescence marks a time of self-discovery and is characterized by profound physical, cognitive, psychological, and sociocultural changes (Sawyer et al., 2012). Within this unique developmental context, the exploration and construction of an adolescent's sexuality is believed to be one of the most significant and challenging developmental tasks (Fortenberry, 2013). In the literature, sexuality often denominates an inclusive category that refers to how adolescents describe, feel, or express their sexual selves (Diamond & Savin-Williams, 2009).

Sexuality development has received growing attention over the past 40 years, with early studies responding to concerns of educators and parents regarding adolescents' early sexual initiation or negative consequences of sexual activities, such as unwanted pregnancies (Moran, 2000). In recent years, sexuality scholars have increasingly acknowledged adolescents' emerging sexual feelings and behavioral responses as expected and thus developmentally normative without undermining the necessity of exploring sexual risks (e.g., Tolman & McLelland, 2011). In this view, scholars point to the usefulness of studying how adolescents construct a "positive sexuality" (Russell, 2005). Maes et al. (2022), for instance, refer to a positive approach to sexual relationships, acceptance of one's own sexuality, a respectful approach to different sexual expressions of others, the ability to have control over sexual interactions, and resilience against negative sexual experiences. Yet, most research still focuses on negative sexuality and thus addresses indicators such as sexual uncertainty, sexual objectification, and risky sexual behaviors (e.g., Peter & Valkenburg, 2009; 2011). In the current chapter, a focus will be placed on both positive and negative sexuality-related attitudes and behaviors.

Adolescents' sexuality development is typically driven by elevated levels of sexual hormones (e.g., testosterone and estrogen levels) that increase sexual drives and stimulate the development of primary (i.e., menarche for girls and semenarche for boys) and secondary sex characteristics (e.g., enlargement of breasts for girls and deepening of the voice for boys) (Ponton & Judice, 2004). Simultaneously, adolescents' cognitive abilities improve, which, in turn, stimulates abstract thinking and self-reflection (Christie & Viner, 2005). Such self-reflection skills are especially imperative regarding the exploration and construction of one's sexuality (e.g., determining one's sexual orientation) (Ponton & Judice, 2004).

Adolescents typically respond to these developmental changes by communicating about their emerging sexual feelings and engaging in (non)coital sexual behaviors (e.g., self-masturbation) (DeLamater & Friedrich, 2002). Scholars emphasize the active role of peers in these processes as they function as sources of support and inform adolescents on sexual strategies (e.g., how boys and girls flirt) and behavior (e.g., when to "lose" your virginity) (van de Bongardt et al., 2015). However, the sexual socialization that adolescents receive from peers can also reinforce prevailing sexual stereotypes (e.g., sexual passiveness for girls; sexual dominance for boys) and sometimes contains erroneous information about, for instance, sexual protection (Ponton & Judice, 2004). Furthermore, romantic and sexual relationships offer a primary venue in which emerging sexual feelings are explored, experimented with, and responded to (Diamond & Savin-Williams, 2009). During this explorative period adolescents will also further discover their preference for heterosexual, homosexual, and bisexual relationships. This exploration is typically more challenging for non-heterosexual adolescents (Saewyc, 2011).

Although sexuality development is equally significant and profound among adolescent girls and boys, their experiences and perceived consequences do differ (Petersen & Hyde, 2010). Such differences are often argued to be the product of biological and social factors. Biologically, differential hormonal influences bring along different developmental needs and body growth among boys and girls (Perry & Pauletti, 2011). As for social factors, societal pressure typically leads individuals to conform to traditional gender roles (Ponton & Judice, 2004). These traditional gender roles coincide with the idea of a sexual double standard in which girls and women are expected to be sexually attractive and pleasing while ignoring their own sexual needs or even denying and shaming their sexual agency (Hamilton & Armstrong, 2009). At the same time, sexual desire and agency is assumed to be inherent in male sexuality (Murray, 2018).

Digital Media and Adolescents' Sexuality

Over the past two decades, scholars have pointed to the increasing presence of digital media in the everyday lives of adolescents (Guse et al., 2012). Owing to the rapid adoption of mobile devices (Ling & Bertel, 2013), most adolescents have the possibility to be constantly online. Within this online environment, sexually oriented digital media activities take place in accordance to adolescents' sexual development and needs. Such activities can be divided into two underlying themes: sexual health education and entertainment. Sexual health–related digital media activities include the use of websites and other online tools (e.g., social media banners) that cover sexual health information (e.g., contraceptive use, STDs, or menstrual cycles). Existing studies indicate that adolescents often turn to digital media in order to seek sexual information (e.g., Nikkelen et al., 2020).

Entertainment-related sexually oriented digital media encompasses adolescents' uses of social media, sexting (via instant messaging tools of social media or mobile phone messages), and online pornography. Adolescents frequently use social media on a daily basis. When describing social media uses, the literature distinguishes between the private and public sphere in which interactions take place. Within the public sphere of social media, existing research mainly focuses on the posting of sexy selfies (e.g., van Oosten et al., 2018) that encompasses 51.7% of adolescents' self-presentations on social media (Kapidzic & Herring, 2015). Further, the public display of romantic affection and conflicts has also been the focus of existing studies (e.g., Rueda et al., 2015). Private social media use encompasses adolescents' engagement in romantic relational communication (e.g., Young et al., 2017) and even sexting via instant messaging tools (e.g., Van Ouytsel et al., 2019).

The current literature defines sexting as "the sending of self-made sexually explicit messages, pictures or videos through the computer or mobile phone" (Van Ouytsel et al., 2019, p. 216). This particular behavior takes place through instant messaging tools of social media and other digital applications, such as Snapchat, a tool that allows adolescents to send temporary available sexting messages to one (or multiple) person(s). A recent meta-analysis points to the relative commonness of sexting among adolescents, as one in ten adolescents has already engaged in this online behavior (Madigan et al., 2018). This number is higher among girls and older adolescents (K. Cooper et al., 2016).

Apart from producing their own sexual material, adolescents, and especially boys, consume sexually explicit internet material (i.e., online pornography) that can also be described as an intimate sexually oriented digital media activity (Peter & Valkenburg, 2016). Exposure rates differ substantially depending on the examined countries in the literature. For instance, in the USA, 77% of adolescent boys and 33% of adolescent girls indicated that they had watched pornography in the past year (Hardy et al., 2019), while in Croatia, pornography use rates were higher among both adolescent boys (90%) and girls (43%) (Milas et al., 2019).

The Affordances of Sexually Oriented Digital Media

Sexually oriented digital media use is especially imperative in adolescents' sexuality as their unique affordances (i.e., characteristics of digital media that provide the potential for a particular action) support the exploration of one's sexuality. Specifically, Cooper and colleagues (1999) identified three disinhibiting characteristics of online environments: (1) *accessibility*, (2) *anonymity*, and (3) *asynchronous communication*.

First, digital media are characterized by their accessibility to (the creation of) various forms of content related to intimacy, sexuality, and gender identity (e.g., Beals, 2010). Given that some adolescents may lack sexual experiences or may feel too embarrassed to discuss intimate topics with others (in person) (e.g., how to wear a condom), the accessibility to a rich variety of sexual information through the online environment can be particularly helpful (Simon & Daneback, 2013). For example, adolescents can turn to sexual health websites to receive reliable information on intimate topics (e.g., Park & Kwon, 2018). Also, via online pornography, adolescents have access to explicit information about sexual behaviors, attitudes, and gender roles (e.g., Grubbs et al., 2019).

Second, digital media's unique affordance to maintain one's anonymity is useful for adolescents who are still discovering their sexuality. Peter and Valkenburg (2011) point to two forms of anonymity: source anonymity and audiovisual anonymity. With source anonymity, adolescents have the ability to view or even distribute content of a sexual or romantic nature without the possibility to link this type of content to a particular individual or source. This extreme form of anonymity is especially appealing to adolescents when they are searching for sexually explicit content online (i.e., pornography). Specifically, adolescents can explore emerging sexual feelings without the risk of being discovered and, consequently, feeling ashamed afterwards (Shek & Ma, 2016).

With audiovisual anonymity, the lack or the reduction of nonverbal cues (i.e., visual or auditory) in online communication is captured (Peter & Valkenburg, 2011). When adolescents engage in sexting or communicate through instant messaging tools, they can choose to only communicate through linguistic/textual/verbal content or to use visual and/or audio cues. Adolescents typically have high levels of self-awareness and are, as a result, often more shy in traditional face-to-face interactions (e.g., Weil et al., 2013). Within digital contexts, audiovisual anonymity can facilitate discussions about intimate topics or themes, while such discussions may be more likely perceived as awkward in offline environments (Van Ouytsel et al., 2016b).

Third, the ability to communicate asynchronously is another relevant affordance to understand the role of digital media in adolescents' sexuality. Through instant messaging tools, adolescents have the opportunity to (privately) communicate with others about sexual or romantic topics while having a heightened sense of control over their conversations (Le et al., 2014). In contrast to face-to-face communication, adolescents are able to edit and think about how they communicate about their emerging sexual or romantic feelings and, thus, learn at their own pace how to have a proper and respectful conversation about intimate topics (Van Ouytsel et al., 2016b).

The affordances of accessibility, anonymity, and asynchronous communication are shared over differential sexually oriented digital media. Other affordances are more platform specific. For example, when adolescents send photos via Snapchat to another person, the visual content is only accessible to the receiver for a maximum of 30 seconds. On Facebook, on the other hand, pictures sent through Messenger are permanently accessible until the receiver deletes them. The temporary accessibility of posts is described in the literature as *ephemeral content* (Chen & Cheung, 2019). This and other platform-specific affordances are assumed to further play a key role in adolescents' choices to use a certain type of digital media platform as a response to specific sexual or romantic relational needs within a particular context.

Motivations for Adolescents' Digital Media Uses within the Context of Sexuality

Uses and gratifications theory denotes that users' media interactions are driven by differential motivations (Katz et al., 1973). Such motivations are entwined with digital media affordances as some affordances create new motivations when new media are introduced (Sundar & Limperos, 2013). Within the context of sexually oriented digital media and adolescents' sexuality, motivations differ from each other in terms of the motivational source (i.e., internal vs. external). As for internal motivations, research points toward sexual exploration, and relationship initiation and maintenance. As for external (or other-imposed) motivations, pressure and coercion have been identified as motivators. The section below discusses these motivations in terms of their meaning and how digital media use driven by a particular motivation affects adolescents' sexuality.

Sexual Exploration

One of the most commonly reported motivations for adolescents' sexual engagement with digital media is the need to explore one's sexuality and emerging sexual feelings (Cooper et al., 2016). Particularly, heightened levels of *arousal and sexual curiosity* characterize adolescence and are the predominant reasons for using online pornography and engaging in sexting. Gender differences are relevant in this context as boys are more often driven by arousal, pleasure, and sexual curiosity than girls (Cooper et al., 2016; Grubbs et al., 2019).

Apart from arousal and curiosity, adolescents share a desire to learn about sexual practices as many of them are still inexperienced. Adolescents frequently turn to sexually oriented digital media stimulated by the *need for information* about sexual activities (e.g., how to initiate intercourse) (Pascoe, 2011). This information-seeking need is especially relevant in terms of adolescents' online pornography use as this type of digital content explicitly shows how to engage in different types of sexual activities. Moreover, pornographic content can even be used as a source of inspiration for novel sexual behaviors (e.g., learning about different sexual positions) (e.g., Grubbs et al., 2019).

The *need to construct one's sexual and gender identity* is further considered to be a key motivator of adolescents' uses of sexually oriented digital media. Specifically within the online environment, adolescents feel more secure and less prejudiced when exploring and, even, expressing their own sexuality and gender identity (e.g., Pascoe, 2011). On social media, adolescents are exposed to varying types of sexual content (e.g., sexy selfies) shared by peers and other significant actors (e.g., influencers). This content offers insights on how adolescent girls and boys behave and present themselves sexually (e.g., Kapidzic & Herring, 2015; Shafer et al., 2013). These self-presentations stimulate adolescents to explore their own sexuality (van Oosten et al., 2015). Online sexual self-presentations express different sexual beliefs, preferences, and behaviors whilst simultaneously negotiating peer approval and acceptance. For heterosexual boys and girls, these self-presentations often reflect traditional gender stereotypes. Girls are more invested in portraying themselves as sexually attractive and seductive, whereas boys' self-presentations are more varied (e.g., pictures of oneself practicing hobbies) (Kapidzic & Herring, 2015). Indeed, the longitudinal study of van Oosten et al. (2017b) shows that adolescents who hold more gender stereotypical beliefs present themselves online more in a sexy way and, at the same time, are also more exposed to sexy self-presentations.

Further, scholars point to the experimental nature of consensual sexting by which adolescents can establish their sexuality. Adolescents are motivated to *experiment with different sexual experiences* whilst expressing their own sexual preferences (e.g., Dir et al., 2013). Also, through the uses of online pornography, adolescents are exposed to different types of sexual activities that allows them to explore their sexual preferences freely. This exploration of one's sexual preferences facilitates the acceptance and establishment of, for example, one's sexual orientation (Grubb et al., 2019).

Relationship Initiation and Maintenance

One frequently reported motivator of digital media uses is the ability to *initiate a romantic relationship* and even *maintain this relationship*. Adolescents use social media and sexting in order to flirt with someone, ask someone out for a date, or even ask someone to be their boyfriend/girlfriend (Young et al., 2017). For sexual minority groups, relationship initiation through digital media is particularly convenient. These groups often experience difficulties forming romantic relationships offline as they have fewer potential romantic partners and experience stigmatizations or even physical harm (Williams et al., 2009). Within the online environment, sexual minority groups can experience less harassment and feel more secure when establishing a romantic relationship (Korchmaros et al., 2015).

Further, in order to *maintain one's romantic relationship*, adolescents also turn to digital media. Particularly, when a relationship is established, adolescents can advertise the relationship status on Facebook (i.e., "in a relationship" or "engaged"), which can be seen as an important step in their romantic relationship (Van Ouytsel et al., 2016b). Also, instant messaging tools on social media allow romantic partners to stay in contact while being physically distant (Utz & Beukeboom, 2011). Scholars even suggest that digital communication is now an integral part of adolescent couple functioning (Blumer & Hertlein, 2015). In order to maintain a more intimate bond with one's romantic partner, adolescents often use sexting (Cooper et al., 2016). Consensual sexting is considered a normal and contemporary form of sexual expression and intimate communication within relationships (Burkett, 2015; Parker et al., 2013). Further, sexting can initiate offline sexual behaviors with romantic partners. For adolescents who are physically separated or cannot engage in sexual activities with their romantic partners (e.g., because this is forbidden by their religion), sexting can take place as a means of sustaining a level of intimacy (Cooper et al., 2016).

Pressure

Similar to offline sexual behavior, online sexual behavior can also be motivated by external factors such as *peer* and *partner pressure*. Peers become increasingly important in the lives of adolescents as they are experiencing elevated need for autonomy from one's parents and, at the same time, seek out approval from their peers (Lerner et al., 2010). Such dynamics are also relevant when considering sexually oriented digital media uses. Particularly, studies consistently demonstrate that the need to conform to peer norms and even the experience of peer pressure are significant motivators for adolescents' posting of sexy selfies on social media (i.e., mostly among girls) (de Vaate et al., 2018; Mascheroni et al., 2015), online pornography use (i.e., mostly among boys) (Chen et al., 2013; Vanden Abeele et al., 2014), and sexting (Dake et al., 2012; Maheux et al., 2020).

Scholars emphasize that sexting can also be initiated after experiencing *pressure from a partner*. Especially girls experience such (implicit) pressure from partners (Walrave et al., 2014). Girls often believe that they need to send self-produced sexual images to their partners in order to maintain a good relationship. Boys, on the other hand, experience more pressure from other peers as the ability to chat to girls and negotiate access to seeing their bodies proves their dominant sexual status (Crofts et al., 2018). Sexual activities with girls (e.g., receiving girls' sexual pictures and forwarding these pictures without their consent) can thus help boys to gain peer status and popularity (Burén & Lunde, 2018; Ringrose et al., 2013). At the same time, more moral responsibility is attributed to girls for sending a sexting picture than for boys forwarding such pictures without consent. As such, regardless of whether they engage in sexting or not, girls' behavior seems to be consistently evaluated in terms of sexist norms (Lippman & Campbell, 2014; Ringrose et al., 2013).

Sexual Coercion

A growing body of literature indicates that the uses of sexually oriented digital media can also take place in a context of abusive dating behaviors (Van Ouytsel et al., 2016a). Reed and colleagues (2017) distinguished three different types of digital dating abuse among adolescents: *digital monitoring and controlling*, *direct aggression*, and *sexual coercion*. Digital monitoring/controlling is the most frequently reported digital abusive behavior. This particular type of abusive behavior entails the intrusion of a partner's privacy via controlling their online activities and relationships (Dracker & Martsolf, 2010). Girls have reported a higher frequency of digital monitoring than boys (Reed et al., 2017).

Further, digital direct aggression toward one's romantic partner or dating interest can also be a motivation for adolescents' engagement with digital media. Such direct aggression can, for example, be expressed by posting a hurtful public/private message or the threat to physically harm one's partner (Borrajo et al., 2015).

Lastly, scholars stress the occurrence of digital sexual coercion among adolescents. This behavior encompasses the use of sexually oriented digital media to pressure someone to send intimate pictures, redistributing intimate pictures without consent, and even threatening with sexual harm (Hellevik, 2019). Boys engage more regularly in digital sexual aggression and coercion (Reed et al., 2017, 2018). In terms of digital sexual coercion, the previous section has already addressed partner pressure being a detrimental motivator for, mostly girls', sexting behaviors. When addressing sexting behavior in adolescents and its problematic motivators, it is especially crucial to emphasize the occurrence of grooming. This online behavior is often considered a criminal offence and entails a process in which an adult manipulates a minor via digital media in order to obtain sexual materials from them or to sexually abuse them (Machimbarrena et al., 2018). For instance, 16.6% of adolescents indicated that they had experienced grooming online (Machimbarrena et al., 2018).

Theoretical Frameworks for Effects of Sexually Oriented Digital Media Use

Several theoretical frameworks can be used to clarify how the effects of sexually oriented digital media take place. Within the literature, social cognitive theory, sexual script theory, and self-effects literature are typically proposed to explain the effects of the uses of these media (i.e., social media, sexting, and online pornography).

Social cognitive theory (Bandura, 2001) is frequently referred to as a traditional theoretical model that is consistently adopted by scholars examining the sexual effects of traditional media (e.g., television). Over the past two decades, this theoretical framework has also proven to be useful to explain digital media effects as the tenets of this theory are transferable to an online environment. Social cognitive theory argues that behavioral and attitudinal effects are contingent on expectancies of such behaviors and attitudes. Within the context of digital media, expectancies are shaped by the observation of attractive models being rewarded for the engagement in or sharing of certain sexual behaviors online or the expression of particular sexual beliefs. For example, digital media users can observe peers on social media or actors of pornographic videos which operate as "attractive models." These models are rewarded, for example through likes (for peers on social media) or sexual satisfaction (for actors in pornographic videos) for the engagement in or sharing of certain sexual behaviors or beliefs. Peers can, for example, share a status update that implies that they had casual sex or post an article about gender equality, while actors in pornographic movies more explicitly engage in casual sex. By observing these rewarded sexual behaviors as well as beliefs promoted by attractive models, digital media users learn which behaviors and beliefs are socially acceptable and positively reinforced. As such, these behaviors and beliefs have a higher chance of being adopted by digital media users. Social cognitive theory further points to the mechanisms explaining the adoption of certain sexual behaviors. In this context, sexual media effects are not produced immediately but operate via underlying processes. Sexual cognitions, such as sexual self-efficacy (i.e., one's beliefs about one's ability to control a sexual behavior or situation), often operate as factors explaining the link between media use and behavioral outcomes.

Building on the principles of social cognitive theory, *sexual script theory* (Gagnon & Simon, 1973) offers an additional theoretical framework conceptualizing how sexual media messages shape users' sexual behaviors. Although this theory was initially created to explain the impact of sexual content in traditional media, its tenets can also be adopted to explore the implications of sexual messages in the digital environment. Within the context of digital media uses, sexual script theory argues that online sexual content is stored in users' memories and operates as a "script" to guide their future sexual behavior. For example, when digital media users observe how other couples behave on social media (e.g., expressing their love for each other), they can "store" this information and use it to guide their (online) behaviors within a romantic relationship. In pornographic content, these sexual scripts are shown more explicitly, offering digital media users more practical guidelines on how to engage in sexual activities. The retrieval of these sexual scripts from one's memory is facilitated through activation and recency processes. In particular, the more often and/or the more recently sexual scripts are observed, the more likely users are to engage in such behaviors endorsed by the scripts.

Although these two traditional theoretical frameworks can explain exposure effects of digital media, they cannot clarify all effects and processes within the online environment. Social media and sexting allow users to create and distribute content themselves. This ability to create and distribute online sexual content can also have substantial implications for the media users themselves. In recent years, scholars have recognized such effects and described them as *self-effects*, which generally constitutes "the effects of messages on the cognitions, emotions, attitudes and behavior of the message creators/senders themselves" (Valkenburg, 2017, p. 478).

Two mechanisms, namely self-perception and self-presentation processes, are especially relevant when clarifying these sexual self-effects. In terms of *self-perception processes*, Bem (1972) argues that individuals ascertain their self-concepts by retrospectively observing their own behaviors. Within the context of digital media, self-perception processes are triggered by the observations of the content media users share or the behavior they depict online. For example, through the sharing of sexy selfies online or the description of certain adventurous sexual behaviors via sexting, digital media users can verify that they are respectively sexy or sexually adventurous (e.g., van Oosten et al., 2018).

Another key mechanism of self-effects of the online environment, namely the occurrence of *self-presentation processes*, is especially relevant within the context of social media. In particular, digital media users have the ability to carefully select which information to share on social media platforms regarding their sexual beliefs and/or behaviors. Therefore, media users will first reflect elaborately on how to present themselves online by engaging in a process called biased scanning. Particularly, by envisioning their desired and ideal online sexual selves, media users will search for information about certain sexual characteristics in their memory that can help to create such desired self-presentations online (Valkenburg, 2017). For example, when adolescents focus on certain physical attributes when sharing sexy selfies (e.g., for girls their cleavage, for boys their muscles) the evaluation of these characteristics makes them more accessible in media users' memories that can, in turn, affect self-evaluations (Schlenker et al., 1994). Moreover, individuals tend to strive for consistency in terms of the way they present themselves to others. This need for consistency can increase the likelihood that online self-presenters will continue to express the same sexual beliefs and/or engage in the same sexual behaviors as they do online (i.e., public commitment; Kelly & Rodriguez, 2006).

Digital Media and Its Implications for Adolescents' Sexuality

A vast and still growing body of literature has examined adolescents' sexually oriented digital media uses and their effects on adolescents' sexuality. Below, the conclusions of this body of work are summarized regarding four types of sexual self-development outcomes (i.e., sexual self-concept, sexual agency, sexual certainty, and sexual satisfaction), three types of attitudinal outcomes (i.e., sexually permissive attitudes, gender stereotypical sexual beliefs, and sexual objectification), two relationship quality indicators (i.e., commitment and sexual attraction), and three types of behavioral outcomes (i.e., sexual activities, risky sexual behavior, and sexual aggression). These outcomes are all significant aspects in the context of adolescents' sexuality development. We also discuss existing literature on underlying processes (e.g., sexual arousal) that can explain the relationship between sexually oriented digital media use and sexual outcomes. Further, if relationships were conditional (e.g., a stronger effect based on adolescents' gender) this will also be addressed.

Sexual Self-Development Outcomes

Sexual Self-Concept

The construction of the *sexual self-concept* can be described as adolescents' understanding of their sexual selves and attributes that define them as a sexual person.

The literature shows that social media and sexting play an important role in the construction of this self-concept and, therefore, guide adolescents in their understanding of their sexual selves. Particularly, with regards to social media, sexy online self-presentations appear to be especially relevant. The study of van Oosten et al. (2018) demonstrated that such self-presentations can define adolescents' sexual self-concept over the course of six months, and are also driven by one's sexual self-concept. This means that not only are sexy self-presentations on social media used as guidance for adolescents to understand their own sexual selves, but the way adolescents view themselves sexually also guides the way they present themselves online (Bobkowski et al., 2016). Relatedly, when it comes to sexting, the literature has demonstrated that when adolescents sext, they have a more developed sexual self-concept in comparison to adolescents who do not sext (Marengo et al., 2019). As such, this implies that sexting may help adolescents in their understanding and exploration of their own sexual selves, such as discovering to whom they are attracted to.

Sexual Agency

As for *sexual agency*, which entails the ability to communicate and negotiate about one's sexuality, the literature seems to be relatively scarce when it comes to adolescents' sexually orientated digital media uses. Only the study of Klein et al. (2020) has explored this sexual outcome in relation to adolescents' pornography uses. They demonstrated that the more girls view pornography online, the more sexually agentic they feel over time. This outcome is especially relevant for girls, as scholars have previously highlighted girls' lack of attention for their own sexual desires (Cheng et al., 2014). Therefore, pornography may offer a useful tool for girls to take ownership of their own sexual desires and express what they want sexually. In contrast, social media may be detrimental for adolescents' sexual agency. Among young adults, Facebook involvement appears to predict a decreased sexual assertiveness through mechanisms of objectified body consciousness (Manago et al., 2015). These findings suggest that similar processes can occur among adolescents. However, this assumption has not been tested yet among adolescents, nor can conclusions be made about the directionality of this relationship given that the research has primarily been correlational at just one time point.

Sexual Certainty

A large body of online pornography studies has explored how this online sexual media use can affect other important factors of adolescents' sexuality, such as their *sexual certainty*. Studies show that the more adolescents watch pornography online, the more they feel uncertain about their sexual beliefs and values (e.g., Peter & Valkenburg, 2008, 2010; van Oosten et al., 2016a).

This relationship has been demonstrated to occur via adolescents' involvement with pornographic content (Peter & Valkenburg, 2010), and girls appear to be more affected than boys (Peter & Valkenburg, 2010; van Oosten et al., 2016a).

Sexual Satisfaction

In terms of *sexual satisfaction* (i.e., the degree to which one is satisfied with one's sexual life), scholars point to the likelihood that adolescents' sexting behavior can promote a greater sexual satisfaction in adolescents (Van Ouytsel et al., 2019) as such relations have been found among adults (Galovan et al., 2018). However, as of yet, no research has explored this particular question in youth. In terms of pornography, on the other hand, it appears that adolescents' uses of this online sexual media negatively affects their sexual satisfaction in the long term (Doornwaard et al., 2014; Peter & Valkenburg, 2006). This means that the more adolescents view online pornography, the less satisfied they are with their own sexual lives. This link is stronger for adolescents who have little to no sexual experience and adolescents who perceive that the majority of their peers are sexually inexperienced.

Attitudinal Outcomes

Sexually Permissive Attitudes

In different types of online sexual content (e.g., sexual self-presentations or pornographic content), sexual activities are predominantly portrayed or referred to as casual and risk-free, without paying attention to the emotional (e.g., fear of being rejected) and physical complexities (e.g., properly using a condom) of these activities (e.g., Carrotte et al., 2020). Such content has been demonstrated to have a significant impact on the development of sexually permissive attitudes among adolescents. Sexually permissive attitudes can be conceptualized as an inclusive category, generally constituting positive attitudes toward sex with casual partners.

The literature indicates that social media and pornography use contribute to the development of such permissive attitudes. Longitudinal research shows a long-term link over the course of one year between adolescents' time looking at sexual online self-presentations of others and increased willingness to engage in casual sex (van Oosten et al., 2017a). Thus, the more adolescents are exposed to sexy online presentations of others, the more they hold positive attitudes toward sex with casual partners. Moreover, looking at others' self-presentation on social media predicts an increase in adolescents' perception of the amount of same-aged friends engaging in casual sex, which in turn predicts an increase in their own willingness to engage in casual sex themselves. Finally, the more adolescents watch pornographic content online, the more they hold positive attitudes toward casual sex (e.g., Baams et al., 2015;

Brown & L'Engle, 2009; Doornwaard et al., 2015) especially among adolescents who perceive pornography as realistic (Baams et al., 2015) and among boys (Doornwaard et al., 2015; Brown & L'Engle, 2009).

Gender Stereotypical Beliefs

Digital media also reinforces traditional sexual gender stereotypes. These gender stereotypical beliefs include the assumption that men are more sexually assertive and dominant, and that women lack sexual agency and are more passive. Double standards are commonly embedded within these gender stereotypes as, for example, women are expected to be sexually reluctant while, simultaneously, they are also highly sexualized and valued based on their sexual attractiveness (Popa & Gavriliu, 2015).

Pornography use contributes to the development of gender stereotypes as these beliefs are reflected in the content and uses of online pornography. Not only do studies point to online pornography depicting men and women in a gender stereotypical manner (e.g., Klaassen & Peter, 2015), but its uses are also highly gendered as online pornography is typically targeted at men and perceived by both boys and girls as "manly" behaviors (e.g., Scarcelli, 2015). Cross-sectional (To et al., 2012) and longitudinal studies (Brown & L'Engle, 2009) consistently find that the more adolescents are exposed to online pornography, the more they hold gender-stereotypical and, even, sexist beliefs.

Sexual Objectification

Although a growing body of literature points to the occurrence of sexualizing practices in digital media, especially toward women (Ringrose, 2011), few studies have addressed how digital media can contribute to the development of adolescents' sexually objectifying beliefs. These beliefs generally constitute the evaluation of an individual based on their sexual attractiveness and sexually instrumental value (Fredrickson & Roberts, 1997).

In terms of social media use, while holding more sexually objectifying beliefs increased exposure to sexy self-presentations of others for young adolescents in one study, this exposure did not further increase such beliefs (van Oosten et al., 2015). Further, in terms of adolescents' engagement in sexting behavior, scholars have expressed concerns regarding the possible sexually objectifying practices that may occur when one sends or receives sexually explicit pictures (Ringrose & Harvey, 2015). Nevertheless, no research has yet explored such possible mechanisms (K. Cooper et al., 2016).

As for online pornography, existing content analytical research stresses that pornographic content is saturated with sexually objectifying practices (especially toward women) (Carrotte et al., 2020; Klaassen & Peter, 2015). Both cross-sectional (e.g., Maes et al., 2019) and longitudinal studies (e.g.,

Peter & Valkenburg, 2009, 2011) have documented that the more adolescents watch online pornography, the more they sexually objectify women. Such beliefs even explain the relationship between exposure to online pornography and acceptance of rape myths (Burt, 1980; Maes et al., 2019). The acceptance of rape myths can have negative implications for adolescents' future sexuality since it can be related to sexual coercion perpetration (Trottier et al., 2021).

Relationship Quality Indicators

Commitment

To understand romantic relational outcomes of adolescents' digital media uses, digital media applications can be distinguished by users' abilities to communicate, create content, or be exposed to content within a public sphere (e.g., Facebook wall or online pornography) versus a private sphere (e.g., instant messaging tools of social media or sexting behavior). These different contexts shape the occurrence of different romantic relational outcomes in adolescents. With regards to the private sphere of instant messaging tools or sexting behavior, scholars point to its beneficial implications for adolescents' perceived romantic relationship quality. Specifically, a growing body of studies has emphasized that adolescents' online communication with romantic partners improves levels of trust, commitment, communication, and security (e.g., Blais et al., 2008; Morey et al., 2013). Moreover, as previously mentioned, the ability to post about one's relationship in the public online sphere allows adolescents to express their love for their partners (Utz & Beukeboom, 2011). However, research is lacking regarding the possible negative or positive implications of such online behavior among adolescents.

Existing research does emphasize that when adolescents are active in the online public sphere, they can also be confronted with other profiles that can be perceived as "romantic competition." Both qualitative and quantitative research has demonstrated that such online experiences evoke feelings of jealousy and distrust among adolescents (e.g., Rueda et al., 2015). Moreover, the literature also points to the possibility that the exposure to alternative partners on social media may have negative implications for adolescents' relationship commitment (de Lenne et al., 2018).

Sexual Attraction

Another indicator of relationship quality is one's sexual attraction to one's partner. In this view, sexting may be especially relevant for adolescents' sexual attraction for their partner. For instance, the more adolescents engage in this online sexual behavior, the higher their feelings of sexual attraction, passion, and sexual arousal toward their partner (van Ouytsel et al., 2019).

Behavioral Outcomes

Sexual Behavior

Sexually oriented digital media can play an important role in adolescents' engagement in sexual activities. Longitudinal studies have concluded that the more adolescents use social media, the more sexually experienced they are (Reitz et al., 2015; van Oosten et al., 2015). Sexting seems to promote sexual behavior in adolescents including higher sexual activity (e.g., MacDonald et al., 2018) and having multiple sexual partners (e.g., Romo et al., 2017). In terms of having multiple sexual partners, the literature indicates that this link is stronger among boys than girls (Mori et al., 2019).

As for adolescents' uses of online pornography, both cross-sectional (e.g., Donevan & Mattebo, 2017) and longitudinal studies (Brown & L'Engle, 2009) have demonstrated that the more adolescents watch such sexual content online, the higher their likelihood of having (casual) sexual intercourse with multiple sexual partners.

Risky Sexual Behavior

In regard to risky sexual behaviors, the current chapter refers to sexual behaviors (under the influence of drugs) that contribute to unintended pregnancy and the transmission of STIs. A recent meta-analysis points to the role of adolescents' social media use in the engagement in risky sexual behaviors (Vannucci et al., 2020). Furthermore, consistent correlational evidence has emerged that the more adolescents sext, the less they use contraception during sexual interactions (e.g., Rice et al., 2018). When it comes to adolescents' online pornography use, results regarding risky sexual behavioral outcomes are inconsistent. Specifically, some studies find that the more adolescents view pornography, the riskier their sexual behaviors (e.g., Luder et al., 2011), while others indicated that there is no such link (e.g., Peter & Valkenburg, 2011).

Sexually Aggressive Behavior

Within the field of sexting research, specific attention has been paid to the occurrence of this online behavior as a form of sexual coercion or harassment (K. Cooper et al., 2016). Specifically, sexting can entail forms of sexual aggression, sexual pressure, and harassment (e.g., through nonconsensual forwarding of sexually explicit pictures). However, limited knowledge exists regarding the offline consequences of negative forms of sexting behavior. In one study, Choi and colleagues (2016) highlighted the association between offline sexual coercion (e.g., being pressured to engage in sexual activities) and sexting behavior among girls.

In terms of adolescents' online pornography use, a link was found with sexual harassment perpetration among boys (Brown & L'Engle, 2009).

Further, the literature points to the necessity of addressing the type of online pornographic content in the context of sexual aggression research. For instance, only exposure to violent online pornography predicts higher sexual assault perpetration among adolescents (Ybarra et al., 2011).

Challenges and Future Directions

For the past two decades, growing attention has been given to adolescents' sexually oriented digital media uses. Not only has the literature pointed to positive motivations of these online media applications (e.g., construction of sexuality), but also to harmful and negative reasons to use sexually oriented digital media (e.g., relationship monitoring). These uses have been demonstrated to shape different outcomes related to sexual self-development (e.g., sexual agency), sexual attitudes (e.g., gender stereotypical beliefs), relationship quality (e.g., commitment), and sexual behaviors (e.g., risky behaviors). By focusing on the unique developmental context of adolescents and, thus, stressing their receptiveness for sexual content, the majority of the studies have pointed to detrimental sexual outcomes of digital media uses. However, scholars have recently emphasized that the predominant attention to negative outcomes and, simultaneously, a systematic inattention to positive outcomes, cannot provide a comprehensive and nuanced understanding of digital media effects (de Leeuw & Buijzen, 2016). As such, it may be possible that positive digital media effects in the context of adolescents' sexuality are undiscovered. This shortcoming introduces our first and most important suggestion for future research.

Specifically, we first encourage future research to explore *beneficial implications* of digital media uses for adolescents' sexuality and future sexual identity and experiences. Future studies are recommended to adopt a positive psychology framework when exploring adolescents' digital media uses. In this framework, positive and beneficial experiences, traits, and underlying mechanisms facilitating such experiences are explored (Seligman & Csikszentmihalyi, 2014). It is fundamental to note, however, that the adoption of this positive psychology paradigm should be considered as an addition to the current knowledge in order to present a balanced and more exhaustive understanding of adolescents' digital media uses. With the occurrence of different social movements striving for, for example, LGBTQ+ rights (e.g., #pride), adolescents are exposed to online prosocial sexual content (e.g., messages that promote a positive sexuality). Such exposure may have a beneficial impact on adolescents' understanding of others' sexualities. Moreover, with the engagement in sexting or the uses of online pornography, adolescents may be more aware and accepting of their own physical sexual feelings. Other positive influences of sexual digital media on young users may include sexual empowerment, an increased sexual knowledge, or other outcomes related to the adolescent's well-being.

As for gender stereotypical beliefs, social media, and in particular online videosharing sites (e.g., YouTube), despite still being restricted by standards of femininity or masculinity (Molyneaux et al., 2008; Wotanis & McMillan, 2014), have shown to be spaces that support a change in gendered ideology among youth (Morris & Anderson, 2015). For instance, male vloggers challenge masculine stereotypes by being emotionally open and embracing of their femininity, supporting gender equality and homosexual rights (Morris & Anderson, 2015), in particular by using satire and parody (Maloney et al., 2018; Wotanis & McMillan, 2014).

Second, the current chapter draws attention to the limited knowledge on *underlying processes*, such as peer norms or physical responses (e.g., arousal), which may explain the (possible) link between adolescents' digital media uses and detrimental and beneficial sexuality outcomes. The lack of longitudinal and experimental research, which is needed to interpret complex response states elicited by digital media uses, may explain this gap in the literature. The exploration of underlying processes explaining sexual digital media effects is crucial though, as it can provide a more comprehensive understanding of key processes explaining why certain media effects occur. Thus, future research, more specifically longitudinal and experimental studies, is strongly recommended to further examine such indirect processes.

Lastly, studies have largely adopted cross-sectional designs, especially in terms of exploring adolescents' sexting behavior and their effects. By following such designs, the literature has only examined the unidirectional nature of sexual digital media effects. More importantly, due to these designs, the direction of the relationships often cannot be established. Moreover, it is likely that the link between adolescents' digital media uses and sexuality is reciprocal and bi-directional. Specifically, we point to adolescents' agency to select digital media or create digital content shaped by their personal characteristics (e.g., pubertal status), sociocultural context (e.g., peers or Western culture), lived experiences, and expectancies of such media uses and content creation. Scholars postulate that adolescents' selection of digital media and content creation and the outcomes of such media uses are two interacting processes. As such, it could be possible that adolescents' existing sexual attitudes, experiences, or behaviors guide the selection of specific digital media applications (e.g., instant messaging tools) or the creation of sexual content (e.g., sexy self-presentations) that, in turn, can strengthen such sexual attitudes or behaviors or make them more susceptible to other attitudinal, experiential, and/or behavioral influences. As such, the third recommendation for future research is to examine the possible *bidirectional nature of links* between adolescents' digital media uses and sexuality-related outcomes.

In sum, the literature shows that sexually oriented digital media use can play an important role in adolescents' sexual socialization. Unique affordance of these media, such as its accessibility, invite to use sexually oriented digital media for the development of sexual selves, relationships, sexual attitudes, and behaviors. Several theories, such as social cognitive theory, can explain why adolescents use such media and how it may shape their sexuality. This chapter advises future research to explore, next to antisocial effects, the beneficial implications of digital media uses for adolescents' sexuality. Moreover, attention needs to be paid to underlying processes explaining the overall sexual socialization of adolescents via the uses of sexually oriented digital media. Lastly, the bidirectional nature of the link between such media uses and sexual outcomes needs to be further explored.

References

Baams, L., Overbeek, G., Dubas, J. S., Doornwaard, S. M., Rommes, E., & Van Aken, M. A. (2015). Perceived realism moderates the relation between sexualized media consumption and permissive sexual attitudes in Dutch adolescents. *Archives of Sexual Behavior, 44*(3), 743–754.

Bandura, A. (2001). Social cognitive theory of mass communication. *Media Psychology, 3*(3), 265–299.

Beals, L. M. (2010). Content creation in virtual worlds to support adolescent identity development. *New Directions for Youth Development, 2010*(128), 45–53.

Bem, D. J. (1972). Self-perception theory. In L. Berkowitz (Ed.), *Advances in experimental social psychology* (Vol. 6, p. 1–62). Elsevier.

Blais, J. J., Craig, W. M., Pepler, D., & Connolly, J. (2008). Adolescents online: The importance of internet activity choices to salient relationships. *Journal of Youth and Adolescence, 37*(5), 522–536.

Blumer, M., & Hertlein, K. M. (2015). The technological genogram: A tool for exploring intergenerational communication patterns around technology use. In C. Breuss (Ed.), *Family communication in the digital age* (pp. 471–490). Peter Lang International Publishers.

Bobkowski, P. S., Shafer, A., & Ortiz, R. R. (2016). Sexual intensity of adolescents' online self-presentations: Joint contribution of identity, media consumption, and extraversion. *Computers in Human Behavior, 58*, 64–74.

Borrajo, E., Gámez-Guadix, M., & Calvete, E. (2015). Cyber dating abuse: Prevalence, context, and relationship with offline dating aggression. *Psychological Reports, 116*(2), 565–585.

Brown, J. D., & L'Engle, K. L. (2009). X-rated: Sexual attitudes and behaviors associated with US early adolescents' exposure to sexually explicit media. *Communication Research, 36*(1), 129–151.

Burén, J., & Lunde, C. (2018). Sexting among adolescents: A nuanced and gendered online challenge for young people. *Computers in Human Behavior, 85*, 210–217.

Burkett, M. (2015). Sex(t) talk: A qualitative analysis of young adults' negotiations of the pleasures and perils of sexting. *Sexuality & Culture: An Interdisciplinary Quarterly, 19*(4), 835–863.

Burt, M. R. (1980). Cultural myths and supports for rape. *Journal of Personality and Social Psychology, 38*(2), 217–230.

Carrotte, E. R., Davis, A. C., & Lim, M. S. (2020). Sexual behaviors and violence in pornography: Systematic review and narrative synthesis of video content analyses. *Journal of Medical Internet Research, 22*(5), e16702.

Chen, A. S., Leung, M., Chen, C. H., & Yang, S. C. (2013). Exposure to internet pornography among Taiwanese adolescents. *Social Behavior and Personality: An International Journal, 41*(1), 157–164.

Chen, K. J., & Cheung, H. L. (2019). Unlocking the power of ephemeral content: The roles of motivations, gratification, need for closure, and engagement. *Computers in Human Behavior, 97*, 67–74.

Cheng, S., Hamilton, L., Missari, S., & Ma, J. (2014). Sexual subjectivity among adolescent girls: Social disadvantage and young adult outcomes. *Social Forces, 93*(2), 515–544.

Choi, H., Van Ouytsel, J., & Temple, J. R. (2016). Association between sexting and sexual coercion among female adolescents. *Journal of Adolescence, 53*, 164–168.

Christie, D., & Viner, R. (2005). Adolescent development. *BMJ, 330*(7486), 301–304.

Collins, R. L., Martino, S., & Shaw, R. (2010). *Influence of new media on adolescent sexual health* (Working Paper WR-761). Rand Health.

Cooper, A., Scherer, C. R., Boies, S. C., & Gordon, B. L. (1999). Sexuality on the internet: From sexual exploration to pathological expression. *Professional Psychology: Research and Practice, 30*(2), 154–164.

Cooper, K., Quayle, E., Jonsson, L., & Svedin, C. G. (2016). Adolescents and self-taken sexual images: A review of the literature. *Computers in Human Behavior, 55*, 706–716.

Crofts, T., Lee, M., McGovern, A., & Milivojevic, S. (2018). Sexting pleasures: Young people, fun, flirtation, and child pornography. In L. Grealy, C. Driscoll, & A. Hickey-Moody (Eds.), *Youth, technology, governance, experience: Adults understanding young people* (pp. 103–122). Routledge.

Dake, J. A., Price, J. H., Maziarz, L., & Ward, B. (2012). Prevalence and correlates of sexting behavior in adolescents. *American Journal of Sexuality Education, 7*(1), 1–15.

Davis, K. (2013). Young people's digital lives: The impact of interpersonal relationships and digital media use on adolescents' sense of identity. *Computers in Human Behavior, 29*(6), 2281–2293.

de Leeuw, R. N., & Buijzen, M. (2016). Introducing positive media psychology to the field of children, adolescents, and media. *Journal of Children and Media, 10*(1), 39–46.

de Lenne, O., Vandenbosch, L., Eggermont, S., Karsay, K., & Trekels, J. (2018). Picture-perfect lives on social media: A cross-national study on the role of media ideals in adolescent well-being. *Media Psychology, 23*(1), 1–27.

de Vaate, A. J. N. B., Veldhuis, J., Alleva, J. M., Konijn, E. A., & van Hugten, C. H. (2018). Show your best self(ie): An exploratory study on selfie-related motivations and behavior in emerging adulthood. *Telematics and Informatics, 35*(5), 1392–1407.

DeLamater, J., & Friedrich, W. N. (2002). Human sexual development. *Journal of Sex Research, 39*(1), 10–14.

Diamond, L. M., & Savin-Williams, R. C. (2009). Adolescent sexuality. In M. Lerner & L. Steinberg (Eds.), *Handbook of adolescent psychology* (pp. 479–523). John Wiley & Sons, Inc.

Dir, A. L., Coskunpinar, A., Steiner, J. L., & Cyders, M. A. (2013). Understanding differences in sexting behaviors across gender, relationship status, and sexual identity, and the role of expectancies in sexting. *Cyberpsychology, Behavior, and Social Networking, 16*(8), 568–574.

Donevan, M., & Mattebo, M. (2017). The relationship between frequent pornography consumption, behaviours, and sexual preoccupancy among male adolescents in Sweden. *Sexual & Reproductive Healthcare: Official Journal of the Swedish Association of Midwives, 12*, 82–87.

Doornwaard, S. M., Bickham, D. S., Rich, M., ter Bogt, T. F., & van den Eijnden, R. J. (2015). Adolescents' use of sexually explicit internet material and their sexual attitudes and behavior: Parallel development and directional effects. *Developmental Psychology, 51*(10), 1476–1488.

Doornwaard, S. M., Bickham, D. S., Rich, M., Vanwesenbeeck, I., van den Eijnden, R. J., & ter Bogt, T. F. (2014). Sex-related online behaviors and adolescents' body and sexual self-perceptions. *Pediatrics, 134*(6), 1103–1110.

Draucker, C. B., & Martsolf, D. S. (2010). The role of electronic communication technology in adolescent dating violence. *Journal of Child and Adolescent Psychiatric Nursing, 23*(3), 133–142.

Fortenberry, J. D. (2013). Sexual development in adolescents. In D. S. Bromberg & W. T. O'Donohue (Eds.), *Handbook of child and adolescent sexuality: Developmental and forensic psychology* (p. 171–192). Elsevier Academic Press.

Fredrickson, B. L., & Roberts, T. A. (1997). Objectification theory: Toward understanding women's lived experiences and mental health risks. *Psychology of Women Quarterly, 21*(2), 173–206.

Gagnon, J. H., & Simon, W. (1973). *Sexual conduct.* Aldine.

Galovan, A. M., Drouin, M., & McDaniel, B. T. (2018). Sexting profiles in the United States and Canada: Implications for individual and relationship well-being. *Computers in Human Behavior, 79*, 19–29.

Grubbs, J. B., Wright, P. J., Braden, A. L., Wilt, J. A., & Kraus, S. W. (2019). Internet pornography use and sexual motivation: A systematic review and integration. *Annals of the International Communication Association, 43*(2), 117–155.

Guse, K., Levine, D., Martins, S., et al. (2012). Interventions using new digital media to improve adolescent sexual health: A systematic review. *Journal of Adolescent Health, 51*(6), 535–543.

Hamilton, L., & Armstrong, E. A. (2009). Gendered sexuality in young adulthood: Double binds and flawed options. *Gender & Society, 23*(5), 589–616.

Hardy, S. A., Hurst, J. L., Price, J., & Denton, M. L. (2019). The socialization of attitudes about sex and their role in adolescent pornography use. *Journal of Adolescence, 72*, 70–82.

Hellevik, P. M. (2019). Teenagers' personal accounts of experiences with digital intimate partner violence and abuse. *Computers in Human Behavior, 92*, 178–187.

Kapidzic, S., & Herring, S. C. (2015). Race, gender, and self-presentation in teen profile photographs. *New Media & Society, 17*(6), 958–976.

Katz, E., Blumler, J. G., & Gurevitch, M. (1973). Uses and gratifications research. *The Public Opinion Quarterly, 37*(4), 509–523.

Kelly, A. E., & Rodriguez, R. R. (2006). Publicly committing oneself to an identity. *Basic and Applied Social Psychology, 28*(2), 185–191.

Klaassen, M. J., & Peter, J. (2015). Gender (in) equality in internet pornography: A content analysis of popular pornographic internet videos. *The Journal of Sex Research*, *52*(7), 721–735.

Klein, V., Šević, S., Kohut, T., & Štulhofer, A. (2020). Longitudinal assessment of the association between the use of sexually explicit material, hyperfemininity, and sexual agency in adolescent women. *Psychology & Sexuality*, 1–15.

Korchmaros, J. D., Ybarra, M. L., & Mitchell, K. J. (2015). Adolescent online romantic relationship initiation: Differences by sexual and gender identification. *Journal of Adolescence*, *40*, 54–64.

Le, V. D., Temple, J. R., Peskin, M., Markham, C., & Tortolero, S. (2014). Sexual behavior and communication. In W. J. Weins & T. C. Hiestand (Eds.), *Sexting and youth: A multidisciplinary examination of research, theory, and law* (pp. 63–94). Carolina Academic Press.

Lerner, R. M., Boyd, M. J., & Du, D. (2010). Adolescent development. In I. B. Weiner & W. E. Craighead (Eds.), *The Corsini encyclopedia of psychology* (4th ed.; pp. 35–36). Wiley.

Ling, R., & Bertel, T. (2013). Mobile communication culture among children and adolescents. In D. Lemish (Ed.), *The Routledge international handbook of children, adolescents and media* (pp. 153–159). Routledge.

Lippman, J. R., & Campbell, S. W. (2014). Damned if you do, damned if you don't... if you're a girl: Relational and normative contexts of adolescent sexting in the United States. *Journal of Children and Media*, *8*(4), 371–386.

Luder, M. T., Pittet, I., Berchtold, A., Akré, C., Michaud, P. A., & Surís, J. C. (2011). Associations between online pornography and sexual behavior among adolescents: Myth or reality?. *Archives of Sexual Behavior*, *40*(5), 1027–1035.

MacDonald, K., Imburgia, T. M., Auerswald, C., & Ott, M. A. (2018). Sexting among adolescent urban males. *Journal of Adolescent Health*, *62*(2), S126.

Machimbarrena, J. M., Calvete, E., Fernández-González, L., Álvarez-Bardón, A., Álvarez-Fernández, L., & González-Cabrera, J. (2018). Internet risks: An overview of victimization in cyberbullying, cyber dating abuse, sexting, online grooming and problematic internet use. *International journal of Environmental Research and Public Health*, *15*(11), 2471.

Madigan, S., Ly, A., Rash, C. L., Van Ouytsel, J., & Temple, J. R. (2018). Prevalence of multiple forms of sexting behavior among youth: A systematic review and meta-analysis. *JAMA Pediatrics*, *172*(4), 327–335.

Maes, C., Schreurs, L., van Oosten, J. M., & Vandenbosch, L. (2019). #(Me) too much? The role of sexualizing online media in adolescents' resistance towards the metoo-movement and acceptance of rape myths. *Journal of Adolescence*, *77*, 59–69.

Maes, C., Trekels, J., Impett, E., & Vandenbosch, L. (2022). The Development of the Positive Sexuality in Adolescence Scale (PSAS). *The Journal of Sex Research*, 1–17. https://doi.org/10.1080/00224499.2021.2011826

Maheux, A. J., Evans, R., Widman, L., Nesi, J., Prinstein, M. J., & Choukas-Bradley, S. (2020). Popular peer norms and adolescent sexting behavior. *Journal of Adolescence*, *78*, 62–66.

Maloney, M., Roberts, S., & Caruso, A. (2018). 'Mmm ... I love it, bro!': Performances of masculinity in YouTube gaming. *New Media and Society*, *20*, 1697–1714.

Manago, A. M., Ward, L. M., Lemm, K. M., Reed, L., & Seabrook, R. (2015). Facebook involvement, objectified body consciousness, body shame, and sexual assertiveness in college women and men. *Sex Roles, 72*(1–2), 1–14.

Marengo, D., Settanni, M., & Longobardi, C. (2019). The associations between sex drive, sexual self-concept, sexual orientation, and exposure to online victimization in Italian adolescents: Investigating the mediating role of verbal and visual sexting behaviors. *Children and Youth Services Review, 102*, 18–26.

Mascheroni, G., Vincent, J., & Jimenez, E. (2015). "Girls are addicted to likes so they post semi-naked selfies": Peer mediation, normativity and the construction of identity online. *Cyberpsychology: Journal of Psychosocial Research on Cyberspace, 9*(1).

Milas, G., Klarić, I. M., Malnar, A., Šupe-Domić, D., & Slavich, G. M. (2019). Socioeconomic status, social-cultural values, life stress, and health behaviors in a national sample of adolescents. *Stress and Health, 35*(2), 217–224.

Molyneaux, H., O'Donnell, S., Gibson, K., & Singer, J. (2008). Exploring the gender divide on YouTube: An analysis of the creation and reception of vlogs. *American Communication Journal, 10*, 1–13.

Moran, J. (2000) *Teaching sex: The shaping of adolescence in the 20th century*. Harvard University Press.

Morey, J. N., Gentzler, A. L., Creasy, B., Oberhauser, A. M., & Westerman, D. (2013). Young adults' use of communication technology within their romantic relationships and associations with attachment style. *Computers in Human Behavior, 29*(4), 1771–1778.

Mori, C., Temple, J. R., Browne, D., & Madigan, S. (2019). Association of sexting with sexual behaviors and mental health among adolescents: A systematic review and meta-analysis. *JAMA Pediatrics, 173*(8), 770–779.

Morris, M., & Anderson, E. (2015). 'Charlie is so cool like': Authenticity, popularity and inclusive masculinity on YouTube. *Sociology, 49*(6), 1200–1217.

Murray, S. H. (2018). Heterosexual men's sexual desire: Supported by, or deviating from, traditional masculinity norms and sexual scripts?. *Sex Roles, 78*(1–2), 130–141.

Nikkelen, S. W. C., van Oosten, J. M. F., & van den Borne, M. M. J. J. (2020). Sexuality education in the digital era: Intrinsic and extrinsic predictors of online sexual information seeking among youth. *Journal of Sex Research, 57*(2), 189–199.

Park, E., & Kwon, M. (2018). Health-related internet use by children and adolescents: Systematic review. *Journal of Medical Internet Research, 20*(4), e7731.

Parker, T. S., Blackburn, K. M., Perry, M. S., & Hawks, J. M. (2013). Sexting as an intervention: Relationship satisfaction and motivation considerations. *The American Journal of Family Therapy, 41*(1), 1–12.

Pascoe, C. J. (2011). Resource and risk: Youth sexuality and new media use. *Sexuality Research and Social Policy, 8*(1), 5–17.

Perry, D. G., & Pauletti, R. E. (2011). Gender and adolescent development. *Journal of Research on Adolescence, 21*(1), 61–74.

Peter, J., & Valkenburg, P. M. (2006). Adolescents' exposure to sexually explicit online material and recreational attitudes toward sex. *Journal of Communication, 56*(4), 639–660.

Peter, J., & Valkenburg, P. M. (2008). Adolescents' exposure to sexually explicit internet material, sexual uncertainty, and attitudes toward uncommitted sexual exploration: Is there a link?. *Communication Research, 35*(5), 579–601.

Peter, J., & Valkenburg, P. M. (2009). Adolescents' exposure to sexually explicit internet material and notions of women as sex objects: Assessing causality and underlying processes. *Journal of Communication, 59*(3), 407–433.

Peter, J., & Valkenburg, P. M. (2010). Adolescents' use of sexually explicit internet material and sexual uncertainty: The role of involvement and gender. *Communication Monographs, 77*(3), 357–375.

Peter, J., & Valkenburg, P. M. (2011). The use of sexually explicit internet material and its antecedents: A longitudinal comparison of adolescents and adults. *Archives of Sexual Behavior, 40*(5), 1015–1025.

Peter, J., & Valkenburg, P. M. (2016). Adolescents and pornography: A review of 20 years of research. *The Journal of Sex Research, 53*(4–5), 509–531.

Petersen, J. L., & Hyde, J. S. (2010). A meta-analytic review of research on gender differences in sexuality, 1993–2007. *Psychological Bulletin, 136*(1), 21–38.

Ponton, L. E., & Judice, S. (2004). Typical adolescent sexual development. *Child and Adolescent Psychiatric Clinics of North America, 13*(3), 497–511.

Popa, D., & Gavriliu, D. (2015). Gender representations and digital media. *Procedia – Social and Behavioral Sciences, 180*, 1199–1206.

Reed, L. A., Tolman, R. M., & Ward, L. M. (2017). Gender matters: Experiences and consequences of digital dating abuse victimization in adolescent dating relationships. *Journal of Adolescence, 59*, 79–89.

Reed, L. A., Ward, L. M., Tolman, R. M., Lippman, J. R., & Seabrook, R. C. (2018). The association between stereotypical gender and dating beliefs and digital dating abuse perpetration in adolescent dating relationships. *Journal of Interpersonal Violence, 36*(9–10), NP5561–NP5585.

Reitz, E., van de Bongardt, D., Baams, L., et al. (2015). Project STARS (Studies on Trajectories of Adolescent Relationships and Sexuality): A longitudinal, multi-domain study on sexual development of Dutch adolescents. *European Journal of Developmental Psychology, 12*(5), 613–626.

Rice, E., Craddock, J., Hemler, M., et al. (2018). Associations between sexting behaviors and sexual behaviors among mobile phone-owning teens in Los Angeles. *Child Development, 89*(1), 110–117.

Ringrose, J. (2011). Are you sexy, flirty, or a slut? Exploring 'sexualization'and how teen girls perform/negotiate digital sexual identity on social networking sites. In R. Gill & C. Scharf (Eds.), *New femininities* (pp. 99–116). Palgrave Macmillan.

Ringrose, J., & Harvey, L. (2015). Boobs, back-off, six packs and bits: Mediated body parts, gendered reward, and sexual shame in teens' sexting images. *Continuum, 29*(2), 205–217.

Ringrose, J., Harvey, L., Gill, R., & Livingstone, S. (2013). Teen girls, sexual double standards and "sexting": Gendered value in digital image exchange. *Feminist Theory, 14*(3), 305–323.

Romo, D. L., Garnett, C., Younger, A. P., et al. (2017). Social media use and its association with sexual risk and parental monitoring among a primarily

Hispanic adolescent population. *Journal of Pediatric and Adolescent Gynecology*, *30*(4), 466–473.

Rueda, H. A., Lindsay, M., & Williams, L. R. (2015). "She posted it on Facebook": Mexican American adolescents' experiences with technology and romantic relationship conflict. *Journal of Adolescent Research*, *30*(4), 419–445.

Russell, S. T. (2005). Conceptualizing positive adolescent sexuality development. *Sexuality Research and Social Policy*, *2*(3), 4–12.

Saewyc, E. M. (2011). Research on adolescent sexual orientation: Development, health disparities, stigma, and resilience. *Journal of Research on Adolescence*, *21*(1), 256–272.

Sawyer, S. M., Afifi, R. A., Bearinger, L. H., et al. (2012). Adolescence: A foundation for future health. *The Lancet*, *379*(9826), 1630–1640.

Scarcelli, C. M. (2015). 'It is disgusting, but...': Adolescent girls' relationship to internet pornography as gender performance. *Porn Studies*, *2*(2–3), 237–249.

Schlenker, B. R., Dlugolecki, D. W., & Doherty, K. (1994). The impact of self-presentations on self-appraisals and behavior: The power of public commitment. *Personality and Social Psychology Bulletin*, *20*(1), 20–33.

Schlenker, B. R., Wowra, S. A., Johnson, R. M., & Miller, M. L. (2008). The impact of imagined audiences on self-appraisals. *Personal Relationships*, *15*(2), 247–260.

Seligman, M. E., & Csikszentmihalyi, M. (2014). Positive psychology: An introduction. In M. Csikszentmihalyi, *Flow and the foundations of positive psychology* (pp. 279–298). Springer.

Shafer, A., Bobkowski, P., & Brown, J. D. (2013). Sexual media practice: How adolescents select, engage with, and are affected by sexual media. In K. E. Dill (Ed.), *The Oxford handbook of media psychology* (pp. 223–251). Oxford University Press.

Shek, D. T., & Ma, C. M. (2016). A six-year longitudinal study of consumption of pornographic materials in Chinese adolescents in Hong Kong. *Journal of Pediatric and Adolescent Gynecology*, *29*(1), 12–21.

Simon, L., & Daneback, K. (2013). Adolescents' use of the internet for sex education: A thematic and critical review of the literature. *International Journal of Sexual Health*, *25*(4), 305–319.

Sundar, S. S., & Limperos, A. M. (2013). Uses and grats 2.0: New gratifications for new media. *Journal of Broadcasting & Electronic Media*, *57*(4), 504–525.

To, S., Ngai, S. S., & Iu Kan, S. (2012). Direct and mediating effects of accessing sexually explicit online materials on Hong Kong adolescents' attitude, knowledge, and behavior relating to sex. *Children and Youth Services Review*, *34*(11), 2156–2163.

Tolman, D. L., & McClelland, S. I. (2011). Normative sexuality development in adolescence: A decade in review, 2000–2009. *Journal of Research on Adolescence*, *21*(1), 242–255.

Trottier, D., Benbouriche, M., & Bonneville, V. (2021). A meta-analysis on the association between rape myth acceptance and sexual coercion perpetration. *The Journal of Sex Research*, *58*(3), 375–382.

Utz, S., & Beukeboom, C. J. (2011). The role of social network sites in romantic relationships: Effects on jealousy and relationship happiness. *Journal of Computer-Mediated Communication*, *16*(4), 511–527.

Valkenburg, P. M. (2017). Understanding self-effects in social media. *Human Communication Research, 43*(4), 477–490.

Valkenburg, P. M., & Peter, J. (2011). Online communication among adolescents: An integrated model of its attraction, opportunities, and risks. *Journal of Adolescent Health, 48*(2), 121–127.

Van de Bongardt, D., Yu, R., Deković, M., & Meeus, W. H. (2015). Romantic relationships and sexuality in adolescence and young adulthood: The role of parents, peers, and partners. *European Journal of Developmental Psychology, 12*(5), 497–515.

Van Oosten, J. M., de Vries, D. A., & Peter, J. (2018). The importance of adolescents' sexually outgoing self-concept: Differential roles of self-and other-generated sexy self-presentations in social media. *Cyberpsychology, Behavior, and Social Networking, 21*(1), 5–10.

Van Oosten, J. M., Peter, J., & Boot, I. (2015). Exploring associations between exposure to sexy online self-presentations and adolescents' sexual attitudes and behavior. *Journal of Youth and Adolescence, 44*(5), 1078–1091.

Van Oosten, J. M., Peter, J., & Vandenbosch, L. (2017a). Adolescents' sexual media use and willingness to engage in casual sex: Differential relations and underlying processes. *Human Communication Research, 43*(1), 127–147.

Van Oosten, J. M., Vandenbosch, L., & Peter, J. (2017b). Gender roles on social networking sites: Investigating reciprocal relationships between Dutch adolescents' hypermasculinity and hyperfemininity and sexy online self-presentations. *Journal of Children and Media, 11*(2), 147–166.

Van Ouytsel, J., Ponnet, K., Walrave, M., & Temple, J. R. (2016a). Adolescent cyber dating abuse victimization and its associations with substance use, and sexual behaviors. *Public Health, 135*, 147–151.

Van Ouytsel, J., Van Gool, E., Walrave, M., Ponnet, K., & Peeters, E. (2016b). Exploring the role of social networking sites within adolescent romantic relationships and dating experiences. *Computers in Human Behavior, 55*, 76–86.

Van Ouytsel, J., Walrave, M., & Ponnet, K. (2019). Sexting within adolescents' romantic relationships: How is it related to perceptions of love and verbal conflict? *Computers in Human Behavior, 97*, 216–221.

Vanden Abeele, M., Campbell, S. W., Eggermont, S., & Roe, K. (2014). Sexting, mobile porn use, and peer group dynamics: Boys' and girls' self-perceived popularity, need for popularity, and perceived peer pressure. *Media Psychology, 17*(1), 6–33.

Vannucci, A., Simpson, E. G., Gagnon, S., & Ohannessian, C. M. (2020). Social media use and risky behaviors in adolescents: A meta-analysis. *Journal of Adolescence, 79*, 258–274.

Walrave, M., Heirman, W., & Hallam, L. (2014). Under pressure to sext? Applying the theory of planned behaviour to adolescent sexting. *Behaviour & Information Technology, 33*(1), 86–98.

Weil, L. G., Fleming, S. M., Dumontheil, I., et al. (2013). The development of metacognitive ability in adolescence. *Consciousness and Cognition, 22*(1), 264–271.

Williams, T., Connolly, J., Pepler, D., & Craig, W. (2009). Questioning and sexual minority adolescents: High school experiences of bullying, sexual harassment and physical abuse. *Canadian Journal of Community Mental Health, 22*(2), 47–58.

Wotanis, L., & McMillan, L. (2014). Performing gender on YouTube: How Jenna Marbles negotiates a hostile online environment. *Feminist Media Studies, 14*(6), 912–928.

Ybarra, M. L., Mitchell, K. J., Hamburger, M., Diener-West, M., & Leaf, P. J. (2011). X-rated material and perpetration of sexually aggressive behavior among children and adolescents: Is there a link? *Aggressive Behavior, 37*(1), 1–18.

Young, R., Len-Ríos, M., & Young, H. (2017). Romantic motivations for social media use, social comparison, and online aggression among adolescents. *Computers in Human Behavior, 75*, 385–395.

7 Culture and Digital Media in Adolescent Development

Adriana M. Manago and Jessica McKenzie

Digital media are integrated into the lives of adolescents in almost every corner of the globe, yet the extent of integration, how media are used, and the effects of media in development are anything but universal. Much of what is known about adolescent digital media use and its consequences center on high-income economies – particularly in the USA and Western Europe (e.g., Twenge et al., 2019; Vanden Abeele, 2016). Comparatively less is known about media use in lower- and middle-income economies, where digital media use has risen exponentially – especially among youth – in a short period of time (Silver et al., 2019). Between 2000 and 2022, internet growth rates in Africa, Asia, Latin America/Caribbean, and the Middle East ranged from 2,300% to 13,000%, compared to 200–600% internet growth rates in Europe, North America, and Oceana/Australia during the same period of time (Internet Usage Statistics, 2022). Indeed, the increase in digital media use is now led by emerging and developing world regions (Poushter et al., 2018).

The international perspective on digital media and adolescent development we provide in this chapter is important for a number of reasons. First, international perspectives help Western-based developmental psychologists such as ourselves appreciate human diversity and understand our own WEIRD (Western, Educated, Individualistic, Rich, Democratic; Henrich et al., 2010) perspectives on technology and human development. Second, cross-cultural research helps us to see how digital media such as mobile devices and social media platforms are cultural tools in the sociocultural tradition of Lev Vygotsky, rather than separate, disconnected, "virtual" places. Cultural tools are material and symbolic resources that accumulate through social processes across generations and that mediate human thinking and action (Cole & Scribner, 1978). Tools enable children to master psychological functions like memory, attention, and interpretation, which become implicated in a culture's definition of intelligence (Maynard et al., 2005). Although Vygotsky's theory is generally applied to cognitive development, the idea that digital media are cultural tools transforming human activity and psychological functioning can also be applied to social skills and identity development during the transition to adulthood (Manago et al., 2008).

In conceptualizing digital media as cultural tools, we can examine the affordances or "opportunities for action" they offer, which are materially and socially constituted (Hutchby, 2001). That is to say, the design of a social media platform or mobile device suggests to users how the technology should be used, but at the same time, these tools may be employed by communities in ways designers may have never imagined (Kling, 2007). Cultural beliefs, values, and institutions influence how and for what purpose adolescents use digital media, and thus the psychological outcomes of use. A relational perspective on affordances suggests that the design of digital tools structure (constrain and enable) certain actions (e.g., one-to-many communication) but have differing ramifications for psychological development depending on social constructions of digital media use (e.g., what is communicated). Furthermore, cultural tools are transformative in the process of mediation and adolescents are uniquely positioned in societies to be brokers of cultural change across generations (Manago et al., 2022). In short, we view youth as active participants in their socialization, and in cultural evolution more broadly, through their use of digital media to negotiate their everyday social lives.

In this chapter, we present cultural perspectives on adolescent development and digital media deriving from international research. Although our focus is international, many of the issues we touch upon can be applied to variability within multicultural societies such as the USA. In keeping with our transactional view, we explore how shared values, structures of community, and notions of selfhood shape, and are shaped by, digital media use. To balance the disproportionate representation of survey research with samples in North America and Western Europe, we looked to anthropological and ethnographic research, including our own fieldwork in Thailand (McKenzie) and a Maya community in Mexico (Manago).

Cultural Values and Digital Media Use around the World

Research suggests that digital communication technologies promote individualistic values and mobility, individual expression, and stimulation (Hansen et al., 2014; Manago & Pacheco, 2019; Pathak-Shelat & DeShano, 2014). But to what extent do such values displace collectivistic values and traditional models of interpersonal relationships – particularly in emerging and developing world regions, where values of collectivism, age-based hierarchy, and family obligation dominate? In the paragraphs that follow, we discuss how digital media are used and the effects of digital media in world regions experiencing a rapid rise in internet and social media use. We focus on how cultural values shape adolescent digital media use, and on how adolescents reshape cultural values through their digital media use. We also consider the implications of this digital media-inspired cultural value reshaping on adolescent well-being.

Africa

Quantitative research in Nigeria suggests that social media reshapes core values of respect for old age, traditional ways of dress, and language use (Asemah et al., 2013). The authors argue that Facebook, Twitter, and 2go are "potent tools of cultural imperialism" (Asemah et al., 2013, p. 67), for they encourage Nigerian youth to pattern their lives after foreign culture and drive the loss of traditional values. Yet the authors also highlight the potential utility of these social media in promoting traditional Nigerian values among youth. Certainly, digital media are powerful tools of globalization insofar as they reduce the distance between practices, values, and people from geographically distant world regions. Yet digital media may also encourage localization (the counterforce of globalization) by encouraging the maintenance and even expansion of local values and practices (Hermans & Dimaggio, 2007) in rapidly changing cultural contexts.

In Ethiopia, Hansen and colleagues' quantitative work points to continuity and change in cultural values with the experimental introduction of laptops. In one study, Hansen et al. (2012) found that after one year of laptop use, adolescents more strongly endorsed individualistic values, yet there was no reduction in collectivistic value endorsement. In another study, Hansen et al. (2014) found that children and adolescents – particularly in rural regions – who were given laptops became significantly more positive about gender equality over time than those without laptops. Those with laptops also endorsed other "modern" cultural values (e.g., achievement, self-direction, universalism). Interestingly, though, they found that traditional values (i.e., religion, family) were also strengthened by the introduction of laptops. The effects of internet and social media use were not assessed in these studies because the laptops given were not connected to the Internet, but it is telling that even the use of offline laptops alter the cultural values endorsed by Ethiopian youth.

Asia

Although digital media are marketed as giving youth power and agency, Pathak-Shelat and DeShano's (2014) qualitative research illustrates that traditional Indian values of obedience to elders are also reinforced by rural Indian adolescents' internalization of parental moral panic about media as risky. They do so by modeling their digital media use around parental concerns ranging from interacting with strangers to developing cancer from new media technologies. Yet adolescents also subtly (re)negotiate age-based hierarchies and power by, for instance, friending those with whom they are unfamiliar (engaging in "risky" behavior) and not friending distant relatives (not respecting familial ties). Importantly, adolescents in this rural Indian context experience media as peripheral rather than central to their lives. Rural Indian youth have less access to mobile phones and computers with internet access

(Pathak-Shelat & DeShano, 2014); they also use digital media in ways that are distinct from youth in urban India – where media use reshapes adolescent cultural practices such as clothing and music choices (Rao et al., 2013).

Research in Thailand, too, points to gaps in media use across rural and urban contexts. The second author's mixed-methods study found that urban-dwelling Thais spend more time on digital media than rural-dwelling Thais, and that adolescents spend more time on digital media than their parents (McKenzie et al., 2022). The media-based opportunities and challenges experienced across generation and geographic location speak to continuity in cultural values. Rural and urban adolescents and parents alike perceive connecting with proximal others (e.g., friends, children) as a key technological affordance. That urban adolescents – who spend the most time on digital media – emphasize collectivistic goals illustrates that media are used in ways that align with and promote traditional cultural values. Yet the media-based challenges highlighted point to digital media paradoxes among those who spend the most time online. Urban adolescents simultaneously experience social media as expanding their presence in the world and restricting real-world experiences, and as enabling connections with, and fostering rejection from, friends. Their parents experience media both as tools for achieving closeness with their children and as endangering family bonds by cheapening time spent together.

In urban Thailand, qualitative research indicates that adolescents' media expertise renders them cultural brokers for their parents (McKenzie et al., 2019). Adolescents in this society traditionally marked by deference to elders train their parents to use digital technologies, which reshapes traditional power dynamics and hierarchical family relationships. It is noteworthy, though, that parents reassert their position of authority (e.g., by mobilizing their children's technological desires as opportunities to teach culturally salient lessons about necessity) and that adolescents use their digital media expertise to assist and serve their parents. This points to continuity of Thai values for age-based hierarchy, moderation, and filial piety, even in the face of rapid technological change.

Latin America/Caribbean

The work of Ferguson and colleagues highlights the influence of digital media on adolescent values and identity in Jamaica. Across two studies, they found that roughly one-third of urban Jamaican adolescents were remotely acculturated to American culture (Ferguson & Bornstein, 2012, 2015). One key avenue through which this remote acculturation occurs is indirect intercultural contact with the United States via media – including social media. Their quantitative research indicates that, compared to their "traditional Jamaican" counterparts, "Americanized Jamaican" adolescents are more affiliated with European American identity, hold weaker beliefs about family obligations, and experience greater conflict with their parents.

The first author's mixed-methods research with young adults in a Maya community in Mexico indicates that cultural values shape how young people think about the benefits and risks of information communication technologies (ICTs) (Manago & Pacheco, 2019). Examining indigenous beliefs about ICTs shortly after the installation of a communication tower, the study found that a commonly discussed ICT benefit was enabling frequent family communication and family closeness and that a commonly discussed ICT risk was their danger in drawing attention away from the family. That ICTs are perceived as promoting and hindering family relationships underscores the role of traditional, collectivistic values in shaping youth perspectives of digital media. ICT benefits also highlighted – particularly among those with higher educational attainment – values of stimulation and self-expression, which involve seeking new information and exploring outside of traditional community structures. Here we see the influence of exposure to Western values of individualism, which are spread via ICTs.

Middle East

For each of the preceding world regions discussed, it was possible to highlight research on adolescent media use and values in nations experiencing dramatic digital media expansion. Though the Middle East includes high-income nations with relatively long-standing digital media integration and low-income nations with dramatic digital media expansion in recent years (Internet Usage in the Middle East, 2022; World Bank Country and Lending Groups, n.d.), most relevant research focuses on the former. Mixed-methods research in high-income Israel, however, points to the role of digital media in reshaping cultural values and family relationships.

Abu Aleon et al. (2019) assessed values among three generations of Bedouins with vignettes that involved a disagreement between two characters: one that endorsed traditional values (family obligation, interdependence, and gender hierarchy) and other that endorsed modern Western values (individual achievement, independence, and gender equality). They found that younger generations of Bedouins were more likely to endorse gender equality than were older generations, and that females were a generation ahead of males in endorsing gender equality and independence. Importantly, time spent on the Internet and watching television were identified as "motors of change" toward Western value endorsement. Mesch's (2006) quantitative examination of Israeli adolescent internet use points to how adolescent internet use affects family cohesion. They found that the more time adolescents spent online, the less time they spent with their parents, and that the purpose of adolescent internet use mattered where family conflict is concerned. While adolescent internet use for social purposes was positively associated with intergenerational family conflict, internet use for educational purposes was not.

Summary

Cultural values influence how digital media are used and the effects of digital media. On the one hand, adolescents use and perceive digital media in ways that align with cultural values. On the other hand, adolescent digital media use reshapes cultural values and interpersonal relationships. The research discussed also illustrates how risks and opportunities of digital media are customized by developmental period, generational cohort, and cultural context. In emerging and developing world regions where technological change is particularly rapid, risks include the potential loss of traditional cultural values and an emergent cultural gap between adolescents and parents. Opportunities include emergent adolescent agency in shaping their development and in reshaping cultural values deemed incongruent with their lived 21st-century realities.

Considering adolescent well-being as it intersects with cultural values, digital media may act as a double-edged sword. The psychological task of encountering and reconciling diverse value systems likely facilitates adolescent perspective-taking and the development of multifaceted, dynamic thinking that is adaptive in our multifaceted and dynamic world. Yet the task of coherently integrating local and global value systems likely presents unique challenges for adolescents (McKenzie, 2020). The difficulties associated with knitting together potentially incompatible value systems and identities may render adolescents more at risk of developing bifurcated or differentiated selves (McKenzie, 2019), thereby threatening the development of an integrated self – a key task of adolescence (Erikson, 1963).

The effects of digital media in world regions experiencing rapid technological growth in some ways mirror the effects in the culturally diverse USA. As explained in this section, adolescent digital media use reshapes cultural values and parent–child power dynamics in India and Thailand. Among rural teenage girls in the Midwestern USA, especially rural girls of color, social media is used to gain and assert power and control, which is perceived as lacking in their offline lives (Rickman, 2018). Like Thai adolescents who act as media-based cultural brokers for their parents, lower-socioeconomic-status American youth frequently assist their parents with technology (Rideout & Katz, 2016) – likely renegotiating parent–child power dynamics in the process. Also highlighted in this section is that adolescent media use does not completely unroot traditional cultural values. From Nigeria and Ethiopia to India, Thailand, and Mexico, media are avenues for localization and local value reassertion. This aligns with Latino families in the USA, who often use digital media in ways that center collectivism (e.g., collaborative father–son searches, sister and brother producing media together) (Levinson & Barron, 2018). Research explicitly addressing the overlapping consequences between and within cultural communities would sharpen the cultural study of adolescent digital media use.

Structures of Community: The Nature of Social Ties in Digital Societies

Many sociological theorists have pondered questions about the impacts of digital communication on structures of community and the ways in which social relations are organized (Castells, 1996; Rainie & Wellman, 2012). One perspective is that communication technologies, particularly social network sites, have greatly reduced the time costs of maintaining relationships such that youth today have more opportunities to interact with larger swaths of diverse others than was possible in the past (Manago & Vaughn, 2015). Yet, much of our thinking on this issue is grounded in evidence from WEIRD samples and Western philosophical traditions. In this section, we interrogate a common framework for understanding social ties in digital societies and present alternative possibilities that may better account for the impact social media is having on the organization of adolescents' social relations.

The Mobility Narrative

Western theories regarding the consequences of communication technologies for human social relations often reflect a mobility narrative (Hampton, 2016). In this narrative, industrialization, transportation systems, urbanization, and communication technologies have brought about greater migration, occupational specialization, and shifts in social structures away from permanent, tight-knit groups grounded in shared geography, to impermanent, heterogenous, and expansive person-centered networks spread across various contexts (e.g., Greenfield, 2009; Rainie & Wellman, 2012). Mobile devices and social media amplify historical trends toward increasing individual mobility by introducing new affordances into social life such as communication at a distance and asynchronous one-to-many (masspersonal) communication that allow people to transcend the limitations of time and space to construct looser networks of associations (Donath, 2008; Wellman, 2002). Digital communication technologies also extend individuals' capacities to connect through shared personal interests, rather than ascribed relationships such as kinship, and to overcome the constraints of social bonds while still deriving social resources from them (Rainie & Wellman, 2012).

The mobility narrative is useful for explaining certain patterns in the international social media research literature. In the West, Facebook has facilitated more extensive webs of associations with social resources for personal exploration and self-expression (Brandtzaeg, 2012; Ito et al., 2009; Manago et al., 2012). Bridging social capital resources such as nonredundant information and novel perspectives are more abundant in social structures with many weak ties (Granovetter, 1973; Williams, 2006) and studies have shown positive associations between social media use, network size, and bridging social capital among US college students (Ellison et al., 2007; Mariek et al., 2018), adolescents in

Australia (J. Y. Lee et al., 2016), and early adolescents in the Netherlands (Antheunis et al., 2016). Similar associations have also been found outside the West, among university students in Karachi, Pakistan (Raza et al., 2017), South Africa (Johnston et al., 2013), Beijing, China (Liu et al., 2013), and adolescents in South Korea (J. Y. Lee et al., 2016). In Manago's field site in the Maya community of Zinacantán, emerging adults who began using the Internet after a communication tower was installed in 2010 constructed social networks through a paper and pencil mapping activity (Antonucci, 1986) comprising greater proportions of nonpermanent social connections (nonkin) compared to emerging adults who did not have access to the Internet (Manago & Pacheco, 2019).

Nevertheless, some patterns in the research literature are not well understood through a mobility narrative. The degree to which young people use social media to build large networks of bridging social capital varies around the world and depends on other relational structures in their cultural contexts. Research has shown that in social contexts outside the USA where it is less normative to sever old ties and form new ones such as in France (Brown & Michinov, 2017), Japan (Thomson et al., 2015), South Korea (Cho, 2010), and among Palestinians in Israel (Abbas & Mesch, 2015), adolescents and emerging adults tend to use social media to construct smaller and more intimate networks based on their face-to-face relationships. The problem of "context collapse" identified in the West as the mixing of multiple, distinct, and even unknown audiences on social network sites leading to the disintegration of contextual cues for self-presentation (boyd, 2008; Vitak, 2012) is a nonissue in southeast Turkey, where people use Facebook to construct multiple closed groups for social interaction and make extensive use of the private chat feature (Costa, 2018). Even adolescents and emerging adults in the USA and UK who construct large online networks tend to use social network sites to maintain connections with existing face-to-face contacts, rather than to meet new people and expand social horizons (Livingstone & Sefton-Green, 2016; Manago et al., 2012; Subrahmanyam et al., 2008).

Additionally, a networked structure of social ties is not endemic to the design of social media. On Renren in China and Cyworld and Kakaostory in Korea, relationships are organized in closed structures of concentric circles, and norms of reciprocity and mutual obligations are central to activities on the site (Hjorth, 2010; J. Y. Lee et al., 2016; Li & Chen, 2014). As social media continue to evolve and proliferate, youth are increasingly alternating between different platforms and tools to manage different kinds of relationships in an integrated environment of affordances, what Madianou and Miller (2013) call "polymedia" environments. For example, US college students use Twitter and Instagram to generate bridging social capital, Facebook for family, and Snapchat to increase intimacy with close others (Phua et al., 2017; Shane-Simpson et al., 2018) while Chinese international students use Facebook as a tool for generating bridging capital and Renren for maintaining connections to home life (Li & Chen, 2014).

Alternatives to a Mobility Narrative

Hampton (2016) proposes that *meta-modernity* is a better narrative metaphor for understanding social media and social structures in contemporary times. In his view, both individual mobility and social accountability are becoming amplified with social media. Communicative affordances for persistent contact and pervasive awareness are reinstating some preindustrial relational structures that counteract growing individual mobility. Mobile devices and social media amplify social obligations and commitments, making people constantly accessible in the present and to people of the past, connecting us *more permanently* across lifespans and generations. Indeed, studies with adolescents in Europe (Mascheroni & Vincent, 2016) and college students in the USA (Hall & Baym, 2012) exemplify how mobile phones have increased norms for perpetual communication, creating new pressures that promote dependence and satisfaction with close others but also feelings of overdependence and dissatisfaction. In addition, one-to-many forms of asynchronous communication via status updates on social media supply everlasting streams of social information that persist and scale (boyd, 2010), recreating the passive informal watchfulness of small, tight-knit communities where the audience is ambiguous and the watchers are also being watched (Hampton, 2016; Marwick, 2012). Pervasive awareness can be found in the ways youth often exhibit heightened conformity to community expectations for gender in their photographs on social media, whether those expectations involve carefully curating sexually attractive selfies in the south of Italy (Nicolescu, 2016) or upholding modesty and family honor in New Delhi (Mishra & Basu, 2014), rural China (McDonald, 2016), and southeast Turkey (Costa, 2016).

Another theoretical perspective is scalable sociality, posited by Miller and colleagues (2016) in a multivolume series of ethnographies on social media use in southeast Turkey, south Italy, northern Chile, south India, rural China, industrial China, emergent Brazil, an English village, and Trinidad. These authors argue that social media have "colonized a space of group sociality between the private and the public" (Miller et al., 2016, p. 286), introducing new structures of relations and genres of communication at various points on continuums from small groups and intimacy to large groups and publicness. To illustrate, Miller et al. show how 11- to 18-year-olds in the English village use dyadic mobile phone messages to talk to their best friends, Snapchat to develop trust in small groups, WhatsApp to communicate with classmates (often same-sex groups discussing other-sex classmates), Twitter to engage in school-wide banter, Facebook to interact with groups outside school such as family, neighbors, and workmates, and Instagram to entertain strangers with visual images. Sociality can also be scaled within a single platform through various functionalities (e.g., use of privacy settings) or through communication strategies themselves (e.g., social steganography – embedding private, hidden messages in public communication, Marwick & boyd, 2014).

Connecting the idea of scalable sociality back to cultural tools, we can see how social media would extend adolescents' capacities to develop skills for social relations at various scales of interaction.

Importantly, the consequences of social media for adolescent development depend on what is being scaled relative to youths' social contexts. Just as Facebook in the USA and QQ in China have scaled public broadcasting (e.g., TV, newspapers, radio) down to individuals contributing to large groups, WhatsApp in Latin America and WeChat in China have scaled intimacy up from face-to-face interactions and the telephone (Miller et al., 2016). In some cases, mobile devices and social media have intensified intimacy by creating new genres of intimate romantic relations, particularly in cultures with greater family mediation in romantic partnering such as south India (Venkatraman, 2016), rural China (McDonald, 2016), Muslim southeast Turkey (Costa, 2016), and in Zinacantán, Mexico (de Leon-Pasquel, 2018). Intimacy and mobility can also be scaled together as is the case with social media facilitating reinforcement of emotional bonds in cross-national families in Trinidad (Sinanan, 2017), allowing families to stay connected when miners are absent for long periods of time in Chile (Haynes, 2016), and helping migratory industrial workers maintain stable connections in industrial China (Wang, 2016). Social media also introduce new opportunities to reinforce and scale traditional social structures, such as in south India where symbolic kinship structures of extended families in caste traditions have become a metaphor for how youth arrange contacts on social media (Venkatraman, 2016). Counter to the linear direction of cultural change toward individualism in the mobility narrative, new scales of sociality may have unexpected consequences for psychological development. For example, Miller and colleagues (2016) found a new kind of openness to strangers with the introduction of social media in rural China but wariness of strangers through social media in Italy and England.

Summary

A mobility narrative may not be comprehensive enough to capture the multi-faceted structures of community that are evolving with the spread of digital tools. Digital tools afford customizable sociality and mobility, but also introduce new kinds of communities, as well as social pressures and constraints at different scales of interaction. Moreover, the ramifications of digital media for adolescent development depend on what is being scaled relative to youths' everyday lives, which is quite different across the globe and across groups in a multicultural society such as the USA. For example, social media create new opportunities for community and critical consciousness raising among racial and ethnic minority youth (Tynes et al., 2011) but also new capacities for racial and ethnic discrimination to occur (Lozada et al., 2021). For LGBTQ+ youth, social media are new avenues for intimacy (Marston, 2019) and also public visibility (Rubin & McClelland, 2015). As adolescents negotiate risks and opportunities at various scales of sociality they are learning new kinds of social skills adaptive for digitally mediated societies that contribute to their identity development and well-being.

The Culturally and Digitally Mediated Self

Western ideals and notions of personhood tend to dominate developmental science on the digitally mediated self. Optimistically, we see interactive media as offering enhanced opportunities for exploration, expression, reflection, and curation in the process of self-construction in the transition to adulthood (Ito et al., 2009; Manago et al., 2008). A more pessimistic view blames social media for narcissism in the USA and greater preoccupation with superficiality and external validation among young people (Twenge, 2013). As we hope to make clear in the following paragraphs, these opportunities and risks for self-development are not functions of digital tools themselves; instead, they reflect social constructions of digital media use, including hopes, fears, and expectations for how the self should be represented. In this section, we compare Western-based norms and meanings for digital self-presentation with those outside the West. This comparison will call into question universal claims about the impact of digital media on self-development and highlight how digital tools are used for both cultural reproduction and transformation.

Is Social Media an Identity Playground?

The popular *New Yorker* cartoon published in 1993, "on the internet nobody knows you're a dog," cleverly illustrates early perspectives in the USA regarding the Internet's impact on identity. Research at this time suggested that the disembodied nature of computer-mediated communication (i.e., reduced social cues, asynchrony, and geographical distance) would facilitate anonymity, pretense, exploration, and transcendence of offline limitations in self-presentations (McKenna & Bargh, 2000; Rodino, 1997; Turkle, 1997). But as the social media landscape evolved, becoming more visual and less anonymous (e.g., Facebook's real-name policy), concerns shifted to adolescents' self-disclosures and risks to their personal privacy (Livingstone, 2008; Tufekci, 2008). Research also began to emphasize how authenticity in combination with positive curation in online self-presentations generated audience support and greater self-regard (Marwick & boyd, 2011; Yang & Brown, 2016). Other studies, both in the USA and Europe, showed that the presentation of false selves online was an indication of lower degrees of identity synthesis (Michikyan et al., 2015) or a response to offline dysfunction, occurring at higher rates among lonely adolescents (Valkenburg & Peter, 2008) and those with poor social skills and social anxiety (Harman et al., 2005).

Ethnographic approaches during this period of time documented more nuanced combinations of authenticity and experimentation happening among adolescents online. Fieldwork in the USA (boyd, 2014) and the UK (Livingstone & Sefton-Green, 2016) captured the polymedia nature of adolescents' lived experiences with social media and how they were learning to express different sides of themselves depending on affordances for visibility and privacy in various social milieus. For example, Livingstone and Sefton-Green described how teenagers in a London secondary school used Tumblr to explore emerging facets of the self anonymously while using Facebook to perform "civil" selves that conformed to expectations of the school community and that engendered shallow social acceptance. Case studies of adolescents in the USA have also depicted different genres or conventions of participation across platforms including "hanging out," "messing around," and "geeking out" – the latter of which involves in-depth identity exploration of niche interests (Ito et al., 2009).

A different story of the digitally mediated self has emerged in South Korea and Japan. In South Korea, the first country in the world where widespread use of a social networking site (Cyworld) occurred among youth, digital self-presentation has not been about the exploration of new horizons but about the mundane (Hjorth, 2007; D. Lee, 2010). In her ethnographic research with university students in Korea in the early 2000s, Hjorth found Cyworld was used to create reels of everyday lived content that could be shared, mimicking the gift-giving in Korean culture that reinforces social ties. Youth used digital tools to capture the ordinary and thus deeply personal aspects of themselves to overcome, rather than exploit, the lack of social presence in computer-mediated communication. This finding is similar to studies with Japanese youth at this time who used early forms of social media to foster a new kind of co-presence and shared perspective of daily life, akin to the intimacy of being together without having to say anything (Ito & Okabe, 2005). The greater emphasis on tethering in these studies is also present in the language for digital tools; in contrast to the term "mobile phone" in the West that means a device that travels, the term "keitai" in Japan signifies a device connected to the body as an appendage, the emphasis on attachment (Ito et al., 2005). Similarly in Singapore, the term is "hand phone," suggesting alternative social constructions of self in relation to digital media that may reflect broad differences between Eastern and Western cultures.

A cross-cultural perspective on mobile devices and social media reveals how these tools are not generally used to escape social norms for self-representation but to conform to them. Kim and Papacharissi (2003) analyzed US and Korean Yahoo! Geocities home pages and found US virtual actors were more likely to present themselves with text-based communication and to describe themselves directly (i.e., stating personality traits) – a reflection of low-context communication in which independent selves transmit explicit and direct messages that can be separated from the context without loss of meaning. Korean virtual actors tended to communicate their identities through more ambiguous multimedia imagery – a reflection of high-context communication where interdependent selves are less direct and more implicit, relying on contextual factors to transmit meaning (see also Gudykunst et al., 1996). A departure from individualistic self-presentation norms of the USA has also been documented more recently in Turkey. Comparing Turkish and American adolescents' self-presentations on Facebook, researchers found adolescents in the USA were more likely to use promotion strategies in their self-representations, conforming to ideals for exalting the self, while those in Turkey tended to conform to Turkish ideals by presenting themselves through exemplification strategies that demonstrated their moral principles (Boz et al., 2016).

Conformity to gender norms on social media is widely observed in the research literature and further demonstrates how cultural expectations for self-presentation are projected to screens. Some researchers have interpreted consistent international gender differences in Facebook profiles (e.g., men present objects to convey status, women present family photos) as due to biology and natural selection (e.g., Tifferet & Vilanai-Yavets, 2014). However, this interpretation fails to recognize historical formations of the patriarchal arc that has spread east and west from the invention of the plow in the Middle East, and through colonization, shaping hierarchical gender relations in particular ways (Quinn, 2019). Within the patriarchal arc there are also cultural differences in gender that are translated into digitally mediated contexts. One content analysis comparing photos of US and Chinese athletes at the 2016 Rio Olympics on Twitter and Sina Weibo found that Chinese female athletes were more likely to incorporate smiling and a tilted head position compared to their Chinese male counterparts; US female athletes were more likely to depict themselves posed on a knee or body arched compared to their male counterparts, who tended to post photos of themselves upright (Xu & Armstrong, 2019). This study also found evidence of greater egalitarianism in US photos compared to Chinese photos, which could be due to the ongoing influence of Confucian ideals for male dominance in China and the attenuating effects of Title IX on male dominance in US sports.

Research on gender self-presentation via digital media reveals cultural continuity but also cultural change. Studies on Facebook use in Muslim cultural contexts show how young women resist traditional constraints such as sexual purity and responsibility for family reputation by segmenting their audiences on social media (Al-Saggaf, 2011; Shen & Khalifa, 2010). One interview study with Muslim university students in New Delhi found that young women negotiated multiple audiences on Facebook, presenting themselves as "nice" and virtuous to uphold their family's honor but also using privacy settings to restrict surveillance and judgment from more conservative parts of their kin networks and express themselves outside traditional norms (Mishra & Basu, 2014). Similarly, ethnographic research in South Korea describes how young women presented themselves on their Cyworld mini-homepages to achieve conventional patriarchal definitions of submissive female beauty in South Korea; yet, in the process of framing, editing, manipulating, and curating their images, the young women also took control of the gaze, which opened up new experiences of power in their identity development (D. Lee, 2005).

Is the Selfie Narcissistic?

A variety of studies have found associations between narcissistic personality traits and social media use, mostly among college students on Facebook but also among social media users in China, Japan, Europe, Australia, and Russia (see meta-analysis by McCain & Campbell, 2018). The assumption in the framing and interpretation of these studies is that posting photos and status updates on social media is ultimately self-promotional and therefore cultivates an unrealistic, self-serving, entitled, and inflated sense of self as special and unique (Gentile et al., 2012). The so-called selfie, a photo taken by the self of the self, has been an emblem of this assumption, construed as an indication of vanity and often employed to accuse young women of self-indulgence, triviality, and attention-seeking (Burns, 2015).

International research has brought to light the existence of alternative paradigms surrounding the selfie that likely have very different consequences for youth self-development. In a favela of Brazil, adolescents post selfies on Facebook to reflect on themselves and the violence in their neighborhoods and to send a signal to their parents (who regularly check the site) that they are safe as they navigate daily life (Nemer & Freeman, 2015). Selfies in this context are not fostering narcissism but instead helping youth contest the power and surveillance of local drug lords. The banal self-portraits that Japanese and South Korean youth exchanged in early iterations of social media created ongoing togetherness in daily life, not inflated sense of selves (Hjorth, 2007; Ito & Okabe, 2005; D. Lee, 2010). However, relational selfies are not just found outside of WEIRD contexts. American and British university students also use selfies relationally when they exchange unedited and disappearing images on Snapchat as a form of intimate conversation; as one participant in a study said, "I've literally had a ten-minute conversation with my friend just doing facial expressions" (Katz & Crocker, 2015, p. 1869). Katz and Crocker report that Chinese university students used WeChat in similar ways but instead of facial expressions, animations symbolizing emotions and actions were used to maintain visual conversations. It is impossible to disentangle whether this observed difference is due to the alternative affordances via Snapchat versus WeChat or due to cultural differences in ideals for emotional expression (see Tsai, 2017).

Understandably, selfies in more public social media contexts tend to involve greater deliberation and curation. But does crafting favorable social impressions through selfies in more public contexts equate to an unrealistic and inflated sense of self? In their compilation of international ethnographies, Miller and colleagues (2016) show that, indeed, posting idealized versions of the self occurred throughout their field sites; yet what the ideal looks like and what it means to people vary widely. While young factory workers in industrial China posted aspirational photos of economic wealth and consumption on the platform QQ, their counterparts in rural China posted photos of family life that combined collectivistic (gratitude to elders) and individualistic (romantic love) aspirations. Selfies among evangelicals in their Brazilian field site showcased material wealth to signify one's religiosity, and in Trinidad, to demonstrate the virtue of hard work. Sometimes the ideal self, such as those presented in selfies in Chile and in an English village, was about demonstrating authenticity through conformity to the ordinary. The authors describe the "footsie" version of the selfie that was popular in Chile where photographers take photos of their feet in a lounging position watching television or playing video games. The footsie is curated to communicate authenticity out of casualness. The footsie would not travel well to Chinese selfie celebrity culture, where photoshopping is an expected and normative courtesy such that *not* using software editing applications to enhance one's images and those of one's friends is considered impolite (see Fan, 2017).

Summary

This section illustrates that social media are not generally used to escape norms and construct an inflated sense of self but instead, to construct a self in line with cultural norms and ideals. Universal claims about the impacts of digital media on adolescent self-development are problematic because norms and ideals for online self-presentation differ across cultures. In a multicultural society such as the USA, race, class, and gender shape how adolescents present themselves through social media and how those self-presentations are interpreted and evaluated (e.g., Daniels & Zurbriggen, 2016; Kapidzic & Herring, 2015). Senft and Baym (2015) argue that although selfies are an expression of human agency, they are also "created, displayed, distributed, tracked, and monetized through an assemblage of nonhuman agents" (p. 1589). Once an image is digitized, it takes up space in the "digital superpublic" and persists outside of the context in which it was first produced, shared, and viewed. As adolescents negotiate online self-presentations and make decisions about who they are and how they want to appear, they contribute to the cultural artefacts circulating in their communities.

Challenges and Future Directions in the Study of Culture and Digital Media

Digital media are cultural tools that at once reflect the cultural values and biases of the creators (Manago et al., 2022) and whose use is shaped by the cultural values of the users (McKenzie et al., 2019). As reflected in this chapter, adolescents and emerging adults – who lead digital and social media use around the world (Pew Research Center, 2019; Silver et al., 2019) – also contribute to cultural change through their media use. Given the inherently cultural nature of digital media, foregrounding culture in media studies is critical.

Cultural Challenges

Popular discourse and research articles alike are awash with broad claims about how digital and social media affect teens (e.g., Crone & Konijn, 2018; Schrobsdorff, 2016; Twenge, 2017), without adequately attending to how culture shapes media use and its effects. When culture is attended to by media scholars, it is often treated as synonymous with "nation." This treatment of nations as monolithic cultural entities is problematic for media studies, as significant within-nation heterogeneity exists in media access and use, and in its effects on adolescents (McKenzie et al., 2022; Sheldon et al., 2020). Although within-culture variation sometimes exceeds between-culture variation (Sheldon et al., 2020), digital media research that takes culture into account typically ignores variations within cultural groups (Cardon et al., 2009). In our increasingly multicultural world, we must go beyond investigating the influence of national culture to examine the roles of ethnicity, race, religion, generation, and geographic location in adolescent digital media use and its consequences. With globalization, we must also consider processes of remote acculturation that may increasingly apply to European-American youth (i.e., the rising popularity of K-pop in the USA) and the unique perspectives of immigrant and bicultural youth, who are negotiating multiple worldviews across different social media platforms (Bae, 2010; Bae-Dimitriadis, 2015).

Another cultural challenge is that adolescent digital media use is typically examined in wealthy nations with more established digital media integration. Findings from these populations tend to be interpreted in terms of a universal biologically governed individual, which masks the way that culture is operating in the West. Moreover, a significant gap exists in our understanding of digital media use and its influence on adolescents in poorer nations experiencing a rapid rise in digital media integration. For example, adolescent media use studies in the Middle East overwhelmingly focus on Israel (e.g., Abu Aleon et al., 2019; Mesch, 2006), a high-income economy with a 451% internet growth rate from 2000 to 2021; far less is known about media use in low-income Yemen (with a staggering 52,592% internet growth rate during that time) and in middle-income Iraq and Iran (with 196,100% and 31,135% internet growth rates during that time, respectively) (Internet Usage in the Middle East, 2021). In nations with a dramatic rise in digital media integration, such as Yemen, Iraq, and Iran, we are likely to see cultural clashes between values promoted by digital media (e.g., individualism, self-expression, and stimulation) and indigenous cultural values. Such clashes, in turn, likely reshape adolescent development, well-being, and intergenerational relation-ships in these nations in rather profound ways. Alternatively, adolescents in these regions may be using social media as cultural tools to reproduce and reshape culture. These possibilities should be of great interest to adolescent media scholars, as an estimated 84% of the world's population reside in low- and middle-income countries experiencing a rapid rise in digital media use among youth (Ortiz-Ospina, 2017; Silver et al., 2019).

Finally, cultural and cross-cultural adolescent media scholars are tasked with prioritizing youth perspectives. Though helpful, survey-based research typically enters with a priori assumptions about what constitutes risk and opportunity, what identity development looks or should look like, what friendship looks like, what well-being looks like, and so on. But conceptions of risk and opportunity are culturally constructed (Manago & Pacheco, 2019; McKenzie et al., 2022); so too are pathways of identity development (e.g., Sugimura, 2020), definitions of and meanings ascribed to friendship (e.g., French, 2015), and conceptions of well-being (Weisner, 2014). Tuning ourselves to the meanings that adolescents themselves ascribe to these concepts is a critical starting point in furthering our understanding of digital media use and its consequences across diverse cultural communities. Doing so will push us to particularize our claims about how digital and social media affect adolescents and ensure that our research aligns with the lived realities of those we aim to represent.

Future Directions

To address the challenges raised above, media scholars must work to under-stand how culture operates in the lives of adolescents, and how culture structures their digital media use and perspectives of digital media. To be sure, experimental, survey-based, and quantitative approaches to cross-cultural studies of adolescent media offer important insights. The work of Hansen and colleagues, for example, illustrated that cultural panic about the eradication of traditional values with the integration of new media are not entirely founded, as traditional Ethiopian values are not threatened by (Hansen et al., 2012) and even increase with (Hansen et al., 2014) the intro-duction of laptops. This begs an important question, though: Why is this the case? In order to understand the processes whereby cultural values change via, and are maintained through, media use, ethnographic research that fore-grounds culture and works to understand how it interacts with digital and social media in the lives of young people will provide invaluable insights.

Cultural foregrounding at each stage of studying adolescent media use – including study design, data collection instruments and procedures, and inter-pretation – is also essential. This requires that researchers calibrate to, and design measures and materials that are grounded in an understanding of local cultural norms, which may be in flux. Such cultural attunement may require that qualitative data collection methodologies (e.g., interviews, focus groups, social network mapping) be used in place of surveys. This is likely to be especially important when researchers are interacting with marginalized populations in multicultural societies, such as racial, ethnic, sexual, and gender minority youth who may operate on a different set of assumptions from researchers. Such methods are also generally useful for cross-cultural examinations of adolescent digital media use, given the potential for cross-cultural differences in survey response styles to be mistakenly interpreted as cultural differences in the measures being compared (Johnson et al., 2010). This cultural foregrounding is promising in deepening our understanding of the diverse experiences adolescents have with digital media.

Conversely, we must consider how cultural change is inhibited – and adolescent development is controlled – by governments through digital and social media. This is achieved by way of broad-scale internet bans, censorship, and mass surveillance. In North Korea, for example, the government allows only tightly controlled domestic intranet (King, 2019). In Iran, government-issued internet blackouts aim to quell internal unrest and protest (Wolff, 2019). It is also achieved by denying and controlling the use of certain social media platforms. Iran, China, and North Korea have a 100% ban on Facebook (Frenkel, 2018; King, 2019; Leskin, 2019); China further bans Instagram, WhatsApp, Twitter, Snapchat, Reddit, Pinterest, YouTube, and Google (Leskin, 2019). Finally, it is achieved by using digital media to surveil its citizens and reassert cultural values. Egypt, for instance, has come under international spotlight in recent years for police use of dating apps to locate, imprison, and torture LGBT citizens (AP News, 2020; Culzac, 2014) – thereby limiting sexual expression and exploration and enforcing homophobia. China's "social credit" system also restricts freedom of expression by using social media surveillance to reassert cultural values of collectivism, conformity, and reputation maintenance (Chen & Zhou, 2019; Wong & Dobson, 2019). In 2019, 23 million Chinese citizens were banned from traveling due to poor social credit scores (Reisinger, 2019). Also in the West, digital algorithms encode and perpetuate racial inequalities (Benjamin, 2019) while media companies are increasingly exploiting personal data for profit, trading on human behavioral futures in what Zuboff (2019) calls "surveillance capitalism." Each example provided here serves to limit or deny intercultural and intracultural contact, thereby inhibiting cultural change and limiting youth agency over their own development.

We set out in this chapter to explore how digital media are cultural tools in adolescent social development. In bringing together alternative cultural perspectives on digital media use and adolescents' values, social ties, and self-development, we have begun to shed light on cultural processes in digital media use that often go unacknowledged in developmental psychology research with WEIRD samples. By examining international research and questioning dominant Western paradigms, we hope to inspire more contextual and critical approaches to understanding the effects of social media for adolescent development.

References

Abbas, R., & Mesch, G. S. (2015). Cultural values and Facebook use among Palestinian youth in Israel. *Computers in Human Behavior*, *48*, 644–653.

Abu Aleon, T., Weinstock, M., Manago, A. M., & Greenfield, P. M. (2019). Social change and intergenerational value differences in a Bedouin community in Israel. *Journal of Cross-Cultural Psychology*, *50*, 708–727.

Al-Saggaf, Y. (2011). Saudi females on Facebook: An ethnographic study. *International Journal of Emerging Technologies and Society*, *9*(1), 1–19.

Antheunis, M. L., Schouten, A. P., & Krahmer, E. (2016). The role of social networking sites in early adolescents' social lives. *Journal of Early Adolescence*, *36*(3), 348–371.

Antonucci, T. C. (1986). Social support networks: A hierarchical mapping technique. *Generations*, *10*(4), 10–12.

AP News. (2020, October 1). *Egypt police arbitrarily arrest, torture LGBT people.* https://bit.ly/3iGdAEU

Asemah, E. S., Ekhareafo, D. O., & Olaniran, S. (2013). Nigeria's core values and the use of social media to promote cultural values. *International Journal of Information and Communication Technology Education*, *9*(4), 58–69.

Bae, M. S. (2010). Go Cyworld! Korean diasporic girls producing new Korean femininity. In S. R. Mazzarella (Ed.), *Girl wide web 2.0: Revisiting girls, the internet and the negotiation of identity* (pp. 91–116). Peter Lang.

Bae-Dimitriadis, M. (2015) Performing "planned authenticity": Diasporic Korean girls' self-photographic play. *Studies in Art Education*, *56*(4), 327–340.

Benjamin, R. (2019). Assessing risk, automating racism. *Science*, *366*(6464), 421–422.

boyd, d. (2008). Facebook's privacy trainwreck: Exposure, invasion, and social convergence. *Convergence*, *14*(1), 13–20.

boyd, d. (2010). Social network sites as networked publics: Affordances, dynamics, and implications. In Z. Papacharissi (Ed.), *Networked self: identity, community, and culture on social network sites* (pp. 39–58). Routledge.

boyd, d. (2014). *It's complicated: The social lives of networked teens.* Yale University Press.

Boz, N., Uhls, Y. T., & Greenfield, P. M. (2016). Cross-cultural comparison of adolescents' online self-presentation strategies: Turkey and the United States. *International Journal of Cyber Behavior, Psychology and Learning (IJCBPL)*, *6*(3), 1–16.

Brandtzaeg, P. (2012). Social networking sites: Their users and social implications – A longitudinal study. *Journal of Computer-Mediated Communication*, *17*(4), 467–488.

Brown, G., & Michinov, N. (2017). Cultural differences in garnering social capital on Facebook: French people prefer close ties and Americans prefer distant ties. *Journal of Intercultural Communication Research*, *46*(6), 579–593.

Burns, A. L. (2015). Self(ie)-discipline: Social regulation as enacted through the discussion of photographic practice. *International Journal of Communication*, *9*, 1716–1733.

Cardon, P. W., Marshall, B., Choi, J., et al. (2009). Online and offline social ties of social network website users: An exploratory study in eleven societies. *Journal of Computer Information Systems*, *50*(1), 54–64.

Castells, M. (1996). *The rise of the network society*. Blackwell.

Chen, S. H., & Zhou, Q. (2019). Cultural values, social status, and Chinese American immigrant parents' emotional expressivity. *Journal of Cross-Cultural Psychology*, *50*(3), 381–395.

Cho, S. E. (2010). *Cross-cultural comparison of Korean and American social network sites: Exploring cultural differences in social relationships and self-presentation* [Doctoral dissertation, Rutgers University-Graduate School-New Brunswick].

Cole, M., & Scribner S. (1978). Introduction. In M. Cole, S. Scribner, V. John-Steiner, & E. Souberman (Eds.), *Mind in society* (pp. 1–15). Harvard University Press.

Costa, E. (2016). *Social media in Southeast Turkey: Love, kinship and politics*. UCL Press.

Costa, E. (2018). Affordances-in-practice: An ethnographic critique of social media logic and context collapse. *New Media & Society*, *20*(10), 3641–3656.

Crone, E. A., & Konijn, E. A. (2018). Media use and brain development during adolescence. *Nature Communications*, *9*, 1–10.

Culzac, N. (2014, September 17). Egypt's police 'using social media and apps like Grindr to trap gay people.' *Independent*. https://bit.ly/2GA6ViL

Daniels, E. A., & Zurbriggen, E. L. (2016). The price of sexy: Viewers' perceptions of a sexualized versus nonsexualized Facebook profile photograph. *Psychology of Popular Media Culture*, *5*(1), 2–14.

de León-Pasquel, L. (2018). Between romantic texting and Ethnorock on YouTube: Repertoires of identity in the virtual landscapes of Tsotsil Mayan youth. *Revista LiminaR. Estudios Sociales y Humanísticos*, *16*(1), 40–55.

Donath, J. (2008). Signals in social supernets. *Journal of Computer-Mediated Communication*, *13*(1), 231–251.

Ellison, N. B., Steinfield, C., & Lampe, C. (2007). The benefits of Facebook "friends": Social capital and college students' use of online social network sites. *Journal of Computer-Mediated Communication*, *12*(4), 1143–1168.

Erikson, E. H. (1963). *Childhood and society* (2nd ed.). Norton.

Fan, J. (2017, December 18). China's selfie obsession. *The New Yorker*. https://www.newyorker.com/magazine/2017/12/18/chinas-selfie-obsession

Ferguson, G. M., & Bornstein, M. H. (2012). Remote acculturation: The "Americanization" of Jamaican islanders. *International Journal of Behavioral Development*, *36*(3), 167–177.

Ferguson, G. M., & Bornstein, M. H. (2015). Remote acculturation of early adolescents in Jamaica towards European American culture: A replication and extension. *International Journal of Intercultural Relations*, *45*, 24–35.

French, D. (2015). Cultural templates for child and adolescent friendships. In L. A. Jensen (Ed.), *The Oxford handbook of human development and culture: An interdisciplinary perspective* (pp. 425–437). Oxford University Press.

Frenkel, S. (2018, January 2). Iranian authorities block access to social media tools. *The New York Times*. https://nyti.ms/3jEgv2k

Gentile, B., Twenge, J. M., Freeman, E. C., & Campbell, W. K. (2012). The effect of social networking websites on positive self-views: An experimental investigation. *Computers in Human Behavior*, *28*(5), 1929–1933.

Granovetter, M. S. (1973). The strength of weak ties. *American Journal of Sociology*, *78*(6), 1360–1380.

Greenfield, P. M. (2009). Linking social change and developmental change: Shifting pathways of human development. *Developmental Psychology, 45*(2), 401–418.

Gudykunst, W. B., Matsumoto, Y., Ting-Toomey, S., Nishida, T., Kim, K., & Heyman, S. (1996). The influence of cultural individualism-collectivism, self construals, and individual values on communication styles across cultures. *Human Communication Research, 22*(2), 510–543.

Hall, J. A., & Baym, N. K. (2012). Calling and texting (too much): Mobile maintenance expectations, (over) dependence, entrapment, and friendship satisfaction. *New Media & Society, 14*(2), 316–331.

Hampton, K. (2016). Persistent and pervasive community: New communication technologies and the future of community. *American Behavioral Scientist, 60,* 101–124.

Hansen, N., Postmes, T., Tovote, K. A., & Bos, A. (2014). How modernization instigates social change: Laptop usage as a driver of cultural value change and gender equality in a developing country. *Journal of Cross-Cultural Psychology, 45*(8), 1229–1248.

Hansen, N., Postmes, T., van der Vinne, N., & van Thiel, W. (2012). Technology and cultural change: How ITC changes self-construal and values. *Social Psychology, 43*(4), 222–231.

Harman, J. P., Hansen, C. E., Cochran, M. E., & Lindsey, C. R. (2005). Liar, liar: Internet faking but not frequency of use affects social skills, self-esteem, social anxiety, and aggression. *CyberPsychology & Behavior, 8,* 1–6.

Haynes, N. (2016). *Social media in Northern Chile: Posting the extraordinarily ordinary.* UCL Press.

Henrich, J., Heine, S. J., & Norenzayan, A. (2010). The weirdest people in the world? *Behavioral and Brain Sciences, 33*(2–3), 61–83.

Hermans, H. J., & Dimaggio, G. (2007). Self, identity, and globalization in times of uncertainty: A dialogical analysis. *Review of General Psychology, 11*(1), 31–61.

Hjorth, L. (2007). Snapshots of almost contact: The rise of camera phone practices and a case study in Seoul, Korea. *Continuum, 21*(2), 227–238.

Hjorth, L. (2010). The game of being social: Web 2.0, social media, and online games. *Iowa Journal of Communication, 42*(1), 73–92.

Hutchby, I. (2001). Technologies, texts and affordances. *Sociology, 35*(2), 441–456.

Internet Usage in the Middle East. (2021, May 27). *Internet world stats: Usage and population statistics.* Retrieved March 10, 2022, from https://bit.ly/2I8jL8r

Internet Usage Statistics. (2022, March 8). *Internet world stats: Usage and population statistics.* Retrieved March 10, 2022, from https://bit.ly/34xUfky

Ito, M., Baumer, S., Bittanti, M., et al. (2009). *Hanging out, messing around, and geeking out: Kids living and learning with new media.* MIT Press.

Ito, M., Matsuda, M., & Okabe, D. (2005). *Personal, portable, pedestrian: Mobile phones in Japanese life.* MIT Press.

Ito, M., & Okabe, D. (2005). *Intimate visual co-presence.* Paper presented at UbiComp 2005, Takanawa Prince Hotel, Tokyo, 11–14 September. http://www.itofisher.com/mito/

Johnson, T., Shavitt, S., & Holbrook, A. (2010). Survey response styles across cultures. In D. Matsumoto & F. Van de Vijver (Eds.), *Cross-cultural research methods in psychology* (pp. 130–176). Cambridge University Press.

Johnston, K., Tanner, M., Lalla, N., & Kawalski, D. (2013) Social capital: The benefit of Facebook 'friends.' *Behaviour & Information Technology*, *32*(1), 24–36.

Kapidzic, S., & Herring, S. C. (2015). Race, gender, and self-presentation in teen profile photographs. *New Media & Society*, *17*(6), 958–976.

Katz, J. E., & Crocker, E. T. (2015). Selfies and photo messaging as visual conversation: Reports from the United States, United Kingdom and China. *International Journal of Communication*, *9*, 1861–1872.

Kim, H., & Papacharissi, Z. (2003). Cross-cultural differences in online self-presentation: A content analysis of personal Korean and US home pages. *Asian Journal of Communication*, *13*(1), 100–119.

King, R. R. (2019, May 15). North Koreans want external information, but Kim Jong-Un seeks to limit access. *Center for Strategic and International Studies*. https://bit.ly/3nlK6jk

Kling, R. (2007). What is social informatics and why does it matter? *The Information Society*, *23*(4), 205–220.

Lee, D. (2005). Women's creation of camera phone culture. *Fibreculture Journal*, *6*(6), 1–11.

Lee, D. (2010). Digital cameras, personal photography and the reconfiguration of spatial experiences. *The Information Society*, *26*(4), 266–275.

Lee, J. Y., Park, S., Na, E., & Kim, E., (2016). A comparative study on the relationship between social networking site use and social capital among Australian and Korean youth. *Journal of Youth Studies*, *19*(9), 1164–1183.

Leskin, P. (2019, October 10). Here are all the major US tech companies blocked behind China's 'Great Firewall.' *Business Insider*. https://bit.ly/2SxDRe8

Levinson, A. M., & Barron, B. (2018). Latino immigrant families learning with digital media across settings and generations. *Digital Education Review*, *33*, 150–169.

Li, X., & Chen, W. (2014). Facebook or Renren? A comparative study of social networking site use and social capital among Chinese international students in the United States. *Computers in Human Behavior*, *35*, 116–123.

Liu, H., Shi, J., Liu, Y., & Sheng, Z. (2013). The moderating role of attachment anxiety on social network site use intensity and social capital. *Psychological Reports: Relationships & Communication*, *112*(1), 252–265.

Livingstone, S. (2008). Taking risky opportunities in youthful content creation: Teenagers' use of social networking sites for intimacy, privacy and self-expression. *New Media & Society*, *10*(3), 393–411.

Livingston, S., & Sefton-Green, J. (2016). *The class: Living and learning in the digital age*. New York University Press.

Lozada, F. T., Seaton, E. K., Williams, C. D., & Tynes, B. M. (2021). Exploration of bidirectionality in African American and Latinx adolescents' offline and online ethnic-racial discrimination. *Cultural Diversity and Ethnic Minority Psychology*, *27*(3), 386–396.

Madianou, M., & Miller, D. (2013). Polymedia: Towards a new theory of digital media in interpersonal communication. *International Journal of Cultural Studies*, *16*(2), 169–187.

Manago, A. M., Graham, M. B., Greenfield, P. M., & Salimkhan, G. (2008). Self-presentation and gender on MySpace. *Journal of Applied Developmental Psychology*, *29*(6), 446–458.

Manago, A. M., & Pacheco, P. (2019). Globalization and the transition to adulthood in a Maya community in Mexico: Communication technologies, social networks, and views on gender. [In J. McKenzie (Ed.), Globalization as a Context for Youth Development Special Issue] *New Directions for Child and Adolescent Development*, 164, 11–25.

Manago, A. M., Santer, N. D., Barsigian, L. L., & Walsh, A. S. (2022). Social media as tools for cultural change in the transition to adulthood. In K. C. McLean (Ed.), *Cultural methods in psychology: Describing and transforming cultures* (pp. 146–173). Oxford University Press.

Manago, A., Taylor, T., & Greenfield, P. (2012). Me and my 400 friends: The anatomy of college students' Facebook networks, their communication patterns, and well-being. *Developmental Psychology*, 48(2), 369–380.

Manago, A. M., & Vaughn, L. (2015). Social media, friendship and happiness in the millennial generation. In M. Demir (Ed.), *Friendship and happiness: Across the lifespan and in different cultures* (pp. 187–206). Springer.

Mariek, M. P., Vanden, A., Marjolijn, L. A., et al. (2018). Does Facebook use predict college students' social capital? A replication of Ellison, Steinfield, and Lampe's (2007) study using the original and more recent measures of Facebook use and social capital. *Communication Studies*, 69(3), 272–282.

Marston, K. (2019). Researching LGBT+ youth intimacies and social media: The strengths and limitations of participant-led visual methods. *Qualitative Inquiry*, 25(3), 278–288.

Marwick, A. (2012). The public domain: Surveillance in everyday life. *Surveillance & Society*, 9(4), 378–393.

Marwick, A. E., & boyd, d. (2011). I tweet honestly, I tweet passionately: Twitter users, context collapse, and the imagined audience. *New Media & Society*, 13(1), 114–133.

Marwick, A. E., & boyd, d. (2014). Networked privacy: How teenagers negotiate context in social media. *New Media & Society*, 16(7), 1051–1067.

Mascheroni, G., & Vincent, J. (2016). Perpetual contact as a communicative affordance: Opportunities, constraints, and emotions. *Mobile Media & Communication*, 4(3), 310–326.

Maynard, A. E., Subrahmanyam, K., & Greenfield, P. M. (2005). Technology and the development of intelligence. In R. J. Sternberg & D. Preiss (Eds.), *Intelligence and technology: The impact of tools on the nature and development of human abilities* (pp. 54–97). Erlbaum.

McCain, J. L., & Campbell, W. K. (2018). Narcissism and social media use: A meta-analytic review. *Psychology of Popular Media Culture*, 7(3), 308–327.

McDonald, T. (2016). *Social media in Rural China*. UCL Press.

McKenna, K. Y. A., & Bargh, J. A. (2000). Plan 9 from Cyberspace: The implications of the internet for personality and social psychology. *Personality and Social Psychology Review*, 4(1), 57–75.

McKenzie, J. (2019). Shifting practices, shifting selves: Negotiations of local and global cultures among adolescents in northern Thailand. *Child Development*, 90(6), 2035–2052.

McKenzie, J. (2020). Negotiating local and global values in a globalized world: The envisioned futures of Thai adolescents. *Journal of Research on Adolescence*, 30(4), 856–874.

McKenzie, J., Castellón, R., Willis-Grossmann, E., Landeros, C., Rooney, J., & Stewart, C. (2022). Digital divides and dyadic gaps: A portrait of media use and perspectives of media in Thailand. [Under review].

McKenzie, J., Rooney, J., Stewart, C., Castellón, R., Landeros, C., & Willis, E. (2019). Brokering culture and power in a media-driven world: Parents of adolescents in northern Thailand. *Journal of Cross-Cultural Psychology*, *50*, 972–990.

Mesch, G. S. (2006). The family and the internet: Exploring a social boundaries approach. *Journal of Family Communication*, *6*(2), 119–138.

Michikyan, M., Dennis, J., & Subrahmanyam, K. (2015). Can you guess who I am? Real, ideal, and false self-presentation on Facebook among emerging adults. *Emerging Adulthood*, *3*(1), 55–64.

Miller, D., Sinanan, J., Wang, X., et al. (2016). *How the world changed social media.* UCL Press.

Mishra, S., & Basu, S. (2014). Family honor, cultural norms, and social networking: Strategic choices in the visual self-presentation of young Indian Muslim women. *Cyberpsychology: Journal of Psychosocial Research on Cyberspace*, *8*, Article 3.

Nemer, D., & Freeman, G. (2015). Empowering the marginalized: Rethinking selfies in the slums of Brazil. *International Journal of Communication*, *9*(1), 1832–1847.

Nicolescu, R. (2016). *Social media in Southeast Italy.* UCL Press.

Ortiz-Ospina, E. (2017, February 22). *Children and poverty: Evidence from new World Bank data.* Our World in Data. https://bit.ly/33CjpPu

Pathak-Shelat, M., & DeShano, C. (2014). Digital youth cultures in small town and rural Gujarat, India. *New Media & Society*, *16*(6), 983–1001.

Pew Research Center. (2019, June 12). *Social media fact sheet.* https://pewrsr.ch/30KLm5V

Phua, J., Jin, S. V., & Kim, J. J. (2017). Uses and gratifications of social networking sites for bridging and bonding social capital: A comparison of Facebook, Twitter, Instagram, and Snapchat. *Computers in Human Behavior*, *72*, 115–122.

Poushter, J., Bishop, C., & Chwe, H. (2018, June 19). *Social media use continues to rise in developing countries but plateaus across developed ones.* Pew Research Center. https://pewrsr.ch/30KH3rh

Quinn, N. (2019). Historical circumstances and biological proclivities surrounding patriarchy. In H. Mathews & A. Manago (Eds.), *The psychology of women under patriarchy* (pp. 31–50). SAR Press.

Rainie, L., & Wellman, B. (2012). *Networked: The new social operating system.* MIT Press.

Rao, M. A., Berry, R., Gonsalves, A., Hastak, Y., Shah, M., & Roeser, R. W. (2013). Globalization and the *identity remix* among urban adolescents in India. *Journal of Research on Adolescence*, *23*(1), 9–24.

Raza, S. A., Qazi, W., & Umer, A. (2017). Facebook is a source of social capital building among university students: Evidence from a developing country. *Journal of Educational Computing Research*, *55*(3), 295–322.

Reisinger, D. (2019, February 22). China banned 23 million people from traveling last year for poor 'social credit' scores. *Fortune*. https://bit.ly/30Ip9Fv

Rickman, A. (2018). *Adolescence, girlhood, and media migration: US teens' use of social media to negotiate offline struggles.* Lexington Books.

Rideout, V. J., & Katz, V. S. (2016). *Opportunity for all? Technology and learning in lower-income families.* A report of the Families and Media Project. The Joan Ganz Cooney Center at Sesame Workshop.

Rodino, M. (1997). Breaking out of binaries: Reconceptualizing gender and its relationship to language in computer-mediated communication. *Journal of Computer-Mediated Communication, 3*(3), JCMC333.

Rubin, J. D., & McClelland, S. I. (2015). 'Even though it's a small checkbox, it's a big deal': Stresses and strains of managing sexual identity(s) on Facebook. *Culture, Health & Sexuality, 17*(4), 512–526.

Senft, T. M., & Baym, N. K. (2015). What does the selfie say? Investigating a global phenomenon. *International Journal of Communication, 9*, 1588–1606.

Schrobsdorff, S. (2016, October 27). Teen depression and anxiety: Why the kids are not alright. *Time.* https://bit.ly/3jGr4Sv

Shane-Simpson, C., Manago, A., Gaggi, N., & Gillespie-Lynch, K. (2018). Why do college students prefer Facebook, Twitter, or Instagram? Site affordances, tensions between privacy and self-expression, and implications for social capital. *Computers in Human Behavior, 86*, 276–288.

Sheldon, P., Herzfeldt, E., & Rauschnabel, P. A. (2020). Culture and social media: The relationship between cultural values and hashtagging styles. *Behaviour & Information Technology, 39*(7), 758–770.

Shen, K. N., & Khalifa, M. (2010). *Facebook usage among Arabic college students: Preliminary findings on gender differences.* University of Wollongong Research Online. http://ro.uow.edu.au/cgi/viewcontent.cgi?article=1074&context=dubaipapers

Silver, L., Smith, A., Johnson, C., Jiang, J., Anderson, M., & Rainie, L. (2019, March 7). *Use of smartphones and social media is common across most emerging economies.* Pew Research Center. https://pewrsr.ch/2SCSMDL

Sinanan, J. (2017). *Social media in Trinidad.* UCL Press.

Subrahmanyam, K., Reich, S. M., Waechter, N., & Espinoza, G. (2008). Online and offline social networks: Use of social networking sites by emerging adults. *Journal of Applied Developmental Psychology, 29*(6), 420–433.

Sugimura, K. (2020). Adolescent identity development in Japan. *Child Development Perspectives, 14*(2), 71–77.

Thomson, R., Yuki, M., & Ito, N. (2015). A socio-ecological approach to national differences in online privacy concern: The role of relational mobility and trust. *Computers in Human Behavior, 51*, 285–292.

Tifferet, S., & Vilnai-Yavetz, I. (2014). Gender differences in Facebook self-presentation: An international randomized study. *Computers in Human Behavior, 35*, 388–399.

Tsai, J. L. (2017). Ideal affect in daily life: Implications for affective experience, health, and social behavior. *Current Opinion in Psychology, 17*, 118–128.

Tufekci, Z. (2008). Can you see me now? Audience and disclosure regulation in online social network sites. *Bulletin of Science Technology & Society, 28*(1), 20–36.

Turkle, S. (1997). *Life on the screen: Identity in the age of the internet.* Simon & Schuster.

Twenge. J. M. (2013). Does online social media lead to social connection or social disconnection?. *Journal of College and Character, 14*(1), 11–20.

Twenge, J. M. (2017). *iGen: Why today's super-connected kids are growing up less rebellious, less happy – and completely unprepared for adulthood.* Simon & Schuster.

Twenge, J. M., Martin, G. N., & Spitzberg, B. H. (2019). Trends in U.S. adolescents' media use, 1976–2016: The rise of digital media, the decline of TV, and the (near) demise of print. *Psychology of Popular Media Culture, 8*(4), 329–345.

Tynes, B. M., Garcia, E. L., Giang, M. T., & Coleman, N. E. (2011). The racial landscape of social network sites: Forging identity, community, and civic engagement. *I/S: A Journal of Law and Policy for the Information Society, 7,* 71–100.

Valkenburg, P., & Peter, J. (2008). Adolescents' identity experiments on the internet: Consequences for social competence and self-concept unity. *Communication Research, 35*(2), 208–231.

Vanden Abeele, M. M. P. (2016). Mobile lifestyles: Conceptualizing heterogeneity in mobile youth culture. *New Media & Society, 18*(6), 908–926.

Venkatraman, S. (2016). *Social media in South India.* UCL Press.

Vitak, J. (2012). The impact of context collapse and privacy on social network site disclosures. *Journal of Broadcasting & Electronic Media, 56*(4), 451–470.

Wang, X. (2016). *Social media in industrial China.* UCL Press.

Weisner, T. S. (2014). Culture, context, and child well-being. In A. Ben-Arieh, F. Casas, I. Frønes, & J. Korbin (Eds.), *Handbook of child well-being* (pp. 87–103). Springer.

Wellman, B. (2002). Little boxes, globalization, and networked individualism. In M. Tanabe, P. van den Besselaar, & T. Ishida (Eds.), *Digital cities II: Computational and sociological approaches* (pp. 10–25). Springer.

Williams, D. (2006). On and off the 'net: Scales for social capital in an online era. *Journal of Computer-Mediated Communication, 11*(2), 593–628.

Wolff, J. (2019, December 9). Iran cutting off its internet wasn't a show of strength. It was a sign of panic. The Washington Post. https://wapo.st/2GIiEf0

Wong, K. L. X., & Dobson, A. S. (2019). We're just data: Exploring China's social credit system in relation to digital platform ratings cultures in Westernised democracies. *Global Media and China, 4*(2), 220–232.

World Bank Country and Lending Groups. (n.d.). *The World Bank.* https://bit.ly/3d6b21X

Xu, Q., & Armstrong, C. L. (2019). # SELFIES at the 2016 Rio Olympics: Comparing self-representations of male and female athletes from the US and China. *Journal of Broadcasting & Electronic Media, 63*(2), 322–338.

Yang, C. C., & Brown, B. B. (2016). Online self-presentation on Facebook and self development during the college transition. *Journal of Youth and Adolescence, 45*(2), 402–416.

Zuboff, S. (2019). *The age of surveillance capitalism: The fight for a human future at the new frontier of power.* Public Affairs Books.

8 Marginalized and Understudied Populations Using Digital Media

Linda Charmaraman, J. Maya Hernandez, and Rachel Hodes

The current generation of adolescents were born into an omnipresent digital world in which offline and online societal and cultural contexts can influence one's developing sense of belonging and identity. Rapid technological advancements, such as widespread adoption of smartphones, streaming technologies, and online influencers, have changed the way adolescents have been primed and groomed to adapt to the shifting environment. As the field of digital media and social technologies continues to grow, the attention to digital divides becomes less about access to digital technologies and more about how young populations use these technologies in healthy (or unhealthy) ways. By 2013, the vast majority of youth had access to the Internet, including Black (92%), Hispanic (88%), and even youth in low-income neighborhoods (89%; Madden et al., 2013). However, the scholarly reporting of cultural, racial, and economic differences in digital media use typically covers access to the Internet, mobile phones, and favorite social media sites rather than how youth from different marginalized groups actually use technology.

To date, most research has been conducted on White and college samples (Zhang & Leung, 2014). This further deepens the knowledge gap (or a "second-level digital divide"; Hargittai & Hinnant, 2008) in understanding how overlooked populations, such as racial-ethnic minorities, sexual and gender minorities, and other vulnerable adolescent populations, may be not only accessing digital media in different ways but also using and repurposing them to subvert the dominant mainstream narratives. Unlike the mainstream media of the 20th century, this socially networked age of the 21st century provides users opportunities to co-construct their identities in the same social

Research reported in this publication was supported by the Eunice Kennedy Shriver National Institute of Child Health and Human Development of the National Institutes of Health under award number 1R15HD094281–01. The content is solely the responsibility of the authors and does not necessarily represent the official views of the National Institutes of Health. We wish to thank Amanda M. Richer for data management, Alyssa Gramajo for project coordination, Julie Parker for help with translation to a broader audience, and our undergraduate students (Teresa Xiao, Emily Zhai, Kensy Jordan, and Tulani Reeves-Miller) for their contributions to the Diversity Challenge and copyediting assistance.

and entertainment environments as where they receive their commercial media programming (Manago, 2015). Since most US-based studies have focused on White or college-based samples to understand social media use (but see Chapter 7 for discussion of cultural differences across the world), there is a silencing of voices that exemplify the diverse identity factors among understudied subgroups of our youth's digital worlds (Stevens et al., 2017). This chapter will discuss the role of digital media on marginalized identity development during adolescence, risk and resilience experiences of social media within these understudied adolescent groups, and challenges and future directions in researching the experiences of these subgroups.

Much like the mainstream televised media messages that dominated past generations, the ever-evolving landscape of digital media is a persistent source of societal messages for adolescents to digest – from unacceptable and acceptable behavior to peer and family relationships to gender and sexual roles to stereotypes and values (Mayhew & Weigle, 2018). Two major developmental tasks for adolescents aged 10–24 are exploring intimacy with others and developing stable personal, social, and collective identities that incorporate gender, racial/ethnic, sexual, moral/religious, and political components (Subrahmanyam et al., 2006). In the sections below, we will explore the role of social media in developing marginalized identities pertaining to race, ethnicity, sexual orientation, homelessness, and disability. Because the emergent development of marginalized identities such as sexual orientation (e.g., Pew Research Center, 2013) or race/ethnicity (e.g., Umaña-Taylor et al., 2014) more often developmentally crystalizes in later adolescence and into emerging adulthood (ages 18–24), there is a limited understanding in the literature on how these identity explorations and formations prospectively develop in early and mid-adolescence (ages 10–17), often relying on retrospective accounts (e.g., Charmaraman, Grossman, & Richer, 2021). Many of the studies in this chapter illustrate the experiences of older youth to shed some light on how tweens or teens may have similar experiences. The less common studies that focused on younger teens and tween experiences are highlighted whenever available.

Role of Digital Media in Development of Marginalized Racial-Ethnic Identities

One form of identity that becomes an integral part of the adolescent developmental period is racial and ethnic identity formation. This particular identity formation is stratified into periods of *exploration* and *commitment* (Phinney & Ong, 2007; Umaña-Taylor et al., 2014), all of which are considered a point of cultural strength contributing to minority youth resiliency (Masten & Reed, 2002). Early (ages 10–13) and mid-adolescence (ages 14–17) is a key period for the exploration of racial-ethnic identity prior to commitment, which occurs during development in conjunction with heightened priorities of social impact, connectedness, and autonomy (Williams et al., 2014). Theoretical research has positioned racial and ethnic identity as an internalized feeling of belonging to a particular racial-ethnic group and is thought to be formed in later adolescence and young adulthood (Phinney, 1990; Yip et al., 2006). Compared to children's conceptions, adolescents' notions of race and ethnicity are more abstract and complex, which is marked by a heightened group consciousness perspective (Quintana, 1994). It is worth noting for this chapter that in the context of the United States, racial and ethnic minorities are individuals who identify as non-White.[1] There are unique histories (e.g., slavery, internment and incarceration, segregation) tied to the individual subgroups of racial and ethnic minorities in the USA, which contribute to the upbringing and identity formation of young people today. With these histories being told and readily accessible in the era of the Internet, exposure from an earlier age of these perceptions is bound to influence the development and well-being of children and teens.

While adolescence is a salient time for exploring racial-ethnic identity, it is a complex process that involves the influence of nested ecologies surrounding an adolescent, such as family (more proximal), school, community, and political climate (more distal) (Charmaraman & Grossman, 2010; Spencer et al., 1997), all of which also influence youth outcomes. One might consider the ubiquitous use of technology, especially social media, among young people as an additional digital ecology that has become a larger part of the processes in racial-ethnic identity exploration. The dominance of digital media exposure and social media use in adolescence across all races and ethnicities (Anderson & Jiang, 2018) has potential consequences, both negative and positive, for youth exploration of what it means to be a person of color in their communities and its effects on mental health.

Risk for Racial-Ethnic Minority Youth

Racial-ethnic differentiation inherently creates opportunities for discrimination and negative stereotypes of minoritized groups to become perpetuated through digital media, which is a well-documented stressor and risk factor for poorer outcomes (Berry, 2000; Trent et al., 2019). As offline risk factors are shown to be mirrored online (Przybylski & Bowes, 2017), discrimination on digital media, and especially social media, has increased stress during an already dynamic time of development. Racial-ethnic discrimination online comes in many forms and may include racial slurs or jokes, negative stereotyping such as "criminals" or "thugs," body shaming of skin tone or body figure, and even threat of harm, simply due to racial-ethnic profiles. Tynes and colleagues (2020) conducted the first study of its kind to investigate the mental health implications of online discrimination among Black and Latinx adolescents (6th–12th grade) over time. This novel study reveals that increases in experienced individual and vicarious online racial discrimination among Black and Latinx adolescents increases risks for higher levels of depressive and anxiety symptoms. Uniquely, older Black adolescent males were more likely to report high exposure to online discrimination at a younger age with decreasing discrimination over time compared to Latinx adolescent males. Yet, those who experienced high and stable vicarious online discrimination and those who were exposed to high levels of individual racial discrimination online at an early age experienced worse psychological outcomes over time, regardless of gender. This example shows the distinct experience of racial-ethnic online discrimination risks of Black and Latinx adolescents. In our work at the Youth, Media, & Wellbeing Research Lab, we demonstrated that Black and Latinx adolescents (5th–9th grade) adopt social media younger than their White peers, further exposing them to behavioral health difficulties such as sleep disruption due to screen content they were exposed to (Zhai et al., 2020).

Much like the historical contexts of racial-ethnic discrimination against Black and Latinx populations in the USA, individuals of Asian heritage have been subjected to severe historical discrimination (Gee et al., 2009). Despite having the highest reported accessibility to the Internet and social media (Spooner, 2001), Asian American youth still remain underrepresented in the literature around digital media and well-being. Asian Americans are often subject to stereotypes such as the "model minorities," "honorary Whites," or even the perpetual foreigners (Kiang et al., 2013, p. 1714), which may have damaging effects on the racial-ethnic exploration among youth. For instance, Asian Americans in later adolescence (18–24 years) are more likely to be cyberbullied compared to White or Hispanic counterparts (Charmaraman et al., 2018). At the same time, Asian Americans are the least likely to report negative occurrences on social media in order to reduce "losing face" and maintain a positive image to the external world. Studies have demonstrated that Asian Americans experience stigma and shame when it comes to their mental health problems and treatment (Surgeon General, 2001; Wang et al., 2020), with cultural stereotypes implying that seeking professional help is a sign of weakness, lack of self-discipline, or may cause shame to the family name (Uba, 1994). Thus, it is unsurprising that Asian American youth would withhold their emotional turmoil from the public eye on social media platforms.

A more recent example of Asian Americans feeling targeted is through the current implications of the global pandemic, which has caused a rapid resurgence of hate and racial profiling among the Asian American communities (Croucher et al., 2020). According to the Integrated Threat Theory (Stephan & Stephan, 2000), this poses a realistic threat and generalized out-group stereotypes of this given event has driven the increases in discriminatory behaviors against Asian Americans, specifically Chinese Americans. Asian American adolescents are among those with highest access to the Internet and social media that leads to early exposures to these racial-ethnic discriminations online. There is emerging evidence indicating that a strong racial-ethnic and/or immigrant identity can protect against the negative effects of online harassment and depression in early adolescence (e.g., Hernandez & Charmaraman, 2021).

Indigenous and Native American adolescents are heavy consumers of digital media (Rushing & Stephens, 2011) but are also a population vastly affected by mental health problems such as substance abuse and suicide (Park-Lee et al., 2018). Racial-ethnic identity exploration among current Indigenous youth is often met with an internal conflict of relating immediate relevant experiences with historical cultures and traumas (Wexler, 2009, p. 272) that contributes to outcomes of well-being. Among Indigenous adolescents, it has been shown that perceived discrimination and historical oppression of Native American populations have been strong indicators of poor mental health outcomes such as alcohol abuse and depression (Cheadle & Whitbeck, 2011). Taking into consideration that offline discrimination is likely to be transferred online (Przybylski & Bowes, 2017), it can be hypothesized that exposure to racial-ethnic discrimination on digital platforms such as social media may also amplify the risk of poor mental health outcomes among Indigenous adolescents. Yet research remains extremely limited in the digital media domain for the population and should be further explored.

Resilience for Racial-Ethnic Minority Youth

As the counternarrative to risks, there is a growing body of literature focused on protective mechanisms of social technologies for youth of color. Among a cohort of racial-ethnic minority adolescents (i.e., Black, Latinx, Asian, and multiracial), research has shown a stronger sense of racial and ethnic identity centrality among Black and Latinx adolescent females showing greater identity centrality compared to males (Charmaraman & Grossman, 2010). This is consistent with the theoretical groundwork of the phenomenological and ecological framework (PVEST) that has been applied to race and ethnic identity formation (Spencer et al., 1997). A scoping review by Williams and Moody (2019) uses the PVEST framework to understand the role of identifying as a Black and female youth and its impacts on well-being in the digital age. Young Black girls are among the highest consumers of social media, and their identities are being supported in ways that are mirrored among other non-Black youth, such as elevating self-esteem and peer affirmations. But because of a long-standing history of stereotypic media portrayal of the young Black female (e.g., nurturing, aggressive, hypersexualized), these messages and stereotypes have translated onto social media that makes identity exploration increasingly complex. This exemplifies that exposure to an online space helps to amplify marginalized youths' voices, but also amplifies the systemic issues surrounding the Black community today that plays a significant role in racial identity exploration.

A developmental consideration during adolescence is the prioritization of social connectedness, and this connectedness through shared heritage, culture, and histories can be strengthened by digital connection. Despite the systemic risk factors related to race and ethnicity that exist in the USA, there is a shift in focus away from deficit-based approaches and toward recognizing the assets and strength within these communities, especially among young people, which help them thrive in a difficult system. In terms of combating the isolation that many adolescents feel, our Youth, Media, & Wellbeing Research Lab demonstrated that Black and Latinx youth aged 11–15 were more likely than White and Asian adolescents to join online groups that made them feel less lonely and isolated (Zhai et al., 2020). These online communities included group chats on Snapchat, House Party, WhatsApp, Discord, anime fandom, and sports or hobby-related groups. In addition, Black youth preferred YouTube video content that was about relationships or friendships, whereas Latinx youth were more likely to seek opportunities to learn how to cope with stress and anxiety and to use social media to stay in touch with family and relatives compared to White youth.

Another powerful example of racial-ethnic based online communities is the *Black Twitter* culture that erupted in 2015. This online culture was a profound way that millions of Black community members came together to share experiences, but more importantly to create a form of resistance to the marginalization that has long-standing impacts to justice and well-being in the Black community (Florini, 2014). A more recent study highlighted that Black adolescents are among the vast users of these online spaces to increase their social capital, but also to facilitate connections to such identity-based communities while amplifying their voices and representation online (Borough et al., 2020).

Latinx adolescents often feel the need to suppress the expression of their culture on social media due to potential discrimination or not enough affirmation (e.g., "likes") compared to when they post more "Americanized" cultures like Thanksgiving or Christmas holiday posts (Borough et al., 2020). Despite this finding, Latinx adolescents still sought out positive aspects of expanding social capital on social media platforms that supported the prospects of job and education opportunities, which is an important factor tied to identity and well-being outcomes for this marginalized group. Another example of the strength in racial-ethnic identity in the digital age for Latinx youth is ethnic identity exploration, such that expressing higher levels of connectedness to the culture via the exploration of their identity is a protective factor against problematic externalizing and internalizing behaviors related to online racial-ethnic discrimination (Umaña-Taylor et al., 2015).

There are still limited accounts of research that emphasize the opportunities and experiences of Asian American and Indigenous adolescents' racial-ethnic identity exploration, especially during early (ages 10–13) and mid-adolescence (ages 11–17), and the role that social media and other digital ecosystems play in this process. In a mixed-method study among older adolescents (ages 18–25), Asian Americans reported using social media as a way of seeking out social support during difficult times in more privatized online channels, which is thought to be a way of navigating the stigma around mental health and impression management that reigns as a priority in many Asian cultures (Charmaraman et al., 2018). Recent findings in response to the rise in racism among Asian Americans have shown online spaces to be a space of demonstrating comradery and resistance to such discrimination, similarly seen in *Black Twitter*, thus preventing harmful outcomes (Abidin & Zeng, 2020). While this work has yet to be shown in the adolescent developmental period, this is another exemplar of the power of collective racial-ethnic identity in an online community.

Among Indigenous youth and resiliency online, while empirical work is vastly minimal, the work of an online space *WeRNative* to support Native teens exemplifies the unique affordances digital media can have to support the identities and well-being with a greater reach than before (Rushing et al., 2018). To support Indigenous youth during a conflict in ethnic identity, there is an opportunity for digital technologies to bridge the gaps between historical contexts and current experiences to enhance the connection to the heritage of Indigenous communities. Work with Indigenous youth in content creation to address health literacy via digital media (e.g., videos) shows that this not only promotes healthy behaviors, but is also a mechanism to address stressors related to culture and ethnic identity (Stewart et al., 2008). Indigenous teens and emerging adults have taken to social media as a means for creative expression of the Native racial-ethnic identity and solidarity, which is said to be a way of reconnecting with the heritage and reaching a broader population of youth in this community (Monkman, 2020; Noor, 2020). Such strength in racial-ethnic identification among a high-risk group of youth is imperative for support of well-being, and the expanded reach and social capital that social media provides can be vastly beneficial for developing Indigenous adolescents.

It is evident that there are risks associated with online discrimination exposure for youth of color, yet there are vast opportunities through social capital, connectedness, and empowerment that youth of color experience with social technologies. Mirroring of risks in online and offline environments can be taken into consideration when building a digital ecosystem that supports diverse groups of adolescents during this time of identity development.

Role of Digital Media in Development of Sexual and Gender Minority Identities

For a subset of youth, referred to in this chapter as LGBT+,[2] processes of identity formation and development during adolescence center around sexual orientation and gender. In this context, identity development is understood as the process by which an individual attaches labels and meaning to their experiences of sexual attraction and gendered existence (Gordon & Silva, 2014; Robertson, 2013). Among social scientists, sexuality and gender are understood as social constructions; much like race, rather than manifesting in the individual as innate biological traits, they are influenced by the social forces that define normative and nonnormative behaviors (Gordon & Silva, 2014; Robertson, 2013). For instance, an adolescent attempting to articulate a minority sexual orientation might be deterred from doing so by *compulsory heterosexuality*, the set of societal norms that presume and dictate heterosexual behavior and identity (Robertson, 2013). Sexual identity development is a highly variable process, but integration of a sexual identity with other aspects of the self is often signified when individuals become comfortable with others knowing their sexuality, actively disclose their identity to others, or engage with the broader LGBT+ community (Rosario et al., 2008). Gender identity is often developed through intrapersonal processes, and alongside other aspects of gender-related experience, including gender presentation and self-image. While gender norms are often even more rigid than those pertaining to sexuality, the ability to express one's gender identity both internally and to an external social world has positive associations with well-being (Kuper et al., 2018). Although young adults often face significant interpersonal consequences when they express marginalized sexual and gender identities, group identification can also be a source of protection and well-being for LGBT+ youth (Scroggs & Vennum, 2020).

Since the Internet's early days, digital media has provided LGBT+ users with spaces to gather, construct identity, and share content with one another. In many respects, various niche online communities today constitute "queer cultural archipelagos" (Ghaziani, 2014, p. 137): concentrated areas that, some argue, have replaced gay bars and "gayborhoods" as safe spaces for those who identify as LGBT+ (Cavalcante, 2019). As this migration online occurs, LGBT+ adolescents are being exposed to these digital spaces – and simultaneously helping to construct the cultures that define them. One study found that LGBT+ adolescents as young as 13 years old, on average, spend more time online than their heterosexual, cisgender counterparts (Palmer et al., 2013). Another study, although it did not find differences in time spent online and excluded transgender youth from its sample, was able to show that sexual minority youth aged 18–24 tended to use the Internet differently than heterosexual youth, expanding their activity across a greater variety of social networking sites and engaging more purposefully in identity development online (Ceglarek & Ward, 2016). While existing scholarship has begun to examine the ways in which LGBT+ young adults navigate cyberspace, LGBT+ youth, especially those under 18 years old, are still a critically understudied population. Research on the ways transgender youth navigate social media remains especially rare.

Often, the ways in which LGBT+ youth learn about themselves and their communities online are directly related to identity development. This type of online engagement may take many forms, including *traditional learning*, in which users seek out information about identity-related terminology and then apply these to their own experiences; *social learning*, in which users observe and identify LGBT+ role models on social media; *experiential learning*, which involves active participation in the online LGBT+ community, especially through the use of dating apps; and *teaching others*, which occurs when LGBT+ individuals use social media platforms to provide others with information on LGBT+ issues, including experiences with coming out (Fox & Ralston, 2016). While each of these processes allow LGBT+ youth to better define their personal, social, and collective identities, this digital learning also incorporates an understanding of the stressors that LGBT+ youth may face when they actively express and practice their gender and sexuality online.

A commonly used term used to discuss social networking's impact on LGBT+ youth well-being is *context collapse*: a phenomenon that occurs when the individual, by sharing content on a social media platform, exposes that content to a variety of different audiences, some of whom may not respond positively (Fox & Ralston, 2016; McConnell et al., 2018). For LGBT+ youth, this conflict is particularly salient, since people they know in various social contexts may have drastically different levels of awareness about their sexuality or gender identity. Context collapse can therefore profoundly impact the ways in which young LGBT+ people navigate disclosure and the coming out process. Coming out itself has complex associations with well-being; while it can positively influence the lives of LGBT+ youth in certain relational contexts, in other contexts it can limit identity formation or negatively impact mental health (McConnell et al., 2018, p. 3).

Many LGBT+ individuals seem able to circumvent some of the difficulties associated with context collapse by dividing their online activity between a variety of social media sites. DeVito et al. (2018) argue that for LGBT+ users, social media activity should be conceptualized as an ecosystem, that is, users are able to manage their self-presentation by targeting content to different audiences on different platforms, in addition to the use of privacy controls within one platform. Examining interactions on specific platforms allows researchers to define some of the key characteristics of the LGBT+ adolescents' online ecosystems. For instance, on Facebook, a platform where users primarily interact with people they already have relationships with offline, LGBT+ youth seem to subscribe to the *lowest common denominator* model, in which they tailor identity presentations toward whichever audiences are most likely to express disapproval toward them (McConnell et al., 2018). Tumblr, meanwhile, has had success engaging young LGBT+ users, which is often attributed to its features that enable LGBT+ youth to connect to others in the LGBT+ community with minimal threat of exposing their identities, such as anonymity and the privileging of content sharing over content creation (Cavalcante, 2019).

As LGBT+ youth come of age on the Internet, social media provides a space for them to cultivate personal, social, and collective identities. In some cases, this process occurs as learning, primarily positive interactions that allow individuals to practice being LGBT+ in relative safety and connection with others. However, LGBT+ participation online coexists with the awareness that nonnormative experiences of sexuality and gender may incur negative social responses. This danger forces LGBT+ youth to navigate coming out and expressing identity with care, manifesting in differential usage of social media platforms, which itself can affect adolescent well-being.

Risk for Sexual/Gender Minority Youth

Existing scholarship on LGBT+ populations' activity online has identified the Internet as a space where youth can be exposed to harassment, discrimination, and other forms of bullying that may be easier to perpetrate in online spaces. Multiple studies have found that LGBT+ youth are more likely to be harassed online than non-LGBT+ youth (Palmer et al., 2013; Ybarra et al., 2015). Cyberbullying is perpetrated against LGBT+ youth in a variety of ways, including *verbal victimization, relational victimization,* and *electronic actions,* all of which are often combined with in-person harassment (Varjas et al., 2013). These distinctions highlight the variety of modes through which the cyberbullying of LGBT+ youth can occur, including sexual harassment, the use of slurs, purposeful social exclusion, and the targeting of social media content using viruses. It is also notable that, in a sample that did not include gender minority youth, several instances were identified in which the LGB adolescents interviewed were themselves perpetrators of bullying, including online verbal harassment (Varjas et al., 2013); this finding complicates the assumption that sexual minority youth are solely victims in their online interactions.

The effects of online harassment include increased depression and suicidality among LGBT+ youth (Schimmel-Bristow & Ahrens, 2018), dangers that are especially salient given that LGBT+ youth are particularly vulnerable to cybervictimization, since revealing their experiences to parents may mean that they risk coming out or losing access to digital technologies (Cooper & Blumenfeld, 2012). However, it is possible that the role of cyberbullying in LGBT+ adolescents' digital landscape may be shifting. Data collected in the fall of 2019 by our Youth, Media, and Wellbeing Lab, for instance, found no difference between the amount of heterosexual and sexual minority youth who reported experiencing cyberbullying online. Our sample included children under 13, of which 25% experienced nonheterosexual attraction (Charmaraman, Hodes, & Richer, 2021). However, there are several indicators that sexual minority youth today may experience more social isolation online than their peers do. These youth tended to have fewer friends on social media, and were less likely to use social media to engage positively with friends, including sharing content that was comedic or that they enjoyed. They also were less likely to be friends with family members, peers, or acquaintances on their social media networks, indicating that the links between in-person and online communities may be weaker for LGBT+ youth than other adolescents. Sexual minority youth also reported feeling isolated more often than heterosexual youth. Therefore, there is reason to be concerned that even when young LGBT+ populations are not directly attacked online, they still experience victimization via structural exclusion from the heteronormative social circles that make up their real-world contacts.

As a consequence of context collapse, LGBT+ youth also often find themselves at heightened risk when they share personal information online. Our Youth, Media, and Wellbeing Lab found that sexual minority youth were less likely to have private settings on their social media accounts (Charmaraman, Hodes, & Richer, 2021), and Varjas et al. (2013) discussed sexual minority teenagers' willingness to share personal information with those they talked to virtually as a possible drawback of online activity. Panizo (2018), in a study of teenagers aged 14–19 in Spain who identified as gay, also noted the recurrence of anecdotes in which teenagers' disclosure of their sexual orientation online was discovered by relatives, forcing them "out of the closet indirectly and involuntarily" (p. 67). While these results are open to further interpretation, they do imply that LGBT+ youth place themselves at higher risk when sharing information about themselves through digital media due to the stark division that sometimes exists between their expression of identity online and offline.

Finally, Youth, Media, and Wellbeing Lab data shows that sexual minority youth report seeing more content related to self-harm on social media and are more likely to have actually attempted self-harm (Charmaraman, Hodes, & Richer, 2021). These sexual minority youth were also found to have higher depressive scores. These findings are in line with concerns about the potential of specific sites, like Tumblr, to foster dangerous subcultures that correspond with social isolation and poor mental health outcomes (Cavalcante, 2019).

Resilience for Sexual/Gender Minority Youth

Despite its documented risks, digital media use often provides numerous ways for LGBT+ youth to build resilience. Many forms of online resilience-building are closely related to the process of identity formation. Hillier and Harrison (2007) were among the first to argue that internet communities constitute *safe spaces* for LGBT+ youth who face hostile environments at home or school. In their study of same-sex attracted Australian youth aged 14–21, they assert that in digital spaces, anonymity and the lack of geographic boundaries provide the ideal practice ground for constructing coming out narratives, engaging with a communal gay culture, experimenting with nonheterosexual intimacy, and socializing with other same-sex-attracted youth. Sexual minority youth have been found to perceive their online friends as significantly more socially supportive than their in-person friends, and LGBT+ youth are more likely to have friends they only know online. Despite the finding that youth across sexual and gender identities feel relatively safe online, researchers note that strong online social support still does not appear to reduce the likelihood of online or in-person harassment and victimization (Ybarra et al., 2015). The Youth, Media, and Wellbeing Lab also found that sexual minority youth they surveyed were more likely to join an online group in order to reduce social isolation or feelings of loneliness (Charmaraman, Hodes, & Richer, 2021), which similarly implies that LGBT+ youth have been able to engage with social media networks in supportive and fortifying ways.

Hillier and Harrison (2007) also note that accessing resources pertaining to sexual orientation, sexual health, and sexual identity can be a critical form of internet use for same-sex-attracted youth, a utility that is echoed in other studies of LGBT+ adolescents. Fox and Ralston (2016) reported that participants used online resources to educate themselves about terminology related to sexual orientation and gender identity, to learn about gender transition, and, in a crossover with their offline context, to identify LGBT+ spaces in physical proximity to them. The Internet can also be a useful tool to identify LGBT+-friendly physicians, therapists, and other care providers (Schimmel-Bristow & Ahrens, 2018).

A final form of resilience-building, also with its roots in identity development, is the use of online platforms as springboards for LGBT+ activism. Education nonprofit GLSEN reported that LGBT+ youth aged 13–18 were about twice as likely as non-LGBT+ youth to participate in civic engagement activities, and 77% had been part of an online community in support of a social cause (Palmer et al., 2013). Connection to online community fosters *sexual citizenship*, which occurs when one's politicized identity prompts one to engage in social activism (Robards et al., 2019). Thus, social media often serves as a tool for LGBT+ youth to communicate about social issues that impact them, and allows them to build strengthened connections to both their immediate and virtual communities.

Ultimately, it is clear that despite the potential of facing victimization, LGBT+ youth wield considerable agency in their online interactions. Much of the time, their vulnerabilities coexist with a demonstrated ability to navigate digital space, in ways that positively supplement or contrast with their offline environments.

Role of Digital Media in the Development of Other Marginalized Youth Identities

In this section, we explore how digital media influences the identities, risk, and resilience of youth from other marginalized backgrounds, ranging from those living in disadvantaged neighborhoods to homeless and neurodiverse youth.

In the case of youth in disadvantaged neighborhoods, Oldenburg (1989) argues that high levels of poverty, decreased employment prospects, and the lack of safe gathering spaces without threat of violence or drug activity lead to a problem of place. These urban youth often have a dilemma of geographic identity – at once proud and connected to one's neighborhood but needing a third space to feel safe and secure to hang out. Soukup (2006) articulated a "digital third space" wherein online communities are key to developing one's neighborhood identity and can be located within a local geographic area, allowing participants to be fully immersed in a computer-mediated environment contributing to a sense of connectedness and sense of refuge.

Homelessness is often an invisible identity that is intentionally hidden from outsiders such as classmates at school or future employers (Whitbeck & Hoyt, 1999). The majority of research on the digital media use of homeless youth focuses on health information seeking (Eyrich-Garg, 2010) and less on social connections with others. Prior research on nonhomeless youth suggests that having a cell phone in one's possession increases feelings of safety and security while on the move, and merely owning a cell phone makes youth feel socially connected (Wei & Lo, 2006). This may be a particularly salient part of homeless youths' identities – having a lifeline to a networked world may be more critical to maintain those connections they most value.

Prior research has demonstrated that social media has provided people with intellectual disabilities an opportunity to express their preferred personal and social identities (Caton & Chapman, 2016), which may include reflections on their identities as neurodiverse, but also serves as an online space where they can be just like everyone else. For instance, in a study with people with Down syndrome, online profiles were places to be vocal about their thoughts, feelings, and needs (Seale, 2007). Studies have shown those with intellectual disabilities publicize their disability in blogs, even when these online venues provided space to focus on other aspects of their lives (McClimens & Gordon, 2008). Other research has observed that some individuals with intellectual disabilities prefer to not mention the label of intellectual disability in an online profile, providing a chance to escape the identity stigma associated with these disabilities (Löfgren-Mårtenson, 2008).

Risk of Other Marginalized Youth

Adolescents from lower-income households have been found to spend on average an hour and a half more on screens than their higher-income peers (George et al., 2020).They are also more likely to be passively viewing content and less frequently using screens for research and learning (OECD, 2016). In the new digital divide of remote learning (Odgers & Robb, 2020), lower-income households not only have less digital access but also fewer adults who can scaffold digital support, which is critical given the increased risk for mental health symptoms.

In a study by VonHoltz and colleagues (2018), individuals who do not have easy access to the Internet, such as may be the case with youth experiencing homelessness, demonstrate the need to be more purposeful when using public computers. For instance, using the Internet for social media is limited when other basic needs are not being met, such as housing, food, and unemployment. When youth do not have easy access to health care or resources to understand their health ailments, they turn to the Internet to self-diagnose, often finding the terminology and sheer volume of information to be too complex. In terms of being connected with others online, young homeless women have been found to be less likely to stay in touch with friends and less likely to post public messages, signaling a weaker social network to rely on and a greater likelihood of social isolation (Guadagno et al., 2013).

Prior research on social technology use among adolescents with physical or intellectual health conditions, such as autism spectrum disorder, have focused on their unique challenges in understanding social situations and managing peer relationships. This can lead individuals with disabilities to turn to technology as a less threatening way of interacting with others (Davidson, 2008). Unfortunately, having a noticeable or visible disability increases the chances of being a victim of cyberbullying, particularly for those who use the Internet more frequently and are already bullied in person (Kowalski et al., 2016). People with intellectual disabilities have also been found to disclose more personal information about themselves and photos online, increasing the potential for financial, sexual, and personal safety threats (Holmes & O'Loughlin, 2014). Adolescents with a diagnosis of attention deficit hyperactivity disorder (ADHD) have been shown to not only be likely victims but also perpetrators of cyberbullying peers. Those with ADHD who were victimized reported higher incidents of loneliness and lower levels of self-efficacy and social support compared to nonvictims (Heiman et al., 2014).

Resilience of Other Marginalized Youth

Digital media and mobile technology access may be especially difficult for homeless youth who are also at increased risk for behavioral and mental health problems associated with substance abuse and violence, compared to housed youth (Rice et al., 2005). Despite the barriers, studies have dispelled the myth of a digital divide for homeless youth, such that around 85% of the homeless population access the Internet at least once a week and 62% of homeless youth had a cell phone, mostly related to instrumental purposes, such as looking for jobs or staying connected with social workers trying to track them down (Rice et al., 2011). Besides using their personal devices, homeless youth are accessing the Internet through social service agencies (60%), public libraries (54%), and internet cafes (14%) (Pollio et al., 2013). Only 9% of homeless youth indicated that they did not have a social media profile (Young & Rice, 2011). Rice and colleagues (2011) found that homeless youth are most likely to stay in touch via cell phones with friends they knew before they were homeless, followed by siblings, parents, and street-based peers, which underlines the critical social network that friends can provide for these youth. Besides studies on digital access and seeking health-related information, there is limited research examining what homeless youth actually communicate about on their social media sites. These studies have found that youth discussed both risk-taking behaviors such as having sex with someone they met online or drug use, but also prosocial discussion topics such as school, family, work, setting goals, and even their homelessness (Barman-Adhikari et al., 2016).

Studies focused on youth with intellectual or socioemotional disabilities are almost always centered on cyberbullying and the promise of technology-facilitated interventions (Schimmel-Bristow & Ahrens, 2018), rather than how these young people use social media in resilient ways. A recent review suggested that potential benefits of social media use in young people with intellectual disabilities include increased opportunities to make and maintain relationships, decreased loneliness (Kydland et al., 2012), increasing self-confidence and self-esteem through learning new technical skills, and having fun (Caton & Chapman, 2016).

Challenges and Future Directions

Moving Beyond Differential Access

Researchers have recently made a call to action on moving away from quantity of time spent on digital technologies, and more toward understanding the quality of experiences online that may have larger impacts to youth well-being (Ito et al., 2020; Odgers & Jensen, 2020). In doing so, the research will be able to provide evidence for how the most pervasive forms of digital media in the current moment is impacting the lives of adolescents, especially those who are marginalized and understudied. In the case of youth who are homeless, access to digital technologies (e.g., mobile phones and public computers) and being able to keep in touch with loved ones is a primary concern for both the research participants and the researchers who study them. However, little is known about which social media platforms are being accessed by this vulnerable population and for what purposes, how often, etc.

Hard to Reach and Hidden Subpopulations

Racial-ethnic identity formation during adolescence is met with many challenges and opportunities in the digital age, especially among the growing diversity in the population. While we have only scratched the surface of the possible implications that this identity development process can have in online and social media spaces, there is still much to be explored. A major challenge that research has going forward is accounting for the wide range of races and ethnicities within the USA, and accounting for bi- and multiracial-ethnic identities. There are also many approaches to mapping out the racial-ethnic identity development during this critical period of adolescence, and prior research has had a stronger focus on the identity commitment during late adolescence and young adulthood (e.g., college samples). As digital media and social media adopters are becoming younger at a rapid rate, we must further explore how the pervasive nature of constant exposure and use affects racial and ethnic identity development in the earlier stages of adolescence. Parents and educators might consider discussions with youth from marginalized backgrounds to prepare for biased language and to arm them with the tools to be proactive with learning about and/or establishing their social identities online.

Despite the fact that some youth may identify as LGBT+ at ages as young as 9 (Calzo & Blashill, 2018), research about LGBT+ adolescent behavior online is extremely limited for populations under 18 years old. Information about the digital media use of LGBT+ children under 13 years old is virtually nonexistent, and the Youth, Media, and Wellbeing Lab's data is among the only to date that include children in middle school. Much of the existing research also fails to include transgender youth in its samples, or frames its analyses of this population as secondary to findings about LGB individuals. Thus, future research on LGBT+ social media use has an opportunity to focus on each of these vulnerable populations. As children gain access to social media earlier in middle school, and even in late elementary school, information about how they begin to develop LGBT+ identity or learn about gender and sexuality can provide important context for parents and teachers. Transgender youth, meanwhile, face unique barriers to positive identity formation throughout their developmental years (Palmer et al., 2013); therefore, research devoted to the mental health impacts of transgender digital media use, especially as compared to other members of the LGBT+ community, is a valuable area for future exploration.

Adolescent development may also be compounded with intersectional identity formations. In a diverse mixed-method study of adolescents and young adults aged 12–25, Charmaraman and colleagues (2015) found that girls and women of color participated in more online blogs and were more likely to report revealing their stress on social media compared to both White and male participants. The unique issues faced by LGBT+ youth who are racial minorities or have other marginalized identities are also understudied, such that race overlaps with terms used and content posted about sexuality (e.g., Wargo, 2016). More expansive qualitative and mixed-method research is necessary to understand how particular experiences of sexual orientation and gender are racialized differently online. GLSEN also suggests that lack of internet access for LGBT+ youth living in rural areas merits future investigation, since many of these adolescents are already isolated from any form of LGBT+ community (Palmer et al., 2013).

Social Media Site Affordances/Hindrances

As noted in earlier sections, it is shown that collective online spaces for interactive and passive use such as social media platforms (e.g., Twitter, Instagram, Facebook, TikTok) have proven to be a space of racial-ethnic empowerment for young people and a way to promote the social capital needed to support well-being during adolescent development. Despite the dark side of the online ecosystems related to racial discrimination and injustices in the algorithmic makeup of these social media spaces, there are vast opportunities for these tools to be utilized to support historically marginalized racial and ethnic youth to navigate and build their identities to promote mental well-being. For instance, Facebook conspicuously does not allow users to define their race on their profiles, but users can display their cultural background through their photos or interests. The opportunities must also be promoted by the industry by deviating away from a color-blind and utiopic cyberspace approach, which often further perpetuates the visual classification of other and hampers empowerment of cultural identities (Grasmuck et al., 2009). More collaborative research with tech industry user experience teams will improve evidence-based decisions around marginalized youth who are primary users of these apps.

LGBT+ activity on newer social media sites, and the ongoing evolution of these communities' online presence, also provide fertile ground for future research. For instance, the video-sharing app TikTok has experienced a surge of popularity among adolescents and corners of the app are primarily devoted to LGBT+ social support and resource sharing (Carey, 2020; Ohlheiser, 2020). At the same time, several sites, including Tumblr and YouTube, have received criticism for implementing guidelines that, while intended to prevent youth from seeing pornographic content, restrict access to LGBT+ media and resources (Romano, 2019; Sybert, 2021); these actions could significantly impact LGBT+ engagement on these platforms. Simpson and Semaan (2020) have detailed the affirming yet fraught relationship many LGBT+ users form with TikTok specifically, and the platform's potential for *algorithmic exclusion*. Finally, certain platforms provide researchers with the opportunity to gather data that is more representative of LGBT+ populations, as demonstrated by Salk et al. (2020); their methodology, in which transgender youth were recruited via targeted social media advertising, has exciting implications for investigators committed to more effectively understanding the unique factors that impact LGBT+ young adults' digital media use.

Across all of the marginalized populations in this chapter, there are untapped research avenues regarding identity work in online spaces. It is worth recognizing, like many other vulnerable youth communities, offline risk factors such as bullying, victimization and behavioral problems spill over into online spaces, which reinforces heightened risks for negative experiences on social media. It is critical that researchers and technology developers recognize the potential amplification of risks tied to one's identity of being a part of this particular vulnerable adolescent population (Odgers, 2018). Moving beyond the deficits-based discourse, future research and practice can capitalize on assets-based and empowerment approaches to positive minority youth development in digital spaces. Being a member of a group that is overlooked or faced with discrimination can galvanize individuals with a sense of purpose, tackling a mutual goal of collective sense-making and more authentic visibility, which, in turn, can promote healthy youth development (Wexler et al., 2009). Partnerships with educators, families, clinicians, and the sociotechnical industry can further increase understanding about how to design inclusive online environments and circumstances that can lead to a digital ecosystem that ultimately supports identity development and emotional well-being.

Notes

[1] Race categorization is largely a social construct that is linked to the history of segregation and racism of non-White individuals in the USA. Ethnicity is more often considered as a point of identification with individuals' heritage, traditions, and in many instances, language spoken. Currently, race and ethnicity are viewed interchangeably as social constructs and continue to be a part of historic and persistent disparities, especially among minority youth. The racial-ethnic identity among minority adolescents is increasingly fluid and has yet to be well understood, but remains a critical component to the experiences of development and well-being. Diversity within the USA continues to grow as youth under the age of 15 who identify as a racial-ethnic minority (e.g., non-White) are now emerging as the majority of youth populations (US Census Bureau, 2019).

[2] A wide range of terminology is used to refer to individuals who do not identify as either heterosexual or cisgender, especially in the context of academic research. In this chapter, we use the acronym *LGBT+* to describe the unique ways that these populations interact with digital media. *LGBT+* highlights the specific identities *lesbian*, *gay*, *bisexual*, and *transgender*, while also acknowledging that many other experiences of sexuality and gender are considered nonnormative. In addition to the more general term *queer*, other studies shorten the acronym to *LGB* or use the terms *same-sex attracted* and *sexual minority* to specifically discuss sexual orientation. We note these differences to contextualize the variety of terminology that appears in this chapter. When discussing specific studies, we use the terms the authors have chosen, but use *LGBT+* to describe the general population in question.

References

Abidin, C., & Zeng, J. (2020). Feeling Asian together: Coping with #COVIDRacism on subtle Asian traits. *Social Media + Society*, 6(3). https://doi.org/10.1177/2056305120948223

Anderson, M., & Jiang, J. (2018, May 31). *Teens, social media & technology 2018*. Pew Research Center: Internet, Science & Tech. https://www.pewresearch.org/internet/2018/05/31/teens-social-media-technology-2018/

Barman-Adhikari, A., Rice, E., Bender, K., Lengnick-Hall, R., Yoshioka-Maxwell, A., & Rhoades, H. (2016). Social networking technology use and engagement in HIV-related risk and protective behaviors among homeless youth. *Journal of Health Communication, 21*(7), 809–817. https://doi.org/10.1080/10810730.2016.1177139

Berry, G. L. (2000). Multicultural media portrayals and the changing demographic landscape: The psychosocial impact of television representations on the adolescent of color. *Journal of Adolescent Health, 27*(2, Suppl. 1), 57–60. https://doi.org/10.1016/S1054-139X(00)00133-6

Borough, M., Literat, I., & Ikin, A. (2020). "Good social media?": Underrepresented youth perspectives on the ethical and equitable design of social media platforms. *Social Media + Society, 6*(2). https://doi.org/10.1177/2056305120928488

Calzo, J. P., & Blashill, A. J. (2018). Child sexual orientation and gender identity in the adolescent brain cognitive development cohort study. *JAMA Pediatrics, 172*(11), 1090–1092. https://doi.org/10.1001/jamapediatrics.2018.2496

Carey, E. (2020, October 1). *TikTok's Queer "It Girls" are creating new LGBTQ+ safe spaces*. them. https://www.them.us/story/tiktoks-queer-it-girls-create-lgbtq-safe-spaces

Caton, S., & Chapman, M. (2016). The use of social media and people with intellectual disability: A systematic review and thematic analysis. *Journal of Intellectual & Developmental Disability, 41*(2), 125–139. https://doi.org/10.3109/13668250.2016.1153052

Cavalcante, A. (2019). Tumbling into queer utopias and vortexes: Experiences of LGBTQ social media users on Tumblr. *Journal of Homosexuality, 66*(12), 1715–1735. https://doi.org/10.1080/00918369.2018.1511131

Ceglarek, P., & Ward, L. (2016). A tool for help or harm? How associations between social networking use, social support, and mental health differ for sexual minority and heterosexual youth. *Computers in Human Behavior, 65*, 201–209. https://doi.org/10.1016/j.chb.2016.07.051

Charmaraman, L., Chan, H. B., Chen, S., Richer, A., & Ramanudom, B. (2018). Asian American social media use: From cyber dependence and cyber harassment to saving face. *Asian American Journal of Psychology, 9*(1), 72–86. https://doi.org/10.1037/aap0000109

Charmaraman, L., Chan, H., Price, T., & Richer, A. (2015). Women of color cultivating virtual social capital: Surviving and thriving. In K. E. Tassie & S. M. Brown (Eds.), *Women of color and social media multitasking: Blogs, timelines, feeds, and community* (pp. 1–19). Lexington Books.

Charmaraman, L., & Grossman, J. M. (2010). Importance of race and ethnicity: An exploration of Asian, Black, Latino, and multiracial adolescent identity. *Cultural Diversity and Ethnic Minority Psychology, 16*(2), 144–151. https://doi.org/10.1037/a0018668

Charmaraman, L., Grossman, J. M., & Richer, A. M. (2021). Same-sex attraction disclosure and sexual communication topics within families. *Journal of GLBT Family Studies, 17*(2), 118–134. https://doi.org/10.1080/1550428X.2020.1820414

Charmaraman, L., Hodes, R., & Richer, A. (2021). Young sexual minority adolescent experiences of self-expression and isolation on social technology: A cross-sectional survey. *JMIR Mental Health, 8*(9), e26207. https://doi.org/10.2196/26207

Cheadle, J. E., & Whitbeck, L. B. (2011). Alcohol use trajectories and problem drinking over the course of adolescence: A study of North American Indigenous youth and their caretakers. *Journal of Health and Social Behavior, 52*(2), 228–245. https://doi.org/10.1177/0022146510393973

Cooper, R. M., & Blumenfeld, W. J. (2012). Responses to cyberbullying: A descriptive analysis of the frequency of and impact on LGBT and allied youth. *Journal of LGBT Youth, 9*(2), 153–177. https://doi.org/10.1080/19361653.2011.649616

Croucher, S. M., Nguyen, T., & Rahmani, D. (2020). Prejudice toward Asian Americans in the Covid-19 pandemic: The effects of social media use in the United States. *Frontiers in Communication, 5*(39). https://doi.org/10.3389/fcomm.2020.00039

Davidson, J. (2008). Autistic culture online: Virtual communication and cultural expression on the spectrum. *Social Cultural Geography, 9*(7), 791–806. https://doi.org/10.1080/14649360802382586

DeVito, M. A., Walker, A. M., & Birnholtz, J. (2018). "Too gay for Facebook": Presenting LGBTQ+ identity throughout the personal social media ecosystem. *Proceedings of the ACM on Human-Computer Interaction, 2*(44), 1–23. https://doi.org/10.1145/3274313

Eyrich-Garg, K. M. (2010). Mobile phone technology: A new paradigm for the prevention, treatment, and research of the non-sheltered "street" homeless? *Journal of Urban Health, 87*(3), 365–380. https://doi.org/10.1007/s11524-010-9456-2

Florini, S. (2014). Tweets, tweeps, and signifyin': Communication and cultural performance on "Black Twitter." *Television & New Media, 15*(3), 223–237. https://doi.org/10.1177/1527476413480247

Fox, J., & Ralston, R. (2016). Queer identity online: Informal learning and teaching experiences of LGBTQ individuals on social media. *Computers in Human Behavior, 65*, 635–642. https://doi.org/10.1016/j.chb.2016.06.009

Gee, G. C., Ro, A., Shariff-Marco, S., & Chae, D. (2009). Racial discrimination and health among Asian Americans: Evidence, assessment, and directions for future research. *Epidemiologic Reviews, 31*(1), 130–151. https://doi.org/10.1093/epirev/mxp009

George, M. J., Jensen, M. R., Russell, M. A., et al. (2020). Young adolescents' digital technology use, perceived impairments, and well-being in a representative sample. *Journal of Pediatrics, 219*, 180–187. https://doi.org/10.1016/j.jpeds.2019.12.002

Ghaziani, A. (2014). *There goes the gayborhood?* Princeton University Press.

Gordon, L. E., & Silva, T. J. (2014). Inhabiting the sexual landscape: Toward an interpretive theory of the development of sexual orientation and identity. *Journal of Homosexuality, 62*(4), 495–530. https://doi.org/10.1080/00918369.2014.986417

Grasmuck, S., Martin, J., & Zhao, S. (2009). Ethno-racial identity displays on Facebook. *Journal of Computer-Mediated Communication, 15*(1), 158–188. https://doi.org/10.1111/j.1083-6101.2009.01498.x

Guadagno, R. E., Muscanell, N. L., & Pollio, D. E. (2013). The homeless use Facebook?! Similarities of social network use between college students and homeless young adults. *Computers in Human Behavior, 29*(1), 86–89. https://doi.org/10.1016/j.chb.2012.07.019

Hargittai, E., & Hinnant, A. (2008) Digital inequality differences in young adults' use of the internet. *Communication Research, 35*(5), 602–621. https://doi.org/10.1177/0093650208321782

Heiman, T., Olenik-Shemesh, D., & Eden, S. (2014). Cyberbullying involvement among students with ADHD: Relation to loneliness, self-efficacy, and social support. *European Journal of Special Needs Education, 30*(1), 15–29. https://doi.org/10.1080/08856257.2014.943562

Hernandez, J. M., & Charmaraman, L. (2021). Conceptualizing the role of racial-ethnic identity in US adolescent social technology use and wellbeing. [Unpublished manuscript].

Hillier, L., & Harrison, L. (2007). Building realities less limited than their own: Young people practicing same-sex attraction on the internet. *Sexualities, 10*(1), 82–100. https://doi.org/10.1177/1363460707072956

Holmes, K. M., & O'Loughlin, N. (2014). The experiences of people with learning disabilities on social networking sites. *British Journal of Learning Disabilities, 42*(1), 3–7. https://doi.org/10.1111/bld.12001

Ito, M., Odgers, C., Schueller, S., et al. (2020). *Social media and youth wellbeing: What we know and where we could go.* Connected Learning Alliance.

Kiang, L., Witkow, M. R., & Champagne, M. C. (2013). Normative changes in ethnic and American identities and links with adjustment among Asian American adolescents. *Developmental Psychology, 49*(9), 1713–1722. https://doi.org/10.1037/a0030840

Kowalski, R. M., Morgan, C. A., Drake-Lavelle, K., & Allison, B. (2016). Cyberbullying among college students with disabilities. *Computers in Human Behavior, 57*, 416–427. https://doi.org/10.1016/j.chb.2015.12.044

Kuper, L. E., Wright, L., & Mustanski, B. (2018). Gender identity development among transgender and gender nonconforming emerging adults: An intersectional approach. *International Journal of Transgenderism, 19*(4), 436–455. https://doi.org/10.1080/15532739.2018.1443869

Kydland, F., Molka-Danielsen, J., & Balandin, S. (2012). Examining the use of social media tool 'Flickr' for impact on loneliness for people with intellectual disability. In T. Fallmyr (Ed.), *NOKOBIT2012: Proceedings of the 2012 Norsk konferanse for organisasjoners bruk av informasjonsteknologi* (pp. 253–264). Akademika forlag.

Löfgren-Mårtenson, L. (2008). Love in cyberspace: Swedish young people with intellectual disabilities and the internet. *Scandinavian Journal of Disability Research, 10*(2), 125–138. https://doi.org/10.1080/15017410701758005

Madden, M., Lenhart, A., Duggan, M., Cortesi, S., & Gasser, U. (2013). *Teens and technology 2013.* Pew Research Center. http://www.pewinternet.org/~/media//Files/Reports/2013/PIP_Teensand Technology2013.pdf

Manago, A. M. (2015). Media and the development of identity. In R. Scott & S. Kosslyn (Eds.), *Emerging trends in the social and behavioral sciences* (pp. 1–14). Wiley & Sons, Inc.

Masten, A. S., & Reed, M. G. J. (2002). Resilience in development. In C. R. Snyder, & S. J. Lopez (Eds.), *Handbook of positive psychology* (pp. 74–88). Oxford University Press.

Mayhew, A. & Weigle, P. (2018). Media engagement and identity formation among minority youth. *Child and Adolescent Psychiatric Clinics of North America, 27*(2), 269–285. https://doi.org/10.1016/j.chc.2017.11.012

McClimens, A., & Gordon, F. (2008). Presentation of self in everyday life: How people labelled with intellectual disability manage identity as they engage the blogosphere. *Sociological Research Online, 13*(4), 1. https://doi.org/10.5153/sro.1774

McConnell, E., Néray, B., Hogan, B., Korpak, A., Clifford, A., & Birkett, M. (2018). "Everybody puts their whole life on Facebook": Identity management and the online social networks of LGBTQ youth. *International Journal of Environmental Research and Public Health, 15*(6), Article 1078. https://doi.org/10.3390/ijerph15061078

Monkman, L. (2020, April 13). *First Nations TikTok users hope to inspire youth to learn more about their cultures.* CBC. https://www.cbc.ca/news/indigenous/tiktok-inspire-indigenous-youth-1.5528667

Noor, P. (2020, July 1). The Navajo teenager who went viral reporting on coronavirus: "I just want us to be seen." *The Guardian.* https://www.theguardian.com/us-news/2020/may/22/navajo-teenager-tiktok-reporting-coronavirus

Odgers, C. (2018). Smartphones are bad for some teens, not all. *Nature, 554*, 432–434.

Odgers, C. L., & Jensen, M. R. (2020). Annual research review: Adolescent mental health in the digital age: Facts, fears, and future directions. *Journal of Child Psychology and Psychiatry, 61*(3), 336–348. https://doi.org/10.1111/jcpp.13190

Odgers, C., & Robb, M. B. (2020). *Tweens, teens, tech, and mental health: Coming of age in an increasingly digital, uncertain, and unequal world, 2020.* Common Sense Media.

OECD. (2016). *Are there differences in how advantaged and disadvantaged students use the internet?* http://dx.doi.org/10.1787/5jlv8zq6hw43-en

Ohlheiser, A. (2020, January 28). TikTok has become the soul of the LGBTQ Internet. *Washington Post.* https://www.washingtonpost.com/technology/2020/01/28/tiktok-has-become-soul-lgbtq-internet/

Oldenburg, R. (1989). *The great good place: Cafés, coffee shops, community centers, beauty parlors, general stores, bars, hangouts, and how they get you through the day.* Paragon House.

Palmer, N. A., Kosciw, J. G., Greytak, E. A., Ybarra, M. L., Korchmaros, J., & Mitchell, K. J. (2013). *Out online: The experiences of lesbian, gay, bisexual and transgender youth on the internet.* GLSEN.

Panizo, L. C. (2018). Gay teenagers in the digital age: Orientations for educators. Alteridad. *Revista de Educación, 14*(1), 62–72. https://doi.org/10.17163/alt.v14n1.2019.05

Park-Lee, E., Lipari, R. N., Bose, J., et al. (2018, July). *Substance use and mental health issues among U.S.-born American Indians or Alaska Natives residing on and off tribal lands.* Center for Behavioral Health Statistics and Quality. https://www.samhsa.gov/data/sites/default/files/cbhsq-reports/DRAIANTribalAreas2018/DRAIANTribalAreas2018.pdf

Pew Research Center. (2013). *A survey of LGBT Americans*. Retrieved April 11, 2021. https://www.pewsocialtrends.org/2013/06/13/a-surveyof-lgbt-americans/

Phinney, J. S. (1990). Ethnic identity in adolescents and adults: Review of research. *Psychological Bulletin, 108*(3), 499–514. https://doi.org/10.1037/0033-2909 .108.3.499

Phinney, J. S., & Ong, A. D. (2007). Conceptualization and measurement of ethnic identity: Current status and future directions. *Journal of Counseling Psychology, 54*(3), 271–281. https://doi.org/10.1037/0022-0167.54.3.271

Pollio, D. E., Batey, D. S., Bender, K., Ferguson, K., & Thompson, S. (2013). Technology use among emerging adult homeless in two US cities. *Social Work, 58*(2), 173–175. https://doi.org/10.1093/sw/swt006

Przybylski, A. K., & Bowes, L. (2017). Cyberbullying and adolescent well-being in England: A population-based cross-sectional study. *The Lancet Child & Adolescent Health, 1*(1), 19–26. https://doi.org/10.1016/S2352-4642(17)30011-1

Quintana, S. M. (1994). A model of ethnic perspective-taking ability applied to Mexican-American children and youth. *International Journal of Intercultural Relations, 18*(4), 419–448. https://doi.org/10.1016/0147-1767(94)90016-7

Rice, E., Lee, A., & Taitt, S. (2011). Cell phone use among homeless youth: Potential for new health interventions and research. *Journal of Urban Health, 88*(6), 1175–1182. https://doi.org/10.1007/s11524-011-9624-z

Rice, E., Milburn, N. G., Rotheram-Borus, M. J., Mallett, S., & Rosenthal, D. (2005). The effects of peer group network properties on drug use among homeless youth. *The American Behavioral Scientist, 48*(8), 1102–1123. https://doi.org/ 10.1177/0002764204274194

Robards, B., Churchill, B., Vivienne, S., Hanckel, B., & Byron, P. (2019). Twenty years of 'cyberqueer': The enduring significance of the internet for young LGBTIQ+ people. In P. Aggleton, R. Cover, D. Leahy, D. Marshall, & M. L. Rasmussen (Eds.), *Youth, sexuality, and sexual citizenship* (pp. 151–167). Routledge. https://doi.org/10.4324/9781351214742-15

Robertson, M. A. (2013). "How do I know I am gay?": Understanding sexual orientation, identity and behavior among adolescents in an LGBT youth center. *Sexuality and Culture, 18*(1), 385–404. https://doi-org.ezproxy.wellesley.edu/ 10.1007/s12119-013-9203-4

Romano, A. (2019, October 10). *A group of YouTubers is trying to prove the site systematically demonetizes queer content*. Vox. https://www.vox.com/culture/ 2019/10/10/20893258/youtube-lgbtq-censorship-demonetization-nerd-city-algorithm-report

Rosario, M., Schrimshaw, E. W., & Hunter, J. (2008). Predicting different patterns of sexual identity development over time among lesbian, gay, and bisexual youths: A cluster analytic approach. *American Journal of Community Psychology, 42*(3–4), 266–282. https://doi-org.ezproxy.wellesley.edu/10.1007/ s10464-008-9207-7

Rushing, S. C., & Stephens, D. (2011). Use of media technologies by Native American teens and young adults in the pacific northwest: Exploring their utility for designing culturally appropriate technology-based health interventions. *The Journal of Primary Prevention, 32*(3), Article 135. https://doi.org/10.1007/ s10935-011-0242-z

Rushing, S. N., Stephens, D., & Dog, T. L. G. (2018). We R Native: Harnessing technology to improve health outcomes for American Indian and Alaska Native youth. *Journal of Adolescent Health, 62*(2), S83–S84. https://doi.org/10.1016/j.jadohealth.2017.11.168

Salk, R. H., Thoma, B. C., & Choukas-Bradley, B. (2020). The gender minority youth study: Overview of methods and social media recruitment of a nationwide sample of U.S. cisgender and transgender adolescents. *Archives of Sexual Behavior, 49*(7), 2601–2610. https://doi.org/10.1007/s10508-020-01695-x

Schimmel-Bristow, A., & Ahrens, K. R. (2018). Technology use among special populations. In M. A. Moreno & A. Radovic (Eds.), *Technology and adolescent mental health* (pp. 43–55). Springer. https://doi.org/10.1007/978-3-319-69638-6

Scroggs, B., & Vennum, A. (2020). Gender and sexual minority group identification as a process of identity development during emerging adulthood. *Journal of LGBT Youth, 18*(3), 287–304. https://doi.org/10.1080/19361653.2020.1722780

Seale, J. K., (2007). Strategies for supporting the online publishing activities of adults with learning difficulties. *Disability & Society, 22*(2), 173–186. https://doi.org/10.1080/09687590601141626

Simpson, E., & Semaan, B. (2020). For you, or for "you"?: Everyday LGBTQ+ encounters with TikTok. *Proceedings of the ACM on Human-Computer Interaction, 4*(252), 1–34. https://doi.org/10.1145/3432951

Soukup, C. (2006). Computer-mediated communication as a digital third place: Building Oldenburg's great good places on the world wide web. *New Media & Society, 8*(3), 421–440. https://doi.org/10.1177/1461444806061953

Spencer, M. B., Dupree, D., & Hartmann, T. (1997). *A phenomenological variant of ecological systems theory (PVEST): A self organization perspective in context.* UPenn. http://repository.upenn.edu/gse_pubs/4

Spooner, T. (2001, December 12). *Asian-Americans and the internet.* Pew Research Center: Internet, Science & Tech. https://www.pewresearch.org/internet/2001/12/12/asian-americans-and-the-internet/

Stephan, W., & Stephan, C. W. (2000). An integrated threat theory of prejudice. In S. Oskamp (Ed.). *Reducing prejudice and discrimination* (pp. 23–46). Lawrence Erlbaum Associates.

Stevens, R., Gilliard-Matthews, S., Dunaev, J., Woods, M. K., & Brawner, B. M. (2017). The digital hood: Social media use among youth in disadvantaged neighborhoods. *New Media & Society, 19*(6), 950–967. https://doi.org/10.1177/1461444815625941

Stewart, S., Riecken, T., Scott, T., Tanaka, M., & Riecken, J. (2008). Expanding health literacy: Indigenous youth creating videos. *Journal of Health Psychology, 13*(2), 180–189. https://doi.org/10.1177/1359105307086709

Subrahmanyam, K., Smahel, D., & Greenfield, P. (2006). Connecting developmental constructions to the internet: Identity presentation and sexual exploration in online teen chat rooms. *Developmental Psychology, 42*, 395–406. https://doi.org/10.1037/0012-1649.42.3.395

Surgeon General. (2001). *Mental health: Culture, race, ethnicity. Supplement to mental health: A report of the Surgeon General.* US Government Printing Office.

Sybert, J. (2021). The demise of #NSFW: Contested platform governance and Tumblr's 2018 adult content ban. *New Media & Society.* https://doi.org/10.1177/1461444821996715

Trent, M., Dooley, D. G., & Dougé, J. (2019). The impact of racism on child and adolescent health. *Pediatrics, 144*(2), e20191765. https://doi.org/10.1542/peds .2019-1765

Tynes, B. M., English, D., Del Toro, J., Smith, N. A., Lozada, F. T., & Williams, D. R. (2020). Trajectories of online racial discrimination and psychological functioning among African American and Latino adolescents. *Child Development, 91*(5), 1577–1593. https://doi.org/10.1111/cdev.13350

Uba, L. (1994). *Asian Americans: Personality patterns, identity, and mental health.* Guilford Press.

Umaña-Taylor, A. J., Quintana, S. M., Lee, R. M., et al. (2014). Ethnic and racial identity during adolescence and into young adulthood: An integrated conceptualization. *Child Development, 85*(1), 21–39. https://doi.org/10.1111/cdev.12196

Umaña-Taylor, A. J., Tynes, B. M., Toomey, R. B., Williams, D. R., & Mitchell, K. J. (2015). Latino adolescents' perceived discrimination in online and offline settings: An examination of cultural risk and protective factors. *Developmental Psychology, 51*(1), 87–100. https://doi.org/10.1037/a0038432

US Census Bureau. (2019, October 2). *Population estimates show aging across race groups differs.* https://www.census.gov/newsroom/press-releases/2019/esti mates-characteristics.html

Varjas, K., Meyers, J., Kiperman, S., & Howard, A. (2013). Technology hurts? Lesbian, gay, and bisexual youth perspectives of technology and cyberbullying. *Journal of School Violence, 12*(1), 27–44. https://doi.org/10.1080/15388220.2012.731665

VonHoltz, L. A. H., Frasso, R., Golinkoff, J. M., Lozano, A. J., Hanlon, A., & Dowshen, N. (2018). Internet and social media access among youth experiencing homelessness: Mixed-methods study. *Journal of Medical Internet Research, 20*(5), e184. https://doi.org/10.2196/jmir.9306

Wang, C., Barlis, J., Do, K. A., et al. (2020). Barriers to mental health help seeking at school for Asian- and Latinx-American adolescents. *School Mental Health, 12*(1), 182–194. https://doi.org/10.1007/s12310-019-09344-y

Wargo, J. M. (2016). "Every selfie tells a story . . .": LGBTQ youth lifestreams and new media narratives as connective identity texts. *New Media & Society, 19*(4), 560–578. https://doi.org/10.1177/1461444815612447

Wei, R., & Lo, V. H. (2006). Staying connected while on the move: Cell phone use and social connectedness. *New Media & Society, 8*(1), 53–72. https://doi.org/10 .1177/1461444806059870

Wexler, L. (2009). The importance of identity, history, and culture in the wellbeing of Indigenous youth. *The Journal of the History of Childhood and Youth, 2*(2), 267–276. https://doi.org/10.1353/hcy.0.0055

Wexler, L. M., DiFluvio, G., & Burke, T. K. (2009). Resilience and marginalized youth: Making a case for personal and collective meaning-making as part of resilience research in public health. *Social Science & Medicine, 69*(4), 565–570.

Whitbeck, L. B., & Hoyt, D. R. (1999). *Nowhere to grow: Homeless and runaway adolescents and their families.* Aldine de Gruyter.

Williams, J., Bolland, K. A., Hooper, L., Church, W., Tomek, S., & Bolland, J. (2014). Say it loud: The Obama effect and racial/ethnic identification of adolescents. *Journal of Human Behavior in the Social Environment, 24*(7), 858–868. https://doi.org/10.1080/10911359.2014.909343

Williams, W. S., & Moody, A. L. (2019). Analyzed selfie: Stereotype enactment, projection, and identification among digitally native Black girls. *Women & Therapy*, *42*(3–4), 366–384. https://doi.org/10.1080/02703149.2019.1622901

Ybarra, M. L., Mitchell, K. J., Palmer, N. A., & Reisner, S. L. (2015). Online social support as a buffer against online and offline peer and sexual victimization among U.S. LGBT and non-LGBT youth. *Child Abuse & Neglect*, *39*, 123–136. https://doi.org/10.1016/j.chiabu.2014.08.006

Yip, T., Seaton, E. K., & Sellers, R. M. (2006). African American racial identity across the lifespan: Identity status, identity content, and depressive symptoms. *Child Development*, *77*(5), 1504–1517. https://doi.org/10.1111/j.1467-8624.2006.00950.x

Young, S. D., & Rice, E. (2011). Online social networking technologies, HIV knowledge, and sexual risk and testing behaviors among homeless youth. *AIDS and Behavior*, *15*(2), 253–260. https://doi.org/10.1007/s10461-010-9810-0

Zhai, E., Jordan, K., Reeves-Miller, T., Xiao, T., & Charmaraman, L. (2020). *Self-care and wellbeing on social media for adolescents of color*. Panel presented at the Diversity Challenge, Boston College, Boston, MA.

Zhang, Y., & Leung, L. (2014). A review of social networking service (SNS) research in communication journals from 2006 to 2011. *New Media & Society*, *17*(7), 1007–1024.

PART III

Digital Media and Adolescent Mental Disorders

9 Depression and Anxiety in the Context of Digital Media

Megan A. Moreno and Anna F. Jolliff

Over the past two decades, scientists have strived to understand the relationship between digital media use and two common mental illnesses in adolescents: depression and anxiety. The lifetime prevalence of depression or anxiety among youth increased from 5.4% in 2003, to 8% in 2007, to 8.4% in 2012 (Bitsko et al., 2018). In this chapter we begin by defining depression and anxiety, and addressing the state of the science around the relationship between these two mental illnesses and social media use. We then consider both potential problematic digital media behaviors for depression and anxiety, as well as potential benefits of social media for youth with these conditions. Throughout this chapter we consider other factors that may influence the proposed relationships among digital media use, depression, and anxiety. We conclude the chapter with considerations of clinical implications and future research directions.

Theories of Depression and Anxiety

This chapter will frequently discuss symptoms of major depressive disorder (MDD) and symptoms of generalized anxiety disorder (GAD). We will refer to these as "depression" and "anxiety" for short, but keep in mind that, first, there are many types of depression and anxiety; and second, the research described here is not limited to participants with clinically significant MDD or GAD, but often simply with depressive or anxious symptoms.

The fifth edition of the *Diagnostic and Statistical Manual* (DSM-5) defines a major depressive episode as a period of at least two weeks during which an individual experiences either a depressed mood or a markedly diminished interest in normal activities (American Psychiatric Association, 2013). In adolescents, the depressed mood many manifest as irritability. Also key to the diagnosis of depression is decreased performance or increased distress in a major area of life, such as school, work, or relationships. In contrast, GAD is characterized as a period of at least six months during which a child experiences excessive and uncontrollable worry, worry that is inappropriate or out of proportion to the anticipated event. In children, this worry is often about competence or performance. Additional symptoms of GAD include restlessness, difficulty concentrating, or sleep disturbance.

There are many theories to explain the development, maintenance, and treatment of depression and anxiety. It will be helpful to have a working theory of depression and anxiety to understand its relationship to digital media use; as such, we will describe two example theories here. However, keep in mind that there are many qualified theories to describe the etiology and maintenance of mental illness – many more than can be discussed in this handbook.

One such theory is cognitive theory. According to cognitive theory, "cognition is at the core of human suffering" (Sommers-Flanagan & Sommers-Flanagan, 2018, p. 273). Factors such as early life events, genetic predisposition, and caregiver modeling lead individuals to develop rigid and negative beliefs about the self, other people, and the world at large. When faced with a life stressor, an individual's core beliefs are triggered and present as automatic thoughts. Over time, the repeated activation of automatic thoughts results in information processing, emotions, and behaviors that are consistent with depression or anxiety. Core beliefs consistent with depression or anxiety might include "I'm unlovable," "I'm powerless," or "I'm defective." There are many critical events during adolescence – and, relevant to this chapter, events on social media – that might activate thoughts like these. According to cognitive theory, depression and anxiety can be reduced through the conscious revision of automatic thoughts and the core beliefs underlying them. This "validity testing" is often performed in partnership with a therapist or another trusted person.

A second theory through which we will view depression and anxiety, in relation to digital media use, is multicultural theory. This is not so much a theory for the etiology of illness as it is a lens, or an orientation, that all theorists must integrate in order to effectively explain and diagnose illness as well as guide treatment (Bitsko et al., 2018). In short, multicultural theory suggests that mental illness develops in response to the oppressive nature of the dominant culture. According to multicultural theorist Derald Wing Sue, "people of color from the moment of birth are subjected to multiple racial micro-aggressions, from the media, peers, neighbors, friends, teachers and even in the educational process" (Sue et al., 2010, p. 212). It is easy to imagine how symptoms of depression and anxiety might silently develop in response to these social forces. Although multicultural counseling does not emphasize diagnosis (in part because psychopathology has been defined using Westernized notions of normativity) treatment *is* possible. Healing from depression and anxiety, from a multicultural lens, must integrate culturally responsive processes and practices, often in community with culturally competent others.

State of the Science: Social Media, Depression, and Anxiety

Over the past decade, the empirical literature and lay news media have addressed at length associations between social media, depression, and anxiety. The sheer volume of studies in this area has led to a recent upswing in published systematic reviews on this topic. Two such systematic reviews found a small positive association between social media use and these two mental illnesses; however, these reviews noted that the quality and practical significance of these studies are often low, and they are typically not designed to capture the nuance of the effect (Keles et al., 2019; Piteo & Ward, 2020). Another 2016 systematic review analyzed 70 studies looking at the relationship between social media use and depression or anxiety, and found that while passive use of social media was not associated with depression, specific behaviors (e.g., self-comparison) were (Seabrook et al., 2016). In sum, recent systematic reviews indicate that research to date is not designed to piece apart the nuanced relationship between social media use and mental health.

Challenges in Studying Depression and Social Media

The relationship between social media, depression, and anxiety is a challenging area of research for several reasons. As illnesses that wax and wane over time, assessments of depression or anxiety at a single time point may not fully capture the illness experience. A critical approach is to use measurements of mental illness that are shown to be valid measurements of the illness in question, such as the Center for Epidemiologic Studies.

The Depression Scale for Children (CES-DC), the Patient Health Questionnaire-9 (PHQ 9), the Generalized Anxiety Disorder scale – 7 (GAD 7), and the Screen for Child Anxiety Related Emotional Disorders (SCARED) are all empirically supported measures of depression or anxiety in adolescents and young adults (Cannon et al., 2007; Keles et al., 2019; Kroenke et al., 2001; Piteo & Ward, 2020; Richardson et al., 2010; Weissman et al., 1980). Despite the availability of valid and reliable screening tools for depression and anxiety, some studies have not employed such tools and have selected instead ad hoc measurement tools, making the results of these studies difficult to interpret (Twenge & Campbell, 2019).

A second challenge when studying depression and social media is determining a measurement approach for social media use. Most commonly, studies focus on *quantity* of social media use in terms of hours or minutes. Screen time is typically measured using self-reported estimates, which are often inaccurate (Ellis, 2019; Moreno, Jelenchick, et al., 2012). Other studies have employed passive observation to understand screen time, which involves asking a participant to download an application on their phone to track their social media use (Messner et al., 2019). However, these studies tend to capture time on a specific device, and adolescent technology use is known to incorporate multiple devices. It is recommended that future studies focus on other aspects of adolescents' technology experiences, such as *quality* or *importance* placed on use. These measurement approaches are less common, and present new ways to examine media's relationship to adolescent health.

Third, many studies examining social media use, depression, and anxiety do not focus on normative social media use. There is a wealth of studies measuring problematic social media use or social media "addiction," specifically, as opposed to various qualities of normative use (Duradoni et al., 2020; Hussain et al., 2020). While these constructs are relevant to adolescent mental health, positive associations between *problematic* social media use and mental illness may not apply to *normative* social media use (Przepiorka & Blachnio, 2020). Thus, much of the research on social media use and depression or anxiety among adolescents actually comments on nonnormative use, and the implications for the general population of adolescents cannot be inferred.

Key Hypotheses on the Relationship between Social Media, Depression, and Anxiety

As we consider several key hypotheses in the literature on the relationship between social media screen time, depression, and anxiety, we ask you to keep in mind the measurement and study design issues that may influence these study findings.

The first hypothesis posits that there is a positive linear relationship between social media, depression, and anxiety. That is, as social media use increases, so does risk for anxiety and depression. From a cognitive theoretical perspective, it may be that exposure to certain stimuli on social media (e.g., a photoshopped image, a photo from a party to which one was not invited, a heartbreaking news story) might activate or reinforce existing negative beliefs about oneself ("I'm worthless") or the world ("everything is out of control"). Further, time spent on social media might *displace* time spent on other behaviors, behaviors that may have resulted in mental health-promoting thoughts (e.g., "I have a knack for piano" or "I'm a good teammate"). The "crowding out" hypothesis explains positive associations between depression and screen time by saying that screen time is related to depression when it occurs at the expense of other beneficial activities (McDool et al., 2020; Twenge, Joiner, Martin, & Rogers, 2018). As discussed, multiple systematic reviews support a weak positive relationship between social media use and adolescent depression or anxiety. However, because the studies reviewed are often cross-sectional, it is difficult to ascertain whether social media use causes depression or anxiety, or whether the presence of anxiety or depression makes one more prone to use social media (and less prone, for example, to activities such as exercise, in-person socialization, vocational pursuits, or recreation).

Certain studies have detected greater risk for anxiety and depression after a certain threshold of social media use is met, which has been cited as three hours per day (Riehm et al., 2019), four hours per day (Barman et al., 2018), and nearly five hours per day (O'Keeffe et al., 2011).

A second hypothesis states that a U-shaped curve best captures the relationship between internalizing symptoms and social media use, with negative mental health associated with very low or very high use. There is some empirical support for this hypothesis (Belanger et al., 2011; Liu et al., 2016; Moreno, Jelenchick, et al., 2012). From a multicultural perspective on anxiety or depression, adolescents with nonnormative (very high or very low) use may be in other ways alienated from the dominant culture. High social media use might indicate a lack of participation in other areas of life, while very low social media involvement might signify estrangement from what now constitutes a developmentally appropriate activity: social media. Further, youth at the very high and very low ends of social media may be socioeconomically disadvantaged; they may live in low-resource settings, without consistent access to the Internet, or in contexts where social media use is the only activity available. Financial hardship, or disempowerment, is associated with depression and anxiety (Selfhout et al., 2009). Further, the U-shaped curve may also result from the stimuli encountered on social media. Frequent social media use puts minority youth at risk of daily, and sometimes hourly, evidence of minority oppression in the form of news media. Similarly, those who choose to stay off of social media may be trying to avoid these stimuli. Importantly, detecting the U-shaped curve requires the use of analytic approaches beyond traditional linear regression. Therefore, it is possible that studies presumed to support a linear positive relationship actually support the U-shaped curve hypothesis.

A third hypothesis is that there is no relationship between social media and depression, or social media and anxiety. More specifically, this hypothesis suggests that there is no *population-level clinically significant* relationship between these illnesses and social media use. Rather, certain subgroups may be at elevated risk for depression and anxiety due to social media use (Radovic et al., 2017) while for others there is no relationship, and for still others social media use actually *promotes* mental health. At a population level, this variability cannot be detected. From a multicultural perspective, this makes sense; one would never expect to find a "population level" effect of social media on depression or anxiety, in a world where oppression (and consequential mental illness) is not equally distributed. A white, cisgender child from a middle-class household is likely to see aspects of their own life reflected online; in contrast, those with any number of minority identities may feel "othered" by going online. The "no relationship" hypothesis is supported by several studies that have identified no population-level statistically significant association between social media use and depression or emotional problems (Anjum et al., 2019; Fardouly et al., 2018; Ferguson, 2021; Jelenchick et al., 2013). Given the additional difficulty of publishing statistically insignificant findings, it may be that more studies have detected the "null" relationship than have been published.

The fourth and final hypothesis is "it's complicated," which mirrors a common relationship status adolescents themselves like to use. The majority of studies focus on screen time as a measure of social media use, and it may be that other aspects of social media use relate more to depression and anxiety than does screen time. This hypothesis finds theoretical support from a cognitive perspective of anxiety and depression. Different online behaviors generate different thoughts, thoughts that may either reinforce or challenge beliefs about the self. Cognitive theory further states that *avoidance* is a key behavior maintaining illnesses like anxiety and depression. If an adolescent scrolls through social media primarily as a means of avoiding – rather than confronting – dreaded stimuli, social media use would likely contribute to the maintenance of anxiety. In contrast, a youth who uses their Finsta (Fake Instagram) to air the "less acceptable" sides of themselves may learn over time, through this online "validity testing," that what they thought were unacceptable features are warmly received by peers. Last, children who already have depression or anxiety might assign social media different worth; they may compulsively check social media for evidence in support of their own worth, while a child who affords social media no such power would not feel this attachment toward use.

Few studies have been designed to test Hypothesis 4; that is, few assess the specific features or intentions underlying adolescents' social media use. As such, it remains to be seen how the specific uses of social media differentially relate to depression and anxiety. A recently developed tool to measure the quality of use, the Adolescents' Digital Technology Interactions and Importance scale, is a promising means of evaluating the importance that adolescents assign to different affordances of technology, including technology to bridge online/offline experiences and preferences, technology to go outside one's identity or offline environment. and technology for social connection (Moreno et al., 2020). Tools like these are needed to understand the nuanced relationship between social media use on depression and anxiety in adolescents.

Where Are We Now?

A 2020 paper synthesized data from systematic reviews and meta-analyses between 2014 and 2019. This included cohort, longitudinal, and ecological momentary assessment studies (Odgers & Jensen, 2020). They authors concluded that most research has been correlational, focused on adults, and has led to a mix of conflicting results. They also observed that most studies report "small associations ... that do not offer a way of distinguishing cause from effect and, as estimated, are unlikely to be of clinical or practical significance" (p. 336). It has become increasingly evident that the current literature may not support Hypothesis 1, but that Hypotheses 2–4 above remain available for more nuanced and high-quality studies to address.

Potentially Problematic Digital Media Behaviors for Depression and Anxiety

As discussed, the relationship between screen time and depression and anxiety in adolescents is not straightforward. Thus, rather than focusing on time spent on social media, an alternative approach is to focus on specific digital behaviors and their relationships to depression and anxiety. Problematic or addictive social media use is discussed elsewhere in this handbook. The present chapter will discuss problematic aspects of *normative* use that are associated with depression and anxiety among adolescents. As a reminder, depression is often characterized by symptoms such as low mood, fatigue, diminished pleasure in activities, and thoughts of death, while anxiety is characterized by symptoms like excessive worry, sleep disturbance, and restlessness. In this section, we will examine how symptoms of depression and anxiety are related to specific adverse experiences on social media, including exposure to cyberbullying, troubling news media, and certain types of highly visual social media. Next, we will consider other variables that strengthen the observed relationships between social media use, depression, and anxiety, including fear of missing out, sleep, and gender.

Risk 1: Adverse Online Experiences

Cyberbullying

The majority of teens have experienced an instance of cyber-victimization at some point. The most common categories of cyber-victimization include name-calling, spreading of rumors, and receiving explicit or unwanted images. However, cyberbullying is less common – and often more serious (Anderson, 2018). Cyberbullying has occurred when cyber-victimization is repeated, intentional, and unwanted (Ansary, 2020). Unsurprisingly, experiencing cyberbullying is linked to depression and anxiety (Alhajji et al., 2019; Barry et al., 2019; Tian et al., 2018; Willenberg et al., 2020). Indeed, a previous study found that online harassment was key to explaining the observed relationship between social media use and depressive symptoms (Kelly et al., 2018). From a cognitive theoretical perspective, experiences of cyber-victimization may cause or reinforce core beliefs associated with depression and anxiety (e.g., "I am unlovable," "I am powerless").

It is also important to adopt a multicultural perspective when understanding the relationship between cyberbullying and depression or anxiety. Adolescents of color frequently experience online racism, including online micro-aggressions, discrimination, and hate crimes (Moreno et al., 2016). Some research suggests, however, that racial minority adolescents are actually *less* likely to report cyberbullying (Alhajji et al., 2019; Edwards et al., 2016). It is unclear whether this finding is due to a real difference in the prevalence of cyberbullying; increased stigma in certain racial or ethnic groups around *reporting* cyberbullying; or because racism is so common to minority adolescents' online experience that they do not recognize it as cyberbullying. Just as offline experiences of racism and bullying are linked to symptoms of depression and anxiety, so these symptoms can emerge from the same interactions online (Cannon et al., 2007).

Adolescent females and members of sexual minority groups are also more at risk of upsetting experiences online (Kroenke et al., 2001; Richardson et al., 2010). Research suggests females are more likely to report cyberbullying and are more negatively affected by it (Alhajji et al., 2019; Rice et al., 2015). Adolescent females are also more likely to be victims of digital intimate partner violence (Burns et al., 2016). In combination with poor sleep, experiences of cyberbullying have been shown to fully explain the relationship between high social media use and psychological distress among females (Kelly et al., 2018).

News Media

Research shows that 77% of adolescents obtain their news through social media (Robb, 2020). The news is frequently troubling and, as such, exposure to it, via social media, may elevate symptoms of anxiety and depression for certain adolescents. This may be especially true for members of stigmatized or disenfranchised groups, as well as people with existing depressive or anxiety symptoms (Caporino et al., 2020; Sahoo et al., 2020; Weinstein, 2018). In the year 2020, for example, adolescents in the United States could not open their most-used social media apps without confronting news of a global pandemic, racial injustice, wildfires across California and Oregon, and a highly contentious election. Black and Hispanic or Latino teens describe finding the news to be more important, and feeling more affected by the news, than their white counterparts (Mundt et al., 2018). Adolescents living in the United States who identify as black, transgender, or undocumented risk facing news of injustice against themselves or others with their same identities nearly every time they log into social media (Campbell & Valera, 2020; Ince et al., 2017; Leopold & Bell, 2017; Robb, 2020). While social media is a platform on which many people can and do effectively advocate for social justice and raise awareness about social injustice, both cognitive and multicultural theories help to explain why encounters with news on social media might perpetuate depression and anxiety. The news can reinforce negative beliefs about the world (*it's dangerous*), oneself (*I'm powerless*), and one's future (*people like me don't make it very far*).

Risk 2: Highly Visual Social Media

Exposure to certain highly visual social media (HVSM) is a risk factor for depression and anxiety in some adolescents. Undoubtedly, visual social media can be positive. However, in this section, we use HVSM as shorthand for *risky* HVSM – for example, media that enables users to modify or "improve" their appearance before uploading (Weissman et al., 1980). Many of the most popular social media platforms for adolescents (Instagram, Snapchat, and most recently TikTok) are visual platforms that allow for appearance modification (Anderson & Jiang, 2018). While use of HVSM has also been associated with disordered eating, the relationship between social media and disordered eating is covered elsewhere in this handbook. The present section will explore the relationship between HVSM and depression and anxiety.

Some of the thoughts and feelings that characterize depression and anxiety may be triggered by exposure to HVSM. Feelings of worthlessness or fears of inadequacy may be sparked or exacerbated by frequent exposure to visually "perfected" images.

Youth may compare themselves to the people they "follow," and find themselves lacking (Marengo et al., 2018). From a multicultural perspective, visual media are uniquely able to transmit messages from the dominant culture: how to look, how to behave, and the types of people and behaviors that are deserving of praise.

People with existing tendencies toward poor body image are at particular risk of depression or anxiety as a result of exposure to HVSM (Kelly et al., 2018; Marengo et al., 2018). The tendency to be bothered if tagged in an unflattering picture is associated with depression among college students (Robinson et al., 2019). HVSM also allows for taking, editing, and uploading pictures of oneself online, which has been linked to anxiety in college students (Mills et al., 2018; Wick & Keel, 2020). Appearance-related social comparisons, which are uniquely afforded by HVSM, have been associated with depression (Choukas-Bradley et al., 2020; Hawes et al., 2020). Engaging with "pro-ana" (pro-anorexia) media or "thinspiration," which often contains depictions of thinness, "clean" foods, and calorie-deficient diets, has been linked with depression and anxiety (Fitzsimmons-Craft et al., 2020; Jennings et al., 2020). From a cognitive perspective, social media may reinforce the negative belief that one's worth is tied to bodily appearance. If viewers perceive themselves as failing to meet these standards, depressive or anxious symptoms may increase. It may also be that adolescents who are anxious or depressed *and* dissatisfied with their bodies are more likely to engage with HVSM in pursuit of information (a like, comment, or share) challenges or confirms of their self-beliefs.

However, despite the theoretical justification and some empirical support, a recent scoping review on HVSM and depression found that the relationship between HVSM and depression is inconclusive (McCrory et al., 2020). It may be that the relationships between HVSM and depression are simply better explained by other variables. The absence of an effect may also be due in part to a lack of research studies designed to detect this effect: research on social media use does not always distinguish between HVSM and other social media, let alone differentiate between *positive* and *negative* forms of visual social media. Further, research typically relies on quantitative methods to evaluate the relationship between HVSM and depression and anxiety, which lacks richness and possibility for participants to elaborate on their experiences.

The relationship between social media use and depression or anxiety also may be dependent on a variety of factors that increase risk for internalizing symptoms. Several of these potential moderators are discussed below.

Fear of Missing Out

Fear of missing out, or FOMO, is defined as the "pervasive apprehension that others might be having rewarding experiences from which one is absent" (Przybylski et al., 2013, p. 1841). FOMO in adolescents has been independently associated with both depression and anxiety and, less consistently, with social media use (Barry et al., 2017; Franchina et al., 2018; Przybylski et al., 2013). Given that social media is a place where the (often enviable) experiences of others are constantly on display, it is not difficult to explain the link between social media use and FOMO. More complex is to explain why adolescents who are higher in FOMO are more at risk for depression or anxiety as a consequence of social media use (Fabris et al., 2020). It may be that, for adolescents with tendencies toward FOMO, exposure to friends' and influencers' "highlight reels" creates feelings of worthlessness, worry, and dissatisfaction with one's own daily life. From a cognitive perspective, scrolling through social media might trigger automatic thoughts, such as "no one invites me to anything" or "my life sucks in comparison with hers." The action of scrolling through social media may also be motivated by FOMO, as depressed or anxious adolescents search for evidence to assuage or confirm the belief that they are missing out.

At present, research is mixed on whether FOMO affects the relationship between social media use and depression or anxiety in adolescents. While there is ample evidence that FOMO is associated with *problematic* social media use and problematic smartphone use (Franchina et al., 2018; Przepiorka & Blachnio, 2020), there is insufficient evidence that FOMO explains or strengthens the relationship between typical use and depression or anxiety at a population level. In some cases, this absence of an effect may be due to insufficient measures of social media; as discussed, insufficient measures focus solely on time spent, rather than activities performed or experiences had while online.

Sleep

Sleep is critical to consider in any study of social media and mental illness. Indeed, sleep is perhaps the most consistently supported variable to explain the relationship between social media use and depression or anxiety (Alonzo et al., 2019; Kelly et al., 2018; Lemola et al., 2015; Oshima et al., 2012). However, studies suggesting that sleep explains the relationship between social media use and depression and anxiety have been largely cross-sectional, meaning directionality is subject to interpretation. Before exploring these hypotheses, it is important to note that poor sleep (e.g., sleeping too much or too little, trouble falling asleep) is actually a *symptom* of both depression and anxiety. Thus, sleep trouble is central to the experience of depression and anxiety for many people.

One hypothesis suggests that social media use *causes* sleeplessness, which in turn causes or exacerbates symptoms of depression or anxiety. Social media may cause sleeplessness by displacing sleeping hours and delaying bedtime (Quante et al., 2019). The blue light exposure associated with social media use may disrupt melatonin and cause wakefulness (Blass et al., 2006; Levenson, 2016; Wahnschaffe et al., 2013). It may be that social media is uniquely stimulating as compared to nonsocial online activities, given that it contains a wealth of self-relevant social information and capacity for social interaction.

A second hypotheses interprets the association in the reverse direction. That is, it may be that adolescents who are already depressed or anxious are more prone to sleep disruption. In turn, disrupted sleep leads to social media use, perhaps as adolescents seek distraction or support online. However, this hypothesis is contentious. Some research has shown that the relationship between poor sleep and social media use cannot be explained by existing depression or anxiety (Twenge & Campbell, 2019; Woods & Scott, 2016). Thus, *all* teens – not just those who are anxious or depressed – may benefit from finding soothing activities that are less stimulating than social media, and from following the American Academy of Pediatrics' recommendations to keep devices out of bedrooms at nighttime (Moreno et al., 2016).

Gender

Some studies have suggested that gender may influence the effect of social media use on depression and anxiety. Several individual studies have found that adolescent females are more likely than males to experience depression associated with social media use (Barthorpe et al., 2020; Kelly et al., 2018; Twenge, Joiner, Rogers, & Martin, 2018; Twenge & Martin, 2020; Waterloo et al., 2018). From a multicultural theoretical perspective, the potentially unique negative effects of social media for adolescent females finds support. The design of social media (including affordances for appearance feedback and negative self-comparison) may be uniquely oppressive to adolescent females, particularly females of color, who face great pressure from the dominant culture to conform to a certain beauty ideal (Coyne et al., 2019; Messner et al., 2019). Under multicultural theory, symptoms of anxiety and depression (e.g., guilt, worry, restlessness, diminished pleasure) should not be understood as reflecting psychopathology, but instead reflecting reasonable reactions to the dominant culture.

However, summaries of research found in recent systematic reviews conclude no consistent effect of gender on the relationship between social media use and internalizing symptoms, and typically conclude that more research is needed on this topic (Keles et al., 2019; Piteo & Ward, 2020). A meta-analysis evaluated 67 independent samples of a combined 19,652 participants, and found that the effect of gender on the relationship between time spent on social media and psychological well-being was insignificant (Huang, 2017). A recent review of reviews reported something slightly different: after controlling for confounding variables, the least-depressed adolescent females in the sample had "slightly increased risk for depressive symptoms with daily social media use"(Odgers & Jensen, 2020, p. 341).

While the moderating effect of gender is inconclusive, research supports that males and females do use social media differently (Boyle et al., 2016). Research suggests that females spend more time online and are more likely to say they are nearly constant online users compared to adolescent males (50% vs. 39%) (Anderson & Jiang, 2018; Duggan, 2013). Females are more likely than males to use social media for self-expression, including expression of joy and pride, as well as expression of negative emotions, such as worry, stress, and depression (Egan & Moreno, 2011; Moreno, Christakis, et al., 2012; Waterloo et al., 2018). Given that females compared to males are likely to use online platforms for emotional expression, it is also possible that females with depression turn to social media more readily for support. Thus, it may be that social media use does not predict depressive symptoms, but greater depressive symptoms predict more frequent social media use, especially among females (Heffer et al., 2019).

Potentially Beneficial Digital Media Behaviors for Depression and Anxiety

Certain uses of social media may promote mental health among adolescents. As previously mentioned, cognitive theory would suggest that online experiences that confirm positive beliefs about the self, and those that challenge or invalidate negative beliefs, are likely to reduce depression or anxiety. From a multicultural perspective, uses of social media that create identity-affirming alternatives to offline spaces may mitigate depression and anxiety. However, the hypothesis that social media use directly reduces anxiety or depression is difficult to test. Similar to studies that try to assess whether social media use directly increases depression or anxiety, there are methodologic barriers to these assessments. That being said, empirical research does support a positive association between social media use and adolescents' mental health. This is especially true for adolescents with depression and anxiety, adolescents with unique and marginalized identities, as well as typical adolescents who seek to maintain or promote mental wellness online.

Benefits of Social Media for the Typical Adolescent

Typical adolescents report using social media in ways that may ward off depressive and anxious symptoms, both by seeking information related to these symptoms and by finding support and connection online (Rideout et al., 2018). Research has shown that adolescents often feel happy, amused, or closer to friends while using social media (Weinstein, 2018; Wenninger et al., 2019). While studies over the years have repeatedly demonstrated social networks and support contribute to overall and mental health, too much online social networking may put one at risk for negative experiences, cognitions, and emotions (Ahn, 2012; Longobardi et al., 2020; Negriff, 2019; Rajani et al., 2011). Those who experience isolation, stress, and unmet needs in their offline worlds may find corrective experiences or buffering effects by going online (Nick et al., 2018; Prochnow et al., 2020). One qualitative interview study found that young people naturally and organically developed close-knit communities of close friends, often in the form of private Instagram accounts, on which privacy was a priority and emotional disclosure was safe and commonplace (Gibson & Trnka, 2020). These findings support the positive, adaptive, and strategic use of social media for typical adolescents.

Benefits of Social Media for Adolescents with Depression and Anxiety

Adolescents with depression and anxiety use social media differently than their mentally well peers (Radovic et al., 2017). Thus, the commonly cited associations between social media use, depression, and anxiety may be explained in part by the unique offerings of social media for depressed and anxious youth. Youth have described feeling motivated to share their depression online because it is perceived as easier than sharing in-person, and because they are hoping to connect with others who understand and have had similar experiences (Carey et al., 2018; Rideout et al., 2018). A systematic narrative review of 28 studies on online help-seeking among adolescents found that adolescents commonly cited anonymity, ease of access, and sense of community as driving motivators to find mental health support online (Pretorius et al., 2019). Thus, youth who are already experiencing depression and anxiety may find particular mental health benefits by going online.

Benefits of Social Media for Marginalized Adolescents

Social media may be particularly beneficial to marginalized adolescents, for whom it may not be safe, feasible, or appealing to find support in the offline world. This may include homeless youth, as well as racial, sexual, and gender minority youth. From a multicultural perspective, the possibility of finding support for mental illness while remaining anonymous may help adolescents to overcome shame and stigma, imposed by the dominant culture, around help-seeking. Further, in the wide world of online support, adolescents may be more likely to find support that is tailored to their cultural values and worldview.

A scoping review of 19 studies on individuals experiencing homelessness and their social media use found that for homeless youth, seeking help online minimized barriers and prejudices often encountered in-person (Calvo & Carbonell, 2019). Perhaps for the same reason, sexual and gender minority youth are significantly more likely than straight and cisgender youth to go online for information about depression and anxiety (Marengo et al., 2018; Rideout et al., 2018). Transgender youth have affirmed that social media is a place to garner emotional, informational, and "appraisal" support, or the validation in seeing their same experience reflected in others (Selkie et al., 2020). In sum, both qualitative and quantitative research studies support that homeless youth, as well as sexual and gender minority youth, use social media to find affirming communities and avoid discrimination (Craig et al., 2015; Escobar-Viera et al., 2020; Jenzen, 2017).

Another area of study has focused on experiences of racial minority youth. Perhaps due to a lack of culturally competent healthcare providers offline, black youth are more likely to go online to share their health stories (Rideout et al., 2018). One study interviewed 25 racially and economically diverse undergraduate students to understand the empowering and disempowering aspects of social media (Brough et al., 2020). Interviewees noted that social media allowed them to find and connect with similar others (e.g., by using the #blackLGBTQ hashtag), as well as to represent their voice both by sharing their own stories and observing as others share theirs. However, the same youth noted that social media can have the opposite effect, encouraging conformity to the dominant culture and exposing them to lifestyles that were not relatable (Brough et al., 2020). Thus, while social media may have unique affordances for marginalized youth, its potential to "other" its end users could also worsen mental health symptoms.

With the exception of the studies mentioned above, there is less support for the differential use of social media by racial or ethnic minorities. None of the recent systematic reviews on the relationship between social media use and internalizing symptoms mention race, although two call for more diverse samples (Odgers & Jensen, 2020; Orben, 2020). This suggests that there is little conclusive evidence on the differential use of social media by race, as well as any differences in associated mental health outcomes, whether positive or negative. Given that certain racial and ethnic groups may have fewer opportunities for culturally competent in-person mental health care and support, it is important to understand how they have built alternative spaces online.

Future Research Directions

After describing the literature to date, including studies that examine the relationships between depression and social media, problematic behaviors and experiences on social media, variables that may affect the relationship between social media and mental health, as well as the ways in which social media may alleviate symptoms of depression and anxiety, it is time to consider future research directions. The content above has noted gaps in the current understanding of these topics and exciting opportunities for future research in this area.

From the evidence surrounding depression and social media, we conclude with four critical considerations to move the research forward. These include improved assessments, advanced and nuanced analysis approaches, interpreting results with regard to their practical significance, and improving transparency in linking findings to conclusions. Further, we recommend that future studies incorporate measurements and hypotheses to address potential positive and negative associations between social media use, depression, and anxiety.

First, for improved assessments, many studies of depression do not use validated measurements for depression, leading to findings with limited clinical implications. Further, assessing technology use has most often focused on self-reported quantity of use, leading to biased and inaccurate assessments. Knowing that the vast majority of youth carry smartphones in their pockets, and often use devices passively (for example, walking while listening to music) and other devices simultaneously (for example, performing schoolwork on one's laptop while using a smartphone as a calculator), accurately reporting the time spent on technology is next to impossible and not always meaningful. Improving technology assessments may involve further considerations of quality of use, such as through understanding emotional investment in use, importance placed on use, and the extent to which device use displaces other activities. Further, because offline activities are limited (either due to availability of resources or, the reality of offline discrimination, or recently, by the global COVD-19 pandemic), technology use may not be a marker of risk so much as a necessary path for education, entertainment, support, and connection.

Second, for advanced and nuanced analytic approaches, many previous studies have used population-level analyses such as linear or logistic regression across single populations. Future studies should consider more nuanced analysis approaches, such as quadratic analysis or latent class analysis to identify differences within groups. This approach would allow for detection and appreciation of individual differences that shape interactions with technology (Orben, 2020).

Understanding of practical significance, represented by statistical effect sizes, is also important, as many studies of media identify small effect sizes that are unlikely to drive clinical illness states. Putting these results into context is critical to help readers understand what behaviors are necessary to modify, and what behaviors lose practical significance in the context of an adolescent's whole health.

Finally, we recommend that researchers evaluating social media, depression, and anxiety consider hypotheses that incorporate the potential for both positive and negative health effects, especially within at-risk subgroups. One study using this approach found that 46% of adolescent participants indicated that social media had a positive effect on their mood, while 41% reported neither a positive nor negative effect, and only 6% reported a negative effect (Wright et al., 2020). Measuring diverse uses and motivations for use, alongside validated measures of depression and anxiety, would allow for fuller consideration of social media's effects on a study population, subgroup or individual. Specifically, the social media use among racial minority youth is underexplored. Thus, research should aim to understand the effects of social media on mental health within subgroups and individuals, especially individuals who are frequent targets of discrimination.

Clinical and Intervention Resources

Resources to promote healthy social media use may benefit both clinicians working with adolescents, and interventionists seeking new approaches to test.

There are several key tools and concepts that can be considered toward these goals:

1. The American Academy of Pediatrics policy statement, "Media Use among School-aged Children and Adolescents," recommended that parents establish media use rules to promote safe and healthy media use (Moreno et al., 2016). The policy statement proposed that families create a Family Media Use Plan to select and engage with media use rules. This plan is available online and includes a Media Use Plan in which families can select family rules and expectations around media use. It also includes a Media Time Calculator that allows teens to plan and consider how they spend their time during a given day, including time for media use.
2. Healthy Internet Use Model. The Healthy Internet Use Model focuses on three key concepts: balance, boundaries, and communication (Moreno, 2013).

- Balance: The balance between online and offline time is a critical concept to discuss with youth. Spending time offline, including hanging out with friends, exercising, or spending time outside, is critical to adolescent development. Further, achieving balance provides protection against concerns such as problematic technology use.
- Boundaries: Boundaries refers to setting limits around what youth are willing to display about themselves online or on social media, as well as setting limits in where adolescents spend their time online. Discussing guidelines on what types of personal information are not appropriate to post on social media sites with teens can help prevent them from several online safety risks. These risks include being targets of bullying, unwanted solicitation, or embarrassment.
- Communication: Just as with many tenets of adolescent health, parents should discuss social media and technology with their adolescents early and often. Establishing home rules for social media and technology use as soon as the child begins using these tools is an important way to promote healthy technology use from the beginning.

Further, adolescents should be advised that social media can promote mental health but can also make it worse. Social media can negatively affect health when it displaces other health-promoting activities, like sleep and physical activity. However, social media use that falls within normative ranges should not be the focus of modification. Rather, adolescent patients should be encouraged to pursue those aspects of social media use that research suggests promote mental health, while reducing or eliminating social media use associated with depression and anxiety.

References

Ahn, J. (2012). The effect of social network sites on adolescents' social and academic development: Current theories and controversies. *Journal of the American Society for Information Science and Technology, 62*(8), 1435–1445. https://doi.org/10.1002/asi.21540

Alhajji, M., Bass, S., & Dai, T. (2019). Cyberbullying, mental health, and violence in adolescents and associations with sex and race: Data from the 2015 Youth Risk Behavior Survey. *Global Pediatric Health, 6,* Article 2333794X19868887. https://doi.org/10.1177/2333794X19868887

Alonzo, R. T., Hussain, J., Anderson, K., & Stranges, S. (2019). Interplay between social media use, sleep quality and mental health outcomes in youth: A systematic review. *Sleep Medicine, 64*(64), S365–S365. https://doi.org/10.1016/j.smrv.2020.101414

American Psychiatric Association. (2013). *Diagnostic and statistical manual of mental disorders (DSM-5®)* (5th ed.). http://www.psych.org/MainMenu/Research/DSMIV.aspx

Anderson, M. (2018, September 27). *A majority of teens have experienced some form of cyberbullying.* https://www.pewresearch.org/internet/2018/09/27/a-majority-of-teens-have-experienced-some-form-of-cyberbullying/

Anderson, M., & Jiang, J. (2018, May 31). *Teens, social media, and technology 2018.* Pew Research Center. http://www.pewinternet.org/2018/05/31/teens-social-media-technology-2018/

Anjum, A., Hossain, S., Sikder, T., Uddin, M. E., & Rahim, D. A. (2019, November 6). Investigating the prevalence of and factors associated with depressive symptoms among urban and semi-urban school adolescents in Bangladesh: A pilot study. *International Health.* https://doi.org/10.1093/inthealth/ihz092

Ansary, N. S. (2020). Cyberbullying: Concepts, theories, and correlates informing evidence-based best practices for prevention. *Aggression and Violent Behavior, 50*, Article 101343. https://doi.org/ARTN 101343 10.1016/j.avb.2019.101343

Barman, L., Mukhopadhyay, D. K., & Bandyopadhyay, G. K. (2018). Use of social networking site and mental disorders among medical students in Kolkata, West Bengal. *Indian Journal of Psychiatry, 60*(3), 340–345. https://doi.org/10.4103/psychiatry.IndianJPsychiatry_210_18

Barry, C. T., Briggs, S. M., & Sidoti, C. L. (2019). Adolescent and parent reports of aggression and victimization on social media: Associations with psychosocial adjustment. *Journal of Child and Family Studies, 28*(8), 2286–2296. https://doi.org/10.1007/s10826-019-01445-1

Barry, C. T., Sidoti, C. L., Briggs, S. M., Reiter, S. R., & Lindsey, R. A. (2017). Adolescent social media use and mental health from adolescent and parent perspectives. *Journal of Adolescence, 61*, 1–11. https://doi.org/10.1016/j.adolescence.2017.08.005

Barthorpe, A., Winstone, L., Mars, B., & Moran, P. (2020). Is social media screen time really associated with poor adolescent mental health? A time use diary study. *Journal of Affective Disorders, 274*, 864–870. https://doi.org/10.1016/j.jad.2020.05.106

Belanger, R. E., Akre, C., Berchtold, A., & Michaud, P. A. (2011). A U-shaped association between intensity of internet use and adolescent health. *Pediatrics, 127*(2), e330–335. https://doi.org/10.1542/peds.2010-1235

Bitsko, R. H., Holbrook, J. R., Ghandour, R. M., et al. (2018). Epidemiology and impact of health care provider-diagnosed anxiety and depression among US children. *Journal of Developmental and Behavioral Pediatrics, 39*(5), 395–403. https://doi.org/10.1097/Dbp.0000000000000571

Blass, E. M., Anderson, D. R., Kirkorian, H. L., Pempek, T. A., Price, I., & Koleini, M. F. (2006). On the road to obesity: Television viewing increases intake of high-density foods. *Physiology & Behavior, 88*(4–5), 597–604. https://doi.org/10.1016/j.physbeh.2006.05.035

Boyle, S. C., LaBrie, J. W., Froidevaux, N. M., & Witkovic, Y. D. (2016). Different digital paths to the keg? How exposure to peers' alcohol-related social media content influences drinking among male and female first-year college students. *Addictive Behaviors, 57*, 21–29. https://doi.org/10.1016/j.addbeh.2016.01.011

Brough, M., Literat, I., & Ikin, A. (2020). "Good social media?": Underrepresented youth perspectives on the ethical and equitable design of social media platforms. *Social Media + Society, 6*(2). https://doi.org/10.1177/2056305120928488

Burns, J. M., Birrell, E., Bismark, M., et al. (2016). The role of technology in Australian youth mental health reform. *Australian Health Review*, *40*(5), 584–590. https://doi.org/10.1071/AH15115

Calvo, F., & Carbonell, X. (2019). Is Facebook use healthy for individuals experiencing homelessness? A scoping review on social networking and living in the streets. *Journal of Mental Health*, *28*(5), 505–519. https://doi.org/10.1080/09638237.2019.1608927

Campbell, F., & Valera, P. (2020). "The only thing new is the cameras": A study of US college students' perceptions of police violence on social media. *Journal of Black Studies*, *51*(7), 654–670. https://doi.org/Artn 0021934720935600 10.1177/0021934720935600

Cannon, D. S., Tiffany, S. T., Coon, H., Scholand, M. B., McMahon, W. M., & Leppert, M. F. (2007). The PHQ-9 as a brief assessment of lifetime major depression. *Psychological Assessment*, *19*(2), 247–251. https://doi.org/10.1037/1040-3590.19.2.247

Caporino, N. E., Exley, S., & Latzman, R. D. (2020). Youth anxiety about political news. *Child Psychiatry & Human Development*, *51*(5), 683–698. https://doi.org/10.1007/s10578–020-00972-z

Carey, J. L., Carreiro, S., Chapman, B., et al. (2018). SoMe and self harm: The use of social media in depressed and suicidal youth. *Proceedings of the 51st Annual Hawaii International Conference on System Sciences*, *2018*, 3314–3319. https://doi.org/10.24251/HICSS.2018.420

Choukas-Bradley, S., Nesi, J., Widman, L., & Galla, B. M. (2020). The Appearance-Related Social Media Consciousness Scale: Development and validation with adolescents. *Body Image*, *33*, 164–174. https://doi.org/10.1016/j.bodyim.2020.02.017

Coyne, S. M., Padilla-Walker, L. M., Holmgren, H. G., & Stockdale, L. A. (2019). Instagrowth: A longitudinal growth mixture model of social media time use across adolescence. *Journal of Research on Adolescence*, *29*(4), 897–907. https://doi.org/10.1111/jora.12424

Craig, S. L., McInroy, L., McCready, L. T., & DeCesare, D. M. (2015). Connecting without fear: Clinical implications of the consumption of information and communication technologies by sexual minority youth and young adults. *Clinical Social Work*, *43*, 159–168. https://doi.org/10.1007/s10615-014-0505-2

Duggan, M. (2013). *Social networking fact sheet*. Pew Research Center's Internet Project library survey. http://www.pewinternet.org/fact-sheets/social-networking-fact-sheet/

Duradoni, M., Innocenti, F., & Guazzini, A. (2020). Well-being and social media: A systematic review of Bergen Addiction Scales. *Future Internet*, *12*(2), Article 24. https://doi.org/ARTN 24 10.3390/fi12020024

Edwards, L., Kontostathis, A. E., & Fisher, C. (2016). Cyberbullying, race/ethnicity and mental health outcomes: A review of the literature. *Media and Communication*, *4*(3), 71–78. https://doi.org/10.17645/mac.v4i3.525

Egan, K. G., & Moreno, M. A. (2011). Prevalence of stress references on college freshmen Facebook profiles. *Computers, Informatics, Nursing*, *29*(10), 586–592. https://doi.org/10.1097/NCN.0b013e3182160663

Ellis, D. A. (2019). Are smartphones really that bad? Improving the psychological measurement of technology-related behaviors. *Computers in Human Behavior, 97*, 60–66. https://doi.org/10.1016/j.chb.2019.03.006

Escobar-Viera, C., Shensa, A., Hamm, M., et al. (2020). "I don't feel like the odd one": Utilizing content analysis to compare the effects of social media use on well-being among sexual minority and nonminority US young adults. *American Journal of Health Promotion, 34*(3), 285–293. https://doi.org/10.1177/0890117119885517

Fabris, M. A., Marengo, D., Longobardi, C., & Settanni, M. (2020). Investigating the links between fear of missing out, social media addiction, and emotional symptoms in adolescence: The role of stress associated with neglect and negative reactions on social media. *Addictive Behaviors, 106*. https://doi.org/ARTN 106364 10.1016/j.addbeh.2020.106364

Fardouly, J., Magson, N. R., Johnco, C. J., Oar, E. L., & Rapee, R. M. (2018). Parental control of the time preadolescents spend on social media: Links with preadolescents' social media appearance comparisons and mental health. *Journal of Youth and Adolescence, 47*(7), 1456–1468. https://doi.org/10.1007/s10964–018-0870-1

Ferguson, C. J. (2021). Links between screen use and depressive symptoms in adolescents over 16 years: Is there evidence for increased harm? *Developmental Science, 24*(1), e13008. https://doi.org/10.1111/desc.13008

Fitzsimmons-Craft, E. E., Krauss, M. J., Costello, S. J., Floyd, G. M., Wilfley, D. E., & Cavazos-Rehg, P. A. (2020). Adolescents and young adults engaged with pro-eating disorder social media: Eating disorder and comorbid psychopathology, health care utilization, treatment barriers, and opinions on harnessing technology for treatment. *Eating and Weight Disorders, 25*(6), 1681–1692. https://doi.org/10.1007/s40519–019-00808-3

Franchina, V., Vanden Abeele, M., van Rooij, A. J., Lo Coco, G., & De Marez, L. (2018). Fear of missing out as a predictor of problematic social media use and phubbing behavior among Flemish adolescents. *International Journal of Environmental Research and Public Health, 15*(10), Article 2319. https://doi.org/10.3390/ijerph15102319

Gibson, K., & Trnka, S. (2020). Young people's priorities for support on social media: "It takes trust to talk about these issues". *Computers in Human Behavior, 102*, 238–247. https://doi.org/10.1016/j.chb.2019.08.030

Hawes, T., Zimmer-Gembeck, M. J., & Campbell, S. M. (2020). Unique associations of social media use and online appearance preoccupation with depression, anxiety, and appearance rejection sensitivity. *Body Image, 33*, 66–76. https://doi.org/10.1016/j.bodyim.2020.02.010

Heffer, T., Good, M., Daly, O., MacDonell, E., & Willoughby, T. (2019). The longitudinal association between social-media use and depressive symptoms among adolescents and young adults: An empirical reply to Twenge et al. (2018). *Clinical Psychological Science, 7*(3), 462–470. https://doi.org/10.1177/2167702618812727

Huang, C. (2017). Time spent on social network sites and psychological well-being: A meta-analysis. *Cyberpsychology, Behavior, and Social Networking, 20*(6), 346–354. https://doi.org/10.1089/cyber.2016.0758

Hussain, Z., Wegmann, E., Yang, H. B., & Montag, C. (2020). Social networks use disorder and associations with depression and anxiety symptoms: A systematic review of recent research in China. *Frontiers in Psychology*, 11, Article 211. https://doi.org/ARTN 21110.3389/fpsyg.2020.00211

Ince, J., Rojas, F., & Davis, C. A. (2017). The social media response to Black Lives Matter: How Twitter users interact with Black Lives Matter through hashtag use. *Ethnic and Racial Studies*, *40*(11), 1814–1830. https://doi.org/10.1080/01419870.2017.1334931

Jelenchick, L. A., Eickhoff, J. C., & Moreno, M. A. (2013). "Facebook depression?": Social networking site use and depression in older adolescents. *Journal of Adolescent Health*, *52*(1), 128–130. https://doi.org/10.1016/j.jadohealth.2012.05.008

Jennings, A. F., LeBlanc, H., Kisch, K., Lancaster, S., & Allen, J. (2020). Blurred boundaries between pro-anorexia and fitspiration media? Diverging cognitive and emotional effects. *Eating Disorders*, 1–11. https://doi.org/10.1080/10640266.2020.1712634

Jenzen, O. (2017). Trans youth and social media: Moving between counterpublics and the wider web. *Gender, Place and Culture*, *24*(11), 1626–1641. https://doi.org/10.1080/0966369X.2017.1396204

Keles, B., McCrae, N., & Grealish, A. (2019). A systematic review: The influence of social media on depression, anxiety and psychological distress in adolescents. *International Journal of Adolescence and Youth*, *25*(1), 79–93. https://doi.org/10.1080/02673843.2019.1590851

Kelly, Y., Zilanawala, A., Booker, C., & Sacker, A. (2018). Social media use and adolescent mental health: Findings from the UK Millennium Cohort Study. *EClinicalMedicine*, *6*, 59–68. https://doi.org/10.1016/j.eclinm.2018.12.005

Kroenke, K., Spitzer, R. L., & Williams, J. B. (2001). The PHQ-9: Validity of a brief depression severity measure. *Journal of General Internal Medicine*, *16*(9), 606–613. https://doi.org/10.1046/j.1525-1497.2001.016009606.x

Lemola, S., Perkinson-Gloor, N., Hagmann-von Arx, P., et al. (2015). Morning cortisol secretion in school-age children is related to the sleep pattern of the preceding night. *Psychoneuroendocrinology*, *52*, 297–301. https://doi.org/10.1016/j.psyneuen.2014.12.007

Leopold, J., & Bell, M. P. (2017). News media and the racialization of protest: An analysis of Black Lives Matter articles. *Equality, Diversity and Inclusion*, *36*(8), 720–735. https://doi.org/10.1108/Edi-01-2017-0010

Levenson, J. C. (2016). The association between social media use and sleep disturbance among young adults. *Preventative Medicine*, *85*, 36–41. https://doi.org/10.1016/j.ypmed.2016.01.001

Liu, M., Wu, L., & Yao, S. (2016). Dose-response association of screen time-based sedentary behaviour in children and adolescents and depression: A meta-analysis of observational studies. *British Journal of Sports Medicine*, *50*(20), 1252–1258. https://doi.org/10.1136/bjsports-2015-095084

Longobardi, C., Settanni, M., Fabris, M. A., & Marengo, D. (2020). Follow or be followed: Exploring the links between Instagram popularity, social media addiction, cyber victimization, and subjective happiness in Italian adolescents. *Children and Youth Services Review*, *113*, Article 104955. https://doi.org/10.1016/j.childyouth.2020.104955

Marengo, D., Longobardi, C., Fabris, M. A., & Settanni, M. (2018). Highly-visual social media and internalizing symptoms in adolescence: The mediating role of body image concerns. *Computers in Human Behavior*, *82*, 63–69. https://doi .org/10.1016/j.chb.2018.01.003

McCrory, A., Best, P., & Maddock, A. (2020). The relationship between highly visual social media and young people's mental health: A scoping review. *Children and Youth Services Review*, *115*. https://doi.org/ARTN 105053 10.1016/j. childyouth.2020.105053

McDool, E., Powell, P., Roberts, J., & Taylor, K. (2020). The internet and children's psychological wellbeing. *Journal of Health Economics*, *69*, Article 102274. https://doi.org/10.1016/j.jhealeco.2019.102274

Messner, E. M., Sariyska, R., Mayer, B., et al. (2019). Insights: Future implications of passive smartphone sensing in the therapeutic context. *Verhaltenstherapie*, *29*(3), 155–165. https://doi.org/10.1159/000501735

Mills, J. S., Musto, S., Williams, L., & Tiggemann, M. (2018). "Selfie" harm: Effects on mood and body image in young women. *Body Image*, *27*, 86–92. https:// doi.org/10.1016/j.bodyim.2018.08.007

Moreno, M. A. (2013). *Sex, drugs 'n Facebook: A parent's toolkit for promoting healthy internet use*. Hunter House, Inc.

Moreno, M. A., Binger, K., Zhao, Q., & Eickhoff, J. (2020). Measuring interests not minutes: Development and validation of the Adolescents' Digital Technology Interactions and Importance Scale (ADTI). *Journal of Medical Internet Research*, *22*(2), e16736. https://doi.org/10.2196/16736

Moreno, M. A., Chassiakos, Y. R., Cross, C., et al. (2016). Media use in school-aged children and adolescents. *Pediatrics*, *138*(5). https://doi.org/ARTNe2016 259210.1542/peds.2016-2592

Moreno, M. A., Christakis, D. A., Egan, K. G., et al. (2012). A pilot evaluation of associations between displayed depression references on Facebook and self-reported depression using a clinical scale. *Journal of Behavioral Health Services & Research*, *39*(3), 295–304. https://doi.org/10.1007/s11414–011-9258-7

Moreno, M. A., Jelenchick, L., Koff, R., & Eickhoff, J. (2012). Depression and internet use among older adolescents: An experience sampling approach. *Psychology*, *3*(9), 743–748. https://doi.org/10.4236/psych.2012.329112

Mundt, M., Ross, K., & Burnett, C. M. (2018). Scaling social movements through social media: The case of Black Lives Matter. *Social Media + Society*, *4*(4). https://doi.org/Artn 2056305118807911 10.1177/2056305118807911

Negriff, S. (2019). Depressive symptoms predict characteristics of online social networks. *Journal of Adolescent Health*, *65*(1), 101–106. https://doi.org/10.1016/j .jadohealth.2019.01.026

Nick, E. A., Cole, D. A., Cho, S. J., Smith, D. K., Carter, T. G., & Zelkowitz, R. L. (2018). The Online Social Support Scale: Measure development and validation. *Psychological Assessment*, *30*(9), 1127–1143. https://doi.org/10.1037/ pas0000558

O'Keeffe, G. S., Clarke-Pearson, K., & Council on Communications & Media. (2011). The impact of social media on children, adolescents, and families. *Pediatrics*, *127*(4), 800–804. https://doi.org/10.1542/peds.2011-0054

Odgers, C. L., & Jensen, M. R. (2020). Annual research review: Adolescent mental health in the digital age: Facts, fears, and future directions. *Journal of Child Psychology and Psychiatry*, *61*(3), 336–348. https://doi.org/10.1111/jcpp.13190

Orben, A. (2020). Teenagers, screens and social media: A narrative review of reviews and key studies. *Social Psychiatry and Psychiatric Epidemiology*, *55*(4), 407–414. https://doi.org/10.1007/s00127–019-01825-4

Oshima, N., Nishida, A., Shimodera, S., et al. (2012). The suicidal feelings, self-injury, and mobile phone use after lights out in adolescents. *Journal of Pediatric Psychology*, *37*(9), 1023–1030. https://doi.org/10.1093/jpepsy/jss072

Piteo, E. M., & Ward, K. (2020). Review: Social networking sites and associations with depressive and anxiety symptoms in children and adolescents – A systematic review. *Child and Adolescent Mental Health*, *25*(4), 201–216. https://doi.org/10.1111/camh.12373

Pretorius, C., Chambers, D., & Coyle, D. (2019). Young people's online help-seeking and mental health difficulties: Systematic narrative review. *Journal of Medical Internet Research*, *21*(11), e13873. https://doi.org/10.2196/13873

Prochnow, T., Patterson, M. S., & Hartnell, L. (2020). Social support, depressive symptoms, and online gaming network communication. *Mental Health and Social Inclusion*, *24*(1), 49–58. https://doi.org/10.1108/Mhsi-11-2019-0033

Przepiorka, A., & Blachnio, A. (2020). The role of Facebook intrusion, depression, and future time perspective in sleep problems among adolescents. *Journal of Research on Adolescence*, *30*(2), 559–569. https://doi.org/10.1111/jora.12543

Przybylski, A. K., Murayama, K., DeHaan, C. R., & Gladwell, V. (2013). Motivational, emotional, and behavioral correlates of fear of missing out. *Computers in Human Behavior*, *29*(4), 1841–1848. https://doi.org/10.1016/j.chb.2013.02.014

Quante, M., Khandpur, N., Kontos, E. Z., Bakker, J. P., Owens, J. A., & Redline, S. (2019). "Let's talk about sleep": A qualitative examination of levers for promoting healthy sleep among sleep-deprived vulnerable adolescents. *Sleep Medicine*, *60*, 81–88. https://doi.org/10.1016/j.sleep.2018.10.044

Radovic, A., Gmelin, T., Stein, B. D., & Miller, E. (2017). Depressed adolescents' positive and negative use of social media. *Journal of Adolescence*, *55*, 5–15. https://doi.org/10.1016/j.adolescence.2016.12.002

Rajani, R., Berman, D. S., & Rozanski, A. (2011). Social networks: Are they good for your health? The era of Facebook and Twitter. *QJM*, *104*(9), 819–820. https://doi.org/10.1093/qjmed/hcr078

Rice, E., Petering, R., Rhoades, H., et al. (2015). Cyberbullying perpetration and victimization among middle-school students. *American Journal of Public Health*, *105*(3), E66–E72. https://doi.org/10.2105/Ajph.2014.302393

Richardson, L. P., McCauley, E., Grossman, D. C., et al. (2010). Evaluation of the Patient Health Questionnaire-9 item for detecting major depression among adolescents. *Pediatrics*, *126*(6), 1117–1123. https://doi.org/10.1542/peds.2010-0852

Rideout, V., Fox, S., & Trust, T. W. (2018). *Digital health practices, social media use, and mental well-being among teens and young adults in the US*. https://digitalcommons.psjhealth.org/publications/1093

Riehm, K. E., Feder, K. A., Tormohlen, K. N., et al. (2019). Associations between time spent using social media and internalizing and externalizing problems among US youth. *JAMA Psychiatry, 76*(12), 1266–1273. https://doi.org/10.1001/jamapsychiatry.2019.2325

Robb, M. B. (2020). *Teens and the news: The influencers, celebrities, and platforms they say matter most*. Common Sense Media. https://www.commonsensemedia.org/research/teens-and-the-news-the-influencers-celebrities-and-platforms-they-say-matter-most-2020

Robinson, A., Bonnette, A., Howard, K., et al. (2019). Social comparisons, social media addiction, and social interaction: An examination of specific social media behaviors related to major depressive disorder in a millennial population. *Journal of Applied Biobehavioral Research, 24*(1), e12158. https://doi.org/ARTNe1215810.1111/jabr.12158

Sahoo, S., Rani, S., Shah, R., Singh, A. P., Mehra, A., & Grover, S. (2020). COVID-19 pandemic-related anxiety in teenagers. *Indian Journal of Psychiatry, 62*(3), 328–330. https://doi.org/10.4103/psychiatry.IndianJPsychiatry_327_20

Seabrook, E. M., Kern, M. L., & Rickard, N. S. (2016). Social networking sites, depression, and anxiety: A systematic review. *JMIR Mental Health, 3*(4), e50. https://doi.org/10.2196/mental.5842

Selfhout, M. H., Branje, S. J., Delsing, M., ter Bogt, T. F., & Meeus, W. H. (2009). Different types of internet use, depression, and social anxiety: The role of perceived friendship quality. *Journal of Adolescence, 32*(4), 819–833. https://doi.org/10.1016/j.adolescence.2008.10.011

Selkie, E., Adkins, V., Masters, E., Bajpai, A., & Shumer, D. (2020). Transgender adolescents' uses of social media for social support. *Journal of Adolescent Health, 66*(3), 275–280. https://doi.org/10.1016/j.jadohealth.2019.08.011

Sommers-Flanagan, J., & Sommers-Flanagan, R. (2018). *Counseling and psychotherapy theories in context and practice: Skills, strategies, and techniques*. John Wiley & Sons.

Sue, D. W., Rivera, D. P., Capodilupo, C. M., Lin, A. I., & Torino, G. C. (2010). Racial dialogues and White trainee fears: Implications for education and training. *Cultural Diversity and Ethnic Minority Psychology, 16*(2), 206–214. https://doi.org/10.1037/a0016112

Tian, L., Yan, Y., & Huebner, E. S. (2018). Effects of cyberbullying and cybervictimization on early adolescents' mental health: Differential mediating roles of perceived peer relationship stress. *Cyberpsychology, Behavior, and Social Networking, 21*(7), 429–436. https://doi.org/10.1089/cyber.2017.0735

Twenge, J. M., & Campbell, W. K. (2019). Media use is linked to lower psychological well-being: Evidence from three datasets. *Psychiatric Quarterly, 90*(2), 311–331. https://doi.org/10.1007/s11126-019-09630-7

Twenge, J. M., Joiner, T. E., Martin, G., & Rogers, M. L. (2018). Amount of time online is problematic if it displaces face-to-face social interaction and sleep. *Clinical Psychological Science, 6*(4), 456–457. https://doi.org/10.1177/2167702618778562

Twenge, J. M., Joiner, T. E., Rogers, M. L., & Martin, G. N. (2018). Increases in depressive symptoms, suicide-related outcomes, and suicide rates among U.S. adolescents after 2010 and links to increased new media screen time. *Clinical Psychological Science, 6*(1), 3–17. https://doi.org/10.1177/2167702617723376

Twenge, J. M., & Martin, G. N. (2020). Gender differences in associations between digital media use and psychological well-being: Evidence from three large datasets. *Journal of Adolescence*, *79*, 91–102. https://doi.org/10.1016/j.adolescence.2019.12.018

Wahnschaffe, A., Haedel, S., Rodenbeck, A., et al. (2013). Out of the lab and into the bathroom: Evening short-term exposure to conventional light suppresses melatonin and increases alertness perception. *International Journal of Molecular Science*, *14*(2), 2573–2589. https://doi.org/10.3390/ijms14022573

Waterloo, S. F., Baumgartner, S. E., Peter, J., & Valkenburg, P. M. (2018). Norms of online expressions of emotion: Comparing Facebook, Twitter, Instagram, and WhatsApp. *New Media & Society*, *20*(5), 1813–1831. https://doi.org/https://doi.org/10.1177/1461444817707349

Weinstein, E. (2018). The social media see-saw: Positive and negative influences on adolescents' affective well-being. *New Media & Society*, *20*(10), 3597–3623. https://doi.org/10.1177/1461444818755634

Weissman, M. M., Orvaschel, H., & Padian, N. (1980). Children's symptom and social functioning self-report scales: Comparison of mothers' and children's reports. *Journal of Nervous Mental Disease*, *168*(12), 736–740. https://doi.org/10.1097/00005053-198012000-00005

Wenninger, H., Krasnova, H., & Buxmann, P. (2019). Understanding the role of social networking sites in the subjective well-being of users: A diary study. *European Journal of Information Systems*, *28*(2), 126–148. https://doi.org/10.1080/0960085x.2018.1496883

Wick, M. R., & Keel, P. K. (2020). Posting edited photos of the self: Increasing eating disorder risk or harmless behavior? *International Journal of Eating Disorders*, *53*(6), 864–872. https://doi.org/10.1002/eat.23263

Willenberg, L., Wulan, N., Medise, B. E., et al. (2020). Understanding mental health and its determinants from the perspective of adolescents: A qualitative study across diverse social settings in Indonesia. *Asian Journal of Psychiatry*, *52*, Article 102148. https://doi.org/10.1016/j.ajp.2020.102148

Woods, H. C., & Scott, H. (2016). #Sleepyteens: Social media use in adolescence is associated with poor sleep quality, anxiety, depression and low self-esteem. *Journal of Adolescence*, *51*, 41–49. https://doi.org/10.1016/j.adolescence.2016.05.008

Wright, B., Garside, M., Allgar, V., Hodkinson, R., & Thorpe, H. (2020). A large population-based study of the mental health and wellbeing of children and young people in the North of England. *Clinical Child Psychology and Psychiatry*, *25*(4), 877–890. https://doi.org/10.1177/1359104520925873

10 The Role of Digital Media in Adolescents' Body Image and Disordered Eating

Savannah R. Roberts, Anne J. Maheux,
Brianna A. Ladd, and Sophia Choukas-Bradley

Social media is a normal part of life for adolescents in the United States. According to nationally representative data, the majority of adolescents (83%) use social media, and of those who do, 70% of teen girls and 56% of teen boys check it every day (Rideout & Robb, 2018). Research on social media has been rapidly increasing, as scholars attempt to understand how social media could both help and harm adolescents' well-being. Prior research suggests that social media has an effect on users' body image, with individuals simultaneously sharing images of themselves at their most attractive while experiencing preoccupation over how their appearance will be perceived by others. The effects of social media on body image may be heightened during adolescence, a developmental stage in which individuals often prioritize their physical attractiveness over other domains of self-worth. In this chapter, we first describe the developmental features of adolescence, and how they intersect with social media, with implications for body image and disordered eating. Next, we provide an introduction to relevant theoretical frameworks for considering social media's effect on body image. Then, we examine how specific features of social media affect adolescents' body image and disordered eating. Finally, we explore specific social media platforms and content devoted to body image concerns and disordered eating.

The Adolescent Developmental Period

Adolescence is a developmental period marked by substantive changes in interpersonal relationships, identity, and autonomy (Dahl et al., 2018). Biological, interpersonal, and sociocultural factors intersect to increase adolescents' concerns about body image and physical appearance. These concerns may take the form of body dissatisfaction, when individuals dislike some element of their appearance, or disordered eating, when individuals engage in eating pathology in an attempt to modify their weight or shape. One key developmental feature of adolescence is the heightened focus on peer relationships (Brechwald & Prinstein, 2011). Increased sensitivity to social reward makes adolescents highly attuned to their peers (Kilford et al., 2016). Importantly, social status among peers is closely tied to appearance, as adolescents perceived to be the most attractive are often also the most popular (Kennedy, 1990; Lease et al., 2002). Concomitantly, adolescents experience increased self-focus and self-consciousness, including the *imaginary audience* – a sense that one's peers are watching one's every move (Elkind, 1967). When peer evaluation centers on appearance, the imaginary audience may increase adolescents' body image disturbances.

Gender differences in sociocultural and biological factors produce differences in adolescents' body dissatisfaction and disordered eating. Girls in particular are socialized to prioritize physical appearance (Daniels et al., 2020; Fredrickson & Roberts, 1997), and adolescent girls experience higher levels of body dissatisfaction and disordered eating than do boys (Neumark-Sztainer et al., 2006). Although ideal beauty standards differ by cultural context and by race/ethnicity, the average ideal body type for women in the USA is unattainably thin yet curvy, while the average ideal body type for men is muscular (Deighton-Smith & Bell, 2018; Edwards et al., 2016). Biologically, patterns of weight gain and fat distribution during adolescence bring girls on average further from the thin beauty ideal, while increased muscularity brings boys on average closer to the muscular beauty ideal. Many girls experience body dissatisfaction due to the perceived discrepancy between one's body and the ideal feminine body, and may engage in disordered eating in an effort to reduce this discrepancy (Halliwell & Harvey, 2006). Adolescent boys may engage in muscle-building behaviors or excessive exercise in pursuit of the masculine ideal (Calzo et al., 2016). These developmental features considered together, adolescence is a period marked by increased risk for body image disturbances and disordered eating. Social media may increase the likelihood of these phenomena by allowing for social support and connection, while leaving adolescents vulnerable to exposure from negative social influences (Dahl et al., 2018). At a time when peer approval and status are of the utmost importance, social media allows for more frequent peer interactions, leading to increased appearance-related feedback (de Vries et al., 2016). Indeed, among adolescents, more frequent social media use is associated with higher investment in one's appearance (de Vries et al., 2014). With increased frequency of appearance-related feedback and higher investment in this feedback, social media use may lead to increased body image concerns.

These concerns occur on a spectrum, ranging from low levels of body dissatisfaction to extreme preoccupation with weight and shape. Body dissatisfaction can be conceptualized as negative evaluations of one's body, typically resulting from a discrepancy between one's ideal and perceived appearance (Grogan, 2016). Body dissatisfaction has been identified as the most powerful predictor and risk factor for the development of disordered eating (Stice et al., 2011). Once disordered eating reaches the level at which it significantly impairs an individual's physical health or daily functioning, that person may meet criteria for an eating disorder, such as anorexia nervosa (AN), bulimia nervosa (BN), or binge eating disorder (BED) (American Psychological Association, 2013). While few adolescents may receive a diagnosis of an eating disorder, the prevalence of body dissatisfaction and disordered eating is relatively common (Swanson et al., 2011). Across three large population-based studies, approximately 81% of adolescent girls and 63% of adolescent boys report body dissatisfaction (Kelly et al., 2018; Lawler & Nixon, 2011; Neumark-Sztainer et al., 2006). Further, population-based studies indicate that disordered eating is highly prevalent among adolescents, estimating that approximately 54–57% of adolescent girls and 30–33% of adolescent boys engage in at least one disordered eating behavior (Croll et al., 2002; Neumark-Sztainer et al., 2011). This chapter will focus primarily on how social media contributes to body dissatisfaction and disordered eating across the general adolescent population.

Relevant Theoretical Frameworks

There are a number of psychological theories relevant to understanding associations among social media use, body image disturbances, and disordered eating. While many of these theories were developed before the advent of social media, they nonetheless explore concepts that are implicated in social media use. The following section details leading theoretical frameworks for the development of body image disturbances and disordered eating, all of which have robust empirical support. Further, we explore a newly developed psychological theory, the transformation framework, which describes the ways in which social media has transformed adolescents' lives and further increased the importance of physical appearance.

Objectification Theory

Objectification theory was proposed as a framework for explaining the psychological consequences women experience from growing up in a society that sexually objectifies the female body (Fredrickson & Roberts, 1997). It argues that women and girls in Western society learn to adopt an observer's perspective of their own bodies – a process called *self-objectification* – after being exposed to frequent sexual objectification, which reinforces the societal message that a woman's interpersonal value is based primarily on her physical appearance (Fredrickson & Roberts, 1997). Self-objectification is linked to body shame, depression, anxiety, and the development of disordered eating (Butkowski et al., 2019; Calogero et al., 2011; Erchull et al., 2013). Research now suggests that boys and men also experience self-objectification, as they are also exposed to sociocultural appearance pressures and may experience sexual objectification (Vandenbosch & Eggermont, 2013). The act of curating one's social media profile can be thought of as a behavioral manifestation of self-objectification, as the user is specifically creating content about one's identity that is meant to be consumed by others (Choukas-Bradley et al., 2019, 2020, 2021). In this way, social media users are encouraged to adopt an observer's perspective of themselves and post social media content that will elicit positive feedback from their social media audience. Later in this chapter, we discuss specific behaviors and experiences on social media that are associated with self-objectification.

Social Comparison Theory

Adolescents who derive self-esteem from their physical attractiveness are likely to engage in social comparison, evaluating their attractiveness by comparing it to other social media users. Festinger's (1954) *social comparison theory* argues that individuals engage in social comparison in order to estimate their own social status relative to others. While this is a natural process, it can be problematic in the case of physical attractiveness. Festinger's seminal paper on social comparison theory (1954) argues that individuals have a tendency to make upward appearance comparisons when evaluating physical attractiveness (i.e., individuals tend to compare themselves to people they perceive as more attractive than themselves), resulting in worse body image. Furthermore, when engaging in social comparison, people try to compare themselves to similar others. Taken together, peers on social media may be perceived as realistic comparison targets, but by presenting highly edited images, these "similar" comparison targets may in fact serve as upward comparison reference groups depicting unattainable attractiveness. Regardless of whether adolescents compare themselves to individuals perceived to be more or less attractive, engaging in social comparison is associated with body dissatisfaction, especially among adolescent girls (Jones, 2001). Indeed, social appearance comparisons appear to be a primary mechanism through which social media exerts influence on body image disturbances and disordered eating during adolescence. Later in this chapter, we describe specific features of social media that encourage social comparison.

Tripartite Influence Model

A third theory relevant to understanding social media's influence on adolescents' body image and disordered eating is the *tripartite influence model* (Thompson et al., 1999), which was developed to explain the mechanisms through which body dissatisfaction originates. This model proposes that through peers, parents, and the media, adolescents are frequently exposed to unattainable standards of beauty. After encountering such exposure, adolescents internalize an unattainable appearance ideal and, like in social comparison theory, engage in appearance comparisons, processes known to lead to greater body dissatisfaction (Keery et al., 2004; Thompson et al., 1999).

Internalization of an appearance ideal (often the "thin ideal" for adolescent girls and the "muscular ideal" for adolescent boys) refers to the extent to which an individual ascribes to culturally defined standards of beauty. Social media perpetuates these unattainable ideals and encourages social appearance comparisons through comments, images, and interactions that communicate societal expectations for adolescents' bodies, ultimately fostering body dissatisfaction because these appearance ideals are unattainable for the majority of individuals (Thompson & Stice, 2001). Given its ubiquity, social media has become a primary source of appearance pressure in adolescents' lives.

The Transformation Framework

The aforementioned theories were all developed before the advent of social media. However, scholars have recently identified features of social media directly implicated in the development of body image disturbances. The *transformation framework* argues that widespread adoption of social media among today's adolescents has fundamentally changed the ways in which they are interacting with one another (Choukas-Bradley et al., 2021; Nesi et al., 2018a, 2018b). Here, we discuss three of the seven specific features of the transformation framework that are most relevant to understanding social media's effects on body image: visualness, publicness, and quantifiability.

First, social media is characterized by *visualness* and *publicness*, meaning that users rely on photographs and videos to communicate to broad, public audiences (Nesi et al., 2018a). This reliance on visual forms of communication can make adolescents hyperaware of their own physical appearance. Currently, highly visual social media (HVSM) – such as Instagram, Snapchat, and TikTok – is the most popular type of social media among adolescents (Anderson & Jiang, 2018). When adolescents use HVSM, they increase their focus on others' attractiveness, are exposed to unattainable beauty standards, and may engage in appearance-driven self-presentation techniques to elicit positive peer feedback in the form of "likes" or comments. These "likes" and comments represent *quantifiability*, or the Numerical indicators of popularity and attractiveness indicated by one's peers and social media audience. We have provided a specific section later in the chapter describing how quantifiability of appearance-based feedback influences adolescents' body image and disordered eating. Collectively, these features of social media may encourage self-objectification and social comparison.

Social Media Behaviors

The unique features of social media offer opportunities to engage in new, social media-specific behaviors, some of which have been linked to body image disturbances and disordered eating. The visual, public, and quantifiable aspects of social media contribute to a heightened focus on appearance and peer feedback. Below we discuss how specific behaviors on social media, including taking, posting, and editing "selfies," and giving and receiving "likes" and comments on one's content, may be implicated in adolescents' body image and disordered eating.

Selfies

Social media offers adolescents the opportunity to take, edit, and post photos of themselves – "selfies" (Lim, 2016). Selfie behaviors, including taking and posting selfies, are relatively common among adolescents (Dhir et al., 2016; McLean et al., 2019), with nationally representative US data reporting that 45% of adolescents often or sometimes post selfies (Anderson & Jiang, 2018). The association between selfie behaviors and body image and disordered eating outcomes is not yet fully understood. Some evidence from adolescent girls and young adult women in China and Australia suggests an association between selfie posting and body dissatisfaction, overvaluation of shape and weight, greater internalization of the thin ideal (McLean et al., 2015), greater engagement in appearance comparisons (Mingoia et al., 2019), self-objectification (Meier & Gray, 2014; Zheng et al., 2019), and restrained eating (Niu et al., 2020). Among samples with both adolescent boys and girls, posting a selfie is associated with self-objectification (Meier & Gray, 2014), body shame (Salomon & Brown, 2019), and restrained eating (Wilksch et al., 2020). Interestingly, other research has found that disordered eating behaviors are associated with greater *avoidance* of posting selfies among adolescent boys and girls (Lonergan et al., 2020), and that Singaporean adolescent girls with greater body esteem are more likely to post selfies than those with lower body esteem (Chang et al., 2019). Some research with adolescent boys and girls in the USA (Nesi et al., 2021) and China (Wang et al., 2019) has found no association between selfie posting and body esteem. Experimental research with adolescent girls and adult women in lab settings shows that those assigned to take and post a selfie to social media report heightened anxiety, less confidence, and feeling less physically attractive afterwards (Mills et al., 2018). Notably, these outcomes were found whether participants were uploading an unedited selfie or had the opportunity to edit and choose a preferred selfie, highlighting that simply focusing on one's appearance and posting it to a semi-public audience may help explain this association. The somewhat conflicting results suggest a need for more research in this area, particularly with mixed-gender samples.

Photo Editing

Social media allows for adolescents to manage their online self-presentation by editing and applying filters to photos before posting. Editing one's photos and selfies, including applying filters, cropping, and modifying one's appearance directly, is not uncommon among adolescents and is more common among girls than boys (see McLean et al., 2015). Qualitative work suggests that adolescent girls engage in "meticulous backstage planning," spending hours planning and editing their photos to meet societal beauty norms, a practice that many consider "necessary" to be "pretty enough" online (Chua & Chang, 2016, p. 193). Editing one's own photos may exacerbate the deleterious effects of social media by encouraging self-objectification, social comparison, and internalization of the thin ideal. Research with adolescents has shown that editing one's photos is associated with self-objectification, which in turn is linked to appearance anxiety, body shame, negative appearance evaluation (Terán et al., 2020), and body image concerns (Wang et al., 2019). Photo-editing encourages social appearance comparisons (Mingoia et al., 2019) and disordered eating behaviors (Lonergan et al., 2020), even when controlling for time on social media and internalization of the thin ideal (McLean et al., 2015). Additionally, some qualitative work suggests that, especially for girls, the curation of one's photos and selfies happens before the editing phase, including scrupulous photo planning and taking of multiple photos to ensure a desired outcome (Chua & Chang, 2016; Mascheroni et al., 2015), processes that some adolescents girls describe as "work" (Yau & Reich, 2019, p. 203).

Exposure to Others' Photos

Emerging evidence suggests photo-based social media activity, rather than total time spent on social media, contributes to adolescents' body image disturbances (Choukas-Bradley et al., 2020; Cohen et al., 2017; Marengo et al., 2018; Meier & Gray, 2014). HVSM in particular allows adolescents unprecedented opportunities to view the idealized and edited photos of their peers. Viewing others' photos on social media is thought to engender risk for disordered eating and body dissatisfaction through internalization of cultural appearance ideals and social appearance comparisons (see Rodgers et al., 2020). Indeed, recent research with adolescents has shown that engaging in social appearance comparisons with others' photos on social media is associated with body dissatisfaction (Chang et al., 2019) and disordered eating (Zimmer-Gembeck et al., 2020), and that monitoring peers' attractiveness on social media is associated with internalization of cultural appearance ideals (Vandenbosch & Eggermont, 2015). Further, adolescent girls high in trait social comparison (those who engage in greater social comparison than their peers) may be especially vulnerable to the deleterious effects of viewing others' photos on body image (Kleemans et al., 2018).

Peer Approval: "Likes" and Comments

Adolescents are also highly attuned to quantifiable metrics of peer approval in the form of "likes," comments, friends, and followers. Neuroimaging studies have demonstrated greater activation in the brain's reward circuitry (e.g., the nucleus accumbens) when adolescents view photos that receive high numbers of "likes," especially when these were their own photos (Sherman et al., 2016; Sherman, Greenfield, et al., 2018; Sherman, Hernandez, et al., 2018), suggesting that quantifiable approval of one's online self-presentation may be especially rewarding. Among adolescent girls in Australia, number of friends on social media has been shown to positively correlate with body image concerns (Tiggemann & Slater, 2013) and dieting (Tiggemann & Slater, 2014).

Peer approval can also be conveyed through comments on adolescents' posts. As expected, longitudinal evidence suggests that social media use generally is associated with more appearance-related peer feedback (i.e., comments) on adolescents' social media posts, though the same study found that the reception of peer appearance-related feedback is unrelated to body dissatisfaction (de Vries et al., 2016). Interestingly, positive appearance-related comments (compliments) have been implicated in adolescent girls' self-objectification, possibly more so than negative comments or "teasing" (Slater & Tiggemann, 2015). However, negative appearance-related comments may be linked to adolescent girls' lower self-esteem and depression and to boys' tendency to act out (Berne et al., 2014). Some work with young adults suggests that the link between social media use and social comparison may be exacerbated by adolescents' viewing "likes" and comments on others' posts (Fardouly et al., 2017; Fox & Vendemia, 2016), to which they ostensibly compare their own peer feedback. Some longitudinal work also suggests that more liking and commenting on others' social media content is associated with decreased appearance self-esteem across development (Steinsbekk et al., 2021).

No prior work to our knowledge has examined the experience of receiving or giving likes on adolescents' disordered eating outcomes specifically, though research with adult women has demonstrated that Facebook use is implicated in the maintenance of disordered eating by providing reinforcement of shape and weight concerns (Mabe et al., 2014). Theoretically, if adolescents receive "likes" and comments on photos that have been edited, or promote an idealized version of their appearance, adolescents may infer that they receive positive feedback for altering their appearance, reinforcing their body dissatisfaction. For adolescents who engage in disordered eating, these "likes" and comments may provide reinforcement for disordered eating behaviors, though this should be studied directly in future research. Indeed, social reinforcement plays a role in adolescents' disordered eating behaviors, and research has demonstrated that adolescent girls in particular encourage dieting and disordered eating among one another, and that girls who engage in disordered eating are more likely to be perceived as popular by their peers, despite having lower body esteem (Lieberman et al., 2001).

Subjective Social Media Experiences

Although social media-specific behaviors clearly play a role in adolescents' body image and disordered eating, researchers are increasingly turning toward subjective, psychological experiences on social media to explain individual differences in these outcomes. Indeed, *investment*, or the degree of importance adolescents place on social media experiences, has been more strongly linked to negative outcomes than merely engaging in the behavior. Below we describe the roles of investment in one's appearance online, investment in peer feedback on one's posts, and heightened appearance-related social media consciousness (ASMC).

Investment in Appearance

Likely due to the sociocultural emphasis on appearance, aspects of adolescent development, features of social media, and, for girls, gender socialization, adolescents are highly invested in how they present themselves online. Although girls report generally placing more importance on appearing attractive online, boys report investment in their online appearance as well (e.g., de Vries et al., 2014; Mingoia et al., 2019; Yau & Reich, 2019). Investment in one's selfies, including putting in more effort to take and edit selfies, is associated with greater body dissatisfaction and dietary restraint, even after controlling for overall social media use and internalization of the thin ideal, among adolescent girls in Australia (McLean et al., 2015), and with greater appearance comparisons among adolescent girls and boys in Australia (Mingoia et al., 2019). Work with young adult women is more extensive and finds a similar pattern (e.g., Cohen et al., 2018; Lonergan et al., 2019). Importantly, photo editing and investment in photos are highly correlated among adolescents and young adults (Cohen et al., 2018; Mingoia et al., 2019; McLean et al., 2015), suggesting that photo editing may be a behavioral manifestation of appearance investment.

Investment in Peer Feedback

Adolescents are also often highly invested in receiving peer feedback on their social media posts in the form of "likes," followers, friends, and comments. Qualitative work suggests that adolescents, especially girls, post selfies for the primary purpose of appearing attractive or favorable to peers and ultimately receiving positive peer feedback (Burnette et al., 2017; Chua & Chang, 2016; Yau & Reich, 2019). Research also shows that adolescents and young adults engage in various behaviors to earn more "likes" on their content, including editing their photos, uploading photos at certain times of day, deleting photos when they do not get enough likes and reposting at a later time, purchasing followers and likes, asking their friends to like their photos, and liking others' photos in exchange for more likes (Dumas et al., 2017; Yau & Reich, 2019).

Among adolescents, this behavior is associated with negative mental and behavioral health outcomes (Nesi & Prinstein, 2019), problematic social media use (e.g., using social media to cope with negative emotions; Martinez-Pecino & Garcia-Gavilán, 2019), and lower global self-esteem (Meeus et al., 2019). Some preliminary work suggests that concern about peer feedback on one's selfies specifically is associated with worse body esteem (Nesi et al., 2021). Among young adult women, greater investment in selfie feedback from peers was associated with body surveillance, body dissatisfaction, and drive for thinness, but not bulimic tendencies (Butkowski et al., 2019). Notably, young adults who engage in negative feedback seeking (i.e., eliciting negative feedback to confirm negative perceptions of oneself) and who receive more negative comments on Facebook are more likely to report disordered eating concerns and behaviors a month later (Hummel & Smith, 2015).

Appearance-Related Social Media Consciousness

The visual nature of social media that leads to a focus on physical appearance, such as HVSM, may manifest as a broader preoccupation with one's social media self-presentation, even in offline spaces. *Appearance-related social media consciousness* (ASMC) has been proposed as a novel subjective experience among adolescents and adults, defined as a preoccupation with one's attractiveness to a real or potential social media audience (Choukas-Bradley et al., 2019, 2020). ASMC is common among both adolescents and young adults, especially among young women (Choukas-Bradley et al., 2019, 2020). In some ways, this experience reflects the extension of self-objectification to a social media audience, whereby adolescents and young adults imagine how their social media photos look to outside observers, overvalue their physical appearance on social media relative to other social media experiences, and even remain vigilant during in-person social interactions with the knowledge that at any moment a photo could be taken and posted to a larger social media audience (Choukas-Bradley et al., 2019, 2020). ASMC is correlated with self-objectification, body surveillance, body shame, body comparison, depressive symptoms, and disordered eating among adolescents (Choukas-Bradley et al., 2020). Additionally, even when controlling for body surveillance (a behavioral manifestation of self-objectification) and overall time on social media, ASMC is associated with greater disordered eating behaviors for adolescent girls (Choukas-Bradley et al., 2020), suggesting the unique effect of social media-specific appearance cognitions.

Social Media Devoted to Body Image Concerns

The prior sections demonstrate how social media plays a role in adolescents' body image and disordered eating. Adolescents may also turn to social media for guidance or inspiration on attaining their desired body type. In addition to universal features such as edited photos, "likes," and comments, social media includes content designed specifically for the purpose of encouraging users to attain a specific body shape or appearance, and influences users' perceptions of body image.

Weight Loss and Fitness Social Media Content

"Thinspiration" and "fitspiration" refer to social media images meant to inspire viewers to be thin or fit, respectively. While social media users may believe this content teaches viewers healthy lifestyle and dieting techniques, it can be problematic if it encourages inaccurate, or even dangerous, health content (Carrotte et al., 2015). Thinspiration and fitspiration images frequently depict weight loss techniques or fitness regimens, though there is no guarantee that these messages come from certified health professionals. More likely, the images have been posted by celebrities, models, influencers, or peers. Moreover, teenage girls with preexisting body image concerns are especially likely to seek out this type of content, hoping to gain inspiration for changing their own weight or appearance (Carrotte et al., 2015). The presentation of these images on social media, where adolescents frequently see the personal life experiences of their peers, may make them appear more relatable and thus attainable, despite many negative outcomes related to viewing these images. Alarmingly, companies that manufacture "wellness" products such as FlatTummyShakes and FitTea hire popular social media influencers and celebrities to advertise their products, though these supplements contain appetite suppressants and laxatives, and thereby facilitate disordered eating (Auguste et al., 2019; Wong, 2018). Studies examining young adults' exposure to and posting of such content consistently show associations with body dissatisfaction and disordered eating behaviors (e.g., Griffiths & Stefanovski, 2019; Holland & Tiggemann, 2017), often mediated by appearance comparisons (e.g., Tiggemann & Zaccardo, 2015). To our knowledge, only one study on the topic has included adolescents, finding that participants with a diagnosed eating disorder were more than twice as likely to view fitness-related social media content, and consumption of such content was highest among adolescent girls relative to boys and young adult women (Carrotte et al., 2015).

Social Media Content Encouraging Eating Disorders

Taken to the extreme, some social media content is dedicated to promoting and encouraging eating disorders. This content, often referred to "pro-ED" (pro-eating disorder), "pro-ana" (pro-anorexia nervosa), or "pro-mia" (pro-bulimia nervosa), facilitates community discussion by individuals with these disorders to maintain their disordered eating behaviors and cognitions. The majority of followers of pro-ED profiles are adolescent girls

(Bert et al., 2016). Content includes images of emaciated figures to inspire extreme thinness, challenges and competitions for caloric restriction, techniques for avoiding treatment, and anti-recovery messages (Arseniev-Koehler et al., 2016; Bert et al., 2016; Ging & Garvey, 2018). Eating disorders may be acquired or exacerbated through social learning processes. Indeed, research on group treatments for adolescent eating disorders demonstrates that patients may bond over their weight loss goals, share tricks for preventing effective care, vomit together, or compete with one another for the most severe case presentation (McGilley, 2006; Vandereycken, 2011). Whereas in clinical contexts, trained clinicians are able to monitor and address these phenomena, such an opportunity is unavailable on social media. Adolescents who are most at risk for disordered eating and who are more easily impressionable may be especially at risk for valuing the potential social support these pro-ED platforms provide (Arseniev-Koehler et al., 2016). At a developmental stage when peer evaluation and feedback is of paramount importance, these platforms pose a dangerous threat for encouraging and exacerbating adolescent eating disorders.

Body Positivity Social Media Content

In response to the increased popularity of appearance-focused photo and video sharing on social media (Anderson & Jiang, 2018), there has been an emergence of body positive content that focuses on challenging the unrealistic beauty standards depicted on social media by reconceptualizing body acceptance. More specifically, the social movement known as "the body positivity movement" has developed on social media with the intention of increasing body acceptance through broad definitions of beauty and the depiction of a greater range of body types and appearances, along with limited photo editing and manipulation (Cohen, Irwin, et al., 2019; Lazuka et al., 2020; Tylka & Wood-Barcalow, 2015; Webb et al., 2017). Indeed, content analyses indicate that posts related to body positivity present varying constructs of beauty (Lazuka et al., 2020), and have gained popularity on mainstream online communities (see Rodgers et al., 2020). Research has begun to examine the potential benefits of exposure to this content, with recent experimental studies finding associations between young women's exposure to body positive images and boosts in body satisfaction and body appreciation, when compared to viewing thin-ideal images (Cohen, Fardouly, et al., 2019; Williamson & Karazsia, 2018). Despite this promising evidence, there is debate regarding how body positive content may continue to place value on physical appearance and may increase shame for individuals who have lower body acceptance (see Cohen et al., 2020). Consistent with this critique, studies have found that despite women's frequently encouraging responses to body positive images, such exposure is associated with higher levels of self-objectification and salience of physical appearance (e.g., describing the self through the lens of physical appearance rather than other attributes; Betz & Ramsey, 2017; Cohen, Fardouly, et al., 2019). The numerous negative outcomes associated with self-objectification (Fredrickson & Roberts, 1997) pose the possibility that body positive posts may have long-term negative impacts that need to be further investigated.

From a theoretical standpoint, there are also potential benefits of body positive social media. For example, the tripartite influence model (Thompson et al., 1999) offers another framework for evaluating the relationship between body positive social media content and body image concerns. Exposure to a more diverse range of bodies may lead to a decrease in the internalization of media's unrealistic appearance ideals (i.e., the thin and muscular ideals), improving viewers' body image. Additionally, it is possible that social media users' engagement in social comparisons with more inclusive and realistic social media targets may positively affect body image outcomes. Since much is currently unknown regarding the impacts of body positive content, future research should investigate the short- and long-term benefits and consequences associated with exposure to body positive social media content, especially among adolescent girls, who may be distinctly vulnerable to these associated effects.

Future Directions, Implications, and Conclusions

Social media has transformed the lives of adolescents. Although research is mixed regarding the overall effect of social media on adolescents' well-being, extant research suggests that the highly visual nature of social media may lead to body image concerns and disordered eating. It may be useful to assess the ways in which an adolescent is using social media, and whether it is causing disruption to their well-being or body image. Given the ubiquity of social media use among adolescents, it is imperative that scholars and mental health care providers consider the effect of social media on adolescents' body image and disordered eating.

While many novel social media behaviors have been linked to body dissatisfaction and disordered eating, social media is constantly evolving. New behaviors and opportunities beyond posting and viewing others' posts are rapidly becoming central for adolescent social media use. For example, many adolescents now have two Instagram accounts – one on which they post polished posts fit for a more public audience and another – a "finsta" or fake Instagram – where they post more private, personal topics and photos (McGregor & Li, 2019). Additionally, Snapchat, a social media site used by approximately 70% of adolescents (Anderson & Jiang, 2018), allows for ephemeral sending where, unlike on more permanent platforms, photos are seen by interaction partners but then immediately deleted (Bayer et al., 2016). With the increasing popularity of TikTok, video-based sites also require increased research attention. It is unclear how these sites may affect adolescents' body image and disordered eating behaviors, and more research is needed to investigate the role of these novel behaviors.

An additional key priority for future research includes applying intersectionality theory (Crenshaw, 1989) when investigating the relationship between photo activity on social media and body image concerns. To this point, the majority of literature in this area focuses heavily on presumably heterosexual White cisgender girls, despite social media use being ubiquitous among all adolescents, regardless of gender, racial/ethnic identity, and sexual orientation. Future research should examine the unique intersection of marginalized identities across race/ethnicity, class, gender, and sexual identity to determine social media's particular effects on specific populations, such as Black girls and young women.

Conclusion

This chapter describes theoretical and empirical work on adolescents' social media use, body image, and disordered eating. Although a few examples highlight the potential benefits of social media for adolescents' body image, the majority of work in this area underscores the role of social media in perpetuating and encouraging body dissatisfaction and disordered eating behaviors, particularly among adolescent girls, by overemphasizing physical attractiveness and body ideals on HVSM. Many of the social media behaviors and experiences described in this chapter are normative and thus insidious in potentially causing harm. Others, such as pro-ED sites, are more flagrant. Adolescents, their parents, and clinicians should be made aware of the potential detriments and dangers of these platforms. Future research should continue to investigate these processes and develop intervention, prevention, and dissemination strategies to foster adolescents' healthy body image and eating behaviors across development.

References

American Psychiatric Association. (2013). *Diagnostic and statistical manual of mental disorders* (5th ed.). https://doi.org/10.1176/appi.books.9780890425596

Anderson, M., & Jiang, J. (2018). *Teens, social media & technology 2018*. Pew Research Center: Internet, Science & Tech. https://www.pewresearch.org/internet/2018/05/31/teens-social-media-technology-2018/

Arseniev-Koehler, A., Lee, H., McCormick, T., & Moreno, M. A. (2016). #Proana: Pro-eating disorder socialization on Twitter. *The Journal of Adolescent Health: Official Publication of the Society for Adolescent Medicine, 58*(6), 659–664. https://doi.org/10.1016/j.jadohealth.2016.02.012

Auguste, K., Bradshaw, A., Bajalia, A., et al. (2019). Detox tea advertising on social media: Examining the content of popular detox tea brands on Instagram.

Journal of Nutrition Education and Behavior, 51(7, Supplement), S125. https://doi.org/10.1016/j.jneb.2019.05.581

Bayer, J. B., Ellison, N. B., Schoenebeck, S. Y., & Falk, E. B. (2016). Sharing the small moments: Ephemeral social interaction on Snapchat. *Information, Communication & Society, 19*(7), 956–977. https://doi.org/10.1080/1369118X.2015.1084349

Berne, S., Frisén, A., & Kling, J. (2014). Appearance-related cyberbullying: A qualitative investigation of characteristics, content, reasons, and effects. *Body Image, 11*(4), 527–533. https://doi.org/10.1016/j.bodyim.2014.08.006

Bert, F., Gualano, M. R., Camussi, E., & Siliquini, R. (2016). Risks and threats of social media websites: Twitter and the Proana movement. *Cyberpsychology, Behavior, and Social Networking, 19*(4), 233–238. https://doi.org/10.1089/cyber.2015.0553

Betz, D. E., & Ramsey, L. R. (2017). Should women be "All About That Bass?": Diverse body-ideal messages and women's body image. *Body Image, 22*, 18–31. https://doi.org/10.1016/j.bodyim.2017.04.004

Brechwald, W. A., & Prinstein, M. J. (2011). Beyond homophily: A decade of advances in understanding peer influence processes. *Journal of Research on Adolescence, 21*(1), 166–179. https://doi.org/10.1111/j.1532-7795.2010.00721.x

Burnette, C. B., Kwitowski, M. A., & Mazzeo, S. E. (2017). "I don't need people to tell me I'm pretty on social media:" A qualitative study of social media and body image in early adolescent girls. *Body Image, 23*, 114–125. https://doi.org/10.1016/j.bodyim.2017.09.001

Butkowski, C. P., Dixon, T. L., & Weeks, K. (2019). Body surveillance on Instagram: Examining the role of selfie feedback investment in young adult women's body image concerns. *Sex Roles, 81*(5), 385–397. https://doi.org/10.1007/s11199-018-0993-6

Calogero, R. M., Tantleff-Dunn, S., & Thompson, J. K. (Eds.). (2011). Objectification theory: An introduction. In *Self-objectification in women: Causes, consequences, and counteractions* (pp. 3–21). American Psychological Association. https://doi.org/10.1037/12304-001

Calzo, J. P., Horton, N. J., Sonneville, K. R., et al. (2016). Male eating disorder symptom patterns and health correlates from 13 to 26 years of age. *Journal of the American Academy of Child & Adolescent Psychiatry, 55*(8), 693–700. https://doi.org/10.1016/j.jaac.2016.05.011

Carrotte, E. R., Vella, A. M., & Lim, M. S. (2015). Predictors of "liking" three types of health and fitness-related content on social media: A cross-sectional study. *Journal of Medical Internet Research, 17*(8), e205. https://doi.org/10.2196/jmir.4803

Chang, L., Li, P., Loh, R. S. M., & Chua, T. H. H. (2019). A study of Singapore adolescent girls' selfie practices, peer appearance comparisons, and body esteem on Instagram. *Body Image, 29*, 90–99. https://doi.org/10.1016/j.bodyim.2019.03.005

Choukas-Bradley, S., Nesi, J., Widman, L., & Galla, B. M. (2020). The Appearance-Related Social Media Consciousness Scale: Development and validation with adolescents. *Body Image, 33*, 164–174. https://doi.org/10.1016/j.bodyim.2020.02.017

Choukas-Bradley, S., Nesi, J., Widman, L., & Higgins, M. K. (2019). Camera-ready: Young women's appearance-related social media consciousness. *Psychology of Popular Media Culture, 8*(4), 473–481. https://doi.org/10.1037/ppm0000196

Choukas-Bradley, S., Roberts, S. R., Maheux, A. J., & Nesi, J. (2021). The perfect storm: A developmental-sociocultural framework for the role of social media in adolescent girls' body image concerns and mental health. *PsyArXiv.* https://doi.org/10.31234/osf.io/ju92a

Chua, T. H. H., & Chang, L. (2016). Follow me and like my beautiful selfies: Singapore teenage girls' engagement in self-presentation and peer comparison on social media. *Computers in Human Behavior, 55*, 190–197. https://doi.org/10.1016/j.chb.2015.09.011

Cohen, R., Fardouly, J., Newton-John, T., & Slater, A. (2019). #BoPo on Instagram: An experimental investigation of the effects of viewing body positive content on young women's mood and body image. *New Media & Society, 21*(7), 1546–1564. https://doi.org/10.1177/1461444819826530

Cohen, R., Irwin, L., Newton-John, T., & Slater, A. (2019). #bodypositivity: A content analysis of body positive accounts on Instagram. *Body Image, 29*, 47–57. https://doi.org/10.1016/j.bodyim.2019.02.007

Cohen, R., Newton-John, T., & Slater, A. (2017). The relationship between Facebook and Instagram appearance-focused activities and body image concerns in young women. *Body Image, 23*, 183–187. http://dx.doi.org/10.1016/j.bodyim.2017.10.002

Cohen, R., Newton-John, T., & Slater, A. (2018). 'Selfie'-objectification: The role of selfies in self-objectification and disordered eating in young women. *Computers in Human Behavior, 79*, 68–74. https://doi.org/10.1016/j.chb.2017.10.027

Cohen, R., Newton-John, T., & Slater, A. (2020). The case for body positivity on social media: Perspectives on current advances and future directions. *Journal of Health Psychology, 26*(13), 2365–2373. https://doi.org/10.1177/1359105320912450

Crenshaw, K. (1989). Demarginalizing the intersection of race and sex: A Black feminist critique of antidiscrimination doctrine, feminist theory and antiracist politics. *University of Chicago Legal Forum, 1989*(1), 139–167. https://chicagounbound.uchicago.edu/uclf/vol1989/iss1/8

Croll, J., Neumark-Sztainer, D., Story, M., & Ireland, M. (2002). Prevalence and risk and protective factors related to disordered eating behaviors among adolescents: Relationship to gender and ethnicity. *Journal of Adolescent Health, 31*(2), 166–175. https://doi.org/10.1016/S1054–139X(02)00368-3

Dahl, R. E., Allen, N. B., Wilbrecht, L., & Suleiman, A. B. (2018). Importance of investing in adolescence from a developmental science perspective. *Nature, 554*(7693), 441–450. https://doi.org/10.1038/nature25770

Daniels, E. A., Zurbriggen, E. L., & Monique Ward, L. (2020). Becoming an object: A review of self-objectification in girls. *Body Image, 33*, 278–299. https://doi.org/10.1016/j.bodyim.2020.02.016

de Vries, D. A., Peter, J., de Graaf, H., & Nikken, P. (2016). Adolescents' social network site use, peer appearance-related feedback, and body dissatisfaction: Testing a mediation model. *Journal of Youth and Adolescence, 45*(1), 211–224. https://doi.org/10.1007/s10964-015-0266-4

de Vries, D. A., Peter, J., Nikken, P., & de Graaf, H. (2014). The effect of social network site use on appearance investment and desire for cosmetic surgery among adolescent boys and girls. *Sex Roles, 71*(9–10), 283–295. https://doi.org/10.1007/s11199-014-0412-6

Deighton-Smith, N., & Bell, B. T. (2018). Objectifying fitness: A content and thematic analysis of #fitspiration images on social media. *Psychology of Popular Media Culture, 7*(4), 467–483. https://doi.org/10.1037/ppm0000143

Dhir, A., Pallesen, S., Torsheim, T., & Andreassen, C. S. (2016). Do age and gender differences exist in selfie-related behaviours? *Computers in Human Behavior, 63*, 549–555. https://doi.org/10.1016/j.chb.2016.05.053

Dumas, T. M., Maxwell-Smith, M., Davis, J. P., & Giulietti, P. A. (2017). Lying or longing for likes? Narcissism, peer belonging, loneliness and normative versus deceptive like-seeking on Instagram in emerging adulthood. *Computers in Human Behavior, 71*, 1–10. https://doi.org/10.1016/j.chb.2017.01.037

Edwards, C., Tod, D., Molnar, G., & Markland, D. (2016). Perceived social pressures and the internalization of the mesomorphic ideal: The role of drive for muscularity and autonomy in physically active men. *Body Image, 16*, 63–69. https://doi.org/10.1016/j.bodyim.2015.11.003

Elkind, D. (1967). Egocentrism in adolescence. *Child Development, 38*(4), 1025–1034. https://doi.org/10.2307/1127100

Erchull, M. J., Liss, M., & Lichiello, S. (2013). Extending the negative consequences of media internalization and self-objectification to dissociation and self-harm. *Sex Roles, 69*(11–12), 583–593. https://doi.org/10.1007/s11199–013-0326-8

Fardouly, J., Pinkus, R. T., & Vartanian, L. R. (2017). The impact of appearance comparisons made through social media, traditional media, and in person in women's everyday lives. *Body Image, 20*, 31–39. https://doi.org/10.1016/j.bodyim.2016.11.002

Festinger, L. (1954). A theory of social comparison processes. *Human Relations, 7*(2), 117–140. https://doi.org/10.1177/001872675400700202

Fox, J., & Vendemia, M. A. (2016). Selective self-presentation and social comparison through photographs on social networking sites. *Cyberpsychology, Behavior, and Social Networking, 19*(10), 593–600. https://doi.org/10.1089/cyber.2016.0248

Fredrickson, B. L., & Roberts, T.-A. (1997). Objectification theory. *Psychology of Women Quarterly, 21*(2), 173–206. https://doi.org/10.1111/j.1471-6402.1997.tb00108.x

Ging, D., & Garvey, S. (2018). 'Written in these scars are the stories I can't explain': A content analysis of pro-ana and thinspiration image sharing on Instagram. *New Media & Society, 20*(3), 1181–1200. https://doi.org/10.1177/1461444816687288

Griffiths, S., & Stefanovski, A. (2019). Thinspiration and fitspiration in everyday life: An experience sampling study. *Body Image, 30*, 135–144. https://doi.org/10.1016/j.bodyim.2019.07.002

Grogan, S. (2016). *Body image: Understanding body dissatisfaction in men, women and children.* Taylor & Francis.

Halliwell, E., & Harvey, M. (2006). Examination of a sociocultural model of disordered eating among male and female adolescents. *British Journal of Health Psychology, 11*(2), 235–248. https://doi.org/10.1348/135910705X39214

Holland, G., & Tiggemann, M. (2017). "Strong beats skinny every time": Disordered eating and compulsive exercise in women who post fitspiration on Instagram. *International Journal of Eating Disorders*, *50*(1), 76–79. https://doi.org/10.1002/eat.22559

Hummel, A. C., & Smith, A. R. (2015). Ask and you shall receive: Desire and receipt of feedback via Facebook predicts disordered eating concerns. *International Journal of Eating Disorders*, *48*(4), 436–442. https://doi.org/10.1002/eat.22336

Jones, D. C. (2001). Social comparison and body image: Attractiveness comparisons to models and peers among adolescent girls and boys. *Sex Roles*, *45*(9), 645–664. https://doi.org/10.1023/A:1014815725852

Keery, H., van den Berg, P., & Thompson, J. K. (2004). An evaluation of the Tripartite Influence Model of body dissatisfaction and eating disturbance with adolescent girls. *Body Image*, *1*(3), 237–251. https://doi.org/10.1016/j.bodyim.2004.03.001

Kelly, Y., Zilanawala, A., Booker, C., & Sacker, A. (2018). Social media use and adolescent mental health: Findings from the UK millennium cohort study. *EClinicalMedicine*, *6*, 59–68. https://doi.org/10.1016/j.eclinm.2018.12.005

Kennedy, J. H. (1990). Determinants of peer social status: Contributions of physical appearance, reputation, and behavior. *Journal of Youth and Adolescence*, *19*(3), 233–244. http://doi.org/10.1007/BF01537889

Kilford, E. J., Garrett, E., & Blakemore, S. J. (2016). The development of social cognition in adolescence: An integrated perspective. *Neuroscience & Biobehavioral Reviews*, *70*, 106–120. https://doi.org/10.1016/j.neubiorev.2016.08.016

Kleemans, M., Daalmans, S., Carbaat, I., & Anschütz, D. (2018). Picture perfect: The direct effect of manipulated instagram photos on body image in adolescent girls. *Media Psychology*, *21*(1), 93–110. http://dx.doi.org/10.1080/15213269.2016.1257392

Lawler, M., & Nixon, E. (2011). Body dissatisfaction among adolescent boys and girls: The effects of body mass, peer appearance culture and internalization of appearance ideals. *Journal of Youth and Adolescence*, *40*(1), 59–71. https://doi.org/10.1007/s10964-009-9500-2

Lazuka, R. F., Wick, M. R., Keel, P. K., & Harriger, J. A. (2020). Are we there yet? Progress in depicting diverse images of beauty in Instagram's Body Positivity Movement. *Body Image*, *34*, 85–93. https://doi.org/10.1016/j.bodyim.2020.05.001

Lease, A. M., Kennedy, C. A., & Axelrod, J. L. (2002). Children's social constructions of popularity. *Social Development*, *11*(1), 87–109. https://doi.org/10.1111/1467-9507.00188

Lieberman, M., Gauvin, L., Bukowski, W. M., & White, D. R. (2001). Interpersonal influence and disordered eating behaviors in adolescent girls: The role of peer modeling, social reinforcement, and body-related teasing. *Eating Behaviors*, *2*(3), 215–236. https://doi.org/10.1016/S1471-0153(01)00030-7

Lim, W. M. (2016). Understanding the selfie phenomenon: Current insights and future research directions. *European Journal of Marketing*, *50*(9/10), 1773–1788. https://doi.org/10.1108/EJM-07-2015-0484

Lonergan, A. R., Bussey, K., Fardouly, J., et al. (2020). Protect me from my selfie: Examining the association between photo-based social media behaviors and self-reported eating disorders in adolescence. *International Journal of Eating Disorders*, *53*(5), 755–766. https://doi.org/10.1002/eat.23256

Lonergan, A. R., Bussey, K., Mond, J., et al. (2019). Me, my selfie, and I: The relationship between editing and posting selfies and body dissatisfaction in men and women. *Body Image, 28*, 39–43. https://doi.org/10.1016/j.bodyim.2018.12.001

Mabe, A. G., Forney, K. J., & Keel, P. K. (2014). Do you "like" my photo? Facebook use maintains eating disorder risk. *International Journal of Eating Disorders, 47*(5), 516–523. https://doi.org/10.1002/eat.22254

Marengo, D., Longobardi, C., Fabris, M. A., & Settanni, M. (2018). Highly-visual social media and internalizing symptoms in adolescence: The mediating role of body image concerns. *Computers in Human Behavior, 82*, 63–69. https://doi.org/10.1016/j.chb.2018.01.003

Martinez-Pecino, R., & Garcia-Gavilán, M. (2019). Likes and problematic Instagram use: The moderating role of self-esteem. *Cyberpsychology, Behavior, and Social Networking, 22*(6), 412–416. https://doi.org/10.1089/cyber.2018.0701

Mascheroni, G., Vincent, J., & Jimenez, E. (2015). "Girls are addicted to likes so they post semi-naked selfies": Peer mediation, normativity and the construction of identity online. *Cyberpsychology: Journal of Psychosocial Research on Cyberspace, 9*(1), Article 5. https://doi.org/10.5817/CP2015-1-5

McGilley, B. H. (2006). Group therapy for adolescents with eating disorders. *Group, 30*(4), 321–336. http://www.jstor.org/stable/41719135

McGregor, K. A., & Li, J. (2019). Fake Instagrams for real conversation: A thematic analysis of the hidden social media life of teenagers. *Journal of Adolescent Health, 64*(2), S39–S40. https://doi.org/10.1016/j.jadohealth.2018.10.088

McLean, S. A., Jarman, H. K., & Rodgers, R. F. (2019). How do "selfies" impact adolescents' well-being and body confidence? A narrative review. *Psychology Research and Behavior Management, 12*, 513–521. https://doi.org/10.2147/PRBM.S177834

McLean, S. A., Paxton, S. J., Wertheim, E. H., & Masters, J. (2015). Photoshopping the selfie: Self photo editing and photo investment are associated with body dissatisfaction in adolescent girls. *International Journal of Eating Disorders, 48*(8), 1132–1140. https://doi.org/10.1002/eat.22449

Meeus, A., Beullens, K., & Eggermont, S. (2019). Like me (please?): Connecting online self-presentation to pre- and early adolescents' self-esteem. *New Media & Society, 21*(11–12), 2386–2403. https://doi.org/10.1177/1461444819847447

Meier, E. P., & Gray, J. (2014). Facebook photo activity associated with body image disturbance in adolescent girls. *Cyberpsychology, Behavior, and Social Networking, 17*(4), 199–206. https://doi.org/10.1089/cyber.2013.0305

Mills, J. S., Musto, S., Williams, L., & Tiggemann, M. (2018). "Selfie" harm: Effects on mood and body image in young women. *Body Image, 27*, 86–92. https://doi.org/10.1016/j.bodyim.2018.08.007

Mingoia, J., Hutchinson, A. D., Gleaves, D. H., & Wilson, C. (2019). The relationship between posting and photo manipulation activities on social networking sites and internalization of a tanned ideal among Australian adolescents and young adults. *Social Media + Society, 5*(1). https://doi.org/10.1177/2056305118820419

Nesi, J., Choukas-Bradley, S., Maheux, A. J., et al. (2021). Selfie appearance investment and peer feedback concern: A multi-method investigation of adolescent selfie practices and psychosocial adjustment. *Psychology of Popular Media*, *10*(4), 488–499. https://doi.org/10.1037/ppm0000342

Nesi, J., Choukas-Bradley, S., & Prinstein, M. J. (2018a). Transformation of adolescent peer relations in the social media context: Part 1 – A theoretical framework and application to dyadic peer relationships. *Clinical Child and Family Psychology Review*, *21*(3), 267–294. https://doi.org/10.1007/s10567-018-0261-x

Nesi, J., Choukas-Bradley, S., & Prinstein, M. J. (2018b). Transformation of adolescent peer relations in the social media context: Part 2 – Application to peer group processes and future directions for research. *Clinical Child and Family Psychology Review*, *21*(3), 295–319. https://doi.org/10.1007/s10567-018-0262-9

Nesi, J., & Prinstein, M. J. (2019). In search of likes: Longitudinal associations between adolescents' digital status seeking and health-risk behaviors. *Journal of Clinical Child & Adolescent Psychology*, *48*(5), 740–748. https://doi.org/10.1080/15374416.2018.1437733

Neumark-Sztainer, D., Paxton, S. J., Hannan, P. J., Haines, J., & Story, M. (2006). Does body satisfaction matter? Five-year longitudinal associations between body satisfaction and health behaviors in adolescent females and males. *Journal of Adolescent Health*, *39*(2), 244–251. https://doi.org/10.1016/j.jadohealth.2005.12.001

Neumark-Sztainer, D., Wall, M., Larson, N. I., Eisenberg, M. E., & Loth, K. (2011). Dieting and disordered eating behaviors from adolescence to young adulthood: Findings from a 10-year longitudinal study. *Journal of the American Dietetic Association*, *111*(7), 1004–1011. https://doi.org/10.1016/j.jada.2011.04.012

Niu, G., Sun, L., Liu, Q., Chai, H., Sun, X., & Zhou, Z. (2020). Selfie-posting and young adult women's restrained eating: The role of commentary on appearance and self-objectification. *Sex Roles*, *82*(3), 232–240. https://doi.org/10.1007/s11199-019-01045-9

Rideout, V., & Robb, M. B. (2018). *Social media, social life: Teens reveal their experiences*. Common Sense Media. https://www.commonsensemedia.org/sites/default/files/uploads/research/2018_cs_socialmediasociallife_executive summary-final-release_3_lowres.pdf

Rodgers, R. F., Slater, A., Gordon, C. S., McLean, S. A., Jarman, H. K., & Paxton, S. J. (2020). A biopsychosocial model of social media use and body image concerns, disordered eating, and muscle-building behaviors among adolescent girls and boys. *Journal of Youth and Adolescence*, *49*(2), 399–409. https://doi.org/10.1007/s10964-019-01190-0

Salomon, I., & Brown, C. S. (2019). The selfie generation: Examining the relationship between social media use and early adolescent body image. *The Journal of Early Adolescence*, *39*(4), 539–560. https://doi.org/10.1177/0272431618770809

Sherman, L. E., Greenfield, P. M., Hernandez, L. M., & Dapretto, M. (2018). Peer influence via Instagram: Effects on brain and behavior in adolescence and young adulthood. *Child Development*, *89*(1), 37–47. https://doi.org/10.1111/cdev.12838

Sherman, L. E., Hernandez, L. M., Greenfield, P. M., & Dapretto, M. (2018). What the brain 'likes': Neural correlates of providing feedback on social media. *Social Cognitive and Affective Neuroscience*, *13*(7), 699–707. https://doi.org/10.1093/scan/nsy051

Sherman, L. E., Payton, A. A., Hernandez, L. M., Greenfield, P. M., & Dapretto, M. (2016). The power of the like in adolescence: Effects of peer influence on neural and behavioral responses to social media. *Psychological Science*, *27*(7), 1027–1035. https://doi.org/10.1177/0956797616645673

Slater, A., & Tiggemann, M. (2015). Media exposure, extracurricular activities, and appearance-related comments as predictors of female adolescents' self-object-ification. *Psychology of Women Quarterly*, *39*(3), 375–389. https://doi.org/10.1177/0361684314554606

Steinsbekk, S., Wichstrøm, L., Stenseng, F., Nesi, J., Hygen, B. W., & Skalická, V. (2021). The impact of social media use on appearance self-esteem from child-hood to adolescence: A 3-wave community study. *Computers in Human Behavior*, *114*, Article 106528. https://doi.org/10.1016/j.chb.2020.106528

Stice, E., Marti, C. N., & Durant, S. (2011). Risk factors for onset of eating disorders: Evidence of multiple risk pathways from an 8-year prospective study. *Behaviour Research and Therapy*, *49*(10), 622–627. https://doi.org/10.1016/j.brat.2011.06.009

Swanson, S. A., Crow, S. J., Le Grange, D., Swendsen, J., & Merikangas, K. R. (2011). Prevalence and correlates of eating disorders in adolescents: Results from the national comorbidity survey replication adolescent supplement. *Archives of General Psychiatry*, *68*(7), 714–723. https://doi.org/10.1001/archgenpsychiatry.2011.22

Terán, L., Yan, K., & Aubrey, J. S. (2020). "But first let me take a selfie": U.S. adolescent girls' selfie activities, self-objectification, imaginary audience beliefs, and appearance concerns. *Journal of Children and Media*, *14*(3), 343–360. https://doi.org/10.1080/17482798.2019.1697319

Thompson, J. K., Heinberg, L. J., Altabe, M., & Tantleff-Dunn, S. (1999). *Exacting beauty: Theory, assessment, and treatment of body image disturbance*. American Psychological Association. https://doi.org/10.1037/10312-000

Thompson, J. K., & Stice, E. (2001). Thin-ideal internalization: Mounting evidence for a new risk factor for body-image disturbance and eating pathology. *Current Directions in Psychological Science*, *10*(5), 181–183. https://doi.org/10.1111/1467-8721.00144

Tiggemann, M., & Slater, A. (2013). NetGirls: The internet, Facebook, and body image concern in adolescent girls. *International Journal of Eating Disorders*, *46*(6), 630–633. https://doi.org/10.1002/eat.22141

Tiggemann, M., & Slater, A. (2014). NetTweens: The internet and body image con-cerns in preteenage girls. *The Journal of Early Adolescence*, *34*(5), 606–620. https://doi.org/10.1177/0272431613501083

Tiggemann, M., & Zaccardo, M. (2015). "Exercise to be fit, not skinny": The effect of fitspiration imagery on women's body image. *Body Image*, *15*, 61–67. https://doi.org/10.1016/j.bodyim.2015.06.003

Tylka, T. L., & Wood-Barcalow, N. L. (2015). What is and what is not positive body image? Conceptual foundations and construct definition. *Body Image*, *14*, 118–129. https://doi.org/10.1016/j.bodyim.2015.04.001

Vandenbosch, L., & Eggermont, S. (2013). Sexualization of adolescent boys: Media exposure and boys' internalization of appearance ideals, self-objectification, and body surveillance. *Men and Masculinities*, *16*(3), 283–306. https://doi.org/10.1177/1097184X13477866

Vandenbosch, L., & Eggermont, S. (2015). The role of mass media in adolescents' sexual behaviors: Exploring the explanatory value of the three-step self-objectification process. *Archives of Sexual Behavior*, *44*(3), 729–742. https://doi.org/10.1007/s10508-014-0292-4

Vandereycken, W. (2011). Can eating disorders become 'contagious' in group therapy and specialized inpatient care? *European Eating Disorders Review*, *19*(4), 289–295. https://doi.org/10.1002/erv.1087

Wang, Y., Xie, X., Fardouly, J., Vartanian, L. R., & Lei, L. (2019). The longitudinal and reciprocal relationships between selfie-related behaviors and self-objectification and appearance concerns among adolescents. *New Media & Society*, *23*(1), 56–77. https://doi.org/10.1177/1461444819894346

Webb, J. B., Vinoski, E. R., Bonar, A. S., Davies, A. E., & Etzel, L. (2017). Fat is fashionable and fit: A comparative content analysis of Fatspiration and Health at Every Size® Instagram images. *Body Image*, *22*, 53–64. https://doi.org/10.1016/j.bodyim.2017.05.003

Wilksch, S. M., O'Shea, A., Ho, P., Byrne, S., & Wade, T. D. (2020). The relationship between social media use and disordered eating in young adolescents. *International Journal of Eating Disorders*, *53*(1), 96–106. http://dx.doi.org/10.1002/eat.23198

Williamson, G., & Karazsia, B. T. (2018). The effect of functionality-focused and appearance-focused images of models of mixed body sizes on women's state-oriented body appreciation. *Body Image*, *24*, 95–101. https://doi.org/10.1016/j.bodyim.2017.12.008

Wong, J. C. (2018, August 29). How Flat Tummy Co gamed Instagram to sell women the unattainable ideal. *The Guardian*. https://www.theguardian.com/media/2018/aug/29/flat-tummy-instagram-women-appetite-suppressant-lollipops

Yau, J. C., & Reich, S. M., (2019). "It's just a lot of work": Adolescents' self-presentation norms and practices on Facebook and Instagram. *Journal of Research on Adolescence*, *29*(1), 196–209. http://dx.doi.org/10.1111/jora.12376

Zheng, D., Ni, X., & Luo, Y. (2019). Selfie posting on social networking sites and female adolescents' self-objectification: The moderating role of imaginary audience ideation. *Sex Roles: A Journal of Research*, *80*(5–6), 325–331. http://dx.doi.org/10.1007/s11199-018-0937-1

Zimmer-Gembeck, M. J., Webb, H. J., Kerin, J., Waters, A. M., & Farrell, L. J. (2020). Risk factors and temporal patterns of disordered eating differ in adolescent boys and girls: Testing gender-specific appearance anxiety models. *Development and Psychopathology*, *33*(3), 856–867. https://doi.org/10.1017/S0954579420000188

11 Digital Media in Adolescent Health Risk and Externalizing Behaviors

Michaeline Jensen, Mariani Weinstein, Morgan T. Brown, and Jessica Navarro

Adolescent externalizing and health risk behaviors are some of the leading causes of morbidity and mortality among young people (Blum & Qureshi, 2011; Kann et al., 2018) and are of significant public health concern. Adolescence is a key period for understanding these types of behaviors, as they tend to emerge and peak in this stage (Claxton & van Dulmen, 2013; Krieger et al., 2018). Importantly, adolescence is not only a key risk corridor for risky and problem behaviors, but also for entry into new social and digital spaces; most social networking sites (and their regulators) set age 13 as the age at which youth can have their own accounts (Jargon, 2019). Co-construction theory (Subrahmanyam et al., 2006) asserts that adolescents create (and co-create) their online worlds and experiences to match developmental needs, and thus we should not be surprised that adolescents' developmentally appropriate affinities for risk taking, boundary testing, and affiliation would all manifest in some form in digital spaces, and that digital activities and offline behaviors would be mutually influential.

How youth digital media use and externalizing/risk-taking behaviors intersect is somewhat more complicated. In many domains, adolescent rates of health risk behaviors (substance use, sexual risk taking, violence perpetration) are at their lowest levels in decades (Lewycka et al., 2018; Twenge & Park, 2017), which some have asserted may be related to the proliferation of digital media and *displacement* of time (previously spent engaging in risk behaviors) in favor of time online and new forms of leisure, entertainment, and relationship formation (Kraut et al., 1998). Others have posited that youth engagement in online communities allows for covert or hidden coordination or reinforcement of deviancy and rule breaking, and thus technology may be linked with increased problem behavior (Ehrenreich & Underwood, 2016). In fact, the associations are not always straightforward, and thus this chapter seeks to summarize and integrate the research findings that have been published to date on these mutual influences and the mechanisms that underlie them.

State of the Evidence on the Role of Digital Media Use in Externalizing Behaviors

Here, we consider the intersections of digital technologies and several domains of externalizing and health risk behaviors (including delinquency, aggression, sexual risk taking, and substance use). For each externalizing or risk-taking behavior, we will review the research around two key questions: 1) Does the *quantity* of engagement with digital media impact adolescents' externalizing and health risk behaviors? 2) What is the role of adolescents' *qualitative* experiences online in these behaviors?

Problem Behavior and Delinquency

Problem behavior is generally conceptualized to include rule breaking, delinquency, antisocial behavior, and other acts that go against societal norms. In the digital age, problem behavior can (and does) occur online, and thus here we attend both to online manifestations of problem behavior alongside the ways in which adolescent engagement with digital media is associated with offline delinquency. As with all the externalizing and health risk behavior outcomes included here, we first consider whether there are consistent associations between the *quantity* of adolescent digital media engagement (e.g., screen time) and their problem behaviors before turning our attention to the *quality/nature* of online experiences.

Quantity of Digital Media Use and Problem Behavior

Some recent studies have suggested that more frequent social media use is tied to more concurrent conduct problems and delinquency among both younger (Ohannessian & Vannucci, 2020) and older (Galica et al., 2017) adolescents. However, these cross-sectional associations have not entirely held up in longitudinal research, as seen in a recent study where time online was linked to later internalizing symptoms and to comorbid internalizing and externalizing symptoms, but not externalizing symptoms in the absence of internalizing (where externalizing was measured as a combination of inattention, impulsivity, and antisocial behavior; Riehm et al., 2020). Similarly, our own research suggests that social media use and phone ownership in early adolescence are not associated with later conduct problems (once baseline conduct problems are accounted for) and that days on which young adolescents use more technology for a variety of purposes do not tend to be days when they report a greater likelihood of conduct problems (Jensen et al., 2019). However, some longitudinal associations have been found: Research with Korean adolescents suggests that technology use for entertainment is related with later online and offline delinquency, and internet use for communication is related to later offline delinquency (though internet use for information seeking seems to protect against offline delinquency; Lim et al., 2019). Other studies have investigated the opposite direction of effects (that earlier conduct problems might increase later social media engagement), which has been supported from adolescence (delinquency) into young adulthood (social media use; Galica et al., 2017) but not from childhood (behavior problems) into adolescence (screen time; Männikkö et al. 2020). Taken together, the displacement hypothesis is not strongly supported by the literature (i.e., there is little evidence that those youth who are online most are getting into *less* trouble) and there is considerable inconsistency in findings around whether digital media engagement might be linked with higher problem behaviors over time. More experimental, longitudinal, and ecologically valid research is needed in this domain.

Overlap between Online and Offline Delinquency

Online delinquent and problem behavior can take many forms. A commonly used typology classifies cybercrime and cyberdeviance into four types: cyber-tresspass (e.g., malware), cyberpornography, cyberviolence (e.g., cyberbullying, trolling, flaming), and cyberdeception and theft (e.g., digital piracy; Graham & Smith, 2019; Wall, 2001). For instance, some youth trespass into off-limits online spaces in ways that could have severe criminal penalties (e.g., cracking into bank accounts) whereas others trespass in ways that are less likely to be prosecuted but nonetheless problematic (e.g., hacking into a peer's social media account). The prevalence of these (usually covert) behaviors among teenagers is understudied and hard to ascertain, but surveys from the security industry suggest that up to 40% of youth have hacked into a social media account, email, or bank account (primarily "for fun" and "out of curiosity;" Richet, 2013).

In reality, the line between online and offline spaces in delinquency is a blurry one. Indeed, emerging evidence suggests that long-standing types of offline delinquency now also manifest online, and the two contexts are not entirely separable. For example, qualitative interviews with ex-gang members and violence-prevention workers have revealed the existence of so-called digitalist gangs (Whittaker et al., 2020) who use social media as a tool for attention for themselves and their gang. These gangs are more likely to be newer and less established (compared to less digitally connected "traditionalist" gangs), and to engage in activities like boasting, taunting, and posting videos of violent confrontations online. These types of online posts can serve to spark very real offline violence, as seen in the so-called Twitter feuds covered by the popular press (Patton et al., 2013). In a recent study of Black youth involved in gangs in Chicago, 11% of posts included a picture of a gun, although not all these pictures were necessarily shared with aggressive intent (Patton et al., 2019). Further, research suggests that gang members are more likely than nongang members to engage online in piracy, harassment, threats, and the facilitation of drug sales, assault, theft, and robbery (Pyrooz et al., 2015), suggesting considerable overlap between online and offline crime.

Youth who engage in delinquent behavior in both online and offline formats may be at particular risk. A recent study found that those adolescents (ages 12–17) who committed both online and offline delinquency were the most likely to experience increased risk factors and fewer protective factors, whereas the online delinquency only group had fewer risk and more protective factors and the offline delinquency only group fell in between the two (Rokven et al., 2018). In a rare longitudinal study, Korean youth who engaged in cyber-delinquency were more likely to report more engagement in later offline delinquency (Nam, 2020), which may suggest that, at least for some, online delinquency may serve as a gateway to later offline (and potentially higher consequence) crime.

Online Depictions of Offline Delinquency

In addition to delinquent acts performed online, social media can be used to portray delinquent acts performed offline. A study of undergraduate students revealed that exposure to online depictions of delinquency (including abusing an intimate partner, illegally carrying a weapon, physical fighting, selling drugs, driving while under the influence, setting fire to property, stealing, and vandalism) was frequent, with 81% of students being exposed to at least one offending behavior online (McCuddy & Vogel, 2015). Furthermore, those students who viewed more delinquency in their online social networks were more likely to engage in delinquent behaviors themselves (though this was a much stronger association in smaller social networks). Unfortunately, the cross-sectional nature of this study does not allow us to ascertain the direction of effects (i.e., whether youth who engage in delinquent behaviors are more likely to affiliate with other youth who do so and post about it online, or whether exposure to online depictions of delinquency may shift youth norms and behaviors).

In an innovative program of research, the Blackberry project (Underwood et al., 2012) has followed a sample of students (and their text messages) over the course of high school. Qualitative coding of real, naturalistic text message data has revealed that most of these teens engaged in at least some antisocial text messaging, and that this text messaging about antisocial activities was associated with increases in multiple reporters' accounts of rule-breaking behavior (Ehrenreich et al., 2014). Furthermore, findings suggest that the reason for associations between peer network delinquent texting topics and youth externalizing problems might be better characterized as selection (externalizing adolescents choosing deviant peer groups) rather than socialization (deviant peer groups driving externalizing behavior; Ehrenreich et al., 2019).

Aggression, Bullying, and Violence

Here, we consider how digital media use may relate to both physical and social/relational forms of aggression (the latter of which is particularly relevant online; Archer & Coyne, 2005). Indeed, aggression online can take a number of forms, including online bullying, harassment, and discrimination. Prevalence estimates vary widely and range from 1.0% to 61.1% of youth experiencing cyber-victimization and 3.0% to 39.0% of youth engaging in cyber-perpetration of aggression, suggesting that social media is a prominent context for cyberbullying (Brochado et al., 2017; Kowalski et al., 2019; Thomas et al., 2015).

Research suggests that many of the social roles that serve to instigate and sustain traditional/offline bullying also can be seen online. Sterner and Felmlee (2019) identified distinct roles of Perpetrator, Reinforcer, Victim, Defender, Bystander, and Informer around cyberbullying on Twitter. Reinforcers and defenders tended to enact these roles by commenting or by liking posts of the perpetrator or victim respectively, whereas informers tended to alert a site administrator to the cyberbullying incident. Interestingly, there were an average of 12 people directly involved (in one of the above roles) in each case of aggression on Twitter, suggesting that some features of social media (e.g., its permanence; Nesi et al., 2018a, 2018b) may increase the reach of cyberbullying experiences beyond those typically seen in face-to-face bullying.

Quantity of Digital Media Use and Online and Offline Aggression

Some have asked whether level of engagement with digital media (e.g., time spent online) presents a risk factor for cyber and traditional aggression. In a recent meta-analysis, links between general social media use and offline violence-related behaviors could not be formally synthesized because only three studies were available; however, the available studies each show that youth who are using social media more frequently tend to report more concurrent violence-related behaviors (Vannucci et al., 2020). Some cross-sectional research has also suggested that adolescents who spent more time online were more likely to be cyberbullying perpetrators (Hinduja & Patchin, 2008), with those who spend particularly high and problematic levels of time online being at the most risk (Kircaburun et al., 2020) and those with particularly low levels of time being (understandably) at very low risk of cyber-perpetration (Zych et al., 2019). It may be that in the average range of technology use, time online and time on social media are not closely related to cyberbullying perpetration.

Overlap between Online and Offline Aggression

Youth who perpetrate bullying online appear to mostly be the same youth who perpetrate bullying offline (Fanti et al., 2012; Hinduja & Patchin, 2008;

Olweus, 2012; Sourander et al., 2010) as confirmed by a meta-analysis that concluded that traditional bullying perpetration is among the strongest predictors of online bullying perpetration (Kowalski et al., 2014). It is common for cyberbullying perpetrators and victims to know one another in person – for example in 57% of the cyberbullying cases at a high school the victim reported that the perpetrator was a schoolmate (P. K. Smith et al., 2008). In a profile analysis, youth who engaged in cyberbullying tended to engage in all other types of bullying as well (relational, verbal, and physical offline bullying) and were at elevated risk for other externalizing behaviors (e.g., using substances and carrying weapons; Wang et al., 2012). A longitudinal analysis of the transactional associations between face-to-face bullying perpetration and cyberbullying perpetration found that higher levels of earlier offline bullying perpetration predicted increases in cyberbullying perpetration (controlling for previous cyberbullying perpetration), but cyberbullying perpetration did not predict increases in offline bullying perpetration (Espelage et al., 2012); this suggests that cyberbullying does not appear to be a first foray that grows into later offline bullying perpetration, but rather that offline bullying perpetration may come to extend to online environments.

Exposure to Online Violent Content and Offline Aggression

The impact of exposure to violent content in video games has been much talked of and controversial. Scholars have proposed that violent video games normalize aggression and can elicit and reward aggressive cognitions (e.g., hostile attributions), quick violent reactions, and aggressive fantasies (Gentile et al., 2014), though others have noted that selection effects are also likely at play (Breuer et al., 2015; Heiden et al., 2019). Early in the field's history, a meta-analysis of early video game research concluded that evidence strongly supports exposure to violence in video games as a causal risk factor for increased aggressive behavior (Anderson et al., 2010), but this finding has not entirely held up over time, with more recent registered reports (e.g., Przybylski & Weinstein, 2019) and meta-analyses of high-quality longitudinal studies finding zero to tiny associations between violent video gaming and later violent behavior (Drummond et al., 2020). One domain that has not yet been extensively researched is that of the potential intersections between social aspects of online gaming and in-game aggression, which has gained growing attention with the advent of online multiplayer gaming (with live video, audio, and or/chat streams; Freeman, 2018). More information is needed on whether the synchronous and semi-anonymous online multiplayer gaming context may socialize and/or reinforce youth verbal (e.g., hate speech, insults) or even serious physical aggression (e.g., the phenomena of SWATting; Lamb, 2020) in ways not yet captured in the literature to date.

Sexual Risk Taking

In adolescence, high risk sexual behaviors include behaviors that increase risk of unintended pregnancy, HIV infection, and other STIs, including early age at first intercourse, multiple sexual partners, concurrent sexual partners, having one-night stands, using drugs or alcohol prior to having sexual intercourse, having sex in exchange for money, and lack of pregnancy prevention methods (Kann et al., 2018). Sex and sexual risk taking have always been salient in adolescence, and in the digital age they are increasingly also taking shape in online spaces.

Social media and platforms that allow private messages are prevalent among youth to develop and maintain their romantic relationships, with only a small minority of adolescents accessing formal dating apps (which are meant to be illegal for minors; Vandenbosch et al., 2016). About 8% of all teens have met a romantic partner online (Lenhart et al., 2015) and 30% of sexually experienced adolescents have met a sexual partner online, with those who met partners online more likely to engage in unprotected sex and with multiple concurrent sexual partners (Ybarra & Mitchell, 2016). In this domain, social media may also contribute to health, safety, and privacy risks. Youth are exposed to and engage with sexual content in media, including pornography and sexting, that may impact their offline sexual behavior. In addition, youth may engage in online sexual behaviors such as cybersex or coordinating encounters with potential partners (including strangers). People have been very concerned about the risk that children will be targeted by sexual predators online, but empirical research suggests that this is in actuality very rare (Ybarra & Mitchell, 2016).

Quantity of Digital Media Use and Sexual Risk Taking

In a recent meta-analysis, the average association (across 14 cross-sectional studies) between social media use and sexual risk taking was $r = 0.21$ (95% CI 0.15, 0.28), representing a small to medium significant association, with stronger associations for younger adolescents and very small associations for later adolescents (Vannucci et al., 2020). Three of these studies included in the meta-analysis captured online sexual acts, including frequency of sexy online presentation (Vandenbosch et al., 2016), frequency of risky sexual online self-presentation (Koutamanis et al., 2015), and frequency of sending sexts (Gregg et al., 2018) whereas the remaining 11 studies captured more traditional indicators of adolescent risky sexual behavior. It does, then, appear that social media use and sexual risk taking tend to co-occur, though the cross-sectional nature of all studies makes it impossible to parse the direction of effects.

Exposure to Online Sexual Content and Offline Sexual Risk Taking

Exposure to sexual content online (e.g., internet pornography) has been linked to offline sexual risk taking, though, as with much research reviewed in this chapter, a lack of longitudinal or experimental designs limits ability for causal inference. For instance, a meta-analysis of six cross-sectional studies revealed that exposure to sexually explicit websites was linked to higher odds of intercourse without a condom in two studies and was perhaps related to having ever had sexual intercourse and having had multiple partners, though significant statistical heterogeneity made meta-analysis difficult, and most studies were weakened by their limited accounting for important potential confounding variables (L. W. Smith et al., 2016). In a relevant experiment on social norms, young adults who were assigned to and viewed sexual content posted by "peers" in a lab-generated Facebook feed tended to estimate that more of their peers engaged in sex without a condom, and in turn expressed higher willingness to engage in this risky behavior themselves (relative to young adults assigned to view nonsexual content on the Facebook feed; S. D. Young & Jordan, 2013). This highlights the important role of descriptive norms in intentions around risky behaviors and is consistent with longitudinal research that shows that adolescents' self-report of exposure to online sexual content is related to normative beliefs and, in turn, increased likelihood of intentions to engage in and actual sexual behavior (Bleakley et al., 2011).

Sexting, Cybersex and Offline Sexual Risk

Sexting refers to the exchange of sexually explicit text or images, usually via private messaging, in a way that need not be synchronous or reciprocal (Daneback et al., 2005). Cybersex is a related concept that can occur via computer (rather than just by text or private message) and encompasses synchronous sexual talk and/or behaviors with a partner over video, voice, or text chat and that often includes an element of sexual gratification through masturbation (Daneback et al., 2005; Judge & Saleh, 2013). Although sexting and cybersex share some features with other types of exposure online to sexual content (e.g., pornography), they are also distinct, as they are usually characterized as more interactive as opposed to one-sided consumption.

Sexting is prevalent in adolescence, with between a quarter to a half of teens reporting engaging in sexting to some extent (Baiden et al., 2020; Frankel et al., 2018; Maheux et al., 2020). Sexting can take many forms, with qualitative research with emerging adults revealing that sexting occurs in various relational contexts including casual sexual, dating and intimate relationships, and nonsexual peer contexts (Burkett, 2015). A study conducted in Belgium found high rates of textual and visual online sexual behavior (with consistently higher rates among boys than girls); about half of teens (55% of boys, 40.6% of girls) had attempted to sexually arouse their romantic partner via online communication, 20% of teens reported sending sexy pictures to a dating partner, and 7.6% of adolescents reported undressing in front of a webcam for a romantic partner (Beyens & Eggermont, 2014). A profile analysis of adolescent women revealed that they tended to follow one of four patterns with relation to online sexual behavior: abstinent, participating in multiple behaviors including risky behaviors, mostly seeking sexual content, and mostly receiving sexual contacts (Maas et al., 2018). Motivations for sexting include sexual arousal, humor, flirtation, and seeking reassurance about appearance. Sexting and cybersex are in some ways normative (and present little risk for negative outcomes like STI and unintended pregnancy) but can also carry their own risks, including receiving unwanted and unsolicited sexts, privacy violations, and feeling pressured to engage in sexting (Burkett, 2015).

Cross-sectional research seems to suggest that those youth who are more sexually active and (to a somewhat lesser extent) who engage in certain types of sexual risk behaviors are also more likely to be engaged in sexting (Frankel et al., 2018; Romo et al., 2017), with photo-based sexting being more strongly tied to offline sexual activity than text-based sexting (Houck et al., 2014). A meta-analysis of 8 studies that examined sexting risk for sexual and risky sexual behaviors concluded that those youth who sexted were significantly more likely to be sexually active, to have had multiple past year partners, and to have used alcohol or drugs before sex (L. W. Smith et al., 2016). A separate meta-analysis of 15 studies (14 cross-sectional) with a wider age span (including adolescents and young adults) found that youth who engage in sexting are moderately more likely to have lifetime and recent sexual experience, and slightly more likely to engage in unprotected sex and have more sexual partners (Kosenko et al., 2017). Rare longitudinal studies on this topic suggest that sexting may serve to increase risk for later offline sexual activity and risk taking. For instance, one study concluded that sexting is associated with later sexual activity but not with later risky sexual activity (sex without a condom, substance use before sex, and multiple sexual partners; Temple & Choi, 2014). Similarly, degree of engagement with chat rooms, dating websites, and erotic contact websites has been associated with later sexual activity in both sexually experienced and nonsexually experienced Belgian adolescents (Vandenbosch et al., 2016). Finally, a study of objectively coded text message content suggests that evidence of sexting at age 16 was associated with reporting an early sexual debut, having sexual intercourse, having multiple sex partners, and engaging in drug use in combination with sexual activity two years later (Brinkley et al., 2017). This is consistent with a profile analysis that suggested that youth who engaged in the riskiest behavior over time engaged in both online sexual risk behaviors (e.g., sexting or arranging a sexual encounter with someone met only online) and offline sexual risk behaviors (e.g., hooking up and unprotected sex; Baumgartner et al., 2012).

As with the other outcomes reviewed here, more longitudinal and experimental research is needed to ascertain what drives these associations: Are sexually active youth more likely to also express that sexuality in sexting? Does sexting serve as a gateway to later in-person sexual behaviors and risk taking? Are sexting, sexual activity, and sexual risk taking driven by other risk factors (e.g., disinhibition; Dir & Cyders, 2015)? Only well-designed empirical studies will tell.

Substance Misuse

Substance misuse is a major public health concern among adolescents, with implications for long-term mental and physical health (Grant & Dawson, 1998; Substance Abuse and Mental Health Services Administration, 2019). Here, we consider research at the intersection of technology and all classes of substance use (including alcohol, prescription and over-the-counter medicine, tobacco, marijuana, and other illicit drugs), though the existing literature (and thus too our review) focuses most closely on the most prevalent adolescent substance use type: alcohol use and misuse.

As with the other externalizing and health risk outcomes considered here, we will review studies on both the quantity of engagement with digital media (and its potential implications for adolescent substance misuse) and research on how adolescents engage around alcohol online. Unlike previously considered outcomes of problem behavior/delinquency, aggression, and sexual risk taking, substance use does not have an online analogue. Although teens can (and do) engage in online expression of sexual behavior and risk (e.g., sexting), delinquency (e.g., hacking and cracking), and aggression (e.g., cyberbullying), there is as of yet no way that adolescents can consume alcohol or other substances online. They do, however, post in both text and pictures (Moreno et al., 2015) about offline alcohol and drug consumption, view such posts from their friends, and use digital media to glorify, rehash, coordinate, and even lament drinking episodes online (D'Angelo et al., 2014; Hebden et al., 2015; Jensen et al., 2018). We will thus here consider whether engaging with digital media in these different ways is associated with riskier adolescent substance use outcomes. Although alcohol-related marketing does occur online, research suggests that most adolescent exposure to alcohol-related content online is noncommercial (posted by individuals in the social network; Cavazos-Rehg et al., 2015) and thus alcohol marketing is not considered here.

Quantity of Digital Media Use and Substance Use

On the whole, research does seem to suggest that those youth who are most engaged with digital media are at least somewhat more likely to misuse alcohol and other substances. This is captured in a recent meta-analysis that identified 14 cross-sectional studies of amount social media use and adolescent substance misuse, with an average pooled effect size of $r = 0.19$, in the small to moderate range (Vannucci et al., 2020). Individual study findings suggested that adolescents who are more engaged with social media are also more likely to report regular alcohol use and binge drinking, tobacco use, and marijuana use compared to those who are less digitally connected (Gommans et al., 2014;

Kaufman et al., 2014; Ohannessian et al., 2017; Sampasa-Kanyinga & Chaput, 2016; Spilková et al., 2017). These associations also seem to persist in adolescents even once potential confounds of impulsivity, sensation seeking, peer relationships, and symptoms of depression are controlled for (Brunborg et al., 2017). One recent longitudinal study suggested that frequency of social media posting and "checking in" on social media was associated with greater likelihood of subsequent initiation of tobacco and cannabis use, though other types of digital media use (e.g., "chatting and shopping" and "reading news/articles and browsing photos) were less consistently linked to risk of subsequent tobacco and cannabis initiation (Kelleghan et al., 2020). Of note, some research has suggested that much of these observed associations may be due to exposure to alcohol-related content on social media, and that once this mediator is partialed out there is no unique association between digital media engagement and alcohol use (Erevik et al., 2017). We thus turn our attention next to the types of alcohol-related content posted and viewed on social media.

Alcohol- and Drug-Related Posting and Substance Use Behaviors

Adolescents post about substance use on social media in a myriad of ways and for various purposes. These can include text-based posts describing alcohol attitudes, intentions, and behaviors (that make up over half of youth alcohol-related posts) as well as image-based alcohol depictions (Moreno et al., 2015). For the most part, when images featuring alcohol or other substances are shared on social media, they tend to be posted by someone in the picture rather than others (Morgan et al., 2010). and alcohol depictions tend to be incidental images (e.g., a person holding a drink while a photo is taken) rather than the primary focus of the image (e.g., a picture of drinking games or a person visibly drunk; Hendriks et al., 2017). Among this sample of Dutch young people aged 12–30, alcohol posting among adolescents under age 18 (legal drinking age) was rare, but young adults endorsed mostly posting images that include alcohol for "entertainment" and choosing *not to post* alcohol-related images because they thought it was "stupid," because they drank little, to reduce risk of a future employer seeing it, and because it was not consistent with their identities (Hendriks et al., 2017). A distinction between legality or illegality of behavior is also relevant for marijuana depictions on social media, which an even larger majority of youth see as inappropriate to post (Lauckner et al., 2019). Nonetheless, when adolescents post about substance use on social media, posts are usually positive in nature, pro-alcohol posts outnumber anti-alcohol posts by a factor of more than 10, and negative consequences of use (e.g., hangovers or embarrassment) are rarely depicted (Cavazos-Rehg et al., 2015; Moreno et al., 2010, 2013).

It is quite clear from the literature that adolescents who post more alcohol-related content on social media tend to drink more (Roberson et al., 2018; Stoddard et al., 2012; Westgate & Holliday, 2016). In a meta-analysis of

19 studies on alcohol-related social media use (that included posting, viewing, and liking others' alcohol-related posts), alcohol-related social media use was moderately and significantly related to alcohol consumption and alcohol-related problems, with stronger associations emerging in cross-sectional and self-report (of alcohol-related social media use) studies compared to longitudinal and observational research (Curtis et al., 2018). Indeed, posting about alcohol is associated with self-reported drinking frequency, heavy drinking, drinking quantity, and likelihood of alcohol use disorder (Glassman, 2012; Marczinski et al., 2016; Moreno & Whitehill, 2014).

Although far less studied, there is also some evidence that similar linkages may be at play for other substances as well. For tobacco, adolescents who posted positive tobacco-related content on Twitter were more likely to report past month cigarette and any tobacco use relative to those who did not post about tobacco on Twitter (Unger et al., 2018), and although posting about tobacco use is much less common than alcohol use among Dutch emerging adults, cigarette-related social media posts are nonetheless associated with real-life cigarette use (Van Hoof et al., 2014). For marijuana, research in young adults suggests that they do indeed post cannabis-related images on Instagram (Cavazos-Rehg et al., 2016) and that posting marijuana-related content to social media is associated with more pro-marijuana attitudes and actual marijuana use among racial-ethnic minority college students from low-income areas; however, no such associations emerged for alcohol depictions, alcohol attitudes, and alcohol use, which may suggest that these associations are most relevant when a behavior is illegal or less normative (Lauckner et al., 2019). Recent research suggests that marijuana-related posting is not uncommon even in adolescence, however, which underscores the necessity of more research in this domain. For instance, in Washington (a state where cannabis is legal for recreational use among adults over the age of 21), nearly a third of adolescents reported sharing marijuana-related content on social media, with about 11–13% sharing images or videos of people smoking marijuana and 24% sharing marijuana-related memes (Willoughby et al., 2020).

Nearly all of the above research has examined the role of alcohol- and drug-related posting to public (e.g., Twitter) or semi-public (e.g., Facebook, Instagram) platforms, but much less research has attended to the role of private communications (e.g., private direct messaging and text messages). However, the research that has examined private messaging suggests it plays a key role. One study found that about a quarter of late adolescents (in the summer after 12th grade) reported discussing substance use on public social media, whereas nearly half report doing so via private digital channels (George et al., 2019). In our own work (Jensen et al., 2018) college students in the USA and Korea have reported that they prefer private text messages to public-facing social networking sites to facilitate alcohol involvement, and private text messaging was more related than public social media to frequency of alcohol use and heavy episodic drinking. We have also shown that counts of alcohol-related words in sent and received private text messages are associated with higher odds of same-day drinking (Jensen & Hussong, 2019). Longitudinal research suggests that these associations may be bidirectional, with those youth who had previously been using substances being more likely to evidence later public and private substance-related discussions, and public and private conversations predicting later increases in marijuana use (but not alcohol or tobacco use; George et al., 2019). Taken together, these findings highlight the importance of future research that attends to how private digital communication channels may be uniquely indicative of substance use risk.

Exposure to Others' Alcohol- and Drug-Related Posts and Substance Use Behavior

In addition to adolescents' own posting behaviors being associated with substance use and misuse, so too is there a sizable body of evidence to suggest that adolescents' peers' posts also have the potential to impact their behavior. The majority of studies seem to support the hypothesis that exposure to others' substance use online is related to pro-substance attitudes and actual substance use behavior (Cabrera-Nguyen et al., 2016; Curtis et al., 2018; Pegg et al., 2018). Results from recent longitudinal designs are particularly informative. Even after controlling for developmental risk factors for initiation of alcohol use, exposure to peers' alcohol-related social media content predicted an adolescent's likelihood of drinking initiation one year later (Nesi et al., 2017). Similarly, adolescent exposure to alcohol-related social media content predicted alcohol consumption six months after exposure after accounting for both the adolescent's and their peers' drinking habits (Boyle et al., 2016). Some studies suggest that different types of exposures may be more influential and long-lasting: Adolescents who had more exposure to pictures (but not text) about friends partying or drinking in their social networks were more likely to increase or maintain their smoking levels over time (Huang, Unger, et al., 2014). This is consistent with findings that image-based alcohol-related content posted by college freshmen may be more related to substance use intentions down the road than purely text posts on social media (D'Angelo et al., 2014). Among young adults in Norway, disclosure of and exposure to alcohol-related content online was tied to later alcohol use, though the strength and consistency of these associations were reduced once relevant covariates were accounted for (Erevik et al., 2017).

An innovative experiment confirms this pattern: Litt and Stock (2011) created two Facebook profiles, one that portrayed alcohol use as normal and a control that displayed no alcohol; after viewing one of the two profiles participants were assessed on willingness to use alcohol and alcohol attitudes. Participants who viewed the alcohol normative profile had higher levels of willingness to use alcohol, more favorable images of alcohol users, more positive attitudes toward alcohol, and lower perceived vulnerability to the consequences of alcohol use, suggesting that exposure affects attitudes concerning alcohol. Results from Roberson and colleagues (2018) build on this idea – higher numbers of people who display drinking in an individual's online network predict more pro-alcohol attitudes. Taken together, it does appear that exposure to substance use in adolescents' online peer networks is associated with increased risk for substance use and misuse, and we thus turn next to potential explanatory mechanisms for this association.

Mechanisms

As seen above, largely separate literatures suggest that adolescent externalizing (aggression and delinquency) and health risk (substance use and sexual risk taking) behaviors intersect with digital media use in myriad ways, with more support for the importance of *activities* youth engage in online rather than just the *amount* of time they spend on screens in co-occurring with and potentially impacting their risky behaviors. Here, we consider several potential mechanisms for these observed associations (shared vulnerability, peer selection and socialization/influence, identity expression, and whether there are unique predictions to be gained) that largely apply across the spectrum of externalizing and health risk outcomes.

Shared Vulnerabilities

A long body of research suggests that externalizing and health risk behaviors (e.g., sexual risk taking, substance use, aggression, and problem behavior) frequently co-occur, and are likely driven by the same vulnerabilities (S. E. Young et al., 2009). So too we are beginning to find that youth who are engaged in online risky or externalizing behaviors are likely to be involved in other behaviors on the externalizing spectrum. For instance, we have seen that perpetrators of online bullying are more likely to engage in substance use and offline conduct behaviors (Sourander et al., 2010; Ybarra & Mitchell, 2004). We also see that sexting is related to nonsexual risk-taking behavior, with adolescents who engage in sexting having higher odds of tobacco and alcohol use (Kosenko et al., 2017).

One compelling explanation for this co-occurrence is that the same risk factors likely predispose youth to multiple types of (online and offline) externalizing spectrum and health risk behaviors. For instance, online antisocial behaviors are associated with many of the same risk factors for in-person antisocial behaviors (i.e., narcissism, exhibitionism, and exploitativeness; Carpenter, 2012). Online aggression and cyberbullying seem to be facilitated by long-known individual (e.g., low agreeableness, moral disengagement, hyperactivity), family (e.g., low parental monitoring), peer (e.g., deviant peer group), and community factors (e.g., low school safety; Espelage et al., 2012; Kowalski et al., 2014; Marín-López et al., 2020). Likewise, similar risks are associated with youth engagement in online and offline sexual behavior: sensation seeking, low levels of education, less parental monitoring, and less family cohesion (Baumgartner et al., 2012; Ševčíková et al., 2014). In particular, risk factors for externalizing problems that are developmentally salient in adolescence (like behavioral disinhibition and its sister concepts of impulsivity, sensation seeking, and low self-control; Steinberg, 2010) stand out as contributors to both offline and online behaviors. This pattern of shared risk across outcomes highlights the importance of accounting for relevant covariates in studies that seek to parse the nature of associations between digital media and externalizing and health risk behaviors and for ensuring that observed associations are meaningful and interpretable, and not just a result of a "third variable" problem.

In fact, some theorize that the online environment may be particularly well-suited for disinhibition. The online disinhibition effect theory posits that a confluence of factors that facilitate disinhibition are inherent in the online space (dissociative anonymity, invisibility, asynchronicity, solipsistic introjections, dissociative imagination, and minimization of authority; Suler, 2004). Although social media is increasingly dropping some of these features (e.g., synchronous dyadic or group conversations via video or voice chat are increasingly common), it still may be the case that the Internet provides some psychological distance from the impact of one's actions and lowers the threshold to rash action to a lower point than what would be present in face-to-face interactions.

Peer Selection

One of the most potent predictors of youth risk taking and externalizing behavior is the peer context, whether that be digital or in traditional, face-to-face spaces (Chan et al., 2019; Leung et al., 2014). Adolescence lies at the nexus of susceptibility to peer influence, concern for social reward, and engagement with digital peer contexts. Some features of digital media and online social networks make them particularly powerful conduits for peer influence: This is articulated in Nesi, Choukas-Bradley, and Prinstein's transformation framework (Nesi et al., 2018a, 2018b), which asserts that traditional peer relations constructs are *transformed* via the features of social media.

We know from decades of research that adolescents tend to be similar to their peers (homophily), with support for similarly minded peers choosing one another as friends (selection) as well as social influence by adolescents on their peers' attitudes and behavior (socialization). The classic question of whether peer similarity is driven by selection or socialization (e.g., Kandel, 1978) is equally relevant in the digital age. That is, are the many associations seen here between peers' online behaviors and adolescents' own online and offline behaviors a result of selection (i.e., choosing people with shared interests and behaviors) or socialization (i.e., peer influence)? Although peer socialization processes are the most frequent intervention target for preventing externalizing and health risk behaviors (Henneberger et al., 2020), selection is often also at play, and it can be difficult to disentangle the two and their influences (Gallupe et al., 2019; Samek et al., 2016). Selection and socialization processes are often mutually influential, such that youth select into antisocial networks and then they reinforce each other over time (Brechwald & Prinstein, 2011). Modern statistical methods like social network analysis and stochastic actor-partner modeling have allowed for scholars to parse the two more finely than ever before, and in fact, selection has been shown to be a stronger explanation for peer similarity in substance use behaviors than socialization effects (Rebellon, 2012).

In some ways, digital media is well-suited to help us better understand homophily, as online communication and social networks leave behind digital traces of the selection and socialization processes that we suspect are at work. Ehrenreich and colleagues (2019) used adolescent text messages over the course of high school, which were coded for antisocial content, to delve deeper into this very question. They found that those youth who were engaging in more externalizing behaviors (a combination of aggression and rule breaking) at each grade were more likely to be exchanging antisocial text messages (about substance use and rule breaking) with a larger proportion of their peers in the *subsequent grade* (evidence of a selection effect), but the proportion of antisocial dyads did not predict next-grade externalizing (lack of support for a socialization effect). Interestingly, they did find some evidence of a socialization effect when they homed in specifically on the first year of high school, such that the proportion of peers exchanging antisocial texts in the 9th grade was associated with one's own rule-breaking behaviors a year later. A study using social network analysis showed that both selection and socialization processes were relevant to adolescent substance use: Teens tended to select friends with similar social media use and substance use behaviors, but exposure to photos of substance use online also seemed to socialize adolescents' later smoking behavior (Huang, Soto, et al., 2014).

Peer Socialization

Although studies of digital media and traditional peer interactions suggest that selection is likely more important than it is often given credit for, socialization is still relevant to understanding peer processes in externalizing behavior. Adolescent susceptibility to peer influence is evolutionarily driven (Ellis et al., 2012) and evident even in their neurobiology (e.g., Chein et al., 2011); adolescence is a period in which youth are keenly motivated for social affiliation (including romantic), and thus highly motivated to seek social approval. We review several forms of peer influence/socialization here.

Deviancy Training

Socialization takes many forms, and deviancy training is one mechanism of peer socialization (Dishion et al., 1996). The process often plays out with a youth discussing an antisocial topic, which is reinforced by the peer's response (e.g., by laughter, encouragement, or more antisocial discussion; Piehler & Dishion, 2007). One of the central difficulties of studying deviancy training in youth is the difficulty of capturing their interactions as they play out, and thus a promising direction for future research is the time-linked analysis of deviancy training in naturalistic peer-to-peer interactions via digital media. Digital communication offers an unprecedented window of opportunity to observe and understand how youth communicate and reinforce one another in their real interactions. Evidence gleaned from the content of youth text messages suggests that those youth whose antisocial text messages are reinforced by peers' positive responses are more likely to see increases in their problem behavior over time. A study of adolescents' text message exchanges noted that antisocial comments in text are often met with laughter (e.g., "lol" and "haha") from their conversational partners, which is similar to the deviancy training observed in past face-to-face observational research (Ehrenreich et al., 2014). Furthermore, these antisocial conversations were associated with increases in rule-breaking behavior a year later.

Some social networking sites include features that can serve to amplify the ability of peers to positively reinforce youth behavior. The Facebook Influence Model (Moreno et al., 2013) posits that peer influence is amplified within the online social networking environment, which in turn shapes downstream cognitions and behaviors around risk. Whereas the seminal studies on deviancy training in face-to-face interactions pinpointed communication features like laughing or encouragement as powerful (albeit minimal) reinforcers of deviant talk, Facebook and Instagram allow youth to send the same message with the click of a "like" or a "♥". In fact, research suggests that the "like" is a powerful reinforcer (Sherman et al., 2016).

Social Norms

Selection and socialization processes on social media can alter perceptions of peer norms over time (David et al., 2006). Descriptive norms capture perceptions of how many of or how often peers *engage* in the relevant behavior (e.g., substance use, delinquency) and injunctive norms capture perceptions of how much peers *approve* of the behavior; both are strongly linked to adolescent behavior (Rimal & Real, 2005). Super Peer Theory (Strasburger et al., 2013) asserts that media can serve as a "super peer" in that it can expose teens to information that makes risk-taking behaviors seem normative, and that this normative influence will in turn cause youth to take risks themselves.

Research is generally supportive of the thesis that exposure to risky content online operates by reshaping youth perceptions of normativity. Qualitative studies with adolescents (Moreno et al., 2009) and college students (Moreno et al., 2012) tend to suggest that peers' references to alcohol use on social media are indicative of their actual alcohol use behaviors offline, with younger youth perhaps being most susceptible to the impact of online depictions on normative beliefs. Our research suggests that the amount of "alcohol talk" in received (but not sent) text messages from college students' entire text messaging network over the course of two weeks is associated with greater perceptions of peer descriptive and injunctive substance use norms, in addition to sent and received alcohol talk being tied to frequency of heavy episodic drinking (Jensen & Hussong, 2019). A longitudinal study of adolescents showed the exposure to sexual content in media increased youth perceptions of normative pressure (which captured both injunctive and descriptive norms), which in turn increased sexual activity intentions and behavior (Bleakley et al., 2011). This is highly consistent with experimental evidence that exposure to sexually suggestive photos impacts adolescents' perception that more of their peers engage in sexual risk taking (S. D. Young & Jordan, 2013) and that college students who viewed a social networking site with alcohol-related content estimated that the average college student drinks more frequently than participants who did not view the alcohol-related content (Fournier et al., 2013).

Status

Adolescents have been known to engage in certain types of problem behaviors (e.g., carrying a weapon, substance use, physical aggression) in service of gaining the status that these behaviors confer (Dijkstra et al., 2010; Osgood et al., 2013; Rulison et al., 2013). Nesi and colleagues (2018b) assert that some features of social media (e.g., its publicness and widespread availability) may amplify youths' quest for status through online spaces through selective self-presentation. Although there have been relatively few studies to date that explicitly test the role of status striving as a driver of youth externalizing and risk-taking behavior, some new research suggests that some adolescents are (and are known by peers for) engaging in "digital status seeking" behaviors (behaviors intended to increase "likes" and approval) online, and that these digital status seeking behaviors are longitudinally tied to later increases in substance use and sexual risk behavior (Nesi & Prinstein, 2019). Indeed, the Internet's culture of "micro-celebrity" may facilitate the extent to which high-status "peers" can impact norms and exert influence (Marwick & boyd, 2011).

We are beginning to see the role of status in peer influence across the externalizing and risk-taking spectrum. For instance, partying is considered by many teens as a high-status activity, and attendance (and subsequent publishing online) of images and text about parties may boost status by association (Marwick & boyd, 2011; Nesi et al., 2018b). Students in a rural high school in the United States tended to drastically overestimate how many of their popular peers were sexting (and those who believed that popular peers had sexted were more likely to have sexted themselves than those who did not hold that perceived norm; Maheux et al., 2020). As reviewed earlier, digitalist gangs are also capitalizing on the attention and status that social media can afford (Whittaker et al., 2020). There is even some evidence that being a perpetrator of cyberbullying is predictive of increased peer status over time (Wegge et al., 2016).

Interestingly, youths' search for status and desire to be perceived positively could also exert a "chilling effect" wherein adolescents may self-censor their real-life behaviors to avoid unfavorable exposure on social media (Marder et al., 2016). A mixed-methods study of the chilling effect revealed that teens do engage in impression management around depictions of substance use (e.g., hiding their drink/cigarette when they know a photo will be taken and likely end up online, presumably to avoid potential consequences if it is seen by a parent) but that they rarely alter their actual substance use behaviors (e.g., choosing not to drink or smoke at the party in the first place; Marder et al., 2016). Further research on impression management, status seeking, and behavior change will certainly better elucidate the nature of these associations in the years to come.

Unique Online Influences?

As reviewed here, online peer influence does seem to be a predictor of youth externalizing and health risk behaviors. An important question, though, is whether online peers exert *unique* influence, over and above that which would be expected (or is seen) from real-life, face-to-face peers (i.e., from school or neighborhood). Recent studies have tested this hypothesis, and overall, it seems that, although peers (in general) are still highly influential, there is significant overlap between online and offline networks, and online-only peer relationships seem to exert none to small effects. For instance, McCuddy (2021) sought to parse influence by adolescents' peers who are known in person (and also sometimes online) from those peers who are uniquely known online (and not in person). They uncovered little evidence that online peers expose adolescents to new/unique support for delinquency (e.g., only 7% of those exposed to any general delinquency in a peer network saw this influence from online-only peers, whereas 64% were exposed to both online and offline peer delinquency). Rates were similar for violence (8% exposed only via online peers) and slightly higher for theft (17%) and substance use (21%). Exposure to online peer support for general delinquency and violence were not associated with adolescent problem behaviors in these domains, though online peers appeared slightly more influential for theft and substance use behaviors. In all cases, online peer influence was of lesser magnitude than traditional (face-to-face) peer influence. Another study has similarly failed to find support for unique influence by online-only friends on marijuana use (Negriff, 2019).

Identity

Adolescent online and offline experiences are increasingly interwoven and often indistinguishable into what Granic and colleagues (2020) call "hybrid realities" that are both important for the attainment of developmental tasks like identity development. The Media Practice Model asserts that adolescents choose to interact with media in ways that are most consistent with their identity (or what they aspire for their identity to be; Brown, 2000). We must consider, then, that adolescents' online engagement in and depiction of risk-taking and externalizing behaviors (e.g., sexting, depictions of substance use, cyber-aggression) are best understood through the lens of identity development and intentional self-presentation.

This thesis is supported by evidence that adolescents engage in sexting and cybersex in ways that are consistent with sexual identity exploration and development (Eleuteri et al., 2017) and that depictions of alcohol use online are related to one's identity as a "drinker" (Thompson & Romo, 2016; Westgate & Holliday, 2016). This is also consistent with research in college students that suggests that depictions of substance use in highly visible areas (i.e., a profile or cover photo, which may seem more tied to identity) are more strongly tied to alcohol use and binge drinking than depictions elsewhere on social media (e.g., in a status update or a photo post; Moreno et al., 2015).

Digital Media as a Tool in Reducing Externalizing and Health Risk Behavior

Although schools and community programs have traditionally been main avenues for health information and education, virtual spaces are also a growing venue for the delivery of educational information, interventions, and support related to externalizing and risk-taking behaviors. Particularly in 2020–2021, when most adolescents in the USA have been engaged in distance learning due to COVID-19 and many in-person intervention programs shuttered, the delivery of health information through social media is increasingly relevant. Social media platforms, text messaging, and web-based platforms offer three key affordances for the delivery of health information: accessibility, anonymity, and credibility. Adolescents often want answers to questions about risk-taking behavior in the moment (Selkie et al., 2011), and the temporal and spatial accessibility of information and support via social media offer youth this proximity and flexibility. Further, online spaces can offer the anonymity teens may need to seek out information related to the use of drugs or alcohol or sexual activity without worrying about their parents' or peers' reactions (Best et al., 2016). Social media also offers a degree of credibility to health information; adolescents can see who originally posted the information as well as those who have shared it, which may help them to determine the validity of the information (Dunn et al., 2018; Stevens et al., 2017).

While existing research on the use of social media as a tool for health information is promising, further research is required, especially given the rapidly changing online mores of the adolescent population.

Health Information

Social media can be a powerful tool in disseminating public health information to adolescents, particularly given the omnipresence of social media in the lives of youth. Even before the advent of social media, the Internet was the primary source of health information for adolescents, especially those with few alternative accurate sources of information and for sensitive topics (Borzekowski et al., 2006; Gray et al., 2005). More recently, a number of qualitative studies with adolescents have confirmed that social media and text messaging are accessible and appealing sources of public health information (e.g., sexual health), though youth are also wary of potentially inaccurate or uncredible online sources (and have encountered barriers like inadvertently opening pornographic content; Selkie et al., 2011). In a study of African American and Latinx youth, Stevens et al. (2017) found that social media was an important source of sexual health information, and that participants felt social media was a more credible source than internet searches. Further, exposure to sexual health information on social media was significantly associated with reductions in sexual risk-taking behaviors (Stevens et al., 2017).

Delivery of Prevention Messaging

In addition to health information, social media can also be utilized to convey prevention messages to adolescents. Another qualitative study with US adolescents found that teens differentiate between social media platforms when engaging with drug prevention content and are highly conscious of how their peers might perceive their behavior (Dunn et al., 2018). Consequently, participants reported reading and liking prevention content, but were not likely to share it with their peers or create antidrug content themselves. Participants in this study recommended using short and humorous videos on platforms away from adult eyes, where teens might feel more comfortable, and the authors thus conclude that it is crucial to involve adolescents in creating effective prevention messaging on social media.

Numerous studies have found that internet-based interventions can reduce risk-taking behavior, albeit with small effects. Adolescent women who participated in a web-based drug prevention intervention were less likely to use drug and alcohol six months after the intervention than their peers in the control group. Further, participants in the intervention group also saw increases in understanding of normative beliefs and self-efficacy (Schwinn et al., 2010). A text-based intervention study of youth seen in the emergency department for drinking-related outcomes found that youth in the intervention group engaged in fewer binge-drinking episodes and drank fewer drinks per day than their peers in the control group at the three-months post-test (Suffoletto et al., 2014).

A 2014 systematic review of 11 intervention studies that examined social media and text messaging as a mechanism for sexual health education concluded that these mediums can increase knowledge of STI prevention and may reduce risky sexual behaviors (Jones et al., 2014). For example, a Facebook-based intervention saw small gains in condom use among adolescents in the intervention group at two months, though this difference diminished by the six-month follow-up (Bull et al., 2012).

Online Support

Although many studies have documented the benefits of online support groups (using a variety of modalities including social media, text messaging, and internet browser) for adolescents with health problems (e.g., cancer, asthma, type I diabetes), very few studies have analyzed the efficacy of online support groups as strategy to reduce adolescents' externalizing and risk-taking behaviors (Selkie et al., 2011). We do know that adolescent participants report utilizing anonymous online chat rooms to discuss sensitive topics (e.g., drug and alcohol use), and that these anonymous interactions can yield feelings of emotional support (Gray et al., 2005).

Research with adults suggests that online support communities could also be a useful tool in mitigating risk-taking and externalizing behaviors in adolescents. Indeed, studies of adults suggest that web-based support through Adult Child of Alcoholic (ACoA) online support groups afford desired anonymity, accessibility, and support from any location or at any time of day (Haverfield & Theiss, 2014). Likewise, a 2020 study of adults in an online recovery group found that the social support offered through the online group interactions seemed to reduce social isolation and the risk of drug addiction alongside helping build "recovery capital" to aid in maintaining sobriety (Bliuc et al., 2020).

While further research with adolescent populations is needed to investigate the potential and efficacy of online support groups in mitigating risk-taking behaviors, we can likely assume that the affordances of online support (i.e., accessibility and anonymity) will also be prized by young people. The need for accessible and high-quality recovery and support services has never been as salient as it is today when most substance abuse recovery and mental health programs have been pushed online due to the COVID-19 pandemic.

Conclusions and Future Directions

Although research on digital media and adolescent externalizing and risk-taking behaviors is still in its infancy, we have already accumulated evidence of several fairly consistent patterns. Adolescents are dual citizens of both online and offline spaces, and as such their identities and risk profiles manifest in both spheres as well. We are increasingly seeing that the *amount of time* adolescents spend online seems to be less important than *the ways in which they* spend that time, which can provide a valuable window into adolescent behavior and risk. Our glimpses into that window thus far suggest that adolescent disclosures and self-presentation online largely overlap with their offline identities and behaviors; our next challenge will be to devise ways to harness this information to enhance the efficacy and reach of interventions targeting these risky behaviors. For example, digital indicators of risk may be useful in targeting of public health messaging, invitations to prevention programming, or even timing of interventions. We have also seen that peer influence is alive and well online, that it largely overlaps with and operates similarly to the offline peer influence processes we have long studied, and that online peers do not seem to be presenting much unique risk compared to the peer influences adolescents encounter in their schools and neighborhoods.

These insights and implications notwithstanding, we still have much to learn. The field requires longitudinal and experimental research that allows for causal inference; only armed with this strength of evidence will we truly be able to parse the direction of effects in observed associations between digital media engagement and externalizing risk. This causal inference will only be possible in well-designed studies that adequately account for shared risk factors (e.g., disinhibition) that may potentially confound associations. Similarly, we require studies that use representative samples from diverse populations that allow us to generalize findings beyond just specific subsets of youth. Understandably, much of the research to date has focused on late adolescents, emerging adults, and college students (populations that are more easily accessible and more amenable to research on sensitive topics like sex, drugs, and crime). The next wave of research, however, must make sure to assess the range of experiences across the full span of adolescence (10–24; Sawyer et al., 2018), with particular attention to how the experiences of early adolescents (who are more likely to be newer residents of the digital world) may differ from those of late adolescents and early adults (Vannucci et al., 2020). We must also ensure that our research speaks to the experiences of youth from diverse backgrounds and identities, with attention to unique ways in which different groups of youth may engage in both online and offline spaces. Finally, we require more research-informed recommendations for how prevention and intervention scientists can best harness adolescents' deep attraction to and engagement with their online social networks in service of sustainable health behavior change.

As the digital world evolves, so too must our science. Researchers must be nimble to adapt their research questions and designs to the ever-changing digital landscape and adolescents' shifting preferences, though it is worth noting that we likely stand to learn the most from studies that tap digital manifestations of well-supported, theoretically driven processes that are much more stable than the platforms on which we study them.

References

Anderson, C. A., Shibuya, A., Ihori, N., et al. (2010). Violent video game effects on aggression, empathy, and prosocial behavior in Eastern and Western countries: A meta-analytic review. *Psychological Bulletin, 136*(2), 151–173. https://doi.org/10.1037/a0018251

Archer, J., & Coyne, S. M. (2005). An integrated review of indirect, relational, and social aggression. *Personality and Social Psychology Review, 9*(3), 212–230. https://doi.org/10.1207/s15327957pspr0903_2

Baiden, F., Amankwah, J., & Owusu, A. (2020). Sexting among high school students in a metropolis in Ghana: An exploratory and descriptive study. *Journal of Children and Media, 14*(3), 361–375. https://doi.org/10.1080/17482798.2020.1719854

Baumgartner, S. E., Sumter, S. R., Peter, J., & Valkenburg, P. M. (2012). Identifying teens at risk: Developmental pathways of online and offline sexual risk behavior. *Pediatrics, 130*(6), e1489–e1496. https://doi.org/10.1542/peds.2012-0842

Best, P., Gil-Rodriguez, E., Manktelow, R., & Taylor, B. J. (2016). Seeking help from everyone and no-one: Conceptualizing the online help-seeking process among adolescent males. *Qualitative Health Research, 26*(8), 1067–1077. https://doi.org/10.1177/1049732316648128

Beyens, I., & Eggermont, S. (2014). Prevalence and predictors of text-based and visually explicit cybersex among adolescents. *YOUNG, 22*(1), 43–65. https://doi.org/10.1177/0973258613512923

Bleakley, A., Hennessy, M., Fishbein, M., & Jordan, A. (2011). Using the integrative model to explain how exposure to sexual media content influences adolescent sexual behavior. *Health Education & Behavior, 38*(5), 530–540. https://doi.org/10.1177/1090198110385775

Bliuc, A.-M., Best, D., & Moustafa, A. A. (2020). Accessing addiction recovery capital via online and offline channels: The role of peer-support and shared experiences of addiction. In A. A. Moustafa (Ed.), *Cognitive, clinical, and neural aspects of drug addiction.* Elsevier Inc. https://doi.org/10.1016/b978-0-12-816979-7.00012-1

Blum, R., & Qureshi, F. (2011). *Morbidity and mortality among adolescents and young adults in the United States: AstraZeneca fact sheet 2011.* https://www.jhsph.edu/research/centers-and-institutes/center-for-adolescent-health/_images/_pre-redesign/az/US%20Fact%20Sheet_FINAL.pdf

Borzekowski, D. L. G., Fobil, J. N., & Asante, K. O. (2006). Online access by adolescents in Accra: Ghanaian teens' use of the internet for health information. *Developmental Psychology, 42*(3), 450–458. https://doi.org/10.1037/0012-1649.42.3.450

Boyle, S. C., LaBrie, J. W., Froidevaux, N. M., & Witkovic, Y. D. (2016). Different digital paths to the keg? How exposure to peers' alcohol-related social media content influences drinking among male and female first-year college students. *Addictive Behaviors, 57*, 21–29. https://doi.org/10.1016/j.addbeh.2016.01.011

Brechwald, W. A., & Prinstein, M. J. (2011). Beyond homophily: A decade of advances in understanding peer influence processes. *Journal of Research on Adolescence, 21*(1), 166–179. https://doi.org/10.1111/j.1532-7795.2010.00721.x

Breuer, J., Vogelgesang, J., Quandt, T., & Festl, R. (2015). Violent video games and physical aggression: Evidence for a selection effect among adolescents.

Psychology of Popular Media Culture, *4*(4), 305–328. https://doi.org/10.1037/ppm0000035

Brinkley, D. Y., Ackerman, R. A., Ehrenreich, S. E., & Underwood, M. K. (2017). Sending and receiving text messages with sexual content: Relations with early sexual activity and borderline personality features in late adolescence. *Computers in Human Behavior*, *70*, 119–130. https://doi.org/10.1016/j.chb.2016.12.082

Brochado, S., Soares, S., & Fraga, S. (2017). A scoping review on studies of cyberbullying prevalence among adolescents. *Trauma, Violence, and Abuse*, *18*(5), 523–531. https://doi.org/10.1177/1524838016641668

Brown, J. D. (2000). Adolescents' sexual media diets. *Journal of Adolescent Health*, *27*(2), 35–40. https://doi.org/10.1016/s1054-139x(00)00141-5

Brunborg, G. S., Andreas, J. B., & Kvaavik, E. (2017). Social media use and episodic heavy drinking among adolescents. *Psychological Reports*, *120*(3), 475–490. https://doi.org/10.1177/0033294117697090

Bull, S. S., Levine, D. K., Black, S. R., Schmiege, S. J., & Santelli, J. (2012). Social media-delivered sexual health intervention: A cluster randomized controlled trial. *American Journal of Preventive Medicine*, *43*(5), 467–474. https://doi.org/10.1016/j.amepre.2012.07.022

Burkett, M. (2015). Sex(t) talk: A qualitative analysis of young adults' negotiations of the pleasures and perils of sexting. *Sexuality and Culture*, *19*(4), 835–863. https://doi.org/10.1007/s12119–015-9295-0

Cabrera-Nguyen, E., Cavazos-Rehg, P., Krauss, M., Bierut, J., & Moreno, M. A. (2016). Young adults' exposure to alcohol- and marijuana-related content on Twitter. *Journal of Studies on Alcohol and Drugs*, *77*(2), 349–353. https://doi.org/10.15288/jsad.2016.77.349

Carpenter, C. J. (2012). Narcissism on Facebook: Self-promotional and anti-social behavior. *Personality and Individual Differences*, *52*(4), 482–486. https://doi.org/10.1016/j.paid.2011.11.011

Cavazos-Rehg, P. A., Krauss, M. J., Sowles, S. J., & Bierut, L. J. (2015). "Hey everyone, I'm drunk": An evaluation of drinking-related Twitter chatter. *Journal of Studies on Alcohol and Drugs*, *76*(4), 635–643. https://doi.org/10.15288/jsad.2015.76.635

Cavazos-Rehg, P. A., Krauss, M. J., Sowles, S. J., & Bierut, L. J. (2016). Marijuana-related posts on Instagram. *Prevention Science*, *17*(6), 710–720. https://doi.org/10.1007/s11121–016-0669-9

Chan, M., Jensen, M., & Dishion, T. J. (2019). Mechanisms and processes of peer contagion. In *Oxford bibliographies in psychology*. Oxford University Press. https://doi.org/10.1093/OBO/9780199828340-0165

Chein, J. M., Albert, D., O'Brien, L., Uckert, K., & Steinberg, L. (2011). Peers increase adolescent risk taking by enhancing activity in the brain's reward circuitry. *Developmental Science*, *14*(2), F1–F10. https://doi.org/10.1111/j.1467-7687.2010.01035.x

Claxton, S. E., & van Dulmen, M. H. M. (2013). Casual sexual relationships and experiences in emerging adulthood. *Emerging Adulthood*, *1*(2), 138–150. https://doi.org/10.1177/2167696813487181

Curtis, B. L., Lookatch, S. J., Ramo, D. E., et al. (2018). Meta-analysis of the association of alcohol-related social media use with alcohol consumption and alcohol-related problems in adolescents and young adults. *Alcoholism: Clinical and Experimental Research*, *42*(6), 978–986. https://doi.org/10.1111/acer.13642

D'Angelo, J., Zhang, C., Eickhoff, J., & Moreno, M. A. (2014). Facebook influence among incoming college freshmen. *Bulletin of Science, Technology & Society*, *34*(1–2), 13–20. https://doi.org/10.1177/0270467614538002

Daneback, K., Cooper, A., & Månsson, S. A. (2005). An internet study of cybersex participants. *Archives of Sexual Behavior*, *34*(3), 321–328. https://doi.org/10.1007/s10508–005-3120-z

David, C., Cappella, J. N., & Fishbein, M. (2006). The social diffusion of influence among adolescents: Group interaction in a chat room environment about antidrug advertisements. *Communication Theory*, *16*(1), 118–140. https://doi.org/10.1111/j.1468-2885.2006.00008.x

Dijkstra, J. K., Lindenberg, S., Veenstra, R., et al. (2010). Influence and selection processes in weapon carrying during adolescence: The roles of status, aggression, and vulnerability. *Criminology*, *48*(1), 187–220.

Dir, A. L., & Cyders, M. A. (2015). Risks, risk factors, and outcomes associated with phone and internet sexting among university students in the United States. *Archives of Sexual Behavior*, *44*(6), 1675–1684. https://doi.org/10.1007/s10508–014-0370-7

Dishion, T. J., Spracklen, K. M., Andrews, D. W., & Patterson, G. R. (1996). Deviancy training in male adolescent friendships. *Behavior Therapy*, *27*(3), 373–390. https://doi.org/10.1016/S0005–7894(96)80023-2

Drummond, A., Sauer, J. D., & Ferguson, C. J. (2020). Do longitudinal studies support long-term relationships between aggressive game play and youth aggressive behaviour? A meta-analytic examination. *Royal Society Open Science*. https://doi.org/10.1098/rsos.200373

Dunn, H. K., Pearlman, D. N., Beatty, A., & Florin, P. (2018). Psychosocial determinants of teens' online engagement in drug prevention social media campaigns: Implications for public health organizations. *Journal of Primary Prevention*, *39*(5), 469–481. https://doi.org/10.1007/s10935–018-0522-y

Ehrenreich, S. E., Meter, D. J., Jouriles, E. N., & Underwood, M. K. (2019). Adolescents' externalizing behaviors and antisocial text messaging across the broader peer network: Implications for socialization and selection effects. *Development and Psychopathology*, *31*(5), 1619–1631. https://doi.org/10.1017/S0954579419001020

Ehrenreich, S. E., & Underwood, M. K. (2016). Peer coercion and electronic messaging. In T. J. Dishion & J. Snyder (Eds.), *The Oxford handbook of coercive relationship dynamics* (pp. 140–153). Oxford University Press. https://doi.org/10.1093/oxfordhb/9780199324552.013.12

Ehrenreich, S. E., Underwood, M. K., & Ackerman, R. A. (2014). Adolescents' text message communication and growth in antisocial behavior across the first year of high school. *Journal of Abnormal Child Psychology*, *42*(2), 251–264. https://doi.org/10.1007/s10802–013-9783-3

Eleuteri, S., Saladino, V., & Verrastro, V. (2017). Identity, relationships, sexuality, and risky behaviors of adolescents in the context of social media. *Sexual and Relationship Therapy*, *32*(3–4), 354–365. https://doi.org/10.1080/14681994.2017.1397953

Ellis, B. J., Del Giudice, M., Dishion, T. J., et al. (2012). The evolutionary basis of risky adolescent behavior: Implications for science, policy, and practice. *Developmental Psychology, 48*(3), 598–623. https://doi.org/10.1037/a0026220

Erevik, E. K., Torsheim, T., Andreassen, C. S., Vedaa, Ø., & Pallesen, S. (2017). Disclosure and exposure of alcohol on social media and later alcohol use: A large-scale longitudinal study. *Frontiers in Psychology, 8*. https://doi.org/10.3389/fpsyg.2017.01934

Espelage, D. L., Rao, M. A., & Craven, R. G. (2012). Theories of cyberbullying. In S. Bauman, D. Cross, & J. Walker (Eds.), *Principles of cyberbullying research: Definitions, measures, and methodology* (pp. 49–67). Routledge. https://doi.org/10.4324/9780203084601

Fanti, K. A., Demetriou, A. G., & Hawa, V. V. (2012). A longitudinal study of cyberbullying: Examining risk and protective factors. *European Journal of Developmental Psychology, 9*(2), 168–181. https://doi.org/10.1080/17405629.2011.643169

Fournier, A. K., Hall, E., Ricke, P., & Storey, B. (2013). Alcohol and the social network: Online social networking sites and college students' perceived drinking norms. *Psychology of Popular Media Culture, 2*(2), 86–95. https://doi.org/10.1037/a0032097

Frankel, A. S., Bass, S. B., Patterson, F., Dai, T., & Brown, D. (2018). Sexting, risk behavior, and mental health in adolescents: An examination of 2015 Pennsylvania Youth Risk Behavior Survey data. *Journal of School Health, 88*(3), 190–199. https://doi.org/10.1111/josh.12596

Freeman, G. (2018). *Multiplayer online games: Origins, players, and social dynamics.* CRC Press.

Galica, V. L., Vannucci, A., Flannery, K. M., & Ohannessian, C. M. C. (2017). Social media use and conduct problems in emerging adults. *Cyberpsychology, Behavior, and Social Networking, 20*(7), 448–452. https://doi.org/10.1089/cyber.2017.0068

Gallupe, O., McLevey, J., & Brown, S. (2019). Selection and influence: A meta-analysis of the association between peer and personal offending. *Journal of Quantitative Criminology, 35*(2), 313–335. https://doi.org/10.1007/s10940-018-9384-y

Gentile, D. A., Li, D., Khoo, A., Prot, S., & Anderson, C. A. (2014). Mediators and moderators of long-term effects of violent video games on aggressive behavior practice, thinking, and action. *JAMA Pediatrics, 168*(5), 450–457. https://doi.org/10.1001/jamapediatrics.2014.63

George, M. J., Ehrenreich, S. E., Burnell, K., Kurup, A., Vollet, J. W., & Underwood, M. K. (2019). Emerging adults' public and private discussions of substance use on social media. *Emerging Adulthood, 9*(4), 408–414. https://doi.org/10.1177/2167696819867533

Glassman, T. (2012). Implications for college students posting pictures of themselves drinking alcohol on Facebook. *Journal of Alcohol and Drug Education, 56*(1), 38–58. http://search.proquest.com/docview/1030281740?accountid=10382%5Cnhttp://link.library.curtin.edu.au/openurl??url_ver=Z39.88-2004&rft_val_fmt=info:ofi/fmt:kev:mtx:journal&genre=article&sid=ProQ:ProQ%3Acriminaljusticeperiodicalsshell&atitle=Implications+for+

Gommans, R., Stevens, G. W. J. M., Finne, E., Cillessen, A. H. N., Boniel-Nissim, M., & ter Bogt, T. F. M. (2014). Frequent electronic media communication with friends is associated with higher adolescent substance use. *International Journal of Public Health*, *60*(2), 167–177. https://doi.org/10.1007/s00038–014–0624-0

Graham, R. S., & Smith, S. K. (2019). *Cybercrime and digital deviance*. Routledge.

Granic, I., Morita, H., & Scholten, H. (2020). Beyond screen time: Identity development in the digital age. *Psychological Inquiry*, *31*(3), 195–223. https://doi.org/10.1080/1047840X.2020.1820214

Grant, B. F., & Dawson, D. A. (1998). Age of onset of drug use and its association with DSM-IV drug abuse and dependence: Results from the national longitudinal alcohol epidemiologic survey. *Journal of Substance Abuse*, *10*(2), 163–173. https://doi.org/10.1016/S0899–3289(99)80131-X

Gray, N. J., Klein, J. D., Noyce, P. R., Sesselberg, T. S., & Cantrill, J. A. (2005). Health information-seeking behaviour in adolescence: The place of the internet. *Social Science and Medicine*, *60*(7), 1467–1478. https://doi.org/10.1016/j.socscimed.2004.08.010

Gregg, D., Somers, C. L., Pernice, F. M., Hillman, S. B., & Kernsmith, P. (2018). Sexting rates and predictors from an urban midwest high school. *Journal of School Health*, *88*(6), 423–433. https://doi.org/10.1111/josh.12628

Haverfield, M. C., & Theiss, J. A. (2014). A theme analysis of experiences reported by adult children of alcoholics in online support forums. *Journal of Family Studies*, *20*(2), 166–184. https://doi.org/10.1080/13229400.2014.11082004

Hebden, R., Lyons, A. C., Goodwin, I., & McCreanor, T. (2015). "When you add alcohol, it gets that much better": University students, alcohol consumption, and online drinking cultures. *Journal of Drug Issues*, *45*(2), 214–226. https://doi.org/10.1177/0022042615575375

Heiden, J. M. Von Der, Braun, B., Müller, K. W., & Egloff, B. (2019). The association between video gaming and psychological functioning. *Frontiers in Psychology*, *10*, 1–11. https://doi.org/10.3389/fpsyg.2019.01731

Hendriks, H., Gebhardt, W. A., & Van Den Putte, B. (2017). Alcohol-related posts from young people on social networking sites: Content and motivations. *Cyberpsychology, Behavior, and Social Networking*, *20*(7), 428–435. https://doi.org/10.1089/cyber.2016.0640

Henneberger, A. K., Mushonga, D. R., & Preston, A. M. (2020). Peer influence and adolescent substance use: A systematic review of dynamic social network research. *Adolescent Research Review*, *6*, 57–73. https://doi.org/10.1007/s40894-019-00130-0

Hinduja, S., & Patchin, J. W. (2008). Cyberbullying: An exploratory analysis of factors related to offending and victimization. *Deviant Behavior*, *29*(2), 129–156. https://doi.org/10.1080/01639620701457816

Houck, C. D., Barker, D., Rizzo, C., Hancock, E., Norton, A., & Brown, L. K. (2014). Sexting and sexual behavior in at-risk adolescents. *Pediatrics*, *133*(2), e276–e282. https://doi.org/10.1542/peds.2013-1157

Huang, G. C., Soto, D., Fujimoto, K., & Valente, T. W. (2014). The interplay of friendship networks and social networking sites: Longitudinal analysis of selection and influence effects on adolescent smoking and alcohol use. *American Journal of Public Health*, *104*(8), 51–60. https://doi.org/10.2105/AJPH.2014.302038

Huang, G. C., Unger, J. B., Soto, D., et al. (2014). Peer influences: The impact of online and offline friendship networks on adolescent smoking and alcohol use. *Journal of Adolescent Health, 54*(5), 508–514. https://doi.org/10.1016/j.jadohealth.2013.07.001

Jargon, J. (2019, June 18). How 13 became the internet's age of adulthood. *The Wall Street Journal.* https://www.wsj.com/articles/how-13-became-the-internets-age-of-adulthood-11560850201

Jensen, M., George, M. J., Russell, M. R., & Odgers, C. L. (2019). Young adolescents' digital technology use and mental health symptoms: Little evidence of longitudinal or daily linkages. *Clinical Psychological Science, 7*(6), 1416–1433. https://doi.org/10.1177/2167702619859336

Jensen, M., & Hussong, A. (2019). Text message content as a window into college student drinking: Development and initial validation of a dictionary of "alcohol talk." *International Journal of Behavioral Development, 45*(1), 3–10. https://doi.org/10.1177/0165025419889175

Jensen, M., Hussong, A. M., & Baik, J. (2018). Text messaging and social network site use to facilitate alcohol involvement: A comparison of U.S. and Korean college students. *Cyberpsychology, Behavior, and Social Networking, 21*(5), 311–317. https://doi.org/10.1089/cyber.2017.0616

Jones, K., Eathington, P., Baldwin, K., & Sipsma, H. (2014). The impact of health education transmitted via social media or text messaging on adolescent and young adult risky sexual behavior: A systematic review of the literature. *Sexually Transmitted Diseases, 41*(7), 413–419. https://doi.org/10.1097/OLQ.0000000000000146

Judge, A. M., & Saleh, F. M. (2013). Sexting, cybersex, and internet use: The relationship between adolescent sexual behavior and electronic technologies. In R. Rosner (Ed.), *Clinical handbook of adolescent addiction* (pp. 377–389). Wiley.

Kandel, D. B. (1978). Homophily, selection, and socialization in adolescent friendships. *American Journal of Sociology, 84*(2), 427–436.

Kann, L., Eaton K., D., Kinchen, S., et al. (2018). Youth risk behavior surveillance: United States, 2017. *MMWR Surveillance Summaries, 67*(8), 1–162. http://ezproxy.cul.columbia.edu/login?url=http://search.ebscohost.com/login.aspx?direct=true&db=cin20&AN=2011717026&site=ehost-live&scope=site

Kaufman, Z. A., Braunschweig, E. N., Feeney, J., et al. (2014). Sexual risk behavior, alcohol use, and social media use among secondary school students in informal settlements in Cape Town and Port Elizabeth, South Africa. *AIDS and Behavior, 18*(9), 1661–1674. https://doi.org/10.1007/s10461-014-0816-x

Kelleghan, A. R., Leventhal, A. M., Cruz, T. B., et al. (2020). Digital media use and subsequent cannabis and tobacco product use initiation among adolescents. *Drug and Alcohol Dependence, 212*, Article 108017. https://doi.org/https://doi.org/10.1016/j.drugalcdep.2020.108017

Kircaburun, K., Demetrovics, Z., Király, O., & Griffiths, M. D. (2020). Childhood emotional trauma and cyberbullying perpetration among emerging adults: A multiple mediation model of the role of problematic social media use and psychopathology. *International Journal of Mental Health and Addiction, 18*(3), 548–566. https://doi.org/10.1007/s11469-018-9941-5

Kosenko, K., Luurs, G., & Binder, A. R. (2017). Sexting and sexual behavior, 2011–2015: A critical review and meta-analysis of a growing literature.

Journal of Computer-Mediated Communication, 22(3), 141–160. https://doi .org/10.1111/jcc4.12187

Koutamanis, M., Vossen, H. G. M., & Valkenburg, P. M. (2015). Adolescents' comments in social media: Why do adolescents receive negative feedback and who is most at risk? *Computers in Human Behavior, 53*, 486–494. https://doi.org/10.1016/j.chb.2015.07.016

Kowalski, R. M., Giumetti, G. W., Schroeder, A. N., & Lattanner, M. R. (2014). Bullying in the digital age: A critical review and meta-analysis of cyberbully- ing research among youth. *Psychological Bulletin, 140*(4), 1073–1137. https://doi.org/10.1037/a0035618

Kowalski, R. M., Limber, S. P., & McCord, A. (2019). A developmental approach to cyberbullying: Prevalence and protective factors. *Aggression and Violent Behavior, 45*, 20–32. https://doi.org/10.1016/j.avb.2018.02.009

Kraut, R., Patterson, M., Lundmark, V., et al. (1998). Internet paradox: A social technol- ogy that reduces social involvement and psychological well-being? *American Psychologist, 53*(9), 1017–1031. https://doi.org/10.1037/0003-066X.53.9.1017

Krieger, H., Young, C. M., Anthenien, A. M., & Neighbors, C. (2018). The epidemi- ology of binge drinking among college-age individuals in the United States. *Alcohol Research: Current Reviews, 39*(1), 23–30.

Lamb, J. B. (2020). Death by swat: The three elements of swatting. In C. Kelly, A. Lynes, & K. Hoffin (Eds.), *Video games crime and next-gen deviance: Reorienting the debate* (pp. 73–89). Emerald Publishing Limited.

Lauckner, C., Desrosiers, A., Muilenburg, J., Killanin, A., Genter, E., & Kershaw, T. (2019). Social media photos of substance use and their relationship to attitudes and behaviors among ethnic and racial minority emerging adult men living in low-income areas. *Journal of Adolescence, 77*, 152–162. https://doi .org/10.1016/j.adolescence.2019.10.013

Lenhart, A., Smith, A., & Anderson, M. (2015, October 1). *Teens, technology and romantic relationships*. Pew Research Center. https://www.pewresearch.org/ internet/2015/10/01/teens-technology-and-romantic-relationships/

Leung, R. K., Toumbourou, J. W., & Hemphill, S. A. (2014). The effect of peer influence and selection processes on adolescent alcohol use: A systematic review of longitudinal studies. *Health Psychology Review, 8*(4), 426–457. https://doi.org/10.1080/17437199.2011.587961

Lewycka, S., Clark, T., Peiris-John, R., et al. (2018). Downwards trends in adolescent risk-taking behaviours in New Zealand: Exploring driving forces for change. *Journal of Paediatrics and Child Health, 54*(6), 602–608. https://doi.org/10 .1111/jpc.13930

Lim, S. A., Kim, E. K., & You, S. (2019). The effects of internet use on school adjustment and delinquency. *Current Psychology, 38*(3), 901–907. https://doi.org/10.1007/ s12144-017-9668-7

Litt, D. M., & Stock, M. L. (2011). Adolescent alcohol-related risk cognitions: The roles of social norms and social networking sites. *Psychology of Addictive Behaviors, 25*(4), 708–713. https://doi.org/10.1037/a0024226

Maas, M. K., Bray, B. C., & Noll, J. G. (2018). A latent class analysis of online sexual experiences and offline sexual behaviors among female adolescents. *Journal of Research on Adolescence, 28*(3), 731–747. https://doi.org/10.1111/ jora.12364

Maheux, A. J., Evans, R., Widman, L., Nesi, J., Prinstein, M. J., & Choukas-Bradley, S. (2020). Popular peer norms and adolescent sexting behavior. *Journal of Adolescence*, *78*, 62–66. https://doi.org/10.1016/j.adolescence.2019.12.002

Männikkö, N., Ruotsalainen, H., Miettunen, J., & Kääriäinen, M. (2020). Associations between childhood and adolescent emotional and behavioral characteristics and screen time of adolescents. *Issues in Mental Health Nursing*, *41*(8), 700–712. https://doi.org/10.1080/01612840.2020.1725195

Marczinski, C. A., Hertzenberg, H., Goddard, P., Maloney, S. F., Stamates, A. L., & O'Connor, K. (2016). Alcohol-related Facebook activity predicts alcohol use patterns in college students. *Addiction Research and Theory*, *24*(5), 398–405. https://doi.org/10.3109/16066359.2016.1146709

Marder, B., Joinson, A., Shankar, A., & Houghton, D. (2016). The extended 'chilling' effect of Facebook: The cold reality of ubiquitous social networking. *Computers in Human Behavior*, *60*, 582–592. https://doi.org/10.1016/j.chb.2016.02.097

Marín-López, I., Zych, I., Ortega-Ruiz, R., Monks, C. P., & Llorent, V. J. (2020). Empathy online and moral disengagement through technology as longitudinal predictors of cyberbullying victimization and perpetration. *Children and Youth Services Review*, *116*, Article 105144. https://doi.org/10.1016/j.childyouth.2020.105144

Marwick, A. E., & boyd, d. (2011). I tweet honestly, I tweet passionately: Twitter users, context collapse, and the imagined audience. *New Media & Society*, *13*(1), 114–133. https://doi.org/10.1177/1461444810365313

McCuddy, T. (2021). Peer delinquency among digital natives: The cyber context as a source of peer influence. *Journal of Research in Crime and Delinquency*, *58*(3), 306–342. https://doi.org/10.1177/0022427820959694

McCuddy, T., & Vogel, M. (2015). Beyond traditional interaction: Exploring the functional form of the exposure-offending association across online network size. *Journal of Criminal Justice*, *43*(2), 89–98. https://doi.org/10.1016/j.jcrimjus.2015.01.002

Moreno, M. A., Briner, L. R., Williams, A., Brockman, L., Walker, L., & Christakis, D. A. (2010). A content analysis of displayed alcohol references on a social networking web site. *Journal of Adolescent Health*, *47*(2), 168–175. https://doi.org/10.1016/j.jadohealth.2010.01.001

Moreno, M. A., Briner, L. R., Williams, A., Walker, L., & Christakis, D. A. (2009). Real use or "real cool": Adolescents speak out about displayed alcohol references on social networking websites. *Journal of Adolescent Health*, *45*(4), 420–422. https://doi.org/10.1016/j.jadohealth.2009.04.015

Moreno, M. A., Cox, E. D., Young, H. N., & Haaland, W. (2015). Underage college students' alcohol displays on Facebook and real-time alcohol behaviors. *Journal of Adolescent Health*, *56*(6), 646–651. https://doi.org/10.1016/j.jadohealth.2015.02.020

Moreno, M. A., Grant, A., Kacvinsky, L., Egan, K. G., & Fleming, M. F. (2012). College students' alcohol displays on Facebook: Intervention considerations. *Journal of American College Health*, *60*(5), 388–394. https://doi.org/10.1080/07448481.2012.663841

Moreno, M. A., Kota, R., Schoohs, S., & Whitehill, J. M. (2013). The Facebook influence model: A concept mapping approach. *Cyberpsychology, Behavior, and Social Networking*, *16*(7), 504–511. https://doi.org/10.1089/cyber.2013.0025

Moreno, M. A., & Whitehill, J. M. (2014). Influence of social media on alcohol use in adolescents and young adults. *Alcohol Research: Current Reviews*, *36*(1), 91–100. http://www.arcr.niaaa.nih.gov/arcr/arcr361/article08.htm

Morgan, E. M., Snelson, C., & Elison-Bowers, P. (2010). Image and video disclosure of substance use on social media websites. *Computers in Human Behavior*, *26*(6), 1405–1411. https://doi.org/10.1016/j.chb.2010.04.017

Nam, S. J. (2020). The longitudinal relationships between cyber delinquency, aggression, and offline delinquency: An autoregressive cross-lagged model. *Journal of Early Adolescence*, *41*(4), 634–652. https://doi.org/10.1177/0272431620939187

Negriff, S. (2019). The influence of online-only friends on the substance use of young adults with a history of childhood maltreatment. *Substance Use & Misuse*, *54*(1), 120–129. https://doi.org/10.1080/10826084.2018.1508299

Nesi, J., Choukas-Bradley, S., & Prinstein, M. J. (2018a). Transformation of adolescent peer relations in the social media context: Part 1 – A theoretical framework and application to dyadic peer relationships. *Clinical Child and Family Psychology Review*, *21*(3), 267–294. https://doi.org/10.1007/s10567-018-0261-x

Nesi, J., Choukas-Bradley, S., & Prinstein, M. J. (2018b). Transformation of adolescent peer relations in the social media context: Part 2 – Application to peer group processes and future directions for research. *Clinical Child and Family Psychology Review*, *21*(3), 295–319. https://doi.org/10.1007/s10567-018-0262-9

Nesi, J., & Prinstein, M. J. (2019). In search of likes: Longitudinal associations between adolescents' digital status seeking and health-risk behaviors. *Journal of Clinical Child & Adolescent Psychology*, *48*(5), 740–748. https://doi.org/10.1080/15374416.2018.1437733

Nesi, J., Rothenberg, W. A., Hussong, A. M., & Jackson, K. M. (2017). Friends' alcohol-related social networking site activity predicts escalations in adolescent drinking: Mediation by peer norms. *Journal of Adolescent Health*, *60*(6), 641–647. https://doi.org/10.1016/j.jadohealth.2017.01.009

Ohannessian, C. M. C., & Vannucci, A. (2020). Social media use and externalizing behaviors during early adolescence. *Youth and Society*, *53*(6), 871–893. https://doi.org/10.1177/0044118X20901737

Ohannessian, C. M. C., Vannucci, A., Flannery, K. M., & Khan, S. (2017). Social media use and substance use during emerging adulthood. *Emerging Adulthood*, *5*(5), 364–370. https://doi.org/10.1177/2167696816685232

Olweus, D. (2012). Invited expert discussion paper cyberbullying: An overrated phenomenon? *European Journal of Developmental Psychology*, *9*(5), 520–538. https://doi.org/10.1080/17405629.2012.682358

Osgood, D. W., Ragan, D. T., Wallace, L., Gest, S. D., Feinberg, M. E., & Moody, J. (2013). Peers and the emergence of alcohol use: Influence and selection processes in adolescent friendship networks. *Journal of Research on Adolescence*, *23*(3), 500–512. https://doi.org/10.1111/jora.12059

Patton, D. U., Eschmann, R. D., & Butler, D. A. (2013). Internet banging: New trends in social media, gang violence, masculinity and hip hop. *Computers in Human Behavior*, *29*(5), A54–A59. https://doi.org/10.1016/j.chb.2012.12.035

Patton, D. U., Frey, W. R., & Gaskell, M. (2019). Guns on social media: Complex interpretations of gun images posted by Chicago youth. *Palgrave Communications*, *5*(1), 1–8. https://doi.org/10.1057/s41599-019-0330-x

Pegg, K. J., O'Donnell, A. W., Lala, G., & Barber, B. L. (2018). The role of online social identity in the relationship between alcohol-related content on social networking sites and adolescent alcohol use. *Cyberpsychology, Behavior, and Social Networking*, *21*(1), 50–55. https://doi.org/10.1089/cyber.2016.0665

Piehler, T. F., & Dishion, T. J. (2007). Interpersonal dynamics within adolescent friendships: Dyadic mutuality, deviant talk, and patterns of antisocial behavior. *Child Development*, *78*(5), 1611–1624. https://doi.org/10.1111/j.1467-8624.2007.01086.x

Przybylski, A. K., & Weinstein, N. (2019). Violent video game engagement is not associated with adolescents' aggressive behaviour: Evidence from a registered report. *Royal Society Open Science*, *6*(2). https://doi.org/10.1098/rsos.171474

Pyrooz, D. C., Decker, S. H., & Moule, R. K. (2015). Criminal and routine activities in online settings: Gangs, offenders, and the internet. *Justice Quarterly*, *32*(3), 471–499. https://doi.org/10.1080/07418825.2013.778326

Rebellon, C. J. (2012). Differential association and substance use: Assessing the roles of discriminant validity, socialization, and selection in traditional empirical tests. *European Journal of Criminology*, *9*(1), 73–96. https://doi.org/10.1177/1477370811421647

Richet, J.-L. (2013). From young hackers to crackers. *International Journal of Technology and Human Interaction*, *9*(3), 53–62. https://doi.org/10.4018/jthi.2013070104

Riehm, K. E., Feder, K. A., Tormohlen, K. N., et al. (2020). Associations between time spent using social media and internalizing and externalizing problems among US youth. *JAMA Psychiatry*, *76*(12), 1266–1273. https://doi.org/10.1001/jamapsychiatry.2019.2325

Rimal, R. N., & Real, K. (2005). How behaviors are influenced by perceived norms: A test of the theory of normative social behavior. *Communication Research*, *32*(3), 389–414. https://doi.org/10.1177/0093650205275385

Roberson, A. A., McKinney, C., Walker, C., & Coleman, A. (2018). Peer, social media, and alcohol marketing influences on college student drinking. *Journal of American College Health*, *66*(5), 369–379. https://doi.org/10.1080/07448481.2018.1431903

Rokven, J. J., Weijters, G., Beerthuizen, M. G. C. J., & van der Laan, A. M. (2018). Juvenile delinquency in the virtual world: Similarities and differences between cyber- enabled, cyber-dependent and offline delinquents in the Netherlands. *International Journal of Cyber Criminology*, *12*(1), 27–46. https://doi.org/10.5281/zenodo.1467690

Romo, D. L., Garnett, C., Younger, A. P., et al. (2017). Social media use and its association with sexual risk and parental monitoring among a primarily Hispanic adolescent population. *Journal of Pediatric and Adolescent Gynecology*, *30*(4), 466–473. https://doi.org/10.1016/j.jpag.2017.02.004

Rulison, K. L., Gest, S. D., & Loken, E. (2013). Dynamic social networks and physical aggression: The moderating role of gender and social status among peers. *Journal of Research on Adolescence*, *23*(3), 437–449. https://doi.org/10.1111/jora.12044

Samek, D. R., Goodman, R. J., Erath, S. A., McGue, M., & Iacono, W. G. (2016). Antisocial peer affiliation and externalizing disorders in the transition from adolescence to young adulthood: Selection versus socialization effects. *Developmental Psychology, 52*(5), 813–823. https://doi.org/10.1037/dev0000109

Sampasa-Kanyinga, H., & Chaput, J. P. (2016). Use of social networking sites and alcohol consumption among adolescents. *Public Health, 139*, 88–95. https://doi.org/10.1016/j.puhe.2016.05.005

Sawyer, S. M., Azzopardi, P. S., Wickremarathne, D., & Patton, G. C. (2018). The age of adolescence. *The Lancet Child & Adolescent Health, 2*(3), 223–228. https://doi.org/10.1016/S2352-4642(18)30022-1

Schwinn, T. M., Schinke, S. P., & Di Noia, J. (2010). Preventing drug abuse among adolescent girls: Outcome data from an internet-based intervention. *Prevention Science, 11*(1), 24–32. https://doi.org/10.1007/s11121–009-0146-9

Selkie, E. M., Benson, M., & Moreno, M. A. (2011). Adolescents' views regarding uses of social networking websites and text messaging for adolescent sexual health education. *American Journal of Health Education, 42*(4), 205–212. https://doi.org/10.1080/19325037.2011.10599189

Ševčíková, A., Šerek, J., Barbovschi, M., & Daneback, K. (2014). The roles of individual characteristics and liberalism in intentional and unintentional exposure to online sexual material among European youth: A multilevel approach. *Sexuality Research and Social Policy, 11*(2), 104–115. https://doi.org/10.1007/s13178–013-0141-6

Sherman, L. E., Payton, A. A., Hernandez, L. M., Greenfield, P. M., & Dapretto, M. (2016). The power of the like in adolescence: Effects of peer influence on neural and behavioral responses to social media. *Psychological Science, 27*(7), 1027–1035. https://doi.org/10.1177/0956797616645673

Smith, L. W., Liu, B., Degenhardt, L., et al. (2016). Is sexual content in new media linked to sexual risk behaviour in young people? A systematic review and meta-analysis. *Sexual Health, 13*(6), 501–515. https://doi.org/10.1071/SH16037

Smith, P. K., Mahdavi, J., Carvalho, M., Fisher, S., Russell, S., & Tippett, N. (2008). Cyberbullying: Its nature and impact in secondary school pupils. *Journal of Child Psychology and Psychiatry and Allied Disciplines, 49*(4), 376–385. https://doi.org/10.1111/j.1469-7610.2007.01846.x

Sourander, A., Klomek, A. B., Ikonen, M., et al. (2010). Psychosocial risk factors associated with cyberbullying among adolescents: A population-based study. *Archives of General Psychiatry, 67*(7), 720–728. https://doi.org/10.1001/archgenpsychiatry.2010.79

Spilková, J., Chomynová, P., & Csémy, L. (2017). Predictors of excessive use of social media and excessive online gaming in Czech teenagers. *Journal of Behavioral Addictions, 6*(4), 611–619. https://doi.org/10.1556/2006.6.2017.064

Steinberg, L. (2010). A dual systems model of adolescent risk-taking. *Developmental Psychobiology, 52*(3), 216–224. https://doi.org/10.1002/dev.20445

Sterner, G., & Felmlee, D. (2019). The social networks of cyberbullying on Twitter. In Information Resources Management Association (Ed.), *Multigenerational online behavior and media use* (pp. 905–922). IGI Global. https://doi.org/10.4018/978-1-5225-7909-0.ch049

Stevens, R., Gilliard-Matthews, S., Dunaev, J., Todhunter-Reid, A., Brawner, B., & Stewart, J. (2017). Social media use and sexual risk reduction behavior among minority youth: Seeking safe sex information. *Nursing Research, 66* (5), 368–377. https://doi.org/10.1097/NNR.0000000000000237

Stoddard, S. A., Bauermeister, J. A., Gordon-Messer, D., Johns, M., & Zimmerman, M. A. (2012). Permissive norms and young adults' alcohol and marijuana use: The role of online communities. *Journal of Studies on Alcohol and Drugs*, *73*(6), 968–975. https://doi.org/10.15288/jsad.2012.73.968

Strasburger, V. C., Wilson, B. J., & Jordan, A. B. (2013). *Children, adolescents, and the media*. Sage Publications.

Subrahmanyam, K., Smahel, D., & Greenfield, P. (2006). Connecting developmental constructions to the internet: Identity presentation and sexual exploration in online teen chat rooms. *Developmental Psychology*, *42*(3), 395–406. https://doi.org/10.1037/0012-1649.42.3.395

Substance Abuse and Mental Health Services Administration. (2019). *Key substance use and mental health indicators in the United States: Results from the 2018 National Survey on Drug Use and Health*. HHS Publication No. PEP19–5068, NSDUH Series H-54 (Vol. 170). https://doi.org/10.1016/j.drugalcdep.2016.10.042

Suffoletto, B., Kristan, J., Callaway, C., et al. (2014). A text message alcohol intervention for young adult emergency department patients: A randomized clinical trial. *Annals of Emergency Medicine*, *64*(6), 664–672. https://doi.org/10.1016/j.annemergmed.2014.06.010

Suler, J. (2004). The online disinhibition effect. *Cyberpsychology & Behavior*, *7*(3), 321–326. https://doi.org/10.1089/1094931041291295

Temple, J. R., & Choi, H. J. (2014). Longitudinal association between teen sexting and sexual behavior. *Pediatrics*, *134*(5), e1287–e1292. https://doi.org/10.1542/peds.2014-1974

Thomas, H. J., Connor, J. P., & Scott, J. G. (2015). Integrating traditional bullying and cyberbullying: Challenges of definition and measurement in adolescents – A review. *Educational Psychology Review*, *27*(1), 135–152. https://doi.org/10.1007/s10648–014-9261-7

Thompson, C. M., & Romo, L. K. (2016). College students' drinking and posting about alcohol: Forwarding a model of motivations, behaviors, and consequences. *Journal of Health Communication*, *21*(6), 688–695. https://doi.org/10.1080/10810730.2016.1153763

Twenge, J. M., & Park, H. (2017). The decline in adult activities among U.S. adolescents, 1976–2016. *Child Development*, *90*(2), 638–654. https://doi.org/10.1111/cdev.12930

Underwood, M. K., Rosen, L. H., More, D., Ehrenreich, S. E., & Gentsch, J. K. (2012). The Blackberry project: Capturing the content of adolescents' text messaging. *Developmental Psychology*, *48*(2), 295–302. https://doi.org/10.1037/a0025914

Unger, J. B., Urman, R., Cruz, T. B., et al. (2018). Talking about tobacco on Twitter is associated with tobacco product use. *Preventive Medicine*, *114*, 54–56. https://doi.org/https://doi.org/10.1016/j.ypmed.2018.06.006

Van Hoof, J. J., Bekkers, J., & Van Vuuren, M. (2014). Son, you're smoking on Facebook! College students' disclosures on social networking sites as indicators of real-life risk behaviors. *Computers in Human Behavior*, *34*, 249–257. https://doi.org/10.1016/j.chb.2014.02.008

Vandenbosch, L., Beyens, I., Vangeel, L., & Eggermont, S. (2016). Online communication predicts Belgian adolescents' initiation of romantic and sexual activity.

European Journal of Pediatrics, *175*(4), 509–516. https://doi.org/10.1007/s00431-015-2666-6

Vannucci, A., Simpson, E. G., Gagnon, S., & Ohannessian, C. M. C. (2020). Social media use and risky behaviors in adolescents: A meta-analysis. *Journal of Adolescence*, *79*, 258–274. https://doi.org/10.1016/j.adolescence.2020.01.014

Wall, D. (2001). *Crime and the internet*. Routledge.

Wang, J., Iannotti, R. J., & Luk, J. W. (2012). Patterns of adolescent bullying behaviors: Physical, verbal, exclusion, rumor, and cyber. *Journal of School Psychology*, *50*(4), 521–534. https://doi.org/10.1016/j.jsp.2012.03.004

Wegge, D., Vandebosch, H., Eggermont, S., & Pabian, S. (2016). Popularity through online harm: The longitudinal associations between cyberbullying and sociometric status in early adolescence. *Journal of Early Adolescence*, *36*(1), 86–107. https://doi.org/10.1177/0272431614556351

Westgate, E. C., & Holliday, J. (2016). Identity, influence, and intervention: The roles of social media in alcohol use. *Current Opinion in Psychology*, *9*, 27–32. https://doi.org/10.1016/j.copsyc.2015.10.014

Whittaker, A., Densley, J., & Moser, K. S. (2020). No two gangs are alike: The digital divide in street gangs' differential adaptations to social media. *Computers in Human Behavior*, *110*, Article 106403. https://doi.org/10.1016/j.chb.2020.106403

Willoughby, J. F., Hust, S. J. T., Li, J., Couto, L., Kang, S., & Domgaard, S. (2020). An exploratory study of adolescents' social media sharing of marijuana-related content. *Cyberpsychology, Behavior, and Social Networking*, *23*(9), 642–646. https://doi.org/10.1089/cyber.2019.0721

Ybarra, M. L., & Mitchell, K. J. (2004). Youth engaging in online harassment: Associations with caregiver-child relationships, internet use, and personal characteristics. *Journal of Adolescence*, *27*(3), 319–336. https://doi.org/10.1016/j.adolescence.2004.03.007

Ybarra, M. L., & Mitchell, K. J. (2016). A national study of lesbian, gay, bisexual (LGB), and non-LGB youth sexual behavior online and in-person. *Archives of Sexual Behavior*, *45*(6), 1357–1372. https://doi.org/10.1007/s10508-015-0491-7

Young, S. D., & Jordan, A. H. (2013). The influence of social networking photos on social norms and sexual health behaviors. *Cyberpsychology, Behavior, and Social Networking*, *16*(4), 243–247. https://doi.org/10.1089/cyber.2012.0080

Young, S. E., Friedman, N. P., Miyake, A., et al. (2009). Behavioral disinhibition: Liability for externalizing spectrum disorders and its genetic and environmental relation to response inhibition across adolescence. *Journal of Abnormal Psychology*, *118*(1), 117–130. https://doi.org/10.1037/a0014657

Zych, I., Farrington, D. P., & Ttofi, M. M. (2019). Bullying and cyberbullying: Protective factors and effective interventions. *Aggression and Violent Behavior*, *45*, 1–3. https://doi.org/10.1016/j.avb.2018.08.006

12 Problematic Digital Media Use and Addiction

Sarah E. Domoff, Aubrey L. Borgen, Bonny Rye, Gloria Rojas Barajas, and Katie Avery

Adolescents spend considerable amounts of time using digital media and social media. Although risks and benefits exist, clinicians, teachers, and parents have grown concerned about problematic use, or excessive use that interferes with adolescents' health, well-being, and development. In this chapter, we explain the difference between problematic and typical media use; detail the measurement of problematic media use; review existing prevention and treatment approaches for problematic use; and provide recommendations for clinicians working with adolescents. As this research is still in its early stages, we conclude with directions for future research.

Problematic vs. Normative Digital Media Use

Historically, conceptualizations of pathological use of digital media have relied on other behavioral disorders, such as pathological gambling. Indeed, Dr. Kimberly Young pioneered early studies on internet addiction (e.g., Young, 1998a), forging the path for subsequent research on identifying how one's use of digital/electronic communication and media may contribute to poor functioning and well-being. Adapting criteria from the DSM-IV-TR (American Psychiatric Association [APA], 2000)'s description of pathological gambling, Young created one of the first known measures of such problematic use: the Internet Addiction Scale (Young, 1998a). Since then, several measures using a similar paradigm have been developed targeting a range of electronic communication and digital media uses, ranging from pathological video game use (Gentile, 2009) to instant messaging addiction (Huang & Leung, 2009) to compulsive texting (Lister-Landman et al., 2017).

Across these measures, a constant is that pathological or problematic use is defined as excessively using digital media or internet/electronic communication to the point of dysfunction. In other words, similar to other "addictions" or "abuse," frequency of use is not the defining or sole factor. It should be reiterated that *how* one uses digital or social media and the impact of such use on one's functioning (e.g., in relationships, at work or school, with peers) delineates problematic versus normative use. Put in other terms, an adolescent may use social media very frequently and not have it negatively impact their life, whereas another adolescent may use social media to a lesser extent and it could have dire consequences for their well-being. Duration or amount of use may matter to a degree (i.e., of course, problematic social media use correlates with higher amounts of use); however, only considering duration of social media use misses the mark for capturing this idea. In this chapter, we discuss this conceptualization further, and explicate current research on assessing, preventing, and treating problematic social media use. We also highlight clinical practices carried out at the Problematic Media Assessment and Treatment Clinic (www.sarahdomoff.com) and other best practices for mental health clinicians seeking to more routinely assess and treat these concerns.

Internet Addiction, Social Media Addiction, and Other Problematic Digital Media Use

Prior to the release of the most recent edition of the DSM – the DSM-5 (APA, 2013), the majority of research on problematic use of digital media used internet addiction criteria (Young, 1998b; based on pathological gambling criteria from the DSM-IV-TR) to conceptualize dysregulated or "addictive" media use (Domoff, Borgen, et al., 2019). Currently, definitions of dysregulated (also termed "addictive" or "excessive") digital media use draw from the DSM-5 criteria for internet gaming disorder (APA, 2013) or theories rooted in behavioral addiction (Domoff, Foley, & Ferkel, 2020). Since then, research has expanded the term "problematic" to encapsulate both one's own dysregulated use *and* digital media use or internet/electronic communication that may harm individuals other than the user themself.

For example, Billieux et al. (2015) proposed a Pathway Model of Problematic Mobile Phone Use, which consists of pathways to three types of problematic mobile phone use: (1) addictive patterns of use (i.e., the primary focus of this chapter); (2) antisocial patterns of use (e.g., cyber-bullying or use in situations that would be deemed socially inappropriate); and (3) risky patterns of use (e.g., phone use while driving or in other situations where physical harm may ensue and unsafe sexting). Although the majority of the following sections will focus on dysregulated use, researchers and clinicians should be aware of these other components of social media interactions and excessive phone use. We elaborate further on antisocial and risky use of social media or digital devices in the clinical implications sections. Similarly, although online gaming is outside the scope of this chapter, it should be noted that many popular games are social in nature and involve multiple players (e.g., massively multiplayer online games). We refer readers to Gentile et al. (2017) for a review of internet gaming disorder and clinical implications for adolescents.

In addition to recent theoretical advances in defining problematic media use, there is a growing body of literature indicating that reward systems in the brain are activated when adolescents use digital media (e.g., gaming disorder; Wegmann & Brand, 2020) and social media (e.g., Nasser et al., 2020) – providing a compelling basis for concerns about their addiction potential. For example, Sherman et al. (2016) examined adolescents' brain reactivity when viewing pseudo Instagram photos. They found that seeing photos with many "likes" was associated with reactivity of several regions of the brain, including those connected to reward processing (interestingly, these authors also found reward regions were activated when "liking" photos, as well, see Sherman et al., 2018). Although this area of research is still new, the initial evidence suggests that engaging with social media (and other types of digital media) are rewarding to adolescents.

Assessing, Preventing, and Treating Problematic Digital Media Use

Assessing Problematic Digital Media Use

There are several measures of various types of problematic digital media use with strong psychometric properties. Although most have been validated with adult samples, we review three that have been developed for adolescents and are specific to social media use. One measurement that has been used to assess problematic digital media use is the Bergen Social Media Addiction Scale (BSMAS), previously known as the Bergen Facebook Addiction Scale (Andreassen et al., 2012). This scale assesses how social media is used rather than the social media platform specifically (Lin et al., 2017) and social media use is assessed over the past year (Watson et al., 2020). The BSMAS is comprised of 18 items that assess 6 symptoms of addiction: salience, mood modification, withdrawal symptoms, tolerance, conflict, and relapse (Andreassen et al., 2012).

The BSMAS' Cronbach's alpha is 0.83 (Andreassen et al., 2012), suggesting strong internal consistency. Regarding convergent validity, this scale associated with the Addictive Tendencies Scale, the Facebook Attitudes Scale, and the Online Sociability Scale (Andreassen et al., 2012).

The Addictive Patterns of Use (APU) Scale is another reliable and valid measure that can be used to screen for smartphone addiction (Domoff, Foley, & Ferkel, 2020). The scale consists of nine items that ask adolescents to rate their frequency of symptoms of addictive phone use (Domoff, Foley, & Ferkel, 2020), based on criteria for internet gaming disorder from the DSM-5, adapted to smartphones. Items include "During the last year, how often have there been times when all you could think about was using your phone?" and "Have you experienced serious conflicts with family, friends, or partner because of your phone use?" (Domoff, Foley, & Ferkel, 2020). In addition to completing the nine items, adolescents are asked to list the features of their phone that they use the most, allowing researchers to identify the types of apps or smartphone functions that may be most problematic. Recently, additional research further supports the validity of APU, with this measure associating with media use (e.g., TV viewing frequency; Domoff, Sutherland, et al., 2020a) and other dysregulated behaviors (e.g., food addiction, dysregulated eating; Domoff, Sutherland, et al., 2020b).

Finally, the Social Media Disorder (SMD) Scale (van den Eijnden et al., 2016) similarly uses criteria of internet gaming disorder, but applied to social media use, to assess symptoms of dysregulated social media use. The developers recognize nine criteria to define disordered social media use within the adolescent population: preoccupation, tolerance, withdrawal, relapse, mood modification, external consequences, deception, displacement, and conflict (van den Eijnden et al., 2016). This scale is made up of 27 items, 3 items for each of the 9 criteria listed previously; a short version that consist of 9 items was also developed that selected the highest loading items on each of the 9 criteria (van den Eijnden et al., 2016). A cut-off score for disordered use was identified as endorsement of at least five of the nine criteria on the scale (van den Eijnden et al., 2016). Positive correlations between social media disorder symptoms on this scale and depressive mood, hyperactivity, and inattention have been demonstrated (van den Eijnden et al., 2016).

Rates of problematic social media use (or high scores on measures of "addictive" or disordered social media use) tend to fall around 7%, across 29 countries (Boer et al., 2020; consistent with gaming disorder rates, Gentile et al., 2017). That is, based on data from countries in Europe, the Middle East, and North America, approximately 7% of adolescent social media users experience impairment due to their use (Boer et al., 2020), such as trouble sleeping/poor quality sleep (e.g., Vernon et al., 2016) and poorer academic functioning (Domoff, Foley, & Ferkel, 2020). Given how recently problematic social media use measures were developed, there is limited research on whether this prevalence has changed over time. However, in terms of how the COVID-19 pandemic is impacting rates, early evidence suggests that burden caused by COVID-19 is associated with greater addictive social media use (Brailovskaia & Margraf, 2021) and some evidence that problematic social media use has increased in some samples from before to during the pandemic (among adolescents in Italy; Muzi et al., 2021). Future research should prioritize examining longitudinal trajectories of problematic social media use, particularly given drastic increases in media use during the COVID-19 pandemic.

Preventing Problematic Social Media Use

Due to the burgeoning interest in social media and smartphone use among adolescents, there has been a vast amount of research highlighting correlates of social media use overall. However, there has been limited research investigating correlates or contributors to problematic social media use. Many researchers have hypothesized that there is a relationship between problematic social media use and adverse mental health symptoms, with the most consistent research supporting links via disrupted sleep and shortened sleep duration (e.g., Vernon et al., 2016). There have also been various studies outlining demographic factors and social factors that are associated with dysregulated social media use. Across the studies described, it is critical to note that we focus on dysregulated use (often called *problematic* in subsequent research) and not amount of social media use. The research on duration or amount of social media use and various correlates is mixed and inconsistent (Odgers et al., 2020), and is too indiscriminate to adequately capture the scope of adolescents' social media interactions. It is also important to note that, unless specified, most research is correlational and should not be inferred as causal.

Internalizing symptoms, such as depressive and anxiety symptoms, correlate with disordered social media use. Bányai et al. (2017) conducted a longitudinal study assessing how problematic social media use and depressive symptoms were related. It was found that both problematic social media use and depressive symptoms grew over a two-year span and that changes in problematic use correlated with changes in depressive symptoms (Bányai et al., 2017). Another study found direct associations between problematic social media use and depressive symptoms and indirect associations between problematic social media use and self-esteem (Kircaburun et al., 2019). It has also been found that those with a higher baseline of depressive symptoms showed a sharper incline in problematic use (Raudsepp & Kais, 2019).

Various demographic factors such as gender and age have shown differing associations with problematic social media use. Gender has been found to have an impact on how social media impacts adolescents. That is, for boys, anxiety was a predictor for higher social media use while for girls, problematic social media use associates with depression (Oberst et al., 2017). For adolescent girls, it is suggested that problematic social media use and depressive symptoms work in a cyclical fashion, whereas depressive symptoms exacerbate problematic social media use, which then further worsens depressive symptoms (Kuss & Griffiths, 2017). This suggests a possibility that adolescent girls with depressive symptoms may struggle to identify adequate coping techniques and instead use social media to ineffectively manage their symptoms (Gámez-Guadix, 2014). Another study found that younger adolescents and female adolescents had higher levels of problematic social media use (Kircaburun et al., 2019). Additionally, the type of social media behavior plays a role in how it impacts the social media user. There is a relationship between passive social media use (e.g., scrolling, low social interaction) and anxiety and depression symptoms, while active social media use (e.g., commenting, liking, communicating with peers) was related to lower symptoms of depression and anxiety in adolescents (Thorisdottir et al., 2019).

Several social factors have been shown to relate to problematic use in adolescents. Social norms and friends' social media use frequency was directly associated with frequency of social media use, leading to an association with problematic use (Marino et al., 2020). Another study found that social connectedness and general belongingness were indirectly related to problematic social media use (Kircaburun et al., 2019). Fear of missing out and perceived academic competence predicted addiction to social media among high school students in one study (Tunc-Aksan & Akbay, 2019).

Regarding protective factors, self-esteem has been shown to be a moderator of problematic social media use and depression in adolescents (Wang et al., 2018). It has been proposed that adolescents with higher levels of self-esteem feel more confident in coping with adversity and are therefore less likely to have depression and subsequent problematic social media use (Wang et al., 2018). For girls who use Facebook actively and have perceived online social support have shown to benefit from social media use, and perceived online social support was found to have a negative association with adolescent girls' depressed moods (Frison & Eggermont, 2016).

Treating Problematic Digital Media Use

Prevention Programs

Given the limited research on risk and protective factors of problematic social media use, it is not surprising that we could not identify any published, empirically supported problematic social media use prevention programs. However, the authors of this chapter have developed and have recently tested the Developing Healthy Social Media Practices (DHSMP) Prevention to address this gap. The DHSMP Prevention program was developed to promote healthy social media use and mitigate risks associated with social media use among youth in grades 6–8. DHSMP Prevention is a classroom-based prevention program, consisting of 6 classes, approximately 45 minutes per session. The program consists of providing adolescents with psycho-education on: (1) positive and negative effects of social media use (i.e., content of social media and user engagement); (2) the impact of various social media use practices on adolescent health and well-being (i.e., context of use); (3) how to critically evaluate content provided via social media (i.e., deciphering whether social media posts/shares are legitimate or "fake news"; (4) how to cope with cyber-bullying; (5) privacy and safety online; and (6) social gaming-specific risks and benefits (e.g., loot boxes and financial risks; app/game design principles to encourage longer game play; fostering positive interactions when gaming).

The DHSMP Prevention program has been piloted with approximately 160 6th graders in one public middle school in the Midwest. Acceptability and efficacy of this program indicate high acceptability based on student ratings, and increased skills in healthy social media use. Specifically, youth reported (on a scale from 1 to 5, with 5 being more confident/likely): feeling confident in their ability to recognize when social media use is harmful (M = 3.84, SD = 1.26); feeling more confident in identifying times and places when they shouldn't be using social media (M = 4.18, SD = 0.96); being likely to reduce their use of social media around bedtime, mealtime, while talking with friends and family, during class, and while doing homework (M = 4.04, SD = 1.22); being likely to use the privacy tips they learned (M = 3.85, SD = 1.14); feeling more confident in recognizing what cyber-bullying is (M = 4.48, SD = 0.84); and a greater likelihood to use strategies to cope with being cyber-bullied (M = 3.58, SD = 1.26). Although not a randomized clinical trial (RCT), preliminary results suggest that a school-based psycho-education program on how to use social media in healthy ways may increase relevant skills in early adolescents. Currently this program is being tested in a nonrandomized trial to further establish its potential efficacy.

Treating Problematic Digital Media Use

Even though problematic digital media use is a significant issue among adolescents, there are no validated treatment options specific to social media use. Research in this area has focused on treating internet gaming disorder (IGD) or internet addiction (IA), with very few studies investigating the treatment of problematic social media use (Pluhar et al., 2019). However, the research about IGD and IA treatment provides a basis for future directions in helping adolescents improve their social media use.

Cognitive Behavioral Therapy: Many research studies investigating the treatment of IA have focused on methods influenced by cognitive behavioral therapy (CBT). One of these investigated treatments is CBT for IA (CBT-IA; Young, 2013). The first phase of CBT-IA focuses on the behavior of individuals with IA, particularly time management and engagement in offline activities. The second phase focuses on the cognitive aspects of IA, introducing participants to challenging and restructuring their maladaptive cognitions about internet use. Finally, the third phase of CBT-IA uses concepts of harm reduction therapy to address any other environmental or psychological problems that are associated with IA (Young, 2011). This treatment model has been tested in a sample of individuals meeting criteria for IA. Adult participants engaged in the 12-week treatment, and a significant majority (70%) were able to manage their symptoms 6 months after completing treatment (Young, 2013).

Using concepts of CBT-IA, a recent study investigated the effectiveness of a treatment model for social media addiction. This treatment model focused primarily on the cognitive aspects of social media addiction, using the methods of cognitive reconstruction, reminder cards, and diary techniques (Hou et al., 2019). College students with high scores on the BSMAS (Andreassen et al., 2017) engaged in a short-term intervention that took place over two weeks. Compared to a group that did not receive the intervention, those in the treatment group experienced decreases in symptoms related to social media addiction, increased self-esteem, and increased sleep quality (Hou et al., 2019). While this study included a small sample of college students, it provides a basis for future research of using CBT to treat problematic social media use.

Abstinence Treatments: As with other types of addictive or problematic behaviors, abstinence from social media has been proposed as a potential treatment option for problematic use. Research about abstinence from social media has mixed results: Some studies have found that withdrawing from Facebook for a week can benefit individual well-being (Tromholt, 2016), while other suggest that complete withdrawal from social media can result in negative effects on highly addicted individuals (Stieger & Lewetz, 2018). Using an ecological momentary intervention, researchers found that abstaining from social media for an entire week can result in frequent relapse and withdrawal symptoms such as craving, boredom, and increased social pressure to be on social media. Long-term abstinence of social media, especially among heavy users, may have just as many (or more) negative effects than positive effects.

However, integrating CBT components and short-term abstinence may result in a useful treatment for problematic social media use. Instead of instructing participants to take a week-long break from social media, researchers for one study instructed adults to take eight 2.5-hour breaks from social media over the course of two weeks (Zhou et al., 2020). As identified by these researchers, the main goal of abstinence is for the participant to begin engaging in substitution behaviors, which can just as easily be accomplished in short breaks from media. During the two-week intervention, participants also recorded their behaviors, feelings, and thoughts in daily records; the researchers included a control group that only completed these diaries, without participating in the abstinence process. Participants who engaged in both abstinence and daily records reported the largest increase in life satisfaction after the intervention. While this study still included a small sample (33 adults in the intervention group), this provides preliminary evidence for combining short-term abstinence and aspects of CBT in treating problematic social media use (Zhou et al., 2020).

Other Treatment Modalities: Additional research about treatment with adolescents indicates that group therapy and parent involvement may be particularly useful. Group therapy with other adolescents provides a form of offline social support that is beneficial to those experiencing IA (Kim, 2008). Meta-analyses of IA group therapy have provided support for this type of treatment, especially in groups of approximately 9–12 adolescents (Chun et al., 2017). In addition, parent training targeted at managing behavior associated with IA can be a helpful treatment component (Du et al, 2010). Both of these treatment modalities should be assessed in future research with adolescents experiencing problematic digital media use.

Clinical Implications

Because of the possible negative consequences of problematic digital media use, it is important that mental health care providers for adolescents are aware of risk factors and early indicators. The American Academy of Pediatrics has recommended that clinicians conduct routine screenings for problematic internet use and has also provided useful recommendations for how to go about initiating a screening routine (D'Angelo & Moreno, 2020). Three areas of competency are important for clinicians screening adolescents for problematic use: knowing risk factors, using a validated screening tool, and identifying when screening will occur. There are multiple factors that indicate an adolescent may be at risk for developing problematic digital media use, which include being male (Widyanto & Griffiths, 2006). Other studies have suggested that some mental health diagnoses can be risk factors for problematic use, most notably ADHD and depression (Pluhar et al., 2019). However, anxiety, sleep disorders, and autism spectrum disorder have also been found to be common diagnoses among adolescents with other types of problematic digital media use. When first meeting with a teen, other risk factors to keep in mind include: dependence on the Internet for relationships and managing mood, narcissistic traits, experiences of FOMO (fear of missing out), dissatisfaction with family relationships, or mental health issues among parents (D'Angelo & Moreno, 2020).

Once a clinician is aware of risk factors affecting their adolescent client, it is important to use a validated screening measure (see Domoff, Borgen, & Robinson, 2020 for additional screening questions for overall problematic digital media use). One of these screening measures is the Problematic Media Use Measure (PMUM; Domoff, Harrison, et al., 2019). The PMUM contains 27 items that were created based on criteria for IGD, and measure how media use is interfering with individual functioning. The PMUM is a parent-report measure that has been validated for use with children aged 4–11 years. Additionally, a short-form (PMUM-SF) has been validated with nine items. Both the original and PMUM-SF are helpful for screening young adolescents for problematic media use. Currently, a self-report version of the PMUM is being validated in the USA and internationally to facilitate screening of problematic media use in older adolescents. Additionally, the APU scale is useful for screening for problematic smartphone and social media use, specifically. Both the PMUM and APU are freely available for clinicians (request access via www.sarahdomoff.com).

Researchers at the University of Wisconsin have provided two screening instruments on their website: the Adolescents' Digital Technology Interactions and Importance (ADTI) Scale and the Problematic and Risky Internet Use Screening Scale (PRIUSS). While the PRIUSS is meant to be used as a screener for adolescent problematic digital media use, it has primarily been validated among older adolescents and young adults, including samples of 18- to 25-year-olds (Jelenchick et al., 2015). The ADTI has been validated among a sample of 12- to 18-year-old adolescents (Moreno et al., 2020). Both of these screening instruments may be useful to clinicians in determining need for intervention services, and can be found at http://smahrtresearch.com/use-our-methods/. Additionally, a three-item PRIUSS has been validated (PRIUSS-3; Moreno et al., 2016).

After screening for problematic digital media use, we recommend administering narrow-band measures of media-specific problems, combined with a clinical interview. For example, at the Problematic Media Assessment and Treatment Clinic (www.sarahdomoff.com), we use the Video Game Addiction Scale (revised; Gentile, 2009) and the Social Media Disorder Scale (van den Eijnden et al., 2016) to further assess criteria for gaming disorder and problematic social media use, respectively. As mentioned, we also screen for other types of risky digital media use, including assessing the content that youth are exposed to, the individuals with whom youth interact online, the context of use (e.g., around bedtime, during other important activities), and parental management of adolescents' digital media use. Although these implications are specific to screening and assessment in outpatient settings, mental health clinicians in the inpatient setting should review clinical recommendations outlined by Burke et al. (2020) for hospitalized youth and social media use in this setting.

Limitations and Future Research Directions

Measures and Consistency of Terminology

Assessing problematic digital media use has proven to be a difficult task because of the inconsistency in terminology and conceptualization of "problematic." We argue that problematic should not be defined by amount of use – instead, clinicians should screen for dysregulated use ("addictive"), risky use (i.e., while driving, intimate/private interactions with unknown individuals), and antisocial use (cyber-bullying, trolling, etc.) routinely with each adolescent. An additional limitation is that screening tools, such as the APU (Domoff, Foley, & Ferkel, 2020) and PMUM (Domoff, Harrison, et al., 2019), do not yet have clinical cut-off scores, necessitating their validation in clinical samples to better identify youth at risk.

Research Design

As research in the area of problematic digital media use continues to grow, many limitations in this area of investigation have come evident. One of the primary limitations is accurate reporting of digital media use, particularly among adolescents. Research suggests that individuals of every age find it difficult to accurately report how much time they are spending using digital media each day (Ohme, 2020). While accurate reporting of screen time is important for research, it is even more important for researchers to measure how adolescents are using digital media and what daily activities the use is interfering with, as those are the primary concerns when determining problematic use.

To get around the limitations of adolescent self-report, some researchers are beginning to use technology to track technology use. Passive sensing technology in smartphones is gaining traction as a convenient way to measure adolescent behavioral patterns like app usage or interactions on social media, in addition to physical health indicators such as movement and sleep (see Trifan et al., 2019 for a review of passive sensing research). The first validated passive sensing app that measures adolescents' mobile device use (e.g., type of app used, duration, timing of use) has recently been supported as feasible to use and acceptable to adolescents and their parents (Domoff et al., 2021). This app, eMoodie, has ecological momentary assessment (EMA) capacity and uses gamification principles to foster completion of surveys and EMA on adolescents' mobile devices (see www.emoodie.com for more information). Using research designs that include objective, accurate measures of problematic digital media use will bring researchers closer to the goal of determining etiology and planning treatment.

Clinical Trials

Another area for improvement in this area of research is increased implementation of clinical trial studies. As the conceptualization and assessment of problematic digital media use expands, opportunities for clinical trial research will become more feasible. One of the few RCTs that has been conducted concerning treatment for problematic digital media use in adolescents was primarily aimed at internet addiction (Du et al., 2010). While the study provided evidence for using CBT to treat internet addiction in adolescents, they identified their limitation of only including participants without comorbid disorders. Anecdotally, problematic digital media use commonly occurs among adolescents who have been diagnosed with other mental health disorders. In order for clinical trials to be generalizable to clinic settings, samples should include adolescents who have comorbid disorders. Additionally, it is important that clinical trials include broader types of problematic digital media use, instead of only internet addiction. The lack of treatment options for these adolescents, in addition to the growing prevalence of problematic digital media use, indicate the need for increased clinical trial research.

Sample Demographics and Diversity

Research into problematic digital media use and internet/social media addiction is being propelled forward by the growing need for identification and resource development. This is most apparent within the growing population of youth who are native to the digital social networking world as well as among those learning to incorporate these new dimensions of their virtual selves into their social networking immigrant lifestyles (Prensky, 2001). Future investigation should seek to address the research limitations of clinical studies in order to maximize generalizability, while also parsing out what may be facilitating differential susceptibility for risks or rewards related to social media usage. In examining the limitations of samples, there is a need for validation of aforementioned screeners and assessment in non-WEIRD (Western, educated, industrialized, rich, and democratic) populations; further, problematic social media research has quite limited samples in terms of racial/ethnic diversity and across socioeconomic strata. Given that lower-income youth and racially/ethnically diverse youth have higher rates of digital media use (and may have different risks related to social media use; e.g., harassment, victimization), future research must address this major limitation of social media research.

References

Andreassen, C. S., Pallesen, S., & Griffiths, M. D. (2017). The relationship between addictive use of social media, narcissism, and self-esteem: Findings from a large national survey. *Addictive Behaviors*, *64*, 287–293. https://doi.org/10.1016/j.addbeh.2016.03.006

Andreassen, C. S., Torbjørn, T., Brunborg, G. S., & Pallesen, S. (2012). Development of a Facebook addiction scale. *Psychological Reports*, *110*(2), 501–517. https://doi.org/10.2466/02.09.18.PR0.110.2.501-517

American Psychiatric Association (2000). *Diagnostic and statistical manual of mental disorders* (4th ed., revised). APA.

American Psychiatric Association (2013). *Diagnostic and statistical manual of mental disorders* (5th ed.). APA.

Bányai, F., Zsila, Á., Király, O., et al. (2017). Problematic social media use: Results from a large-scale nationally representative adolescent sample. *PLoS ONE*, *12*(1), Article e0169839. https://doi.org/10.1371/journal.pone.0169839

Billieux, J., Maurage, P., Lopez-Fernandez, O., et al. (2015). Can disordered mobile phone use be considered a behavioral addiction? An update on current evidence and a comprehensive model for future research. *Current Addiction Reports*, *2*, 156–162. https://doi.org/10.1007/s40429-015-0054-y

Boer, M., van den Eijnden, R. J., Boniel-Nissim, M., et al. (2020). Adolescents' intense and problematic social media use and their well-being in 29 countries.

Journal of Adolescent Health, *66*(6), S89–S99. https://doi.org/10.1016/j.jadohealth.2020.02.014

Brailovskaia, J., & Margraf, J. (2021). The relationship between burden caused by coronavirus (Covid-19), addictive social media use, sense of control and anxiety. *Computers in Human Behavior*, *119*, Article 106720. https://doi.org/10.1016/j.chb.2021.106720

Burke, T. A, Nesi, J., Domoff, S. E, Romanowicz, M., & Croarkin, P. E. (2020). Titrating social media use during adolescent inpatient psychiatric hospitalization. *Journal of the American Academy of Child and Adolescent Psychiatry*, *59*(9), 1007–1009. https://doi.org/10.1016/j.jaac.2020.06.008

Chun, J., Shim, H., & Kim, S. (2017). A meta-analysis of treatment interventions for internet addiction among Korean adolescents. *Cyberpsychology, Behavior, and Social Networking*, *20*(4), 225–231. https://doi.org/10.1089/cyber.2016.0188

D'Angelo, J., & Moreno, M. A. (2020). Screening for problematic internet use. *Pediatrics*, *145*, S182–S185. https://doi-org.cmich.idm.oclc.org/10.1542/peds.2019-2056F https://doi.org/10.3109/00048670903282725

Domoff, S. E.,Banga, C. A., Borgen, A. L., et al. (2021). Use of passive sensing to quantify adolescent mobile device usage: Feasibility, acceptability, and preliminary validation of the eMoodie application. *Human Behavior and Emerging Technologies*, *3*(1), 63–74. https://doi.org/10.1002/hbe2.247

Domoff, S. E., Borgen, A. L., Foley, R. P., & Maffett, A. (2019). Excessive use of mobile devices and children's physical health. *Human Behavior & Emerging Technologies*, *1*(2), 169–175. https://doi.org/10.1002/hbe2.145

Domoff, S. E., Borgen, A. L., & Robinson, C. (2020). Problematic use of screen media and mobile devices. In M. Knox (Ed.), Clinician's toolkit for children's behavioral health (pp. 175–198). Academic Press. https://doi.org/10.1016/B978-0-12-816024-4.00008-5

Domoff, S. E., Foley, R. P., & Ferkel, R. (2020). Addictive phone use and academic performance in adolescents. *Human Behavior and Emerging Technologies*, *2*(1), 33–38. https://doi.org/10.1002/hbe2.171

Domoff, S. E., Harrison, K., Gearhardt, A. N., Gentile, D. A., Lumeng, J. C., & Miller, A. L. (2019). Development and validation of the Problematic Media Use Measure: A parent report measure of screen media "addiction" in children. *Psychology of Popular Media Culture*, *8*(1), 2–11. https://doi.org/10.1037/ppm0000163

Domoff, S. E., Sutherland, E. Q., Yokum, S., & Gearhardt, A. N. (2020a). The association of adolescents' television viewing with Body Mass Index percentile, food addiction, and addictive phone use. *Appetite*, *157*, Article 104990. https://doi.org/10.1016/j.appet.2020.104990

Domoff, S. E., Sutherland, E. Q., Yokum, S., & Gearhardt, A. N. (2020b). Adolescents' addictive phone use: Associations with eating behaviors and adiposity. *International Journal of Environmental Research and Public Health*, *17*(8), Article 2861. https://doi.org/10.3390/ijerph17082861

Du, Y. S., Jiang, W., & Vance, A. (2010). Longer term effect of randomized, controlled group cognitive behavioural therapy for internet addiction in adolescent students in Shanghai. *Australian & New Zealand Journal of Psychiatry*, *44*(2), 129–134. https://doi.org/10.3109/00048670903282725

Frison, E., & Eggermont, S. (2016). Exploring the relationships between different types of Facebook use, perceived online social support, and adolescents' depressed mood. *Social Science Computer Review*, *34*(2), 153–171. https://doi.org/10.1177/0894439314567449

Gámez-Guadix, M. (2014). Depressive symptoms and problematic internet use among adolescents: Analysis of the longitudinal relationships from the cognitive-behavioral model. *Cyberpsychology, Behavior, and Social Networking*, *17*(11), 714–719. https://doi.org/10.1089/cyber.2014.0226

Gentile, D. (2009). Pathological video-game use among youth ages 8 to 18: A national study. *Psychological Science*, *20*(5), 594–602. https://doi.org/10.1111/j.1467-9280.2009.02340.x

Gentile, D. A., Bailey, K., Bavelier, D., et al. (2017). Internet gaming disorder in children and adolescents. *Pediatrics*, *140*(Suppl. 2), S81–S85. https://doi.org/10.1542/peds.2016-1758H

Hou, Y., Xiong, D., Jiang, T., Song, L., & Wang, Q. (2019). Social media addiction: Its impact, mediation, and intervention. *Cyberpsychology: Journal of Psychosocial Research on Cyberspace*, *13*, Article 4. https://doi.org/10.5817/CP2019-1-4

Huang, H., & Leung, L. (2009). Instant messaging addiction among teenagers in China: Shyness, alienation, and academic performance decrement. *CyberPsychology & Behavior*, *12*(6), 675–679. https://doi.org/10.1089/cpb.2009.0060

Jelenchick, L. A., Eickhoff, J., Zhang, C., Kraninger, K., Christakis, D. A., & Moreno, M. A. (2015). Screening for adolescent problematic internet use: Validation of the Problematic and Risky Internet Use Screening Scale (PRIUSS). *Academic Pediatrics*, *15*, 658–665. https://doi-org.cmich.idm.oclc.org/10.1016/j.acap.2015.07.001

Kim, J. U. (2008). The effect of a R/T group counseling program on the internet addiction level and self-esteem of internet addiction university students. *International Journal of Reality Therapy*, *27*(2), 1–12.

Kircaburun, K., Griffiths, M. D., & Billieux, J. (2019). Childhood emotional maltreatment and problematic social media use among adolescents: The mediating role of body image dissatisfaction. *International Journal of Mental Health and Addiction*, *18*, 1536–1547. https://doi.org/10.1007/s11469–019-0054-6

Kuss, D. J., & Griffiths, M. D. (2017). Social networking sites and addiction: Ten lessons learned. *International Journal of Environmental Research and Public Health*, *14*(3). https://doi.org/10.3390/ijerph14030311

Lin, C. Y., Broström, A., Nilsen, P., Griffiths, M. D., & Pakpour, A. H. (2017). Psychometric validation of the Persian Bergen social media addiction scale using classic test theory and Rasch models. *Journal of Behavioral Addictions*, *6*(4), 620–629. https://doi.org/10.1556/2006.6.2017.071

Lister-Landman, K. M., Domoff, S. E., & Dubow, E. F. (2017). The role of compulsive texting in adolescents' academic functioning. *Psychology of Popular Media Culture*, *6*(4), 311–325. https://doi.org/10.1037/ppm0000100

Marino, C., Gini, G., Angelini, F., Vieno, A., & Spada, M. M. (2020). Social norms and e-motions in problematic social media use among adolescents. *Addictive Behaviors Reports*, *11*, Article 100250. https://doi.org/10.1016/j.abrep.2020.100250

Moreno, M. A., Arseniev-Koehler, A., & Selkie, E. (2016). Development and testing of a 3-item screening tool for problematic internet use. *The Journal of Pediatrics, 176*, 167–172. https://doi.org/10.1016/j.jpeds.2016.05.067

Moreno, M. A., Binger, K., Zhao, Q., & Eickhoff, J. (2020). Measuring interests not minutes: Development and validation of the Adolescents' Digital Technology Interactions and Importance Scale (ADTI). *Journal of Medical Internet Research, 22*(2), e16736. https://doi.org/10.2196/16736

Muzi, S., Sansò, A., & Pace, C. S. (2021). What's happened to Italian adolescents during the COVID-19 pandemic? A preliminary study on symptoms, problematic social media usage, and attachment: Relationships and differences with pre-pandemic peers. *Frontiers in Psychiatry, 12*, Article 590543. https://doi.org/10.3389/fpsyt.2021.590543

Nasser, N. S., Sharifat, H., Rashid, A. A., et al. (2020). Cue-reactivity among young adults with problematic Instagram use in response to Instagram-themed risky behavior cues: A pilot fMRI study. *Frontiers in Psychology, 11*, Article 2386. https://doi.org/10.3389/fpsyg.2020.556060

Oberst, U., Wegmann, E., Stodt, B., & Brand, M. (2017). Negative consequences from heavy social networking in adolescents: The mediating role of fear of missing out. *Journal of Adolescence, 55*, 51–60. https://doi.org/10.1016/j.adolescence.2016.12.008

Odgers, C. L., Schueller, S. M., & Ito, M. (2020). Screen time, social media use, and adolescent development. *Annual Review of Developmental Psychology, 2*, 485–502. https://doi.org/10.1146/annurev-devpsych-121318-084815

Ohme, J. (2020). Mobile but not mobilized? Differential gains from mobile news consumption for citizens' political knowledge and campaign participation. *Digital Journalism, 8*(1), 103–125. https://doi.org/10.1080/21670811.2019.1697625

Pluhar, E., Kavanaugh, J. R., Levinson, J. A., & Rich, M. (2019). Problematic interactive media use in teens: Comorbidities, assessment, and treatment. *Psychology Research and Behavior Management, 12*, 447–455. https://doi.org/10.2147/PRBM.S208968

Prensky, M. (2001). Digital natives, digital immigrants. In *On the horizon*. MCB University Press. https://www.marcprensky.com/writing/Prensky%20-%20Digital%20Natives,%20Digital%20Immigrants%20-%20Part1.pdf

Raudsepp, L., & Kais, K. (2019). Longitudinal associations between problematic social media use and depressive symptoms in adolescent girls. *Preventive Medicine Reports, 15*, Article 100925. https://doi.org/10.1016/j.pmedr.2019.100925

Sherman, L. E., Hernandez, L. M., Greenfield, P. M., & Dapretto, M. (2018). What the brain 'likes': Neural correlates of providing feedback on social media. *Social Cognitive and Affective Neuroscience, 13*(7), 699–707. https://doi.org/10.1093/scan/nsy051

Sherman, L. E., Payton, A. A., Hernandez, L. M., Greenfield, P. M., & Dapretto, M. (2016). The power of the like in adolescence: Effects of peer influence on neural and behavioral responses to social media. *Psychological Science, 27*(7), 1027–1035. https://doi.org/10.1177/0956797616645673

Stieger, S., & Lewetz, D. (2018). A week without using social media: Results from an ecological momentary intervention study using smartphones. *Cyberpsychology,*

Behavior, and Social Networking, 21(10), 618–624. https://doi.org/10.1089/cyber.2018.0070

Thorisdottir, I. E., Sigurvinsdottir, R., Asgeirsdottir, B. B., Allegrante, J. P., & Sigfusdottir, I. D. (2019). Active and passive social media use and symptoms of anxiety and depressed mood among Icelandic adolescents. *Cyberpsychology, Behavior, and Social Networking, 22*(8), 535–542. https://doi.org/10.1089/cyber.2019.0079

Trifan, A., Oliveira, M., & Oliveira, J. L. (2019). Passive sensing of health outcomes through smartphones: Systematic review of current solutions and possible limitations. *JMIR mHealth and uHealth, 7*(8), e12649. https://doi.org/10.2196/12649

Tromholt, M. (2016). The Facebook experiment: Quitting Facebook leads to higher levels of well-being. *Cyberpsychology, Behavior, and Social Networking, 19*(11), 661–666. https://doi.org/10.1089/cyber.2016.0259

Tunc-Aksan, A., & Akbay, S. E. (2019). Smartphone addiction, fear of missing out, and perceived competence as predictors of social media addiction of adolescents. *European Journal of Educational Research, 8*(2), 559–566. https://doi.org/10.12973/eu

van den Eijnden, R. J. J. M., Lemmens, J. S., & Valkenburg, P. M. (2016). The Social Media Disorder Scale. *Computers in Human Behavior, 61*, 478–487. https://doi.org/10.1016/j.chb.2016.03.038

Vernon, L., Modecki, K. L., & Barber, B. L. (2016). Tracking effects of problematic social networking on adolescent psychopathology: The mediating role of sleep disruptions. *Journal of Clinical Child & Adolescent Psychology, 46*(2), 269–283. https://doi.org/10.1080/15374416.2016.1188702

Wang, P., Wang, X., Wu, Y., et al. (2018). Social networking sites addiction and adolescent depression: A moderated mediation model of rumination and self-esteem. *Personality and Individual Differences, 127*, 162–167. https://doi.org/10.1016/j.paid.2018.02.008

Watson, J. C., Prosek, E. A., & Giordano, A. L. (2020). Investigating psychometric properties of social media addiction measures among adolescents. *Journal of Counseling and Development, 98*(4), 458–466. https://doi.org/10.1002/jcad.12347

Wegmann, E., & Brand, M. (2020). Cognitive correlates in gaming disorder and social networks use disorder: A comparison. *Current Addiction Reports, 7*, 356–364. https://doi.org/10.1007/s40429-020-00314-y

Widyanto, L., & Griffiths, M. (2006). 'Internet addiction': A critical review. *International Journal of Mental Health and Addiction, 4*(1), 31–51. https://doi.org/10.1007/s11469-006-9009-9

Young, K. S. (1998a). *Caught in the net: How to recognize the signs of internet addiction and a winning strategy for recovery.* John Wiley & Sons.

Young, K. S. (1998b). Internet addiction: The emergence of a new clinical disorder. *CyberPsychology & Behavior, 1*(3), 237–244. https://doi.org/10.1089/cpb.1998.1.237

Young, K. S. (2011). CBT-IA: The first treatment model for internet addiction. *Journal of Cognitive Psychotherapy, 25*(4), 304–312. https://doi.org/10.1891/0889-8391.25.4.304

Young, K. S. (2013). Treatment outcomes using CBT-IA with internet-addicted patients. *Journal of Behavioral Addictions, 2*(4), 209–215. https://doi.org/10 .1556/JBA.2.2013.4.3

Zhou, X., Rau, P. L. P., Yang, C. L., & Zhou, X. (2020). Cognitive behavioral therapy-based short-term abstinence intervention for problematic social media use: Improved well-being and underlying mechanisms. *Psychiatric Quarterly, 92*(2), 761–779. https://doi.org/10.1007/s11126–020-09852-0

13 The Effects of Digital Media and Media Multitasking on Attention Problems and Sleep

Susanne E. Baumgartner

With the rise of social and mobile media, not only has the amount of media use changed but also how and when adolescents use media. Almost half of US American adolescents claim that they are almost always online (Anderson & Jiang, 2018). Being constantly online also leads to new forms of media use, such as media multitasking. Media multitasking is commonly defined as using two types of media simultaneously, or using media while engaging in other non-media activities, such as using media while doing homework, during dinner, or during face-to-face conversations (Jeong & Hwang, 2012; van der Schuur et al., 2015). Media multitasking is highly prevalent, particularly among young people (Carrier et al., 2015).

The rise of digital media and media multitasking has led to concerns whether these forms of media use deteriorate adolescents' attention. The main assumption is that if adolescents get used to using media wherever they are and whenever they want, they might have difficulties sustaining their attention, for example when doing their homework or when attending school (Ralph et al., 2015). Moreover, the constant use of digital media has been linked to sleep problems among adolescents (Hale et al., 2019). Since sleep is crucial for the healthy development of adolescents, including their attention and level of sleepiness in school, it is important to understand the ways in which digital media affects sleep. This chapter provides an overview of the current state of the field on the effects of digital media and media multitasking on attention and sleep.

Digital Media and Attention Problems: What Do We Know?

There is a long tradition in media effects research studying the effects of media on attention problems and ADHD-related behaviors. The focus was long on the effects of watching television or playing video games that have been the most popular forms of media use among adolescents in the past. For example, a meta-analysis from 2014 shows that there is indeed a small but significant association between the time children and adolescents spent watching TV and video games and ADHD-related behaviors (Nikkelen et al., 2014). This is further supported in a more recent review of the literature

(Beyens et al., 2018). The effects of TV and video games on attention problems have been typically attributed to two main characteristics of these media types: their fast-paced and potentially violent content. It has been assumed that both of these characteristics might lead to higher arousal states to which adolescents potentially habituate (e.g., see Beyens et al., 2018). In the past decade, however, the media landscape and the types of media that are popular among adolescents have changed dramatically. This has resulted in a research shift away from the effects of traditional types of media (i.e., TV and video games) toward understanding the potential effects of social media and media multitasking on attention.

Media Multitasking and Attention

In 2009, Ophir, Nass, and Wagner published a seminal paper on differences in cognitive processing styles between heavy and light media multi-taskers. Specifically, heavy media multitaskers were more easily distracted than light media multitaskers during a cognitive task they performed in the laboratory. It was the first study explicitly investigating the potential effects of media multitasking on cognitive processes. The authors interpreted their findings as an indication that people who multitask with media frequently have a completely different processing style than people who do this less frequently. Following this study, a plethora of studies have been conducted to understand the relationship between media multitasking and various aspects of attention (for reviews, see Uncapher & Wagner, 2018; van der Schuur et al., 2015). The literature can be differentiated into studies using self-report-based measures of attention in everyday life, and studies using cognitive tasks to measure the level of sustained attention in laboratory settings. It is, however, important to note that most of these studies focused on young adults (i.e., university students), and very few studies focused specifically on adolescents.

Studies using self-reports for attention problems in everyday life have consistently shown that adolescents who media multitask more frequently have more problems focusing their attention (for a review see van der Schuur et al., 2015). For example, media multitasking is positively related to increased attentional failures and mind wandering in young adults (i.e., undergraduate students; Ralph et al., 2013). Moreover, adolescents who media multitask more frequently have more attention problems and higher levels of impulsivity (Baumgartner et al., 2014, 2018). A recent meta-analysis supported these findings by showing that media multitasking and attention problems in everyday life are significantly positively related, with small to moderate effect sizes (Wiradhany & Koerts, 2019).

In contrast to the studies on everyday functioning, studies that tested differences in sustained attention with cognitive tasks in the laboratory show more mixed results. Whereas some find no differences between heavy and light media multitaskers on various tasks related to sustained attention or distractibility (e.g., Baumgartner et al., 2014; Ralph et al., 2015; Wiradhany et al., 2019), others find small effects (e.g., Cain & Mitroff, 2010; Madore et al., 2020; Moisala et al., 2016). Overall, the findings based on cognitive tasks are less consistent than those based on self-reports, and are more difficult to compare as different cognitive tasks are used across studies. Although the existing findings are rather mixed, a recent review of the literature concludes that for tasks measuring sustained attention, evidence points toward performance detriments for heavy media multitaskers in comparison to light media multitaskers (Uncapher & Wagner, 2018).

Despite rather mixed findings for performance differences in cognitive tasks, overall, the existing studies support the idea that adolescents who media multitask more frequently show more attention problems in their everyday lives. However, almost all of these studies are cross-sectional and therefore conclusions about the direction of the effect cannot be drawn. Notably, it is also possible that media multitasking does not lead to attention problems, but that adolescents who are more easily distracted in their everyday lives are more likely to engage in media multitasking. To date, only a few longitudinal studies exist that tried to establish the causal direction of these effects. One longitudinal study found that adolescents who used media more often during academic activities (such as while doing homework) reported increased difficulties in focusing their attention during academic activities over time (van der Schuur et al., 2015). Another study found effects of media multitasking on attention problems only among early adolescents (12–13 years old) but not among middle adolescents (Baumgartner et al., 2018). Thus, there is some but limited evidence for long-term effects of media multitasking on attention. In line with media effects theories, such as reinforcing spiral models (Slater, 2007), it has been proposed that the effects of media multitasking on attention problems might be reciprocal, with adolescents suffering from attention problems being more drawn to media multitasking, and media multitasking in the long run further exacerbating their attention problems (Baumgartner et al., 2018). However, more longitudinal research is needed to empirically test this proposition.

Social Media Use and Attention

Evidence for a relationship between social media use and attention is even more scarce. Only a few studies to date have specifically examined the relationship between the frequency of social media use and attention problems. These studies tentatively point toward a relationship between the use of social media and inattentiveness with adolescents using social media more frequently showing more signs of attention problems (Barry et al.,

2017: Boer et al., 2020). The evidence for a relationship between attention problems and *problematic* or *addictive* social media use is more compelling. Several studies showed that adolescents who use social media in obsessive or problematic ways, also report more attention problems (e.g., Boer et al., 2020; Mérelle et al., 2017; Settanni et al., 2018; Yen et al., 2007). For example, one study found associations between problematic social media use and hyperactivity among a large sample of more than 20,000 Dutch adolescents (Mérelle et al., 2017), and another study found cross-sectional correlations between problematic social media use and attention deficits, impulsivity, and hyperactivity (Boer et al., 2020).

The question of causality across these studies is key. Does the use of social media deteriorate adolescents' attention capacities or are those adolescents who have difficulties sustaining their attention more drawn to social media? Due to the scarcity of longitudinal studies in this realm this question cannot yet be conclusively answered. One longitudinal study investigating the reciprocal relationships between ADHD and social media use found no evidence for an effect of social media use frequency on ADHD over time but an effect of *addictive* social media use on ADHD (Boer et al., 2020). This indicates that not the frequency of use per se but more problematic usage patterns (such as uncontrollability of usage or displacement of social activities) might be detrimental to adolescents' attention. Although this study found no evidence for attention problems being a predictor of developing problematic social media use patterns, another study found that ADHD symptoms in adolescents were the strongest predictor for developing internet addiction two years later (Ko et al., 2009).

Taken together, it seems likely that adolescents with attention problems are more drawn to social media in general, and that they are also more likely to show problematic usage patterns. The stimulating and arousing nature of digital media is particularly appealing to individuals showing symptoms of ADHD as they have a higher need for stimulation (Weiss et al., 2011). Digital media might provide the optimal level of stimulation to them. However, it is still unknown how far the (problematic) use of digital media further increases attention problems. The existing studies indicate that there is indeed a possibility that problematic usage patterns further deteriorate attention. However, due to the small amount of longitudinal studies, it is difficult to draw definite conclusions.

How Do Social Media and Media Multitasking Affect Attention?

To understand how social media and media multitasking affect attention problems among adolescents, it is important to identify theoretical explanations for such effects. Three potential explanations have been put forward to explain the potential effects of media multitasking on attention: 1) habituation to high arousal levels, 2) becoming increasingly sensitive to irrelevant information, and 3) deterioration of attentional control processes (see Baumgartner et al., 2018).

Similarly to the mechanism that was proposed for the effects of violent and fast-paced TV on attention, habituation to high arousal levels might also play a role in the effects of media multitasking and social media use on attention. Media multitasking is considered an arousing activity, and it has been shown that switching between media activities increases arousal levels (Yeykelis et al., 2014). Thus, it can be assumed that when adolescents engage frequently in media multitasking, they habituate to these rather high arousal levels. This in turn makes them favor stimulating and arousing activities in the future. That individuals can habituate to media stimuli has been previously shown for video games with gamers physiologically habituating to arousal levels after repeated video game play (Grizzard et al., 2015). In the context of media multitasking this could mean that adolescents habituate to the arousing nature of multitasking, and as a consequence find less stimulating single-task environments less appealing (e.g., sitting in class or listening to a lecture).

The second potential explanation is that media multitasking affects basic cognitive processes. Ever since Ophir et al. (2009) showed differences in cognitive processing among heavy and light media multitaskers, it has been suspected that engaging in media multitasking may cause these different processing patterns. Engaging in media multitasking requires individuals to attend to multiple streams of information. It has thus been argued that this type of information processing may train the brain to become more sensitive to irrelevant information (Ophir et al., 2009). If individuals get used to continuously attending to several streams of information, they might be more easily distracted by irrelevant external (and potentially internal) distractions (Adler & Benbunan-Fich, 2012).

The third mechanism that has been suggested is that by engaging in media multitasking, adolescents deteriorate their basic attentional control processes. This has been called the "deficit-producing hypothesis" (Ralph et al., 2013). The main assumption is that media multitasking might deteriorate adolescents' ability to regulate their attention internally as they get used to external stimulations. A similar mechanism has previously been assumed for the effects of fast-paced TV content for which it was suggested that fast-paced content captures attention in a bottom-up fashion and does not train adolescents' volitional attention processes (e.g., Lillard & Peterson, 2011). Thus, by engaging in media multitasking frequently, adolescents might not train their ability to guide their attention. This may lead to deficits in these attentional control processes over time (Rothbart & Posner, 2015).

Next to these three cognitive mechanisms, others have argued that digital media use may increase symptoms of ADHD among adolescents by replacing time spent with more developmentally beneficial activities (Weiss et al., 2011). Thus, even if digital media use has no direct effect on cognitive processes, it may still interfere with the healthy development of these skills because it replaces developmentally important activities, such as playing or having conversations with friends and family (Pea et al., 2012).

Importantly, although all of these mechanisms are theoretically plausible, empirical research assessing the mediating role of these mechanisms is still missing. Understanding the underlying mechanisms, however, is crucial as this will help to develop intervention studies that target the problematic aspects of digital media use rather than restricting digital media use in general.

Are There Any Positive Effects of Digital Media on Attention?

If digital media has the potential to affect attentional processes, the question is warranted whether digital media use may not also have positive effects on cognition and attention. Indeed, it has been argued that engagement in media multitasking may also train attentional processes (i.e., trained attention hypothesis: Kobayashi et al., 2020; van der Schuur et al., 2015). It has been assumed that people who engage frequently in media multitasking may improve their task switching skills and lower their switching costs by training these skills. Evidence for this trained attention hypothesis for media multitasking is scarce. However, one brain imaging study found some evidence for improved attentional brain activity among heavy media multitaskers (Kobayashi et al., 2020), and another study found better task switching performance among heavy media multitaskers (Alzahabi et al., 2013). Interestingly, it has been recently suggested that there are curvilinear relationships in that intermediate media multitaskers have better attentional control than low or heavy media multitaskers (Cardoso-Leite et al., 2016). More research is needed to establish whether such positive or curvilinear effects do indeed occur.

In contrast to the rather mixed findings on potential beneficial effects of media multitasking, research on the positive effects of playing action video games are more consistent. These studies show positive effects of playing action video games on several attentional skills, such as focused attention, selected attention, and sustained attention (for a recent meta-analysis, see Bediou et al., 2018, and for a review focusing specifically on attention, see C. S. Green & Bavelier, 2012). These effects were shown for cross-sectional studies but also for intervention studies that showed improvements in these cognitive skills after playing games for 20–40 hours. Most of these studies focused on young adults; however, a few also corroborated these effects for children and adolescents (Dye et al., 2009). Action video games pose a high demand on divided attention, information filtering, and motor control. It is therefore assumed that engaging in these games trains these attentional processes and can therefore benefit attentional control (e.g., Bediou et al., 2018).

In sum, there is some evidence that digital media has positive effects on attention skills. However, this highly depends on the content and type of media used. Particularly, first-person action video games seem to be beneficial. Moreover, effects are dependent on the amount of time spent with particular media. Extant literature suggests possible curvilinear relationships with moderate amounts of exposure being more beneficial than no exposure or too much exposure (Cardoso-Leite et al., 2016; Schmidt & Vandewater, 2008).

Future Research Directions for the Effects of Digital Media on Attention

Overall, research so far has found supporting evidence for a relationship between the amount of media multitasking and social media on the one hand and attention problems on the other hand. Adolescents who engage more frequently in media multitasking and who show more problematic social media use patterns, are also more likely to have attention problems in their everyday lives. The key endeavor for future research is to establish the causality of this relationship. It is yet unclear whether adolescents with attention problems are more drawn to engage in media multitasking, or whether media multitasking affects attention over time. Tentative evidence suggests a reciprocal relationship in that adolescents with attention problems are more drawn to specific types of media and media use patterns, and that spending too much time with these digital media further increases their attention problems (Baumgartner et al., 2018).

Next to the fundamental question of causality, it is crucial to understand the characteristics and affordances of digital media that lead to potential effects on attention. Which characteristics of social media and media multitasking impair attention, and how do these differ from other types of media? Understanding these characteristics is important for several reasons. First, this may help our understanding of the underlying mechanisms through which they are at work. Despite several theoretical assumptions about these mechanisms, empirical evidence is clearly lacking. Understanding these mechanisms might help adolescents to find more beneficial ways to use digital media without banning these completely from their lives. Moreover, a theoretical understanding of which characteristics are problematic would have crucial advantages in the current fast-changing media landscape. Currently, research lags behind new technological developments, and the same questions emerge with every new type of media. To create a more sustainable research agenda it would be helpful to understand the key characteristics of media that drive these effects, and compare and differentiate these among different media types (Orben, 2020).

Digital Media Use and Sleep: What Do We Know?

Sleep plays a critical role in the development of adolescents. Insufficient sleep has been linked to decreased cognitive functioning, increased risk of obesity, and diminished well-being, such as depressive symptoms and perceived stress (e.g., Shochat et al., 2014; Short et al., 2013). From late childhood to early adolescence sleep-related problems increase (Mitchell et al., 2020), with approximately 75% of students in their last year of high school getting insufficient sleep in comparison to only 16% of 6th graders (i.e., fewer than eight hours per night; National Sleep Foundation, 2006). Due to the importance of sleep for healthy psychological and physical development, it is concerning that so many adolescents today get insufficient sleep. Digital media are often seen as one of the main culprits for insufficient sleep and sleep problems, especially among adolescents (e.g., Bhat et al., 2018; Mireku et al., 2019). Particularly smartphones and social media are used extensively by adolescents, and frequently when already in bed or even during the night (e.g., Scott & Woods, 2019; van den Bulck, 2003, 2007).

There is consensus in the field that digital media use is linked to insufficient sleep in adolescents. Several reviews and meta-analyses support this notion (see, e.g., Carter et al., 2016; Hale et al., 2019; LeBourgeois et al., 2017). For example, a meta-analysis on the effects of mobile media devices on sleep, concluded – based on 20 studies with a total of more than 125,000 children and adolescents – that the use of media devices was consistently linked to insufficient sleep quantity, lower sleep quality, and increased daytime sleepiness (Carter et al., 2016). Similarly, in a more recent review of the literature, digital media use was related to adolescents going to bed later, needing more time to fall asleep, waking up during the night, showing signs of sleep problems, and daytime sleepiness (Hale et al., 2019). These effects have been shown for the general time that adolescents spent with media, but particularly for bedtime media use (Hale et al., 2019) and are consistent across various countries and cultural backgrounds (Hale et al., 2019).

Despite this strong evidence for cross-sectional relationships between digital media use and sleep, there are only a few longitudinal and experimental studies, and evidence from these studies is rather mixed. Some longitudinal studies found that digital media use was related to less sleep one or two years later (Johnson et al., 2004; Mazzer et al., 2018; Poulain et al., 2019). In contrast, others did not find longitudinal effects of media use on sleep (Tavernier & Willoughby, 2014), or only for specific subgroups (van der Schuur et al., 2018). For example, media multitasking was over time only related to increased sleep problems among girls but not among adolescent boys (van der Schuur et al., 2018).

To further establish the causality of the relationship, a few intervention studies exist that encouraged adolescents or young adults to reduce the use of specific media before bedtime to examine whether this improves sleep length and quality. These studies typically show improvements in sleep quality during intervention. For example, engaging in a smartphone app-based slow-breathing exercise improved subsequent sleep in comparison to using social media before going to bed (Laborde et al., 2019). Similarly, reducing adolescents' screen time after 9pm on school nights was related to increased sleep duration and improved daytime vigilance (Perrault et al., 2019). A recent meta-analysis on 11 intervention studies concluded that interventions can be successful in reducing screen time and improving sleep time (on average by 11 minutes per day) among children and adolescents (Martin et al., 2020). These studies are promising as they show that reducing screen time can have beneficial effects on sleep. Longer intervention studies, however, are needed to further test the long-term effectiveness and willingness to comply among adolescent samples.

Why and How Do Digital Media Affect Sleep?

Three underlying mechanisms are typically put forward in the literature to explain the effects of digital media use on sleep (e.g., Bartel & Gradisar, 2017). First, the use of digital media before bedtime or when already in bed might displace sleep time. Second, the blue light emitted from digital devices might interfere with the secretion of the sleep hormone, melatonin. Third, the arousing content of digital media might make it difficult for adolescents to fall asleep after media use.

Sleep displacement may occur in two stages: it may lead adolescents to go to bed later and, once in bed, media use may delay the time when adolescents close their eyes and try to fall asleep (Exelmans & van den Bulck, 2017a). Evidence for sleep displacement is consistent for adolescent samples, and has been shown to occur for various types of digital media, such as smartphone, social media, video games, and TV (e.g., Hysing et al., 2015; Kubiszewski et al., 2013). Overall, the literature clearly points toward later bedtimes for adolescents who use digital devices in the evening. Delayed bedtimes and sleep times might be particularly problematic for adolescents who have strict school starting times and cannot easily sleep in. For adult samples, it has been shown that digital media use might lead to later bedtimes but in turn also to later rise times (Custers & van den Bulck, 2012).

Particularly for the use of smartphones, sleep displacement might also occur after sleep onset during the night, when incoming messages interrupt sleep. Several studies reported that smartphones lead to nighttime awakenings (Fobian et al., 2016; van den Bulck, 2003), and these nighttime awakenings might negatively influence sleeping patterns in the long run (Foerster et al., 2019). Therefore, adolescents who take their devices to bed might not only fall asleep later but might also be awakened by these devices during the night. Based on the existing literature, it is very likely that sleep displacement is a contributing factor for the detrimental impact of digital media on sleep. However, it is likely not the only factor because sleep displacement can only account for effects on sleep quantity but to a lesser account for the effects on sleep quality.

The bright screen light emitted by electronic devices has also been considered one of the main culprits for the effects of digital media on sleep. It has been argued that the artificial light emitted by electronic devices may lead to a disruption of the circadian rhythm, leading to increased alertness, and deteriorating sleep quality (Cho et al., 2015). When considering the effects of artificial light on sleep at least three factors need to be considered: the intensity of the emitted light, the duration of light exposure, and the type of light (Cho et al., 2015). Bright light is more disruptive for sleep, as well as short-wave and blue light. Electronic devices, such as smartphones, emit short-wave blue light that is said to suppress the production of the hormone melatonin, which plays an important role in making people sleepy and supporting healthy sleep.

Several studies found negative effects of screen light on subsequent sleepiness and sleep quality (Cajochen et al., 2011; Chang et al., 2015; A. Green et al., 2017). For example, exposure to a very bright LED-backlit computer screen affected melatonin levels and sleepiness of male adults (Cajochen et al., 2011). Similarly, negative effects of reading an e-reader before going to sleep were found (Chang et al., 2015). Importantly, the effects of screen light might be stronger for adolescents than for adults, as adolescents seem to be more affected by short-wave light than adults (Nagare et al., 2019).

Despite several studies finding effects of screen light on sleep quality, it is still highly debated in the field whether the light emitted from tablets, e-readers, TVs, and smartphones is bright enough to interfere with melatonin secretion and sleep. In a recent study, no or only very small and clinically insignificant effects of a bright tablet screen were found (Heath et al., 2014). Moreover, in those studies that found effects on melatonin secretion and/or sleep, sample sizes were rather small, and participants were exposed to rather extreme artificial light conditions, such as five hours of an extremely bright screen (Cajochen et al., 2011), or four hours of a bright e-reader screen (Chang et al., 2015). The clinical relevance of these findings is therefore still debatable. Overall, it is rather unlikely that the light emitted from digital devices is the only or even the most influential mechanism in explaining the effects of digital media on sleep.

The final mechanism that has been put forward is arousal. It is assumed that specific media content might lead to increased physiological arousal, which in turn makes it difficult for people to fall asleep after media use. This mechanism has received the least research attention, and a comprehensive theoretical conceptualization is missing. More specifically, we lack a clear conceptualization of which content characteristics lead to which effects on which mediator (e.g., physiological arousal, cognitive alertness). Bedtime media use might differ widely among adolescents, and from a media psychological perspective it is likely to assume that not all content is equally detrimental to all adolescents' sleep. Although adolescents might use media for the same amount of time before going to bed, their usage patterns might differ tremendously, and their sleep might be differentially affected by their use. For example, one teenager might be listening to relaxing music on their smartphone when in bed, while another teen is actively posting and reacting on their social media accounts. It is likely that these different types of media use lead to very different effects on arousal and sleep.

Moreover, not only the type of content that adolescents consume might have an effect on sleep but also *how* these media are used. For example, interactive media (i.e., video games) seem to have a stronger negative impact on sleep than the passive use of media (i.e., watching a DVD; McManus et al., 2020; Weaver et al., 2010). Similarly, engaging in media multitasking is also related to sleep problems among adolescents (van der Schuur et al., 2018). These studies stress the importance of investigating not only screen time but examining more specifically the types of digital media use and the ways digital media are used.

There is limited understanding about the mechanisms that link varying content types and usage behaviors to sleep quantity and quality. So far, it has been frequently suggested that digital media use leads to heightened physiological arousal (Exelmans & van den Bulck, 2017b). However, specific types of media content may not necessarily increase physiological arousal but might lead to increased cognitive alertness that prohibits sleep (Weaver et al., 2010; Wuyts et al., 2012). Empirical investigations of these mechanisms for digital media are largely missing. One study showed small effects of video game play on alertness but not on arousal, stressing the importance of differentiating between these two processes (Weaver et al., 2010).

In sum, our current understanding of which digital media content factors are related to sleep, and through which mechanisms, is very limited. We know very little about whether specific content and usage patterns affect the varying sleep indicators differently and through which underlying mechanisms content affects sleep (see also Hale & Guan, 2015).

Future Research Directions for Digital Media and Sleep

Although concerns that media negatively affect the sleep of adolescents have a long tradition, these worries are exacerbated with the rise of smartphones and social media as these media types are used more than any other type of media by youth, and are often carried with them to bed. To avoid negative effects of digital media on sleep, the standard advice to adolescents is not to use any types of digital media in the two hours before going to bed (LeBourgeois et al., 2017). This is also reflected in current intervention studies that solely focus on removing digital media from the bedroom altogether (Martin et al., 2020). Although this advice is common and accepted by many, there are at least two problems related to this advice.

First, this strategy is in stark contrast to adolescents' lived experience and developmental needs, and consequently it is unlikely that adolescents will agree to completely ban these devices from their bedrooms. Second, this advice is based on a rather simplistic view on the effects of digital media on sleep that considers the use of the device as universally detrimental. However, how exactly adolescents use digital media before bedtime can vary tremendously, plausibly resulting in differential effects on their sleep quantity and quality. Despite years of research into the effects of digital media on sleep, there are still important shortcomings in the literature that make it difficult to draw final conclusions about the effects of digital media on sleep. Solving these issues in future research is critical to being able to provide adolescents with effective advice on how to use digital media in healthy ways.

Causality

Although there is consistent evidence in the literature for a negative relationship between digital media use and sleep, the direction of this relationship is less than clear. The vast majority of the existing studies are based on cross-sectional designs, making it impossible to draw conclusions about the direction of the relationship (Exelmans & van den Bulck, 2019). Although it is generally assumed that the use of digital media deteriorates sleep, it could also be that the relationship is reversed in that adolescents who sleep less tend to use more digital media. For example, adolescents who do not sleep well might use digital media as a means to cope with stress and insomnia, or because they are depleted and do not have the capacities for regulating their media use efficiently. For example, university students used more social media on days they had slept less during the previous night (Mark et al., 2016). Similarly, sleep-deprived children watched more TV during the day in an experimental study (Hart et al., 2017).

Findings like this cast doubt on the idea that there is a simple cause-and-effect relationship between digital media and sleep. Recent advancement in media effects theories conceptualize media use and effects as reciprocal, evolving dynamically over time (Slater, 2007). In the case of media use and sleep this could mean that adolescents suffering from sleep problems are more likely to use more media that in turn may further deteriorate their sleep. This dynamic and reciprocal nature for smartphone use and sleep is understudied as it demands assessing use and effects over longer time periods in the natural environment of adolescents. One two-wave study found some evidence by showing that media use and sleep times were reciprocally related in adolescents over a one-year period (Poulain et al., 2019). Understanding the nature of the relationship between digital media use and sleep is of key importance for our understanding of the effects of digital media and for intervention and prevention programs.

Individual Responses and Potential Facilitating Effects

Recent theoretical advances in media effects research stress the importance of individual susceptibilities to media effects (Beyens et al., 2020; Valkenburg & Peter, 2013). Also, for the relationship between sleep and digital media, individual differences are likely to be of importance. First, individuals differ in how they use digital media before sleep. For example, Scott and Woods (2018) showed that adolescents with higher levels of fear of missing out tended to use social media longer before sleep time and were more cognitively aroused before falling asleep. Thus individualized usage patterns might lead to varying effects. This is also important because not all evening media diets might be problematic. Some adolescents might use their smartphones in a way that benefits their sleep by actually decreasing their aroused state. This assumption builds on established media effects paradigms that argue that media are used to regulate arousal levels and to establish physiological homeostasis (Zillmann, 1988). For example, people can use apps to seek out social support, relax, and regulate sensory stimulation (Harrison et al., 2019). Research has shown that some people report that they use media in bed to wind down from the day (Eggermont & van den Bulck, 2006). However, little research has investigated whether digital media can be used in ways that benefit adolescents' sleep. Understanding such effects could help to educate adolescents to use their smartphones in more beneficial ways.

A second reason why it is important to study individual differences is that, while uniform effects of some content are possible, adolescents likely differ in their individual responses to digital media content. For example, one study found that adolescents who used social media more frequently slept less well than those who used social media less frequently. However, this effect disappeared when social media stress was taken into account, showing that only those respondents who experienced high levels of stress from their social media use suffered from sleep problems (van der Schuur et al., 2019). Moreover, this study showed that social media use was more problematic for the sleep of girls and early adolescents. Similarly, others found that only those who were more emotionally invested in their social media use slept less well (Woods & Scott, 2016), and that physiological reactions to violent game play differed depending on previous game experience (Ivarsson et al., 2013). Investigating these individual responses to smartphone use is crucial to understand why specific content is problematic for some adolescents but not for others.

Improved Measurement

The vast majority of existing studies relied on self-reports of media use and/or sleep. Self-reports for media use and sleep have been shown to be unreliable and it is thus likely that existing studies suffer from substantial measurement errors. Luckily recent developments in digital media and sleep tracking make it easier to assess digital media use as well as sleep unobtrusively and objectively. For example, there is a multitude of commercially available sleep trackers available with some studies showing promising results using them. We therefore hope that future research will try to combine self-reports with more objective measures for both digital media use and sleep. Assessing the complexity of digital media use objectively will be a crucial step to move beyond investigating screen time toward understanding differential effects of specific content (Carter et al., 2016; Hale et al., 2019; Scott & Woods, 2019).

Overall Conclusion

Parents, educators, and researchers alike are interested in the effects that our digitalized society has on adolescents. Whether digital media impairs attention and sleep has been investigated in a large amount of studies. Yet, the conclusions that we can draw are still limited. Overall, there is compelling evidence that adolescents who use social media more frequently and who are engaging in media multitasking more frequently are more likely to show attention problems in their everyday lives. Moreover, using digital media before bedtime is related to less sleep and more sleep problems. However, the key question of whether digital media causally impairs attention and sleep cannot yet be conclusively answered. To answer this question, it is crucial for the field to advance the theoretical as well as methodological approaches that we currently employ.

Concerning theory development, it is of key importance to identify content characteristics and affordances of digital media that drive such effects. Extracting these factors is crucial to understand not only the effects of today's digital media landscape but also the effects of future media technologies that will emerge (see also Orben, 2020). Moreover, identifying content characteristics will allow us to differentiate potential detrimental from facilitating digital media use. For some adolescents, specific types of media use might have beneficial effects, for example, when they use relaxing smartphone content before they go to bed. Such beneficial effects are oftentimes neglected in current research.

Once we have a clearer theoretical understanding of the content characteristics that drive effects, we need to employ methodological techniques that are able to empirically test those effects in more precise ways. For this, it is important to move beyond cross-sectional studies relying on self-reports of general "screen time" toward assessing digital media in its complexity. Current technological developments facilitate the tracking of digital media use and sleep unobtrusively, objectively, and continuously. Moreover, current advancements in computational methods allow us to integrate, extract and analyze these types of complex data in more efficient ways. This will pave the way toward more advanced studies that examine the dynamic nature of digital media use, sleep and attention in unprecedented ways, and that will accelerate our knowledge of the effects of digital media on youth.

References

Adler, R. F., & Benbunan-Fich, R. (2012). Juggling on a high wire: Multitasking effects on performance. *International Journal of Human-Computer Studies* *70*(2), 156–168. https://doi.org/10.1016/j.ijhcs.2011.10.003

Alzahabi, R., & Becker, M. W. (2013). The association between media multitasking, task-switching, and dual-task performance. *Journal of Experimental Psychology: Human Perception and Performance*, *39*(5), 1485–1495. https://doi.org/10.1037/a0031208

Anderson, M., & Jiang, J. (2018, May 31). *Teens, social media & technology 2018*. PewResearch Center. https://www.pewresearch.org/internet/2018/05/31/teens-social-media-technology-2018/

Barry, C. T., Sidoti, C. L., Briggs, S. M., Reiter, S. R., & Lindsey, R. A. (2017). Adolescent social media use and mental health from adolescent and parent perspectives. *Journal of Adolescence*, *61*, 1–11. https://doi.org/10.1016/j.adolescence.2017.08.005

Bartel, K., & Gradisar, M. (2017). New directions in the link between technology use and sleep in young people. In S. Nevšímalová & O. Bruni (Eds.), *Sleep disorders in children* (pp. 69–80). Springer. https://doi.org/10.1007/978-3-319-28640-2_4

Baumgartner, S. E., van der Schuur, W. A., Lemmens, J. S., & te Poel, F. (2018). The relationship between media multitasking and attention problems in adolescents: Results of two longitudinal studies. *Human Communication Research*, *44*(1), 3–30. https://doi.org/10.1093/hcre.12111

Baumgartner, S. E., Weeda, W. D., van der Heijden, L. L., & Huizinga, M. (2014). The relationship between media multitasking and executive function in early adolescents. *The Journal of Early Adolescence*, *34*(8), 1120–1144. https://doi.org/10.1177/0272431614523133

Bediou, B., Adams, D. M., Mayer, R. E., Tipton, E., Green, C. S., & Bavelier, D. (2018). Meta-analysis of action video game impact on perceptual, attentional, and cognitive skills. *Psychological Bulletin*, *144*(1), 77–110. https://doi.org/10.1037/bul0000130

Beyens, I., Pouwels, J. L., van Driel, I. I., Keijsers, L., & Valkenburg, P. M. (2020). The effect of social media on well-being differs from adolescent to adolescent. *Scientific Reports*, *10*, Article 10763. https://doi.org/10.1038/s41598-020-67727-7

Beyens, I., Valkenburg, P. M., & Piotrowski, J. T. (2018). Screen media use and ADHD-related behaviors: Four decades of research. *Proceedings of the National Academy of Sciences*, *115*(40), 9875–9881. https://doi.org/10.1073/pnas.1611611114

Bhat, S., Pinto-Zipp, G., Upadhyay, H., & Polos, P. G. (2018). "To sleep, perchance to tweet": In-bed electronic social media use and its associations with insomnia, daytime sleepiness, mood, and sleep duration in adults. *Sleep Health*, *4*(2), 166–173. https://doi.org/10.1016/j.sleh.2017.12.004

Boer, M., Stevens, G., Finkenauer, C., & van den Eijnden, R. (2020). Attention deficit hyperactivity disorder-symptoms, social media use intensity, and social media use problems in adolescents: Investigating directionality. *Child Development*, *91*(4), e853–e865. https://doi.org/10.1111/cdev.13334

Cain, M. S., & Mitroff, S. R. (2010). Distractor filtering in media multitaskers. *Journal of Vision, 10,* 260. https://doi.org/10.1167/10.7.260

Cajochen, C., Frey, S., Anders, D., et al. (2011). Evening exposure to a light-emitting diodes (LED)-backlit computer screen affects circadian physiology and cognitive performance. *Journal of Applied Physiology, 110*(5), 1432–1438. https://doi.org/10.1152/japplphysiol.00165.2011

Cardoso-Leite, P., Kludt, R., Vignola, G., Ma, W. J., Green, C. S., & Bavelier, D. (2016). Technology consumption and cognitive control: Contrasting action video game experience with media multitasking. *Attention, Perception, & Psychophysics, 78*(1), 218–241. https://doi.org/10.3758/s13414–015-0988-0.

Carrier, L. M., Rosen, L. D., Cheever, N. A., & Lim, A. F. (2015). Causes, effects, and practicalities of everyday multitasking. *Developmental Review, 35,* 64–78. https://doi.org/10.1016/j.dr.2014.12.005

Carter, B., Rees, P., Hale, L., Bhattacharjee, D., & Paradkar, M. S. (2016). Association between portable screen-based media device access or use and sleep outcomes: A systematic review and meta-analysis. *JAMA Pediatrics, 170*(12), 1202–1208. https://doi.org/10.1001/jamapediatrics.2016.2341

Chang, A. M., Aeschbach, D., Duffy, J. F., & Czeisler, C. A. (2015). Evening use of light-emitting eReaders negatively affects sleep, circadian timing, and next-morning alertness. *Proceedings of the National Academy of Sciences, 112*(4), 1232–1237. https://doi.org/10.1073/pnas.1418490112

Cho, Y., Ryu, S. H., Lee, B. R., Kim, K. H., Lee, E., & Choi, J. (2015). Effects of artificial light at night on human health: A literature review of observational and experimental studies applied to exposure assessment. *Chronobiology International, 32*(9), 1294–1310. https://doi.org/10.3109/07420528.2015.1073158

Custers, K., & van den Bulck, J. (2012). Television viewing, internet use, and self-reported bedtime and rise time in adults: Implications for sleep hygiene recommendations from an exploratory cross-sectional study. *5Behavioral Sleep Medicine, 10*(2), 96–105. https://doi.org/10.1080/15402002 .2011.596599

Dye, M. W., Green, C. S., & Bavelier, D. (2009). The development of attention skills in action video game players. *Neuropsychologia, 47*(8–9), 1780–1789. https://doi.org/10.1016/j.neuropsychologia.2009.02.002

Eggermont, S., & van den Bulck, J. (2006). Nodding off or switching off? The use of popular media as a sleep aid in secondary-school children. *Journal of Paediatric Child Health, 42*(7), 428–433. https://doi.org/10.1111/j.1440-1754.2006.00892.x

Exelmans, L., & van den Bulck, J. (2017a). Bedtime, shuteye time and electronic media: Sleep displacement is a two-step process. *Journal of Sleep Research, 26*(3), 364–370. https://doi.org/10.1111/jsr.12510

Exelmans, L., & van den Bulck, J. (2017b). Binge viewing, sleep, and the role of pre-sleep arousal. *Journal of Clinical Sleep Medicine, 13*(8), 1001–1008. https://doi.org/10.5664/jcsm.6704

Exelmans, L., & van den Bulck, J. (2019). Sleep research: A primer for media scholars. *Health Communication, 34*(5), 519–528. https://doi.org/10.1111/jsr.12510

Fobian, A. D., Avis, K., & Schwebel, D. C. (2016). Impact of media use on adolescent sleep efficiency. *Journal of Developmental Behavioral Pediatrics, 37*(1), 9–14. https://doi.org/10.1097/DBP.0000000000000239

Foerster, M., Henneke, A., Chetty-Mhlanga, S., & Röösli, M. (2019). Impact of adolescents' screen time and nocturnal mobile phone-related awakenings on sleep and general health symptoms: A prospective cohort study. *International Journal of Environmental Research and Public Health, 16*(3), Article 518. https://doi.org/10.3390/ijerph16030518

Green, A., Cohen-Zion, M., Haim, A., & Dagan, Y. (2017). Evening light exposure to computer screens disrupts human sleep, biological rhythms, and attention abilities. *Chronobiology International, 34*(7), 855–865. https://doi.org/10.1080/07420528. 2017.1324878

Green, C. S., & Bavelier, D. (2012). Learning, attentional control, and action video games. *Current Biology, 22*(6), R197–R206. https://doi.org/10.1016/j.cub.2012.02.012

Grizzard, M., Tamborini, R., Sherry, J. L., et al. (2015). The thrill is gone, but you might not know: Habituation and generalization of biophysiological and self-reported arousal responses to video games. *Communication Monographs, 82*(1), 64–87. https://doi.org/10.1080/03637751.2014.971418

Hale, L., & Guan, S. (2015). Screen time and sleep among school-aged children and adolescents: A systematic literature review. *Sleep Medicine Reviews, 21,* 50–58. https://doi.org/10.1016/j.smrv.2014.07.007

Hale, L., Li, X., Hartstein, L. E., & LeBourgeois, M. K. (2019). Media use and sleep in teenagers: What do we know? *Current Sleep Medicine Reports, 5*(3), 128–134. https://doi.org/10.1007/s40675–019-00146-x

Harrison, K., Vallina, L., Couture, A., Wenhold. H., & Moorman, J. D. (2019). Sensory curation: Theorizing media use for sensory regulation and implications for family media conflict. *Media Psychology, 22*(4), 653–688. https://doi.org/10.1080/15213269.2018.1496024

Hart, C. N., Hawley, N., Davey, A., et al. (2017). Effect of experimental change in children's sleep duration on television viewing and physical activity. *Pediatric Obesity, 12*(6), 462–467. https://doi.org/10.1111/ijpo.12166

Heath, M., Sutherland, C., Bartel, K., et al. (2014). Does one hour of bright or short-wavelength filtered tablet screenlight have a meaningful effect on adolescents' pre-bedtime alertness, sleep, and daytime functioning? *Chronobiology International, 31*(4), 496–505. https://doi.org/10.3109/07420528.2013.872121

Hysing, M., Pallesen, S., Stormark, K. M., Jakobsen, R., Lundervold, A. J., & Sivertsen, B. (2015). Sleep and use of electronic devices in adolescence: Results from a large population-based study. *BMJ Open, 5*(1), e006748. http://dx.doi.org/10.1136/bmjopen-2014-006748

Ivarsson, M., Anderson, M., Åkerstedt, T., & Lindblad, F. (2013). The effect of violent and nonviolent video games on heart rate variability, sleep, and emotions in adolescents with different violent gaming habits. *Psychosomatic Medicine, 75*(4), 390–396. https://doi.org/10.1097/PSY.0b013e3182906a4c

Jeong, S., & Hwang, Y. (2012). Does multitasking increase or decrease persuasion? Effects of multitasking on comprehension and counterarguing. *Journal of Communication, 62*(4), 571–587. https://doi.org/10.1111/j.1460-2466.2012.01659.x

Johnson, J. G., Cohen, P., Kasen, S., First, M. B., & Brook, J. S. (2004). Association between television viewing and sleep problems during adolescence and early adulthood. *Archives of Pediatrics & Adolescent Medicine, 158*(6), 562–568. https://doi.org/10.1001/archpedi.158.6.562

Ko, C. H., Yen, J. Y., Chen, C. S., Yeh, Y. C., & Yen, C. F. (2009). Predictive values of psychiatric symptoms for internet addiction in adolescents: A 2-year prospective study. *Archives of Pediatrics & Adolescent Medicine, 163*(10), 937–943. https://doi.org/10.1001/archpediatrics.2009.159

Kobayashi, K., Oishi, N., Yoshimura, S., et al. (2020). Relationship between media multitasking and functional connectivity in the dorsal attention network. *Scientific Reports, 10,* Article 17992. https://doi.org/10.1038/s41598-020-75091-9

Kubiszewski, V., Fontaine, R., Rusch, E., & Hazouard, E. (2013). Association between electronic media use and sleep habits: An eight-day follow-up study. *International Journal of Adolescence and Youth, 19*(3), 395–407. http://doi.org/10.1080/02673843.2012.751039

Laborde, S., Hosang, T., Mosley, E., & Dosseville, F. (2019). Influence of a 30-day slow-paced breathing intervention compared to social media use on subjective sleep quality and cardiac vagal activity. *Journal of Clinical Medicine, 8*(2), Article 193. https://doi.org/10.3390/jcm8020193

LeBourgeois, M. K., Hale, L., Chang, A. M., Akacem, L. D., Montgomery-Downs, H. E., & Buxton, O. M. (2017). Digital media and sleep in childhood and adolescence. *Pediatrics, 140,* S92–S96. https://doi.org/10.1542/peds.2016-1758J

Lillard, A. S., & Peterson, J. (2011). The immediate impact of different types of television on young children's executive function. *Pediatrics, 128*(4), 644–649. https://doi.org/10.1542/peds.2010-1919

Madore, K. P., Khazenzon, A. M., Backes, C. W., et al. (2020). Memory failure predicted by attention lapsing and media multitasking. *Nature, 587*(7832), 87–91. https://doi.org/10.1038/s41586-020-2870-z

Mark, G., Wang, Y. D. O. I., Niiya, M., & Reich, S. (2016). Sleep debt in student life: Online attention focus, Facebook, and mood. *Proceedings of the 2016 CHI Conference on Human Factors in Computing Systems,* 5517–5528. https://doi.org/10.1145/2858036.2858437

Martin, K. B., Bednarz, J. M., & Aromataris, E. C. (2020). Interventions to control children's screen use and their effect on sleep: A systematic review and meta-analysis. *Journal of Sleep Research, 30*(3), e13130. https://doi.org/10.1111/jsr.13130

Mazzer, K., Bauducco, S., Linton, S. J., & Boersma, K. (2018). Longitudinal associations between time spent using technology and sleep duration among adolescents. *Journal of Adolescence, 66,* 112–119. https://doi.org/10.1016/j.adolescence.2018.05.004

McManus, B., Underhill, A., Mrug, S., Anthony, T., & Stavrinos, D. (2020). Gender moderates the relationship between media use and sleep quality. *Journal of Sleep Research, 30*(4), e13243. https://doi.org/10.1111/jsr.13243

Mérelle, S., Kleiboer, A., Schotanus, M., et al. (2017). Which health-related problems are associated with problematic video-gaming or social media use in adolescents? *Clinical Neuropsychiatry: Journal of Treatments Evaluation, 14*(1), 11–19. hdl.handle.net/1765/98403

Mitchell, J. A., Morales, K. H., Williamson, A. A., et al. (2020). Changes in sleep duration and timing during the middle-to-high school transition. *Journal of Adolescent Health, 67*(6), 829–836. https://doi.org/10.1016/j.jadohealth.2020.04.024

Mireku, M. O., Barker, M. M., Mutz, J., et al. (2019). Night-time screen-based media device use and adolescents' sleep and health-related quality of life. *Environment International*, *124*, 66–78. https://doi.org/10.1016/j.envint.2018.11.069

Moisala, M., Salmela, V., Hietajärvi, L., et al. (2016). Media multitasking is associated with distractibility and increased prefrontal activity in adolescents and young adults. *NeuroImage*, *134*, 113–121. https://doi.org/10.1016/j.neuroimage .2016.04.011

Nagare, R., Plitnick, B., & Figueiro, M. G. (2019). Effect of exposure duration and light spectra on nighttime melatonin suppression in adolescents and adults. *Lighting Research & Technology*, *51*(4), 530–543. https://doi.org/10.1177/ 1477153518763003

National Sleep Foundation. (2006). *Teens and sleep: Sleep in America polls*. National Sleep Foundation.

Nikkelen, S. W. C., Valkenburg, P. M., Huizinga, M., & Bushman, B. J. (2014). Media use and ADHD-related behaviors in children and adolescents: A meta-analysis. *Developmental Psychology*, *50*(9), 2228–2241. https://doi.org/10.1037/ a0037318

Ophir, E., Nass, C., & Wagner, A. D. (2009). Cognitive control in media multitaskers. *Proceedings of the National Academy of Sciences*, *106*(37), 15583–15587. https://doi.org/10.1073/pnas.0903620106

Orben, A. (2020). The Sisyphean cycle of technology panics. *Perspectives on Psychological Science*, *15*(5), 1143–1157. https://doi.org/10.1177/1745691620919372

Pea, R., Nass, C., Meheula, L., et al. (2012). Media use, face-to-face communication, media multitasking, and social well-being among 8- to 12-year-old girls. *Developmental Psychology*, *48*(2), 327–336. https://doi.org/10.1037/a0027030

Perrault, A. A., Bayer, L., Peuvrier, M., et al. (2019). Reducing the use of screen electronic devices in the evening is associated with improved sleep and daytime vigilance in adolescents. *Sleep*, *42*(9), zsz125. https://doi.org/10.1093/sleep/zsz125

Poulain, T., Vogel, M., Buzek, T., Genuneit, J., Hiemisch, A., & Kiess, W. (2019). Reciprocal longitudinal associations between adolescents' media consumption and sleep. *Behavioral Sleep Medicine*, *17*(6), 763–777. https://doi.org/ 10.1080/15402002.2018.1491851

Ralph, B. C. W., Thomson, D. R., Cheyne, J. A., & Smilek, D. (2013). Media multitasking and failures of attention in everyday life. *Psychological Research*, *78*(5), 661–669. https://doi.org/10.1007/s00426–013-0523-7

Ralph, B. C. W., Thomson, D. R., Seli, P., Carriere, J. S. A., & Smilek, D. (2015). Media multitasking and behavior measures of sustained attention. *Attention, Perception, & Psychophysics*, *77*(2), 390–401. https://doi.org/10.3758/s13414– 014-0771-7

Rothbart, M. K., & Posner, M. I. (2015). The developing brain in a multitasking world. *Developmental Review*, *35*, 42–63. https://doi.org/10.1016/j.dr.2014.12.006

Schmidt, M. E., & Vandewater, E. A. (2008). Media and attention, cognition, and school achievement. *The Future of Children*, *18*(1), 63–85. https://doi.org/ 10.1353/foc.0.0004

Scott, H., & Woods, H. C. (2018). Fear of missing out and sleep: Cognitive behavioural factors in adolescents' nighttime social media use. *Journal of Adolescence*, *68*, 61–65. https://doi.org/10.1016/j.adolescence.2018.07.009

Scott, H., & Woods, H. C. (2019). Understanding links between social media use, sleep and mental health: Recent progress and current challenges. *Current Sleep Medicine Reports*, *5*(3), 141–149. https://doi.org/10.1007/s40675-019-00148-9

Settanni, M., Marengo, D., Fabris, M. A., & Longobardi, C. (2018). The interplay between ADHD symptoms and time perspective in addictive social media use: A study on adolescent Facebook users. *Children and Youth Services Review*, *89*, 165–170. https://doi.org/10.1016/j.childyouth.2018.04.031

Shochat, T., Cohen-Zion, M., & Tzischinsky, O. (2014). Functional consequences of inadequate sleep in adolescents: A systematic review. *Sleep Medicine Review*, *18*(1), 75–87. https://doi.org/10.1016/j.smrv.2013.03.005

Short, M. A., Gradisar, M., Lack, L. C., & Wright, H. R. (2013). The impact of sleep on adolescent depressed mood, alertness and academic performance. *Journal of Adolescence*, *36*(6), 1025–1033. https://doi.org/10.1016/j.adolescence.2013.08.007

Slater, M. D. (2007). Reinforcing spirals: The mutual influence of media selectivity and media effects and their impact on individual behavior and social identity. *Communication Theory*, *17*(3), 281–303. https://doi.org/10.1111/j.1468-2885.2007.00296.x

Tavernier, R., & Willoughby, T. (2014). Sleep problems: Predictor or outcome of media use among emerging adults at university? *Journal of Sleep Research*, *23*(4), 389–396. https://doi.org/10.1111/jsr.12132

Uncapher, M. R., & Wagner, A. D. (2018). Minds and brains of media multitaskers: Current findings and future directions. *Proceedings of the National Academy of Sciences*, *115*(40), 9889–9896. https://doi.org/10.1073/pnas.1611612115

Valkenburg, P. M., & Peter, J. (2013). The differential susceptibility to media effects model. *Journal of Communication*, *63*(2), 221–243. https://doi.org/10.1111/jcom.12024

Van den Bulck, J. (2003). Text messaging as a cause of sleep interruption in adolescents, evidence from a cross-sectional study. *Journal of Sleep Research*, *12*(3), 263. https://doi.org/10.1046/j.1365-2869.2003.00362.x

Van den Bulck, J. (2007). Adolescent use of mobile phones for calling and for sending text messages after lights out: Results from a prospective cohort study with a one-year follow-up. *Sleep*, *30*(9), 1220–1223. https://doi.org/10.1093/sleep/30.9.1220

van der Schuur, W. A., Baumgartner, S. E., & Sumter, S. R. (2019). Social media use, social media stress, and sleep: Examining cross-sectional and longitudinal relationships in adolescents. *Health Communication*, *34*(5), 552–559. https://doi.org/10.1080/10410236.2017.1422101

Van der Schuur, W. A., Baumgartner, S. E., Sumter, S. R., & Valkenburg, P. M. (2015). The consequences of media multitasking for youth: A review. *Computers in Human Behavior*, *53*, 204–215. https://doi.org/10.1016/j.chb.2015.06.035

Van der Schuur, W. A., Baumgartner, S. E., Sumter, S. R., & Valkenburg, P. M. (2018). Media multitasking and sleep problems: A longitudinal study among adolescents. *Computers in Human Behavior*, *81*, 316–324. https://doi.org/10.1016/j.chb.2017.12.024

Weaver, E., Gradisar, M., Dohnt, H., Lovato, N., & Douglas, P. (2010). The effect of presleep video-game playing on adolescent sleep. *Journal of Clinical Sleep Medicine*, *6*(2), 184–189. https://doi.org/10.5664/jcsm.27769

Weiss, M. D., Baer, S., Allan, B. A., Saran, K., & Schibuk, H. (2011). The screens culture: Impact on ADHD. *ADHD Attention Deficit and Hyperactivity Disorders*, *3*(4), 327–334. https://doi.org/10.1007/s12402-011-0065-z

Wiradhany, W., & Koerts, J. (2019). Everyday functioning-related cognitive correlates of media multitasking: A mini meta-analysis. *Media Psychology*, *24*(2), 276–303. https://doi.org/10.1080/15213269.2019.1685393

Wiradhany, W., van Vugt, M. K., & Nieuwenstein, M. R. (2019). Media multitasking, mind-wandering, and distractibility: A large-scale study. *Attention, Perception, & Psychophysics*, *82*, 1112–1124. https://doi.org/10.3758/s13414-019-01842-0

Woods, H. C., & Scott, H. (2016). # Sleepyteens: Social media use in adolescence is associated with poor sleep quality, anxiety, depression and low self-esteem. *Journal of Adolescence*, *51*, 41–49. https://doi.org/10.1016/j.adolescence.2016.05.008

Wuyts, J., De Valck, E., Vandekerckhove, M., et al. (2012). The influence of pre-sleep cognitive arousal on sleep onset processes. *International Journal of Psychophysiology*, *83*(1), 8–15. https://doi.org/10.1016/j.ijpsycho.2011.09.016

Yen, J. Y., Ko, C. H., Yen, C. F., Wu, H. Y., & Yang, M. J. (2007). The comorbid psychiatric symptoms of internet addiction: Attention deficit and hyperactivity disorder (ADHD), depression, social phobia, and hostility. *Journal of Adolescent Health*, *41*(1), 93–98. https://doi.org/10.1016/j.jadohealth.2007.02.002

Yeykelis, L., Cummings, J. J., & Reeves, B. (2014). Multitasking on a single device: Arousal and the frequency, anticipation, and prediction of switching between media content on a computer. *Journal of Communication*, *64*, 167–192. https://doi.org/10.1111/jcom.12070

Zillmann, D. (1988). Mood management through communication choices. *American Behavioral Scientist*, *31*(3), 327–340. https://doi.org/10.1177/000276488031003005

14 Digital Media, Suicide, and Self-Injury

Kaylee Payne Kruzan and Janis Whitlock

While interest in the relationship between media use and young people's mental health is not new, the complexity of newer media technologies present novel research challenges – largely due to the interactive, multidimensional nature of contemporary communication technologies, such as those typified by social media environments. While early media studies focused primarily on effects of "screen time," studies of modern-day social media must grapple with a number of overlapping and influential factors since effects are no longer related to mere exposure to potentially harmful content, but to the interactions that take place as individuals use and shape these platforms, as well.

The relationship between social media and self-injurious behaviors – specifically suicidal thoughts and behaviors and nonsuicidal self-injury (NSSI) – emerged as a primary research focus soon after social media came into widespread use, perhaps due to the well-established links between both media exposure and well-being (Wartella & Reeves, 1985) and to media effects and suicidal thoughts and behaviors (Phillips, 1974). This focus was reinforced by studies linking widely covered suicides (Niederkrotenthaler et al., 2012) and popular shows depicting suicide (Swedo et al., 2020) to upticks in self-injury and suicide-related activity.

This chapter is devoted to examining the relationship between social media and self-injurious thoughts and behaviors. Self-injurious thoughts and behaviors (SITB) describe thoughts and behaviors with (e.g., suicidal ideation, suicide plans, gestures, and behaviors) and without (e.g., NSSI) suicidal intent (Miller & Prinstein, 2019). While the developmental trajectories of NSSI and suicidal thoughts and behaviors differ from one another (Fox et al., 2015), SITB are not always clearly delineated from one another in the literature, in part because they commonly co-occur and in part because they each contribute to an increased risk for future suicide attempts (Kiekens et al., 2018). Such conflation applies to the literature on which this chapter draws. For simplicity, we will use the term SITB to refer to self-injury with, and without, intent in this chapter and we will refer to more specific constructs within this broader term when studies focus on a narrower sample.

Chapter Aims

This chapter includes two overarching aims: (1) to summarize research on the risks and benefits of social media use for SITB-related outcomes, including what is and is not known about primary mechanisms at play in these relationships and (2) to identify high-level implications, including opportunities and challenges for future research, intervention, and prevention efforts. The first section provides an overview on the prevalence and presentation of SITB in adolescence and the role of social media in SITB, while the second section summarizes findings related to the risks and benefits of social media use for SITB, and key mechanisms involved in these relationships. The final section covers implications for research, practice, and policy, through high-level opportunities and challenges.

Background

Adolescence and SITB

Understanding and addressing SITB is of major public health importance. Suicide is the second leading cause of death among young people between the ages of 10 and 24 globally (Curtin et al., 2016). Among US-based adolescent populations, lifetime prevalence of suicidal thoughts and behaviors is between 3.1% and 8.8% for suicide attempts and between 19.8% and 24.0% for suicidal ideation, with a marked increase in both suicidal ideation and behavior between the ages of 12 and 17 (Nock et al., 2008). Rates of NSSI – "the deliberate, self-inflicted damage of body tissue *without suicidal intent* and for purposes not socially or culturally sanctioned" (International Society for the Study of Self-Injury, 2018) – range from 17% to 37% among adolescents and young adults (Jacobson & Gould, 2007; Swannell et al., 2014).

Self-injurious thoughts and behaviors typically emerge in early- to mid-adolescence, with average age of onset for NSSI between 13 and 15 (Gillies et al., 2018), and mid- to late-adolescence for suicidal thoughts and behaviors (Nock et al., 2013). Older adolescents and young adults are more likely to die by suicide (Cha et al., 2018), when compared to younger adolescents – a pattern consistent with the idea that risk of engagement in serious suicide-related behaviors increases over time as experience of trauma and/or distress accumulates and interacts with bio-psycho-social developmental changes in ways that enhance vulnerability to cognitive and emotional challenges (Steinberg, 2010). Adolescence is also characterized by a highly social orientation, increased propensity for risk taking, and individuation/identity formation – each of which may interact with social media use in ways that amplify, or increase susceptibility to, potential media effects.

The Role of Social Media and SITB

Three decades of experience with, and empirical study of, unidirectional media affirms the potency of media influence on behavior, particularly for adolescents and children (Brown et al., 2006). The empirical link between exposure to violent media content and child and adolescent aggression was central to early media concerns and resulted in coordinated policy responses (US Senate, 2000). More recent efforts to understand the effects of social media on youth mental health retain a heightened focus on the potential adverse effects, such as: cybervictimization (John et al., 2018; Massing-Schaffer & Nesi, 2020), internet addiction (Jasso-Medrano & López-Rosales, 2018), and exposure to graphic self-injury and suicidal content (Arendt et al., 2019). It is thus not surprising that there are serious concerns about the impact that social media may have on individuals who bring preexisting vulnerabilities to online exchanges, such as SITB-vulnerable young people.

While attention to each of these domains has translated into research on social media effects of value to professionals, researchers, and platform designers, it has not yet led to robust understanding of the precise risks that social media pose to youth mental health – largely due to the number of contingencies that require disentangling and a need for methodological innovation (Whitlock & Masur, 2019). Moreover, while concern about the impact of social media on youth continues to be a regular feature of public worry and headlines, it is also recognized that social media offers important support to users, including SITB-vulnerable individuals, by (1) facilitating social connection (Duggan et al., 2012), (2) extending the reach of prevention/intervention efforts (Thorn et al., 2020), (3) linking young people who are already engaging in SITB with much needed information and support (Lavis & Winter, 2020; Lewis & Michal, 2016), and (4) increasing public awareness of SITB and reducing stigma (Li et al., 2018; Nathan & Nathan, 2020). A balanced and nuanced approach that takes into account both the risk and benefits of social media for SITB outcomes is needed to effectively consider the many factors that likely mediate and moderate social media effects.

Brief Overview of Methods Used to Study the Relationship Between SITB and Social Media

A brief historical overview on the methodological approaches most commonly used in social media and SITB research is both helpful in contextualizing the risks and benefits and in surfacing methodological frontiers in this domain. In general, SITB-focused research aims have (1) described online content and activity related to SITB, (2) explored the relationship between online activity and SITB, and (3) identified risks germane to intervention efforts. While these efforts have laid the theoretical and empirical foundations necessary for inferring and anticipating risks and benefits and for understanding key mechanisms, they have been less effective in surfacing and disentangling clear causal relationships between social media use and SITB behaviors or in describing the moderating role preexisting SITB vulnerability plays in these relationships.

In general, research documenting potential effects of SITB-related content and exchange has been more straightforward to generate than research aimed at understanding causal relationships between online activity and SITB; in part because the latter requires innovative methods that balance privacy and ethical concerns with the need for cross-ecological and granular approaches capable of disentangling effects. Moreover, because the nature of communication technologies is so dynamic, the research methods required to understand effects must also be dynamic. Most early work focused on content and thematic analyses to investigate common themes in online discussions about self-injury and suicide (Rodham et al., 2007; Whitlock et al., 2006). Surveys were (and still are) used to assess motives for social media use and to understand the perceived effects of use (Lewis & Michal, 2016).

Recent advances in the application of computational methods to social media research have paved the way for investigation of links between online activities and SITB risk, largely through tracking patterns in linguistic and behavioral markers (De Choudhury et al., 2016; Du et al., 2018). Ecological momentary assessments (EMA), or diary methodologies, have been used to understand the relationship between social media use and outcomes related to mental health. For example, EMA methods were used to understand what behaviors young people engage in instead of self-injury (Fitzpatrick et al., 2020). Longitudinal studies have begun yielding results, but even these are limited by challenges in disentangling between- from within-effects of media use, understanding risks and benefits accrued to vulnerable subgroups, and the way that both developmental stage and specific social media affordances interact with social media use (Schemer et al., 2020). In sum, research focused on the intersection of SITB and social media use has evolved from a focus on more static content in online communities (precursors to social media) to more dynamic interactions between user behaviors, content, and offline markers over time. While important methodological challenges remain, much has been learned; this is the focus of the following sections.

Risks of Social Media for Self-Injury and Suicide

Study of the ways in which use of social media increases SITB risk reveals a complex portrait of effects, some of which clearly enhance risk of SITB behavior and others that may protect against such risk. This section details the dominant categories of risk identified thus far including: (1) exposure to SITB content, (2) normalization and narrative reinforcement, (3) contagion, (4) cyberbullying, and (5) heavy social media use.

Exposure to Suicide and Self-Injury Content

As with traditional media, at least some research documents a link between exposure to suicidal and self-injury social media content and increased risk for SITB experiences. Exposure to digital SITB-related content is not infrequent – in one study, 25% of young people were exposed to suicide stories through social media (Dunlop et al., 2011). This is concerning because increased exposure to self-injury-related content has been associated with decreased aversion to self-injury and to future suicidal ideation in past work (Franklin et al., 2016) and because habituation to SITB content may reduce barriers to, and increase the acquired capability for, suicide (Massing-Schaffer & Nesi, 2020). Moreover, such risks may not diminish over time. For example, in a study of effects of exposure to self-harm content on Instagram, researchers found that lifetime exposure to self-harm content was associated with increased SITB risk. Furthermore, exposure was related to an increase in self-harm behaviors, suicidal ideation, and hopelessness one month later, even when controlling for preexisting SITB vulnerability (Arendt et al., 2019).

While it is possible that well-moderated sites could minimize harm resulting from unregulated exposure to triggering content, empirical evidence suggests that even with site moderation individuals can be exposed to triggering graphic or emotional images or text (Baker & Lewis, 2013; Lewis & Michal, 2016), including tips on concealment, suicidal ideation, or plans (Dyson et al., 2016). Indeed, in the aforementioned Instagram study, only 20% of those who reported seeing self-harm content intentionally searched for it (Arendt et al., 2019). Further, some studies indicate that a subgroup of individuals access online communities in order to sustain or trigger self-injury and share maladaptive techniques (Lewis & Seko, 2016; Whitlock et al., 2006).

Awareness of the potential for social media content to have harmful effects has led to an increase in moderation efforts, often by platform developers themselves. Popular social media platforms like Instagram, for example, have built in "sensitivity screens" (i.e., trigger warnings) that are meant to shield content related to self-injury and other harmful behaviors enabling users to view content if they clear the shield (Carman, 2019). However, even these efforts require empirical study since, in this case, evidence suggests that use of trigger warnings to decrease risk of SITB-related harm has relatively limited effects on distress (Sanson et al., 2019) and may increase anticipatory anxiety in some cases (Gainsburg & Earl, 2018). Effects of what a user does in response to a trigger warning is also less intuitive than it might seem. For example, a study focused on self-injury related activity on TalkLife, a mobile peer-support app, showed that choosing to dismiss a trigger warning and view self-injury content was related both to greater intentions to injure *and* greater ability to resist injuring within a week's time (Kruzan et al., 2021). Notably, posting triggering content was related to increased odds of both self-injury thoughts and behaviors. In sum, more work is needed to explicate both the factors that contribute to effects related to exposure to SITB content and the potential protective value of moderation efforts, like trigger warnings.

The Downside of Social Connection on Social Media: Normalization and Narrative Reinforcement

The fact that self-injury and suicide-related posts so frequently co-occur with themes of loneliness underscores the important role that social connection plays in mental health and well-being (Cavazos-Rehg et al., 2017). Indeed, the promise of rich social connection is one of the factors that makes participation in social media so appealing. However, empirical evidence suggests that the "social" part of social media is simultaneously a risk and a protective factor for SITB. While the perceived and actual social support that comes from social media's ability to connect young people struggling with self-injury and suicide can be beneficial and SITB-protective, regular exposure to SITB content and association with other individuals struggling with SITB may expose vulnerable adolescents to communities where self-injury is normalized or encouraged, even if not overtly or consciously (Rodham et al., 2007; Whitlock et al., 2006). This "normalization effect" is commonly seen in studies of online communication about self-injury where young people discuss self-injury thoughts and behaviors in detail and often minimize the severity of self-injury and its consequences (Dyson et al., 2016). Moreover, the tendency for individuals to co-construct and then reinforce foundational narratives, sometimes termed "narrative reinforcement," that essentially justifies the need for and use of SITB-linked activities, can lead to desensitization and normalization of behavior, especially when self-injury is depicted as painless and effective (Whitlock et al., 2007).

Even when a user is trying to minimize exposure to triggering content, most studies show that it is common for pro-recovery messages and encouragement to occur alongside pro-self-injury posts and comments, such as advice on how to injure safely and how to conceal wounds (Lavis & Winter, 2020; Whitlock et al., 2006). This may not only normalize self-injury, but may also trigger SITB-impulses or discourage use of alternative coping strategies or professional help seeking (Dyson et al., 2016; Smithson et al., 2011). In sum, while the emotional support received through social media sites can positively influence the recovery process, this support may detract from the severity of the behavior, potentially slowing the change process (Dyson et al., 2016).

Contagion: Spread and Scale of Social Media Messages

The idea that exposure to a behavior through media may be "contagious" is a subject of long-standing research interest. Research shows both an increase in the number of SITB themes in on- and offline media, and concomitant concern that such content may contribute to onset or maintenance of SITB among vulnerable individuals, mostly likely through social modelling (Jarvi et al., 2013). While the adverse impact of SITB social media content on individuals with existing vulnerabilities is intuitive, recent work suggests that even individuals without existing vulnerabilities may be at risk of adverse outcomes from SITB-related themes in social media. For example, there is evidence that viewing suicide-cluster-related posts (e.g., vigils, memorials), online news articles related to suicide, and watching the Netflix series *13 Reasons Why* (which features suicidal content) is associated with increased odds of suicidal ideation and attempts, among students both with and without prior self-injury history (Swedo et al., 2020). This study did not control for other known risk factors, like depression or anxiety, and it cannot rule out the possibility that other important preexisting vulnerabilities exist, but it does suggest that even individuals without prior self-injury history are adversely affected by some media content. This possibility is also implicit in research that finds an over 14% increase in population-based suicide trends for young people between 10 and 19 (Niederkrotenthaler et al., 2019) and "excess" hospitalizations for suicide attempts among young people (Cooper et al., 2018) following the release of *13 Reasons Why*.

In a similar vein, research reveals that individuals who post suicidal content are more tightly clustered in friend, or reposting groups, than users who do not post suicide-related content. This supports the idea that individuals tend to gravitate to like-minded others online in ways that may heighten likelihood of narrative reinforcement, and concomitantly, risk of spread among those most vulnerable (Colombo et al., 2016). However, the authors also note that re-tweeting behavior connects users whose posts contain suicidal ideation with users whose posts do not, providing evidence for the potential of contagion across diverse networks.

Contagion and Social Media "Challenges"

Social media challenges allow users to pose a behavioral challenge to followers who then receive online community recognition for meeting the challenge – most often over a series of days or weeks. While potentially harmless, or even beneficial, challenges can also heighten individual SITB risk. The Blue Whale Challenge, which occurred through social media from 2013 to 2017, is purported to encourage youth to participate in a series of tasks over 50 days that involve self-harm and culminate in a suicide challenge (Sumner et al., 2019). Not only is the challenge itself associated with heightened SITB risk, but YouTube media covering this challenge often violated Suicide Prevention Resource Center guidelines (Khasawneh et al., 2020). Such challenges also underscore the ways in which the very features that make social media so attractive also present novel risks.

Cyberbullying

Bullying is a long-standing source of stress for young people and this holds as true in online social settings as it does in offline social settings (John et al., 2018). Cyberbullying, a term used to describe bullying that occurs online, is also associated with heightened risk for SITB. Notably, it is not just the victims of cyberbullying who are at elevated SITB risk. A recent meta-analysis shows that youth victims of cyberbullying are over twice likely to engage in self-harm, to report a suicide attempt, and to report suicidal thoughts, when compared to nonvictims (John et al., 2018). Even one episode of cybervictimization increases risk of suicidal ideation (Hirschtritt et al., 2015). Moreover, the risk of SITB after a cyberbullying incident increases significantly among individuals with existing vulnerabilities. Indeed, in a study of adolescents presenting to Canadian emergency departments for mental health complaints, those reporting histories of cybervictimization were over 11 times more likely to report suicidal ideation (Alavi et al., 2017). Also, being both a victim and perpetrator of cyberbullying doubles the risk of reporting suicidal thoughts when compared to those who have one of these experiences (Bonanno & Hymel, 2013; John et al., 2018).

Heavy Social Media Use

Research has also shown that risk of NSSI and SITB increases with heavy social media use (Lee et al., 2016; Twenge & Campbell, 2019). Indeed, in a study of Canadian high school students, those who spent more than two hours a day on social media had were five times more likely to experience suicidal ideation when compared to peers reporting fewer than two hours of social media use a day (Sampasa-Kanyinga & Lewis, 2015). Similarly, adolescents who report heavy digital media use are twice as likely to report suicidal thoughts, suicide plans, and suicide attempts when compared to light users, according to a large survey study (Twenge & Campbell, 2019). And, in a recent review of seven studies researchers documented a direct association between heavy social media/internet use and suicide attempts (Sedgwick et al., 2019).

Interestingly, some studies show that some social media use is better than no use (Kim, 2012; Lee et al., 2016). These findings are consistent with broader literature on social media use and well-being that suggests curvilinear relationships between social media use and well-being with benefits derived from some use, versus no use, and risks increasing most significantly from low or moderate to heavy use (Kim, 2012; Przybylski & Weinstein, 2017; Twenge & Campbell, 2019). Specifically, risks increase most significantly from low (<1 hour a day) or moderate to heavy use (>5 hours a day) (Twenge & Campbell, 2019). One explanatory theory is that time spent on social media displaces other activities that could be beneficial for mental health, such as physical activity, in-person social interaction, and sleep – all risk factors for suicide (Porras-Segovia et al., 2019; Sedgwick et al., 2019; Verkooijen et al., 2018).

Benefits of Social Media for Reducing Self-Injury and Suicide

While risks associated with social media use are a focus of continued empirical investigation, salutary effects have also been documented. Reviews focused on social media and SITB (deliberate self-harm: Biernesser et al., 2020; Dyson et al., 2016 and self-harm and suicide: Daine et al., 2013; Marchant et al., 2017; Memon et al., 2018) converge in their identification of tangible benefits, including enhanced: (1) social support and connectedness, (2) self-knowledge/expression, and (3) access/exchange of resources/information. Key empirical findings for each area are described below.

Social Support and Connectedness

One of the primary perceived benefits of social media use is the exchange of social support not bounded by time or geography. This is important because social support is known to buffer effects of negative life events, enhance mental health and well-being (Cutrona & Suhr, 1992), decrease feelings of isolation, lead to sense of purpose, and to promote feelings of acceptance or being understood (Daine et al., 2013). Opportunities for social support through social media can be powerful for young people with SITB, since stigma is often an impediment to offline help and support seeking. Online environments allow for anonymity and carry few clear social penalties for candid sharing, which makes such environments particularly attractive to individuals concerned about disclosing SITB-related behaviors or impulses to people in their offline lives (Duggan et al., 2012). And, since social support is a critical protective factor for SITB (Joiner et al., 2012), social exchange in social media forums offers a promising alternative to offline sharing.

It is thus unsurprising that empirical evidence suggests that young people with SITB histories use the Internet more often than their peers (De Riggi et al., 2018; Memon et al., 2018) and that it is a preferred means for seeking and receiving help (Frost & Casey, 2016). For example, youth with suicidal ideation are more likely to report online-only friendships, relative to those without suicidal ideation, and these friendships appear to buffer the harmful effects of relational victimization and stress (Massing-Schaffer et al., 2020). Nearly one-third of young people with a history of self-injury had reported online help seeking in one study – and those who sought help online were more distressed and suicidal than those who had not (Frost & Casey, 2016). Additionally, adolescents with more recent NSSI have higher levels of online support seeking, compared to those with past or no NSSI history (De Riggi et al., 2018). Even when individuals have a strong support system offline, they may have trouble accessing support in times when they need it (Kruzan et al., 2021; Lavis & Winter, 2020). The immediate nature of social support exchange on social media may be important for individuals who struggle with SITB given that intense urges are commonly cited as a key barrier to behavior change (Kruzan & Whitlock, 2019) and findings showing that young people frequently look for, and receive, emotional support online when they are experiencing an urge (Lewis & Michal, 2016; Rodham et al., 2007).

Not all social support is equal, however. While some work suggests that young people perceive benefits from participation (Brown et al., 2020; Lewis & Michal, 2016), others note the "mundane" or safe nature of the advice, which leads to questions of actual utility (Smithson et al., 2011). The availability and immediate accessibility of such support is nonetheless quite appealing – as is the fact that support is exchanged among peers with shared experience and experiential knowledge (Marchant et al., 2017; Thoits, 2011). Research consistently documents a preference for peer versus professional support for NSSI and the tendency for young people to confide SITB in peers versus others in their social network (De Riggi et al., 2018), something social media facilitates organically.

The question of whether such peer support is helpful for SITB outcomes remains nascent. Early work showed positive associations between social support received and decreased self-injury behaviors (Murray & Fox, 2006), but research directly connecting social support through social media use to its effects on SITB outcomes is limited. One experimental study varying exposure to hopeful or hopeless YouTube videos, found that hopeful messages were associated with increased positive attitudes toward recovery, suggesting shifts in recovery-oriented subjective norms (Lewis et al., 2018). Interestingly, there were no attitudinal changes in those viewing hopeless messages.

Self-Knowledge and Expression

Beyond the use of social media as a source of social support is its role in facilitating self-expression and exploration. Being able to connect and provide mutual support, narrate experiences, and self-reflect, while also maintaining autonomy and anonymity, are all identified as clear benefits to social media use among individuals with SITB history (Coulson et al., 2017; Rodham et al., 2013). Indeed, self-oriented motivations such as understanding NSSI experience or expressing oneself through narrative description or other forms of creative expression are potent motives of online activity (Seko et al., 2015). Insight gleaned through sharing one's story and encountering resonance in others' stories is important in recovery and is associated with active information seeking, increased self-efficacy, and enhanced self-awareness (Kruzan & Whitlock, 2019). Since young people frequently provide advice to others online (Seko et al., 2015; Whitlock et al., 2006), it is also possible that seeing oneself as a valued mentor to others with shared struggles may increase commitment to recovery processes. Online self-presentation and expression can assist in developing self-understanding, and be associated with beneficial shifts in self-perceptions (Kruzan & Won, 2019; Valkenburg, 2017).

Exchange of Resources and Information

Use of social media to both identify and exchange coping techniques is also common and potentially beneficial (Duggan et al., 2012) for individuals navigating self-injury or suicidal thoughts and urges (Lavis & Winter, 2020; Lewis & Michal, 2016). Tips on how to reduce the urge or replace self-injury behaviors are also highly salient. For example, in a study of three different social media sites (Reddit, Instagram, Twitter) researchers found a rich exchange of coping advice related to visual, distraction, and sensory techniques effective in reducing urges (Lavis & Winter, 2020). There is also evidence that topics related to professional help seeking for SITB are a feature of some online exchange (Lavis & Winter, 2020), but whether this is common remains unclear since there is work suggesting that online exchange does not lead to increased professional help seeking (R. C. Brown et al., 2020) and because this line of inquiry remains underexplored.

The power of social media exchange to alter offline behavior does open opportunity for development of more formal intervention. Online peers may be uniquely positioned to provide advice on treatment and coping strategies, and this advice may be easier to digest, and apply, when coming from someone who has "been there" (Naslund et al., 2016). Such exchange can be considered a unique and potent form of expertise (Marchant et al., 2017) that can be leveraged to deliver coping- and recovery-supportive messages and resources. Since not all resources exchanged through social media are evidence-based, and some can be harmful or depict self-injury as an effective coping strategy (Lewis & Baker, 2011; Seko & Lewis, 2018), it is crucial that the nature of naturally occurring exchange is understood and mitigated when potentially harmful.

Key Mechanisms: Moderators and Mediators of Effects on SITB

Individual, developmental, and social-contextual factors are all empirically and theoretically relevant when considering susceptibility to SITB and media effects, especially since young people with preexisting vulnerabilities, such as other mental health conditions, are more likely to be exposed to harmful content (Dyson et al., 2016). SITB-specific individual-level factors such as prior SITB history may moderate social media effects (Dyson et al., 2016). Cyberbullying may also moderate or mediate social media effects (John et al., 2018), and while underexplored, factors such as offline support and prior SITB help seeking are likely to moderate the effect of social media on SITB. For example, social media effects, particularly negative effects, might be less damaging to individuals who have rich social supports outside of social media. A review of the most acknowledged likely mediators follows.

Mental Health History

Just as prior mental health history has the potential to moderate the effects of social media use on SITB outcomes, it can also mediate this relationship. In some work, the relationship between heavy social media use and NSSI was mediated by factors such as suicidality, anxiety, and affective and psychotic disorders (Mészáros et al., 2020).

Affect and Intentions

Emotional affect and motives for use are also likely mediators of the relationship between social media and SITB. The connection between NSSI and affect is well established, and may be particularly important in understanding interactions that lead to risks or benefits of social media use, since both NSSI (Klonsky, 2007) and social media use can be ways to modulate emotion (Rideout & Fox, 2018). Indeed, young people can deliberately seek out uplifting, distressing, or neutral messages that reflect, and may impact, their own affective state. While few studies have examined the role of mood in the relationship between SITB and social media use, young people with lived NSSI experience often discuss mood as part of their use of social media and related technologies (Seko et al., 2015).

Interactional Factors

In addition to the amount of use, the way someone uses social media is consistently connected to mental health outcomes (Verduyn et al., 2017). This trend holds for SITB-related studies, as well, but the patterns of effects are not entirely intuitive. In a cross-sectional study of the association between SITB (both NSSI and suicidal thoughts and behavior) and social media use type among Norwegian university students, researchers found that active public social media use (e.g., posting, commenting) was associated with *increased* odds of NSSI ideation and behaviors and suicide attempts, whereas social private use (e.g., messaging friends) was associated with *reduced* odds of all NSSI and suicide outcomes (Kingsbury et al., 2021). Passive nonsocial use (e.g., reading news) was associated with *decreased* odds of NSSI ideation, NSSI, and suicidal ideation, and active nonsocial use (e.g., for studies) was associated with *decreased* odds of suicide attempt. In parallel with the broader literature on social media effects on well-being, these findings suggest a nuanced relationship that differs by types of engagement.

Social Comparison Processes

Social comparison is a primary mechanism through which social media use impacts mental health and well-being (Appel et al., 2016; Kruzan & Won, 2019; Wang et al., 2017). Upward social comparison – wherein individuals compare themselves to those who are perceived as better off – has been associated with reductions in self-esteem, increased negative affect, and envy (Appel et al., 2016; Wang et al., 2017). Consonant with this general trend, Kingsbury et al., (2021) found that the presence of social comparison is associated with increased odds for all NSSI and suicidal outcomes. However, social comparison processes may look slightly different on social media sites or forums that are structured almost entirely around conversations about SITB (e.g., TalkLife) where the general positivity bias documented in mainstream social media does not exist. In light of its influence, the role of social comparison for SITB risk in social media should be explored further.

Opportunities and Challenges

Despite limitations, social media and related platforms, like mobile apps, offer excellent opportunities to leverage modern communication technologies in ways that provide timely and scalable intervention and, ideally, prevention. Such opportunities, however, present unique challenges related to methodological innovation and strategies for effectively addressing privacy and ethical considerations.

Opportunities: Amplifying the Beneficial Potential of Social Media

In addition to the opportunities inherent in the nature of the technology's design, such as the possibility for enhanced social connection and belonging, there are unique opportunities for: (1) identification/detection, (2) intervention, (3) prevention, and (4) awareness/stigma reduction.

Identification/Detection

Automated methods for predicting SITB risk and social media effects are promising as they are capable of considering complex combinations not likely to arise from more traditional assessments (Walsh et al., 2017). Creative use of machine learning has been successful in early efforts to detect and address suicidal content, particularly when used to detect and intervene with novel online risks, such as pro-suicide games (Sumner et al., 2019). This same method can also be used to identify at-risk users. Natural language processing and topic modeling have been leveraged to understand changes in suicide-related content following national reports of celebrity suicides (Kumar et al., 2015) and changes in emotional expression and self-attentional focus are consistently identified as indicators of higher suicide risk, for example (Coppersmith et al., 2018; De Choudhury et al., 2016). However, most work has focused on high-level trends, rather than individual risk patterns, which would be useful for tailoring interventions. An exception to this is a study that was able to differentiate between users who are at risk of transitioning to suicidal ideation (De Choudhury et al., 2016). While discerning posts related to self-injury with, and without, suicidal intent is more difficult, it is a promising area for further investigation.

Intervention

As the ability to detect at-risk users who could benefit from additional resources improves, scalable interventions delivered through social media will be possible. Preliminary evidence suggests that young people would be receptive to digital interventions, such as those through social media (Naslund et al., 2016) and that digital interventions focused on acquisition and implementation of evidence-based SITB coping skills are likely to be efficacious in reducing self-injury (Rizvi et al., 2016; Schroeder et al., 2018). Such interventions could also serve as a decisional tool for future help-seeking behaviors, for both those at risk of SITB and concerned friends and family (Rowe et al., 2018).

Two frameworks particularly promising for early intervention in the social media environment are: (1) single session interventions (Schleider & Weisz, 2017) and (2) digital micro interventions (Baumel et al., 2020). Single session interventions (SSIs) – brief, but potent, treatments designed to last one session – have shown promise in reducing many mental health outcomes in adolescent populations (Schleider & Weisz, 2017). These interventions are scalable, potentially capable of reaching young people who are unlikely to come into contact with more formal/traditional services, and are flexible enough to be disseminated in multiple contexts, including social media. Additionally, the potential value of SSIs in reducing SITB has already been noted (Dobias et al., 2020).

Digital micro interventions (DMIs) are small "bite-sized" interventions designed to fit seamlessly into an individual's natural use of media (Baumel et al., 2020). In contrast to the linear and/or single-platform approach DMIs work across a number of platforms (e.g., social media apps, text messaging) and involve a series of smaller, dynamic touch points that are responsive to young people's media habits. Since at least one suicide prevention study suggests that young users want preventive interventions embedded in the platforms they already frequent (Thorn et al., 2020), DMIs may be particularly well suited for delivering SITB early intervention and prevention.

Prevention

Social media can be leveraged to increase awareness, reduce stigma, and provide psychoeducation at scale (Robinson et al., 2016). Simulation studies in this area demonstrate that suicide prevention efforts on social media have the potential to reach at-risk populations at a much larger scale than traditional methods (Silenzio et al., 2009). Despite this potential, few prevention efforts for SITB to date have been disseminated on social media. Some of the more innovative work in this area engages young social media users in codesigning workshops aimed at developing a social media campaign (the #chatsafe project) focused on safe communication about suicide online (Thorn et al., 2020). The project demonstrated that it is feasible to safely engage young people in codesigning a suicide prevention intervention (Robinson et al., 2018; Thorn et al., 2020). A number of auxiliary but useful key takeaways surfaced through this process, including finding that young people wanted to see guidelines through sharable content – including videos, animations, photographs – and that they want to feel visible in the media campaign (Thorn et al., 2020).

Awareness and Stigma Reduction

Destigmatizing mental health struggles and increasing positive discourse and disclosure is another opportunity for social media to address SITB. Social media can be used to gauge public perceptions of suicide, determine needs for literacy, and deliver psychoeducation when needed (Nathan & Nathan, 2020). Social media mining can also be leveraged to improve the performance of stigma reduction programs (Li et al., 2018). However, more research is needed to better understand how social media can be used to reduce stigma and promote open and nuanced discussions.

Challenges: Minimizing the Negative Potential of Social Media

Some of the challenges of studying and understanding the relationship between social media use and SITB outcomes are broadly related to (1) creating and maintaining a safe environment, (2) methodological innovation, and (3) privacy and ethical considerations.

Creating and Maintaining a Safe Environment

The need to attenuate negative effects of social media use and prevent further "digital harm" – or "online communication and activity that leads to, supports, or exacerbates, non-suicidal yet intentional harm or impairment of an individual's physical well-being" (Pater & Mynatt, 2017) (p. 1501) is critical to creating and maintaining safe online environments. While much of the work focused on social media and SITB risks focuses on moderation, it is also useful to think about how spaces can be designed to facilitate connection and supportive exchanges and to make negative interactions less likely. To accomplish this, however, understanding of how platforms can be designed to protect users against negative experiences (e.g., cyberbullying) without sacrificing opportunities for user agency (including peer-to-peer intervention) at interaction and platform level must be enhanced and leveraged. Researchers in fields like human–computer interaction are particularly well suited to address these concerns due to their person-centered approaches, especially when working in collaboration with experts in both SITB and adolescent development and well-being.

Methodological Innovation

The dynamic nature of social media environments coupled with the broad-reaching messaging power presents new and important methodological challenges for research – all of which merit careful attention from scholars in various technical and clinical disciplines. Social media data has improved our understanding of the needs and struggles of young people with SITB histories and has been linked to markers of SITB risk. However, both automation and platform use preferences evolve rapidly – necessitating a flexible approach. While use of automated methods has powerful potential, algorithms are "black boxes," and utility is not likely to be of universal ease or impact across platforms. Therefore, understanding variations in speed, efficiency, and utility of methods across platforms will be a key component of augmenting utility. It will be similarly important for researchers to consider how to best translate findings from sophisticated detection algorithms into practice and to have a set of guidelines for developing, and validating, social media interventions.

Two of the greatest needs for future research are to examine the temporal relationship between online activities and behavior change, and to discern which mechanisms contribute to desirable outcomes. To do this, it will be important to triangulate different types of data and methods (Lavis & Winter, 2020) and to consider new methodological approaches capable of tracking what participants actually see and do online. Combining EMA with tracking (logging media use), for example, may assess states rather than traits, reduce recall bias, and link fluctuations to the manifold situational factors and circumstances outlined in this chapter (Whitlock & Masur, 2019). Future research should also consider the bi-directional relationships between SITB and social media engagement (Lavis & Winter, 2020). To date, most work has focused on the impact of social media use on SITB risk; however, it is equally important to understand how individual histories of SITB and risk influence social media use.

Privacy and Ethics

Such methodological approaches pose significant ethical challenges and will require care in balancing potential ethical challenges inherent in such methods with the benefits they provide. One of the biggest challenges for platform designers, researchers, and policy-makers is navigating user privacy and ethics while also safeguarding against potential harms of free expression – both in terms of platform affordances and the research needed to better understand the complex interactions between social media use, SITB risk, and individual-level factors such as developmental stage and other risk and protective factors (Whitlock & Masur, 2019). There is also a need to establish universal protocols for how risk detection and accuracy is measured and applied across platforms (Westers et al., 2020). This will likely require continuous monitoring and updating of algorithms as the data available expands and brings with it questions about privacy and opting-in to such monitoring.

Conclusion

Evidence that young people go online, exchange support, and share relatively openly about their experiences is promising in that it presents grounds to understand young people's experiences, detect needs, and design and deliver scalable preventative interventions. However, there are also risks associated with the social media environment such as exposure to, and the quick spread of, potentially harmful content. To better understand how we can best amplify the beneficial potential of social media, while minimizing the negative consequences, further research focused on disentangling factors that contribute most to the SITB–social media relationship is needed.

References

Alavi, N., Reshetukha, T., Prost, E., et al. (2017). Relationship between bullying and suicidal behaviour in youth presenting to the emergency department. *Journal of the Canadian Academy of Child and Adolescent Psychiatry, 26*(2), 70–77.

Appel, H., Gerlach, A. L., & Crusius, J. (2016). The interplay between Facebook use, social comparison, envy, and depression. *Current Opinion in Psychology, 9*, 44–49. https://doi.org/10.1016/j.copsyc.2015.10.006

Arendt, F., Scherr, S., & Romer, D. (2019). Effects of exposure to self-harm on social media: Evidence from a two-wave panel study among young adults. *New Media & Society, 21*(11–12), 2422–2442. https://doi.org/10.1177/1461444819850106

Baker, T. G., & Lewis, S. P. (2013). Responses to online photographs of non-suicidal self-injury: A thematic analysis. *Archives of Suicide Research, 17*(3), 223–235. https://doi.org/10.1080/13811118.2013.805642

Baumel, A., Fleming, T., & Schueller, S. M. (2020). Digital micro interventions for behavioral and mental health gains: Core components and conceptualization of digital micro intervention care. *Journal of Medical Internet Research, 22*(10), e20631. https://doi.org/10.2196/20631

Biernesser, C., Sewall, C. J. R., Brent, D., Bear, T., Mair, C., & Trauth, J. (2020). Social media use and deliberate self-harm among youth: A systematized narrative review. *Children and Youth Services Review, 116*, Article 105054. https://doi.org/10.1016/j.childyouth.2020.105054

Bonanno, R. A., & Hymel, S. (2013). Cyber bullying and internalizing difficulties: Above and beyond the impact of traditional forms of bullying. *Journal of Youth and Adolescence*, *42*(5), 685–697. http://dx.doi.org.turing.library .northwestern.edu/10.1007/s10964–013-9937-1

Brown, J. D., L'Engle, K. L., Pardun, C. J., Guo, G., Kenneavy, K., & Jackson, C. (2006). Sexy media matter: Exposure to sexual content in music, movies, television, and magazines predicts black and white adolescents' sexual behavior. *Pediatrics*, *117*(4), 1018–1027. https://doi.org/10.1542/peds.2005-1406

Brown, R. C., Fischer, T., Goldwich, D. A., & Plener, P. L. (2020). "I just finally wanted to belong somewhere": Qualitative analysis of experiences with posting pictures of self-injury on Instagram. *Frontiers in Psychiatry*, *11*, Article 274. https://doi.org/10.3389/fpsyt.2020.00274

Carman, A. (2019, February). Instagram head admits platform has a problem policing self-harm posts: It'll introduce sensitivity screens this week. *The Verge*. https://www.theverge.com/2019/2/4/18210473/instagram-self-harm-suicide-cutting-posts-molly-russell

Cavazos-Rehg, P. A., Krauss, M. J., Sowles, S. J., et al. (2017). An analysis of depression, self-harm, and suicidal ideation content on Tumblr. *Crisis*, *38*(1), 44–52. https://doi.org/10.1027/0227-5910/a000409

Cha, C. B., Franz, P. J., Guzmán, E. M., Glenn, C. R., Kleiman, E. M., & Nock, M. K. (2018). Annual Research Review: Suicide among youth – Epidemiology, (potential) etiology, and treatment. *Journal of Child Psychology and Psychiatry, and Allied Disciplines*, *59*(4), 460–482. https://doi.org/10.1111/jcpp.12831

Colombo, G. B., Burnap, P., Hodorog, A., & Scourfield, J. (2016). Analysing the connectivity and communication of suicidal users on Twitter. *Computer Communications*, *73*, 291–300. https://doi.org/10.1016/j.comcom.2015.07.018

Cooper, M. T., Bard, D., Wallace, R., Gillaspy, S., & Deleon, S. (2018). Suicide attempt admissions from a single children's hospital before and after the introduction of Netflix series *13 Reasons Why*. *Journal of Adolescent Health*, *63*(6), 688–693. https://doi.org/10.1016/j.jadohealth.2018.08.028

Coppersmith, G., Leary, R., Crutchley, P., & Fine, A. (2018). Natural language processing of social media as screening for suicide risk. *Biomedical Informatics Insights*, *10*. https://doi.org/10.1177/1178222618792860

Coulson, N. S., Bullock, E., & Rodham, K. (2017). Exploring the therapeutic affordances of self-harm online support communities: An online survey of members. *JMIR Mental Health*, *4*(4), e44. https://doi.org/10.2196/mental .8084

Curtin, S. C., Warner, M., & Hedegaard, H. (2016). *Increase in suicide in the United States, 1999–2014*. US Department of Health and Human Services, Centers for Disease Control and Prevention, National Center for Health Statistics.

Cutrona, C. E., & Suhr, J. A. (1992). Controllability of stressful life events and satisfaction with spouse support behaviors. *Communication Research*, *19*(2), 154–174.

Daine, K., Hawton, K., Singaravelu, V., Stewart, A., Simkin, S., & Montgomery, P. (2013). The power of the web: A systematic review of studies of the influence of the internet on self-harm and suicide in young people. *PLoS ONE*, *8*(10), e77555. https://doi.org/10.1371/journal.pone.0077555

De Choudhury, M., Kiciman, E., Dredze, M., Coppersmith, G., & Kumar, M. (2016). Discovering shifts to suicidal ideation from mental health content in social media. *Proceedings of the 2016 CHI Conference on Human Factors in Computing Systems*, 2098–2110. https://doi.org/10.1145/2858036.2858207

De Riggi, M., Lewis, S., & Heath, N. (2018). Brief report: Nonsuicidal self-injury in adolescence: Turning to the internet for support. *Counselling Psychology Quarterly, 31*(3), 397–405. https://doi.org/10.1080/09515070.2018.1427556

Dobias, M., Chen, S., Fox, K., & Schleider, J. L. (2020). Brief interventions for self-injurious thoughts and behaviors in young people: A systematic review [Preprint]. *PsyArXiv*. https://doi.org/10.31234/osf.io/z26ch

Du, J., Zhang, Y., Luo, J., et al. (2018). Extracting psychiatric stressors for suicide from social media using deep learning. *BMC Medical Informatics and Decision Making, 18*(2), Article 43. https://doi.org/10.1186/s12911-018-0632-8

Duggan, J. M., Heath, N. L., Lewis, S. P., & Baxter, A. L. (2012). An examination of the scope and nature of non-suicidal self-injury online activities: Implications for school mental health professionals. *School Mental Health, 4*(1), 56–67. https://doi.org/10.1007/s12310-011-9065-6

Dunlop, S. M., More, E., & Romer, D. (2011). Where do youth learn about suicides on the internet, and what influence does this have on suicidal ideation? *Journal of Child Psychology and Psychiatry, 52*(10), 1073–1080. https://doi.org/10.1111/j.1469-7610.2011.02416.x

Dyson, M. P., Hartling, L., Shulhan, J., et al. (2016). A systematic review of social media use to discuss and view deliberate self-harm acts. *PLoS ONE, 11*(5), e0155813. https://doi.org/10.1371/journal.pone.0155813

Fitzpatrick, S., Kranzler, A., Fehling, K., Lindqvist, J., & Selby, E. A. (2020). Investigating the role of the intensity and duration of self-injury thoughts in self-injury with ecological momentary assessment. *Psychiatry Research, 284*, Article 112761. https://doi.org/10.1016/j.psychres.2020.112761

Fox, K. R., Franklin, J. C., Ribeiro, J. D., Kleiman, E. M., Bentley, K. H., & Nock, M. K. (2015). Meta-analysis of risk factors for nonsuicidal self-injury. *Clinical Psychology Review, 42*, 156–167. https://doi.org/10.1016/j.cpr.2015.09.002

Franklin, J. C., Fox, K. R., Franklin, C. R., et al. (2016). A brief mobile app reduces nonsuicidal and suicidal self-injury: Evidence from three randomized controlled trials. *Journal of Consulting and Clinical Psychology, 84*(6), 544–557. https://doi.org/10.1037/ccp0000093

Frost, M., & Casey, L. (2016). Who seeks help online for self-injury? *Archives of Suicide Research: Official Journal of the International Academy for Suicide Research, 20*(1), 69–79. https://doi.org/10.1080/13811118.2015.1004470

Gainsburg, I., & Earl, A. (2018). Trigger warnings as an interpersonal emotion-regulation tool: Avoidance, attention, and affect depend on beliefs. *Journal of Experimental Social Psychology, 79*, 252–263. https://doi.org/10.1016/j.jesp.2018.08.006

Gillies, D., Christou, M. A., Dixon, A. C., et al. (2018). Prevalence and characteristics of self-harm in adolescents: Meta-analyses of community-based studies 1990–2015. *Journal of the American Academy of Child and Adolescent Psychiatry, 57*(10), 733–741. https://doi.org/10.1016/j.jaac.2018.06.018

Hirschtritt, M. E., Ordóñez, A. E., Rico, Y. C., & LeWinn, K. Z. (2015). Internal resilience, peer victimization, and suicidal ideation among adolescents. *International Journal of Adolescent Medicine and Health*, *27*(4), 415–423. https://doi.org/10.1515/ijamh-2014-0060

International Society for the Study of Self-Injury. (2018). *What is self-injury*. https://itriples.org/about-self-injury/what-is-self-injury

Jacobson, C. M., & Gould, M. (2007). The epidemiology and phenomenology of non-suicidal self-injurious behavior among adolescents: A critical review of the literature. *Archives of Suicide Research*, *11*(2), 129–147. https://doi.org/10.1080/13811110701247602

Jarvi, S., Jackson, B., Swenson, L., & Crawford, H. (2013). The impact of social contagion on non-suicidal self-injury: A review of the literature. *Archives of Suicide Research*, *17*(1), 1–19. https://doi.org/10.1080/13811118.2013.748404

Jasso-Medrano, J. L., & López-Rosales, F. (2018). Measuring the relationship between social media use and addictive behavior and depression and suicide ideation among university students. *Computers in Human Behavior*, *87*, 183–191. https://doi.org/10.1016/j.chb.2018.05.003

John, A., Glendenning, A. C., Marchant, A., et al. (2018). Self-harm, suicidal behaviours, and cyberbullying in children and young people: Systematic review. *Journal of Medical Internet Research*, *20*(4), e129. https://doi.org/10.2196/jmir.9044

Joiner, T. E., Ribeiro, J. D., & Silva, C. (2012). Nonsuicidal self-injury, suicidal behavior, and their co-occurrence as viewed through the lens of the interpersonal theory of suicide. *Current Directions in Psychological Science*, *21*(5), 342–347. https://doi.org/10.1177/0963721412454873

Khasawneh, A., Madathil, K. C., Dixon, E., Wiśniewski, P., Zinzow, H., & Roth, R. (2020). Examining the self-harm and suicide contagion effects of the Blue Whale Challenge on YouTube and Twitter: Qualitative study. *JMIR Mental Health*, *7*(6), e15973. https://doi.org/10.2196/15973

Kiekens, G., Hasking, P., Boyes, M., et al. (2018). The associations between non-suicidal self-injury and first onset suicidal thoughts and behaviors. *Journal of Affective Disorders*, *239*, 171–179. https://doi.org/10.1016/j.jad.2018.06.033

Kim, J. Y. (2012). The nonlinear association between internet using time for non-educational purposes and adolescent health. *Journal of Preventive Medicine and Public Health*, *45*(1), 37–46. https://doi.org/10.3961/jpmph.2012.45.1.37

Kingsbury, M., Reme, B.-A., Skogen, J. C., et al. (2021). Differential associations between types of social media use and university students' non-suicidal self-injury and suicidal behavior. *Computers in Human Behavior*, *115*, Article 106614. https://doi.org/10.1016/j.chb.2020.106614

Klonsky, E. D. (2007). The functions of deliberate self-injury: A review of the evidence. *Clinical Psychology Review*, *27*(2), 226–239. https://doi.org/10.1016/j.cpr.2006.08.002

Kruzan, K. P., & Whitlock, J. (2019). Processes of change and nonsuicidal self-injury: A qualitative interview study with individuals at various stages of change. *Global Qualitative Nursing Research*, *6*. https://doi.org/10.1177/2333393619852935

Kruzan, K. P., Whitlock, J., & Bazarova, N. N. (2021). Examining the relationship between the use of a mobile peer-support app and self-injury outcomes: Longitudinal mixed methods study. *JMIR Mental Health*, *8*(1), e21854. https://doi.org/10.2196/21854

Kruzan, K. P., & Won, A. S. (2019). Embodied well-being through two media technologies: Virtual reality and social media. *New Media & Society*, *21*(8), 1734–1749. https://doi.org/10.1177/1461444819829873

Kumar, M., Dredze, M., Coppersmith, G., & De Choudhury, M. (2015). Detecting changes in suicide content manifested in social media following celebrity suicides. *Proceedings of the 26th ACM Conference on Hypertext & Social Media – HT'15*, 85–94. https://doi.org/10.1145/2700171.2791026

Lavis, A., & Winter, R. (2020). #Online harms or benefits? An ethnographic analysis of the positives and negatives of peer-support around self-harm on social media. *Journal of Child Psychology and Psychiatry*, *61*(8), 842–854. https://doi.org/10.1111/jcpp.13245

Lee, S. Y., Park, E.-C., Han, K.-T., Kim, S. J., Chun, S.-Y., & Park, S. (2016). The association of level of internet use with suicidal ideation and suicide attempts in South Korean adolescents: A focus on family structure and household economic status. *The Canadian Journal of Psychiatry*, *61*(4), 243–251. https://doi.org/10.1177/0706743716635550

Lewis, S. P., & Baker, T. G. (2011). The possible risks of self-injury web sites: A content analysis. *Archives of Suicide Research*, *15*(4), 390–396. https://doi.org/10.1080/13811118.2011.616154

Lewis, S. P., & Michal, N. J. (2016). Start, stop, and continue: Preliminary insight into the appeal of self-injury e-communities. *Journal of Health Psychology*, *21*(2), 250–260. https://doi.org/10.1177/1359105314527140

Lewis, S. P., & Seko, Y. (2016). A double-edged sword: A review of benefits and risks of online nonsuicidal self-injury activities. *Journal of Clinical Psychology*, *72*(3), 249–262. https://doi.org/10.1002/jclp.22242

Lewis, S. P., Seko, Y., & Joshi, P. (2018). The impact of YouTube peer feedback on attitudes toward recovery from non-suicidal self-injury: An experimental pilot study. *Digital Health*, *4*. https://doi.org/10.1177/2055207618780499

Li, A., Huang, X., Jiao, D., O'Dea, B., Zhu, T., & Christensen, H. (2018). An analysis of stigma and suicide literacy in responses to suicides broadcast on social media. *Asia-Pacific Psychiatry*, *10*(1), e12314. https://doi.org/10.1111/appy.12314

Marchant, A., Hawton, K., Stewart, A., et al. (2017). A systematic review of the relationship between internet use, self-harm and suicidal behaviour in young people: The good, the bad and the unknown. *PLoS ONE*, *12*(8), e0181722. https://doi.org/10.1371/journal.pone.0181722

Massing-Schaffer, M., & Nesi, J. (2020). Cybervictimization and suicide risk in adolescence: An integrative model of social media and suicide theories. *Adolescent Research Review*, *5*(1), 49–65. https://doi.org/10.1007/s40894-019-00116-y

Massing-Schaffer, M., Nesi, J., Telzer, E. H., Lindquist, K. A., & Prinstein, M. J. (2020). Adolescent peer experiences and prospective suicidal ideation: The protective role of online-only friendships. *Journal of Clinical Child & Adolescent Psychology*, 1–12. https://doi.org/10.1080/15374416.2020.1750019

Memon, A. M., Sharma, S. G., Mohite, S. S., & Jain, S. (2018). The role of online social networking on deliberate self-harm and suicidality in adolescents: A systematized review of literature. *Indian Journal of Psychiatry*, *60*(4), 384–400.

Mészáros, G., Győri, D., Horváth, L. O., Szentiványi, D., & Balázs, J. (2020). Nonsuicidal self-injury: Its associations with pathological internet use and psychopathology among adolescents. *Frontiers in Psychiatry*, *11*, Article 814. https://doi.org/10.3389/fpsyt.2020.00814

Miller, A. B., & Prinstein, M. J. (2019). Adolescent suicide as a failure of acute stress-response systems. *Annual Review of Clinical Psychology*, *15*, 425–450. https://doi.org/10.1146/annurev-clinpsy-050718-095625

Murray, C. D., & Fox, J. (2006). Do internet self-harm discussion groups alleviate or exacerbate self-harming behaviour? *Australian E-Journal for the Advancement of Mental Health*, *5*(3), 225–233. https://doi.org/10.5172/jamh.5.3.225

Naslund, J. A., Aschbrenner, K. A., Marsch, L. A., & Bartels, S. J. (2016). The future of mental health care: Peer-to-peer support and social media. *Epidemiology and Psychiatric Sciences; Verona*, *25*(2), 113–122. http://dx.doi.org.proxy.library.cornell.edu/10.1017/S2045796015001067

Nathan, N. A., & Nathan, K. I. (2020). Suicide, stigma, and utilizing social media platforms to gauge public perceptions. *Frontiers in Psychiatry*, *10*. https://doi.org/10.3389/fpsyt.2019.00947

Niederkrotenthaler, T., Fu, K., Yip, P. S. F., et al. (2012). Changes in suicide rates following media reports on celebrity suicide: A meta-analysis. *Journal of Epidemiology and Community Health*, *66*(11), 1037–1042. https://doi.org/10.1136/jech-2011-200707

Niederkrotenthaler, T., Stack, S., Till, B., et al. (2019). Association of increased youth suicides in the United States with the release of *13 Reasons Why*. *JAMA Psychiatry*, *76*(9), 933–940. https://doi.org/10.1001/jamapsychiatry.2019.0922

Nock, M. K., Borges, G., Bromet, E. J., et al. (2008). Cross-national prevalence and risk factors for suicidal ideation, plans and attempts. *British Journal of Psychiatry*, *192*(2), 98–105. https://doi.org/10.1192/bjp.bp.107.040113

Nock, M. K., Green, J. G., Hwang, I., et al. (2013). Prevalence, correlates, and treatment of lifetime suicidal behavior among adolescents: Results from the National Comorbidity Survey Replication Adolescent Supplement. *JAMA Psychiatry*, *70*(3), Article 300. https://doi.org/10.1001/2013.jamapsychiatry.55

Pater, J., & Mynatt, E. (2017). Defining digital self-harm. *Proceedings of the 2017 ACM Conference on Computer Supported Cooperative Work and Social Computing*, 1501–1513. https://doi.org/10.1145/2998181.2998224

Phillips, D. P. (1974). The influence of suggestion on suicide: Substantive and theoretical implications of the Werther effect. *American Sociological Review*, *39*(3), 340–354. https://doi.org/10.2307/2094294

Porras-Segovia, A., Pérez-Rodríguez, M. M., López-Esteban, P., et al. (2019). Contribution of sleep deprivation to suicidal behaviour: A systematic review. *Sleep Medicine Reviews*, *44*, 37–47. https://doi.org/10.1016/j.smrv.2018.12.005

Przybylski, A. K., & Weinstein, N. (2017). A large-scale test of the Goldilocks hypothesis: Quantifying the relations between digital-screen use and the mental well-being of adolescents. *Psychological Science*, *28*(2), 204–215. https://doi.org/10.1177/0956797616678438

Rideout, V., & Fox, S. (2018). Digital health practices, social media use, and mental well-being among teens and young adults in the U.S. *Providence St. Joseph Health*. https://digitalcommons.psjhealth.org/publications/1093

Rizvi, S. L., Hughes, C. D., & Thomas, M. C. (2016). The DBT Coach mobile application as an adjunct to treatment for suicidal and self-injuring individuals with borderline personality disorder: A preliminary evaluation and challenges to client utilization. *Psychological Services*, *13*(4), 380–388. https://doi.org/10.1037/ser0000100

Robinson, J., Cox, G., Bailey, E., et al. (2016). Social media and suicide prevention: A systematic review. *Early Intervention in Psychiatry*, *10*(2), 103–121. https://doi.org/10.1111/eip.12229

Robinson, J., Hill, N. T. M., Thorn, P., et al. (2018). The #chatsafe project. Developing guidelines to help young people communicate safely about suicide on social media: A Delphi study. *PLoS ONE*, *13*(11), e0206584. https://doi.org/10.1371/journal.pone.0206584

Rodham, K., Gavin, J., Lewis, S. P., St. Denis, J. M., & Bandalli, P. (2013). An investigation of the motivations driving the online representation of self-injury: A thematic analysis. *Archives of Suicide Research*, *17*(2), 173–183. https://doi.org/10.1080/13811118.2013.776459

Rodham, K., Gavin, J., & Miles, M. (2007). I hear, I listen and I care: A qualitative investigation into the function of a self-harm message board. *Suicide & Life-Threatening Behavior*, *37*(4), 422–430.

Rowe, S. L., Patel, K., French, R. S., et al. (2018). Web-based decision aid to assist help-seeking choices for young people who self-harm: Outcomes from a randomized controlled feasibility trial. *JMIR Mental Health*, *5*(1), e10. https://doi.org/10.2196/mental.8098

Sampasa-Kanyinga, H., & Lewis, R. F. (2015). Frequent use of social networking sites is associated with poor psychological functioning among children and adolescents. *Cyberpsychology, Behavior, and Social Networking*, *18*(7), 380–385. https://doi.org/10.1089/cyber.2015.0055

Sanson, M., Strange, D., & Garry, M. (2019). Trigger warnings are trivially helpful at reducing negative affect, intrusive thoughts, and avoidance. *Clinical Psychological Science*, *7*(4), 778–793. https://doi.org/10.1177/2167702619827018

Schemer, C., Masur, P. K., Geiß, S., Müller, P., & Schäfer, S. (2020). The impact of internet and social media use on well-being: A longitudinal analysis of adolescents across nine years. *Journal of Computer-Mediated Communication*, *26*(1), 1–21. https://doi.org/10.1093/jcmc/zmaa014

Schleider, J. L., & Weisz, J. R. (2017). Little treatments, promising effects? Meta-analysis of single-session interventions for youth psychiatric problems. *Journal of the American Academy of Child & Adolescent Psychiatry*, *56*(2), 107–115. https://doi.org/10.1016/j.jaac.2016.11.007

Schroeder, J., Wilkes, C., Rowan, K., et al. (2018). Pocket skills: A conversational mobile web app to support dialectical behavioral therapy. *Proceedings of the 2018 CHI Conference on Human Factors in Computing Systems – CHI'18*, 1–15. https://doi.org/10.1145/3173574.3173972

Sedgwick, R., Epstein, S., Dutta, R., & Ougrin, D. (2019). Social media, internet use and suicide attempts in adolescents. *Current Opinion in Psychiatry*, *32*(6), 534–541. https://doi.org/10.1097/YCO.0000000000000547

Seko, Y., Kidd, S. A., Wiljer, D., & McKenzie, K. J. (2015). On the creative edge: Exploring motivations for creating non-suicidal self-injury content online.

Qualitative Health Research, *25*(10), 1334–1346. https://doi.org/10.1177/1049732315570134

Seko, Y., & Lewis, S. P. (2018). The self – harmed, visualized, and reblogged: Remaking of self-injury narratives on Tumblr. *New Media & Society*, *20*(1), 180–198. https://doi.org/10.1177/1461444816660783

Silenzio, V. M. B., Duberstein, P. R., Tang, W., Lu, N., Tu, X., & Homan, C. M. (2009). Connecting the invisible dots: Reaching lesbian, gay, and bisexual adolescents and young adults at risk for suicide through online social networks. *Social Science & Medicine*, *69*(3), 469–474. https://doi.org/10.1016/j.socscimed.2009.05.029

Smithson, J., Sharkey, S., Hewis, E., et al. (2011). Problem presentation and responses on an online forum for young people who self-harm. *Discourse Studies*, *13*(4), 487–501. https://doi.org/10.1177/1461445611403356

Steinberg, L. (2010). A dual systems model of adolescent risk-taking. *Developmental Psychobiology*, *52*(3), 216–224. https://doi.org/10.1002/dev.20445

Sumner, S. A., Galik, S., Mathieu, J., et al. (2019). Temporal and geographic patterns of social media posts about an emerging suicide game. *Journal of Adolescent Health*, *65*(1), 94–100. https://doi.org/10.1016/j.jadohealth.2018.12.025

Swannell, S. V., Martin, G. E., Page, A., Hasking, P., & St John, N. J. (2014). Prevalence of nonsuicidal self-injury in nonclinical samples: Systematic review, meta-analysis and meta-regression. *Suicide & Life-Threatening Behavior*, *44*(3), 273–303. https://doi.org/10.1111/sltb.12070

Swedo, E. A., Beauregard, J. L., de Fijter, S., et al. (2020). Associations between social media and suicidal behaviors during a youth suicide cluster in Ohio. *Journal of Adolescent Health*, *68*(2), 308–316. https://doi.org/10.1016/j.jadohealth.2020.05.049

Thoits, P. A. (2011). Mechanisms linking social ties and support to physical and mental health. *Journal of Health and Social Behavior*, *52*(2), 145–161. https://doi.org/10.1177/0022146510395592

Thorn, P., Hill, N. T., Lamblin, M., et al. (2020). Developing a suicide prevention social media campaign with young people (the #chatsafe project): Co-design approach. *JMIR Mental Health*, *7*(5), e17520. https://doi.org/10.2196/17520

Twenge, J. M., & Campbell, W. K. (2019). Media use is linked to lower psychological well-being: Evidence from three datasets. *Psychiatric Quarterly*, *90*(2), 311–331. https://doi.org/10.1007/s11126–019-09630-7

US Senate. (2000). *Joint statement on the impact of entertainment violence on children*. http://www.senate.gov/~brownback/violencel.pdf

Valkenburg, P. M. (2017). Understanding self-effects in social media. *Human Communication Research*, *43*(4), 477–490. https://doi.org/10.1111/hcre.12113

Verduyn, P., Ybarra, O., Résibois, M., Jonides, J., & Kross, E. (2017). A critical review: Do social network sites enhance or undermine subjective well-being? *Social Issues and Policy Review*, *11*(1), 274–302. https://doi.org/10.1111/sipr.12033

Verkooijen, S., de Vos, N., Bakker-Camu, B. J. W., et al. (2018). Sleep disturbances, psychosocial difficulties, and health risk behavior in 16,781 Dutch adolescents. *Academic Pediatrics*, *18*(6), 655–661. https://doi.org/10.1016/j.acap.2018.03.003

Walsh, C. G., Ribeiro, J. D., & Franklin, J. C. (2017). Predicting risk of suicide attempts over time through machine learning. *Clinical Psychological Science*, *5*(3), 457–469. https://doi.org/10.1177/2167702617691560

Wang, J.-L., Wang, H.-Z., Gaskin, J., & Hawk, S. (2017). The mediating roles of upward social comparison and self-esteem and the moderating role of social comparison orientation in the association between social networking site usage and subjective well-being. *Frontiers in Psychology*, *8*. https://doi.org/10.3389/fpsyg.2017.00771

Wartella, E., & Reeves, B. (1985). Historical trends in research on children and the media: 1900–1960. *Journal of Communication*, *35*(2), 118–133. https://doi.org/10.1111/j.1460-2466.1985.tb02238.x

Westers, N. J., Lewis, S. P., Whitlock, J., et al. (2020). Media guidelines for the responsible reporting and depicting of non-suicidal self-injury. *The British Journal of Psychiatry*, *219*(2), 1–4. https://doi.org/10.1192/bjp.2020.191

Whitlock, J., Lader, W., & Conterio, K. (2007). The internet and self-injury: What psychotherapists should know. *Journal of Clinical Psychology*, *63*(11), 1135–1143. https://doi.org/10.1002/jclp.20420

Whitlock, J., & Masur, P. (2019). Disentangling the association of screen time with developmental outcomes and well-being: Problems, challenges, and opportunities. *JAMA Pediatrics*, *173*(11), 1021–1022. https://doi.org/10.1001/jamapediatrics.2019.3191

Whitlock, J. L., Powers, J. L., & Eckenrode, J. (2006). The virtual cutting edge: The internet and adolescent self-injury. *Developmental Psychology*, *42*(3), 407–417. https://doi.org/10.1037/0012-1649.42.3.407

PART IV

Intervention and Prevention in the Digital Age

15 School-Based Initiatives Promoting Digital Citizenship and Healthy Digital Media Use

Emily Weinstein and Carrie James

Supporting adolescents toward healthy digital media use and digital citizenship more broadly "takes a village" (Hollandsworth et al., 2011). Chapters in this volume have touched on different aspects of digital media use and adolescent mental health, pointing to the importance of clinical intervention. Schools are another crucial entry point for delivery of support and prevention of future mental health difficulties. Educators have considerable reach to a captive audience of youth. Examining why, what, and how they teach students about digital media use and well-being is vital. In this chapter, we review leading K–12 digital media curricula that aim to teach students how to lead healthy digital lives. We outline the content and pedagogical approaches present in these materials and distill a set of learning goals apparent across curricular resources: critical awareness, self-reflection, and behavioral change. Given the relative absence of external evaluations of school-based interventions, we draw on relevant research to suggest both promising directions and key questions for future research.

Why do schools take on healthy digital media use and digital citizenship more broadly as a topic of instruction and intervention? At least four distinct drivers are arguably at play: problems, parents, precedent, and policies. First, *problems:* Digital and social media are meaningful venues for young people's learning and lives beyond the classroom (Ito et al., 2020). As adolescents use apps for peer connection, there are meaningful upsides but also inevitable conflicts. Conflicts that start online routinely spill over into schools, creating problems educators must solve through reactive sanctions, proactive classroom lessons, or both (Hinduja & Patchin, 2011). Other problems that educators feel pressed to solve include in-school device misuse, distraction, and inattention in class due to media-linked sleep deprivation (e.g., Klein, 2020; Sparks, 2013).

We are grateful to Chloe Brenner for her exemplary research support and detailed reviews of lesson plans and resources. Thanks also to the program creators and team members who provided us with access to and information about the programs reviewed as part of this chapter. We also acknowledge Anne Collier and Kelly Mendoza for sharing helpful insights about the state of the field of school-based interventions related to healthy digital media use. Finally, we wish to disclose that we are ongoing partners with Common Sense Education, one of the program providers whose curriculum was reviewed as part of this chapter. Both authors have worked closely with Common Sense on research and development related to their Digital Citizenship curriculum.

Second, *parents* are searching for support as they raise the first generation of digital youth (Palfrey & Gasser, 2011). They may turn to schools for guidance, or even demand that schools intervene when issues like digital drama or cyberbullying cases involve their children and fellow students. Third, *precedent*: in many schools, there is a long history of teaching relevant topics, including media literacy, news and information literacy, and health and wellness. Teachers of these topics have naturally (even if reluctantly) had to incorporate digital media into their class content in order to keep it relevant. Fourth, *policies*: The above factors have triggered school device policies to which enrolled students must consent, especially in schools with one-to-one laptop or tablet programs. However, schools are not the only policy drivers. Increasingly, schools themselves are subject to state policies that suggest or even mandate teaching of digital topics (Media Literacy Now, 2020; Phillips & Lee, 2019). For example, in 2019, the state of Texas passed legislation requiring school districts to incorporate digital citizenship (defined as "appropriate, responsible, and healthy online behavior") into curricula and instruction (Media Literacy Now, 2020, p. 12).

In sum, *problems, parents, precedent*, and *policies* create a demand for resources to support digital citizenship and healthy digital media use. Comprehensive curricula and other resources for schools emerged in the 2000s in response, initially with a focus on internet safety and then with the expanded purview and framing of "digital citizenship" (Cortesi et al., 2020). While these curricula center on the Internet and social media, they build on a longer tradition of media literacy education (MLE). MLE has long advocated competences for informed and critical reflection about media. Through MLE, students develop a core recognition that media messages are constructed and a related understanding of the persuasion techniques used in ads and other mass media (Hobbs, 2010). Now expanded to encompass "'the digital," contemporary MLE spans skills and knowledge for critical reflection about digital content (i.e., posts produced by others and oneself) as well as traditional mass media content. Protection and empowerment are dual motivations for digital and media literacy education: building essential literacies to protect youth from potential risks (e.g., harm to their psychological well-being) and empower them to leverage media benefits (e.g., for learning, social connection) (Hobbs, 2017).

Digital citizenship encompasses all of the skills for participation in a digital world – personally, socially, and civically – including essential "new media literacies" (Cortesi et al., 2020; Jenkins, 2009). Mike Ribble and Gerald Bailey, who were among the first to use the term *digital citizenship*, named digital health and wellness as a key aspect of digital citizenship in the first edition of their book, *Digital Citizenship in Schools* (2007). At the time, they emphasized physical health and framed the topic in relation to protection from harms like carpal tunnel, poor posture, and eye strain through improper ergonomics. Ribble and Bailey also referenced psychological well-being and internet addiction, which they acknowledged as "another aspect of digital safety that has not received the attention it deserves" (p. 32).

Psychological well-being is no longer at the margins of discussions about digital life. In recent years, technology overuse and psychological well-being have been a steady focus in both public discourse and academic research. These topics have also been a source of considerable debate among researchers. As discussed throughout this volume, research currently converges around a recognition that young people are differentially susceptible to digital media impacts (See Subrahmanyam & Michikyan, Chapter 1 in this volume; Valkenburg, Chapter 2 in this volume). Individual, social, and contextual risk factors present in adolescents' offline lives are often mirrored or amplified as they use digital media. For example, adolescents who have mental health challenges, those who are victimized, those who have limited family resources, and those who are surrounded by more offline violence in their communities all face digital risks that can impact their health and well-being (e.g., see Nesi et al., 2019; Odgers, 2018; Patton et al., 2016; Underwood & Ehrenreich, 2017). And yet, digital media use can also reduce or mitigate offline risk (Ito et al., 2020). Youth who are ostracized *offline* can find supportive community connections and resources for coping and recovery *online*.

The design features of technologies also shape their use in ways that matter for adolescent health and well-being. Today's apps and devices are designed with features that are intentionally tested, iterated, and deployed to hold users' attention (Center for Humane Technology, 2020a). For example, social media apps provide an endless stream of intermittent rewards (Alter, 2017; Center for Humane Tech, 2020a, 2020b). Features like infinite scrolling remove natural stopping cues. Default push notifications interrupt other activities. And metrics like Snapchat streaks capitalize on social reciprocity. These features leverage psychological vulnerabilities to create powerful habits loops and even, in some cases, behavioral addictions (Alter, 2017).

Although individual youth are differentially vulnerable to these design tactics, from a developmental standpoint all adolescents are in a position of vulnerability given their sensitivity to social feedback and peer acceptance (Steinberg, 2014). At the same time, the neural bases for impulse control are still developing (Dahl, 2004; Tamm et al., 2002). Thus, contemporary adolescents are in a precarious position: the rewards social media offer are compelling *and* their capacities for self-regulation are not yet fully mature. Given that avoiding digital technology all together is neither desirable nor practical, learning how to use it in ways that promote rather than diminish health and well-being is arguably crucial. Schools represent an opportune context for this learning given their reach to a wide audience of youth and the frequent role of schools (whether realized or aspirational) in providing guidance related to matters of health and well-being (e.g., health class and drug and alcohol prevention efforts).

Digital Citizenship and Related Curricula for School-Based Approaches

To examine existing school-based approaches to support healthy digital technology use, we conducted a two-phase review of available curricula. First, we identified and reviewed leading digital citizenship programs and lessons (Table 15.1). Second, we conducted a closer examination of curricular resources identified in Step 1 that addressed healthy digital habits.

In the first phase of our review, we identified 20 relevant programs through (1) Google search, (2) consultation with experts, (3) review of educator resource "round ups" (e.g., via Edutopia), and (4) a recent comprehensive report on digital citizenship frameworks and approaches (Cortesi et al., 2020). With one exception (Center for Humane Technology), all programs we reviewed are framed as curricula, lessons, and/or classroom resources designed for use in K–12 school contexts. All are described as resources for supporting digital media use, often under the label of "digital citizenship." We did not examine programs related to coding or computer science skills, nor did we focus on programs that incorporate but do not center technology use (for example, programs focused on self-harm and suicide prevention that may also cover the role of online communities).

In Table 15.1, we outline for each program (as of Fall 2020) the structure and format of resources, target grade levels, fee structure, and whether each program provides explicit instruction on the following common digital citizenship topics: cyberbullying and drama; identity expression and digital footprints; information quality and news literacy; privacy and safety; sexting; friendship and communication; violent and/or explicit content; and healthy digital habits.

All of these topics are relevant to healthy digital media use and individual well-being. A few examples: Cyberbullying is linked to poor psychosocial functioning, increased likelihood of self-injury, and poor physical health, as well as diminished academic performance (Kowalski et al., 2014). Certain types of sexting are associated with internalizing problems (depression/anxiety) and risky sexual health behaviors, particularly for younger adolescents (Mori et al., 2019). Self-expression and digital footprints are intertwined with identity development, which is a key task of adolescence and healthy psychosocial development for all youth (Davis & Weinstein, 2017). Depressed adolescents also report online self-expression practices like oversharing, "stressed posting," and disclosing their own mental health issues (Nesi et al., 2019; Radovic et al., 2017). These practices may amplify short-term risks (e.g., because they contribute algorithmic inputs that suggest an interest in depressogenic or triggering content) and create lasting digital footprints with sensitive mental health information. Graphic, violent content in video games and pornography is a persistent focus of adult concern, though causal impacts on youth health and behavior remain a source of contention among researchers (Anderson, 2003; Ferguson, 2020; Gentile, 2011; Kohut & Štulhofer, 2018).

Table 15.1 *Digital citizenship curricula and resources*

				Topics addressed[1]							
Program	Resource structure	Target grade levels	Fee structure	Cyber-bullying, drama	Identity, dig. footprints	Info. quality, news literacy	Privacy, safety	Sexting	Communi-cation, Friendship	Violent and/or explicit content	Digital media habits, balance
Be Internet Awesome - Digital Safety & Citizenship Curriculum (Google)	Curriculum of 5 units with 26 lesson activities and an online game (Interland)	2–6	Free	■	■	■	■		■		
Cyberbalance and Healthy Content Choices Curriculum (iKeepSafe)	3 lessons (1 lesson for students in grades K–5, 2 lessons for grades 7–12) with YouTube playlists for each lesson and an illustrated e-book series for elementary students	K–12	Free	■	■	■	■			■	■
Cyber Civics Classroom Curriculum (CyberWise)	3-year middle school curriculum of 50+ lessons organized in 6–8 units per grade level	6–8	Paid (pricing based on number of students)	■	■			■			■
Digital Citizenship Curriculum (Common Sense Education)	Curriculum of 50+ lessons across 6 topical areas with ~1–2 lessons per topic per grade from K–12 and several interactive online games	K–12	Free	■	■	■	■	■	■	■	■

Table 15.1 (*cont.*)

Program	Resource structure	Target grade levels	Fee structure	Topics addressed[1]							
				Cyber-bullying, drama	Identity, dig. footprints	Info. quality, news literacy	Privacy, safety	Sexting	Communi-cation, Friendship	Violent and/or explicit content	Digital media habits, balance
Digital Citizenship+ Resource Platform (Berkman Klein Center at Harvard University)	Resource library of lessons, infographics, videos, podcasts, and guides spanning 17 topics	6–12	Free	■	■	■	■		■		■
Digital Citizenship Collection (BrainPOP)	20 self-guided, interactive online lessons; curriculum for grades 3–5 provides additional lesson supports and sequencing for a selection of these lessons	3–12	Paid subscription	■	■	■	■		■		
Digital Citizenship (Digital Futures Initiative)	3 lessons (1 lesson per grade for grades 7–9) each touching briefly on a range of digital topics; required educator training course	7–9	Free	■	■	■	■	■	■		■
Digital Literacy & Citizenship Curriculum (Google & iKeepSafe)	Curriculum of 3 workshop lesson plans	6–8	Free	■	■	■	■				

Organization	Description	Grade level	Cost
DQ (DQ Institute)	8-week self-directed online digital citizenship course via an interactive adventure game that builds and scores "Digital IQ"	3–6	Free basic plan, paid premium plan
Human Relations Media	Collection of 19 streamable videos with corresponding teacher guides, each on a different topic related to social media and youth	K–12	Paid (each video purchased separately)
InCTRL (Cable Impacts Foundation)	7 lessons, each on a different topic	4–8	Free
Media Education Lab (University of Rhode Island)	Resource library with an assortment of media literacy lesson guides, curricula, and multi-media resources (e.g., podcasts, magazines)	Not specified	Includes both free and paid resources
Media Lessons and Resources (MediaSmarts, Canada's Centre for Digital and Media Literacy)	Resource library with 50+ lessons searchable by grade level and/or topic	K–12	Free

Table 15.1 (*cont.*)

Program	Resource structure	Target grade levels	Fee structure	Topics addressed[1]							
				Cyber-bullying, drama	Identity, dig. footprints	Info. quality, news literacy	Privacy, safety	Sexting	Communication, Friendship	Violent and/or explicit content	Digital media balance
Screenshots Curriculum (Media Power Youth)	Curriculum of 9 lessons organized as 3 units with corresponding podcast, videos, and PowerPoints (note: Media Power Youth's after-school program was not included in this review)	6–8	Free and paid options	■	■	■	■		■	■	■
NetSmartz (National Center for Missing & Exploited Children)	Four PowerPoint-based lessons on online safety (one each per grades K–2, 3–5, 6–8, 9–12); animated video series with lesson activities for K–3 (Into the Cloud); 3 elementary e-books with discussion guides	K–12	Free	■	■		■	■	■	■	
News Literacy Project	E-learning platform (Checkology) with 13 lessons and other resources for teaching news literacy, including misinformation	4-12	Free			■					

Resource	Description	Grade Level	Cost
The Digital Citizenship Handbook for School Leaders: Fostering Positive Interactions Online (Ribble & Park, 2019)	Book with a framework and progression chart that outlines 9 elements of digital citizenship and corresponding classroom activities	K–12	Free tip sheet; book available for purchase
Internet Safety (The Safe Side)	Week-long curriculum with 5 lessons (designed to be taught 1 per day) and an accompanying YouTube video	K–3	Free
Talks and Guidelines for Families & Educators (Center for Humane Technology)	Video-recorded presentation on persuasive technology; "Take Control" tech tips and strategies	Not specified; likely most relevant for 6–12	Free (video of recorded talk available on Vimeo); paid guest speaker talks
White Ribbon Week	4 week-long curriculum units with 5 lessons each; designed for a whole-school approach where school takes on 1 topic per year, 1 lesson per day	K–5	Paid (each unit purchased separately)

Notes: Shading key: *dark grey* = designated topic, covered in depth; *light grey* = topic mentioned or covered to some extent; *white* = not covered based on our review of resources.

[1] These topics reflect common categories based on our review and may not align exactly with the terminology used within a particular resource. In some cases, multiple topics are covered within the context of a particular unit or lesson.

Available school-based programs that address topics relevant to adolescent well-being vary considerably in their approaches. Some programs provide brief coverage of a topic, while others offer multiple lessons for a deeper dive. Some have one resource set that is designed for applicability to students across multiple grade levels, while others are grade differentiated. Programs that have resources framed as applicable across multiple grade levels include: The Center for Humane Technology, which currently has a single signature video-recorded presentation and related technology tips and strategies; Google's Be Internet Awesome curriculum, which has a collection of lessons that are all framed as best-suited for students in grades 2–6; and White Ribbon Week, which also uses the same lessons across a grade band (in their case, all elementary school grade levels). Other programs are grade differentiated: Common Sense Education, for example, has different lessons aligned to every year of school from kindergarten through 12th grade and CyberWise has lessons for each year of middle school. Across programs, some lessons are structured around a lecture-style presentation while others are interactive and use discussion questions, writing prompts, or hypothetical scenarios to engage students through more constructivist approaches (where learners actively make meaning of content and their personal connections to it). Most have mixed-media elements and a few have their own full-fledged online games (e.g., Be Internet Awesome, Common Sense Education, and DQ). Nearly all of the programs have educator tips, guides, or resources to support teaching and several have comprehensive professional development training (e.g., webinars, courses, and certification programs).

Even a brief review of the lessons also reveals considerable variation in how different programs approach the same topic. For example, with respect to cyberbullying, programs vary in how much time they allot to the topic (e.g., is cyberbullying a passing mention or the focus of multiple lessons?); in pedagogical approaches (e.g., do teachers provide students with strategies for dealing with cyberbullying and/or ask students to come up with their own ideas?); and – perhaps most crucially – in both implicit and explicit messages about the topic (e.g., are students primarily encouraged to be *allies* who stand with targets or to be *upstanders* who stand up to aggressors?). Each topic area listed in Table 15.1 could reasonably be the focus of a full review to examine these key messages and approaches and how they map to existing research. Given our focus in this chapter on healthy media use, we conducted a review of lessons that aim to promote healthy digital habits (i.e., those in the far-right column of the table, which is outlined and labeled "Digital Habits, Media Balance").

A Closer Look at School-Based Lessons to Promote Healthy Digital Habits

The second phase of our review was a more focused examination of resources from across these programs that aim to promote healthy digital habits. To our knowledge, none of these lessons has yet been systematically evaluated. We therefore provide a descriptive review of what the available lessons teach about healthy technology use and how they approach this aim. All of the lessons we reviewed on healthy digital habits emphasize one or more of the following learning goals: (1) critical awareness of design features and/or psychological principles that shape technology use; (2) self-reflection on personal digital media use; and (3) strategies for behavioral change. In the following sections, we review these learning goals in turn. We provide examples of how each learning goal is approached in lessons about healthy digital media use, discuss how and why it might help promote healthy media use, and outline relevant questions for future research to build an evidence base for school-based approaches.

Critical Awareness of Design Features and Psychological Principles

One recurring aim of lessons designed to promote healthy digital media use is critical awareness and understanding. These lessons metaphorically pull back the curtain and reveal to students how digital features and design can powerfully intersect with psychological processes to shape technology experiences. Lessons from all but one program included an emphasis on this kind of critical awareness. Examples include teaching students:

- how platforms harness data to push *tailored content* and *targeted ads* based on interests and browsing history;
- how features like *infinite scroll* and *auto-play* intentionally remove friction to make for seamless ongoing use;
- how *metrics*, especially "likes" and "streaks," play off motives related to social status and instincts for social reciprocity;
- how social media contributes to *highlight reels* that are ripe for social comparison and contribute to a common experience of feeling bad when scrolling through a social media feed;
- how social media apps and gaming platforms leverage *variable rewards* much in the same way as casino slot machines to create a compelling unconscious reward structure;
- how social networks can function as *echo chambers* that distort perceptions;
- how *misinformation* is presented in ways that look real and promote circulation;
- how to recognize *active versus passive uses* of technology, which seem to differentially impact well-being; and
- how digital features like notifications and/or content like pornography activate *dopamine reward circuits*.

How and why might this kind of learning promote healthy digital media use? In traditional media literacy education, students learn that media messages are constructed, and they learn to recognize and analyze techniques that influence persuasion (National Association for Media Literacy Education, 2007). Critical thinking is seen as key to "liberating the individual from unquestioning dependence on immediate cultural environment" (Brown, 1998, p. 47). A meta-analysis of 51 traditional media literacy interventions indeed found significant positive effects on students' knowledge and critical understanding (Jeong et al., 2012). More recent experimental research demonstrated that teaching adolescents about "addictive" social media designs and their harmful effects can prompt enduring awareness of design features. It can also motivate young people's interest in regulating their social media use and in learning relevant strategies (Galla et al., 2021).

Jeong and colleagues' meta-analysis of traditional media literacy interventions indicated that: a) passive teaching approaches (e.g., lecture-style) and interactive approaches (e.g., discussion, role playing, games) were both effective, b) that lessons could be successfully delivered by peers or by expert instructors, and c) interventions with a greater number of sessions tended to have larger effect sizes. These insights may prove relevant for curricula aiming to promote healthy digital media use. That is, students may similarly benefit from learning how digital tools and content are constructed and how these constructions influence perception and persuasion. While varied pedagogies and lesson contexts hold potential value, repeated lessons are likely more effective than isolated "one-and-done" approaches. That said, these are still open questions for research on digital habits interventions, and especially so given emerging evidence related to the value of single-session interventions for mental health (Schleider et al., 2020). Further questions include: Do passive versus interactive approaches change learning outcomes related to critical awareness about digital media? Which formats (expert instruction, peer-based, etc.) are most effective? Further, in terms of content, which digital design features and principles are most relevant to include in curricula? And more generally, there is the crucial question of efficacy: Does teaching for critical awareness indeed impact students' digital technology experiences and – if so – how?

Available digital media lessons aim to help students identify features that unconsciously drive their technology use. In addition to building students' knowledge, recognizing these features and design tactics may also motivate their desires to take action toward more control. However, critical understanding alone is likely an insufficient catalyst for behavioral change. Jeong et al.'s (2012) meta-analysis indicated that media literacy interventions seemed to have greater effects on knowledge-related outcomes than on behavior-related outcomes. Relatedly, research from behavioral economics suggests that even when people know a strategy is being used to "nudge" their behavior, this knowledge does not remove its effect (e.g., Bruns et al., 2018). Thus, lessons designed to impact healthy digital media use are likely wise to include a focus on critical understanding, but such understanding may prove insufficient to successfully reroute digital habits.

Self-Reflection about Personal Digital Media Use

Self-reflection is a second prominent learning goal in lessons that target healthy digital media habits. This is driven by fundamentally interactive (rather than lecture-based) activities that typically direct students to consider some aspect of their personal digital media use. In existing lessons within the digital citizenship programs we reviewed, self-reflection ranged from open-ended brainstorming about personal tech habits to the use of more templatized tools for logs and tracking. Such tools differ in both structure and in the focal behaviors they prompt students to consider. For example, CyberCivics provides a "Time Tracker" template where students log every activity (including but not limited to technology use) from morning until night and note the time spent, in minutes, on each activity. Students then bring their trackers to class, total their time on different activities, and use the data to make observations about their "digital diets." InCTRL has a "24/7" log for tracking total technology time each day for a week. White Ribbon Week uses a circle graph divided into 24 slices where students shade in the number of hours they spend on different activities and then discuss what it means to "balance" a day. Common Sense has a "Media Choices Inventory" (embedded in a 7th-grade lesson), which prompts students to reflect on their media use from the prior day: "What media did you use?" "When did you use it?" (e.g., morning), "How much time did you spend?" (in minutes), and "How did you feel?" MediaSmarts offers a "Media Diary" where students fill out a checklist each day for a week to indicate "What I did using screen media" by checking boxes that correspond to digital activities like entertainment, keeping in touch, seeing what people are doing, posting or browsing photos, online learning, and music. Students simultaneously keep a separate "Mood Diary" focused on tracking, for each day, how they "experienced my different relationships and connections today" and then "How I felt today" overall. Other self-reflection lessons do not include logging tools but take approaches like directing students to take stock of all current digital habits and how each habit makes them feel (Common Sense, "Digital Habits Check-up"), or completing a "Digital Stress Self-test" to notice problematic digital habits (Media Smarts, "Dealing with Digital Stress").

The aforementioned lessons share an emphasis on promoting healthy digital media use by building students' awareness of their own technology habits. Keeping a media-use diary is an established approach in traditional media literacy education (Hobbs, 2010). As Hobbs describes, "record-keeping activities help people keep track of media choices and reflect on decisions about sharing and participation, deepening awareness of personal habits" (p. 23). In the context of digital media, negative outcomes from technology use are often mediated by negative experiences people have while using technology (e.g., social comparison, FOMO; Burnell et al., 2019). Noticing and disrupting negative digital experiences may therefore serve a protective function.

Recognizing, for example, that browsing Instagram before bed is contributing to anxious thoughts or that TikTok is a source of unwanted distraction during homework time can set the stage for making different choices. In this vein, Carrier and colleagues (2018) argue for *digital metacognition* as a relevant digital-age coping practice. They argue that critical self-reflection facilitates digital metacognition, which involves thinking intentionally and strategically about one's technology choices. Self-reflection tools that help students draw links between specific digital activities and corresponding emotional reactions ostensibly support digital metacognition. At the same time, research is clear that *how* young people use technology is more important than simply *how much* they use (Reeves et al., 2020). Self-reflection lessons that place heavy emphasis on logging screen time without further differentiation (e.g., of how time is spent or what emotions it evokes) may therefore prove less effective.

These are, for the most part, hypotheses rather than conclusions. That said, one cluster randomized controlled trial of a school-based intervention in German schools showed promising results of a media intervention anchored in self-reflection that was designed to build metacognition related to online gaming activities (Walther et al., 2014). Future research should examine the specific curricular features that support effective digital self-reflection lessons: Does it make a difference if students reflect generally about digital habits versus if they track technology use? If tracking technology use is effective, what is the optimal duration for tracking (e.g., one day, one week) and what, specifically, should students be prompted to track (e.g., time spent, activities, emotional reactions)? How can curricula prompt both a light-bulb-type recognition of digital experiences and, crucially, support dispositional tendencies toward ongoing digital metacognition? Given that young people's cognitive capacities for self-reflection develop over time, it may also be important to explore how different kinds of self-reflective activities align with students' ages and developmental stages.

Behavioral Change for Healthy Digital Habits

Naturally, the end goal of much curriculum is behavioral change outside of the classroom: helping students establish and maintain healthy technology use in their real lives. Nearly all of the existing lessons we reviewed urge "balance" as a key aim. Some lessons utilize metaphors to concretize the finite nature of time and/or help students consider ways to balance technology with other activities or priorities. The Center for Humane Technology uses an "empty glass" metaphor to guide students' thinking about the activities they use to fill their time. iKeepSafe uses the idea of a "rock garden of our life" to help students prioritize time spent on important "boulders" (career goals, friends) and "pebbles" (school work), and "grains of sand" (screen time). MediaSmarts uses the metaphor of a "media diet" with older students (this metaphor is also used by CyberWise); for younger students, the concept of balance is conveyed through an equally divided pie chart that has separate portions students fill out for active time, learning time, and screen time.

One way in which lessons try to help students achieve balance is through intention-setting activities. These involve making commitments that help bound screen time and facilitate other priorities and activities. Templates guide students in making "pledges" about their technology use (e.g., DQ Institute and iKeepSafe) or to work with their parents/guardians on "family media agreements" (e.g., Common Sense). Lessons also seek to support healthy habits in students' lives outside of the classroom by teaching specific behavioral strategies. On-device strategies include, for example:

- using apps to track and manage screen time;
- adding browser extensions that support focused study time;
- unfollowing or muting social media accounts that evoke negative reactions;
- switching phone screens to grey scale;
- turning off push notifications; and
- trying to prioritize active rather than passive activities on social media.

Off-device strategies include practices like:

- putting phones out of sight before bed;
- using a "phone stack" when hanging out with friends to reduce digital distractions during face-to-face socializing;
- scheduling screen time and screen-free time in advance;
- keeping a personal inventory of favorite offline activities (e.g., basketball, coloring, yoga) to refer back to; and
- identifying self-soothing and/or active nondigital activities that relieve boredom or sadness.

Another avenue toward behavioral change is scaffolding more deliberate personal challenges in which students actually try out strategies or plans that change their typical media habits. These challenges take the form of instructor-prompted digital media breaks (CyberWise, "Social Media Vacation"; MediaSmarts, "Disconnection Challenge"; Digital Future Initiative, "Digital Time Out") and student-designed experiments to change a specific digital habit of their choice (Common Sense Education, "Digital Habits Check-Up"; White Ribbon Week, "Device-Free Zone"). Memorable heuristics like rhymes, acronyms, and thinking routines are used in some lessons to encourage retention of key principles. Examples include Common Sense's "pause, breathe, finish up" saying to help younger students wrap up their technology use and Digital Future Initiative's D framework "4 C's" (Count to ten, Consider possible consequences, Careful with moods and emotions, Check for advice).

We still have much to learn about whether, how, and why these approaches actually enable healthy digital media behaviors. Technology pledges and agreements are one type of intervention that warrants focused study. On the one hand, these tools may facilitate proactive planning that supports digital metacognition and establishes valuable boundaries, in addition to catalyzing conversations between youth and their parents/caregivers. Research on rule-setting related to technology use is mixed, though, and generally suggests that compliance (or a lack thereof) is shaped by the *content* of the rules and young people's *relationships* with the adults who are designing, implementing, and enforcing those rules (e.g., Hiniker et al., 2016; Kesten et al., 2015). Technology limits handed down from adults can be ineffective or outright backfire (Samuel, 2015). Further, research on student pledges related to honor codes suggests that asking students to simply make a one-time pledge to follow a preconstructed set of principles is insufficient (LoSchiavo & Shatz, 2011). The idea that students will make commitments about their technology use and then simply follow through on those plans may also overlook the impacts of persuasive design features (Alter, 2017), social pulls and pressures, and developmental changes as students get older. Likely, the value of pledges and media agreements depends on how they are developed and then used. Relevant, too, is the aforementioned experimental research, which demonstrated that education about persuasive tech design features – presented alongside messages about autonomy and social justice – can boost adolescents' motivation to self-regulate social media use (Galla et al., 2021). Yet these experiments also underscore that motivational changes are no guarantees of lasting behavioral change (Galla et al., 2021).

Learning behavioral strategies may build digital agency and support self-regulation. Agency and efficacy – which both involve competence, confidence, and control – are inherently linked to psychological well-being (e.g., Bandura, 1989). Students have *digital agency* when they can control and manage their personal uses of technologies (Passey et al., 2018). The strategies embedded in existing lessons arguably add "friction" to disrupt typical routines and unwanted, automatic behaviors – a crucial principle of habit change (Clear, 2018). For example, strategies like using a phone stack create friction against the habit of instinctively checking messages during a dinner with friends; disabling push notifications reduces the otherwise ongoing diversion of attention that can derail focus during study time. However, it is not clear whether the strategies advocated in current lessons cover the most relevant approaches used by savvy youth. A key area for future research is identifying behavioral strategies that adolescents are already using and/or which resonate with their authentic device struggles and self-identified values and goals. Relatedly, what paves the way from learning about a strategy in class to trying it outside of the classroom, and to deploying it on a routine basis?

Digital Citizenship Education: State of the Field

Above, we describe a suite of potentially promising pedagogies keyed to three crucial learning goals for supporting healthy digital habits. In Figure 15.1, we distill these three distinct learning goals of existing digital habits lessons and

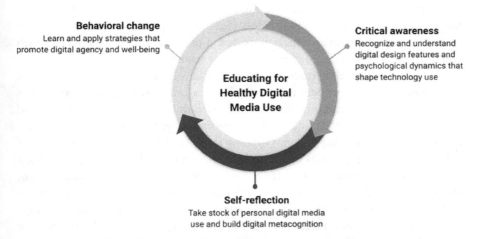

Figure 15.1 *Educating for healthy digital media use: three core learning goals*

propose a cyclical relationship among them. Although we developed this model based on our review of lessons that target digital habits and media balance, it holds broader relevance for other aspects of technology use – such as online sharing and digital footprints. This model may offer a guide for assessing digital citizenship lesson content and pedagogies.

These three focal aims – *critical awareness, self-reflection,* and *behavioral change* – likely have relevance beyond school settings, too, and particularly for mental health professionals who work directly with youth. Consider, for example, a teen whose struggle with depression appears to be exacerbated by social comparison on social media (Nesi & Prinstein, 2015). Building critical awareness could begin with discussion of the ways social media feeds can function as highlight reels that invite comparison (Weinstein, 2017). Self-reflection might then involve engaging the teen in a process of self-identifying whether and when this pattern holds in their personal media use: Are there specific accounts that lead them to compare themself to others in ways that erode their mood or well-being? This self-reflection step could include building digital metacognition so that they begin to self-monitor and recognize when comparative thinking comes up in their everyday media use. Behavioral change could be supported through active strategies, like curating their social media feed(s) by unfollowing accounts that spark toxic comparison and adding accounts that encourage recovery and spark inspiration.

Returning to the context of school-based efforts, our review confirms over-all that there are a number of available resources designed for digital citizen-ship and the intended promotion of healthy digital habits. Many of these resources are free, well-developed materials that are ready for immediate use and accompanied by detailed guidance for facilitators. Educators who are interested in promoting healthy digital media use will likely have little trouble finding relevant supports. What is less clear at this point is whether available resources actually achieve their intended aims and, more generally, which pedagogical approaches are effective and for whom.

We caution, too, that research about digital citizenship topics themselves (e.g., young people's experiences with digital drama, sexting pressures, news and civic life, and creating healthy digital habits) is rapidly evolving and extremely relevant to the content of classroom lessons. Notably, in some cases, research consensus is hard won. Ongoing debates about the interpretations of evidence regarding impacts of technology use on mental health are a relevant example. It is understandable, then, that creators of school programs might struggle to distill the latest empirical research into clear, age-appropriate instructional content and classroom materials. In reviewing the digital habits lessons, we saw at least three instances of decisive curricular messages that are arguably misaligned with current research: (1) using the language of "addiction" to characterize everyday media habits; (2) describing a causal relationship between media activities and mental health issues (e.g., depression, anxiety, suicide risk); and (3) emphasizing total screen time without any attention to the types of digital activities that comprise that time. In addition to including potentially problematic messages, we noted examples of simplistic and likely ineffective instructional approaches (e.g., just telling all students "Don't compare yourself to others on social media") (see Weinstein, 2017 for context on why this approach may fall short). We also observed in some lessons a clear implication that offline activities are inherently more worthwhile than any online activities.

Researchers must also attend to different methods of implementation for school-based interventions. As we have touched on above, research should go beyond analysis of curricular content to consider details like where (e.g., advisory, health class, social studies, whole school assembly), how often (e.g., "one and done" versus multiple lessons across a semester or year), and who facilitates (e.g., classroom teacher, guidance counselor, expert guest speaker, peer mentor). A further question about interventions for healthy digital media use is *by whom and for whom.* Who decides what constitutes healthy versus unhealthy use, particularly given that youth use technologies in ways that reflect dramatically different offline circumstances and access to resources (Ito et al., 2020; Odgers, 2018)? Who actually receives digital citizenship interventions and in which ways do such interventions "meet them where there are" versus miss the mark?

There remain persistent and pernicious inequities across US education (e.g., Jencks & Phillips, 2011; Reardon, 2011). The recent example of remote learning during the COVID-19 pandemic provided yet another illustration of the ways in which young people differentially experience learning on a day-to-day basis in ways that set them up for stark differences in learning, health, and well-being outcomes (MacGillis, 2020). Unsurprisingly, educational inequities play out in the context of technology-related education in ways that disproportionately impact black, Latino, and low-income youth (Watkins & Cho, 2018). A puzzle relates to who is responsible for attending to equity concerns when it comes to teaching digital topics. Should consideration of vulnerable students, and specific vulnerabilities, be "baked into" digital citizenship curricula and associated teacher supports? Or should programs leave it to teachers to make relevant adaptations for their students – whether they be students who have constrained resource access those who face learning challenges, those who have known mental health challenges, or any other number of relevant vulnerabilities? These questions are key for research, relevant to policy, and consequential from an ethical standpoint.

Other School-Based Approaches for Supporting Healthy Digital Media Use

Notably, digital citizenship curricula are but one approach to supporting healthy digital media use. The literature also suggests considerable advantages to integrating internet safety into already well-established and evidence-based programs that address related off-line harms (see Finkelhor et al., 2020 for discussion). This integrative approach recognizes the considerable overlap between offline and online behaviors and corresponding intervention strategies. For example, as Finkelhor et al. (2020) describe, cyberbullying co-occurs with offline victimization and well-established prevention strategies for bullying hold relevance for cyberbullying (e.g., norm-setting about acceptable versus hurtful behaviors, teaching de-escalation strategies, discussing bystander support). Educational interventions that integrate cyberbullying with offline bullying appear effective based on meta-analytic review (Gaffney et al., 2019). Finkelhor and colleagues argue that internet addiction/overuse is another topic best addressed through integration with existing interventions, specifically those that promote mental and physical health for high-risk youth, for example, by developing self-control, time management skills, and parental mediation.

Schools can also model or promote digital citizenship and healthy digital media use beyond the classroom lesson format. Additional venues for extra-curricular, school-based interventions – all of which are potentially relevant to digital citizenship – include whole school assemblies, peer-to-peer mentoring programs, and family engagement events. Acceptable use policies also set overarching guidelines and expectations for at-school technology use and/or the use of school-provided devices. These policies may bear resemblance to the aforementioned use-related "pledges" and represent another school channel for communicating messages and values about technology use.

Conclusion

Today's digital technologies are designed with compelling features that contribute to their allure. These apps and devices are created to capture and hold people's attention: designed and iterated to be "irresistible" (Alter, 2017). Youth readily use these tools, though technologies are rarely created with young people's healthy development front of mind. For adolescents, normative developmental drives and vulnerabilities contribute to heightened interest in the affordances digital media provide, from peer feedback to immediate rewards in gaming and on social media. While debate continues about the specific nature and mechanisms by which screen activities impact mental health, there is little question that digital media use should be a standard component of discussions about youth well-being.

As prior chapters in this handbook address, young people with particular mental health challenges may use digital media in ways that mirror or amplify risks. Clinical intervention represents an important avenue for providing these youth with targeted support. Yet questions about promoting healthy digital media use are widely relevant, and arguably merit attention with any and every young person who uses digital tools. Schools are a natural context for interventions particularly as they increasingly provide students with access to devices and encourage or require digital media use for learning. Our review documents a range of digital citizenship curricula and related resources to guide school-based intervention. These resources vary in their focal topics and in their approaches to those topics, as well as in terms of their formats, target grade levels, fee structures, and messaging. Across lessons that specifically target healthy digital habits, we observed three common learning goals: (1) building critical awareness so that students recognize and understand psychological dynamics and digital affordances that shape technology use; (2) scaffolding self-reflection that prompts students to take stock of their current digital media use and build digital metacognition; and (3) supporting behavioral change through strategies that promote digital agency and well-being. While programs often cover one or two of these learning goals, there is potential power in a three-pronged approach. Overall, relevant research suggests these aims and their corresponding approaches are good bets for supporting healthy digital media use. But, at present, we do not have a sufficient evidence base to guide decision-making about school-based interventions for promoting healthy digital media use. What works, for whom, and under what circumstances? Which topics, messages, and approaches align with current research on digital life and adolescent mental health/well-being? To what extent and how should school-based digital citizenship interventions be designed with an explicit equity lens?

All told, school-based interventions offer tangible ways to reach and support young people. Moving toward a set of well-developed *and* evidence-based curricular resources for digital media use will provide vital direction for the field.

References

Alter, A. (2017). *Irresistible: The rise of addictive technology and the business of keeping us hooked.* Penguin.

Anderson, C. A. (2003). Violent video games: Myths, facts, and unanswered questions. *Psychological Science Agenda, 16*(5), 1–8.

Bandura, A. (1989). Regulation of cognitive processes through perceived self-efficacy. *Developmental Psychology, 25*(5), 729–735.

Brown, J. A. (1998). Media literacy perspectives. *Journal of Communication, 48*(1), 44–57.

Bruns, H., Kantorowicz-Reznichenko, E., Klement, K., Luistro Johnson, M., & Rahali, B. (2018). Can nudges be transparent and yet effective?. *Journal of Economic Psychology, 65*, 41–59.

Burnell, K., George, M. J., Vollet, J. W., Ehrenreich, S. E., & Underwood, M. K. (2019). Passive social networking site use and well-being: The mediating roles of social comparison and the fear of missing out. *Cyberpsychology: Journal of Psychosocial Research on Cyberspace, 13*(3), 5. https://doi.org/10.5817/CP2019-3-5.

Carrier, L. M., Rosen, L. D. & Rokkum, J. N. (2018, January 8). Productivity in peril: Higher and higher rates of technology multitasking. *Behavioral Scientist.* https://behavioralscientist.org/productivity-peril-higher-higher-rates-technology-multitasking/

Center for Humane Technology. (2020a). *Ledger of harms.* https://ledger.humanetech.com/

Center for Humane Technology. (2020b). *Take control: What we as individuals can do.* https://www.humanetech.com/take-control

Clear, J. (2018). *Atomic habits: An easy & proven way to build good habits & break bad ones.* Penguin.

Cortesi, S., Hasse, A., Lombana-Bermudez, A., Kim, S., & Gasser, U. (2020). *Youth and digital citizenship+ (plus): Understanding skills for a digital world.* Berkman Klein Center for Internet & Society.

Dahl, R. E. (2004). Adolescent brain development: A period of vulnerabilities and opportunities. Keynote address. *Annals of the New York Academy of Sciences, 1021*(1), 1–22.

Davis, K., & Weinstein, E. (2017). Identity development in the digital age: An Eriksonian perspective. In M. F. Wright (Ed.), *Identity, sexuality, and relationships among emerging adults in the digital age* (pp. 1–17). IGI Global.

Ferguson, C. J. (2020). Aggressive video games research emerges from its replication crisis (sort of). *Current Opinion in Psychology, 36*, 1–6.

Finkelhor, D., Walsh, K., Jones, L., Mitchell, K., & Collier, A. (2020). Youth internet safety education: Aligning programs with the evidence base. *Trauma, Violence, & Abuse, 22*(5), 1233–1247.

Gaffney, H., Farrington, D. P., Espelage, D. L., & Ttofi, M. M. (2019). Are cyberbullying intervention and prevention programs effective? A systematic and meta-analytical review. *Aggression and Violent Behavior, 45*, 134–153.

Galla, B. M., Choukas-Bradley, S., Fiore, H. M., & Esposito, M. V. (2021). Values-alignment messaging boosts adolescents' motivation to control social media use. *Child Development, 92*(5), 1717–1734.

Gentile, D. A. (2011). The multiple dimensions of video game effects. *Child Development Perspectives*, *5*(2), 75–81.

Hinduja, S., & Patchin, J. W. (2011). Cyberbullying: A review of the legal issues facing educators. *Preventing School Failure: Alternative Education for Children and Youth*, *55*(2), 71–78.

Hiniker, A., Schoenebeck, S. Y., & Kientz, J. A. (2016, February). Not at the dinner table: Parents' and children's perspectives on family technology rules. *Proceedings of the 19th ACM Conference on Computer-Supported Cooperative Work & Social Computing*, 1376–1389.

Hobbs, R. (2010). *Digital and media literacy: A plan of action*. The Aspen Institute.

Hobbs, R. (2017). Measuring the digital and media literacy competencies of children and teens. In F. C. Blumberg & P. J. Brooks (Eds.), *Cognitive development in digital contexts* (pp. 253–274). Academic Press.

Hollandsworth, R., Dowdy, L., & Donovan, J. (2011). Digital citizenship in K-12: It takes a village. *TechTrends*, *55*(4), 37–47.

Ito, M., Odgers, C., Schueller, S., et al. (2020). *Social media and youth wellbeing: What we know and where we could go*. Connected Learning Alliance.

Jencks, C., & Phillips, M. (Eds.). (2011). *The black-white test score gap*. Brookings Institution Press.

Jenkins, H. (2009). *Confronting the challenges of participatory culture: Media education for the 21st century*. MIT Press.

Jeong, S. H., Cho, H., & Hwang, Y. (2012). Media literacy interventions: A meta-analytic review. *Journal of Communication*, *62*(3), 454–472.

Kesten, J. M., Sebire, S. J., Turner, K. M., Stewart-Brown, S., Bentley, G., & Jago, R. (2015). Associations between rule-based parenting practices and child screen viewing: A cross-sectional study. *Preventive Medicine Reports*, *2*, 84–89.

Klein, A. (2020, June 3). Why principals worry about how mobile devices affect students' social skills, attention spans. *Education Week*. https://www.edweek.org/ew/articles/2020/06/03/why-principals-worry-about-how-mobile-devices.html

Kohut, T., & Štulhofer, A. (2018). Is pornography use a risk for adolescent well-being? An examination of temporal relationships in two independent panel samples. *PLoS ONE*, *13*(8), e0202048.

Kowalski, R. M., Giumetti, G. W., Schroeder, A. N., & Lattanner, M. R. (2014). Bullying in the digital age: A critical review and meta-analysis of cyberbullying research among youth. *Psychological Bulletin*, *140*(4), 1073–1137.

LoSchiavo, F. M., & Shatz, M. A. (2011). The impact of an honor code on cheating in online courses. *MERLOT Journal of Online Learning and Teaching*, *7*(2), 179–184.

MacGillis, A. (2020, October 5). The students left behind by remote learning. *The New Yorker* and *ProPublica*. https://www.newyorker.com/magazine/2020/10/05/the-students-left-behind-by-remote-learning

Media Literacy Now. (2020). *U.S. media literacy policy report 2020*. Media Literacy Now.

Mori, C., Temple, J. R., Browne, D., & Madigan, S. (2019). Association of sexting with sexual behaviors and mental health among adolescents: A systematic review and meta-analysis. *JAMA Pediatrics*, *173*(8), 770–779.

National Association for Media Literacy Education. (2007, November). *The core principles of media literacy education.* https://namle.net/publications/core-principles/

Nesi, J., & Prinstein, M. J. (2015). Using social media for social comparison and feedback-seeking: Gender and popularity moderate associations with depressive symptoms. *Journal of Abnormal Child Psychology, 43*(8), 1427–1438.

Nesi, J., Wolff, J. C., & Hunt, J. (2019). Patterns of social media use among psychiatrically hospitalized adolescents who are psychiatrically hospitalized. *Journal of the American Academy of Child & Adolescent Psychiatry, 58*(6), 635–640.

Odgers, C. (2018). Smartphones are bad for some teens, not all. *Nature, 554*, 432–443.

Odgers, C. L., & Jensen, M. R. (2020). Annual Research Review: Adolescent mental health in the digital age: Facts, fears, and future directions. *Journal of Child Psychology and Psychiatry, 61*(3), 336–348.

Palfrey, J., & Gasser, U. (2011). Reclaiming an awkward term: What we might learn from digital natives. *I/S: A Journal of Law and Policy for the Information Society, 7*(1), 33–55.

Passey, D., Shonfeld, M., Appleby, L., Judge, M., Saito, T., & Smits, A. (2018). Digital agency: Empowering equity in and through education. *Technology, Knowledge and Learning, 23*(3), 425–439.

Patton, D. U., Eschmann, R. D., Elsaesser, C., & Bocanegra, E. (2016). Sticks, stones and Facebook accounts: What violence outreach workers know about social media and urban-based gang violence in Chicago. *Computers in Human Behavior, 65*, 591–600.

Phillips, A. L., & Lee, V. R. (2019). Whose responsibility is it? A statewide survey of school librarians on responsibilities and resources for teaching digital citizenship. *School Library Research, 22.*

Radovic, A., Gmelin, T., Stein, B. D., & Miller, E. (2017). Depressed adolescents' positive and negative use of social media. *Journal of Adolescence, 55*, 5–15.

Reardon, S. F. (2011). The widening academic achievement gap between the rich and the poor: New evidence and possible explanations. In G. J. Duncan & R. J. Murnane (Eds.), *Whither opportunity* (pp. 91–116). Russell Sage.

Reeves, B., Robinson, T., & Ram, N. (2020). Time for the Human Screenome Project. *Nature, 577*(7790), 314–317.

Ribble, M. & Bailey, G. (2007). *Digital citizenship in schools.* International Society for Technology in Education.

Samuel, A. (2015, November 4). Parents: Reject technology shame. *The Atlantic.* https://www.theatlantic.com/technology/archive/2015/11/why-parents-shouldnt-feel-technology-shame/414163/

Schleider, J. L., Dobias, M. L., Sung, J.Y., & Mullarkey, M. C. (2020). Future directions in single-session youth mental health interventions. *Journal of Clinical Child and Adolescent Psychology, 49*, 264–278.

Sparks, S. D. (2013, December 11). "Blue light" may impair students' sleep, studies say. *Education Week.* https://www.edweek.org/ew/articles/2013/12/11/14sleep_ep.h33.html

Steinberg, L. (2014). *Age of opportunity: Lessons from the new science of adolescence.* Houghton Mifflin Harcourt.

Tamm, L., Menon, V., & Reiss, A. L. (2002). Maturation of brain function associated with response inhibition. *Journal of the American Academy of Child & Adolescent Psychiatry*, *41*(10), 1231–1238.

Underwood, M. K., & Ehrenreich, S. E. (2017). The power and the pain of adolescents' digital communication: Cyber victimization and the perils of lurking. *American Psychologist*, *72*(2), 144–158.

Walther, B., Hanewinkel, R., & Morgenstern, M. (2014). Effects of a brief school-based media literacy intervention on digital media use in adolescents: Cluster randomized controlled trial. *Cyberpsychology, Behavior, and Social Networking*, *17*(9), 616–623.

Watkins, S. C., & Cho, A. (2018). *The digital edge: How Black and Latino youth navigate digital inequality*. NYU Press.

Weinstein, E. (2017). Adolescents' differential responses to social media browsing: Exploring causes and consequences for intervention. *Computers in Human Behavior*, *76*, 396–405.

16 Digital Media Interventions for Adolescent Mental Health

Jessica L. Hamilton, David M. Siegel, and Matthew M. Carper

The majority of mental health problems first emerge during the adolescent years (Kessler et al., 2005). Thus, adolescence is a critical developmental window for both mental health prevention and intervention. Despite improvements in our understanding and ability to detect and treat youth mental health problems, there remains a persistent need for mental health services among youth, with the majority of youth untreated (Cummings et al., 2013; Merikangas et al., 2011). Among youth who do get treatment, there is often a long gap between the onset of symptoms and when youth first receive treatment (de Girolamo et al., 2012), as well as low treatment attendance and completion in this population. As rates of mental health problems such as depression and suicidality continue to rise during adolescence (Centers for Disease Control, 2018), the gap between those who need and receive mental health services will only continue to grow.

In this chapter, we review the potential for technology to advance our understanding and treatment of mental health problems among adolescents through digital mental health interventions (DMHIs). We first discuss existing barriers to mental health care among adolescents, followed by a discussion of how DMHIs can address these barriers to improve access to and quality of adolescent mental health services. We then review existing research on DMHIs and the digital frameworks that are used to collect and deliver psychoeducation, assessment, and interventions across different hardware (e.g., smartphones, computers) and modalities (e.g., online, text, apps). Finally, we conclude with a discussion of the current limitations of DMHIs and key directions for the field to improve adolescent mental health care using DMHIs.

Barriers to Existing Mental Health Services

Significant, and often systemic, barriers interfere with access and delivery of mental health services for adolescents, including barriers related to cost, geographic proximity, and time, among others. These barriers often

We would like to thank Woanjun Lee, BA for his contributions to the tables for this chapter. Jessica L. Hamilton was supported by funding from the National Institute of Mental Health (K01MH121584; L30MH117642).

result in long waitlists and travel times, as well as a shortage of professionals providing evidence-based care (Andrilla et al., 2018), particularly those who are trained to work with youth (American Psychological Association, 2016). Access to treatment is especially challenging for youth in rural regions (Andrilla et al., 2018) and for adolescents who are racial, ethnic, sexual, and/or gender minorities. These youth often face additional barriers to receive culturally sensitive care (Alegria et al., 2010). Inadequate education about mental illness, distrust of medical providers, and stigma about help-seeking behaviors (i.e., internalizing stigma) and mental health care (i.e., treatment stigma) also prevent adolescents from seeking help (Clement et al., 2015; Gulliver et al., 2010). Teens also often lack awareness and understanding of their symptoms as clinically significant, are uneducated about their treatment options, or are hesitant to share their symptoms with parents or other adults (Gulliver et al., 2010). Even when youth do access mental health care, treatment completion and compliance are often low due to these persistent barriers (e.g., cost, time, transportation, stigma). Thus, there is a critical need for services that are scalable, accessible, and developmentally appropriate for the prevention and intervention of adolescent mental health problems.

Potential Benefits of Digital Mental Health Interventions for Adolescents

Advancing technologies offer novel opportunities to improve the detection, prevention, and treatment of mental health problems. DMHIs have the potential to revolutionize mental health care by providing effective, accessible, scalable, and low-cost interventions. While adolescents are at heightened risk for mental health problems, they also may be uniquely positioned to benefit from DMHIs and novel digital tools (Wong et al., 2020).

DMHIs can overcome many of the aforementioned systemic and individual barriers for youth (e.g., availability, cost, transportation, stigma). There are several factors that suggest DMHIs may be promising for adolescent mental health care. First, certain technologies to deliver DMHIs are already widely in use. For example, smartphones have become nearly ubiquitous among youth, with over 95% of teens owning these regardless of gender, race/ethnicity, or sexual identity (Anderson & Jiang, 2018). Second, adolescents are early adopters of many digital technologies. They report high levels of comfort with and preference for online communication, particularly when discussing mental health (Bradford & Rickwood, 2015). Thus, DMHIs also promote help-seeking behaviors and can serve as a "gateway" to initiating mental health care (Kauer et al., 2014). Third, adolescents also commonly use the Internet for mental health information (Leanza & Alani, 2020; Park & Kwon, 2018), which is especially the case for adolescents who identify as racial/ethnic minorities or have parents that are less health literate (Park & Kwon, 2018).

Finally, as the first point of entry for many adolescents, DMHIs can facilitate treatment by reducing uncertainty about interactions with providers and ambiguity about treatment options (Boydell et al., 2014). Rather than being a passive participant, teens can gain a newfound understanding and agency over their mental health, which may promote treatment seeking and engagement.

Further, while stigma toward help-seeking and mental health care is prominent across age groups (Sharac et al., 2010), adolescents identify stigma as one of the greatest barriers to mental health care (Gulliver et al., 2010). DMHIs can be anonymous, private, and accessible to teens at any time of the day and in any location, thereby allowing teens to access and receive mental health care in the way that is most comfortable for them (Toscos et al., 2019). In this sense, DMHIs can reach diverse groups of adolescents efficiently by connecting with teens where they are (online) and in the digital spaces where they feel most comfortable. DMHIs have the potential to not only reduce the gap in mental health services and delivery, but also reduce mental health disparities that exist across youth who are marginalized or undeserved (Schueller et al., 2019). DMHIs can provide readily available, reliable, and accurate mental health information to adolescents, particularly youth who are traditionally underserved in mental health care. DMHIs may also be more readily adaptable or translated into other languages, which may help with the limited availability of multilingual mental health professionals. However, inequities in access to technology may actually create a digital divide in who has access to DMHIs (Odgers & Jensen, 2020). By collecting and delivering content in real time and in real-world contexts, DMHIs have the potential to inform and deliver timely, flexible, and personalized mental health care, thereby improving detection and treatment of mental health problems across risk stages and demographics (Price et al., 2014).

Modes of Delivery for Digital Health Interventions

As technology evolves, an abundance of novel digital platforms and tools have been developed to improve mental health among youth and adults. DMHIs provide online services for interventions through various hardware (e.g., computer, phone, tablet, wearable) and modalities. These modalities include online/web-based interventions, video conferencing, text messaging, smartphone applications ("apps"), social media sites, game-based approaches (e.g., "serious games") (Lister et al., 2014), virtual reality, as well as emerging technologies like passive sensing (e.g., wearables, digital phenotyping) and artificial intelligence (e.g., chatbots). Yet, technology has far outpaced research on DMHIs. Most work examining DMHIs is heavily skewed toward modalities that have existed longer (e.g., telehealth, online/web-based interventions). Newer modalities of delivering mental health services, such as

Table 16.1 *Suggested readings for understanding DMHIs' effectiveness, implementation, and future directions*

Overall Reviews of DMHIs for Children and Adolescents	
Boydell et al., 2014	Scoping review of 126 studies on the use of technology (teleconferencing, telephone, internet, email, SMS/mobile phone, CD-ROM) to deliver mental health services to children and youth
Clarke et al., 2015	Systematic review of 28 studies on the effectiveness of online mental health promotion and prevention interventions, such as web-based support, for youth (12–25 years old)
Hollis et al., 2017	Meta review of 21 review articles and systematic review of 30 empirical articles on DMHIs (computer assisted therapy, smartphone apps, and wearable technologies) for youth mental health treatment across disorders (e.g., ADHD, autism, anxiety, depression)
Punukollu & Marques, 2019	Review of 4 studies of online mobile-based apps in the detection, management, and maintenance of youth mental health concerns
Reviews on DMHI Implementation and Dissemination	
Wozney et al., 2018	Review of DMHI implementation for anxiety disorders and depression in youth
Garrido et al., 2019	Systematic review, thematic analysis, narrative synthesis, and meta-analysis of DMHIs and their effectiveness in youth with depression and anxiety
Liverpool et al., 2020	Systematic review of 6 modes of DMHI for children and youth (websites, games/computer assisted programs, apps, robots and digital device, virtual reality, and text messages) and intervention-specific and person-specific barriers and facilitators to their implementation
Additional Articles for Understanding DMHIs for Youth and for Underserved Groups	
Schueller et al., 2019	Review of current DMHIs (smartphone apps, text messages, social media) for use in undeserved populations (e.g., individuals who are ethnic, racial, gender, or sexual minorities, live in rural areas, or are experiencing homelessness)
Wong et al., 2020	Affordances-based framework for understanding engagement in DMHIs in the context of adolescent development

Note: Full references are available in the References section.

mobile health (e.g., text messaging, apps), wearables, or games, are still in the earlier phases of testing for treatment effectiveness with youth. Nevertheless, given their promise for reducing the burden of mental health problems in adolescents, the field is rapidly expanding to empirically evaluate DMHIs for adolescent mental health problems. Below, we briefly discuss the potential benefits and effectiveness of a range of specific DMHI modes of delivery. Table 16.1 provides a review of suggested readings about DMHIs' effectiveness and implementation. Later in this chapter, we will discuss potential challenges of these technologies for mental health interventions.

Videoconferencing

Telehealth services (e.g., telephone and videoconferencing) most closely mirror traditional face-to-face assessment and treatment delivery, and also offer new opportunities. Videoconferencing provides synchronous communication between patients and providers, with the increased convenience for patients of eliminating travel. Being in one's natural environment has the potential to improve ecological validity of both assessment and treatment for youth with certain mental health problems (e.g., depression, psychosis, anxiety) compared to traditional treatment in an office or hospital setting. Specifically, videoconferencing may allow the clinician to observe the home environment to better assess a teen's home or provide opportunities to participate in more naturalistic exposures. Therapy conducted using videoconferencing has received empirical support to effectively treat a range of youth mental health problems (Myers et al., 2007, 2008; Nelson et al., 2017). Videoconferencing is now relatively common and accepted in mental health care among professionals, youth, and their caregivers (Boydell et al., 2014). Following the physical distancing practices of the COVID-19 pandemic (Gruber et al., 2021), videoconferencing will likely continue to increase in its use and acceptability as a means of providing mental health care to youth. Despite its more common use in mental health care compared to other DMHIs, empirical research is still underway to provide guidance for the use of videoconferencing (Nelson et al., 2017), including how to ethically navigate patient boundaries in their homes, which will be critical for delivering care using this modality.

Online/Web-Based Interventions

Online or web-based platforms can provide a myriad of services. This includes: access to comprehensive mental health information (e.g., blogs, websites); scalable, affordable, and effective interventions to youth and their families for mental health problems; and translation of existing evidence-based treatments into computerized or online lessons, modules, or sessions accompanied by homework or tasks, among others. Systematic and meta-analytic reviews of randomized control trials (RCTs) support the effectiveness of online/web-based services for treating adolescent mental health problems (Clarke et al., 2015; Hollis et al., 2017). Most studies have been conducted with youth with subclinical or clinical levels of depression and anxiety (Grist et al., 2019; Khanna et al., 2017). To date, online interventions for these clinical problems have garnered the most support. Most online or web-based interventions are based on cognitive behavioral therapy (CBT) (Ebert et al., 2015). The majority of computerized and internet-based CBT programs were found to be of moderate to high quality (Clarke et al., 2015; Wozney et al., 2018). These programs included components of self-monitoring, interactive content (e.g., videos, characters storytelling, games), and both online and offline support. However, online programs now include other treatment modalities and approaches for targeting youth mental health problems (Garrido et al., 2019), such as positive psychology, mindfulness (Ritvo et al., 2019), and problem-solving (Hoek et al., 2012).

Importantly, there is a need to better understand the level of human interaction (if any) needed for online or web-based interventions to be effective with youth mental health treatment, especially to counter low rates of engagement and adherence. Most online or web-based interventions are therapist-assisted, including a virtual or online therapist or to supplement in-person and face-to-face clinician visits. Meta-analytic reviews suggest online interventions that included therapists or clinicians performed better in reducing depression and anxiety symptoms than interventions that were self-guided (Clarke et al., 2015; Hollis et al., 2017). Indeed, some research suggests that self-guided online or web-based interventions were not effective for youth depression (Garrido et al., 2019). Alternatively, some studies indicate that minimal therapist involvement was better for youth anxiety than significant or more extensive therapist involvement (Podina et al., 2016).

Some of the largest barriers for self-guided online treatments for adolescents are low rates of treatment completion and adherence (Clarke et al., 2015; Garrido et al., 2019). To address these concerns, low-intensity web-based interventions have been developed to deliver skill-based interventions in single sessions (Schleider & Weisz, 2018). Self-administered online single-session interventions have demonstrated effectiveness in reducing adolescent depressive symptoms, as well as other core characteristics of depression (e.g., low perceived agency, self-worth, and hopelessness; Schleider & Weisz, 2018; Schleider, Dobias, Sung, & Mullarkey, 2020). One recent trial found that online single-session interventions demonstrate effectiveness in natural settings and also reach a large number of adolescents with one or more marginalized identities (Schleider, Dobias, Sung, Mumper, & Mullarkey, 2020). Thus, online single-session interventions may offer brief, low-intensity, accessible, and scalable mental health interventions for youth who may otherwise not engage in care, possibly serving as tools for universal or indicated prevention or during transitional periods of more intensive care. More research and diversification of these online brief interventions (e.g., length, type) is needed to evaluate the setting and context in which they are most effective (Schleider, Dobias, Sung, Mumper, & Mullarkey, 2020). Further, a recent RCT tested the effectiveness of a web-based decision aid to support young people in help-seeking for their self-harm (Rowe et al., 2018). Youth generally reported the online decision aid to be acceptable, easy to use, and informative for seeking help, which suggests another way in which online or web-based interventions can promote adolescent mental health.

Text Messaging

Text messaging can also be an affordable and effective way of providing interventions, monitoring symptoms, or prompting adolescents to engage in behaviors to promote mental health, such as coping skills during crisis. This type of platform can prompt adolescents to employ skills, as well as provide automated reminders for appointments and medication to improve treatment attendance (Branson et al., 2013). Texts can be personalized and tailored to the adolescent based on their needs and preferences by altering the message frequency, content, and customized interactions. Text-based services may be an especially accessible DMHI. Nearly all youth have mobile phones and smartphones and text messaging does not require internet for delivery. Further, text messaging interventions are not at risk for deletion, which is common for smartphone apps (Baumel et al., 2019), as text capabilities are embedded in phones. Text messaging interventions also may have lower upfront costs for development compared to apps that need to be adapted and delivered for both iOS and Android platforms. Importantly, there is some support for the effectiveness of text interventions for treating youth health problems (Loescher et al., 2018), including substance use and depression (Mason et al., 2015; Whitton et al., 2015). Further, a recent text messaging intervention also improved the mental health literacy of parents of adolescents (Chu et al., 2019), which may subsequently improve mental health care for teens by reducing one potential barrier to treatment.

Smartphone Apps

The widespread ownership of mobile phones, particularly smartphones, provides unparalleled and unobtrusive access to adolescents in real time and in the "real world" to deliver scalable and low-cost mental health interventions. Current mental health apps can serve multiple purposes, including for psychoeducation, monitoring symptoms or behaviors, providing "just in time" or ecological momentary interventions, and as adjunctive or stand-alone treatments. There are many potential benefits to using apps to engage youth in mental health services, including heightened sense of privacy, accessibility, convenience, and integration in daily life. Importantly, apps can be more personalized and tailored to the individual, and can provide more developmentally appropriate and interactive material that engages adolescents (Bakker et al., 2016). For some youth, the very act of mental health monitoring may be beneficial in improving symptoms (Kauer et al., 2012), which can be delivered in a user-friendly manner and can be used as a preventive measure or adjunct to treatment. Monitoring apps that serve as an adjunct to treatment may increase engagement among youth, allowing adolescents to have an increased awareness and sense of agency over their own behavior and mental health symptoms. However, most monitoring apps available for download have received limited empirical support. In general, relatively few apps have been empirically tested to determine their effectiveness in treating youth mental health problems (Melbye et al., 2020; Punukollu & Marques, 2019).

Although research is limited, apps designed to supplement other mental health treatment and aid care between sessions have demonstrated effectiveness, particularly for youth anxiety (Carper, 2017; Pramana et al., 2014; Silk et al., 2020). These apps enhance treatment exposures and skills-based practice, homework compliance, and symptom tracking between sessions. Apps also have the potential to provide adolescents with "just in time" adaptive interventions that are low-intensity and high-impact and when they most need it most, such as times of crisis. Indeed, specific suicide prevention apps have been developed (Martinengo et al., 2019), with preliminary evidence of positive treatment effects (Arshad et al., 2020). While not encouraged to be standalone treatments, digital safety planning and tools (Kennard et al., 2015, 2018) may help adolescents at risk for suicide while youth are in crisis or during high-risk periods by addressing the gap between hospital discharge and outpatient treatment.

Most evidence-based apps developed by researchers are not yet commercially available (Punukollu & Marques, 2019). In contrast, there are tens of thousands of commercially available apps for mental health, highlighting the large divide between apps developed for commercial use compared to those developed by researchers. Few of these available apps have been tested for effectiveness and most popular apps do not include therapeutic elements (Wasil et al., 2019), though empirical evaluation is currently underway for some commercial apps (Bry et al., 2018). There is also very little regulatory oversight of apps and limited available high-quality information on the effectiveness of commercially available apps (Boudreaux et al., 2014). This can leave adolescents vulnerable to mental health misinformation or using DMHIs that offer little therapeutic benefits (and some that could be harmful). Given that adolescents report difficulty distinguishing accurate from inaccurate information sources (Park & Kwon, 2018), user guidance is needed to inform teens, parents, and providers (Palmer & Burrows, 2021). There are several resources available that provide quantitative feedback, rubrics, and recommendations about mobile apps (Table 16.2). However, teens would likely benefit from a readily available tool, available in app stores, to provide information to them on which apps are research-based (Lagan et al., 2020) in a developmentally appropriate manner.

Game-Based Interventions

Another promising domain of DMHIs is video games, which includes those that are entirely focused on mental health (e.g., "serious games" or "mental health games") and components of video games added to DMHIs for

Table 16.2 *Resources for evaluating mental health apps*

Resource	Description	Link
PsyberGuide	Comprehensive collection of reviews and ratings of various apps for mental health. Users can use filters to search through a list of apps.	onemindpsyberguide.org
M-Health Index and Navigation Database (MIND)	Searchable database of various apps for mental health that have been reviewed by trained app reviewers. Uses principles of the American Psychiatric Association's App Evaluation Model.	https://apps.digitalpsych .org/
Mobile App Rating Scale (MARS)	Multidimensional measure for classifying and assessing the quality of mobile health apps.	dx.doi.org/10.2196/ mhealth.3422
ENLIGHT	Comprehensive suite of measures to evaluate mHealth interventions.	dx.doi.org/10.2196/ jmir.7270
Professional Psychological Organizations		
ABCT	Expert reviews of multimedia resources for mental health published online and quarterly journal: *Cognitive and Behavioral Practice*.	abct.org
ADAA	List of apps that have been reviewed by ADAA members over the years.	adaa.org
APA	List of apps and websites that may be helpful for improving mental health. Aimed primarily at clinicians.	apa.org

Notes: ABCT = Association for Behavioral and Cognitive Therapies; ADAA = Anxiety and Depression Association of America; APA = American Psychological Association. Links are directed to the main organization website.

"gamification" of mental health (Fleming et al., 2016). With the components inherent in video games (e.g., levels, challenges, rewards), video games facilitate intrinsic motivation to incentivize adolescent engagement and adherence. Games have the potential to facilitate specific skills that also promote mental health and even improve treatment uptake, such as learning, memory, and coping skills. Games are also highly popular among adolescents (Rideout & Robb, 2019), which may encourage adolescent engagement. Video games can be played on familiar, low-cost platforms that are already integrated into the lives of youth (e.g., smartphones, web browsers, game systems, computers, etc). This may make these DMHIs more easily accessible compared to other cutting-edge platforms (e.g., virtual reality). Many research-based video games are still only available on computers, but gamification of mobile apps or other DMHIs offer promise (Lister et al., 2014).

The majority of research on video games has been conducted on internalizing disorders and demonstrated some effectiveness (Lau et al., 2016; Li et al., 2014), especially in conjunction with other treatments (Merry et al., 2012; Schoneveld et al., 2018). Studies indicate that video games may be especially effective at increasing motivation, teaching cognitive restructuring, imparting relaxation techniques, and providing psychoeducation to ameliorate these types of disorders (Knox et al., 2011; Pramana et al., 2014). These rewarding elements (e.g., levels, positive feedback) also draw on adolescents' cognitive and motivational development (Somerville & Casey, 2010), which may motivate adolescents to participate and engage in treatment. Some recent programs also integrate biofeedback techniques to teach breathing, meditation, and relaxation exercises (Pramana et al., 2014). The use of avatars in gaming also provide a higher level of personalization and engagement, as well as reduce stigma toward mental health (Ferchaud et al., 2020). Personalization may also have the potential to aid youth in identity development, as teens can experiment with different ways of presenting themselves. This may be particularly important for youth who identify as sexual and/or gender minorities, providing safe spaces to anonymously explore and discuss difficult topics related to their identities and mental health (DeHaan et al., 2013). Video games and gamification may be particularly compelling for adolescents with autism spectrum disorder (ASD) or those with attention deficit-hyperactivity disorder (ADHD) due to the existing popularity of video games in these populations (Yerys et al., 2019). Future RCTs and reviews are needed to fully capture the benefits and evaluate the effectiveness of gaming for adolescent mental health.

Virtual and Augmented Realities

Virtual and augmented realities create new opportunities for delivering and enhancing treatments. Virtual reality provides an immersive experience that virtually transports individuals into a real or imaged physical environment. In contrast, augmented realities overlay image and video content on top of reality, enhancing a person's in-person physical environment. Virtual and augmented realities can deliver services in an interactive manner while still remaining under the control of the adolescent and provider (Li et al., 2017). Virtual and augmented reality may be promising for youth with ASD (Berenguer et al., 2020; Vahabzadeh et al., 2018) and for youth with anxiety disorders (Barnes & Prescott, 2018), where sensory input can be tailored to the individual need. For example, virtual realities can simulate experiences found in everyday life or expose youth to fears or situations that may not otherwise be possible in daily life (e.g., fear of flying) or the clinical setting (e.g., public speaking in large crowds). Augmented realities can further extend youth's natural environment to simulate real-world experiences, such as specific phobias (e.g., spiders) and social interactions with peers. To date, virtual reality is more regularly used and examined with adults (Cieslik et al., 2020);

there is still limited empirical support on the effectiveness of virtual and augmented realities for youth mental health treatment (Grist et al., 2019). Despite its initial development nearly two decades ago, there continues to be a lag in the adoption of virtual reality for clinical interventions or in clinical practice, potentially due to its high cost and complex development. However, research may surge in virtual and augmented reality systems as they become more mobile and available on smartphones, commercially available, and as design becomes more centered on its potential clinical utility (Bell et al., 2020).

Social Media

Given the increasing presence of social media in the daily lives of adolescents, researchers have sought to employ social media as novel tools for mental illness detection, prevention, and intervention. Adolescence is a unique developmental period during which individuals are more sensitive to social feedback, peer relationships, and peer influence (Prinstein & Dodge, 2008). Social media provides adolescents with a range of social affordances, including social support, sense of belonging, and access to a network of known and unknown peers (Nesi et al., 2018). Thus, social media-based DMHIs have the power to reduce stigma, increase help-seeking behaviors, connect peers, and provide support and psychoeducation about the benefits of mental health problems (Betton et al., 2015). Social media can also connect adolescents with needed support and information that aids in treatment engagement, symptom reduction, and even as a form of suicide prevention (Robinson et al., 2016). Indeed, social media campaigns targeting mental health awareness and stigma reduction have demonstrated effectiveness in reducing stigma and increasing adolescent treatment engagement (Booth et al., 2018).

Research is still in its nascency for employing existing social media platforms to deliver interventions, with most systematic reviews identifying a need for high-quality studies examining online peer-to-peer support (Ali et al., 2015) or social networking sites (Ridout & Campbell, 2018). Thus far, social media-based interventions that include social networking or peer support components have been found to be acceptable, feasible, and safe for youth across a range of mental health problems (Ridout & Campbell, 2018), including depression (Radovic et al., 2018; Rice et al., 2014) and first-episode psychosis (Alvarez-Jimenez et al., 2013; McEnery et al., 2021). These interventions are professionally mediated to ensure networks remain supportive and informational, while also training some youth to be leaders in these peer networks.

Emerging Digital Tools

There are several new and emerging digital tools, such as passive sensing and artificial intelligence, that may further revolutionize how and in what ways

DMHIs promote adolescent mental health. One exciting avenue for DMHIs is the use of passive sensing from wearables or digital phenotyping of individuals' online or mobile footprints. With the integration of passive sensors from smartphones or wearables, ecological momentary interventions can be developed that provide just-in-time and adaptive treatments (Russell & Gajos, 2020). As smartphones are nearly always with adolescents (Anderson & Jiang, 2018), the rich data collected by smartphone sensors can yield information about location, activity levels, light exposure, social networking activity, and social connection (e.g., calls/messages). This information can be synthesized into clinically meaningful metrics of sleep, physical activity, emotional distress, and upstream clinical presentations (Huckvale et al., 2019; Vaidyam et al., 2019). This field is rapidly evolving for youth (Russell & Gajos, 2020), particularly to address the rising mental health concerns and suicide crisis in this population (Allen et al., 2019; Torous, Larsen, et al., 2018). To date, few apps have been developed that operationalize digital phenotyping data in actual interventions (Wong et al., 2020), though some are currently being developed and tested.

Artificial intelligence has also progressed in recent years, including the development of fully automated conversational agents (e.g., chatbots). Chatbots are able to process text and emojis entered by a participant and provide personalized responses that aim to mimic human conversation. Unlike other DMHIs that are fully automated, chatbots offer a level of direct and synchronous interaction that may motivate users to continue participation and even provide empathic support (Morris et al., 2018). Chatbots can provide daily check-ins for participants' symptoms and behaviors. They can also be readily integrated with other passive sensing metrics to increase awareness and individualization. Since some individuals are more willing to disclose to a machine than other individuals (Lucas et al., 2014), chatbots can serve as moderators or agents when real human interactions are not available. While preliminary studies indicate symptom reduction for adults with the use of chatbots (Fitzpatrick et al., 2017), particularly for psychoeducation and self-guided treatment, there is still much work needed to understand the risks and benefits of using this mode of delivery for DMHIs (Vaidyam et al., 2019). Nevertheless, integrating components of artificial intelligence like chatbots into other DMHIs may enhance connectedness and engagement in care for adolescents.

Challenges and Future Directions to Digital Mental Health Research and Treatment

Although DMHIs demonstrate great potential for delivering scalable and low-cost mental health services to adolescents, many obstacles remain. Simply stated, there is a significant divide between research and technology development. Commercially available technology is far outpacing research on the effectiveness and implementation of DMHIs for youth, as well as the enforcement of data privacy and security measures. The scalability of DMHIs also remains in question to determine whether these tools are actually as cost-effective, accessible, and effective in reaching underserved youth as initially promised. This section outlines the current challenges of the field and critical directions for growth to improve our understanding and use of DMHIs for adolescent mental health care.

Effectiveness of DMHIs: For Whom and in What Contexts?

There is a dearth of research investigating the effectiveness of DMHIs across modalities in adolescents, particularly newer and currently popular modes of delivery (e.g., smartphone apps). While most research has been conducted on web-based/online interventions, more rigorous research is needed to examine the effectiveness of DMHIs delivered via mobile applications, social media, and gaming platforms. These DMHI modalities represent areas of potential high engagement for teens. To date, most research also has focused on DMHIs for youth depression and anxiety. High-quality research is needed to examine DMHIs for specific mental health conditions beyond internalizing disorders (Hollis et al., 2017), such as youth with ASD (Yerys et al., 2019), psychosis (Reilly et al., 2019), and eating disorders (Loucas et al., 2014). Most research is also limited to short-term outcomes, and research on the long-term effects of DMHIs is needed. It also is critical to understand which youth may benefit from DMHIs and in what contexts, such as different stages of clinical severity or treatment progression. For instance, certain modalities may be most appropriate as a gateway to care, during waitlist or transitions to care, or "booster" sessions to supplement prior treatment and prevent relapse. Certain DMHI modalities also may pair better with certain conditions, such as using virtual or augmented realities with youth who have ASD and ADHD (Yerys et al., 2019). While there are concerns noted about using DMHIs clinically with high-risk adolescents (Palmer & Burrows, 2021), recent research suggests DMHIs may be effective in reducing suicidality (Hetrick et al., 2017) and for use in screening, prevention, and intervention with psychosis (Reilly et al., 2019). This research points to the potential utility of DMHIs for higher-risk adolescents as well. However, research would benefit from more systematic examination of how the effectiveness of DMHIs varies across clinical presentations, symptoms, and severity. Research is also needed to evaluate effectiveness of DMHIs by intervention stage (e.g., prevention, intervention) and type (e.g., skill building, CBT, exposure). Further, the active ingredients of DMHIs and fidelity to evidence-based approaches remain to be specified (Hollis et al., 2017). More details about DMHI design and implementation would help isolate the most effective elements, such as short motivational messages, gamification features, or symptom monitoring (Whitton et al., 2015). Research on the dose of clinical/human interaction needed (if at all) to engage and treat adolescents also is imperative, particularly since level of clinician involvement affects both cost-effectiveness and scalability.

Gap between Research and Commercial Technology

The fast pace at which technology is developed presents a major obstacle for the academic and research community. In contrast to commercial technology, research is typically produced at a much slower pace. RCTs are the "gold-standard" approach for determining efficacy and effectiveness. However, RCTs can take 5–7 years from initiation to dissemination (Hollis et al., 2017), and even longer for broader implementation. This length of time may render a DMHI modality irrelevant by the time it is deemed effective. Timing may be particularly important to consider in the context of DMHI research for adolescents, who rapidly adopt new platforms and technology. DMHIs that are specific to a single platform or modality may quickly become obsolete or outgrow their functionality. For instance, text-based interventions may be effective, but it remains unclear to what extent teens will use texting platforms as social media messaging continues to become more common. Thus, revised or alternate approaches to developing and testing DMHIs are needed that balance the need for rigorous testing with the need for evaluations that are timely and relevant (Murray et al., 2016; Pham et al., 2016). One such approach may be reducing the need for reevaluation for revised iterations of DMHIs that do not alter the core therapeutic principles (Torous et al., 2019). Another option to bridge the research-commercial gap is to partner with existing apps that are already popular with teens and test their effectiveness or incorporate evidence-based approaches as needed. This may be a particularly effective method given that teens report that brand familiarity helps with app engagement (Liverpool et al., 2020). Furthermore, systematic and consensus guidelines on DMHIs are needed (Torous et al., 2019), which may help close the gap between commercial and research digital tools and ensure high-quality mental health services for adolescents.

Privacy and Security

One major challenge at the forefront of DMHI research is the privacy and safety of digital spaces (Wong et al., 2020). Indeed, most teens are unaware of who has access to their data or how it is being used. Teen privacy and data security present concerns for providers with recommending or implementing DMHIs with adolescents. While privacy policies may exist for some apps, a recent review of apps targeting teens found that most data privacy statements were written at or above a 12th-grade reading level (Das et al., 2018), which is problematic for adolescents and their parents. Without knowing how their data will be used, adolescents may agree to have their private information sold and marketed to third-party companies. Violations of teens' privacy directly conflict with adolescents' strong preference for mental health privacy in engagement with DMHIs (Park & Kwon, 2018). Uncertainty regarding teens' data privacy also presents ethical concerns for clinicians in recommending or using commercially available digital tools with patients (Kerst et al., 2020; Palmer & Burrows, 2021). Thus, it is critical that researchers take special consideration in ensuring that adolescents are aware of how their digital data will be stored and secured (Torous, 2019). One potential avenue for addressing these concerns could be increasing digital health literacy among adolescents, such as through school-based curricula in childhood and throughout adolescence (see Chapter 15 of this volume). Directly addressing digital mental health literacy with teens may help them navigate the overabundance of digital tools and select DMHIs that are private, safe, and from reliable sources (Park & Kwon, 2018). However, it is also important for researchers to take a more active role in disseminating tools (Lagan et al., 2020) or advocating for policies that will aid teens, providers, and parents in understanding and identifying evidence-based DMHIs as they develop. Research on whether these approaches improve teens' perceived and actual privacy, as well as the reach and engagement of DMHIs, would further inform future directions in this area.

Youth-Centered DMHIs

Most DMHIs are plagued by low rates of adherence from participants (Fleming et al., 2018; Hollis et al., 2017). Programs that are self-guided or that include minimal human (especially clinician) contact suffer the most from low engagement across modalities compared to interventions that include more human and clinician contact. Indeed, most teens stop using mental health apps within days to weeks (Baumel et al., 2019), do not complete all modules of online interventions (Christensen et al., 2009), and do not use video games created by researchers in their daily lives (Fleming et al., 2018). This suggests a large difference between clinical trials in which adolescents are incentivized, which still struggle from lower adherence rates (Clarke et al., 2015), and real-world application.

While there are many factors that contribute to adolescents' poor engagement in DMHIs (Torous, Nicholas, et al., 2018), poor usability and the absence of adolescent-specific design may be key components. Collaborating with experts across disciplines (e.g., design, engineering) is critical in designing DMHIs that are more user-friendly and that integrate components well-received by adolescents, such as the inclusion of graphics, video, personalization, and elements that facilitate social connection (Liverpool et al., 2020). Adolescents' input and preferences, particularly from those with lived experience of mental illness, are especially important in the development of DMHIs (Scholten & Granic, 2019). Furthermore, leveraging developmental science to inform the development, design, and implementation of DMHIs may be particularly effective for adolescents (Giovanelli et al., 2020). For instance, adolescents are highly sensitive to social contexts and, perhaps unsurprisingly, DMHIs that are conducted without any provider interaction are less effective (Hollis et al., 2017). Though social media interventions hold particular promise, there are major challenges for developing DMHIs via social media (Pagoto et al., 2016). For instance there is a need to adapt content to fit specific social media platforms and to stay abreast of evolving norms of the targeted population (Pagoto et al., 2016). This is particularly challenging for teens given the relatively quick adoption and extinction of platforms and norms, which suggests that DMHIs using social media may be best developed across platforms rather than relying on a single medium. However, researchers should also consider the unique affordances of social media, including its social, cognitive, identity, and emotional affordances, in designing mental health interventions for social media that best fit the needs and goals of targeted youth (Moreno & D'Angelo, 2019). However, research is needed to examine the affordances of DMHIs that are most important to adolescents (Wong et al., 2020).

Scalability of DMHIs

Relatedly, research on the scalability and implementation of DMHIs in real-world contexts is sorely needed (Liverpool et al., 2020). Most research has focused on acceptability, adoption, and appropriateness, but the cost and sustainability of DMHIs remain understudied (Wozney et al., 2018). Although there is potential for improving mental health outcomes for adolescents, DMHIs are still not widely employed in clinical practice or within health systems. Thus, research efforts should assess both provider and patient acceptability and intention to use DMHIs. It is also critical to address potential barriers to their implementation, such as comfort level, privacy, and safety concerns (Kerst et al., 2020). Further, the costs of development and maintenance for DMHIs, including long-term maintenance (Hollis et al., 2017), is important for scalability and integration in clinical care (Liverpool et al., 2020). One approach to overcoming barriers in long-term maintenance DMHIs is to increase the use of open-access methods and resource-sharing to ensure DMHIs are accessible and free. Using open-access methods might also increase the reach of DMHIs to underserved populations. Interdisciplinary research teams that include various stakeholders may be most effective in troubleshooting these barriers and improving the implementation and scalability of DMHIs (Torous et al., 2019; Torous, Wisniewski, et al., 2018). Thus, research and development of DMHIs should collaborate across disciplines, including medicine, computer science, engineering, public health, schools, education, policy-makers, and clinical care. Most, importantly, adolescents and their families should play an integral part in improving the scalability of DMHIs.

Culturally Sensitive and Equitable DMHIs

While DMHIs may be able to reduce health disparities through their reach and accessibility, it is important to develop and implement interventions that are equitable and inclusive, and that engage diverse communities in DMHI design and implementation. For instance, most research with DMHIs in youth has been done in developed countries, and consequently, there is much less access to DMHIs in lower- and middle-income countries (Liverpool et al., 2020). Even within developed countries, disparities exist both in access to high-quality mental health services and for adolescents who are racial, ethnic, sexual, or gender minorities. There is a dire need to customize interventions to these minority and historically underserved populations (Schueller et al., 2019). Yet, it is critical that DMHIs engage in participatory designs that reflect the diverse and evolving needs of these populations (Schueller et al., 2019), as some online resources may inadvertently increase feelings of marginalization and misinformation (Steinke et al., 2017). For instance, DMHIs that "group together" all sexual and gender minority youth or all Latinx/Hispanic youth may further alienate individuals from mental health services given the large heterogeneity that exists within these populations (Schueller et al., 2019; Steinke et al., 2017). Further, few to no DMHIs have been specifically designed or implemented that target the unique needs of youth with marginalized and intersecting identities. Thus, DMHIs may have the potential to increase access and delivery of equitable and effective mental health services to youth across demographics; however, research on culturally sensitive DMHIs remains a high-priority area.

Double-Edged Sword of Digital Media

There is a potential irony in using DMHIs with adolescents amid general concerns about adolescents' use of and reliance on digital technology. Using DMHIs for mental health may be especially concerning for youth who may use or experience digital media in ways that further exacerbate their symptoms (Radovic et al., 2017). Thus, a critical future direction will be the development and tailoring of interventions or programs that help youth, particularly those with mental illness, use digital media in a way that promotes mental health. One such example is #chatsafe, which is an international program that helps teens communicate safely online with others about suicide (Robinson et al., 2018). Preliminary results suggest that individuals who participated in #chatsafe felt better equipped to communicate safely about suicide online, as well as to identify and support others who may be at risk for suicide (Robinson et al., 2020; Thorn et al., 2020). To date, there is still limited research on interventions that target media use and behaviors among youth with mental health problems. However, there are several emerging interventions that use mindfulness (Weaver & Swank, 2019) and daily reflection (Hou et al., 2019) as a means to improve mindless scrolling and reduce unwanted use. Further, a recent values-alignment intervention focused on adolescents' own motivations to self-regulate their social media use (Galla et al., 2021), finding that adolescents who participated in the intervention experienced more motivation to self-regulate and independently changed their social media behaviors to be consistent with their values. Thus, it is important to consider the potential for conflicting messages regarding the risks and benefits of digital media when using DMHIs with adolescents. Further, it will be critical to continue designing and implementing interventions, offered both digitally and in other formats, that help adolescents use media in a way that promotes their mental health.

Conclusion

Given the large gap between the need and delivery of mental health services for adolescents, DMHIs have received considerable attention among researchers and providers. The current state of research with youth suggests only preliminary effectiveness of most DMHIs, with the most support for online/web-based interventions for depression and anxiety (Hollis et al., 2017). However, the field is rapidly expanding to evaluate DMHIs and to address the current challenges in research on DMHIs' effectiveness and implementation. Thus, DMHIs continue to hold great promise in delivering accessible, developmentally informed, and scalable interventions for the detection, monitoring, prevention, and treatment of adolescent mental health problems.

References

Alegria, M., Vallas, M., & Pumariega, A. J. (2010). Racial and ethnic disparities in pediatric mental health. *Child and Adolescent Psychiatric Clinics of North America, 19*(4), 759–774. https://doi.org/10.1016/j.chc.2010.07.001

Ali, K., Farrer, L., Gulliver, A., & Griffiths, K. M. (2015). Online peer-to-peer support for young people with mental health problems: A systematic review. *JMIR Mental Health, 2*(2), e19. https://doi.org/10.2196/mental.4418

Allen, N. B., Nelson, B. W., Brent, D., & Auerbach, R. P. (2019, May 1). Short-term prediction of suicidal thoughts and behaviors in adolescents: Can recent developments in technology and computational science provide a breakthrough? *Journal of Affective Disorders, 250*, 163–169. https://doi.org/10.1016/j.jad.2019.03.044

Alvarez-Jimenez, M., Bendall, S., Lederman, R., et al. (2013). On the HORYZON: Moderated online social therapy for long-term recovery in first episode psychosis. *Schizophrenia Research, 143*(1), 143–149. https://doi.org/10.1016/j.schres.2012.10.009

American Psychological Association. (2016). *Strengthening the child and adolescent mental health workforce.* http://www.apa.org/about/gr/issues/cyf/child-workforce.aspx

Anderson, M., & Jiang, J. (2018), May 31). *Teens, social media, and technology.* Pew Research Center. https://www.pewresearch.org/internet/2018/05/31/teens-social-media-technology-2018/

Andrilla, C. H. A., Patterson, D. G., Garberson, L. A., Coulthard, C., & Larson, E. H. (2018). Geographic variation in the supply of selected behavioral health providers. *Americal Journal of Preventative Medicine, 54*(6 Suppl. 3), S199–S207. https://doi.org/10.1016/j.amepre.2018.01.004

Arshad, U., Farhat Ul, A., Gauntlett, J., Husain, N., Chaudhry, N., & Taylor, P. J. (2020). A systematic review of the evidence supporting mobile- and internet-based psychological interventions for self-harm. *Suicide and Life-Threatening Behaviors, 50*(1), 151–179. https://doi.org/10.1111/sltb.12583

Bakker, D., Kazantzis, N., Rickwood, D., & Rickard, N. (2016). Mental health smartphone apps: Review and evidence-based recommendations for future developments. *JMIR Mental Health, 3*(1), e7. https://doi.org/10.2196/mental.4984

Barnes, S., & Prescott, J. (2018). Empirical evidence for the outcomes of therapeutic video games for adolescents with anxiety disorders: Systematic review. *JMIR Serious Games, 6*(1), e3. https://doi.org/10.2196/games.9530

Baumel, A., Muench, F., Edan, S., & Kane, J. M. (2019). Objective user engagement with mental health apps: Systematic search and panel-based usage analysis. *Journal of Medical Internet Research, 21*(9), e14567. https://doi.org/10.2196/14567

Bell, I. H., Nicholas, J., Alvarez-Jimenez, M., Thompson, A., & Valmaggia, L. (2020). Virtual reality as a clinical tool in mental health research and practice. *Dialogues in Clinical Neuroscience, 22*(2), 169–177. https://doi.org/10.31887/DCNS.2020.22.2/lvalmaggia

Berenguer, C., Baixauli, I., Gomez, S., Andres, M. E. P., & De Stasio, S. (2020). Exploring the impact of augmented reality in children and adolescents with autism spectrum disorder: A systematic review. *International Journal of Environmental Research and Public Health, 17*(17), Article 6143. https://doi.org/10.3390/ijerph17176143

Betton, V., Borschmann, R., Docherty, M., Coleman, S., Brown, M., & Henderson, C. (2015). The role of social media in reducing stigma and discrimination. *British Journal of Psychiatry, 206*(6), 443–444. https://doi.org/10.1192/bjp.bp.114.152835

Booth, R. G., Allen, B. N., Bray Jenkyn, K. M., Li, L., & Shariff, S. Z. (2018). Youth mental health services utilization rates after a large-scale social media campaign: Population-based interrupted time-series analysis. *JMIR Mental Health, 5*(2), e27. https://doi.org/10.2196/mental.8808

Boudreaux, E. D., Waring, M. E., Hayes, R. B., Sadasivam, R. S., Mullen, S., & Pagoto, S. (2014). Evaluating and selecting mobile health apps: Strategies for healthcare providers and healthcare organizations. *Translational Behavioral Medicine, 4*(4), 363–371. https://doi.org/10.1007/s13142–014-0293-9

Boydell, K. M., Hodgins, M., Pignatiello, A., Teshima, J., Edwards, H., & Willis, D. (2014). Using technology to deliver mental health services to children and youth: A scoping review. *Journal of the Canadian Academy of Child & Adolescent Psychiatry, 23*(2), 87–99. https://www.ncbi.nlm.nih.gov/pubmed/24872824

Bradford, S., & Rickwood, D. (2015). Young people's views on electronic mental health assessment: Prefer to type than talk? *Journal of Child and Family Studies, 24*(5), 1213–1221. https://doi.org/10.1007/s10826–014-9929-0

Branson, C. E., Clemmey, P., & Mukherjee, P. (2013). Text message reminders to improve outpatient therapy attendance among adolescents: A pilot study. *Psychological Services, 10*(3), 298–303. https://doi.org/10.1037/a0026693

Bry, L. J., Chou, T., Miguel, E., & Comer, J. S. (2018). Consumer smartphone apps marketed for child and adolescent anxiety: A systematic review and content analysis. *Behavior Therapy, 49*(2), 249–261. https://doi.org/10.1016/j.beth.2017.07.008

Carper, M. M. (2017). Multimedia field test thinking about exposures? There's an app for that! *Cognitive and Behavioral Practice, 24*(1), 121–127. https://doi.org/10.1016/j.cbpra.2016.11.001

Centers for Disease Control. (2018). *Injury prevention and control: WISQARS.* https://www.cdc.gov/injury/wisqars/index.html

Christensen, H., Griffiths, K. M., & Farrer, L. (2009). Adherence in internet interventions for anxiety and depression. *Journal of Medical Internet Research, 11*(2), e13. https://doi.org/10.2196/jmir.1194

Chu, J. T. W., Wadham, A., Jiang, Y., et al. (2019). Effect of MyTeen SMS-based mobile intervention for parents of adolescents: A randomized clinical trial. *JAMA Network Open, 2*(9), e1911120. https://doi.org/10.1001/jamanetworkopen.2019.11120

Cieslik, B., Mazurek, J., Rutkowski, S., Kiper, P., Turolla, A., & Szczepanska-Gieracha, J. (2020). Virtual reality in psychiatric disorders: A systematic review of reviews. *Complementary Therapies in Medicine, 52,* Article 102480. https://doi.org/10.1016/j.ctim.2020.102480

Clarke, A. M., Kuosmanen, T., & Barry, M. M. (2015). A systematic review of online youth mental health promotion and prevention interventions. *Journal of Youth and Adolescence, 44*(1), 90–113. https://doi.org/10.1007/s10964–014-0165-0

Clement, S., Schauman, O., Graham, T., et al. (2015). What is the impact of mental health-related stigma on help-seeking? A systematic review of quantitative and qualitative studies. *Psychological Medicine, 45*(1), 11–27. https://doi.org/10.1017/S0033291714000129

Cummings, J. R., Wen, H., & Druss, B. G. (2013). Improving access to mental health services for youth in the United States. *JAMA, 309*(6), 553–554. https://doi.org/10.1001/jama.2013.437

Das, G., Cheung, C., Nebeker, C., Bietz, M., & Bloss, C. (2018). Privacy policies for apps targeted toward youth: Descriptive analysis of readability. *JMIR mHealth uHealth, 6*(1), e3. https://doi.org/10.2196/mhealth.7626

de Girolamo, G., Dagani, J., Purcell, R., Cocchi, A., & McGorry, P. D. (2012). Age of onset of mental disorders and use of mental health services: Needs, opportunities and obstacles. *Epidemiology and Psychiatric Sciences, 21*(1), 47–57. https://doi.org/10.1017/s2045796011000746

DeHaan, S., Kuper, L. E., Magee, J. C., Bigelow, L., & Mustanski, B. S. (2013). The interplay between online and offline explorations of identity, relationships, and sex: A mixed-methods study with LGBT youth. *The Journal of Sex Research, 50*(5), 421–434. https://doi.org/10.1080/00224499.2012.661489

Ebert, D. D., Zarski, A. C., Christensen, H., et al. (2015). Internet and computer-based cognitive behavioral therapy for anxiety and depression in youth: A meta-analysis of randomized controlled outcome trials. *PLoS ONE, 10*(3), e0119895. https://doi.org/10.1371/journal.pone.0119895

Ferchaud, A., Seibert, J., Sellers, N., & Escobar Salazar, N. (2020). Reducing mental health stigma through identification with video game avatars with mental illness. *Frontiers in Psychology, 11*, Article 2240. https://doi.org/10.3389/fpsyg.2020.02240

Fitzpatrick, K. K., Darcy, A., & Vierhile, M. (2017). Delivering cognitive behavior therapy to young adults with symptoms of depression and anxiety using a fully automated conversational agent (Woebot): A randomized controlled trial. *JMIR Mental Health, 4*(2), e19. https://doi.org/10.2196/mental.7785

Fleming, T., Bavin, L., Lucassen, M., Stasiak, K., Hopkins, S., & Merry, S. (2018). Beyond the trial: Systematic review of real-world uptake and engagement with digital self-help interventions for depression, low mood, or anxiety. *Journal of Medical Internet Research, 20*(6), e199. https://doi.org/10.2196/jmir.9275

Fleming, T. M., Bavin, L., Stasiak, K., et al. (2016). Serious games and gamification for mental health: Current status and promising directions. *Frontiers in Psychiatry, 7*, Article 215. https://doi.org/10.3389/fpsyt.2016.00215

Galla, B., Choukas-Bradley, S., Fiore, H. M., & Esposito, M. V. (2021). Values-alignment messaging boosts adolescents' motivation to control social media use. *Child Development, 92*(5), 1717–1734. https://doi.org/10.1111/cdev.13553

Garrido, S., Millington, C., Cheers, D., et al. (2019). What works and what doesn't work? A systematic review of digital mental health interventions for depression and anxiety in young people. *Frontiers in Psychiatry, 10*, Article 759. https://doi.org/10.3389/fpsyt.2019.00759

Giovanelli, A., Ozer, E. M., & Dahl, R. E. (2020). Leveraging technology to improve health in adolescence: A developmental science perspective. *Journal of Adolescent Health, 67*(2S), S7–S13. https://doi.org/10.1016/j.jadohealth.2020.02.020

Grist, R., Croker, A., Denne, M., & Stallard, P. (2019). Technology delivered interventions for depression and anxiety in children and adolescents: A systematic review and meta-analysis. *Clinical Child and Family Psychology Review, 22*(2), 147–171. https://doi.org/10.1007/s10567–018-0271-8

Gruber, J., Prinstein, M. J., Clark, L. A., et al. (2021). Mental health and clinical psychological science in the time of COVID-19: Challenges, opportunities, and a call to action. *American Psychologist, 76*(3), 409–426. https://doi.org/10.1037/amp0000707

Gulliver, A., Griffiths, K. M., & Christensen, H. (2010). Perceived barriers and facilitators to mental health help-seeking in young people: A systematic review. *BMC Psychiatry, 10*, Article 113. https://doi.org/10.1186/1471-244X-10-113

Hetrick, S. E., Yuen, H. P., Bailey, E., et al. (2017). Internet-based cognitive behavioural therapy for young people with suicide-related behaviour (Reframe-IT): A randomised controlled trial. *Evidence-Based Mental Health, 20*(3), 76–82. https://doi.org/10.1136/eb-2017-102719

Hoek, W., Schuurmans, J., Koot, H. M., & Cuijpers, P. (2012). Effects of internet-based guided self-help problem-solving therapy for adolescents with depression and anxiety: A randomized controlled trial. *PLoS ONE, 7*(8), e43485. https://doi.org/10.1371/journal.pone.0043485

Hollis, C., Falconer, C. J., Martin, J. L., et al. (2017). Annual Research Review: Digital health interventions for children and young people with mental health problems – A systematic and meta-review. *Journal of Child Psychology and Psychiatry*, *58*(4), 474–503. https://doi.org/10.1111/jcpp.12663

Hou, Y., Xiong, D., Jiang, T., Song, L., & Wang, Q. (2019). Social media addiction: Its impact, mediation, and intervention. *Cyberpsychology: Journal of Psychosocial Research on Cyberspace*, *13*(1). https://doi.org/10.5817/CP2019-1-4

Huckvale, K., Venkatesh, S., & Christensen, H. (2019). Toward clinical digital phenotyping: A timely opportunity to consider purpose, quality, and safety. *NPJ Digital Medicine*, *2*(1), 1–11. https://doi.org/10.1038/s41746–019-0166-1

Kauer, S. D., Mangan, C., & Sanci, L. (2014). Do online mental health services improve help-seeking for young people? A systematic review. *Journal of Medical Internet Research*, *16*(3), e66. https://doi.org/10.2196/jmir.3103

Kauer, S. D., Reid, S. C., Crooke, A. H., et al. (2012). Self-monitoring using mobile phones in the early stages of adolescent depression: Randomized controlled trial. *Journal of Medical Internet Research*, *14*(3), e67. https://doi.org/10.2196/jmir.1858

Kennard, B. D., Biernesser, C., Wolfe, K. L., et al. (2015). Developing a brief suicide prevention intervention and mobile phone application: A qualitative report. *Journal of Technology in Human Services*, *33*(4), 345–357. https://doi.org/10.1080/15228835.2015.1106384

Kennard, B. D., Goldstein, T., Foxwell, A. A., et al. (2018). As Safe as Possible (ASAP): A brief app-supported inpatient intervention to prevent postdischarge suicidal behavior in hospitalized, suicidal adolescents. *American Journal of Psychiatry*, *175*(9), 864–872. https://doi.org/10.1176/appi.ajp.2018.17101151

Kerst, A., Zielasek, J., & Gaebel, W. (2020). Smartphone applications for depression: A systematic literature review and a survey of health care professionals' attitudes towards their use in clinical practice. *European Archives of Psychiatry and Clinical Neuroscience*, *270*(2), 139–152. https://doi.org/10.1007/s00406–018-0974-3

Kessler, R. C., Berglund, P., Demler, O., Jin, R., Merikangas, K. R., & Walters, E. E. (2005). Lifetime prevalence and age-of-onset distributions of DSM-IV disorders in the National Comorbidity Survey Replication. *Archives of General Psychiatry*, *62*(6), 593–602. https://doi.org/10.1001/archpsyc.62.6.593

Khanna, M. S., Carper, M. M., Harris, M. S., & Kendall, P. C. (2017). Web-based parent-training for parents of youth with impairment from anxiety. *Evidence Based Practice in Child and Adolescent Mental Health*, *2*(1), 43–53. https://doi.org/10.1080/23794925.2017.1283548

Knox, M., Lentini, J., Cummings, T. S., McGrady, A., Whearty, K., & Sancrant, L. (2011). Game-based biofeedback for paediatric anxiety and depression. *Mental Health in Family Medicine*, *8*(3), 195–203.

Lagan, S., Aquino, P., Emerson, M. R., Fortuna, K., Walker, R., & Torous, J. (2020). Actionable health app evaluation: Translating expert frameworks into objective metrics. *NPJ Digital Medicine*, *3*, Article 100. https://doi.org/10.1038/s41746–020-00312-4

Lau, H. M., Smit, J. H., Fleming, T. M., & Riper, H. (2016). Serious games for mental health: Are they accessible, feasible, and effective? A systematic review and meta-analysis. *Frontiers in Psychiatry*, *7*, Article 209. https://doi.org/10.3389/fpsyt.2016.00209

Leanza, F., & Alani, R. (2020). Health information and healthcare seeking online. In M. A. Moreno & A. J. Hoopes (Eds.), *Technology and adolescent health In schools and beyond* (pp. 115–140). Elsevier.

Li, J., Theng, Y. L., & Foo, S. (2014). Game-based digital interventions for depression therapy: A systematic review and meta-analysis. *Cyberpsychology, Behavior, and Social Networking*, *17*(8), 519–527. https://doi.org/10.1089/cyber.2013.0481

Li, L., Yu, F., Shi, D., et al. (2017). Application of virtual reality technology in clinical medicine. *American Journal of Translational Research*, *9*(9), 3867–3880. https://www.ncbi.nlm.nih.gov/pubmed/28979666

Lister, C., West, J. H., Cannon, B., Sax, T., & Brodegard, D. (2014). Just a fad? Gamification in health and fitness apps. *JMIR Serious Games*, *2*(2), e9. https://doi.org/10.2196/games.3413

Liverpool, S., Mota, C. P., Sales, C. M. D., et al. (2020). Engaging children and young people in digital mental health interventions: Systematic review of modes of delivery, facilitators, and barriers. *Journal of Medical Internet Research*, *22*(6), e16317. https://doi.org/10.2196/16317

Loescher, L. J., Rains, S. A., Kramer, S. S., Akers, C., & Moussa, R. (2018). A systematic review of interventions to enhance healthy lifestyle behaviors in adolescents delivered via mobile phone text messaging. *American Journal of Health Promotion*, *32*(4), 865–879. https://doi.org/10.1177/0890117116675785

Loucas, C. E., Fairburn, C. G., Whittington, C., Pennant, M. E., Stockton, S., & Kendall, T. (2014). E-therapy in the treatment and prevention of eating disorders: A systematic review and meta-analysis. *Behaviour Research and Therapy*, *63*, 122–131. https://doi.org/10.1016/j.brat.2014.09.011

Lucas, G. M., Gratch, J., King, A., & Morency, L. P. (2014). It's only a computer: Virtual humans increase willingness to disclose. *Computers in Human Behavior*, *37*, 94–100. https://doi.org/10.1016/j.chb.2014.04.043

Martinengo, L., Van Galen, L., Lum, E., Kowalski, M., Subramaniam, M., & Car, J. (2019). Suicide prevention and depression apps' suicide risk assessment and management: A systematic assessment of adherence to clinical guidelines. *BMC Medicine*, *17*(1), Article 231. https://doi.org/10.1186/s12916–019-1461-z

Mason, M., Ola, B., Zaharakis, N., & Zhang, J. (2015). Text messaging interventions for adolescent and young adult substance use: A meta-analysis. *Prevention Science*, *16*(2), 181–188. https://doi.org/10.1007/s11121–014-0498-7

McEnery, C., Lim, M. H., Knowles, A., et al. (2021). Social anxiety in young people with first-episode psychosis: Pilot study of the EMBRACE moderated online social intervention. *Early Intervention in Psychiatry*, *15*(1), 76–86. https://doi.org/10.1111/eip.12912

Melbye, S., Kessing, L. V., Bardram, J. E., & Faurholt-Jepsen, M. (2020). Smartphone-based self-monitoring, treatment, and automatically generated data in children, adolescents, and young adults with psychiatric disorders: Systematic review. *JMIR Mental Health*, *7*(10), e17453. https://doi.org/10.2196/17453

Merikangas, K. R., He, J. P., Burstein, M., et al. (2011). Service utilization for lifetime mental disorders in U.S. adolescents: Results of the National Comorbidity

Survey-Adolescent Supplement (NCS-A). *Journal of the American Academy of Child and Adolescent Psychiatry, 50*(1), 32–45. https://doi.org/10.1016/j.jaac.2010.10.006

Merry, S. N., Stasiak, K., Shepherd, M., Frampton, C., Fleming, T., & Lucassen, M. F. (2012). The effectiveness of SPARX, a computerised self help intervention for adolescents seeking help for depression: Randomised controlled non-inferiority trial. *British Medical Journal, 344*, e2598. https://doi.org/10.1136/bmj.e2598

Moreno, M. A., & D'Angelo, J. (2019). Social media intervention design: Applying an affordances framework. *Journal of Medical Internet Research, 21*(3), e11014. https://doi.org/10.2196/11014

Morris, R. R., Kouddous, K., Kshirsagar, R., & Schueller, S. M. (2018). Towards an artificially empathic conversational agent for mental health applications: System design and user perceptions. *Journal of Medical Internet Research, 20*(6), e10148. https://doi.org/10.2196/10148

Murray, E., Hekler, E. B., Andersson, G., et al. (2016). Evaluating digital health interventions: Key questions and approaches. *American Journal of Preventative Medicine, 51*(5), 843–851. https://doi.org/10.1016/j.amepre.2016.06.008

Myers, K. M., Valentine, J. M., & Melzer, S. M. (2007). Feasibility, acceptability, and sustainability of telepsychiatry for children and adolescents. *Psychiatric Services, 58*(11), 1493–1496. https://doi.org/10.1176/ps.2007.58.11.1493

Myers, K. M., Valentine, J. M., & Melzer, S. M. (2008). Child and adolescent telepsychiatry: Utilization and satisfaction. *Telemedicine and e-Health, 14*(2), 131–137. https://doi.org/10.1089/tmj.2007.0035

Nelson, E. L., Cain, S., & Sharp, S. (2017). Considerations for conducting telemental health with children and adolescents. *Child and Adolescent Psychiatric Clinics of North America, 26*(1), 77–91. https://doi.org/10.1016/j.chc.2016.07.008

Nesi, J., Choukas-Bradley, S., & Prinstein, M. J. (2018). Transformation of adolescent peer relations in the social media context: Part 1 – A theoretical framework and application to dyadic peer relationships. *Clinical Child and Family Psychology Review, 21*(3), 267–294. https://doi.org/10.1007/s10567–018–0261-x

Odgers, C. L., & Jensen, M. R. (2020). Adolescent development and growing divides in the digital age. *Dialogues in Clinical Neuroscience, 22*(2), 143–149. https://doi.org/10.31887/DCNS.2020.22.2/codgers

Pagoto, S., Waring, M. E., May, C. N., et al. (2016). Adapting behavioral interventions for social media delivery. *Journal of Medical Internet Research, 18*(1), e24. https://doi.org/10.2196/jmir.5086

Palmer, K. M., & Burrows, V. (2021). Ethical and safety concerns regarding the use of mental health-related apps in counseling: Considerations for counselors. *Journal of Technology in Behavioral Science, 6*, 137–150. https://doi.org/10.1007/s41347–020-00160-9

Park, E., & Kwon, M. (2018). Health-related internet use by children and adolescents: Systematic review. *Journal of Medical Internet Research, 20*(4), e120. https://doi.org/10.2196/jmir.7731

Pham, Q., Wiljer, D., & Cafazzo, J. A. (2016). Beyond the randomized controlled trial: A review of alternatives in mHealth clinical trial methods. *JMIR mHealth uHealth, 4*(3), e107. https://doi.org/10.2196/mhealth.5720

Podina, I. R., Mogoase, C., David, D., Szentagotai, A., & Dobrean, A. (2016). A meta-analysis on the efficacy of technology mediated CBT for anxious children and adolescents. *Journal of Rational Emotive Cognitive Behavioral Therapy*, *34*(1), 31–50. https://doi.org/10.1007/s10942-015-0228-5

Pramana, G., Parmanto, B., Kendall, P. C., & Silk, J. S. (2014). The SmartCAT: An m-health platform for ecological momentary intervention in child anxiety treatment. *Telemedicine and e-Health*, *20*(5), 419–427. https://doi.org/10.1089/tmj.2013.0214

Price, M., Yuen, E. K., Goetter, E. M., et al. (2014). mHealth: A mechanism to deliver more accessible, more effective mental health care. *Clinical Psychology & Psychotherapy*, *21*(5), 427–436. https://doi.org/10.1002/cpp.1855

Prinstein, M. J., & Dodge, K. A. (Eds.). (2008). *Understanding peer influence in children and adolescents*. The Guilford Press.

Punukollu, M., & Marques, M. (2019). Use of mobile apps and technologies in child and adolescent mental health: A systematic review. *Evidence Based Mental Health*, *22*(4), 161–166. https://doi.org/10.1136/ebmental-2019-300093

Radovic, A., Gmelin, T., Hua, J., Long, C., Stein, B. D., & Miller, E. (2018). Supporting Our Valued Adolescents (SOVA), a social media website for adolescents with depression and/or anxiety: Technological feasibility, usability, and acceptability study. *JMIR Mental Health*, *5*(1), e17. https://doi.org/10.2196/mental.9441

Radovic, A., Gmelin, T., Stein, B. D., & Miller, E. (2017). Depressed adolescents' positive and negative use of social media. *Journal of Adolescence*, *55*, 5–15. https://doi.org/10.1016/j.adolescence.2016.12.002

Reilly, T., Mechelli, A., McGuire, P., Fusar-Poli, P., & Uhlhaas, P. J. (2019). E-clinical high risk for psychosis: Viewpoint on potential of digital innovations for preventive psychiatry. *JMIR Mental Health*, *6*(10), e14581. https://doi.org/10.2196/14581

Rice, S. M., Goodall, J., Hetrick, S. E., et al. (2014). Online and social networking interventions for the treatment of depression in young people: A systematic review. *Journal of Medical Internet Research*, *16*(9), e206. https://doi.org/10.2196/jmir.3304

Rideout, V., & Robb, M. B. (2019). *The Common Sense census: Media use by tweens and teens*. C. S. Media.

Ridout, B., & Campbell, A. (2018). The use of social networking sites in mental health interventions for young people: Systematic review. *Journal of Medical Internet Research*, *20*(12), e12244. https://doi.org/10.2196/12244

Ritvo, P., Daskalakis, Z. J., Tomlinson, G., et al. (2019). An online mindfulness-based cognitive behavioral therapy intervention for youth diagnosed with major depressive disorders: Protocol for a randomized controlled trial. *JMIR Research Protocols*, *8*(7), e11591. https://doi.org/10.2196/11591

Robinson, J., Cox, G., Bailey, E., et al. (2016). Social media and suicide prevention: A systematic review. *Early Intervention in Psychiatry*, *10*(2), 103–121. https://doi.org/10.1111/eip.12229

Robinson, J., Hill, N. T. M., Thorn, P., et al. (2018). The #chatsafe project. Developing guidelines to help young people communicate safely about suicide on social media: A Delphi study. *PLoS ONE*, *13*(11), e0206584. https://doi.org/10.1371/journal.pone.0206584

Robinson, J., Teh, Z., Lamblin, M., Hill, N. T. M., La Sala, L., & Thorn, P. (2020). Globalization of the #chatsafe guidelines: Using social media for youth suicide prevention. *Early Intervention in Psychiatry*, *15*(5), 1409–1413. https://doi.org/10.1111/eip.13044

Rowe, S. L., Patel, K., French, R. S., et al. (2018). Web-based decision aid to assist help-seeking choices for young people who self-harm: Outcomes from a randomized controlled feasibility trial. *JMIR Mental Health*, *5*(1), e10. https://doi.org/10.2196/mental.8098

Russell, M. A., & Gajos, J. M. (2020). Annual Research Review: Ecological momentary assessment studies in child psychology and psychiatry. *Journal of Child Psychology and Psychiatry*, *61*(3), 376–394. https://doi.org/10.1111/jcpp.13204

Schleider, J., & Weisz, J. (2018). A single-session growth mindset intervention for adolescent anxiety and depression: 9-month outcomes of a randomized trial. *Journal of Child Psychology and Psychiatry*, *59*(2), 160–170. https://doi.org/10.1111/jcpp.12811

Schleider, J. L., Dobias, M. L., Sung, J. Y., & Mullarkey, M. C. (2020). Future directions in single-session youth mental health interventions. *Journal of Clinical Child and Adolescent Psychology*, *49*(2), 264–278. https://doi.org/10.1080/15374416.2019.1683852

Schleider, J. L., Dobias, M., Sung, J., Mumper, E., & Mullarkey, M. C. (2020). Acceptability and utility of an open-access, online single-session intervention platform for adolescent mental health. *JMIR Mental Health*, *7*(6), e20513. https://doi.org/10.2196/20513

Scholten, H., & Granic, I. (2019). Use of the principles of design thinking to address limitations of digital mental health interventions for youth: Viewpoint. *Journal of Medical Internet Research*, *21*(1), 1–14. https://doi.org/10.2196/11528

Schoneveld, E. A., Lichtwarck-Aschoff, A., & Granic, I. (2018). Preventing childhood anxiety disorders: Is an applied game as effective as a cognitive behavioral therapy-based program? *Prevention Science*, *19*(2), 220–232. https://doi.org/10.1007/s11121-017-0843-8

Schueller, S., Hunter, J. F., Figueroa, C., & Aguilera, A. (2019). Use of digital mental health for marginalized and underserved populations. *Current Treatment Options in Psychiatry*, *6*(3), 243–255. https://doi.org/10.1007/s40501-019-00181-z

Sharac, J., McCrone, P., Clement, S., & Thornicroft, G. (2010). The economic impact of mental health stigma and discrimination: A systematic review. *Epidemiology and Psychiatric Society*, *19*(3), 223–232. https://doi.org/10.1017/s1121189x00001159

Silk, J. S., Pramana, G., Sequeira, S. L., et al. (2020). Using a smartphone app and clinician portal to enhance brief cognitive behavioral therapy for childhood anxiety disorders. *Behavior Therapy*, *51*(1), 69–84. https://doi.org/10.1016/j.beth.2019.05.002

Somerville, L. H., & Casey, B. J. (2010). Developmental neurobiology of cognitive control and motivational systems. *Current Opinion in Neurobiology*, *20*(2), 236–241. https://doi.org/10.1016/j.conb.2010.01.006

Steinke, J., Root-Bowman, M., Estabrook, S., Levine, D. S., & Kantor, L. M. (2017). Meeting the needs of sexual and gender minority youth: Formative research on potential digital health interventions. *Journal of Adolescent Health*, *60*(5), 541–548. https://doi.org/10.1016/j.jadohealth.2016.11.023

Thorn, P., Hill, N. T., Lamblin, M., et al. (2020). Developing a suicide prevention social media campaign with young people (the #chatsafe project): Co-design approach. *JMIR Mental Health*, *7*(5), e17520. https://doi.org/10.2196/17520

Torous, J. (2019). Measuring progress in measurement-based care with smartphone tools. *Acta Psychiatrica Scandinavica*, *140*(4), 293–294. https://doi.org/10.1111/acps.13093

Torous, J., Andersson, G., Bertagnoli, A., et al. (2019). Towards a consensus around standards for smartphone apps and digital mental health. *World Psychiatry*, *18*(1), 97–98. https://doi.org/10.1002/wps.20592

Torous, J., Larsen, M. E., Depp, C., et al. (2018). Smartphones, sensors, and machine learning to advance real-time prediction and interventions for suicide prevention: A review of current progress and next steps. *Current Psychiatry Reports*, *20*(7), 51. https://doi.org/10.1007/s11920–018-0914-y

Torous, J., Nicholas, J., Larsen, M. E., Firth, J., & Christensen, H. (2018). Clinical review of user engagement with mental health smartphone apps: Evidence, theory and improvements. *Evidence Based Mental Health*, *21*(3), 116–119. https://doi.org/10.1136/eb-2018-102891

Torous, J., Wisniewski, H., Liu, G., & Keshavan, M. (2018). Mental health mobile phone app usage, concerns, and benefits among psychiatric outpatients: Comparative survey study. *JMIR Mental Health*, *5*(4), e11715. https://doi.org/10.2196/11715

Toscos, T., Coupe, A., Flanagan, M., et al. (2019). Teens using screens for help: Impact of suicidal ideation, anxiety, and depression levels on youth preferences for telemental health resources. *JMIR Mental Health*, *6*(6), e13230. https://doi.org/10.2196/13230

Vahabzadeh, A., Keshav, N. U., Abdus-Sabur, R., Huey, K., Liu, R., & Sahin, N. T. (2018). Improved socio-emotional and behavioral functioning in students with autism following school-based smartglasses intervention: Multi-stage feasibility and controlled efficacy study. *Behavioral Sciences*, *8*(10). https://doi.org/10.3390/bs8100085

Vaidyam, A., Halamka, J., & Torous, J. (2019). Actionable digital phenotyping: A framework for the delivery of just-in-time and longitudinal interventions in clinical healthcare. *mHealth*, *5*, 25. https://doi.org/10.21037/mhealth.2019.07.04

Vaidyam, A. N., Wisniewski, H., Halamka, J. D., Kashavan, M. S., & Torous, J. B. (2019). Chatbots and conversational agents in mental health: A review of the psychiatric landscape. *Canadian Journal of Psychiatry*, *64*(7), 456–464. https://doi.org/10.1177/0706743719828977

Wasil, A. R., Venturo-Conerly, K. E., Shingleton, R. M., & Weisz, J. R. (2019). A review of popular smartphone apps for depression and anxiety: Assessing the inclusion of evidence-based content. *Behavior Research and Therapy*, *123*, Article 103498. https://doi.org/10.1016/j.brat.2019.103498

Weaver, J. L., & Swank, J. M. (2019). Mindful connections: A mindfulness-based intervention for adolescent social media users. *Journal of Child and Adolescent Counseling*, *5*(2), 103–112. https://doi.org/10.1080/23727810.2019.1586419

Whitton, A. E., Proudfoot, J., Clarke, J., et al. (2015). Breaking open the black box: Isolating the most potent features of a web and mobile phone-based intervention for depression, anxiety, and stress. *JMIR Mental Health*, *2*(1), e3. https://doi.org/10.2196/mental.3573

Wong, C. A., Madanay, F., Ozer, E. M., et al. (2020). Digital health technology to enhance adolescent and young adult clinical preventive services: Affordances and challenges. *Journal of Adolescent Health*, *67*(2S), S24–S33. https://doi .org/10.1016/j.jadohealth.2019.10.018

Wozney, L., McGrath, P. J., Gehring, N. D., et al. (2018). eMental healthcare technologies for anxiety and depression in childhood and adolescence: Systematic review of studies reporting implementation outcomes. *JMIR Mental Health*, *5*(2), e48. https://doi.org/10.2196/mental.9655

Yerys, B. E., Bertollo, J. R., Kenworthy, L., et al. (2019). Brief report: Pilot study of a novel interactive digital treatment to improve cognitive control in children with autism spectrum disorder and co-occurring ADHD symptoms. *Journal of Autism and Developmental Disorders*, *49*(4), 1727–1737. https://doi.org/10 .1007/s10803–018-3856-7

Index

Printed in the USA
CPSIA information can be obtained
at www.ICGtesting.com
LVHW081034201023
761430LV00025B/326

9 781108 838726